T0368014

Behavioural Investing

For other titles in the Wiley Finance Series
please see www.wiley.com/finance

Behavioural investing

"For over 20 years, James has had a front row seat at the global investing circus. This compilation of his best essays is full of trenchant observations about the foibles and peccadillos of fund managers – and practical advice on how to improve. It is a must read for anyone interested in the practical application of the insights from the study of behavioural finance. James' essays on the Seven Sins of Fund Management are a modern classic. They should be a touchstone for every active investor seeking to raise their game."

—Hassan Elmasry, CFA, Managing Director, Morgan Stanley Investment Management

"Our investment process owes a great deal to the insights from Montier's writing. His articles challenge the reader to confront their own behavioural frailties, but in such a way that valuable lessons are easily absorbed. All too often investment is a dry and technical subject, but Montier's user-friendly style makes even the most complex issues seem straightforward."

—Stephen Barrow
CIO IronBridge International

"James Montier brings behavioural finance to life with his remarkable insights and vivid prose. He does an admirable job exploring the implications of this literature for investment practice. A list of his 'seven sins' should be reviewed daily by every investment manager."

—Kent Daniel, Managing Director and Director of Equities Research, Quantitative Investment Strategies Group, Goldman Sachs

JAMES MONTIER is Global Strategist at Société Générale. He was previously the global equity strategist at Dresdner Kleinwort. He has been the top rated strategist in the annual Extel survey for the last three years. He is also the author of *Behavioural Finance*, published by Wiley in 2000. James was on the 50 must read analysts list compiled by The Business magazine, and was one of the Financial News' Rising Stars.

James is a regular speaker at both academic and practitioner conferences, and is regarded as the leading authority on applying behavioural finance to investment. He is also a visiting fellow at the University of Durham and a fellow of the Royal Society of Arts. He has been described as a maverick by the Sunday Times, an enfant terrible by the FAZ, and a prophet by the Fast Company! When not writing or reading, he can usually be found blowing bubbles at fish and swimming with sharks.

Behavioural Investing

A practitioner's guide to applying behavioural finance

James Montier

John Wiley & Sons, Ltd

Other Wiley Editorial Offices

John Wiley & Sons Inc., 111 River Street, Hoboken, NJ 07030, USA

Jossey-Bass, 989 Market Street, San Francisco, CA 94103-1741, USA

Wiley-VCH Verlag GmbH, Boschstr. 12, D-69469 Weinheim, Germany

John Wiley & Sons Australia Ltd, 42 McDougall Street, Milton, Queensland 4064, Australia

John Wiley & Sons (Asia) Pte Ltd, 2 Clementi Loop #02-01, Jin Xing Distripark, Singapore 129809

John Wiley & Sons Canada Ltd, 6045 Freemont Blvd, Mississauga, ONT, L5R 4J3, Canada

Wiley also publishes its books in a variety of electronic formats. Some content that appears
in print may not be available in electronic books.

Anniversary Logo Design: Richard J. Pacifico

British Library Cataloguing in Publication Data

A catalogue record for this book is available from the British Library

ISBN 978-0-470-51670-6 (HB)

Typeset in 10/12pt Times by Aptara, New Delhi, India

This book is printed on acid-free paper responsibly manufactured from sustainable forestry
in which at least two trees are planted for each one used for paper production.

To Connor
The best nephew a proud uncle could hope for

Contents

Preface   xvii

Acknowledgments   xxi

SECTION I: COMMON MISTAKES AND BASIC BIASES   1

1   Emotion, Neuroscience and Investing: Investors as Dopamine Addicts   3
   Spock or McCoy?   5
   The Primary of Emotion   5
     Emotions: Body or Brain?   6
     Emotion: Good, Bad of Both?   7
   Self-Control is Like a Muscle   11
   Hard-Wired for the Short Term   13
   Hard-Wired to Herd   14
   Plasticity as Salvation   15

2   Part Man, Part Monkey   17
   The Biases We Face   19
   Bias #1: I Know Better, Because I Know More   19
     The Illusion of Knowledge: More Information Isn't Better Information   20
     Professionals Worse than Chance!   21
     The Illusion of Control   22
   Bias #2: Big ≠ Important   23
   Bias #3: Show Me What I Want to See   23
   Bias #4: Heads was Skill, Tails was Bad Luck   24
   Bias #5: I Knew it all Along   25
   Bias #6: The Irrelevant has Value as Input   25
   Bias #7: I Can Make a Judgement Based on What it Looks Like   27
   Bias #8: That's Not the Way I Remember it   28
   Bias #9: If you Tell Me it Is So, It Must be True   29
   Bias #10: A Loss Isn't a Loss Until I Take It   30
   Conclusions   35

3   **Take a Walk on the Wild Side**   **37**
    Impact Bias   39
    Empathy Gaps   40
    Combating the Biases   44

4   **Brain Damage, Addicts and Pigeons**   **47**

5   **What Do Secretaries' Dustbins and the Da Vinci Code have in Common?** **55**

6   **The Limits to Learning**   **63**
    Self-Attribution Bias: Heads is Skill, Tails is Bad Luck   67
    Hindsight Bias: I Knew it All Along   69
    Skinner's Pigeons   71
    Illusion of Control   72
    Feedback Distortion   73
    Conclusions   76

SECTION II: THE PROFESSIONALS AND THE BIASES   77

7   **Behaving Badly**   **79**
    The Test   81
    The Results   82
    Overoptimism   82
    Confirmatory Bias   83
    Representativeness   84
    The Cognitive Reflection Task (CRT)   85
    Anchoring   87
        Framing   87
        Loss Aversion   89
    Keynes's beauty contest   90
    Monty Hall Problem   92
    Conclusions   94

SECTION III: THE SEVEN SINS OF FUND MANAGEMENT   95

8   **A Behavioural Critique**   **97**
    Sin city   99
        Sin 1: Forecasting (Pride)   99
        Sin 2: The Illusion of Knowledge (Gluttony)   100
        Sin 3: Meeting Companies (Lust)   100
        Sin 4: Thinking You Can Outsmart Everyone Else (Envy)   100
        Sin 5: Short Time Horizons and Overtrading (Avarice)   101
        Sin 6: Believing Everything You Read (Sloth)   101
        Sin 7: Group-Based Decisions (Wrath)   101
    Alternative Approaches and Future Directions   102

Sin 1: Forecasting (Pride) `   103
9 The Folly of Forecasting: Ignore all Economists, Strategists, & Analysts   **105**
    Overconfidence as a Driver of Poor Forecasting   109
    Overconfidence and Experts   110
    Why Forecast When the Evidence Shows You Can't?   114
        Unskilled and Unaware   115
        Ego Defence Mechanism   115
    Why Use Forecasts?   119
    Debasing   120

10 What Value Analysts?   **123**

Sin 2: Illusion of Knowledge (Gluttony)   131
11 The Illusion of Knowledge or Is More Information Better Information?   **133**

Sin 3: Meeting Companies (Lust)   141
12 Why Waste Your Time Listening to Company Management?   **143**
    Managers are Just as Biased as the Rest of Us   145
    Confirmatory Bias and Biased Assimilation   148
    Obedience to Authority   151
    Truth or Lie?   153
    Conclusions   157

Sin 4: Thinking You Can Outsmart Everyone Else (Envy)   159
13 Who's a Pretty Boy Then? Or Beauty Contests, Rationality and Greater
    Fools   **161**
    Background   163
    The Game   163
    The Solution   164
    The Results   165
    A Simple Model of Our Contest   168
    Comparison with Other Experiments   170
    Learning   173
    Conclusions   174

Sin 5: Short Time Horizons and Overtrading (Avarice)   177
14 ADHD, Time Horizons and Underperformance   **179**

Sin 6: Believing Everything You Read (Sloth)   187
15 The Story is The Thing (or The Allure of Growth)   **189**

16 Scepticism is Rare or (Descartes vs Spinoza)   **197**
    Cartesian Systems   199
    Spinozan Systems   199
    Libraries   200
    A Testing Structure   200

The Empirical Evidence   200
Strategies to Counteract Naïve Belief   203

Sin 7:   Group Decisions (Wrath)   207
17 Are Two Heads Better Than One?   **209**
Beating the Biases   215

SECTION IV: INVESTMENT PROCESS AS BEHAVIOURAL DEFENCE   217

18 The Tao of Investing   **219**

PART A: THE BEHAVIORAL INVESTOR   223

19 Come Out of the Closet (or, Show Me the Alpha)   **225**
The Alpha   228
The Evolution of the Mutual Fund Industry   229
Characteristics of the Funds   231
The Average and Aggregate Active Share   231
Persistence and Performance   231
Conclusions   233

20 Strange Brew   **235**
The Long Run   237
Death of Indexing   238
Getting the Long Run Right   238
The Short Run   239
Tactical Asset Allocation   239
Equity Managers   240
Break the Long-Only Constraint   242
Add Breadth   244
Not Just an Excuse for Hedge Funds   245
Truly Alternative Investments   245
Conclusions   246

21 Contrarian or Conformist?   **247**

22 Painting by Numbers: An Ode to Quant   **259**
Neurosis or Psychosis?   261
Brain Damage Detection   262
University Admissions   263
Criminal Recidivism   263
Bordeaux Wine   263
Purchasing Managers   264
Meta-Analysis   264
The Good News   267
So Why Not Quant?   268

23 The Perfect Value Investor   **271**
  Trait I: High Concentration In Portfolios   273
  Trait II: They Don't Need to Know Everything, and Don't Get Caught in the
    Noise   276
  Trait III: A Willingness to Hold Cash   276
  Trait IV: Long Time Horizons   277
  Trait V: An Acceptance of Bad Years   278
  Trait VI: Prepared to Close Funds   278

24 A Blast from the Past   **279**
  The Unheeded Words of Keynes and Graham   281
    On the Separation of Speculation and Investment   281
    On the Nature of Excess Volatility   282
    On the Folly of Forecasting   283
    On the Role of Governance and Agency Problems   284
    On the Importance (and Pain) of Being a Contrarian   285
    On the Flaws of Professional Investors   286
    On the Limits to Arbitrage   286
    On the Importance of the Long Time Horizon   287
    On the Difficulty of Defining Value   288
    On the Need to Understand Price Relative to Value   288
    On Why Behavioural Errors don't Cancel Out   289
    On Diversification   289
    On the Current Juncture   289
    On the Margin of Safety   290
    On Beta   291
    On the Dangers of Overcomplicating   291
    On the Use of History   291

25 Why Not Value? The Behavioural Stumbling Blocks   **293**
  Knowledge ≠ Behaviour   295
  Loss Aversion   296
  Delayed Gratification and Hard-Wiring for the Short Term   297
  Social Pain and the Herding Habit   300
  Poor Stories   301
  Overconfidence   301
  Fun   303
  No, Honestly I Will Be Good   303

PART B: THE EMPIRICAL EVIDENCE: VALUE IN ALL ITS FORMS   **305**

26 Bargain Hunter (or It Offers Me Protection)   **307**
  Written with Rui Antunes
  The Methodology   308
  Does Value Work?   309
  The Anatomy of Value   310
  The Siren of Growth   311
  Growth Doesn't Mean Ignoring Valuation   311

The Disappointing Reality of Growth   313
Analyst Accuracy?   314
Value versus Growth   316
Key points   317
Regional Tables   318
   Global   318
   USA   320
   Europe   323
   Japan   325

27 Better Value (or The Dean Was Right!)   **329**
   Written with Rui Antunes

28 The Little Note that Beats the Market   **337**
   Written with Sebastian Lancetti
The Methodology and the Data   339
The Results   340
   The *Little Book* Works   340
   Value Works   341
   EBIT/EV Better than Simple PE   341
Quality Matters for Value   341
Career Defence as an Investment Strategy   342
What About the Long/Short View?   343
The Future for the *Little Book*   344
Tables and Figures   345
   Regional Results   345

29 Improving Returns Using Inside Information   **355**
Patience is a Virtue   357
Using Inside Information   357
A Hedge Perspective   359
Risk or Mispricing?   359
Evidence for Behavioural Errors   360
Evidence Against the Risk View   361
European Evidence   363
Conclusions   365

30 Just a Little Patience: Part I   **367**

31 Just a Little Patience: Part II   **375**
   Written with Sebastian Lancetti
Value Perspective   377
Growth Perspective   380
Growth and Momentum   381
Value for Growth Investors   382
Value and Momentum   383
Implications   383

32 Sectors, Value and Momentum   **387**
    Value   389
    Momentum   389
    Sectors: Value or Growth   390
    Stocks or Sectors   391

33 Sector-Relative Factors Works Best   **395**
    Written with Andrew Lapthorne
    Methodology   398
    The Results   398
    Conclusion   403

34 Cheap Countries Outperform   **405**
    Strategy by Strategy Information   409

PART C: RISK, BUT NOT AS WE KNOW IT   423

35 CAPM is CRAP (or, The Dead Parrot Lives!)   **425**
    A Brief History of Time   427
    CAPM in Practice   427
    Why Does CAPM Fail?   431
    CAPM Today and Implications   432

36 Risk Managers or Risk Maniacs?   **437**

37 Risk: Finance's Favourite Four-Letter Word   **445**
    The Psychology of Risk   447
    Risk in Performance Measurement   447
    Risk from an Investment Perspective   448

SECTION V: BUBBLES AND BEHAVIOUR   453

38 The Anatomy of a Bubble   **455**
    Displacement   457
    Credit Creation   457
    Euphoria   459
    Critical Stage/Financial Distress   459
    Revulsion   463

39 De-bubbling: Alpha Generation   **469**
    Bubbles in the Laboratory   471
    Bubbles in the Field   472
    Displacement: The Birth of a Boom   473
    Credit Creation: Nurturing the Boom   473
    Euphoria   476
    Critical Stage/Financial Distress   477
    Revulsion   483

Applications   487
   Asset Allocation   487
Alpha Generation   488
   Balance Sheets   489
   Earnings Quality   489
   Capital Expenditure   490
Long-Only Funds   491
Summary   491

40 Running with the Devil: A Cynical Bubble   **493**
The Main Types of Bubble   496
   Rational/Near Rational Bubbles   496
   Intrinsic Bubbles   498
   Fads   499
   Informational Bubbles   499
Psychology of Bubbles   500
Composite Bubbles and the De-Bubbling Process   500
Experimental Evidence: Bubble Echoes   503
Market Dynamics and the Investment Dangers of Near Rational Bubbles   503
Conclusions   505

41 Bubble Echoes: The Empirical Evidence   **507**
Conclusions   516

SECTION VI: INVESTMENT MYTH BUSTERS   519

42 Belief Bias and the Zen Investing   **521**
Belief Bias and the X-System   524
Confidence Isn't a Proxy for Accuracy   528
Belief Bias and the Zen of Investing   528

43 Dividends Do Matter   **529**
Conclusions   540

44 Dividends, Repurchases, Earnings and the Coming Slowdown   **541**

45 Return of the Robber Barons   **549**

46 The Purgatory of Low Returns   **563**

47 How Important is the Cycle?   **573**

48 Have We Really Learnt So Little?   **581**

49 Some Random Musings on Alternative Assets   **587**
Hedge Funds   589

Commodities   590
Which Index?   590
Composition of Commodity Futures Returns   591
The Times They are A-Changin'   591
Conclusions   595

SECTION VII: CORPORATE GOVERNANCE AND ETHICS   597

50 Abu Ghraib: Lesson from Behavioural Finance and for Corporate
    Governance   599
    Fundamental Attribution Error   601
    Zimbardo's Prison Experiment   602
    Milgram: The Man that Shocked the World   604
    Conditions that Turn Good People Bad   608
    Conclusions   609

51 Doing the Right Thing or the Psychology of Ethics   611
    The Ethical Blindspot   613
    The Origins of Moral Judgements   614
    Examples of Bounded Ethicality and Unconscious Biases   617
        Implicit Attitudes (Unconscious Prejudices)   617
        In-Group Bias (Bias that Favours Your Own Group)   619
        Overclaiming Credit (Bias that Favours You)   620
        Conflicts of Interest (Bias that Favours Those Who Can Pay You) 621
    Mechanisms Driving Poor Ethical Behaviour   627
        Language Euphemisms   628
        Slippery Slope   628
        Errors in Perceptual Causation   628
        Constraints Induced by Representations of the Self   629
    Combating Unethical Behaviour   629

52 Unintended Consequences and Choking under Pressure: The Psychology of
    Incentives   631
    Evidence from the Laboratory   635
    Evidence from the Field   638
        Child Care Centres   638
        Blood Donations   638
        Football Penalty Kicks   639
        Basketball Players   640
    Back to the Laboratory   640
    Who is Likely to Crack Under Pressure?   641
    Conclusions   643

SECTION VIII: HAPPINESS   645

53 If It Makes You Happy   647
    Top 10   653

54 Materialism and the Pursuit of Happiness   **655**
   Aspiration Index   657
   Materialism and Happiness: The Evidence   658
   Problems of Materialism   660
   What to Do?   660
   Why Experiences Over Possessions?   663
   Conclusions   665

References   **667**

Index   **677**

Preface

This book represents the first six years of an ongoing research project. The aim of this project was to truly understand the psychology of finance and investing and explore its implications for practitioners. There can be little doubt that behavioural finance has never been more popular among professional investors. Certainly, if my diary is any guideline, the subject is still in much demand. The chart below shows the number of times in a rolling 12-month period the words behavioural (or behavioral) finance appear in the press.

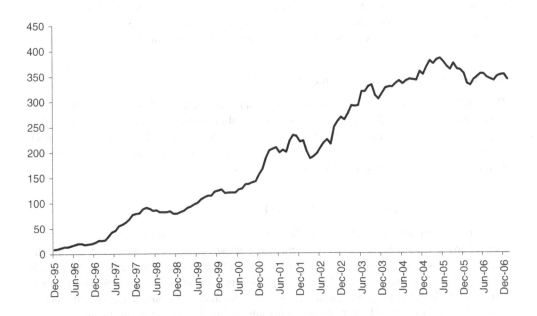

I reached the conclusion that I was a natural pessimist while looking at this chart, as the first thing that entered my mind was – it's a bubble. An optimist would presumably conclude that it was a growth industry! I certainly hope the latter interpretation holds true.

My first book on the subject (*Behavioural Finance*, Wiley, 2002) was really the result of a series of lectures I had given to students. This book draws together research written for a professional audience whose time for reading research is highly limited. For this reason each chapter is written to 'stand alone' to allow the reader to dip in and out at will. Each chapter also aims to deal with a practical issue of relevance to the professional investor. However, despite the independent nature of the chapters, I have chosen to group them together into themes, representing the seven major thrusts of my ongoing research project.

I   Common Mistakes and Basic Biases

The title here gives the gist. In many ways one of the most powerful insights offered by the literature on judgement and decision making is that we are all prone to the potential pitfalls that psychologists have spent years documenting. Indeed, when I give a lecture to professional investors, those who probably get the most out of the talk are those who identify themselves as the perpetrators of behavioural mistakes. The chapters in this section aim to explore some of the most common biases, and suggest some simple ways in which we might be able to mitigate our susceptibility.

II   The Professionals and the Biases

Among some there is a view that the individual investor is the source of all behavioural mispricing. However, I suspect this is far from true. Indeed there are now a number of papers (such as Jackson, Glushkov) that argue convincingly that the professionals may well be the noise traders. The aim of this section is to demonstrate that professional investors are just as likely to suffer behavioural biases as the rest of us. Indeed, in as much as they are experts in their field, they may well be even more overconfident and overoptimistic than lay people.

III   The Seven Sins of Fund Management

The aim of this section was to examine a typical large institutional fund management organization and assess its vulnerabilities to psychological critique. The first step on the road to reform is to be able to identify the areas of weakness in the current structure. Issues such as an overreliance on forecasting, the illusion of trading, wasting time meeting company managements, and the dangers of overtrading are covered here.

IV   An Investment Process as a Behaviour Defence

If the previous section represented a long list of don'ts, then this section is an attempt to provide a list of dos. It is concerned with investment philosophy/process. Since we cannot control the return on an investment (much as we would like to be able to do), then the best we can do is create a process that makes sense. Here we explore contrarian strategies and value investing as a framework for mitigating behavioural biases. As I am also an empirical sceptic, this section contains many empirical chapters based on demonstrating the principles discussed.

V   Bubbles and Behaviour

Of all the areas of behavioural finance none captures the public's imagination like bubbles. This section explores a paradigm for analysing and assessing bubbles and their paths. It is a good demonstration of the constancy of human behaviour. Every bubble in history has been slightly different, but the underlying characteristics and processes are amazingly similar.

VI Investment Myth Busters

A popular TV show concerned two 'mad' scientists who loved nothing more than to explode urban myths. This section represents my attempt to do something similar in finance. We have a bad habit of accepting theories as fact within finance, and of accepting statements as if they were truths. The chapters here try to expose some of the believable but incorrect beliefs that many investors seem to share.

VII Corporate Governance and Ethics

We often interpret other actions as evidence of their underlying nature. However, when people find themselves in a situation, we fail to understand the impact that has on their behaviour. So, rather than bad apples it is more often than not bad barrels, and the chapters here explore how social psychological insights can improve our understanding of corporate governance. We also explore one of economics' most cherished beliefs – that incentives work – from a psychological perspective, and the results are intriguing, suggesting that optimal incentives are more difficult to design than many economists would have us believe.

VIII Happiness

This section deals with two of the most popular and most controversial notes I have written. They tackle the heresy of money not equalling happiness, which is clearly anathema to many who work in finance. These chapters explore the issue of what makes us happy, and what we can do to increase our level of happiness. These may seem like unusual topics for a researcher employed by an investment bank, but they were borne out of a belief that some of the most miserable people in the world seem to work in the field of finance.

Only you as reader will be able to judge how well I have achieved my aim of applying behavioural finance. Your comments and feedback would be most welcome and I can be contacted via my e-mail address: James.Montier@Googlemail.com

Acknowledgments

I am never sure who reads acknowledgements. Notwithstanding, there are several people to whom I owe a debt of gratitude. Firstly, my friend and colleague Albert Edwards. It was Albert who had the foresight to see that behavioural finance would be of interest to professional investors, and was prepared to support me in pushing the boundaries of what might be regarded as acceptable research. He also read most of the papers contained herein, and provided many useful suggestions to improve them, and challenge me.

Next, I must thank my co-authors on numerous of the empirical chapters in Section IV, Rui Antunes and Sebastian Lancetti of the Dresdner Kleinwort Quant team. Both gentlemen have more skill at dealing with data and quant models in their little finger than I have in my entire being. They both helped to take my ideas and turn them into raw hard numbers, to satisfy even the most demanding of empirical sceptics.

The head of the Quant team, Andrew Lapthorne, not only graciously allowed me to publish one of his papers (as Chapter 33) but also read almost every paper in the collection and commented on all of them. Andy has been a great sounding board for my ideas over the years, and I thank him very much.

Kathy Alexandrou deserves special mention. She is responsible for taking my work and turning it into the notes that Dresdner Kleinwort clients have been reading. She is a true wizard of turning charts into works of art, and keeping me on track with my notes.

I am also grateful to the research management at Dresdner Kleinwort who have allowed me to publish research that I believe no other bank would have permitted. They also very kindly allowed me to reproduce the notes you will read between these covers.

Amanda Keogan, Jane Atterbury and Cally Smith deserve applause for managing to get me everywhere on time, and back again. At one time or another all these ladies have had the responsibility for looking after my travel and diary. They have all done a sterling job, and I thank them all.

The many academics who provided the papers (both from finance and psychology) that are quoted within these pages also merit a huge thank you. Without their work this book would not have been possible. As Newton said: "If I have seen further it is by standing on the shoulders of giants."

Jenny Ward of the Dresdner Kleinwort EMIS team has managed to unearth a large number of weird and wonderful papers that I have requested over the years, and I thanks her for all her help.

Also, a huge thank you to all the clients who have expressed their interest in my work over the last six years. Without your support I am under no illusion that I would have been dispensed with years ago. It is your interest in behavioural finance that has kept me employed. Long may it continue!

On a personal note, I would also like to thank my friends and family. They have to put up with me dashing off to scribble down notes and ideas at the oddest of times. A special thanks goes to my parents and my nana for their unconditional love, and to Wendy who encouraged me to write this book and put up with me while I did so. She also read many of the chapters, corrected my English, and questioned me thoroughly. Thanks babes, couldn't have done it without you.

To anyone I have forgotten to mention, my apologies and thanks. All errors and omissions remain the sole responsibility of the author.

SECTION I

Common Mistakes and Basic Biases

1
Emotion, Neuroscience and Investing: Investors as Dopamine Addicts*

> **Understanding what happens in our brain when we make decisions may help us to learn to overcome some of the mistakes we make. Emotions are key. Our ability to exercise self-control over such impulses is limited and decreases with use! Too often we succumb to our hard-wired tendencies to focus on the short term and herd.**

- Emotional decision-making is the default option for our brains. However, we all like to think that we only use logic to arrive at our decisions. In fact without emotion we would be largely incapable of making any decisions, but all too often we allow emotion to rule unchecked. Welcome to the human condition!

- Neuroscientists have recently uncovered two particular traits of significance to investors. The first is that we are hard-wired for the short term. We tend to find the chance of short-term gains very attractive. They appear to stimulate the emotional centres of the brain, and release dopamine. This makes us feel confident, stimulated, and generally good about ourselves.

- The second is that we appear to be hard-wired to herd. The pain of social exclusion (i.e. betting against everyone else) is felt in exactly the same parts of the brain that feel real physical pain. So pursuing contrarian strategies is a little bit like having your arm broken on a regular basis!

- Self-control over these impulses is very hard. Psychologists have found that self-control is a limited resource. The more we use it, the less we have left to deal with the next occasion when self-control is required.

- The good news is that we continue to make brain cells pretty much throughout our lives. And our brains aren't fixed forever, we can rearrange the neurons (a process called plasticity). We aren't doomed, we can learn, but it isn't easy!

---

*This article appeared in *Global Equity Strategy* on 20 January 2005. The material discussed was accurate at the time of publication.

What goes on inside our heads when we make decisions? Understanding how our brains work is vital to understanding the decisions we take. Neuroeconomics is a very new field that combines psychology, economics and neuroscience. That may sound like the unholy trinity as far as many readers are concerned, but the insights that this field is generating are powerful indeed.

Before I head off into the realms of neuroscience I should recap some themes we have explored before that provide the backdrop for much of the discussion that follows. One of the most exciting developments in cognitive psychology over recent years has been the development of dual process theories of thought. All right, stay with me now, I know that sounds dreadful, but it isn't. It is really a way of saying that we tend to have two different ways of thinking embedded in our minds.

SPOCK OR McCOY?

For the Trekkies out there, these two systems can, perhaps, be characterized as Dr McCoy and Mr Spock. McCoy was irrepressibly human, forever allowing his emotions to rule the day. In contrast, Spock (half human, half Vulcan) was determined to suppress his emotions, letting logic drive his decisions.

McCoy's approach would seem to be founded in system X. System X is essentially the emotional part of the brain. It is automatic and effortless in the way that it processes information – that is to say, the X-system pre-screens information before we are consciously aware that it even made an impact on our minds. Hence, the X-system is effectively the default option. The X-system deals with information in an associative way, and its judgements tend to be based on similarity (of appearance) and closeness in time. Because of the way the X-system deals with information it can handle vast amounts of data simultaneously. To computer nerds it is a rapid parallel processing unit. In order for the X-system to believe that something is valid, it may simply need to wish that it were so.

System C is the "Vulcan" part of the brain. To use it requires deliberate effort. It is logical and deductive in the way in which it handles information. Because it is logical, it can only follow one step at a time, and hence in computing terms it is a slow serial processing unit. In order to convince the C-system that something is true, logical argument and empirical evidence will be required, and Table 1.1 provides a summary of the main differences between the two systems.

This dual system approach to the way the mind works has received support from very recent studies by neuroscientists who have begun to attach certain parts of the brain to certain functions. In order to do this, neuroscientists ask experiment participants to perform tasks while their brains are being monitored via electroencephalograms (EEG), positron emission topography (PET) or, most often of late, functional magnetic resonance imaging (fMRI). The outcomes are then compared to base cases and the differences between the scans highlight the areas of the brain that are being utilized.

Table 1.2 lays out some of the major neural correlates for the two systems of thinking that we have outlined in Table 1.1. There is one very important thing to note about these groupings: the X system components are much older in terms of human development. They evolved a long time before the C-system correlates.

THE PRIMACY OF EMOTION

This evolutionary age helps to explain why the X system is the default option for information processing. We needed emotions far before we needed logic. This is perhaps best explained

Table 1.1   Two systems of reasoning

System One/X-system/Reflexive/Intuitive	System Two/C-system/Reflective
Holistic	Analytic
Affective (what feels good)	Logical?
Associative – judgements based on similarity and temporal contiguity	Deductive
Rapid parallel processing	Slow, serial processing
Concrete images	Abstract images
Slower to change	Changes with speed of thought
Crudely differentiated – broad generalization	More highly differentiated
Crudely integrated – context-specific processing	More highly integrated – cross context processing
Experienced passively and preconsciously	Experienced actively and consciously
Automatic and effortless	Controlled and effortful
Self-evidently valid: "Experiencing is believing" or perhaps wishing is believing	Requires justification via logic and evidence

Source: Modified from Epstein (1991).

Table 1.2   Neural correlates of the two reasoning systems

X-system	C-system
Amygdala	Anterior cingulate cortex
Basal ganglia	Prefrontal cortex
Lateral temporal cortex	Medial temporal lobe

Source: DrKW Macro research.

by an example using fear, which is one of the better understood emotions.[1] Fear seems to be served by two neural pathways. One fast and dirty (LeDoux's low road), the other more reflective and logical (the high road), and the links to the two systems of thinking outlined above are hopefully obvious.

Imagine standing in front of a glass vessel that contains a snake. The snake rears up, the danger is perceived, and the sensory thalamus processes the information. From here two signals emerge. On the low road the signal is sent to the amygdala, part of the X system,[2] and the brain's centre for fear and risk. The amygdala reacts quickly, and forces you to jump back.

However, the second signal (taking the high road) sends the information to the sensory cortex, which, in a more conscious fashion, assesses the possible threat. This is the system that points out that there is a layer of glass between you and the snake. However, from a survival viewpoint, a false positive is a far better response than a false negative!

Emotions: Body or Brain?

Most people tend to think that emotions are the conscious response to events or actions. That is, something happens and your brain works out the emotional response – be it sadness, anger,

---

[1] Largely thanks to the work of Joseph LeDoux, see his wonderful book the *Emotional Brain* (1996) for details.
[2] Also know as the limbic system.

happiness, etc. Then your brain tells your body how to react – tear up, pump blood, increase the breathing rate, etc.

William James, the grandfather of modern psychology, was among the first to posit that actually true causality may well flow from the body to the brain. In James's view of the world, the brain assesses the situation so quickly that there simply isn't time for us to become consciously aware of how we should feel. Instead the brain surveys the body, takes the results (i.e. skin sweating, increased heart beat, etc.) then infers the emotion that matches the physical signals the body has generated.

If you want to try this yourself, try pulling the face that matches the emotion you wish to experience. For instance, try smiling (see, we aren't always miserable and bearish despite our reputations). If you sit with a smile on your face, concentrating on that smile, then very soon you are likely to start to feel the positive emotions that one associates with smiling.[3]

An entertaining example of the body's impact upon decisions is provided by Epley and Gilovich (2001). They asked people to evaluate headphones. While conducting the evaluation, participants were asked to either nod or shake their heads. Those who were asked to nod their heads during the evaluation gave much more favourable ratings than those who were asked to shake their heads.

In the words of Gilbert and Gill (2000), we are momentary realists. That is to say, we have a tendency to trust our initial emotional reaction and correct that initial view "only subsequently, occasionally and effortfully". For instance, when we stub a toe on a rock or bang our head on a beam (an easy thing to do in my house), we curse the inanimate object despite the fact it could not possibly have done anything to avoid our own mistake.

Emotions: Good, Bad or Both?

However, emotions may be needed in order to allow us to actually make decisions. There are a group of people who, through tragic accidents or radical surgery, have had the emotional areas of their minds damaged. These individuals did not become the walking optimizers known as *homo economicus*. Rather, in many cases, these individuals are now actually incapable of making decisions. They make endless plans but never get round to implementing any of them.[4]

Bechara *et al.* (1997) devised an experiment to show how the lack of emotion in such individuals can lead them to make suboptimal decisions. They played a gambling game with both controls (players without damage to the emotional centres of the brain) and patients (those with damage to the emotional parts of the brain). Each player was seated in front of four packs of cards (A, B, C and D). Players were given a loan of $2,000 and told that the object of the game was to avoid losing the loan, while trying to make as much extra money as possible. They were also told that turning cards from each of the packs would generate gains and occasional losses. The players were told of the impact of each card after each turn, but no running score was given.

Turning cards from packs A and B paid $100, while those from C and D paid only $50. Unpredictably, the turning of some cards carried a penalty. Consistently playing packs A and B led to an overall loss, while playing C and D led to an overall gain.

---

[3] For more on this see Paul Ekman's *Emotions Revealed* (2003). It is also worth noting that some developmental psychologists have designed programs to teach children to recognize the physical signs of emotions (such as anger) and then use thought to control those emotions. See Mark Greenberg's work on PATHS (www.prevention.psu.edu/projects/PATHScurriculum.htm). Much of the work has focused on teaching children to constrain their anger – a modern-day equivalent of counting to 10.

[4] For more on this see Damasio (1994).

Table 1.3   Progress over the game

	Number of rounds		Percentage	
	Controls	Patients	Controls	Patients
Pre-punishment	0–10	0–10	100	100
Pre-hunch	10–50	9–80	100	100
Hunch	50–80	–	100	–
Conceptual	80+	80+	70	50

Source: Bechara *et al.* (1997).

Performance was assessed at various stages of the game. Four different periods were identified. The first involved no loss in either pack (pre-punishment); the second phase was when players reported they had no idea about the game, and no feeling about the packs; the third was found only in the controls, who started to say they had a hunch about packs A and B being riskier; and finally, the last phase, when (conceptual) players could articulate that A and B were riskier.

Table 1.3 shows the average number of rounds in each phase, and the percentage of players making it through each phase of the game. The patients were unable to form hunches, and far fewer survived the game.

Now cast your eye over Figures 1.1 and 1.2. Figure 1.1 shows the number of cards drawn from packs A and B (bad) and C and D (good) in each phase by the controls. In the pre-hunch phase they are already favouring the good packs marginally. In the hunch phase, controls are clearly favouring the good packs.

Now look at the performance of the patients in Figure 1.2. In the pre-hunch phase they continually chose the bad packs. As noted above, there was no hunch phase. And perhaps most bizarrely of all, even when they had articulated that packs A and B were a bad idea, they still picked more cards from those decks than from C and D! So despite "knowing" the correct

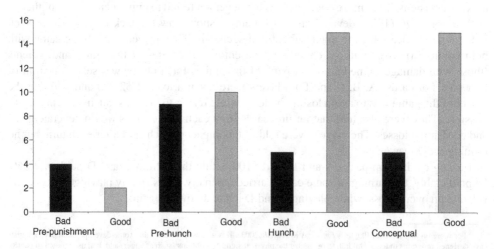

Figure 1.1   Average number of cards drawn from bad and good packs: The controls.
Source: Bechara *et al.* (1997).

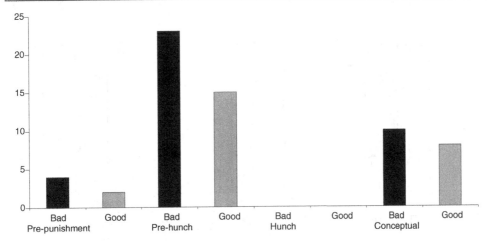

Figure 1.2   Average number of cards drawn from bad and good packs: The patients.
Source: Bechara *et al.* (1997).

conceptual answer, the lack of ability to feel emotion severely hampered the performance of these individuals.

However, similar games can be used to show that emotions can also help us. Bechara *et al.* (2004) played an investment game. Each player was given $20. They had to make a decision each round of the game: invest $1 or not invest. If the decision was not to invest, the task advanced to the next round. If the decision was to invest, players would hand over $1 to the experimenter. The experimenter would then toss a coin in full view of the player. If the outcome was a head, the player lost the dollar, if the coin landed tail up then $2.50 was added to the player's account. The task would then move to the next round. Overall 20 rounds were played.

Bechara *et al.* played this game with three different groups: normals, a group of players with damage to the neural circuitry associated with fear[5] (target patients who can no longer feel fear), and a group of players with other lesions to the brain unassociated with the neural fear circuitry (patient controls).

The experimenters uncovered that the players with damage to the fear circuitry invested in 83.7% of rounds, the normals invested in 62.7% of rounds, and the patient controls in 60.7% of rounds. Was this result attributable to the brain's handling of loss and fear? Figure 1.3 shows a breakdown of the results, based on the result in the previous round. It shows the proportions of groups that invested. It clearly demonstrates that normals and patient controls were more likely to shrink away from risk-taking, both when they had lost in the previous round and when they won!

Players with damaged fear circuitry invested in 85.2% of rounds following losses on previous rounds, while normal players invested in only 46.9% of rounds following such losses.

Bechara *et al.* also found evidence of just how difficult learning actually is. Instead of becoming more optimal as time moves on, normal players actually become less optimal! (See Figure 1.4.) For the record, a rational player would, of course, play in all rounds.

---

[5] Technically speaking this group had suffered lesions to the amygdala, orbitofrontal cortex and insular/somatosensory cortex – all parts of the X-system.

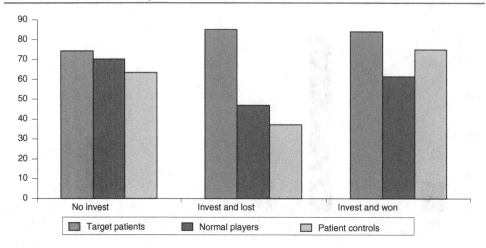

Figure 1.3   Percentage of players investing divided into the outcomes from the previous round. *Source:* Bechara *et al.* (2004).

Emotion, therefore, can both help and hinder us. Without emotion we are unable to sense risk, but with emotion we can't control the fear that risk generates! Welcome again to the human condition!

Camerer *et al.* (2004) argue that the influence of emotions depends upon the intensity of the experience. They note

> At low level of intensity, affect appears to play a largely 'advisory' role. A number of theories posit that emotions carry information that people use as an input into the decisions they face...
>
> ...At intermediate level of intensity, people begin to become conscious of conflicts between cognitive and affective inputs. It is at such intermediate levels of intensity that one observes ... efforts at self-control...

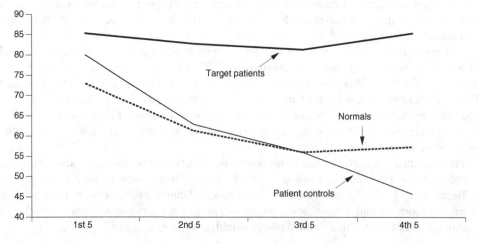

Figure 1.4   Percentage of players investing by groups of rounds. *Source:* Bechara *et al.* (2004).

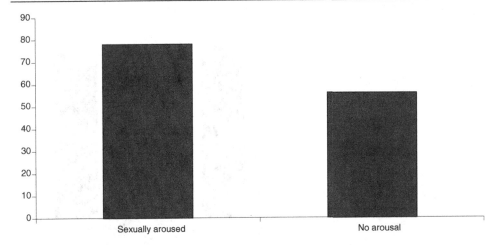

Figure 1.5 Probability of forceful behaviour by arousal state.
Source: Loewenstein *et al.* (1997).

...Finally, at even greater levels of intensity, affect can be so powerful as to virtually preclude decision-making. No one 'decides' to fall asleep at the wheel, but many people do. Under the influence of intense affective motivation, people often report themselves as being 'out of control' ... As Rita Carter writes in *Mapping the Mind*, 'where thought conflicts with emotion, the latter is designed by neural circuitry in our brains to win'.

Camerer et al. (2004)

It is also worth noting that we are very bad at projecting how we will feel under the influence of emotion – a characteristic that psychologists call 'hot-cold empathy gaps'. That is to say, when we are relaxed and emotion free, we underestimate how we would act under the influence of emotion.

For instance, Loewenstein *et al.* (1997) asked a group of male students to say how likely they were to act in a sexually aggressive manner in both a hot and a cold environment. The scenario they were given concerned coming home with a girl they had picked up at a bar, having been told by friends that she had a reputation for being 'easy'. The story went on that the participants and the girl were beginning to get into physical genital contact on the sofa. The participants were then told they had started to try to remove the girl's clothes, and she said she wasn't interested in having sex.

Participants were then asked to assign probabilities to whether they would (1) coax the girl to remove her clothes, or (2) have sex with her even after her protests. Figure 1.5 shows the self-reported probability of sexual aggressiveness (defined as the sum of the probabilities of 1+2). Under the 'no arousal' condition there was an average 56% probability of sexual aggression. After having been shown sexually arousing photos, the average probability of aggression rose to nearly 80%!

SELF-CONTROL IS LIKE A MUSCLE

Unfortunately a vast array of psychological research (Muraven and Baumeister, 2000; Baumeister, 2003) suggests that our ability to use self-control to force our cognitive pro-

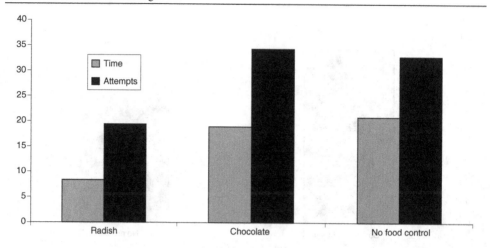

Figure 1.6 Self-control is a draining experience.
Source: Muraven and Baumeister (2000).

cess to override our emotional reaction is limited. Each effort at self-control reduces the amount available for subsequent self-control efforts.

A classic example of Baumeister's work concerns the following experiment. Participants are asked to avoid eating food for three hours before the experiment began (timed to force them to skip lunch). When they arrived they were put into one of three groups.

The first group were taken into a room in which cookies had recently been baked, so the aroma of freshly made chocolate chip delights wafted around. This room also contained a tray laid out with the freshly baked cookies and other chocolate delights, and a tray full of radishes. This group were told they should eat as many radishes as they could in the next five minutes, but they were also told they weren't allowed to touch the cookies. A second group was taken to a similar room with the same two trays, but told they could eat the cookies. The third group was taken to an empty room.

All the food was then removed and the individuals were given problems to solve. These problems took the form of tracing geometric shapes without retracing lines or lifting the pen from the paper. The problems were, sadly, unsolvable. However, the amount of time before participants gave up and the number of attempts made before they gave up were both recorded.

The results were dramatic (see Figure 1.6). Those who had eaten the radishes (and had therefore expended large amounts of self-control in resisting the cookies) gave up in less than half the time that those who had eaten chocolate or eaten nothing had done. They also had far less attempts at solving the problems before giving up.

Baumeister (2003) concludes the survey by highlighting the key findings of their research:

1. Under emotional distress, people shift toward favoring high-risk, high-payoff options, even if these are objectively poor choices. This appears based on a failure to think things through, caused by emotional distress.
2. When self-esteem is threatened, people become upset and lose their capacity to regulate themselves. In particular, people who hold a high opinion of themselves often get quite upset in response to a blow to pride, and the rush to prove something great about themselves overrides their normal rational way of dealing with life.

3. Self-regulation is required for many forms of self-interest behavior. When self-regulation fails, people may become self-defeating in various ways, such as taking immediate pleasures instead of delayed rewards. Self-regulation appears to depend on limited resources that operate like strength or energy, and so people can only regulate themselves to a limited extent.

4. Making choices and decisions depletes this same resource. Once the resource is depleted, such as after making a series of important decisions, the self becomes tired and depleted, and its subsequent decisions may well be costly or foolish.

5. The need to belong is a central feature of human motivation, and when this need is thwarted such as by interpersonal rejection, the human being somehow ceases to function properly. Irrational and self-defeating acts become more common in the wake of rejection.

When I read this list it struck me just how many of these factors could influence investors. Imagine a fund manager who has just had a noticeable period of underperformance. He is likely to feel under pressure to start to focus on high-risk, high-payoff options to make up the performance deficit. He is also likely to feel his self-esteem is under threat as outlined in 2 above. He is also likely to begin to become increasingly myopic, focusing more and more on the short term. All of this is likely to be particularly pronounced if the position run resulting in the underperformance is a contrarian one. Effectively, most of the elements that lead to the psychology of irrationality are likely to be present in large quantities.

HARD-WIRED FOR THE SHORT TERM

Having explored the role of emotions and our ability to moderate their influence, it is now time to turn to some examples of how powerful neuroscience can be in helping us to understand investor behaviour.

The first example suggests that we may be hard-wired to focus on the short term. Economists are all brought up to treasure the concept of utility[6] – the mental reward or pleasure experienced. Traditionally, economists view money as having no direct utility; rather it is held to have indirect utility, that is, it can be used to purchase other goods and services, which do provide direct utility.

Neuroscientists have found that money actually does have 'utility', or at least the brain anticipates receiving money in the same way that other rewards are felt, such as enjoying food or pleasure-inducing drugs (Knutson and Peterson, 2004).

The trouble is that the reward system for the brain has strong links to the X-system. The anticipation of reward leads to the release of dopamine. Dopamine makes people feel good about themselves, confident and stimulated.

Cocaine works by blocking the dopamine receptors in the brain, so the brain cannot absorb the dopamine, and hence nullify its effects. Because the brain cannot absorb the dopamine, it triggers further releases of the drug. So when one takes coke, the dopamine release is increased, taking the user to a high. Neuroscientists have found that the larger the anticipated reward the more dopamine is released.

McClure et al. (2004) have recently investigated the neural systems that underlie decisions about delayed gratification. Much research has suggested that people tend to behave impatiently today but plan to act patiently in the future. For instance, when offered a choice between £10 today and £11 tomorrow, many people choose the immediate option.

---

[6] In fact phychologists have recently argued that there is no single utility. Instead we have experienced utility (actual liking from an outcome), remembered utility (memory of liking), predicted utility (expected liking for the outcome in the future) and decision utility (the actual choice of outcome).

However, if asked today to choose between £10 in a year, and £11 in a year and a day, many people who went for the 'immediate' option in the first case now go for the second option.

In order to see what happens in the brain when faced with such choices, McClure *et al.* measured the brain activity of participants as they made a series of intertemporal choices between early and delayed monetary rewards (like the one above). Some of the choice pairs included an immediate option, others were choices between two delayed options. The results they uncovered are intriguing.

When the choice pair involved an immediate gain, the ventral stratum (part of the basal ganglia), the medial orbitofrontal cortex, and the medial prefrontal cortex were all disproportionately used. All these elements are associated with the X-system. McClure *et al.* also point out that these areas are riddled by the midbrain dopamine system. They note, 'These structures have consistently been implicated in impulsive behaviour, and drug addiction is commonly thought to involve disturbances of dopaminergic neurotransmission in these systems.' Since money is a reward, the offer of money today causes a surge in dopamine that people find very hard to resist.

When the choice involved two delayed rewards, the prefrontal and parietal cortex were engaged (correlates of the C-system). The more difficult the choice, the more these areas seemed to be used. Given the analysis of the limits to self-control that was outlined above, perhaps we should not hold out too much hope for our ability to correct the urges triggered by the X-system. All too often, it looks as if we are likely to end up being hard-wired for the short term.

Keynes was sadly right when he wrote, "Investment based on genuine long-term expectation is so difficult to-day as to be scarcely practicable."

HARD-WIRED TO HERD

In the past, we have mentioned that there is strong evidence from neuroscience to suggest that real pain and social pain are felt in exactly the same places in the brain. Eisenberger and Lieberman (2004) asked participants to play a computer game. Players think they are playing in a three-way game with two other players, throwing a ball back and forth.

In fact, the two other players are computer controlled. After a period of three-way play, the two other 'players' began to exclude the participant by throwing the ball back and forth between themselves. This social exclusion generates brain activity in the anterior cingulate cortex and the insula, both of which are also activated by real physical pain.

Contrarian strategies are the investment equivalent of seeking out social pain. In order to implement such a strategy you will buy the things that everyone else is selling, and sell the stocks that everyone else is buying. This is social pain. Eisenberger and Lieberman's results suggest that following such a strategy is really like having your arm broken on a regular basis – not fun!

> To buy when others are despondently selling and sell when others are greedily buying requires the greatest fortitude and pays the greatest reward
>
> Sir John Templeton

> It is the long-term investor, he who most promotes the public interest, who will in practice come in for the most criticism... For it is in the essence of his behaviour that he should be eccentric, unconventional and rash in the eyes of average opinion
>
> John Maynard Keynes

PLASTICITY AS SALVATION

All of this may make for fairly depressing reading. With emotions we cannot control ourselves, and without them we cannot make decisions. We appear to be doomed to chase short-term rewards and run with the herd. When we try to resist these temptations we suffer subsequent declines in our ability to exercise self-control. Not a pretty picture.

However, all is not lost. For many years it was thought that the number of brain cells was fixed and that they decayed over time. The good news is that this isn't the case. We are capable of generating new brain cells over most of our lifetime.

In addition, the brain isn't fixed into a certain format. The easiest way of thinking about this is to imagine the brain as a cobweb. Some strands of that cobweb are thicker than others. The more the brain uses a certain pathway, the thicker the strand becomes. The thicker the strand, the more the brain will tend to use that path. So if we get into bad mental habits, they can become persistent.

However, we are also capable of rearranging those pathways (neurons). This is how the brain learns. It is properly called plasticity. We aren't doomed, we can learn, but it isn't easy!

2

Part Man, Part Monkey

Leaving the trees could have been our first mistake. Our minds are suited for solving problems related to survival, rather than being optimized for investment decisions. The result of our inheritance is that we are all capable of making mistakes. The list below provides a list of maxims to remember in order to avoid the most common investment pitfalls.

- These biases apply to me, you and everyone else as well.
- Be less certain in your views, especially if they are forecasts.
- You know less than you think you do.
- Try to focus on the facts, not the stories.
- More information isn't better information.
- Listen to those who disagree with you.
- Examine your mistakes, failures aren't just bad luck.
- You didn't know it all along, you just think you did.
- Judge things by how statistically likely they are, not how they appear.
- Big, vivid, easy to recall events are less likely than you think they are.
- Don't confuse good firms with good investments or good earnings growth with good returns.
- Use reverse-engineered models to avoid anchoring on the market prices.
- Don't take information at face value; think carefully about how it was presented to you.
- Sell your losers and ride your winners.

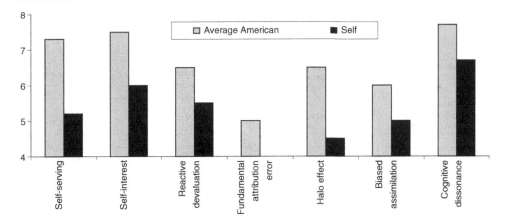

Figure 2.1 The self vs others' susceptibility to biases.
Source: Adapted from Pronin *et al.* (2002).

Perhaps the first step down this path is becoming aware of the fact that we are all likely to suffer from what psychologists call *heuristics* and *biases*. Heuristics are just rules of thumb that allow us to deal with informational deluge. In many cases they work well, but sometimes they lead us far stray from rational decision-making.

Of course, we all like to think that we are immune to the influences of biases. But the reality is, of course, that we are all likely to suffer some of these mental errors on some occasions. For instance, Pronin *et al.* (2002) asked people to rate on a 9-point scale (with 5 being 'somewhat') how likely the average American was to suffer a particular bias, and how likely they were to suffer the same biases. A booklet describing the biases was provided. Figure 2.1 shows the results. In all cases, people rated themselves less likely to suffer a given bias than average. Across the biases, the average score for the average American was 6.75. For those taking part, the average score was 5.31. All the differences were statistically significant. Pronin *et al.* refer to this as the *bias blind spot*.

THE BIASES WE FACE

Psychologists have spent years documenting and cataloging the types of errors to which we are prone. The main results are surprisingly universal across cultures and countries.

Hirschleifer (2001) suggests that most of these mistakes can be traced to four common causes: self-deception, heuristic simplification, emotion, and social interaction. Figure 2.2 tries to classify the major biases along these lines. It outlines the most common of the various biases that have been found, and also tries to highlight those with direct implications for investment.

This may look like a mass of mistakes, and indeed it is; however, for the purposes of exposition, let's focus on the 10 most important biases that we come across.

BIAS #1: I KNOW BETTER, BECAUSE I KNOW MORE

Let me start by asking you three questions. Firstly, are you an above-average driver? Secondly, are you above average at your job? Thirdly, are you above average as a lover?

A taxonomy of biases

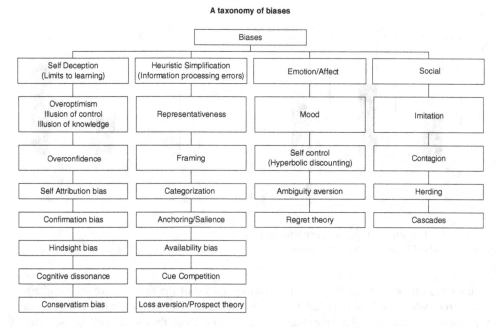

Figure 2.2   Taxonomy of biases.

So far in the countless times that I have conducted those questions I have only had one person answer that he is a below-average lover. For the record, he is one of my colleagues, and obviously desperately needs help! Now, why am I asking you these very strange questions? Well, they go to the heart of the two most common biases that we come across – *overoptimism* and *overconfidence*. Overoptimism and overconfidence tend to stem from the illusion of control and the illusion of knowledge.

The Illusion of Knowledge: More Information Isn't Better Information

The illusion of knowledge is the tendency for people to believe that the accuracy of their forecasts increases with more information. So dangerous is this misconception that Daniel Boorstin opined: 'The greatest obstacle to discovery is not ignorance – it is the illusion of knowledge.' The simple truth is that more information is not necessarily better information; it is what you do with it, rather than how much you have, that matters.

Nowhere is this better shown than in a classic study by Paul Slovic (1973). Eight experienced bookmakers were shown a list of 88 variables found on a typical past performance chart on a horse (e.g. the weight to be carried, the number of races won, the performance in different conditions, etc.). Each bookmaker was then asked to rank the pieces of information by importance.

Having done this, the bookmakers were then given data for 40 past races and asked to rank the top five horses in each race. Each bookmaker was given the past data in increments of the 5, 10, 20, and 40 variables that the bookmaker had selected as being most important. Hence, each bookmaker predicted the outcome of each race four times – once for each of the information sets. For each prediction, the bookmakers were asked to give a degree of confidence ranking in their forecast.

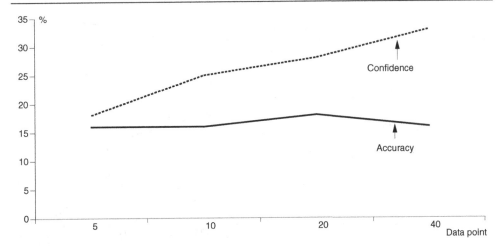

Figure 2.3   Accuracy vs confidence for bookmakers as a function of the information set.
Source: Slovic (1973).

Figure 2.3 shows how both accuracy and confidence change as the information set grows over time. Accuracy is mainly a flat line regardless of the amount of information the bookmakers had at their disposal!

However, look what happened to the bookmakers' confidence. It soared as the information set increased. With five pieces of information, accuracy and confidence were quite closely related. However, by the time 40 pieces of information were being used, accuracy was still around 15%, but confidence has soared to more than 30%! So more information isn't better information; it is what you do with it that truly matters.

That fact doesn't stop the vast majority of investors desperately trying to accumulate more information than their rivals. The evidence suggests that, just like bookmakers, professional investors are generally much too confident.

Professionals Worse than Chance!

Figure 2.4 is based on a study by Torngren and Montgomery (2004). Participants were asked to select the stock they thought would do best each month from a pair of stocks. All the stocks were well-known blue-chip names, and players were given the name, industry, and the prior 12 months' performance for each stock. Laypeople (undergrads in psychology) and professional investors (portfolio managers, analysts, and brokers) both took part in the study. At each selection, players were asked to state how confident they were in the outcome predicted.

The bad news is that both groups were worse than sheer luck. That is to say, you should have been able to beat both groups just by tossing a coin! The even worse news was that the professionals were really dreadful, underperforming laypeople by a large margin. For instance, when the professionals were 100% sure they were correct, they were actually right less than 15% of the time! This fits with the mass of evidence that psychologists have uncovered: *while experts may know more than non-experts, they are also likely to be even more overconfident than non-experts.*

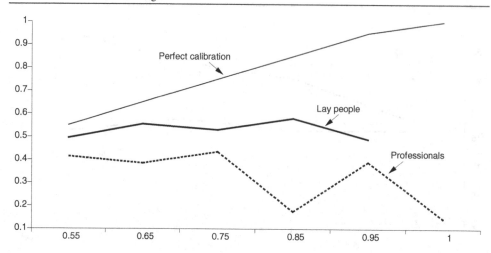

Figure 2.4 Accuracy and confidence on stock selection.
Source: Torngren and Montgomery (2004).

Players were also asked to rank the inputs they used in reaching their decisions. Figure 2.5 shows the average scores for the inputs. Laypeople were essentially just guessing, but were also influenced by prior price performance. In contrast, the professionals thought they were using their knowledge to pick the winners.

The Illusion of Control

The *illusion of control* refers to people's belief that they have influence over the outcome of uncontrollable events. For instance, people will pay four and a half times more for a lottery

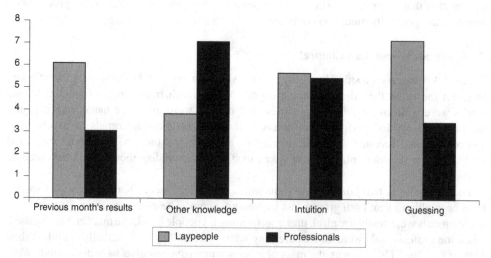

Figure 2.5 Average rating of input importance.
Source: Torngren and Montgomery (2004).

ticket that contains numbers they choose rather than a random draw of numbers. People are more likely to accept a bet on the toss of a coin before it has been tossed, rather than after it has been tossed and the outcome hidden, as if they could influence the spin of the coin in the air! Information once again plays a role. The more information you have, the more in control you will tend to feel.

BIAS #2: BIG $\neq$ IMPORTANT

Every piece of information can be judged along two dimensions – strength and weight. Confusing these two dimensions can easily generate overreaction and underreaction. For instance, let's assume that you have interviewed a potential employee and have taken up his or her references. You receive a letter of recommendation, which is full of glowing testimonials to your potential employee's abilities in almost every walk of life. Sadly, the letter was written by the candidate's mum.

The strength of the information is represented by the high level of the glowing traits talked about; the weight of the information is very low because the author of the letter is a highly biased source.

Tversky and Griffin (1992) have shown that, in general, a combination of high strength and low weight will generate overreaction, whereas low strength and high weight tends to create underreaction (see Table 2.1).

Investors often seem to confuse these two elements of information. For instance, when a firm announces either the introduction or suspension of a dividend payment, investors tend to underreact. They treat the information incorrectly. In fact, changes in dividend policy are very high weight (management doesn't alter dividend policy lightly). However, they also tend to be low strength because investors (incorrectly) don't place much emphasis on dividends.

In contrast, investors seem to almost continually overreact to firms with historically high earnings growth. Investors seem to take tremendous faith from a firm's past history, rather than focusing on the likely prospects in the future (more on this later).

Table 2.1   The dimensions of information

		Weight	
		High	Low
Strength	High	–	*Overreaction*
	Low	*Underreaction*	–

Source: DrKW Macro research.

BIAS #3: SHOW ME WHAT I WANT TO SEE

Consider the following situation: Four cards are laid out in front of you, and each card carries one alphanumeric symbol. The set comprises E, 4, K, 7. If I tell you that if a card has a vowel on one side, then it should have an even number on the other, which card(s) do you need to turn over to see if I am telling the truth?

Give it some thought. Most people select E and 4. The correct answer is E and 7 as only these two cards are capable of proving whether or not I am lying. If you turn the E over and find an odd number, then I was lying, and if you turn the 7 over and find a vowel then you know I was lying. By turning the 4 over you can prove nothing. If it has a vowel then you have found information that agrees with my statement but doesn't prove it. If you turn the 4 over and find a consonant, you have proved nothing. At the outset I stated that a vowel must have an even number. I didn't say an even number must have a vowel!

So why are we drawn to E and 4? We have a very bad habit of looking for information that agrees with us. This thirst for agreement rather than refutation is known as *confirmatory bias*. When Karl Popper wrote his philosophy of science, he stated that the only way of testing a view is to form the hypothesis and then spend the rest of the day looking for all the information that disagrees with it. But that isn't the way most of us work. We tend to form our views and then spend the rest of the day looking for all the information that make us look right.

Our natural tendency is to listen to people who agree with us. It feels good to hear our own opinions reflected back to us. We get those warm, fuzzy feelings of content. Sadly, this isn't the best way of making optimal decisions. What we should do is sit down with the people who disagree with us most. Not to enable us to change our minds (because the odds are staked massively against such an outcome), but rather to make us aware of the opposite point of view. We should look for the logical error in the opposite point of view. If we can't find such an error, then we shouldn't be so sure about holding our own view as strongly as we probably do.

A supplementary problem for trying to follow this path is that we often find ourselves suffering the *hostile media bias*. That is, not only do we look for information that agrees with us, but when we are presented with information that disagrees with us we tend to view the source as having a biased view!

BIAS #4: HEADS WAS SKILL, TAILS WAS BAD LUCK

We have a relatively fragile sense of self-esteem, and one of the key mechanisms for protecting this self-image is *self-attribution bias*. This is the tendency to attribute good outcomes to skill and bad outcomes to sheer bad luck. This is one of the key limits to learning that investors are likely to encounter. This mechanism prevents us from recognizing mistakes as mistakes, and hence often prevents us from learning from those past errors.

To combat this problem we really need to use a matrix diagram similar to Table 2.2. Only by cross-referencing our decisions and the reasons for those decisions with the outcomes can we hope to understand where we are lucky and where we are skilful – that is, was I right for the right reason, or was I right for some spurious reason? In order to use this framework, we need a written record of the decisions we took and the reasoning behind those decisions, so remember to write things down.

Table 2.2   Decision matrix

	Good outcome	Bad outcome
Right reason	Skill (could be luck, but let's be generous)	Bad luck
Wrong reason	Good luck	Mistake

BIAS #5: I KNEW IT ALL ALONG

One of the most dangerous biases we encounter when teaching behavioural psychology is *hindsight bias*. This refers to the fact that after something has happened we are all really sure we knew about it beforehand! The best example of hindsight bias among investors is the dot.com bubble of the late 1990s. Going around talking with investors and telling them it was a bubble used to result in physical threats of violence against us. Yet now, going around and seeing exactly the same set of investors, there has been an Orwellian rewriting of history. Now everyone sits there saying they knew it was a bubble – they were investing in it, but they knew it as a bubble!

Of course, if everyone thinks they can predict the past, they are likely to be far too sure about their ability to predict the future. Hence, hindsight is one of the dynamic generators of overconfidence. I mention that hindsight is one of the most dangerous biases when teaching behavioural psychology, because there is a risk that after reading this you will walk away, saying, 'Well, that was kind of interesting . . . but I knew it all along!'

BIAS #6: THE IRRELEVANT HAS VALUE AS INPUT

When faced with uncertainty we have a tendency to grab on to the irrelevant as a crutch. The incorporation of the irrelevant often happens without any conscious acknowledgment at all (a classic X-system trait).

The classic example of *anchoring* comes from Tversky and Kahneman (1974). They asked people to answer general knowledge questions, such as what percentage of the United Nations is made up of African nations? A wheel of fortune with the numbers 1 to 100 was spun in front of the participants before they answered. Being psychologists, Tversky and Kahneman had rigged the wheel so that it gave either 10 or 65 as the result of a spin. The subjects were then asked if the answer was higher or lower than the number on the wheel, and also asked their actual answer. The median response from the group that saw the wheel spot at 10 was 25, and the median response from the group that saw 65 was 45! Effectively, people were grabbing at irrelevant anchors when forming their opinions. For what it is worth, the percentage today is just under 20%.

Another well-known example concerns solving eight factorial (8!). It is presented in two different ways to the survey participants: as $1 \times 2 \times 3 \times 4 \times 5 \times 6 \times 7 \times 8$ or as $8 \times 7 \times 6 \times 5 \times 4 \times 3 \times 2 \times 1$. The median answer under the first scenario was 512; the median answer under the second scenario was 2250. So people appear to anchor on the early numbers in forming their expectations. By the way, the actual answer is 40,320.

Anchoring has obvious implications for valuations, especially in a world in which we all sit in front of screens that flash prices at us all day long. It is far too easy to latch onto the current market price as an anchor. Analysts are often fearful of announcing target prices that are a long way from current market prices. I know that whenever I tell investors that the S&P 500 would need to fall to around 500 before I would be prepared to buy it, the reaction is usually a grin, as if I had taken leave of my senses (which, in fairness, many have argued I did a long time ago). However, simply dismissing 500 because it is a long way from the current 1181 is a version of anchoring.

Northcraft and Neale (1987) show that real estate agents suffer anchoring when pricing houses. They took two groups of estate agents to the same house, and gave them exactly the same information except that the original listing price of property was different for each

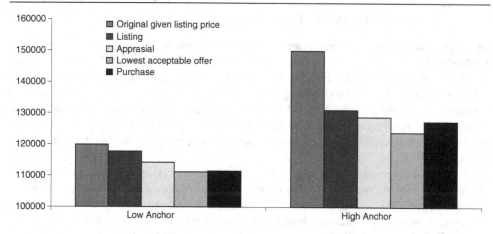

Figure 2.6 Anchoring and housing valuations.
Source: Northcraft and Neale (1987).

group. They were asked to provide a variety of prices. The results are shown in Figure 2.6. On average, the difference between the two groups was more than 12%, despite the fact they looked at the same house!

A further example of anchoring affecting valuation can be found in a paper by Ariely *et al.* (2003). In this study, participants were shown a variety of common(ish) objects. They were then asked whether they would buy the object for a dollar amount equal to the last two digits of their Social Security number. The participants were then asked the maximum price they would pay for each item. The idea of asking the first question was to set up the anchor (i.e. the last two digits of their Social Security number). If people anchor, then there should be some differences between those with a high/low Social Security number.

Figure 2.7 shows the results of Ariely *et al.*'s experiment. The average ratio of high Social Security number participants' maximum purchases prices to low Social Security number

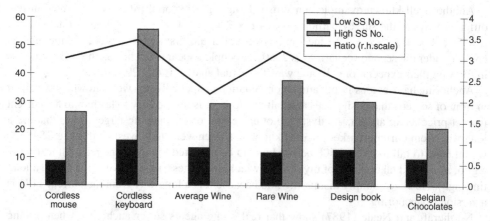

Figure 2.7 Anchoring and valuation (LHS is in $).
Source: Ariely *et al.* (2003).

participants' maximum purchase prices was an incredible $2.7\times$! The highest differential was just under $3.5\times$. So, despite the fact that the Social Security numbers had nothing to do with the objects, they created vast valuation gaps.

The degree of anchoring is heavily influenced by the salience of the anchor; that is to say, the more seemingly relevant the anchor, the more people will tend to cling to it, which helps to explain why analysts are so frequently afraid to have target prices that differ vastly from market prices. However, as already shown, even totally irrelevant anchors can have a massive effect on valuation.

From an aggregate market perspective, what are the likely anchors? Prices are flashed at us all day long – TV ads, newspaper inserts, ticker tape numbers scrolling across the bottom of the TV news channel, stock analysts' e-newsletters, real estate listings, and more. Investors seem to latch onto these price mirages and mistakenly equate them with values. Of course, we can guard against such mistakes by using reverse-engineered models of valuation. Take market prices and check what they imply for growth, then assess whether there is any hope of that growth actually being delivered.

BIAS #7: I CAN MAKE A JUDGEMENT BASED ON WHAT IT LOOKS LIKE

Consider the following: Linda is 31, single, outspoken, and very bright. She majored in philosophy at her university, and as a student was deeply concerned with issues surrounding equality and discrimination. Is it more likely that Linda works in a bank, or is it more likely that Linda works in a bank and is active in the feminist movement?

Somewhat bizarrely, many people go for the latter option. But this can't possibly be true. The second option is a subset of the first option, and a subset can never be larger than one of the contributing sets!

So what is happening? Well, people judge events by how they appear, rather than by how likely they are. This is called *representativeness*. In the example of Linda, people picking the option that Linda works in a bank and is active in the feminist movement are underweighting the base rate that there are simply more people who work in banks than people who work in banks and are active in the feminist movement!

Representativeness has many applications in investment. For example, do investors think that good companies make good investments? If so, this is a potential case of representativeness. A further example of representativeness is outlined in Figure 2.8. It shows portfolios based around long-term earnings growth forecasts for consensus analysts.[1] The first bar shows the per-annum growth rate in the 5 years prior to expectation formation. It also traces out the earnings growth per annum in 1, 3 and 5 years following the forecasts.

The results show that analysts suffer representativeness twice over. Firstly, companies that have seen high growth in the previous 5 years are forecast to continue to see very high earnings growth in the next 5 years. Analysts are effectively looking at the company's past performance and saying 'this company has been great, and hence it will continue to be great', or 'this company is a dog and it will always be a dog'. This is exactly the same logic as the Linda problem!

Secondly, analysts fail to understand that earnings growth is a highly mean-reverting process over a 5-year time period. The base rate for mean reversion is very high. The low-growth

---

[1] It draws on our own research and work by Chan, Karceski and Lakonishok (2003).

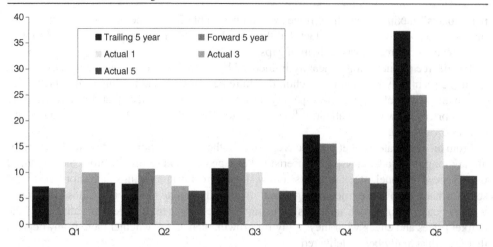

Figure 2.8 Earnings growth isn't persistent.
Source: DrKW, Montier (2002), and Chan, Karceski and Lakonishok (2003).

portfolio generates nearly as much long-term earnings growth as the high-growth portfolio. Effectively, analysts judge companies by how they appear, rather than how likely they are to sustain their competitive edge with a growing earnings base.

BIAS #8: THAT'S NOT THE WAY I REMEMBER IT

Our minds are neither supercomputers nor even good filing cabinets. They bear more resemblance to post-it notes that have been thrown into the bin, and covered in coffee, which we then try to unfold and read! However, we all tend to think of our memories as perfect, like picture postcards or photos. The psychological truth is that memory is a mental process. One input into that process is the truth, but it is certainly not the only, let alone the major, input. In general, people are more likely to recall vivid, well-publicized or recent information.

The *recency effect* is also reinforced by the fact that people tend to rely on their own experiences in preference to statistics or the experiences of others. In a wonderfully titled paper 'The tree of experience in the forest of information', Simonsohn *et al.* (2004) show through a series of experiments that direct experience is frequently much more heavily weighted than general experience, even if the information is equally relevant and objective.

Simonsohn *et al.* hypothesize that one reason for the overweighting of direct experience "is the impact of emotion. .... [D]irectly experienced information triggers emotional reactions which vicarious information doesn't".

They continue, "If people use their direct experience to assess the likelihood of events, they are likely to overweight the importance of unlikely events that have occurred to them, and to underestimate the importance of those that have not." In fact, in one of their experiments, Simonsohn *et al.* find that personal experience is weighted twice as heavily as vicarious experience! All of this means that investors' experience will be a major determinant of their perception of reality.

The emotional impact of information also has its role to play. For instance, when asked which is a more likely cause of death in the United States, shark attacks or lightning strikes, a large number of people opt for shark attacks. Why? Because shark attacks are easy to recall, and they are easily available to the memory. When someone gets nibbled off the coast of Florida we all hear about it, and, to those of us of a certain age, *Jaws* was a truly terrifying film. In fact, the chances of being killed by a lightning strike are 30 times greater than the chance of being killed by a shark. More people die each year from pig attacks or coconuts falling on their head – or even getting their head stuck in an electrically operated car door window – than die of a shark attack!

A less drastic example comes from Kahneman and Tversky (1973), who asked people the following question: In a typical sample of text in the English language, is it more likely that a word starts with the letter k or that k is its third letter? Of the 152 people in the sample, 105 generally thought that words with the letter k in the first position were more probable. In reality, there are approximately twice as many words with k as the third letter as there are words that begin with k. Yet because we index on the first letter, we can recall them more easily.

The shark example has applications in finance. Investors are always looking for the big trigger event. However, in focusing on the 'big trigger', investors often miss the cumulative impact of small pieces of news. The press help to perpetuate the myth that every infinitesimally small wiggle in the markets can be accounted for by some 'rational' explanation. For instance, a recent newspaper contained the following explanation for a significant up-day in the stock market: 'U.S. stocks on Wednesday put up their best one-day showing in almost four months as falling crude prices and some positive corporate news bolstered the bulls in the lead up to the end of the first quarter.'

BIAS #9: IF YOU TELL ME IT IS SO, IT MUST BE TRUE

WYSIWYG (pronounced *wizzy-wig* – what you see is what you get) was a computer term that described the on-screen appearance being identical to the printed version. All too often, financial data isn't WYSIWYG. *Obstrufication* (or obfuscation: confusion resulting from failure to understand) is frequently the name of the game when it comes to financial information. Of course, the financial markets employ a veritable army of analysts to check through the numbers and expose what is really going on. Well, that is the theory, at least!

However, the reality of analysis may be very different. I suspect that investors and analysts frequently suffer from narrow framing or frame dependence. That is to say, we simply don't see through the way in which information is presented to us. Any decent pollster can extract exactly the desired answer simply by framing the question in differing ways.

The following represents a classic example of narrow framing.

Imagine that you are preparing for an outbreak of an unusual Asian disease that is expected to kill around 600 people. Two alternative programmes to combat the disease have been proposed. Scientific estimates of the outcomes from the two programmes are as follows:

If programme A is adopted, 200 people will be saved. If programme B is adopted, there is a one-third probability that 600 people will be saved and a two-thirds probability that none of the 600 people will be saved.

Which programme would you favour?

When Kahneman and Tversky asked this question they found that 72% of subjects favoured programme A. Now consider the same problem, but with the following estimated outcomes:

If programme C is adopted, 400 will die. If programme D is adopted, there is one-third probability that nobody will die, and a two-thirds probability that 600 will die.

Kahneman and Tversky found that only 22% of subjects favoured programme C.

Of course, the astute among you will have quickly spotted that programme A is identical to programme C, and programme B is identical to programme D. However, the way in which the question was presented created this oddity of preference reversal.

The importance of framing is probably due to cognitive limits. Our brains have only a limited ability to deal with information. In particular, we tend to suffer from something known an *inattentional blindness*.[2] Inattentional blindness is a phenomenon in which people fail to notice stimuli appearing in front of their eyes when they are preoccupied with an attentionally demanding task.

My favourite example involves people being asked to watch two groups of players (one dressed in white, the other dressed in black) pass a basketball between members of their own team. Watchers were asked to count the number of passes between players wearing white tops. They were also asked to note if anything unusual occurred during the watching of the video. As the film was played, a gorilla walked into view, faced the camera and beat his chest. Despite the obvious incongruity of this occurrence, 46% of watchers failed to notice anything out of the ordinary! (See Simons and Chabris, 1999.)

Let me give you an example from Finance. In 1996, the FASB asked that firms reflect the cost of options granted to managements in their profit and loss statements. USA Inc. was aghast; they claimed that it would drive them out of business. Eventually a compromise was reached in which firms agreed to expense options but only in the footnotes. If we now fast forward 10 years, the FASB informed firms that they had to transfer the cost from the footnotes into the P&L. There was uproar once again, despite the fact that they had been reporting such a disclosure for 10 years. Such are the powers of framing!

BIAS #10: A LOSS ISN'T A LOSS UNTIL I TAKE IT

Imagine you had bought a bottle of wine for £15 a few years ago. The wine has now appreciated vastly in price so that at auction a bottle would now fetch something north of £150. Would you be prepared to buy a bottle or sell your existing stock? The most frequently encountered answer is a resounding 'no' to both questions. When faced with this situation, people are generally unwilling to either buy or sell the wine.

This inaction inertia is known as *the status quo bias* (which is not a bizarre attachment to an ageing rock group as some may think). It is also an example of the *endowment effect*. Simply put, the endowment effect says that once you own something you start to place a higher value on it than others would.

The endowment effect is relatively easy to demonstrate empirically. The classic format is to randomly give half a class of students a mug (say). Then tell the class that a market will be formed in which students with mugs can sell them to students without mugs who might want them. Presumably, since the mugs were randomly distributed, roughly half the people should wish to trade. So the predicted volume level is 50%.

However, volumes in such markets are usually a fraction of the amount that might be expected. Indeed, in many experiments the actual volume level is closer to 10%! The key reason for the lack of transactions is a massive gap between the would-be buyers and sellers.

---

[2] For more on this see the work of Daniel Simons, the leader in this field. http://viscog.beckman.uiuc.edu/djs_lab/.

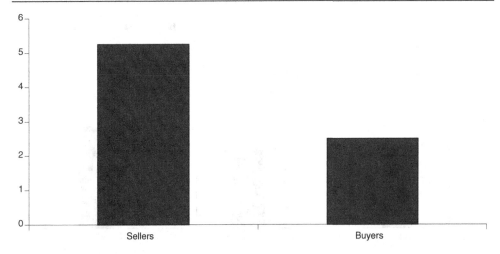

Figure 2.9 The price of a mug: Willingness to accept, willingness to pay.
Source: Kahneman *et al.* (1990).

Figure 2.9 shows the results from a typical experiment (see Kahneman *et al.*, 1990). The object issued was indeed university mugs (a staple in such experiments). These mugs retailed for $6 at the university store. Those who had mugs were willing to sell them from $5.25 on average (known as the willingness to accept, or WTA). Those who didn't have mugs weren't willing to spend more than $2.50 to acquire one (known as the willingness to pay, or WTP).

So, despite being given the mugs only minutes before, the act of ownership led sellers to ask for double the amount that buyers were willing to actually pay for the mug. Ownership seems to massively distort people's perceptions of value.

Does this endowment effect stem from a reluctance to buy or a reluctance to sell? The relative importance of these two factors can be assessed by introducing a third category of player into the market. Rather than having just buyers and sellers, experimenters have introduced *choosers*. As before, mugs are distributed across the class randomly. The sellers were asked if they would be willing to sell their mugs at prices ranging from $0.25 to $9.25. A second group, the buyers, were asked if they would be willing to buy a mug over the same range of prices. A third group, the choosers, were not given a mug but were asked to choose, for each of the prices, whether they would rather receive a mug or the equivalent amount of money.

In theory, the choosers and the sellers are in exactly the same situation – both groups are deciding at each price between the mug and the amount of money. The only difference between the two groups is that the choosers don't have physical possession of a mug. However, Figure 2.10 shows that the theory doesn't really count for very much!

Across three different experiments at three different universities the choosers seem to act much more like buyers than sellers. Across the experiments reported here (Kahneman *et al.*, 1990; Franciosi *et al.*, 1996), choosers' prices were generally higher (on average around 50% higher) than the buyers' prices, but were still well below the prices set by the sellers. Sellers had prices that were on average nearly 3 times greater than the buyers were willing to pay, and nearly double the amount the choosers would have been willing to trade at.

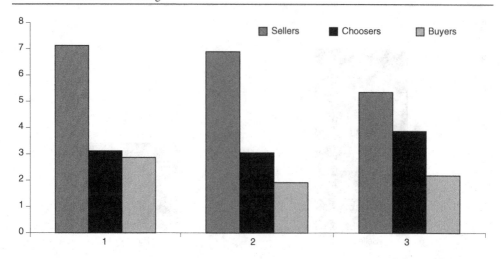

Figure 2.10 The price of a mug: Sellers, choosers and buyers.
Source: Kahneman *et al.* (1990) and Franciosi *et al.* (1996).

This represents clear evidence of the endowment effect being driven by a reluctance of the owners to part with their endowment, even though they may have only actually owned the item in question for a matter of minutes.

Think about these effects the next time you're considering a particular company. If you already hold stock in that company, you may actually impute a higher value than is warranted, simply because you already own the shares. You are likely to enter a meeting with company management expecting to be convinced that any concerns you had are misplaced. Of course, management will never tell you anything other than it is a great business and a great investment. Some very successful fund managers never see companies for this very reason.

Rather than walking into the meeting in a sceptical frame of mind thinking 'unless I hear something that really alters my view then I will sell this stock', we tend to look for all the information that agrees with our stance, which, when we already own a stock, is likely to be, "I'll keep holding this stock."

Both the status quo bias and the endowment effect are part of a more general issue known as *loss aversion*. Psychologists long ago noted that people tend to worry about gains and losses rather than about levels (in direct violation of normal economic theory).[3] In particular, people have been found to dislike losses far more than they like gains.

For example, consider the following: You are offered a bet on the toss of a fair coin. If you lose, you must pay me £100. What is the minimum amount that you need to win in order to make this bet attractive?

Unlike many of the questions from psychology, this one has no right or wrong answer. It is purely a matter of personal choice. Figure 2.11 shows the answers I received when I played this game with some former colleagues from another investment bank.

The average response was well over £200. That fits with all the studies that have been done on loss aversion. In general, people seem to dislike loss 2 to 2.5 times as much as they enjoy gains.

---

[3] Prospect theory is the most frequently used behavioural alternative to classical economics. It incorporates loss aversion neatly.

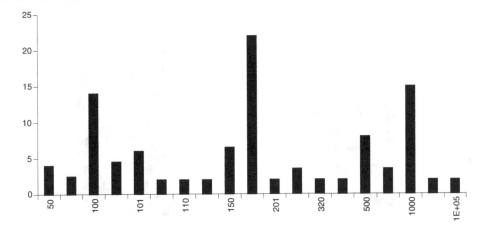

Figure 2.11 Loss aversion among stockbrokers.
Source: Montier (2002).

Shefrin and Statman (1985) predicted that because people dislike incurring losses much more than they enjoy making gains, and people are willing to gamble in the domain of losses, investors will hold onto stocks that have lost value (relative to the reference point of their purchase) and will be eager to sell stocks that have risen in value. Effectively, they argued that people tended to ride losers and cut winners. This has become known as the *disposition effect*.

Odean (1998) obtained data from a discount brokerage for around 10,000 accounts from 1987 to 1993. Each purchase and sale for each account had been recorded. Odean found that investors held losing stocks for a median of 124 days and held winning stocks for a median of 102 days. He also calculated the percentage of losing positions that were realized (as a percentage of all losing stocks held) and the percentage of winning positions that were realized (as a percentage of all winning stocks held).

Lo and behold, Odean uncovered that these individual investors sold an average of 15% of all winning positions and only 9% of all losing positions. That is to say, individual investors are 1.7 times as likely to sell a winning stock than a losing stock (see Figure 2.12).

One of the most common reasons for holding onto a stock is the belief that it will bounce back subsequently. This could be motivated by any number of potential psychological flaws ranging from overoptimism and overconfidence to self-attribution bias (a belief that good outcomes are the result of skill, and bad outcomes are the result of sheer bad luck). Odean decided to investigate whether investors were correctly betting on recovery in the losers they continued to hold. Sadly, he found that the winners that were sold outperformed the losers that continued to be held by an average excess return of 3.4% per annum.

Barber, Odean and Zheng (2001) has also studied the behaviour of investors in mutual funds (rather than direct shares). This time the period covered 1990 to 1996 and encompassed some 32,000 households with holdings of mutual funds. Odean uncovered a very similar pattern to the evidence already presented. When it comes to buys, some 54% of investors' purchases are in the top 20% of mutual funds ranked by past performance (that is to say, investors chase past winners). However, when it comes to selling mutual funds, only 14% of all investors' sales are in the bottom 20% of mutual funds ranked by past performance. In fact, it transpires that

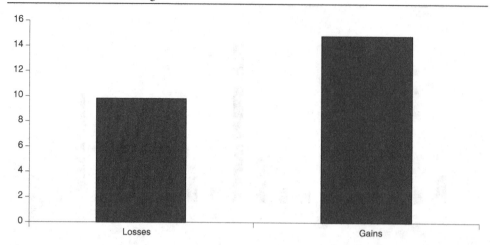

Figure 2.12 Proportion of losses and gains realized: US individual investors.
Source: Odean (1998).

mutual fund investors were more than 2.5 times as likely to sell a winning fund rather than a losing fund (see Figure 2.13).

Professional investors are often very dismissive of such findings. In general, they assume that all of this behavioural finance theorizing applies to individual investors but not to them. This seems to be a classic example of that key behavioural characteristic – overconfidence.

However, such overconfidence seems to be sadly misplaced. Andrea Frazzini (2004) has recently investigated the behaviour of mutual fund managers, and has discovered that even such seasoned professionals seem to suffer loss aversion.

Frazzini analysed the holding and transactions of mutual funds between 1980 and 2002. He ended up with a sample of nearly 30,000 US domestic mutual funds. Just like Odean, he

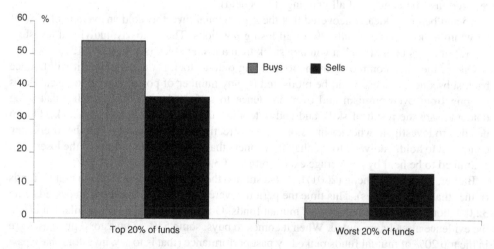

Figure 2.13 Proportion of buys and sells across best and worst funds.
Source: Barber, Odean and Zheng (2001).

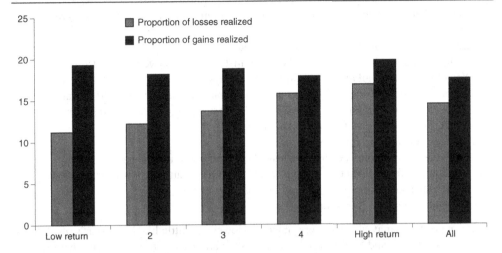

Figure 2.14 Proportion of losses and gains realized: US domestic mutual funds.
Source: Frazzini (2004).

found that professional money managers seemed to suffer loss aversion. Across all funds, he found that 17.6% of all gains were realized, but only 14.5% of all losses were realized. So professional investors were 1.2 times as likely to sell a winning stock rather than a losing stock.

However, Frazzini takes his analysis one step further. He ranks the mutual funds by the performance achieved over the last 12 months. The results are shown in Figure 2.14. The best-performing funds are those with the highest percentage of losses realized (i.e. the least loss averse). The best-performing funds are less than 1.2 times more likely to sell a winning position than a losing position.

The worst-performing funds had the lowest percentage of realized losses. In fact, the worst-performing funds show about the same degree of loss aversion as the individual investors. They are 1.7 times more likely to sell a winning position than a losing position.

Investors would be well advised to be mindful of this strong evidence of loss aversion. As with all biases, everyone is likely to think that they are less likely than everyone else to suffer from loss aversion. The reality of the situation is that we all seem to be liable to the fear of loss. As such, a (formal) sell discipline is likely to be of prime importance within any successful investment process.

CONCLUSIONS

These 10 biases seem to be the most common mental pitfalls that investors stumble into. The following 15 rules are attempts to suggest ways in which we might try to avoid plunging headlong into them:

1. These biases apply to me, you, and everyone else.
2. You know less than you think you do.
3. Try to focus on the facts, not the stories.
4. More information doesn't equal better information.

5. Think whether a piece of information is high strength and low weight, or low strength and high weight.
6. Look for information that disagrees with you.
7. Your failures aren't just bad luck; examine mistakes to improve your performance.
8. You didn't know it all along, you just think you did.
9. If you can't debias, then rebias – we know people will anchor on the irrelevant, so let's replace the unimportant with the relevant. Set up a sensible valuation framework.
10. Judge things by how statistically likely they are, not how they appear.
11. Don't overweight personal experience.
12. Big, vivid, easy to recall events are less likely than you think they are.
13. Don't take information at face value; think carefully about how it was presented to you.
14. Don't value something more, simply because you own it.
15. Sell your losers and ride your winners.

Of course, these may all seem very obvious. However, a little like New Year's resolutions, they are easy to say and hard to implement. Having an investment process that incorporates best mental practice requires you to step back from the hurly burly of day-to-day market turbulence and understand how to apply psychology's findings to your own behaviour.

3

Take a Walk on the Wild Side*

> In the cold light of day, you know when a company issues a profit warning that you *should* sell, because such bad news rarely comes alone. However, when the company issues the statement you don't sell. Rather you start making excuses as to why this stock will be all right. The difference between stated behaviour and actual behaviour is called an empathy gap, and they matter!

- As Dunn puts it, we as a species are unique in our ability to be emotional time travellers. We alone can fast forward to imagine future events and how we will feel and act in those events. However, while we have the ability to perform such acts, we are actually very poor at forecasting both our future feelings and actions.
- In general, people in a cold (unemotional) state tend to overestimate the influence of emotional situations on the intensity and duration of their feelings (impact bias). However, people underestimate the influence of emotional situations on their choices, actions and preferences (empathy gaps).
- Impact bias is easy to see in our behaviour. People predict that they will be very unhappy for a very long time after a romantic relationship ends. In fact, psychologists have found that people quickly return to their baseline level of happiness. The return to 'normal' occurs much faster than people predict.
- Empathy gaps are likely to be more of a problem in financial markets than impact bias. When we are satiated after lunch, we cannot imagine being hungry again. Yet, while we are starving, we cannot imagine feeling bloated. We seem to use simple extrapolation of our current state into the future. So when we are cold and clear headed we think we will behave in one fashion. But, in the heat of the moment, we find ourselves behaving in a completely different way (often to our detriment).
- My favourite example of empathy gaps comes from a paper by Ariely and Loewenstein. A group of men were asked how arousing they found certain ideas such as bondage. When non-aroused the average response was 36%, when aroused this rocketed up to 53%. Men woefully failed to realize that they found almost any sexual act much more interesting once they were aroused!
- Can we combat these biases? Impact biases seem to be relatively easy to deal with. Simply showing people examples of declining lines seems to do the trick. Asking people to remember a wide range of past emotional experiences and their reactions also seems to do the trick.

*This article appeared in *Global Equity Strategy* on 11 May 2005. The material discussed was accurate at the time of publication.

- However, empathy gaps are far harder to overturn. From a market perspective, having simple but non-negotiable precommitment style trading rules may be the best hope of beating the bias. For example, having a house rule that you must sell a stock once it has a profit warning removes the conflict of an empathy gap by removing the possibility of a choice.

Emotions matter. For instance, in a recent study of day-traders, Lo *et al.* (2004) conclude

"That subjects whose emotional reaction to monetary gains and losses was intense on both the positive and negative side exhibited significantly worse trading performance, and large sudden swings in emotional states seemed especially detrimental to cumulative profit-and-losses."

Nor is the evidence limited to day-traders. In their pioneering pilot study of professional traders, Lo and Repin (2002) noted: "Physiological variables associated with the autonomic nervous system (ANS) are highly correlated with market events even for highly experienced professional traders." That is to say, they wired traders up to a machine that measured heartbeat, skin conductance, blood volume pulse, body temperature, etc., while the traders were at work. These variables are all associated with the ANS, which itself is held to be part of the emotional decision-making process (see *Global Equity Strategy*, 20 January 2005, for more on this). Lo and Repin monitored these variables as events hit the market. Significant deviations were observed.

They also found an inverse relationship between trader experience and physiological responses. The more experienced traders had far less reaction to events in terms of the emotional responses than the less experienced traders.

Emotional forecasting is one element that is unique to humans. As a species, we alone are emotional time travellers.[1] Only humans engage in mentally fast forwarding to imagine future events and how we will feel and act during those events. Given the importance of emotions on decision-making, it is perhaps surprising to find that we are really very poor at emotional forecasting. In general, people in a cold (unemotional) state tend to *overestimate* the influence of emotional situations on the intensity and duration of their feelings (impact bias). However, people also *underestimate* the influence of emotional situations on their choices and preferences (empathy gaps).

IMPACT BIAS

Let me give you an example of impact bias. People predict that they will be very unhappy for a very long time after a romantic relationship breaks up but, in fact, psychologists have found that they are back to their baseline levels of happiness in a very brief time, far shorter than the people themselves predict.

Dunn *et al.* (2003) asked students to forecast their overall level of happiness in a year from now if they lived in various houses at their university. This questioning was carried out shortly before the students were randomly assigned to one of the houses. Participants focused too much on the physical qualities of the house in question, such as its beauty or location, rather than on factors that are much more correlated with happiness, such as who might be their roommates. By focusing on the physical aspects, participants significantly mispredicted their happiness ratings (1 = unhappy, 7 = happy) compared to the actual outturn several months later. Indeed, as Figure 3.1 shows, there was actually little difference on happiness ratings regardless of the desirableness or otherwise of the house.

An alternative example comes from Wilson *et al.* (2000). Two months before a game, they asked people to rate how happy they would be if their football team won. Participants were asked how happy they would be on the day itself and on the next 3 days.

---

[1] An expression borrowed from Dunn and Laham (2006).

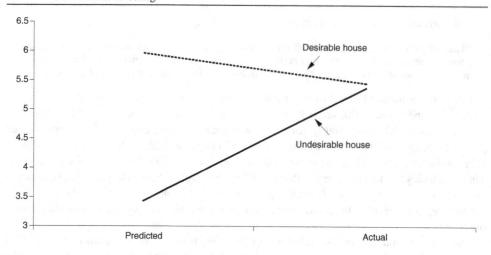

Figure 3.1 Predicted and actual happiness based on house.
Source: Dunn, Wilson and Gilbert (2003).

The day after the game, participants then re-rated their overall happiness. People showed strong evidence of an impact bias. People predicted that they would be above their baseline of happiness right after the game and for each of the next 3 days. In fact, their actual level of happiness was no different from their baseline by the day after the game (Figure 3.2).

EMPATHY GAPS

Whereas people overestimate the influence of emotional situations on the intensity and duration of their feelings (impact bias), they underestimate the influence of emotional situations upon choice (empathy gaps). It is the latter that we are more likely to encounter in financial markets. We can sit here in the cool light of day and say I will sell that stock when it reaches $ZZ

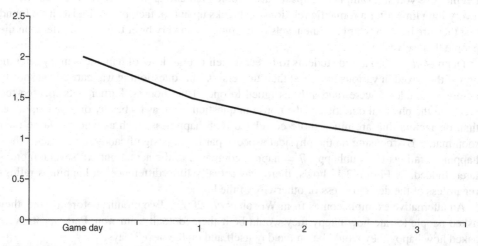

Figure 3.2 Expected deviation from baseline happiness.
Source: Wilson *et al.* (2000).

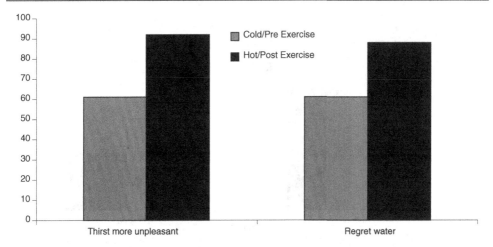

Figure 3.3 Percentage reporting thirst worst and regretting not having extra water most.
Source: Van Boven and Loewenstein (2003).

or I'll sell it if it ever has a profit warning. However, when the stock reaches $ZZ or has a profit warning, we suddenly find our decisions are very different from the ones we set out to implement.

Such empathy gaps have been documented across a wide range of situations. A good example comes from Van Boven and Loewenstein (2003), who asked people to imagine they were lost in some woods. They were then asked if they would find being thirsty more unpleasant than being hungry and whether they would regret not bringing extra water more than extra food. Two groups of people were asked this question and offered a bottle of water as reward for taking part, some of whom had just finished at the gym, others of whom were yet to start their work out.

Figure 3.3 shows the results. When in a cold state (pre-exercise) around 61% of participants thought if they were the lost hikers they would both find the thirst more unpleasant than the hunger, and would regret not taking more water rather than regret not taking more food. However, when the 'hot' group was considered, 92% thought the thirst would be much more unpleasant than the hunger, and 88% thought they would regret not taking more water rather than not taking more food.

A similar result was found by Read and Van Leeuwen (1998). They asked office workers to choose between either healthy snacks (fruit) or unhealthy snacks (crisps and chocolate). The snacks the workers chose would be received in one week's time. Some of the workers would receive their chosen snack late in the afternoon (when they were likely to be hungry); others would receive their snacks directly after lunch (when they were presumably satiated). Some of the workers were asked which snack they would prefer immediately after they had eaten their lunch, others were asked late in the afternoon.

Effectively this methodology gives a two by two sort. The basic idea was that crisps and chocolate would be relatively more attractive when people were hungry. Optimal behaviour should only depend upon future hunger. However, as the results in Figure 3.4 demonstrate, that isn't the case.

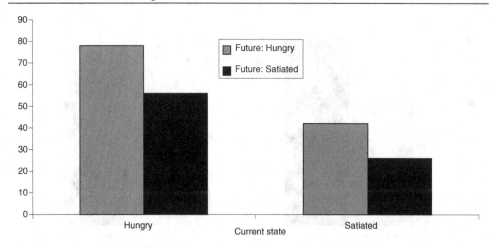

Figure 3.4 Predicting hunger: Dependency upon current condition.
Source: Read and Van Leeuwen (1998).

Even when told they would receive the snack after lunch, those people who were already hungry elected the junk snack much more than those who chose when satiated. The results show that people seem to extrapolate their current emotional stance into the future. The hungry people cannot imagine being satiated, and the satiated cannot imagine being hungry.

Some time ago, we wrote on loss aversion and endowment effects (see *Global Equity Strategy*, 6 April 2005). Endowment effects (valuing something more simply because you happen to own it) can be seen as a form of empathy gap. To illustrate the point, Loewenstein and Adler (1995) showed a class a mug. All the participants were told that they would receive one, and that they would have the opportunity to sell it for money. Half of the subjects predicted how much they'd sell it for. After a delay, all the subjects are given a mug and an opportunity to sell. The results are shown in Figure 3.5. Those who predicted their selling price before they actually 'owned' the mug grossly underpredicted their own selling price.

Our final example (and my personal favourite) comes from a recent paper by Ariely and Loewenstein (2006). A sample of 35 male undergraduates at the University of California were each paid $10 to participate in the study. Each was given a laptop and asked to rate how likely they were to find certain sexual stimuli attractive. (For the sake of decorum and modesty we have omitted the list of acts in question. However, it is, of course, available on request.)

The participants were asked to rate how much they would enjoy each of several acts in the cold light of day. They then repeated the survey while enjoying self-gratification in the privacy of their homes. Participants were told to complete the survey only when they were 75% aroused.

Figure 3.6 shows the average level of interest expressed in non-aroused and aroused states. In the cold light of day the average rating was 36%. However, this rocketed to 53% when the men conducted the survey in an aroused state! Almost every act saw between a 15% and 20% increase in its attractiveness when the participants were aroused. The participants were incredibly bad at predicting how they would feel under 'hot' conditions.

The same group were also asked a set of questions on their likely use of 'morally questionable behaviour to procure sex', such as ensuring that the partner was drunk, proceeding after she

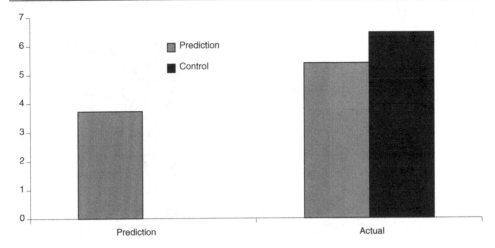

Figure 3.5 Endowment effects: Underestimating the impact of ownership.
Source: Loewenstein and Adler (1995).

has said no, and even drugging her. In the non-aroused state, the average rating across these morally dubious practices was 31%. In the aroused state this rose to 51%, confirming the results of the previous studies (Figure 3.7).

So all the evidence points to the fact that people overestimate the impact of emotions on their feelings, but underestimate its impact on their choices and preferences. From a psychological perspective this differing reaction helps to highlight the difference between feelings and choices.

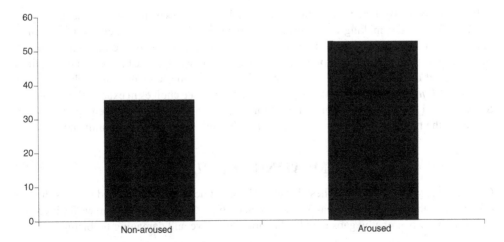

Figure 3.6 The impact of arousal on desire.
Source: Ariely and Loewenstein (2006).

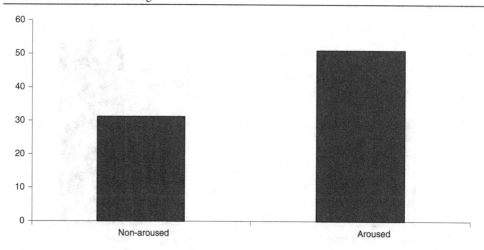

Figure 3.7   The impact of arousal on morally dubious actions.
Source: Ariely and Loewenstein (2006).

Indeed, Van Boven and Kane (2005) suggest that it is the difference between the two that accounts for the differing reactions. They argue that people expect feelings to fluctuate over time, but expect choices to be constant. As they put it:

> "It would not seem off to people if their best friend wakes up cheerful, gets bored during morning classes, grumpy after a lunchtime argument, embarrassed while giving a presentation, and proud after receiving an A on an exam"

but

> "It would seem odd to people if their best friend chose to dance in front of an audience in the morning, refused to dance at lunchtime, and was again ready to show his moves after dinner."

People also believe that choices are dispositional. That is to say, they reflect the underlying nature of the person making the choice, rather than the situation in which the person finds himself. We have previously discussed the fact that we all tend to believe that other people's actions reflect their 'personality' or underlying disposition, whereas we believe our own actions are the result of the situation in which we find ourselves (the fundamental attribution error, see *Global Equity Strategy*, 31 January 2005). We tend to see choices in exactly the same way. Since we tend to believe that choices reflect underlying nature, we expect them not to change. However, the reality is that our choices are unstable, shifting upon visceral influences.[2]

COMBATING THE BIASES

Can we do anything to combat these biases? The good news is yes! The bad news is that we can do more about impact bias than we can about empathy gaps. This is bad news for investors since, of the two, empathy gaps may be the more pervasive and damaging problem.

---

[2] This poses a major problem for the economic theory of revealed preference.

Dunn and Laham (2006) suggest several ways of reducing impact bias:

- *Showing people examples of progression or change.* Simply showing a picture of a declining line seems to be enough to prime people to remember that emotions decline over time!
- *Asking people to remember a wide variety of past emotional events and their feelings.* A single event will not suffice; availability bias ensures that if people are asked to remember a single event they will pick an extreme one. So a wide range of events is needed to combat this problem.
- *Asking people to think about background events and activities rather than the easily available aspects.* In the study mentioned earlier about football fans, when the fans were asked to consider activities they would be doing – i.e. studying, socializing and working – they made far more moderate forecasts of their happiness as a result of their team winning.
- *Structuring choice situations so that options are not compared in a side-by-side fashion.* Side-by-side comparison makes features salient (as in the housing experiment discussed earlier). So preventing this allows people to take in other features. Alternatively, asking people to look for similarities or shared features rather than concentrating on the differences could also help to mitigate the problem.

When it comes to empathy gaps, it is harder to find suggested fixes. Simple monetary incentives have failed to result in any improvement in the ability of people to bridge the empathy gap.

The best approach seems to be trying to put people into the same emotional state that they will be in when the event actually occurs. Sadly for many market applications this isn't a viable approach. Instead, the alternative may be to have predefined courses of action that can be automatically implemented. Simple trading rules may help to prevent the empathy gap from arising by altering the outcome. If we have a rule to sell a stock once it misses an earnings number, for example, then as soon as it misses we sell, rather than pontificating and saying everything will be all right next quarter!

Table 3.1   A summary of impact bias and empathy gaps

	Impact bias	Empathy gap
Biases	Overestimate the influence of emotional situations on the intensity and duration of feelings	Underestimate the influence of emotional situations upon choices, actions and preferences
Example	When a romantic relationship ends, I will feel terrible for ages	When I am stuffed after lunch I can't imagine wanting food again
Solutions	Show pictures of declining lines Ask people to remember a wide variety of past emotional events and their feelings Ask people to think about background events rather than the easily available aspects Ask people to focus on similarities rather than differences	Try to simulate the state in which you will be required to make the decision Use non-negotiable pre-commitment trading rules/try to eliminate future choices

Source: DrKW Macro research.

The final possible mediator of empathy gaps comes from very preliminary results from Brackett, Dunn and Schneiderman quoted in Dunn and Laham (2006). They have found a link between individuals who have high emotional intelligence (EI) and accurate affective forecasts. EI consists of four elements: (i) the ability to perceive emotions accurately, (ii) the ability to use emotions to facilitate thought, (iii) the ability to understand emotions and their meanings, and (iv) the ability to manage emotions.

In their experiment, supporters of John Kerry who had previously completed an EI test were asked to predict how they would feel if George Bush won the 2004 presidential election. They later reported their actual feelings after Bush's win. Predicted and actual feelings were barely correlated among those who had low or near average EI. However, those with high EI scores had strongly correlated predicted and actual feelings. So perhaps our best hope of avoiding impact bias and empathy gaps is to work on developing our emotional intelligence (see Table 3.1).

4

Brain Damage, Addicts and Pigeons*

> So what do the brain damaged, addicts and pigeons have in common? They are all capable of outperforming the rest of us in specific tasks. Where it pays to take risks, those who can't feel fear (brain damaged/addicts) outperform us by taking more on. However, in life they make bad choices. So check your emotions at the door when investing, but remember to pick them up again before you go home.

- Several recent press reports have picked up on a new study by Bechara *et al.* showing that patients with a specific brain lesion, which prevents them from feeling fear, outperform normal players in a simple investment game.
- At the beginning of the game, each player is given $20. They are told that the game will last 20 rounds. At the start of each round, they are asked if they would like to invest. If they say 'yes' then a fair coin is flipped. If it comes up heads they are given $2.50, if it comes up tails they lose $1. It is optimal to invest in all rounds. In fact, you would only stand a 13% chance of ending up with less money than you started with by investing in all rounds.
- We have discussed this study in previous work. However, the basic finding is that the patients who cannot feel fear end up investing much more of the time. They seem largely immune to the effects of losing money. However, the rest of us have a torrid time and tend to pull back from investing once we have suffered a loss.
- However, a subgroup of the authors have written a sequel which uncovers another group who manage to outperform ... addicts! The study examines a group who are addicted to alcohol, cocaine/crack or methamphetamines. Just like the brain-damaged group, the addicts outperform the normals. They choose to invest 82% of the time after a round in which they suffered a loss; the patients with fear lesions are up at around 85%. However, the normals only invested less than 41% of the time after they had suffered a loss! So bad is the pain of losing $1 that they go into some kind of shutdown mode.
- Before you all dash off to hire the brain-damaged and the addicted, it is worth noting that the game is rigged to ensure that risk is related to return. If the tables are turned such that taking risk is a bad outcome then the addicts and the fear lesion patients underperform the rest of us. This helps to provide the reason why these two groups make such poor life choices. In investing, risk is meant to be rewarded, so those who can keep their emotions in check are likely to make the best investors. However, to be the best human beings they have to remember to pick them up on the way out of the door.
- What about pigeons? Well pigeons and rats (indeed most animals) have been found to outperform when it comes to pattern-spotting. Assume, for example, that people are watching

---

*This article appeared in *Global Equity Strategy* on 20 September 2005. The material discussed was accurate at the time of publication.

a random sequence of two flashing light bulbs – one red, the other green. If the red light flashes 70% of the time, and the people are then asked to predict the sequence, they end up trying to find a pattern of frequency matching (i.e. guessing red 70% of the time, and guessing green 30% of the time). The optimal strategy is simply to pick the dominant light all the time. Rats and pigeons show this optimal behaviour! So how about hiring some pigeons?

Given the choice who would you select to run money? Someone who has brain damage, an addict, a pigeon or a professional fund manager? It is a tough choice I know. Several newspaper reports[1] picked up on a study that we first mentioned in October 2004 (see *Behavioural Finance Compendium*, October 2004) and in more detail in a note in 2005 (see *Global Equity Strategy*, 20 January 2005).

The essence of the now much quoted paper is that a group of individuals who have a specific lesion to the emotional areas of the brain manage to outperform a group of normals.

Bechara *et al.* (2005) play an investment game. Each player was given $20. They had to make a decision each round of the game: invest $1 or not invest. If the decision was not to invest, the task advanced to the next round. If the decision was to invest, players would hand $1 to the experimenter. The experimenter would then toss a coin in view of the player. If the outcome was heads, the player lost the dollar, if the coin landed tails up then $2.50 was added to the player's account. The task would then move to the next round. Overall 20 rounds were played. It is, of course, optimal to invest across all rounds, as the expected payoff for accepting the bet is $1.25 versus $1 for not playing. In fact, if one invests in all rounds there is only a 13% chance of obtaining lower earnings than if one abstains from investing at all and just holds the $20.

Bechara *et al.* played this game with three different groups : 'normals', a group of players with damage to the neural circuitry associated with fear[2] (target patients who can no longer feel fear), and a group of players with other lesions to the brain unassociated with the fear circuitry (patient controls).

The experimenters uncovered that the players with damage to the fear circuitry invested in 83.7% of rounds, the 'normals' invested in 62.7% of rounds, and the patient controls 60.7% of rounds. Was this result attributable to the brain's handling of loss and fear? Figure 4.1 shows the breakdown of the results based on the result in the previous round. It shows the proportions of groups that invested. It clearly demonstrates that 'normals' and patient controls were more likely to shrink away from risk-taking, both when they had lost in the previous round and when they won!

Players with damaged fear circuitry invested in 85.2% of rounds following losses on previous rounds, while normal players invested in only 46.9% of rounds following such losses. The effect of this was to ensure that the normals ended up with $22.80 on average, the patient controls with $20.07 on average, while the patients who couldn't feel fear ended up with $25.70 on average.

However, a less well known paper by a subgroup of the same authors finds that addicts perform nearly as well as those with lesions in the fear systems (Shiv *et al.*, 2005). Three different groups of addicts were analysed, although no differences between those who were addicted to alcohol, cocaine/crack or methamphetamines were detected.

Figures 4.1 and 4.2 show the results on a variety of measures across the sample from Bechara *et al.* and Shiv *et al.* Figure 4.1 shows the overall percentage of time that the various groups chose to invest across all rounds. Both the patients who couldn't feel fear and the addicts performed significantly better in terms of the percentage of time they chose to invest. Remember that it is optimal to invest in all rounds; the patients with lesions in the system of

---

[1] It also served as an interesting example of the diffusion of information. The WSJ first ran the story in July, *The Times* in the UK picked up on it on 19 September, and then Bloomberg jumped on the bandwagon as well.

[2] Technically speaking this group had suffered lesions to the amygdala, orbitofrontal and insular/somatosensory cortex – all parts of the X-system.

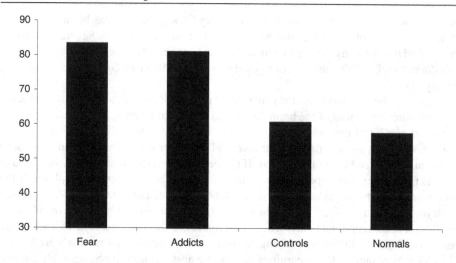

Figure 4.1   Percentage of time of the various groups chose to invest overall.
Source: Adapted from Shiv *et al.* (2005) and Bechara *et al.* (2005).

fear invested in just over 83% of rounds, and the addicts in nearly 81% of rounds. However, the normals and the patient controls invested in only around 58–60% of rounds!

An alternative perspective on the performance of various groups can be gained from looking at the total dollar earnings of each group. As Figure 4.2 shows, once again because of their 'more optimal' behaviour the fear lesion patients and the addicts significantly outperformed the other two groups.

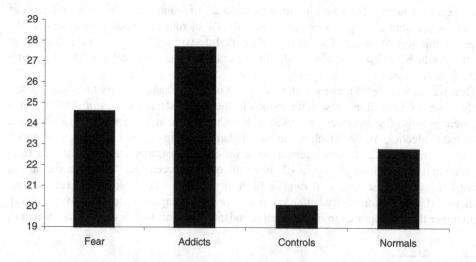

Figure 4.2   Total dollar earnings by group.
Source: Adapted from Shiv *et al.* (2005) and Bechara *et al.* (2005).

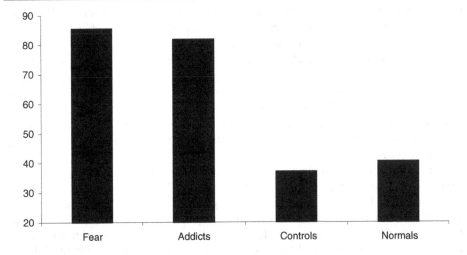

Figure 4.3   Percentage of rounds invest option was chosen after a prior loss outcome.
Source: Adapted from Shiv *et al.* (2005) and Bechara *et al.* (2005).

However, the most telling difference between the groups is the percentage of time that each group was willing to invest after a round in which they had suffered a loss. Of course, in theory, the outcome of a previous round should have no impact on the decision whether one invests in the next round, because the coin has no memory, so each toss is an independent event. Theory is one thing, but reality is something very different.

Figure 4.3 shows the percentage of time that the various groups chose to invest after a round in which they had suffered a loss. The addicts and the fear lesion patients behaved relatively optimally – that is to say, they ignored the prior outcome most of the time, and invested again. However, the patient controls and the normals made appalling choices. So bad was the pain of losing even $1 that they invested only 37% and 41% of the time after a round in which they had suffered a loss (respectively).

So why are the addicts and the fear lesion patients so good at this task? Well, both groups lack the ability to process emotional information normally. Effectively addicts seem to be able to process fear of the negative consequences of their habit. This lack of fear in both groups translates into lower myopic loss aversion (a fear of short-term losses), leading to lower risk aversion and therefore higher returns in situations where risk is rewarded.

Of course, the game to which the players were subjected was designed to ensure that risk-taking was rewarded. However, before investment banks and fund managers start either recruiting those that have no fear or are addicted to drugs[3] it should be noted that both the fear lesion patients and the addicts tend to make pretty poor choices in their lives more generally. That is to say, blind risk-taking is not a great strategy for life in general. Indeed, both fear lesion patients and the addicts have been found to perform worse than normals when the game is altered such that risk-taking is actually a bad idea.[4]

---

[3] The idea of investment banks embarking on a programme of giving traders drugs was mentioned by one client with whom I was discussing these issues. Another pointed out that this behaviour would account for why the 1980s were a great period in markets!

[4] See Bechara *et al.* (1997), discussed in *Global Equity Strategy*, 20 January 2005. See also Stout *et al.* (2004).

Assuming that risk is rewarded in financial markets, then the best investors are likely to be those who can keep their emotional reactions to loss in check. This also offers insights into why it is so hard to be a contrarian investor. If you follow such a strategy you will by definition be buying the assets that everyone else is selling, and selling the assets that everyone else is buying. Buying assets that have gone down is likely to trigger the emotion of fear, and it is this that we need to overcome. However, to be not only a successful investor but a successful human being as well, we need all our emotions, including fear, if we are to avoid making poor life choices. The challenge to each of us is to develop this ability to turn our emotions on and off (or, more accurately, know when to react to them and when to override them) depending on the circumstance.

So we have tackled the brain damaged and the addicted; but what of the pigeons in our title? Well, they are another group that tend to outperform humans on certain tasks. Imagine, if you will, two light bulbs, one red and one green. The lights will flash in a random sequence, but with a fixed probability. One of the lights will flash 70% of the time, the other 30% of the time. If you show people a set of these sequences, and then ask them to predict what the next sequence will look like, most people will come up with an elaborate pattern that contains around 70% red lights and 30% green lights. This is known as frequency matching.

However, as long as the probability of the lights isn't equal, then frequency matching is a suboptimal strategy. Such a strategy will only generate the correct answers 58% of the time $(0.7 \times 0.7 + 0.3 \times 0.3)$. However, a simple strategy of just predicting the dominant light all the time would lead to a 70% success ratio $(1 \times 0.7 + 0 \times 0.3)$.

Bizarrely, rats and pigeons follow the optimal strategy and then manage to outperform most humans! Wolford et al. (2000) suggest that humans do badly because we believe there is a pattern; even if we are told the sequence is random, and because we believe a pattern exists, we try to figure out what it is.

Gazzaniga has long argued that the left hemisphere of the brain plays home to an interpreter function that tries to make sense out of information. He has used split-brain patients to research this concept. Split-brain patients have had the highway between the hemispheres of the brain severed as a cure for chronic epilepsy. Because of this operation, such people can no longer transfer information between the hemispheres of the brain.

For instance, if a split-brain patient is shown a picture only to the left hemisphere and another picture to the right hemisphere, then provided with an array of pictures and asked to point to a picture associated with the presented pictures, something peculiar happens. Let's assume that the left hemisphere saw a chicken, and the right hemisphere saw a picture of snow. The left hemisphere then chooses a chicken claw, and the right hemisphere chooses a shovel. When asked to explain the choices, the patient responded, 'Oh that's simple. The chicken claw goes with the chicken, and you need a shovel to clean out the chicken shed.' In general, the right hemisphere lacks the ability to speak, and with the left hemisphere ignorant of the picture shown to the right hemisphere it is forced to make up a story to support the choices.

Wolford et al. get both split-brain patients and groups who have specific left and right brain damage to participate in a game like the light game outlined above. With the split brain patients, they find that the left hemisphere behaves like most people, it tries to frequency match. In contrast, the right hemisphere behaves like a pigeon or a rat, and approaches the optimum solution of always picking the dominant light. This strongly suggests that the pattern-hunting tendency is embodied within the left hemisphere of the brain.

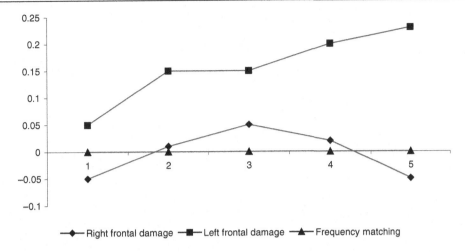

Figure 4.4   Distance from frequency matching.
Source: Wolford *et al.* (2000)

To check this finding, Wolford *et al.* turned to groups of patients who had a significant lesion to the prefrontal cortex after a stroke on either the left- or right-hand side of the brain. They played five rounds of the game, each made up of 100 signals.

The patients who had suffered damage to the right frontal area (i.e. had a left hemisphere intact) behaved just like the rest of us – they frequency matched. However, those with damage to the left hemisphere behaved like most animals and found solutions close to the optimum. Figure 4.4 shows the distance from frequency matching that the two groups achieved.

The presence of the interpreter function of the brain is almost impossible to escape, bar the most drastic surgery. However, if we are at least aware of the brain's desire to make up stories and find patterns we might just be able to guard against it. So the next time you think you spot a pattern, think twice.

Thus, the brain-damaged, the addicts and pigeons all have one thing in common, they are capable of outsmarting us in some circumstances. This serves to highlight the fact that we aren't the supercomputers so loved by finance theorists and economists. We are a bounded rational group, often using rules of thumb that have worked well for us as a species in the past. However, just because something has worked well in our ancient past doesn't mean that it is the best way of thinking in today's world.

We need to strike a balance between trying to control our emotions when it comes to investing, and not forgetting when we leave the office. We also need to be on our guard against the ever-present interpreter residing within our brains.

5
What do Secretaries' Dustbins and the
Da Vinci Code have in Common?*

The justification of near-random moves in markets has spawned a sub-industry of noise generators. People seem to have an inbuilt need to find excuses. Rather than the market declining because of fear over US inflation, the less prosaic (but probably more honest) answer is that this sort of thing tends to happen when you invest in expensive equity markets based largely on momentum.

- The need to find rationales of every market movement has long amused me. Ex-post excuses can be made up to fit almost all situations. But is it really reasonable to say that today thousands of investors woke up and decided that they would all be worried about inflationary fears or Ben Bernanke's credibility?
- However, excuses have a powerful effect on our thought processes. Ellen Langer conducted experiments in the 1970s that showed that people were much more willing to let someone jump in front of them in a queue to use a photocopier if a reason (no matter how banal) was provided.
- We all appear to enjoy having excuses, even if they are largely meaningless – perhaps it is a reflection of our need to mitigate existentialist fears. There are a wealth of psychological studies that show that when people see information in a familiar format, they process it 'mindlessly'. Hence the survival of noise peddlers in financial markets, presumably.
- However, Larry Summers (former US treasury secretary) showed, in a paper written in 1989, that over half of all the largest moves in stock markets appear totally unrelated to fundamentals. Of course, if it isn't fundamentals that are driving markets, then it must surely be sentiment. Maynard Keynes warned long ago, "when disillusion falls upon an overoptimistic and overbought market, it should fall with sudden and even catastrophic force."
- Our fear and greed index remains at very extended levels, suggesting that markets are indeed overoptimistic and overbought. So to us, sudden unexplained declines are to be expected. That is the very nature of a cynical bubble.
- In addition, we are entering the period when equity markets tend to be seasonally weak. Since 1970, across a wide variety of equity markets, the average excess returns (over cash) have been negative between May and October. A new study extends these results to sectors and finds that consumer staples and food sectors outperform during the summer months.

---

* This article appeared in *Global Equity Strategy* on 18 May 2006. The material discussed was accurate at the time of publication.

- Most investors will shun seasonal results, putting them in the same category as reading chicken entrails. However, these same investors will blindly accept the ex-post excuses proffered up by the talking heads. It really is a very strange world.

The markets undergo a bout of jitters and everyone is left scratching around for a reason. For instance, one maven was quoted in the FT of Tuesday 16 May as saying, "Markets had been spooked by fears that rising US inflationary pressures would force the Federal Reserve to keep raising interest rates and hit by a lack of confidence in Ben Bernanke". I have had numerous calls from journalists, salespeople and even (sad to say) a couple of clients asking what was behind the sell-off and, more importantly, if this is just a blip or the start of something more significant. My response was characteristically unhelpful (if honest) – "only time will tell. I really don't have a clue".

I know that markets are expensive and that sentiment is exceptionally high, which is rarely a good combination of events. The most likely outlook for long-term returns is very poor. But is this the beginning of the return of the bear market? Nobody knows and, frankly, anyone who tells you he does, would have been run out of Dodge for being a snake oil salesman.

But this need to find rationales for the mindless moves of markets has long amused me. The justification for near-random moves in markets has spawned a sub-industry of noise generators. They all spend their days telling us why prices moved by 2% yesterday. Does this not strike anyone as a slightly bizarre resource misallocation?

To some extent, brokers exist to deliver what their clients require. So, perhaps we shouldn't be too hard on those whose daily discussions are effectively junk digests. Rather, we should ask, why do we feel the need to explain random fluctuations?

In 1978, Ellen Langer and her co-authors wrote a wonderful paper entitled 'The mindlessness of ostensibly thoughtful action' (Langer *et al.*, 1978). They explore the role of 'placebic' information in people's behaviour. Placebic information is simply words that mean nothing. Could such redundant information really impact anyone's behaviour?

Langer *et al.* set up a clever experiment by waiting for a queue to form at a photocopier and having a confederate try to butt into the queue. Three possible excuses for jumping the queue were provided : (1) 'Excuse me, I have 5 pages. May I use the Xerox machines?' (the no information case); (2) 'Excuse me, I have 5 pages. May I use the Xerox machine, because I have to make copies?' (the placebic case – after all, everyone in the queue needed to make copies or they wouldn't have been in the queue to start with!); (3) 'Excuse me, I have 5 pages. May I use the Xerox machine, because I'm in a rush?' (real information).

Figure 5.1 shows the percentage of people who allowed the confederate to jump the queue. A surprisingly high 60% of people allowed the confederate to jump the queue even without the provision of a reason. However, when either placebic or real information was given, the compliance rate rose to over 90%. So, simply by using 'because' in a sentence, the confederate was able to persuade people to believe that the justification was true and meaningful. We appear to like reasons, however banal they may be.

Langer *et al.* went on to conduct a second experiment in which they rummaged around in the rubbish bins of the secretaries at the Graduate Center of the City University of New York. They collected a sample of memos to give them an idea of the kind of information that the secretaries would face on a daily basis. Having determined this, the experimenters then sent mock memos from a non-existent person. The memo simply asked for the memo itself to be returned to a certain room at the university (a totally futile exercise).

Langer *et al.* hypothesized that when the information arrived in a fashion that the secretaries would regard as 'normal' they would respond in a 'mindless' fashion. Having looked at the style of memos the secretaries regularly received, the experimenters thought that impersonal requests would be the most common form of memo encountered. The results in Figure 5.2 bear out the researchers' viewpoint. When the secretaries received an impersonal request style

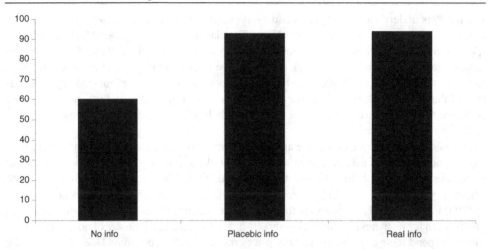

Figure 5.1 Percentage willing to allow queue jumping by information provision group.
Source: Langer *et al.* (1978).

of memo, 90% of them followed the instruction to return the memo to another room in the university via the internal mail.

As I was going to press, I came across another great example of people's malleability. The Catholic Church had conducted a poll of 1000 people, which revealed that those who had read the *Da Vinci Code* were twice as likely to believe that Jesus Christ fathered children, and four times as likely to believe that Opus Dei was a murderous sect, than those who hadn't read the book!

All this evidence strongly suggests that when people see information in a format with which they are familiar, they will 'dumbly' process it. Hence, the survival of the noise peddlers in

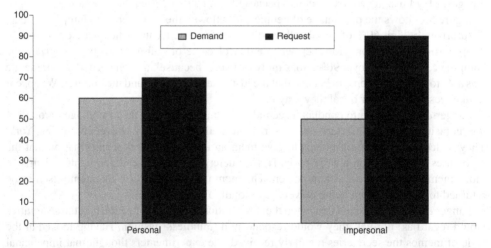

Figure 5.2 Percentage of secretaries returning the pointless memo.
Source: Langer *et al.* (1978).

financial markets, perhaps. Investors faced with chronic uncertainty will turn to any vaguely plausible explanation and seek to find such explanations.

As an anecdote to this 'mindlessness', I regularly refer to the work of Larry Summers (former US treasury secretary and one of the early pioneers of behavioural finance). He published a paper in 1989 (Cutler *et al.*, 1989) which explores the 50 largest moves in the US stock market between 1947 and 1987. Summers and colleagues scoured the press to see if they could find any reason for the market move. They concluded,

> On most of the sizable return days... the information that the press cites as the cause of the market move is not particularly important. Press reports on adjacent days also fail to reveal any convincing accounts of why future profits or discount rates might have changed.

To put it another way, over half of the largest moves in markets are totally unrelated to anything that might be classed as fundamentals.

So if it isn't fundamentals behind the move, what is it? The answer must surely be sentiment. As Maynard Keynes noted:

> It is of the nature of organized investment markets, under the influence of purchasers largely ignorant of what they are buying and of speculators who are more concerned with forecasting the next shift of market sentiment than with a reasonable estimate of the future yield of capital-assets, that, when disillusion falls upon an overoptimistic and overbought market, it should fall with sudden and even catastrophic force.
>
> John Maynard Keynes, Chapter 22, *The General Theory*

We have regularly noted that equity markets are expensive (see *Global Equity Strategy*, 5 April 2005, for details) and we have explored the extended nature of risk tolerance (see *Global Equity Strategy*, 12 April 2005). Figure 5.3 shows the DrKW fear and greed index. This measure continues to show that equity investors are behaving in an irrationally exuberant fashion, buying without any concept of risk or the price they are paying for that risk. A simple change in sentiment is more than enough to damage a market that is being driven simply by cynical momentum-oriented investors.

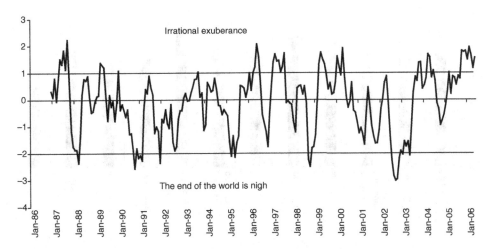

Figure 5.3   DrKW fear and greed index.
Source: DrKW Macro research.

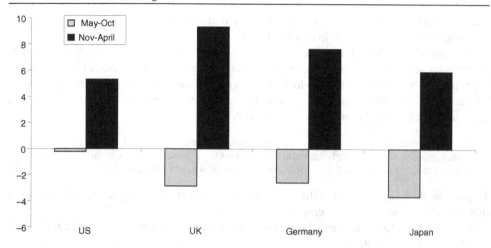

Figure 5.4   Sell in May and go away? Average Excess returns (%) (1970–2005).
Source: DrKW Macro research.

Not only is sentiment exceedingly stretched, but we are now in the seasonally weak period for equity markets. The well-known adage of 'sell in May' looks like good advice on average. Figure 5.4 updates our work on the average excess (over cash) returns for the May–October and November–April periods (see *Global Equity Strategy*, 5 May 2005). On average, investors would have been better off holding cash between May and October, and only investing in the November to April period. So, perhaps we should all take the summer off.

Jacobsen and Visaltanachoti (2006) have recently explored the possibility of a difference in returns at the sector level analogous to those seen at the market level. They use US market data from 1927 to 2005. Figure 5.5 shows the 12 out of 17 sectors in which Jacobsen and

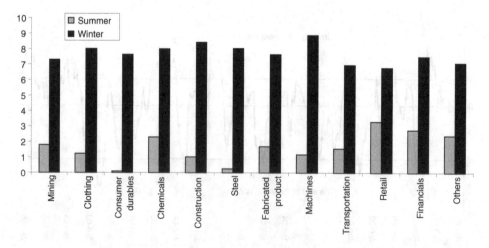

Figure 5.5   Sell in May and go away? Average sector returns (%) (1927–2005).
Source: Jacobsen and Visaltanachoti (2006).

Visaltanachoti found a statistically significant difference between the summer and winter returns.

They found that consumer and food sectors outperform the market during the summer months, whereas durables, chemicals, construction and machines outperform during the winter months. Jacobsen and Visaltanachoti go on to show that a rotation strategy exploiting this finding would significantly outperform the market.

Most investors will shun seasonal results, putting them in the same category as reading chickens entrails. However, these same investors will accept without blinking the idea that suddenly thousands of investors woke up this morning and decided to worry about US inflation or Ben Bernanke's credibility. It really is a very strange world!

6

The Limits to Learning*

Occasionally we get accused of assuming that people don't learn from their mistakes. We make this assumption because there is a wealth of evidence that suggests this exactly. We explore some of the major hurdles that we all face when it comes to learning from our own mistakes.

- We all think we are excellent at learning. After all, most of us have gone through years of university education and got one or more bits of paper showing just how good we are at accumulating knowledge. However, it is learning from past errors that interests me. Here the evidence is compelling: we aren't good at understanding our mistakes. In fact, we generally don't even acknowledge that we have made mistakes, let alone go on to learn from them.
- Our minds have a gamut of mental devices that can be deployed to protect us from the ugly reality of our poor decision-making. Four hurdles in particular stand out. Firstly, self-attribution bias. This is our habit of attributing all good outcomes to skill, and bad outcomes to misfortune. This biased attribution prevents us from recognizing our mistakes as errors. Keeping written records of decisions and the 'logic' behind those decisions can help to mitigate this bias.
- Hindsight bias is a second oft-used mental defence mechanism. Hindsight bias refers to the fact that, after something has happened, we are all really sure that we knew it would happen all along. Once people know the answer, they find it impossible to imagine any other outcome. As with self-attribution, hindsight blinds us to past errors. Orwellian rewriting of history becomes the norm. Simply warning people about this bias has little effect. Explicitly, asking people to think about other alternative outcomes has more impact. Again, written records of previous beliefs can also help to offset this bias.
- Our world is inherently probabilistic. That is to say, we live in an uncertain world where cause and effect are not always transparent. We have a habit of believing that we can control events far more than we can. Thus we attribute outcomes to our actions, even though such outcomes may well have nothing to do with us. The illusion of control is particularly prevalent when lots of choices are available; you have had early success at the task, the task is familiar to you, the amount of information is high and you have a personal involvement. Large portfolios, high turnover and short time horizons are the financial equivalents of these conditions.
- The final major hurdle in learning from our failures stems from our ability to twist the facts to fit our own beliefs. So if we get on the bathroom scales and they show us we have gained

---

* This article appeared in *Global Equity Strategy* on 19 June 2006. The material discussed was accurate at the time of publication.

weight, we get off and try again, just in case we were standing strangely. However, if they gave us a pleasant surprise we would accept it and skip off to the shower. We go through life in much the same fashion, accepting feedback that agrees with us, and scrutinizing any that disagrees with us. Once again; this prevents us learning from our errors.

We all think we are experts at learning. After all, most of us have gone through years of university education and emerged on the other side with a piece of paper 'proving' our ability to assimilate information. However, I'm not concerned with book learning; I am far more interested in learning from our own errors and mistakes or, somewhat more accurately, why we often fail to learn from our own past failures.

But first I ought to present just a couple of examples of the evidence we have of people not learning from past mistakes. The first comes from the work of Max Bazerman of Harvard. He regularly asks people the following question:

> You will represent Company A (the potential acquirer), which is currently considering acquiring Company T (the target) by means of a tender offer. The main complication is this: the value of Company T depends directly on the outcome of a major oil exploration project that it is currently being undertaken. If the project fails, the company under current management will be worth nothing ($0). But if the project succeeds, the value of the company under current management could be as high as $100 per share. All share values between $0 and $100 are considered equally likely.
>
> By all estimates, Company T will be worth considerably more in the hands of Company A than under current management. In fact, the company will be worth 50% more under the management of A than under the management of Company T. If the project fails, the company will be worth zero under either management. If the exploration generates a $50 per share value, the value under Company A will be $75. Similarly, a $100 per share under Company T implies a $150 value under Company A, and so on.
>
> It should be noted that the only possible option to be considered is paying in cash for acquiring 100% of Company T's shares. This means that if you acquire Company T, its current management will no longer have any shares in the company, and therefore will not benefit in any way from the increase in its value under your management.
>
> The board of directors of Company A has asked you to determine whether or not to submit an offer for acquiring company T's shares, and if so, what price they should offer for these shares.
>
> This offer must be made now, before the outcome of the drilling project is known. Company T will accept any offer from Company A, provided it is at a profitable price for them. It is also clear that Company T will delay its decision to accept or reject your bid until the results of the drilling project are in. Thus you (Company A) will not know the results of the exploration project when submitting your price offer, but Company T will know the results when deciding on your offer. As already explained, Company T is expected to accept any offer by Company A that is greater than the (per share) value of the company under current management, and to reject any offers that are below or equal to this value. Thus, if you offer $60 per share, for example, Company T will accept if the value under current management is anything less than $60. You are now requested to give advice to the representative of Company A who is deliberating over whether or not to submit an offer for acquiring Company T's shares, and if so, what price he/she should offer for these shares. If your advice is that he/she should not to acquire Company T's shares, advise him/her to offer $0 per share. If you think that he/she should try to acquire Company T's shares, advise him/her to offer anything between $1 to $150 per share. What is the offer that he/she should make? In other words, what is the optimal offer?

The correct answer is zero for the following reason: Suppose the acquirer offers $60. From the above we know that all points are equally likely, so by offering $60, Company T is assumed on average to be worth $30. Given that the company is worth 50% more to the acquirer, the acquirer's expected value is $1.5 \times \$30 = \$45$. So a bid of $60 has a negative expected value. Any positive offer has a negative expected value, so the acquirer is better off making no offer.

In contrast to this rational logic, the overwhelming majority of responses fall in the range $50–$75. The 'logic' behind this is that on average the company must be worth $50, and thus be worth $75 to the acquirer, so any price in this range is mutually beneficial. However, this ignores the rules of the game. Most obviously, the target can await the result of the

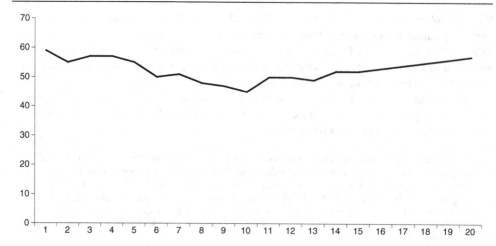

Figure 6.1   20 rounds of acquiring a company.
Source: Ball, Bazerman and Carroll (1991).

exploration before accepting or rejecting, and the target will only accept offers that provide a profit.

Figure 6.1 shows 20 rounds of the game. Across 20 rounds, there is no obvious trend indicating that participants learned the correct response. In fact, Ball *et al.* (1991) find that only five of the 72 participants (MBA students from a top university) learned over the course of the game.

Figure 6.2 shows the results over a 1000 rounds of the game from a study by Grosskopf and Bereby-Meyer (2002). Players didn't learn from hundreds and hundreds of rounds!

The second example of a failure to learn comes from a simple investment game devised by Bechara *et al.* (2004). Each player was given $20. They had to make a decision on each round

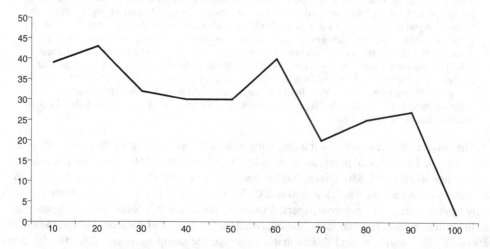

Figure 6.2   1000 rounds of acquiring a company (blocks of 10 games).
Source: Grosskopf and Bereby-Meyer (2002).

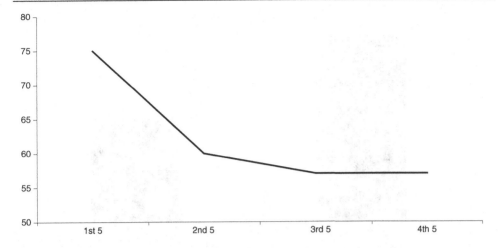

Figure 6.3   Percentage of players investing by groups of rounds.
Source: Bechara *et al.* (2004).

of the game: invest $1 or not invest. If the decision was not to invest, the task advanced to the next round. If the decision was to invest, players would hand over $1 to the experimenter. The experimenter would then toss a coin in view of the players. If the outcome was heads, the player lost the dollar. If the outcome landed tails up then $2.50 was added to the player's account. The task would then move to the next round. Overall, 20 rounds were played.

Figure 6.3 shows that there was no evidence of learning as the game went on. If players learned over time, they would have worked out that it was optimal to invest in all rounds. However, as the game went on, fewer and fewer players continued: they were actually becoming worse off as time went on!

I'm sure you can think back and remember many mistakes from which you should have learned, but didn't (or perhaps I shouldn't judge everybody by my standards). The above is merely setting the scene for our discussion on why people fail to learn. It is the impediments to learning to which we now turn our attention.

The major reason we don't learn from our mistakes (or the mistakes of others) is that we simply don't recognize them as such. We have a gamut of mental devices all set up to protect us from the terrible truth that we regularly make mistakes.

SELF-ATTRIBUTION BIAS: HEADS IS SKILL, TAILS IS BAD LUCK

We have a relatively fragile sense of self-esteem; one of the key mechanisms for protecting this self image is *self-attribution bias*. This is the tendency for good outcomes to be attributed to skill and bad outcomes to be attributed to sheer bad luck. This is one of the key limits to learning that investors are likely to encounter. This mechanism prevents us from recognizing mistakes as mistakes, and hence often prevents us from learning from those past errors.

You can't have helped but notice that the football world cup is under way at the moment. Personally I can't stand the sport, but it might just be worth listening to the post match analysis to see how many examples of self-attribution one can find.

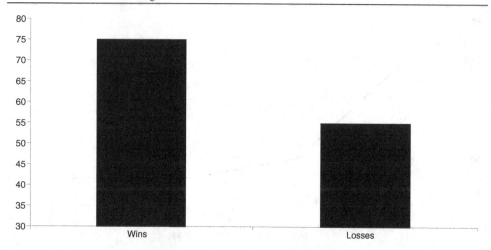

Figure 6.4   Percentage of internal attributions following wins and losses.
Source: Lau and Russell (1980).

Lau and Russell (1980) examined some 33 major sporting events during the autumn of 1977. Explanations of performance were gathered from eight daily newspapers, giving a total of 594 explanations. Each explanation was measured in terms whether it referred to an internal factor (something related to the team's abilities) or an external factor (such as a bad referee).

Unsurprisingly, self-attribution was prevalent: 75% of the time following a win, an internal attribution was made (i.e. the result of skill); whereas only 55% of the time following a loss was an internal attribution made.

The bias was even more evident when the explanations were further categorized as coming from either a player/coach or a sportswriter. Players and coaches attributed their success to an internal factor over 80% of the time. However, internal factors were blamed only 53% of the

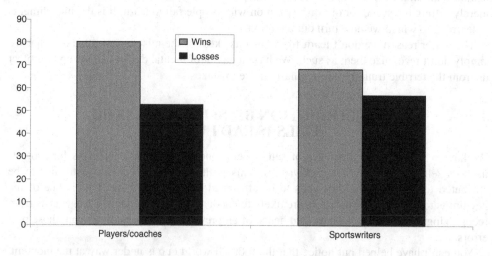

Figure 6.5   Percentage of internal attributions following wins and losses by function.
Source: Lau and Russell (1980).

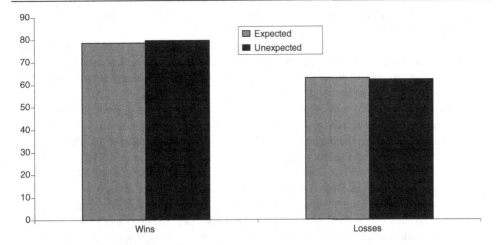

Figure 6.6 Percentage of internal attributions following wins and losses by expected outcome.
Source: Lau and Russell (1980).

Table 6.1 Beating self-attribution

	Good outcome	Bad outcome
Right reason	Skill	Bad luck
Wrong reason	Good luck	Mistake

Source: DrKW Macro research.

time following losses. Sportswriters attributed wins to internal factors 70% of the time when their home team won, and 57% of the time when their home team lost.

The expected outcome of the game had no impact on the post-match explanations that were offered. Even when one team was widely expected to thrash the other, the attributions of the winners referred to internal factors around 80% of the time, and the attributions of the losers referred to an internal factor 63% of the time.

To combat the pervasive problem of self-attribution we really need to keep a written record of the decisions we take and the reasons behind those decisions. We then need to map those into a quadrant diagram, as shown in Table 6.1. That is, was I right for the right reason? (I can claim some skill, it could still be luck, but at least I can claim skill), or was I right for some spurious reason? (In which case I will keep the result because it makes the portfolios look good, but I shouldn't fool myself into thinking that I really knew what I was doing). Was I wrong for the wrong reason? (I made a mistake and I need to learn from it), or was I wrong for the right reason? (After all, bad luck does occur). Only by cross-referencing our decisions and the reasons for those decisions with the outcomes, can we hope to understand when we are lucky and when we have used genuine skill.

HINDSIGHT BIAS: I KNEW IT ALL ALONG

One of the reasons I suggest that people keep a written record of their decisions and the reasons behind their decisions, is that if they don't, they run the risk of suffering from the insidious hindsight bias. This simply refers to the idea that once we know the outcome we tend to think we knew it all the time.

The best example of this from the investment world is probably the bubble in TMT in the late 1990s. Those who were telling people it was a bubble were treated as cretins. However, today there seems to have been an Orwellian rewriting of history, as everyone now thinks they knew it was a bubble (even though they were fully invested at the time).

Barach Fischhoff (1975) was aware of this strong tendency. He gave students descriptions of the British occupation of India and problems of the Gurkas of Nepal. In 1814, Hastings (the governor-general) decided that he had to deal with the Gurkas once and for all. The campaign was far from glorious and the troops suffered in the extreme conditions. The Gurkas were skilled at guerrilla style warfare, and as they were few in number, it offered little chance for full-scale engagements. The British learned caution only after several defeats.

Having read a much longer version of the above, Fischhoff asked one group to assign probabilities to each of the four outcomes: (1) British victory, (2) Gurka victory, (3) military stalemate without a peace settlement, and (iv) military stalemate with a peace settlement.

With the other four groups, Fischhoff provided the 'true' outcome, except that three of the four groups received a false 'true' outcome. Again these groups were asked to assign probabilities to each of the outcomes.

The results are shown in Figure 6.7. The hindsight bias is clear from even a cursory glance at the figure. All the groups who were told their outcome was true assigned it a much higher probability than the group without the outcome information. In fact, there was a 17 percentage point increase in the probability assigned once the outcome was known! That is to say, none of the groups was capable of ignoring the ex-post outcome in their decision-making.

Hindsight is yet another bias that prevents us from recognizing our mistakes. It has been repeatedly found that simply telling people about hindsight and extolling them to avoid it has very little impact on our susceptibility. Rather, Slovic and Fischhoff (1977) found that the best mechanism for fighting hindsight bias was to get people to explicitly think about the counterfactuals: what didn't occur and what could have led to an alternative outcome? In

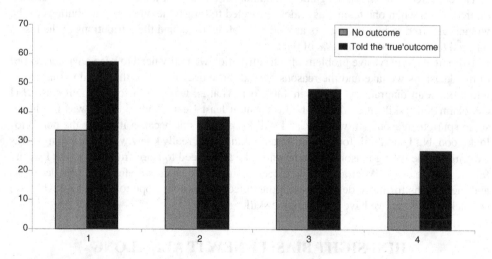

Figure 6.7   Hindsight bias: knowing the outcome influences choices (%).
Source: Fischhoff (1975).

experiments, Slovic and Fischhoff found that hindsight was still present when this was done, but it was much reduced.

SKINNER'S PIGEONS

An additional problem stems from the fact that our world is probabilistic. That is to say, we live in an uncertain world where cause and effect are not always transparent. However, we often fail to accept this fundamental aspect of our existence. In 1947, B.F. Skinner was exploring the behaviour of pigeons. Skinner was the leader of a school of psychology known as behaviouralism, which held that psychologists should study only observable behaviour, not concern themselves with the imponderables of the mind.

Skinner's theory was based around operant conditioning. As Skinner wrote, "The behavior is followed by a consequence, and the nature of the consequence modifies the organism's tendency to repeat the behavior in the future." A more concrete example may be useful here.

One of Skinner's favourite subjects was pigeons. He placed a series of hungry pigeons in a cage attached to an automatic mechanism that delivered food to the pigeon "at regular intervals with no reference whatsoever to the bird's behaviour". He discovered that the pigeons associated the delivery of the food with whatever chance actions they had been performing as it was delivered, and that they continued to perform the same actions:

> One bird was conditioned to turn counter-clockwise about the cage, making two or three turns between reinforcements. Another repeatedly thrust its head into one of the upper corners of the cage. A third developed a 'tossing' response, as if placing its head beneath an invisible bar and lifting it repeatedly. Two birds developed a pendulum motion of the head and body, in which the head was extended forward and swung from right to left with a sharp movement followed by a somewhat slower return.
>
> Skinner (1947)

Skinner suggested that the pigeons believed that they were influencing the automatic mechanism with their 'rituals' and that the experiment also shed light on human behaviour:

> The experiment might be said to demonstrate a sort of superstition. The bird behaves as if there were a causal relation between its behavior and the presentation of food, although such a relation is lacking. There are many analogies in human behavior. Rituals for changing one's fortune at cards are good examples. A few accidental connections between a ritual and favorable consequences suffice to set up and maintain the behavior in spite of many unreinforced instances. The bowler who has released a ball down the alley but continues to behave as if she were controlling it by twisting and turning her arm and shoulder is another case in point. These behaviors have, of course, no real effect upon one's luck or upon a ball halfway down an alley, just as in the present case the food would appear as often if the pigeon did nothing – or, more strictly speaking, did something else.

Indeed, some experiments by Ono (1987) showed that Skinner's findings were also applicable to humans. He placed humans into the equivalent of Skinner boxes: rooms with a counting machine to score points, a signal light and three boxes with levers. The instructions were simple:

> You may not leave the experimental booth... during the experiment. The experimenter doesn't require you to do anything specific. But if you do something, you may get points on the counter. Try to get as many points as possible.

In fact, participants would receive points on either a fixed time interval or a variable time interval. Nothing they did could have influenced the outcome in terms of points awarded. However, Ono recorded some very odd behaviour. Several subjects developed 'persistent idiosyncratic and stereotyped superstitious behaviour'. Effectively they began to try to find patterns of behaviour, such as pulling the left lever four times, and then the right lever twice, and the middle lever once.

My favourite behaviour was displayed by one young lady in Ono's study. He records,

> A point was delivered just as she jumped to the floor (from the table). . . after about five jumps, a point was delivered when she jumped and touched the ceiling with her slipper in her hand. Jumping to touch the ceiling continued repeatedly and was followed by more points until she stopped about 25 minutes into the session, perhaps because of fatigue.

Could it be that investors are like Skinner's pigeons, drawing lessons by observing the world's response to their actions? It is certainly possible. The basic failure with the pigeons and Ono's human experiments is that they only look at the positive co-occurrences, rather than look at the percentage of the times the strategy paid off, relative to all the times they tried.

ILLUSION OF CONTROL

We love to be in control. We generally hate the feeling of not being able to influence the outcome of an event. It is probably this control freak aspect of our nature that leads us to behave like Skinner's pigeons. My favourite example of the illusion of control concerns lottery tickets from the classic paper by Langer (1975). She asked some people to choose their own lottery numbers, while others were given a random assignment of numbers. Those who chose their own numbers wanted, on average, $9 to surrender the ticket. Those who received a random assignment/lucky dip lottery ticket wanted only $2! (see Figure 6.8.)

Another great example comes from Langer and Roth (1975). Subjects were asked to predict the outcome of 30 coin tosses. In reality, the accuracy of the participants was rigged so that

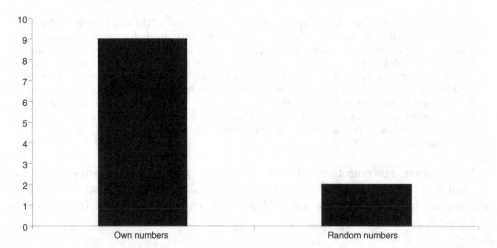

Figure 6.8   The illusion of control: price to sell lottery ticket ($).
Source: Langer (1975).

everyone guessed correctly in 15 of the trials, but roughly one-third of the subjects began by doing very well (guessing correctly on the first four tosses), one-third began very badly, and one-third met with random success. After the 30 tosses, people were asked to rate their performance. Those who started well, rated themselves as considerably better at guessing the outcomes than those who started badly.

In their analysis of a wide range of illusion of control studies, Presson and Benassi (1996) summarize that the illusion is more likely when lots of choices are available, you have early success at the task (as per above), the task you are undertaking is familiar to you, the amount of information available is high, and you have personal involvement. Large portfolios, high turnover and short time horizons all seem to be the financial equivalents of conditions that Presson and Benassi outline. Little wonder that the illusion of control bedevils our industry.

FEEDBACK DISTORTION

Not only are we prone to behave like Skinner's pigeons but we also know how to reach the conclusions we want to find (known as 'motivated reasoning' among psychologists). For instance, if we jump on the bathroom scales in the morning, and they give us a reading that we don't like, we tend to get off and try again (just to make sure we weren't standing in an odd fashion[1]). However, if the scales have delivered a number under our expectations, we would have hopped off the scales into the shower, feeling very good about life.

Strangely enough, we see exactly the same sort of behaviour in other areas of life. Ditto and Lopez (1992) set up a clever experiment to examine just such behaviour. Participants were told that they would be tested for the presence of TAA enzyme. Some were told that the TAA enzyme was beneficial (i.e. 'people who are TAA positive are 10 times less likely to experience pancreatic disease than are people whose secretory fluids don't contain TAA'), others were told that TAA was harmful ('10 times more likely to suffer pancreatic disease').

Half of the subjects in the experiment were asked to fill out a set of questions before they took the test; the other half were asked to answer the questions after the test. In particular two questions were important. The first stated that several factors (such as a lack of sleep) may impact the test, and participants were asked to list any such factors that they had experienced in the week before the test. The other question asked participants to rate the accuracy of the TAA enzyme test on a scale of 0 to 10 (with 10 being a perfect test).

Figures 6.9 and 6.10 show the results that Ditto and Lopez uncovered. In both questions there was little difference in the answers offered by those who were told that having the TAA enzyme was healthy and those who were told it was unhealthy *provided* they were asked before they were given the results. However, massive differences were observed once the results were given.

Those who were told that the enzyme was healthy and answered the questions *after* they had received the test results, gave less life irregularities and thought the test was better than those who answered the questions *before* they knew the test results.

Similarly, those who were told that the enzyme was unhealthy and answered the questions *after* the test results, provided considerably more life irregularities and thought the test was less reliable than those who answered *before* knowing the test results. Both groups behaved exactly as we do on the scales in the bathroom. Thus, we seem to be very good at accepting

---

[1] Of course, once you reach my size you start to regard the scales as the devil's device, and treat them with ignore.

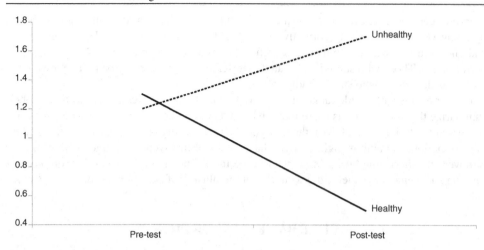

Figure 6.9   Number of test-affecting life irregularities cited.
Source: Ditto and Lopez (1992).

feedback we want to hear while not only ignoring, but actively arguing against, feedback we don't want to hear.

Interestingly, Westen *et al.* (2005) found that such motivated reasoning is associated with parts of the brain that control emotion, rather than logic (the X-system, rather than the C-system, for those who have attended one of my behavioural teach-ins). Committed Democrats and Republicans were shown statements from both Bush and Kerry and a neutral person (Figure 6.11). Then a contradictory piece of behaviour was shown, illustrating a gap between the rhetoric of the candidates and their actions. Participants were asked to rate how contradictory the words and deeds were (on a scale of 1 to 4). An exculpatory statement was then

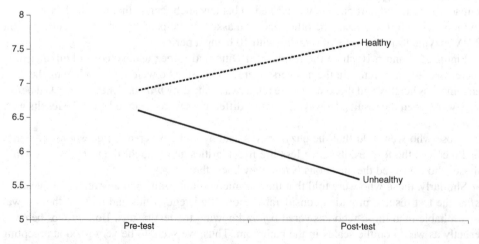

Figure 6.10   Perceived accuracy of TAA enzyme test.
Source: Ditto and Lopez (1992).

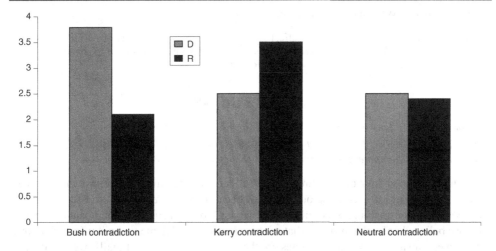

Figure 6.11 Behavioural ratings of the extent of the contradiction (scale 1 to 4, higher equals worse)
Source: Ditto and Lopez (1992).

provided, giving some explanation as to why the mismatch between words and deeds occurred, and finally participants were asked to rate whether the mismatch now seemed so bad in the light of the exculpatory statement.

Strangely enough, the Republicans thought that the Bush contradiction was far milder than the Democrats', and vice versa when considering the Kerry contradiction. Similar findings were reported for the question on whether the exculpatory statement mitigated the mismatched words and deeds (Table 6.2).

Westen *et al.* found that the neural correlates of motivated reasoning were associated with parts of the brain known to be used in the processing of emotional activity rather than logical analysis. They note *'Neural information processing related to motivated reasoning appears to be qualitatively different from reasoning in the absence of a strong emotional stake in the conclusions reached.'*

Furthermore, Westen *et al.* found that after the emotional conflict of the contradiction has been resolved a burst of activity in one of the brain's pleasure centres can be observed (the ventral striatum). That is to say, the brain rewards itself once an emotionally consistent outcome

Table 6.2 Example of statements

Initial	'First of all, Ken Lay is a supporter of mine. I love the man. I got to know Ken Lay years ago, and he has given generously to my campaign. When I'm President, I plan to run the government like a CEO runs a country, Ken Lay and Enron are a model of how I'll do that' – George Bush, 2000.
Contradictory	Mr Bush now avoids any mention of Ken Lay and is critical of Enron when asked.
Exculpatory	People who know the President report that he feels betrayed by Ken Lay, and was genuinely shocked to find that Enron's leadership had been corrupt.

Source: Westen *et al.* (2005).

has been reached. Westen *et al.* conclude:

> The combination of reduced negative affect ... and increased positive affect or reward ... once subjects had ample time to reach biased conclusions, suggests why motivated judgements may be so difficult to change (i.e. they are doubly reinforcing).

CONCLUSIONS

Experience is a dear teacher – Benjamin Franklin
Experience is a good teacher, but she sends in terrific bills – Minna Antrim
Experience is the name that everyone gives their mistakes – Oscar Wilde

We have outlined four major hurdles when it comes to learning from our own mistakes. Firstly, we often fail to recognize our mistakes because we attribute them to bad luck rather than poor decision-making. Secondly, when we are looking back, we often cannot separate what we believed beforehand from what we now know. Thirdly, due to the illusion of control, we often end up assuming that outcomes are the result of our actions. Finally, we are adept at distorting the feedback we do receive, so that it fits into our own view of our abilities.

Some of these behavioural problems can be countered by keeping written records of decisions and the 'logic' behind those decisions. But this requires discipline and a willingness to re-examine our past decisions. Psychologists have found that it takes far more information about mistakes than it should, to get us to change our minds.

As Ward Edwards (1968) notes:

> An abundance of research has shown that human beings are conservative processors of fallible information. Such experiments compare human behaviour with the outputs of Bayes's theorem, the formal optimal rule about how opinions. . . should be revised on the basis of new information. It turns out that opinion change is very orderly, and usually proportional to numbers calculated from Bayes's theorem – but it is insufficient in amount. A convenient first approximation to the data would say that it takes anywhere from two to five observation's to do one observations' worth of work in inducing a subject to change his opinion.

So little wonder that learning from past mistakes is a difficult process. However, as always, being aware of the potential problems is a first step to guarding against them.

SECTION II
The Professionals and the Biases

7

Behaving Badly[*]

> None of us is immune to behavioural biases. Those who have attended my teach-ins on the subject have had a short test inflicted upon them. This note provides both a copy of the test (for you to try) and an analysis of the results from our sample of 300 fund managers. I will say no more to avoid influencing your answers, but my faith in behavioural finance is stronger than ever!

---

* This article appeared in *Global Equity Strategy* on 2 February 2006. The material discussed was accurate at the time of publication.

Before you go any further, try the 17 questions below, but spend no more than 10 minutes on this test.

THE TEST

1. Please write down the last four digits of your telephone number.
2. Is the number of physicians in London higher or lower than this number?
3. What is your best guess as to the number of physicians in London?
4. A bat and a ball together cost $1.10. The bat costs $1.00 more than the ball. How much does the ball cost?
5. A health survey was conducted in a sample of adult males, in New Jersey, of all ages and occupations. Please give your best estimates of the following values:
   - What percentage of the men surveyed have had one or more heart attacks?
   - What percentage of the men surveyed are both over 55 and have had one or more heart attacks?
6. Are you above average at your job?
7. Imagine these are four playing cards laid out in front of you. Each one has a letter on one side and a number on the other. If a card has an E, it should have a 4. Which cards do you need to turn over in order to see if I am telling the truth?

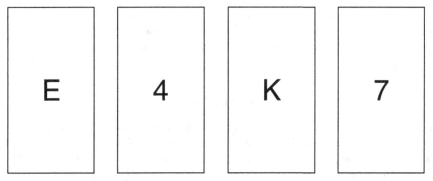

8. Suppose an unbiased coin is flipped three times, and each time the coin lands as heads. If you had to bet $1,000 on the next toss, what side would you choose? Heads, tails or no preference?
9. If it takes 5 machines 5 minutes to make 5 widgets, how long would it take 100 machines to make 100 widgets?
10. If John can drink one barrel of water in 6 days and Mary can drink one barrel of water in 12 days, how long would it take them to drink one barrel of water together?
11. Imagine that the UK is preparing for the outbreak of an unusual disease, which is expected to kill 600 people. Two alternative programmes to combat the disease have been proposed. Assume the exact scientific estimates of the consequences of the programmes are as follows:
    - If programme A is adopted 200 people will be saved.
    - If programme B is adopted there is a one-third probability that 600 people will be saved, and a two-thirds probability that no one will be saved.
    - Which programme do you choose?

12. You are offered the following bet. On the toss of a fair coin, if you lose you must pay £100, what is the minimum amount that you need to win in order to make this bet attractive to you?

13. In a lake, there is a patch of lily pads. Every day the patch doubles in size. If it takes 48 days for the patch to cover the entire lake, how long would it take for the patch to cover half the lake?

14. The same disease from question 11 is back. Only this time the two programmes now have the following payoffs:
    - If programme C is adopted 400 people will die.
    - If programme D is adopted there is a one-third probability that nobody will die, and a two-thirds probability that 600 people will die.
    - Which programme do you support?

15. A student at a university has a Grade Point Average (GPA) of 3.8 in her first semester. The average GPA at the university is 3.1. What will be her GPA percentile when she graduates as a senior? (The better she does the higher the percentile... i.e. 100 would be the top people in the year.)

16. You are on a game show. You are offered a choice of one of three doors. Behind two of the doors there is a goat. Behind one the doors there is a car. When you announce the door you have chosen, the host of the show opens one of the two doors not selected by you, and reveals a goat. After he has done this, he offers you the opportunity to switch your choice. Should you stick or switch?

17. You are now going to play a game against the others sitting in this room. The game is simply this. Pick a number between 0 and 100. The winner of the game will be the person who guesses the number closest to two-thirds of the average number picked. What would be your guess?

THE RESULTS

Nearly 300 professional fund managers have submitted themselves to the unpleasant task of trying to answer these questions. The victims have come from all areas of the globe. I've had the opportunity to administer this test to investors from the UK, the USA, Asia and Europe. Interestingly, the results I've found do not show any geographic distinguishing features; Americans were no more likely to be overoptimistic than the Brits, for instance. I have also been able to test managers at both large and small institutions, and across a variety of asset classes and investment styles. However, there were few discernible differences across different groups. So I will aggregate the answers to provide an overview of the most common biases displayed by professional fund managers.

OVEROPTIMISM

The most common bias we come across is overoptimism – that is, people's tendency to exaggerate their own abilities. That is particularly likely when people suffer the illusion of control (they think they can influence the outcome) or the illusion of knowledge (they think they know more than everyone else). Both of these illusions seem to be writ large in financial markets. Question 6 was obviously an attempt to see just how overoptimistic fund managers were. The results show *that some 74% of our sample thought themselves above average at their jobs* (Figure 7.1). Many wrote comments along the lines of "I know everyone says they

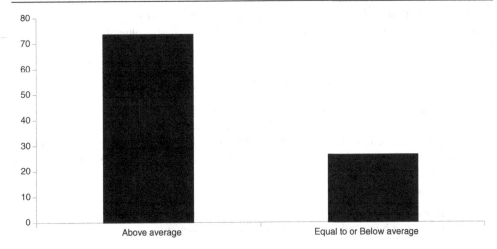

Figure 7.1   The illusion of control: the % of fund managers who believe they are....
Source: DrKW Macro research.

are, but I really am"! Of the remaining 26%, most thought they were average, but very few, if any, said they were below average!

When presenting on behavioural finance I regularly ask the audience whether they are above-average drivers. However, the best response rate comes from the question of whether or not people are above-average lovers. You can always count on one male member of the audience putting up both arms and jumping up and down. Indeed, so far I have found only one person who thinks he is a below-average lover!

CONFIRMATORY BIAS

An amazing 95% of those who took the test failed question 7: the four cards (E, 4, K, and 7) with each card having a number on one side and a letter on the other. You are told if the card has an E it should have a 4 on the reverse, so which card or cards do you need to turn over to see if you were told the truth or not?

The two most common answers are E and 4. However, the correct answer is that you need to turn over the E and 7. The E is pretty obvious, since if you turn it over and there isn't a 4 on the reverse then you were being told a lie. If you turn the 7 over and it has an E on the back you have also proved you were lied to. However, 4 can't tell you anything. The rubric for the question states that an E should have a 4, *not* that a 4 should have an E. So turning the 4 over can't tell you anything at all.

The habit of turning the 4 over is an example of confirmatory bias – the tendency to look for information that agrees with us. When Karl Popper wrote his philosophy of science he argued that the only way of testing a hypothesis was to form the view and then spend the rest of the day looking for the evidence that proves you to be wrong. But that isn't the way we work, instead we form our views and then spend the rest of the day finding all the information that agrees with our view.

So instead of having meetings with those who agree with us, we should actually sit down with those who disagree with us. Not so we change our minds because the odds on changing our minds through straight conversation are essentially zero, but rather so we are aware of the opposite point of view. If we can't identify the logical flaw in their argument then we shouldn't be so sure about our own view.

REPRESENTATIVENESS

One of the other common heuristics (rules of thumb) is judging things by how they appear rather than how statistically likely they are. The classic example comes from the seminal paper by Tversky and Kahneman (1983). It concerns Linda, a 31-year-old who is single, outspoken and very bright. She majored in philosophy. As a student, she was deeply concerned with issues of discrimination and equality.

Which is more likely?

1. Linda works in a bank.
2. Linda works in a bank and is active in the feminist movement.

An alarmingly high percentage of people go for the second option. However, it can't possibly be true, as it represents a conjunction fallacy. That is, there must always be more people who work in banks than there are who work in banks *and* are active in the feminist movement.

So why do so many people get this question wrong? The answer seems to be that the description is biased, it sounds like someone who might plausibly be involved in the feminist movement. People are driven by the narrative of the description rather than by the logic of the analysis.

Our test contained several examples of various elements of representativeness. The first was question 5. The question concerned estimating the percentage of men in New Jersey who had one or more heart attacks, followed by the percentage of men over 55 who had one or more heart attacks. The second part of the question is a conjunction fallacy in the same way as the Linda problem. There are always going to be more men who had one or more heart attacks than there are men over 55 *and* one or more heart attacks.

However, across our 300 fund managers the estimated average percentage of men suffering one or more heart attacks was 12.5%, while the estimated percentage of men over 55 and suffering one or more heart attacks was 16%.

Of course, averages can hide all sorts of things, so looking at the full data set reveals that 40% of the sample suffered from representativeness in as much as they had higher estimates of the latter part of the question compared to the first section answer!

Two other questions also relate to the representativeness heuristic. The first was question 8, the fair coin that has landed on heads for three successive times. You have to bet $1000 on the next toss. What would you call?

The good news is that 81% of the survey correctly said they had no preference. 12.5% displayed the gamblers' fallacy – betting on a reversal when clearly the coin has no memory so each outcome is equally likely. Presumably, these are the same people who stand at roulette tables carefully watching the reds and blacks and betting against the runs of random events. 6.5% suffered the hot hand fallacy – that is, they saw the sequence and took it as evidence that the coin was 'hot' and would thus keep coming up heads.

The other question that is designed to tease out the representativeness heuristic is question 15. This was a highly unpopular question: around 60% of people either couldn't or wouldn't answer the question. It concerns the percentile prediction of a student when she finally graduates using information from her first semester.

In fact, the performance of a student in the first semester is totally uncorrelated with the outcome of a degree course nearly three years later. Given the information available – that the student was above average in the first semester, but nothing else – the optimal prediction is that she will simply perform in an average fashion at the end of her degree, so a 50th percentile forecast would have been rational.

Of the 40% of the fund managers who answered this question, 86% displayed some form of extreme prediction. That is to say, they had a forecast of over 50. In fact the average forecast was for a 74th percentile ranking. This is again a form of the representativeness heuristic, since answers such as these represent the extrapolation of a single (meaningless) data point into the indefinite future!

THE COGNITIVE REFLECTION TASK (CRT)

Questions 4, 9 and 13 collectively form the Cognitive Reflection Task (CRT). This test was designed by Shane Frederick (2005)[1] of MIT. As regular readers will know, I often talk of the brain having two different systems. Using the labels of Lieberman *et al.* (2002) we refer to these as the X-system and the C-system. The X-system is the default option. It is an effortless, fast, parallel-processing system. The C-system requires a deliberate effort to use and is slow but logical. The CRT was designed to see how easy people find it to interrupt their X-system style automatic responses.

Each of the three questions has an obvious but incorrect answer and a less obvious but correct response. For instance, in the bat and the ball question the answer that leaps to mind is 10c. However, even a moment's reflection reveals that the difference between $1 and 10c is only 90c, not $1 as the question states.

The correct answer is, of course, 5c. Just writing down the problem should make this transparent:

Bat + ball = 1.10
Bat − ball = 1
2 Bat = 2.10
Bat = 1.05, therefore ball = 0.05

The answer to question 9 is 5 minutes, but 100 minutes is the oft-cited incorrect answer. And the correct answer to question 13 is 47 days, not 24 days. The idea that the CRT problems generate incorrect 'intuitive' answers is supported by the dominance of a standard set of incorrect answers (i.e. the most common incorrect answers are 10 cents, 100 minutes and 24 days).

Further support comes from Frederick's observation that 'Those who answered 10 cents to the "bat and ball" problem estimated that 92 percent of people would correctly solve it, whereas those who answered "5 cents" estimated that "only" 62 percent would'.

Table 7.1 shows a selection of the results that Frederick uncovered when administering the CRT. I have also shown the overall average (including a long list of studies not reported here) from Frederick's work, plus the comparative line for our sample of professional fund managers. Of the 300 fund managers who have taken the test, *only 40% managed to get all three questions right*. Thus only a minority managed to get the maximum score.

This performance puts professional fund managers above Princeton students, but below the best performing group – the MIT students. Of our sample, 10% didn't manage to get any of

---

[1] My thanks to Daniel Read of Durham University for bringing Shanes' work to my attention.

Table 7.1   CRT scores

Location/institution	Mean CRT score	0 (%)	1 (%)	2 (%)	3 (%)
MIT	2.18	7	16	30	48
Princeton	1.63	18	27	28	26
Boston fireworks display	1.53	24	24	26	26
Carnegie Mellon University	1.51	25	25	25	25
Harvard University	1.43	20	37	24	20
Overall	**1.24**	**33**	**28**	**23**	**17**
Professional fund managers	1.99	10	21	29	40

Source: Frederick (2005), and DrKW Macro research.

the CRT questions right. In terms of the individual questions, 58% got question 4 correct, 68% correctly answered question 9 and 74% managed to figure out question 14.

Frederick finds that the number of CRT questions passed is highly correlated with several behavioural traits. Specifically he finds that those with a high CRT score are more patient. For example, consider the following choice: you can either have $3,400 this month or $3,800 next month, which do you choose?

Of those who scored zero on the CRT, 65% went for the near term lower payout (which implies an annual discount rate of 280%!). In contrast, of those with the highest CRT score, 60% went for the further out higher payout.

A similar finding resulted from asking people how much they would be willing to pay for overnight shipping of a chosen book. Those with a zero CRT score were willing to pay an average $4.54, while those with the maximum score were willing to pay $2.18.

Frederick also found that the CRT was positively correlated with people's attitudes to risk. Table 7.2 shows the results when people were presented with various risks. When the gamble was framed in terms of gains, those with a high CRT score were far more likely to select the riskier option. However, when framed in terms of losses, the high CRT group were markedly less loss averse and selected to take the certain loss rather than gamble.

In many of the behaviour patterns we observe there is a marked difference between the performance of those with high and low scores on the CRT. So, in the sections below I will show the average/overall results and then show the results obtained for the various CRT groups.

Table 7.2   Risk attitudes and the CRT

	Percentage choosing riskier option	
Gamble	Low CRT score	High CRT score
$100 for sure or a 75% chance of $250	19	38
Lose $100 for sure or a 75% chance to lose $250	54	31
$100 for sure or a 3% chance of $7000	8	21
Lose $100 for sure or a 3% chance to lose $7000	63	28

Source: Frederick (2005).

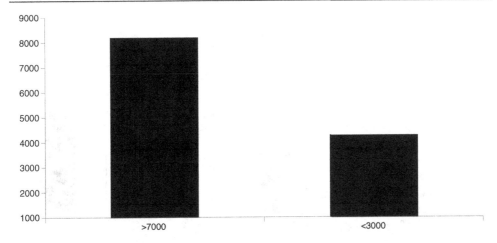

Figure 7.2 Anchoring: Telephone numbers as an input.
Source: DrKW Macro research.

ANCHORING

The very first set of questions were designed to see if fund managers displayed any tendency towards anchoring. Remember that anchoring is our tendency to grab hold of irrelevant and often subliminal inputs in the face of uncertainty. The idea behind the question is to see if people use their phone numbers as an input when trying to estimate the number of doctors in London.

Of course, if people were rational then there would be no difference between those who happened to have high telephone numbers and those with low telephone numbers. Unfortunately, as Figure 7.2 shows, those with telephone numbers above 7000 believe there are on average just over 8000 doctors. Those with telephone numbers below 3000 think there are around 4000 doctors. This represents a very clear difference of opinion driven by the fact that investors are using their telephone numbers, albeit subconsciously, as inputs into their forecast.

From the perspective of the CRT, all the groups except those with the maximum CRT score exhibit noticeable anchoring effects (Figure 7.3). We do not have very many managers in the zero category (thankfully!) so we cannot be sure (statistically speaking) that there is a meaningful difference, but in the other cases we certainly can.

Framing

Framing refers to a situation whereby we fail to see through the way in which information is provided to us. In the test, one question was essentially presented twice. Once framed in terms of saving lives and once in terms of killing people (questions 11 and 14). There is no attempt at trickery – question 14 even refers to question 11. If people were rational then it should make no difference whether the question is stated in terms of saving 200 people or of 400 people dying.

However, Figure 7.4 shows that when the question was framed in terms of saving lives, nearly 80% of respondents chose the certain option. However, when it was framed in terms of people dying, only 56% of people chose the certain option. This is a serious preference

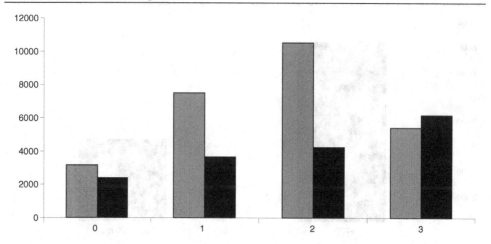

Figure 7.3   Anchoring: by CRT group.
Source: DrKW Macro research.

reversal – and a major problem for economics which claims that people's preferences should be stable.

Equally as worrying from our perspective, 20% of the population were indifferent between options A and B or options C and D. This shows an alarming lack of understanding about risk. Option A results in 200 lives saved for sure, whereas option B only has an expected value of 200 lives saved. A certain value should always be preferred to an exactly equal *expected* payoff! After all it is only *expected*, whereas the certain value is guaranteed. The indifference expressed means that the respondents fail to take into account the risk involved. This lack of understanding of risk is slightly unsettling given that our industry is meant to be vaguely aware of the concept!

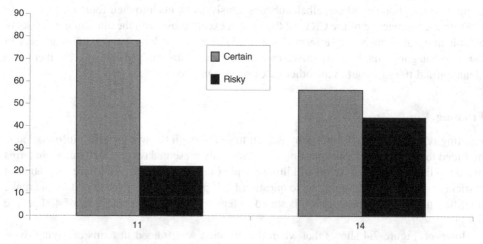

Figure 7.4   Framing: clear evidence of a preference reversal (%).
Source: DrKW Macro research.

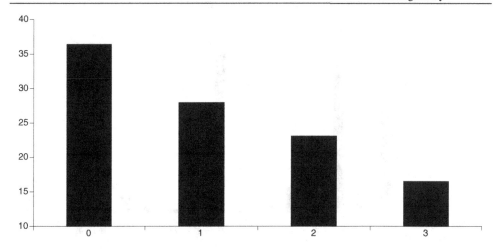

Figure 7.5 Framing effects drop as CRT score rises (%).
Source: DrKW Macro research.

This represents a large preference reversal with 22% of people appearing to change their minds between the two presentations of the problem – a far cry from rationality.

Figure 7.5 shows the percentage of participants showing a preference reversal sorted into CRT groups. The scale of preference reversals is monotonically declining as the success at the CRT increases. So nearly 40% of those who did not get any of the CRT questions correct exhibited a preference switch. This drops to 16.5% by the time we work our way up to the group with the highest CRT score.

Loss Aversion

Loss aversion refers to our tendency to dislike losses far more than we like gains. Question 12 represents a quick and easy way of measuring the scale of loss aversion. On the toss of a fair coin, if you lose you have to pay me £100. What is the minimum you need to win to make that bet attractive?

The frequency of choices is shown in Figure 7.6. The average is £190! That fits pretty well with the vast majority of studies which show that generally people dislike losses somewhere around 2 to $2\frac{1}{2}$ times as much as they enjoy gains.

It is slightly worrying that we got answers below £100! Even I could make money out of these people.

The scale of reward needed to persuade people to accept the bet is also closely related to the CRT. For instance, those who got only one of the CRT questions correct required an average of £275, those with two CRT questions correct £229, those with the maximum CRT score asked for only £165 (Figure 7.7).

Those with zero score on the CRT only asked for £158. However, 60% of them did not answer the question. It remains unclear whether they did not understand the question (which seems unlikely) or whether they simply will not bet at all (i.e. an infinite required payoff). So I do not read much into the low requested amount from the zeros.

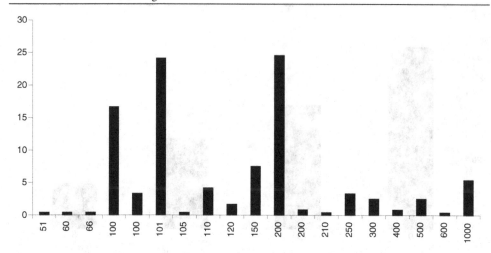

Figure 7.6   Fund managers are just about as loss averse as everyone else (frequency %).
Source: DrKW Macro research.

KEYNES'S BEAUTY CONTEST

When Keynes wrote Chapter 12 of the *General Theory* he likened professional investing to a newspaper beauty contest. He opined:

> The actual, private object of the most skilled investment to-day is 'to beat the gun', to outwit the crowd, and to pass the bad, or depreciating, half-crown to the other fellow.
>
> This battle of wits to anticipate the basis of conventional valuation a few months hence, rather than the prospective yield of an investment over a long term of years, does not even require gulls amongst the public to feed the maws of the professional; — it can be played

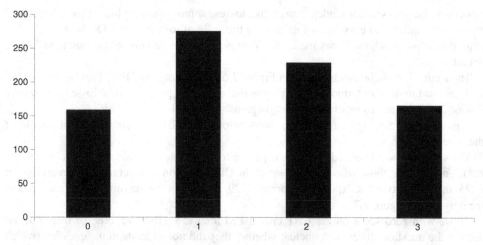

Figure 7.7   Amount needed to play the gamble by CRT score (£).
Source: DrKW Macro research.

by professionals amongst themselves. Nor is it necessary that anyone should keep his simple faith in the conventional basis of valuation having any genuine long-term validity. For it is, so to speak, a game of Snap, of Old Maid, of Musical Chairs — a pastime in which he is victor who says Snap neither too soon nor too late, who passes the Old Maid to his neighbour before the game is over, who secures a chair for himself when the music stops. These games can be played with zest and enjoyment, though all the players know that it is the Old Maid which is circulating, or that when the music stops some of the players will find themselves unseated.

Or, to change the metaphor slightly, professional investment may be likened to those newspaper competitions in which the competitors have to pick out the six prettiest faces from a hundred photographs, the prize being awarded to the competitor whose choice most nearly corresponds to the average preferences of the competitors as a whole; so that each competitor has to pick, not those faces which he himself finds prettiest, but those which he thinks likeliest to catch the fancy of the other competitors, all of whom are looking at the problem from the same point of view. It is not a case of choosing those which, to the best of one's judgment, are really the prettiest, nor even those which average opinion genuinely thinks the prettiest. We have reached the third degree where we devote our intelligences to anticipating what average opinion expects the average opinion to be. And there are some, I believe, who practise the fourth, fifth and higher degrees.

John Maynard Keynes, *General Theory of Employment, Interest and Money* (1936) pp. 155–156.

I have played this game before. Indeed for an in-depth discussion on the subject see *Global Equity Strategy*, 17 February 2004. Question 17 represents a mathematical version of the game. The aim of the task is to pick a number between 0 and 100, the winner being the person who picks the number closest to two-thirds of the average number picked.

The game itself should be simple under the standard assumptions of economics, i.e. rationality *and* common knowledge. Since all players want to choose two-thirds of the average, there is only one number that satisfies the equation $x = 2/3 \times x$, and that is zero. So the only equilibrium[2] answer to this question is zero (as many of you pointed out).

The game can be solved by a process known as 'iterated dominance'. A dominated strategy is one that yields a lower payoff than another, regardless of what other players are doing. For example, choosing a number greater than 67 is a dominated strategy because the highest possible solution to the game is 67 (i.e. if everyone else picks the maximum number 100). However, if no one violates dominance by choosing a number above 67, then the highest outcome is two-thirds of 67 and so on. Deleting dominated strategies in this fashion will eventually lead you to zero.[3]

Of course, this only works under the assumption that everyone you are playing against is rational, and they know that you are rational as well. As soon as we start to see that at least some of the market is not fully rational, then the problem becomes more and more complex.

I originally played this game to show how hard it was to be just one step ahead of everyone else. The findings from playing it again show that this is still a very valid conclusion. Figure 7.8 shows the frequency of answers from our 300 fund managers.

The average number picked was 30 giving a two-thirds average of 20. Rather than using the iterated dominance strategies outlined earlier, most players assume that the starting point should be 50, i.e. the mean from a random draw. Hence level-0 players chose 50 (15% of our total sample). Level-1 players chose the best reaction to the level-0 players, i.e. they picked two-thirds of 50, providing a spike at 33 (14% of our sample). Level-two players "best react"

[2] Technically, zero is the only fixed point Nash equilibrium.
[3] This process is also known as backward induction.

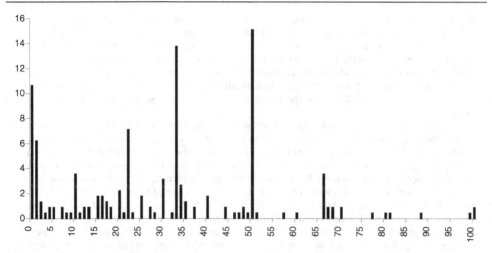

Figure 7.8   Keynes's beauty contest (frequency, %).
Source: DrKW Macro research.

to a 33, yielding the massive spike at 22 (7% of our sample). Level-3 players end up with 15 as their pick (2% of the sample). Once past level 2 or 3 reasoning, players frequently slide down the slippery slope towards the infinite iterations that produce zero (11% of our sample).

It is easy to measure the number of steps of strategic thinking that are being carried out by the following formula (for choices less than 50) $\ln(x/50)/\ln(2/3)$. So with an average of 30, the average level of thinking comes out at 1.3 steps!

People's performance on the CRT was related to the degrees of thinking they displayed when on the beauty contest game (Figure 7.9). Those with a zero score on the CRT selected an average number of 47 in the beauty contest, whereas those with a score of 3 on the CRT had an average selection of 22.

MONTY HALL PROBLEM

The final element examined by our test is the Monty Hall problem. This is one of the most divisive problems that I have ever encountered. It regularly leaves professors of maths purple in the face from arguing about it. It is question 16, the game show with the three doors, behind which are two goats and one car. I am assuming that you want to win the car, as I played this with one person who was Greek and said he wanted to win the goats!

You pick a door, then I will open one of the other doors and reveal a goat. I then offer you the chance to switch from the door you have chosen to the other unopened door. Should you switch?

Of the participants, 47% said they would stick with the door they originally chose; 43% said they would switch; and 11% said they had no preference (Figure 7.10). The correct answer is that you should switch. Now why?

Well consider the pictures on page 100. Each row represents a version of the game. Let us assume that you always choose door 1 (purely for pedagogical reasons). In the first row I can

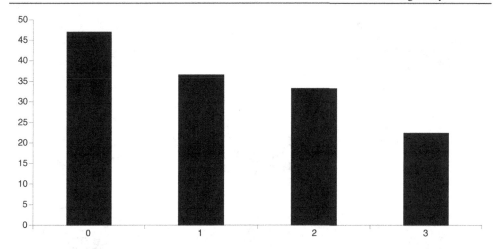

Figure 7.9   Keynes's beauty contest average choice by CRT group.
Source: DrKW Macro research.

then open either door 2 or 3, and if you switch you lose. However, in the other two games switch is the optimal strategy. In the second row you pick door 2, and I will open door 3, if you switch you win. In the third row you pick door 1, and I will open door two, if you switch you win. The hidden piece of information is that I am never going to reveal the car. So the only time you win by sticking is when you pick the car straight off – a one in three chance.

An alternative way of thinking about it is to do the following. The door you pick obviously has a 1 in 3 chance of being the correct door. When I open the door it very clearly has a zero probability attached to it. Thus the other door must have a probability of two-thirds. This can be proved via Bayes' theorem, but I will omit the proof for the sake of readability.

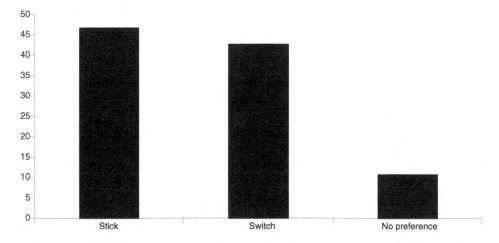

Figure 7.10   Percentage choosing each option in the Monty Hall problem.
Source: DrKW Macro research.

CONCLUSIONS

The purpose of this note was to illustrate that professional fund managers are not a breed apart. They are just as likely as everyone else to suffer behaviour biases. The objective is not to laugh at how foolish others are, but rather to show just how hard it is to avoid falling into cognitive pitfalls.

Even those with the maximum CRT score still appeared to generate exaggerated opinions of themselves, and to have a tendency to look for information that agreed with them.

The challenge facing all of us is to learn to be more reflective rather than reflexive. Of course, learning isn't easy. So designing a framework that is relatively robust to behavioural biases may actually be the easy path – I started down that road with the 'Seven sins of fund management' (see *Global Equity Strategy*, 18 November 2005).

SECTION III

The Seven Sins of Fund Management

8

A Behavioural Critique*

How can behavioural finance inform the investment process? We have taken a hypothetical 'typical' large fund management house and analysed their process. This collection of notes tries to explore some of the areas in which understanding psychology could radically alter the way they structure their businesses. The results may challenge some of your most deeply held beliefs.

- This collection of notes aims to explore some of the more obvious behavioural weaknesses inherent in the 'average' investment process.
- Seven sins (common mistakes) were identified. The first was placing forecasting at the very heart of the investment process. An enormous amount of evidence suggests that investors are generally hopeless at forecasting. So using forecasts as an integral part of the investment process is like tying one hand behind your back before you start.
- Secondly, investors seem to be obsessed with information. Instead of focusing on a few important factors (such as valuations and earnings quality), many investors spend countless hours trying to become experts about almost everything. The evidence suggests that, in general, more information just makes us increasingly overconfident rather than better at making decisions.
- Thirdly, the insistence of spending hours meeting company managements strikes us as bizarre from a psychological standpoint. We are not good at looking for information that will prove us to be wrong. So most of the time, these meetings are likely to be mutual love-ins. Our ability to spot deception is also very poor, so we won't even spot who is lying.
- Fourthly, many investors spend their time trying to 'beat the gun' as Keynes put it. Effectively, everyone thinks they can get in at the bottom and out at the top. However, this seems to be remarkably hubristic.
- Fifthly, many investors seem to end up trying to perform on very short time horizons and overtrade as a consequence. The average holding period for a stock on the NYSE is 11 months! This has nothing to do with investment; it is speculation, pure and simple.
- Penultimately, we all appear to be hard-wired to accept stories. However, stories can be very misleading. Investors would be better served by looking at the facts, rather than getting sucked into a great (but often hollow) tale.

---

*This article appeared in *Global Equity Strategy* on 18 November 2005. The material discussed was accurate at the time of publication.

- And finally, many of the decisions taken by investors are the result of group interaction. Unfortunately groups are far more a behavioural panacea. In general, they amplify rather than alleviate the problems of decision-making.
- Each of these sins seems to be a largely self-imposed handicap when it comes to trying to outperform. Identifying the psychological flaws in the 'average' investment process is an important first step in trying to design a superior version that might just be more robust to behavioural biases.

SIN CITY

Over the last year or so we have produced a series of notes in *Global Equity Strategy* that have sought to provide an 'outside' perspective on the fund management industry. The driving force behind these notes is that whenever I present on behavioural finance to those in the industry, the most frequent response I get is: 'That it is all very interesting but how do I apply it?'

This chapter is my attempt to take some of the basic biases and then demonstrate just where they might crop up. Having been privy to a great many clients and their processes over the last 12 years or so, I decided to create a composite 'typical' large fund management house. As I thought about the various aspects of this firm's investment process, I began to see the areas where behavioural biases may reach their zenith. These became the seven sins of fund management.

Sin 1: Forecasting (Pride)

An enormous amount of evidence suggests that we simply cannot forecast. The core root of this inability to forecast seems to lie in the fact that we all seem to be overoptimistic and overconfident. For instance, we have found that around 75% of fund managers think they are above average at their jobs! It doesn't matter whether it is forecasting bonds, equities, earnings or pretty much anything else, we are simply far too sure about our ability to forecast the future.

Given the dreadful track records that can be seen from even a cursory glance at the data, it begs the question of why we bother to use forecasts let alone put them at the very heart of the investment process? (A mistake that probably 95% of the investment processes I've come across persist in making.)

The answer probably lies in a trait known as anchoring. That is, in the face of uncertainty, we will cling to any irrelevant number as support. Little wonder, then, that investors continue to rely on forecasts.

Some have argued that any forecast is better than no forecast at all. For instance, Joe Nocera, writing in the *New York Times* (1 October 2005) opined

> Indeed, I wound up thinking that forecasting is to the market what gravity is to the earth. As much as we like to poke fun at faulty predictions, we can't function without them. Even if we disagree with, say, the analysts' consensus on Cisco, that consensus gives us to a basis that helps us to form our own judgments about whether it is overvalued or undervalued. Without forecasts, the market would no longer be grounded to anything.

This misses the point on many levels. Firstly, when it comes to anchoring we know that irrelevant numbers can influence people's behaviour. For instance, Englich *et al.* (2005) show that legal experts were influenced by irrelevant anchors when setting jail sentences even when the experts were fully aware of the irrelevance of the input.

In one study, participants (judges) were asked to role dice to determine the sentencing request from the prosecution. The pair of dice they used were loaded to either give a low number (1, 2) or a high number (3, 6). Having rolled the dice, participants were told to sum the scores and this number represented the prosecution's demand. Since the judges themselves rolled the dice, they could clearly see that the input was totally irrelevant. However, the group who received the total score of 3 issued an average sentence of 5.3 months; those who received a total score of 9 issued an average sentence of 7.8 months! So, by even providing a forecast, people are likely to cling to it.

Secondly, and this is a really radical idea, what if we anchor share values in something we can measure like dividends! Since we know people will stumble into the pitfall of anchoring, our best hope is getting them to anchor to something vaguely sensible. Support for this idea is offered by the work of Hirota and Sunder (2003). They show that in experimental markets, bubbles are much more likely to appear when investors lack dividends as an anchor.

Sin 2: The Illusion of Knowledge (Gluttony)

All too often it seems that we thirst for more and more information. Investors appear to believe that they need to know more than everyone else in order to outperform. This belief actually stems from an efficient market's view of the world. If markets are efficient, then the only way they can be beaten is by knowing something that everyone else doesn't know, i.e. knowing more information or knowing the future. It is all the more paradoxical, therefore, to find fund managers regularly displaying such a belief.

The psychological literature suggests that we have cognitive limits to our capacity to handle information. Indeed we seem to make the same decision regardless of the amount of information we have at our disposal. Beyond fairly low amounts of information, anything we gather generally seems to increase our confidence rather than improve our accuracy. So more information isn't better information, it is what you do with it, rather than how much you collect that matters.

Sin 3: Meeting Companies (Lust)

Why does meeting companies hold such an important place in the investment process of many fund managers? Is it because they provide deep insights into why we should invest in them? Or is it because we need to fill our time with something that makes us look busy?

There are at least five psychological hurdles that must be overcome if meeting companies is to add value to an investment process. Firstly, consider the point just made above. More information isn't better information, so why join the futile quest for an informational edge that probably doesn't exist? Secondly, corporate managers are just like the rest of us. They tend to suffer from cognitive illusions, so their views are likely to be highly biased. Thirdly, we all tend to suffer from confirmatory bias – that is, a habit of looking for information that agrees with us. So rather than asking lots of hard questions that test our base case, we tend to ask nice leading questions that generate the answers we want to hear. Fourthly, we have an innate tendency to obey figures of authority. Since company managers have generally reached the pinnacle of their profession, it is easy to envisage situations where analysts and fund managers find themselves effectively overawed.

Finally, the sad truth is that we are simply lousy at telling truth from deception. We all think we are great at spotting liars, but the data shows otherwise, we generally perform in line with pure chance. So even when you meet companies you won't be able to tell whether they are telling the truth or not.

Sin 4: Thinking You Can Outsmart Everyone Else (Envy)

One of the responses I occasionally encounter when teaching behavioural finance is 'now that I understand behavioural finance, I can outsmart everyone else'. To me this fails to learn the two most common behavioural traits mentioned earlier, overoptimism and overconfidence. To try to illustrate just how hard it was to be just one step ahead of everyone else, we played a version of Keynes's beauty contests with our clients. The results illustrate just what a tall order such a strategy actually is. Only three people out of 1000 managed to pick the correct answer!

Sin 5: Short Time Horizons and Overtrading (Avarice)

Because so many investors end up confusing noise with news, and trying to outsmart each other, they end up with ridiculously short time horizons. The average holding period for a stock on the New York Stock Exchange is 11 months! Over 11 months your return is just a function of price changes. It has nothing to do with intrinsic value or discounted cash flow. It is just people punting on stocks, speculating not investing.

Sin 6: Believing Everything You Read (Sloth)

We all love a story. Stock brokers spin stories that act like sirens drawing investors onto the rocks. More often than not these stories hold out the hope of growth, and investors find the allure of growth almost irresistible. The only snag is that all too often that growth fails to materialize.

Sadly, we appear to be hard-wired to accept stories at face value. In fact, evidence suggests that in order to understand something we have to believe it first. Then, if we are lucky, we might engage in an evaluative process. Even the most ridiculous of excuses/stories is enough to get results. For instance, Langer et al. (1978) asked people in a queue for a photocopier if they could push in. Sometimes, they offered the 'placebic' excuse it was because 'they needed to make copies'; on other occasions an excuse was omitted altogether. Even when no excuse was offered, 42% of people let the experimenter push in front of them. When the excuse was included, nearly 60% of people gave way to the experimenter! We need to be sceptical of the stories we are presented with.

Sin 7: Group-Based Decisions (Wrath)

The final sin I've covered in this collection is the generally held belief that groups are better at making decisions than individuals. The dream model of a group is that it meets, exchanges ideas and reaches sensible conclusions. The idea seems to be that group members will offset each other's biases.

Unfortunately, social psychologists have spent most of the last 30 years showing that group decisions are among the worst ever made. Far from offsetting each other's biases, groups usually end up amplifying them! Groups tend to reduce the variance of opinions, and lead members to have more confidence in their decisions after group discussions (without improving accuracy). They also tend to be very bad at uncovering hidden information. Indeed, members of groups frequently enjoy enhanced competency and credibility in the eyes of their peers if they provide information that is consistent with the group view. So using groups as the basis of asset allocation or stock selection seems to be yet another self-imposed handicap on performance.

ALTERNATIVE APPROACHES AND FUTURE DIRECTIONS

Over the course of publishing these notes, some have noticed that they tend to provide a list of 'don'ts', as in don't forecast, don't meet company managements, etc. Personally I have no problem with this, as knowing what not to do should itself be a useful guide. However, some would prefer a list of what to do. I've explored in many notes the possible use of alternative approaches, which generally rely on a quantitative approach to investing (see *Global Equity Strategy*, 16 March 2005) and I will be writing on this later. The seven sins listed here are not the only ones that could occur. Future work will be directed towards other sins, including the illusion of control, the possibility of having too much choice, and benchmarking. But in the meantime we hope the notes selected here provide some hints on how we might construct an investment process that may be slightly more robust to behavioural biases than many currently appear.

SIN 1

Forecasting (Pride)

The Folly of Forecasting: Ignore all Economists, Strategists, & Analysts*

Both an enormous amount of evidence and anecdotal experience suggests that people are very bad at forecasting. This is often because we all tend to be massively overconfident. This begs two questions: firstly, why do we persist in forecasting despite the appalling track record? And, more importantly, why do investors put forecasts at the heart of the investment process?

- Lao Tzu, a sixth-century BC poet, observed: 'Those who have knowledge don't predict. Those who predict don't have knowledge.' Despite these age-old words of wisdom our industry seems to persist in producing and using forecasts. This is all the more puzzling given the easily available data on the appalling nature of track records in forecasting. Economists, strategists and analysts are all guilty. In general, forecasts seem to be a lagged function of actual outcomes – adaptive expectations dominate forecasts.

- The two most common biases are overoptimism and overconfidence. Overconfidence refers to a situation whereby people are surprised more often than they expect to be. Effectively people are generally much too sure about their ability to predict. This tendency is particularly pronounced among experts – that is to say, experts are more overconfident than lay people. This is consistent with the illusion of knowledge driving overconfidence.

- Several studies confirm professional investors to be particularly overconfident. For instance, one recent study found that 68% of analysts thought they were above average at forecasting earnings! I've found that 75% of fund managers think they are above average at their jobs.

- Why do we persist in forecasting, given such appalling track records? There are two avenues to explore – simply put, ignorance and arrogance. Dunning and colleagues have documented that the worst performers are generally the most overconfident. They argue that such individuals suffer a double curse of being unskilled and unaware of it. Dunning *et al.* argue that the skills needed to produce correct responses are virtually identical to those needed to self-evaluate the potential accuracy of responses. Hence the problem.

- Tetlock argues that experts regularly deploy five ego defence mechanisms. Experts use various combinations of these defences to enable them to continue to forecast, despite their poor performance.

- Why do we persist in using forecasts in the investment process? The answer probably lies in behaviour known as anchoring. That is, in the face of uncertainty we will cling to any

---

*This article appeared in *Global Equity Strategy* on 18 November 2005. The material discussed was accurate at the time of publication.

irrelevant number as support. So it is little wonder that investors cling to forecasts, despite their uselessness.

- So what can be done to avoid these problems? Most obviously we need to stop relying on pointless forecasts. There are plenty of investment strategies that don't need forecasts as inputs, such as value strategies based on trailing earnings, or momentum strategies based on past prices. Secondly, we need to redeploy the armies of analysts. They should return to doing what their name suggests: analysing, rather than trying to guess the unknowable!

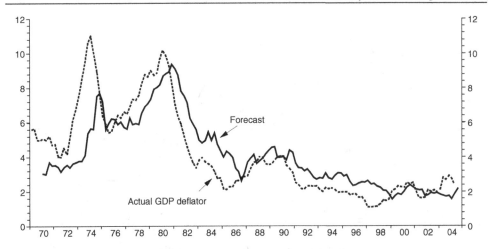

Figure 9.1   US GDP deflator and forecasts.
Source: DrKW Macro research.

Those who have endured one of my behavioural finance presentations will have heard me rant and rave over the pointlessness of forecasting. I have finally got around to putting pen to paper on this subject[1].

The sixth-century BC poet Lao Tzu observed: "Those who have knowledge, don't predict. Those who predict don't have knowledge." Despite these age-old words of wisdom, our industry seems to eternally persist in basing the investment process around forecasts.

Before exploring the reasons for our dependency upon the irrelevant guess of unknowable future, I had better buttress my case by showing just how bad the track record of forecasting actually is. The figures below set out the forecasting performance of so-called professionals. For the ease of data accessibility, all series below are taken from the Federal Reserve Bank of Philadelphia Livingston survey or the Survey of professional forecasters. However, the findings are not the result of a strange data set, I have used different data and found that, similar patterns exist across them all.

Figure 9.1 shows economists' attempts to forecast the rate of inflation as measured by the GDP deflator. Sadly it reveals a pattern that will become all too common in the next few figures. Economists are really very good at telling you what has just happened! They constantly seem to lag reality. Inflation forecasts appear to be largely a function of past inflation rates.

Our second category are the bond forecasters (Figure 9.2). Previously, we have analysed their behaviour in depth (see *Global Equity Strategy*, 22 February 2005). Much like the economists above, their performance is found to be severely lacking. Not only are bond forecasters bad at guessing the *level* of the yield, they can't even forecast the *direction* of yield changes. Table 9.1 shows that when yields were forecast to rise, they actually fell 55% of the time!

In case you think this is just a case of an equity man picking on debt, Figure 9.3 shows the feeble forecasting abilities of equity strategists. They, too, seem to think that the recent past is best extrapolated into the future, and hence end up lagging reality. Acknowledgement

---

[1] I was much inspired to write this after reading Nassim Taleb's 2005 paper 'The Scandal of Prediction'. He renewed my vigour for this subject.

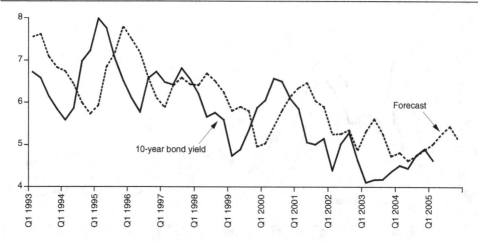

Figure 9.2   Consensus one year ahead bond yield forecasts and reality (%).
Source: DrKW Macro research.

Table 9.1   Predicted vs actual
yield movement (four quarters ahead,
1992–2004) – % of occurrences

		Actual	
		Up	Down
Predicted	Up	45	55
	Down	22	78

Source: DrKW Macro research.

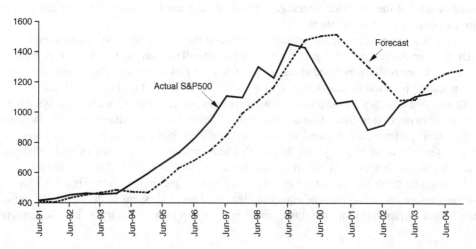

Figure 9.3   S&P 500 and forecasts.
Source: DrKW Macro research.

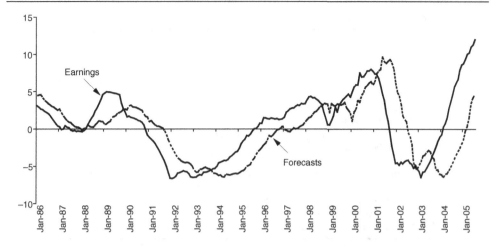

Figure 9.4 Analysts lag reality (Operating earnings and forecasts, deviations from trend, $/Sh).
Source: DrKW Macro research.

of our own limitations is one of the reasons why we don't even attempt to produce index forecasts.

Our last category of truly inept seers are the analysts. Their inability is perhaps the most worrying, as their forecasts are possibly taken far more seriously than the average macro forecast.

Figure 9.4 is constructed by removing the linear time trend from both the operating earnings series for the S&P 500 and the analyst forecasts of those same earnings. In the figure I have simply plotted the deviations from trend. It clearly shows that just like the other forecasters examined here, analysts are very good at telling us what has just happened but of little use in telling us what is going to happen in the future.

OVERCONFIDENCE AS A DRIVER OF POOR FORECASTING

The two most common biases that psychologists have documented are overoptimism and overconfidence. Technically speaking overconfidence refers to a situation where people are surprised more often than they expect to be. Statistically we describe such individuals as 'not well calibrated'. What we really mean by that is if we ask people for a forecast and then ask them for the 98% confidence intervals, so that the true answer should lie outside of the bounds just 2% of the time, it tends to lie outside of the bounds 30–40% of the time! People are simply far too sure about their ability to predict.

Russo and Schoemaker (1989) have devised a simple test. Before you go any further try to answer the questions in Table 9.2 and see how you do.

The answers can be found at the bottom of page 116. If you are properly calibrated only one of the answers to these questions should lie outside of the limits you wrote down. When I took the test two of my answers were outside of the bounds so I, like everyone else, am overconfident. However, compared to Russo and Schoemaker's sample of over 1000 participants I didn't do too badly. Less than 1% got nine or more answers correct, with most respondents missing four to seven items!

Table 9.2   Self-test of overconfidence[2]

	90% confidence range	
	Low	High
Martin Luther King's age at death		
Length of the Nile River		
Number of countries that are members of OPEC		
Number of books in the Old Testament		
Diameter of the moon in miles		
Weight of an empty Boeing 747 in pounds		
Year in which Wolfgang Amadeus Mozart was born		
Gestation period (in days) of an Asian elephant		
Air distance from London to Tokyo		
Deepest (known) point in the ocean (in feet)		

Source: Russo and Schoemaker (1989).

One key finding in the literature on overconfidence is that experts are even more overconfident than lay people. Experts do know more than lay people, but sadly this extra knowledge seems to trigger even higher levels of overconfidence.

OVERCONFIDENCE AND EXPERTS

Figure 9.5 the calibration curves for two groups of experts – weathermen and doctors. Each group is given information relative to their own discipline, so weathermen are given weather patterns and asked to predict the weather, doctors are given case notes and asked to diagnose the patient.

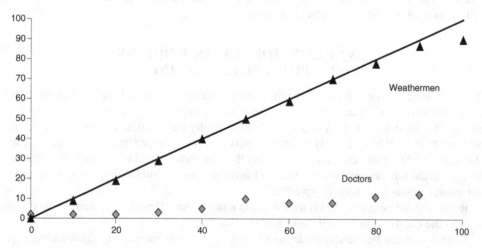

Figure 9.5   Calibration of weathermen and doctors.
Source: Plous (1991).

---

[2] 39 years; 4187 miles; 13 countries; 39 books; 2160 miles: 390,000 pounds; 1756, 645 days; 5959 miles; 36,198 feet.

We are measuring predicted probability (confidence) against actual probability. So the 45° line is a perfect statistical calibration. Weather forecasters actually do remarkably well. In contrast, doctors are a terrifying bunch of people. When they were 90% sure they were correct, they were actually right less than 15% of the time!

So why is there such a difference in the performance of these two groups? It largely appears to relate to the illusion of knowledge (defined as a situation where we think we know more than everyone else). Weathermen get rapid undeniable evidence on their abilities as forecasters; after all, you only have to look out of the window to see if they managed to get it right or not. Doctors, in contrast, often lack feedback so find it far harder to know when they have been right or wrong.

It might be tempting to think of our industry as akin to weathermen; if we make decisions or forecasts we should be able to see in the fairly near term if they were correct or not. However, recent evidence suggests that most investors are more akin to doctors than weathermen, at least in terms of the scale of their overconfidence.

Figure 9.6 is based on a study by Torngren and Montgomery (2004). Participants were asked to select the stock they thought would outperform each month from a pair of stocks. All the stocks were well-known blue-chip names, and players were given the name, industry and prior 12 months' performance for each stock. Laypeople (undergrads in psychology) and professional investors (portfolio managers, analysts and brokers) took part in the study.

Overall, the students were around 59% confident in their stock-picking abilities. However, the professionals averaged 65% confidence. The bad news is that both groups were worse than sheer luck. That is to say, you should have been able to beat both groups just by tossing a coin!

In addition to the overall statistics, at each selection, players were asked to state how confident they were in the outcome predicted (Figure 9.7). The even worse news was that professionals were really dreadful, underperforming laypeople by a large margin. For instance, when the professionals were 100% sure they were correct, they were actually right less than 15% of the time!

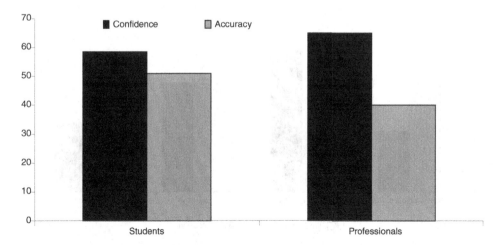

Figure 9.6   Average accuracy and confidence on stock selection (%).
Source: Torngren and Montgomery (2004).

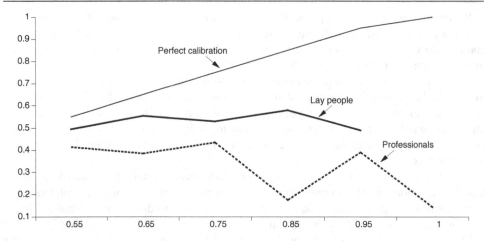

Figure 9.7   Accuracy and confidence on stock selection.
Source: Torngren and Montgomery (2004).

Players were also asked to rank the inputs they used in reaching their decisions. Figure 9.8 shows the average scores for the inputs. Laypeople were essentially just guessing, but were also influenced by prior price performance. In contrast, the professionals thought they were using their knowledge to pick the winners. It is hard to imagine a better example of the illusion of knowledge driving confidence.

Glaser *et al.* (2005) investigate overconfidence in professional investors and laypeople by asking both groups to answer 10 general knowledge questions and 10 finance questions, much like the self-test set out on page 116. If people are well calibrated, the number of correct answers that fall outside the limits should be about 1 in 10. Figure 9.9 shows the actual number of answers that exceeded the confidence limits (the general knowledge and finance questions have been averaged together to give a score out of 10).

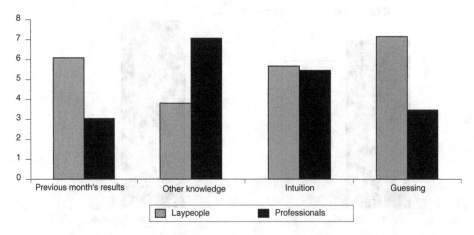

Figure 9.8   Average rating of input importance.
Source: Torngren and Montgomery (2004).

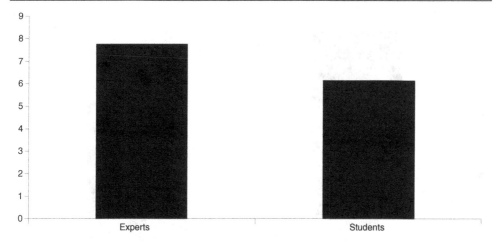

Figure 9.9 Average number of questions outside of the confidence interval.
Source: Glaser, Langer and Weber (2005).

The professional investors had a median of nearly eight questions outside of their confidence intervals; the laypeople (students) had a median six questions outside of their confidence ranges. Once again confirming that experts are more over-confident than the rest of us.

A recent paper by Stotz and Nitzsch (2005) surveyed analysts at major investment banks. They were asked to say how many of their rivals were more accurate and less accurate than they themselves with respect to both earnings forecasts and target prices. Unsurprisingly, the analysts thought that they were all above average. Indeed the average analyst's overconfidence with regard to earnings was 68.44%, and 61.49% with respect to target prices.

Stotz and Nitzsch also asked the analysts to give reasons for their assessment of their ability. They found that when it came to target prices (where analysts were less overconfident) analysts often argued that 'prices sometimes happen by chance', or that they were the result of 'irrational investors', or that successful price forecasts had a large element of luck. In contrast, when it came to explaining their earnings forecasts analysts said 'detailed knowledge of the company or sector' helped to make good forecasts, as did 'experience' and 'hard work'. This would seem to be further evidence of the illusion of control and the illusion of knowledge driving overconfidence (see Figure 9.10).

I have recently been subjecting participants at my behavioural finance seminars to a questionnaire designed to measure their behavioural biases. I've been collating these results and will soon publish a note on the findings. However, as a sneak preview, one of the questions is: 'Are you above average at your job?' I have around 200 respondents; they are all professional fund managers[3]. A stunning 75% of those I have asked think themselves above average at their jobs (Figure 9.11). Many have written such things as, 'I know everyone thinks they are above average, but I am'!

---

[3] If anyone is interested in taking the test, please email me, and I will be able to send you the questionnaire and add your response to the sample. James.Montier@drkw.com.

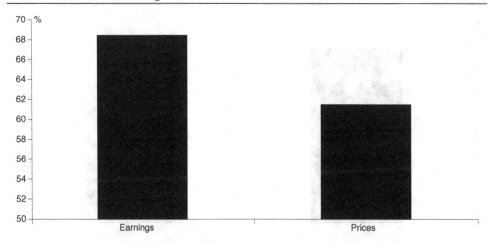

Figure 9.10   Average analysts confidence in their ability to forecast earnings and prices.
Source: Stotz and Nitzsch (2005).

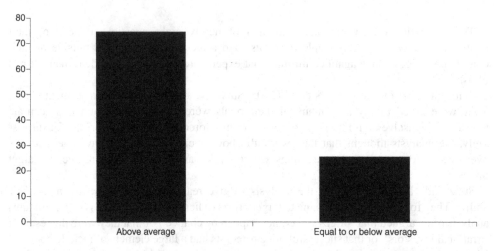

Figure 9.11   Percentage of fund managers who rate themselves as above average at their jobs.
Source: DrKW Macro research.

All of this begs at least two questions. Firstly, why do professionals manage to continue forecasting given that the evidence suggests they can't? Secondly, why do we keep using these useless forecasts? So let's examine each of these in turn.

WHY FORECAST WHEN THE EVIDENCE SHOWS YOU CAN'T?

Two areas of psychology help to explain how forecasters keep forecasting in the face of pretty overwhelming evidence that they are no good at it. This can perhaps be explained as ignorance (not knowing that their overconfidence exists) and arrogance (ego defence mechanism).

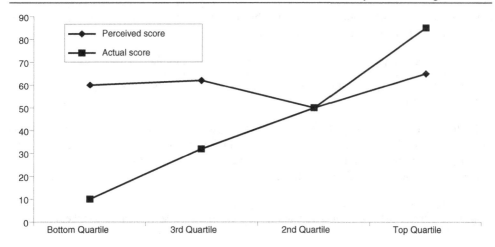

Figure 9.12   Perceived and actual scores: Unskilled and unaware.
Source: Kruger and Dunning (1999).

Unskilled and Unaware

David Dunning and a variety of co-authors over the years have documented a disturbing pattern of behaviour. *Those who are among the worst performers are actually the most overconfident.*

For instance, Kruger and Dunning (1999) asked people to rate how they performed on a logic-reasoning test. Figure 9.12 shows the perceived score and the actual score. Those in the bottom two quartiles by actual score thought they would be in the 60 percentile (i.e. well above average). However, their actual scores put those in the bottom quartile in the tenth percentile. A massive case of overconfidence.

In a follow-up paper, Dunning *et al.* (2003) explore some of the mechanisms that prevent people from realizing just how unskilled they actually are. They note:

> People fail to recognize their own incompetences because that incompetence carries with it a double curse … the skills needed to produce correct responses are virtually identical to those needed to evaluate the accuracy of one's responses… Thus, if people lack the skills to produce correct answers, they are also cursed with an inability to know when their own answers, or anyone else's are right or wrong.

Dunning *et al.* also point out that very often people's estimates of their ability arise from a 'top-down' approach. That is to say, people start with a preconceived belief about their skills or abilities (along the lines of 'I'm good at my job' or 'I'm good at forecasting') and use those beliefs to estimate how well they will do at a specific task.

Unfortunately, all the evidence suggests that people's impressions of their skills and abilities are at best moderately correlated and frequently uncorrelated with their actual performance. Indeed, this is nicely evidenced by the example above where all groups had a perceived score of between 50 and 60% – bearing no relation to the actual outturn!

Ego Defence Mechanism

A second group of techniques deployed by forecasters could be best described as ego defence mechanisms. Philip Tetlock (2002) has investigated the use of 'excuses' for forecast failures among experts on world politics. Tetlock has been monitoring expert's views on world politics in real time for more than a decade. He notes:

> Almost as many experts as not thought that the Soviet Communist Party would remain firmly in the saddle of power in 1993, that Canada was doomed by 1997, that neo-fascism would prevail in Pretoria by 1994, that EMU would collapse by 1997... that the Persian Gulf Crisis would be resolved peacefully.

He found that across the vast array of predictions, with respect to a wide range of political events, experts who reported they were 80% or higher confident in their predictions were actually correct only around 45% of the time. Across all predictions, the experts were little better than coin tossers. As Tetlock notes:

> 'Expertise thus may not translate into predictive accuracy but it does translate into the ability to generate explanations for predictions that experts themselves find so compelling that the result is massive over-confidence.'

After each of the events passed, the forecasts were shown to be either right or wrong, Tetlock returned to the experts and asked them to reassess how well they thought they understood the underlying process and forces at work. Table 9.3 below shows the experts belief in their own abilities both before and after the events. Look at the judged probabilities both pre- and post-events for those whose forecasts were incorrect. They are virtually identical. So despite the incontrovertible evidence that they were wrong, the experts showed no sign of cutting their faith in their own understanding of the situation. A true Bayesian would have slashed their assigned probability (last column in the table). This is prime evidence of the conservatism bias – a tendency to hang on to your views for too long, and only slowly adjust from them.

Tetlock identified five common strategies/defences used to explain the forecast error while preserving the faith in the view (Figure 9.13):

1. The 'if only' defence – if only the Federal Reserve had raised rates, then the US stock price bubble would have been avoided. Effectively, the experts claim they would have

Table 9.3 Subjective probabilities experts assigned to their understanding of the underlying forces at the beginning and end of the forecast periods

Predicting the future of	Status of forecast	Judged prior probability (before the outcome is known)	Judged posterior probability (after the outcome is known)	Bayesian predicted posterior probability
Soviet Union	Inaccurate	0.74	0.70	0.49
	Accurate	0.69	0.83	0.80
South Africa	Inaccurate	0.72	0.69	0.42
	Accurate	0.70	0.77	0.82
EMU	Inaccurate	0.66	0.68	0.45
	Accurate	0.71	0.78	0.85
Canada	Inaccurate	0.65	0.67	0.39
	Accurate	0.68	0.81	0.79

Source: Tetlock (2002).

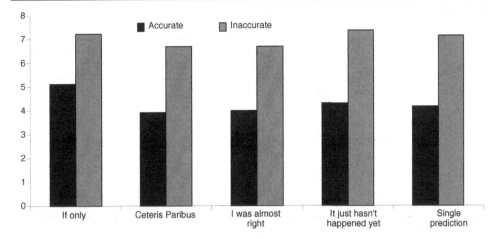

Figure 9.13 Average use of defence mechanism across four cases.
Source: Adapted from Tetlock (2002).

been correct 'if only' their original advice or analysis had been followed. This makes their forecast a historical counterfactual, which is impossible to prove.

2. The 'ceteris paribus' defence – Although the experts' advice or analysis was correct, something else occurred, which was covered in the ubiquitous *ceteris paribus*, that resulted in the forecast being blown off course. So the stock market would have crashed but for the presence of government-led manipulation.

3. The 'I was almost right' defence – Although the predicted outcome did not occur, it 'almost' did. Tetlock gives the examples of so-called close call counterfactuals such as "the hardliners almost overthrew Gorbachev" or "the EU almost disintegrated during the currency crisis of 1992".

4. The 'It just hasn't happened yet' defence – Although the predicted outcome has not yet occurred, it will eventually come to pass. This is one of my favourites! I know that I regularly use this defence to assert that high valuations will inevitably and eventually lead to low returns for investors, thus maintaining my faith in my view of markets.

5. The 'single prediction' defence – Although the conditions of the forecast were met, and the outcome never came close to occurring and now never will, this failure shouldn't be held against the framework/view that inspired it. "Everyone knows (or should know) that forecasting is pointless" thus the analysis is valid, but the act of forecasting was flawed.

These five defence mechanisms are regularly deployed by experts to excuse the dismal failure of their forecasts. Table 9.4 shows scores (on a 9 point scale) of how important these defences are. Unsurprisingly those who gave inaccurate forecasts rely much more heavily upon the mechanisms than those who gave accurate forecasts. In fact, across the four cases used here, those who gave inaccurate forecasts were 1.6 times more likely to reply on one of these defence mechanisms than the accurate forecasters.

Tyska and Zielonka (2002) applied Tetlock's approach to analysts and weathermen. As we have already noted, weathermen are one of those rare groups that are actually well calibrated. Financial analysts, in contrast, have been found to be very overconfident as documented above.

Table 9.4 Average reactions of experts to confirmation and disconfirmation of their conditional forecasts

Predicting the future of	Status of forecast	If only	Ceteris Paribus	I was almost right	It just hasn't happened yet	Single prediction
Soviet Union	Inaccurate	7.0	7.1	6.8	6.4	7.3
	Accurate	4.1	3.9	3.6	5.0	3.1
South Africa	Inaccurate	7.1	7.0	7.3	7.3	7.1
	Accurate	4.5	3.5	3.3	4.0	4.8
EMU	Inaccurate	7.2	5.9	6.2	7.8	7.0
	Accurate	5.1	4.6	4.9	3.8	4.3
Canada	Inaccurate	7.6	6.8	6.5	8.0	7.2
	Accurate	6.8	3.7	4.2	4.4	4.5

Source: Adapted from Tetlock (2002).

Tyska and Zielonka asked financial analysts to predict a stock market level in about a month and half's time. Weathermen were asked to predict the average temperature in April (again around one and half months into the future). In both cases, three mutually exclusive and exhaustive outcomes were specified in such a way that each outcome was roughly equally likely (i.e. had a 0.33 chance of happening). For example, the analysts were asked if the index would be below y, between x and y, or above x? They were also asked how confident they were in their predictions.

Figure 9.14 shows the average scale of overconfidence that was reported. Remember that the three choices were constructed so that each option was roughly equally likely, so a well-calibrated individual would have reported 33% confidence. However, the analysts had an average confidence of just over 58%, and the weathermen had an average confidence of just over 50%. So both groups were, as usual, overconfident, but the analysts were more overconfident.

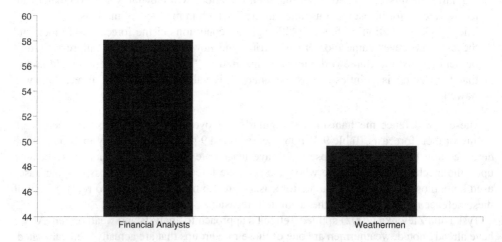

Figure 9.14 Average confidence probability.
Source: Tyszka and Zielonka (2002).

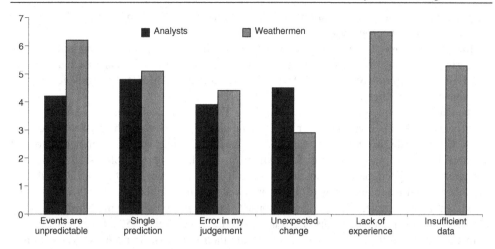

Figure 9.15   Justifications of the forecast failure.
Source: Tyszka and Zielonka (2002).

In fact only around one-third of the analysts were actually correct, and around two-thirds of the weathermen were correct. Those who gave incorrect forecasts were once again contacted and asked to assign importance ratings on a 8-point scale to various reasons for their forecast failure (Figure 9.15).

It is interesting to note that the less confident weathermen's single biggest justification for their forecast failure was a lack of personal experience, followed by an acknowledgement that the weather is inherently unforecastable. Analysts, on the other hand, argued that they shouldn't be judged on the basis of a single prediction (the single prediction defence), and that something else happened to alter the outcome that would have otherwise been achieved (the '*ceteris paribus*' defence from above).

So just like Tetlock's political experts, financial analysts seem to be using mental defence mechanisms to protect themselves from the reality of their appalling bad track record at forecasting.

WHY USE FORECASTS?

Given all the evidence that people are generally dreadful at forecasting[4] why do so many investors use forecasts at the very centre of their investment processes? In part the obsession with forecasts probably stems from the ingrained love of efficient markets. It might seem odd to talk of efficient markets and active managers in the same sentence, but the behaviour of many market participants is actually consistent with market efficiency (EMH). That is, many investors believe they need to know more than everyone else to outperform. This is consistent with EMH because the only way to beat an efficient market is to know something that isn't in

---

[4] Dawes, Faust and Meehl (1991) note that there is an important difference between clinical and actuarial forecasts. Clinical forecasts describe those whereby the decision-maker combines or processed information in his head. Actuarial forecasts rely on well-specified models that have been tested. A vast amount of data shows that actuarial forecasts massively outperform clinical forecasts. We will leave a discussion of what this means for investors until another note, but for the time being recognize that our industry is one in which clinical method often hides behind an actuarial façade.

the price (i.e. non-public information). One way of knowing more is to be able to forecast the future better than everyone else.

However, one psychological trait above all others helps to explain the continued use of forecasts – anchoring. We have discussed anchoring in the context of valuations in a previous note (see *Global Equity Strategy*, 27 August 2004). Anchoring refers to our tendency to grab onto the irrelevant when faced with uncertainty.

The classic example of anchoring comes from Tversky and Kahneman's landmark paper (1974). They asked people to answer general knowledge questions such as what percentage of the UN is made up of African nations? A wheel of fortune with the numbers 1 to 100 was spun in front of the participants before they answered. Being psychologists, Tversky and Kahneman had rigged the wheel so it gave either 10 or 65 as the result of a spin. The subjects were then asked if the answer was higher or lower than the number on the wheel, and also asked their actual answer. The median response from the group that saw the wheel stop at 10 was 25%, and the median response from the group that saw 65 was 45%! Effectively, people were grabbing at irrelevant anchors when forming their opinions. (For the record the correct answer was 20%).

Another well-known example concerns solving 8 factorial (8!), except that it is presented in two different ways, either (i) $1 \times 2 \times 3 \times 4 \times 5 \times 6 \times 7 \times 8$ or (ii) $8 \times 7 \times 6 \times 5 \times 4 \times 3 \times 2 \times 1$. The median answer under case (i) was 512, the median answer under case (ii) was 2250. So people appear to anchor on the early numbers in forming their expectations. By the way, the actual answer is 40,320.

Anchoring is not just a cheap parlour trick. Englich and Mussweiler (2001) take criminal trial judges with an average of more than 15 years of experience as subjects. The judges hear the cases, at the end of which the prosecutor asks for either a 36-month sentence, or a 12-month sentence for exactly the same case. Those prosecutors who asked for a 36-month sentence extracted a jail time that was 8 months longer than those who sought a 12-month sentence. Intriguingly, these findings were independent of whether a true prosecutor or a student played the role of the prosecutor!

One of the questions I have asked on my behavioural finance questionnaire has been for people to write down the last four digits of their telephone number, then say whether the number of doctors in their capital city is higher or lower than the last four digits of their telephone number, and finally make their best guess on the number of doctors in their capital city. The results are shown in Figure 9.16. Those whose last four telephone digits were greater than 7000 on average report 6762 doctors, while those with telephone numbers below 2000 arrived at an average 2270 doctors! So professional fund managers seem to be as liable as everyone else to suffer from anchoring.

When faced with the unknown, people will grasp onto almost anything. So it is little wonder that an investor will cling to forecasts, despite their uselessness.

DEBASING

So what can be done to avoid these problems? The most obvious solution is to stop relying upon pointless forecasts. This comes as anathema to most investors. But there are plenty of strategies that one can implement without the use of forecasts. Many examples of such strategies have appeared on these pages, such as value-based strategies based on trailing earnings or Graham and Dodd PEs (see *Global Equity Strategy*, 16 March 2005 and 28 June 2005, as examples).

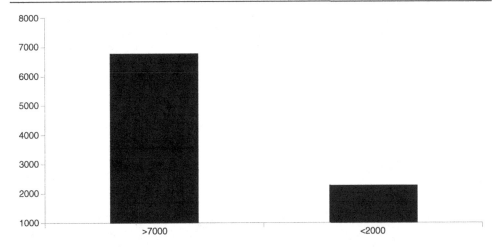

Figure 9.16 Anchoring among fund managers.
Source: DrKW Macro research.

Secondly, we should redirect our efforts away from forecasting. Having armies of analysts and economists who are all forecasting is a complete waste of time. There is a good reason we call analysts analysts not forecasters: they are meant to analyse not guess the unknowable future. They would be better utilized in analysing the present and understanding what that means for the future rather than coming up with spurious anchors for investors. However, this requires a radical rethink of the investment process and, hence, is exceptionally unlikely to occur.

10

What Value Analysts?*

According to a new survey, analysts' favoured valuation measure is the forward PE. However, investors are just as well-off using historic earnings as prospective earnings when it comes to value investing. Additionally, an analysis of analyst recommendations reveals that they do not rate value as an input. Instead they prefer to concentrate on short-term momentum growth stocks.

- A new survey by Dukes *et al.* (2006) reveals that nearly 80% of analysts choose the forward PE as their preferred valuation method. The second most popular valuation technique is relative valuation (either to the stock's historical range or an industry average).
- The least popular method of stock valuation was dividend discount model (or the cash flow equivalent). Yet every finance text, since John Burr Williams wrote the *Theory of Investment Value* in 1938, has argued that DDM/DCF is the 'correct' way to value a stock.
- The survey also revealed the time horizons that analysts used as inputs in their valuation work. According to theory, an equity represents a long-term claim on assets. Yet analysts tend to use only one or two years as inputs! This concentration on the near-term fits with the shrinkage in average holding periods that we have remarked on many times, so analysts may simply be responding to the demands of their client base.
- The wisdom of relying upon analysts forecasts is called into question by some new work from Sebastian Lancetti of our Quant team. He looked at the performance of value strategies based on forecast PE, and trailing PE and found no difference between the two. So investors might as well use freely available trailing information rather than pay for access to analysts.
- An analysis of consensus stock recommendations reveals that analysts pay scant attention to valuation when forming their views. In fact, the stocks they like most are expensive on pretty much every measure — PE, PB, PS, DY and PCF! The stocks most favoured by analysts have high long-term earnings growth forecasts. Unfortunately, the evidence suggests that analysts haven't got a clue about forecasting long-term growth. A cynic might say that analysts are just justifying their conclusions.
- The other hallmark of analyst-favoured stocks is that they have enjoyed good recent performance. Momentum is, of course, a well-known feature of markets. So could it be that analysts are merely exploiting this trait? If so, they are massively overpaid. A computer could generate a list of momentum stocks at a fraction of the cost.
- However, if they were exploiting momentum, they would also care about the long-term momentum picture. Momentum has been shown to work far better when it combines

*This article appeared in *Global Equity Strategy* on 26 September 2006. The material discussed was accurate at the time of publication.

short-term winners with long-term losers (i.e. a trend reversal). However, analysts seem to prefer stocks that have done well both recently and over the longer term.

- All of this seems strange to me, but perhaps the bigger question (to quote Obi Wan Kenobi in *Star Wars*) is, "Who is more foolish? The fool or the fool who follows him?"

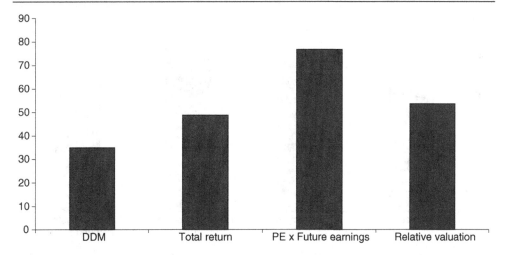

Figure 10.1 Percentage of analysts using each valuation method.
Source: Adapted from Dukes *et al.* (2006). DrKW Macro research.

I recently gave a lecture to a group of finance students working towards their PhDs. The conversation turned to the role of analysts. Having been drilled in the orthodoxy of efficient markets, the students simply couldn't believe that analysts weren't paid to get their earnings forecasts correct. Much as I tried to disabuse them of their strange beliefs, they just couldn't comprehend the idea that analysts existed to sell stories, not to make accurate forecasts.

Regular readers will know that every so often I like to take a look at what the analysts are doing. A new paper in the *Journal of Investing* by Dukes *et al.* (2006) helps to shed some light on one particular aspect of analyst behaviour – valuation.

Dukes *et al.* surveyed 43 analysts at a wide variety of institutions and across differing investment styles in order to gain insight into how analysts approach the problem of valuation. The results they uncovered are disappointing but not surprising. Figure 10.1 shows the percentage of analysts who say they use a particular method of valuation. The favoured method of valuation appears to be taking a PE based upon future earnings (77%[1]) – hardly the stuff of rocket science.

Ever since John Burr Williams wrote the *Theory of Investment Value* in 1938, almost every finance text ever written has told us that the only sensible way to think about stock valuation is a discounted flow of future dividends (or cash flows, if you must). As far as I know, even the CFA teaches the DDM/DCF valuation approach. Despite the overwhelming consensus on the 'proper' use of such methods, a mere 35% of analysts say they use it, and those that do confess to deploying such a valuation say it is "only used as a check on other methods!".

Of those analysts who said they used comparative valuation (the second most popular form of valuation), the most popular choice of comparison benchmark was the historical company PE (44%), followed by an industry average (42%) (Figure 10.2).

The other interesting aspect uncovered by Dukes *et al.* was the time horizon of the analysts' valuation methods. Figure 10.3 shows the number of years used as an input into the various valuation approaches used by analysts. Those who focus on DDM and total return[2] style

---

[1] Percentages will not sum to 100 as analysts could have multiple answers.
[2] Where the estimated dividend yield and growth are estimated and compared to the average stock.

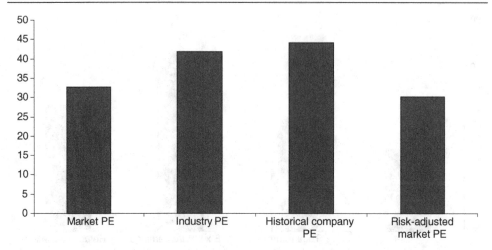

Figure 10.2 When using a comparison measure which measure do you favour?
Source: Adapted from Dukes *et al.* (2006). DrKW Macro research.

valuations tend to have longer time horizons (i.e. 5 years plus). In contrast, the most popular measure (the forward earnings-based PE) is based on the short term (i.e. 1–2 years). So most analysts are content to focus upon the near-term outlook for earnings rather than the flow of returns to investors. This makes sense given the shrinkage in time horizons (as witnessed by holding periods) that we have regularly pointed out in the past.

The wisdom of relying upon analysts' forecasts from an investor perspective is thrown into question by some recent work from Sebastian Lancetti of our Global Quant team. I asked Sebastian to test the performance of a value strategy based on stocks ranked by forecast PE against one with stocks ranked by trailing PE. The results for Europe are shown in Figure 10.4.

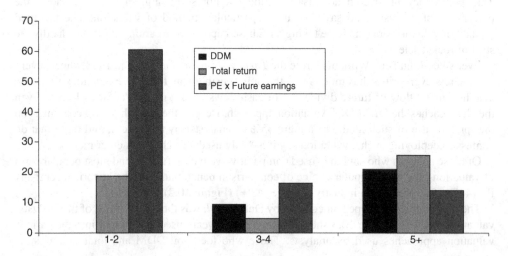

Figure 10.3 Time horizon input into valuation models.
Source: Adapted from Dukes *et al.* (2006). DrKW Macro research.

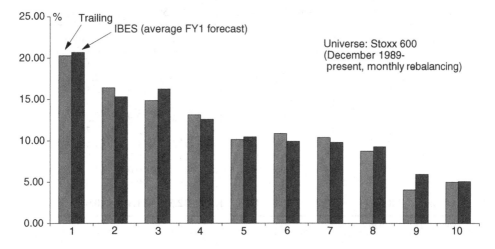

Figure 10.4   Value deciles using trailing and forecast earnings (deciles 1 = cheap, 10 = expensive). *Source:* DrKW Macro research.

Even a cursory glance at the figure reveals that there was no material difference between the use of forecasts and the use of trailing earnings. Thus the analysts added nothing to the performance of the strategy (I guess the good news is that at least they didn't subtract anything). Sebastian's result suggests that value investors would be just as well-off using trailing information (freely available) rather than having to pay for access to analysts.

Over a year ago I examined the properties of consensus analyst recommendations, to see if I could understand what made a stock attractive to an analyst (see *Global Equity Strategy*, 15 June 2005). This chapter provides a good opportunity to update that study.

Consensus recommendations can be translated into numeric terms as per Table 10.1. We can then group stocks into deciles based around the average analyst view. The characteristics of stocks in each basket can then be examined.

Table 10.2 shows the results of such an analysis for the S&P 500. Several things stand out from the table. Firstly, the optimistic bias of analysts shows up with the average rating on a stock being 3.8 (i.e. only just below an Add). Only in the bottom decile do we find stocks with an average recommendation of less than a Hold (i.e. below 3).

Looking at the stocks the analysts favour most, we can see they like expensive stocks in terms of PE, with very low dividend yields, high price to sales, and high price to cash flow.

Table 10.1   Recommendations and numerics

Recommendation	Numeric value
Buy	5
Add	4
Hold	3
Reduce	2
Sell	1

Source: DrKW Macro research.

Table 10.2   Properties of consensus recommendations (S&P 500) (medians)

Recommendation	PE	PB	DY	PS	PCF	LTG	Returns (12m)
4.6	18.9	3.3	0.7	1.7	14.9	13.1	16.1
4.3	19.3	3.3	0.8	2.3	13.4	14.4	9.7
4.2	16.4	2.7	1.6	1.7	12.4	11.6	14.5
4.0	17.4	2.5	1.2	1.6	12.0	11.8	8.3
3.9	17.1	3.0	1.0	1.6	12.8	12.9	10.5
3.8	18.7	2.6	1.1	1.4	11.7	12.4	9.7
3.6	17.8	2.5	1.1	1.4	12.5	11.7	7.4
3.4	18.3	2.9	1.4	1.8	11.5	10.8	8.5
3.2	17.4	2.6	1.7	1.6	11.8	10.0	12.9
2.7	17.2	2.1	1.8	1.3	9.9	9.0	7.6
Average 3.8	**17.8**	**2.8**	**1.2**	**1.6**	**12.3**	**11.8**	**10.5**

Source: DrKW Macro research.

That is, they love expensive stocks in all forms. So the idea that valuation is a key input into analysts' recommendations seems to flounder when confronted with empirical reality.

Their favoured stocks also have very high expected long-term growth rates (LTG in Table 10.2). Of course, this makes sense, as the analysts make up the long-term growth numbers and the recommendations. Sadly, as we have shown many times before, the analysts are not very good at forecasting long-term earnings growth.

Figure 10.5 is one that we have used before but it bears repeating. It shows portfolios sorted into Quintiles, ranked on the basis of long-term earnings growth forecasts for consensus analysts (Q5 being the highest). The first bar shows the per annum growth rate in the 5 years prior to expectation formation (T5). It also traces out the compound earnings growth per annum in the 1, 3 and 5 years following the forecasts.

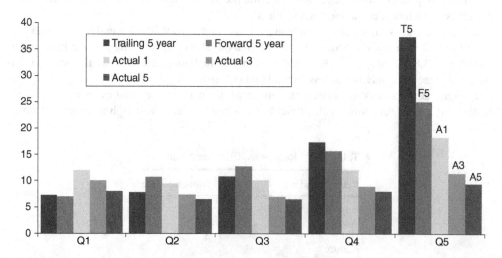

Figure 10.5   Earnings growth isn't persistent (Quintiles sorted by long-term EPS growth forecasts). *Source:* DrKW Macro research and Chan *et al.* (2003).

The low-growth portfolio (Q1) generates nearly as much future EPS growth (A5) as the high-growth portfolio (Q5). In fact the biggest input into forecast long-term earnings growth seems to be past 5-year earnings growth. Isn't extrapolation a marvellous thing! Indeed, a cynic might argue that analysts are just using their long-term growth forecasts to justify their views on the stock.

The other outstanding feature of analysts' recommendations is that they have all done exceptionally well in the past 12 months in terms of returns. That is to say, analysts appear to be little more than momentum players.

Of course, momentum is a perfectly sensible approach to investing. There is a long history of studies showing that momentum investing tends to work. Indeed, Sebastian Lancetti recently published a note that could have easily be called everything you need to know about momentum but were afraid to ask (see *Winners and Losers*, 6 September 2006). However, if analysts have simply decided that their job is running a momentum screen, then they are vastly overpaid. A computer could run a momentum screen in a fraction of the time it takes an analyst to write a report — not to mention that the computer would operate at a fraction of the cost.

Before we conclude that analysts are just rationally exploiting the momentum feature of markets, it is worth considering the long-term price momentum implications of their stock selections. It has long been known that past winner stocks become future losers and vice versa (Thaler and DeBondt, 1985). So if analysts are rationally exploiting momentum, we would expect them to do so with a mind to long-term momentum as well as to short-term momentum. That is to say, they would be better off buying long-term losers that have recently become short-term winners, i.e. stocks that had witnessed a positive trend reversal.

Chan and Kot (2002) have shown that this can be a very profitable strategy. Figure 10.6 is taken from their paper, and shows the performance of four different portfolios, each based on the interaction of long- and short-term momentum. Their data covers the US market from 1965 to 2002. The best performing strategy is the short-term winner long-term loser combination.

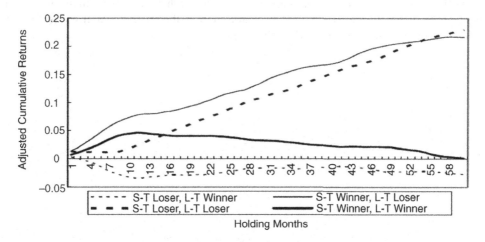

Figure 10.6   % Winners' and losers' long-term performance in momentum strategies (%).
Source: Chan and Kot (2002).

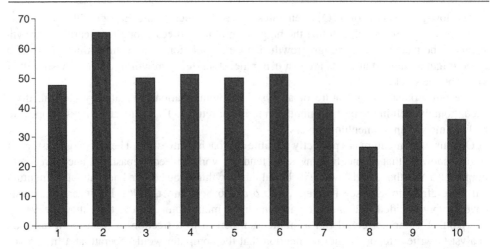

Figure 10.7   Long-term momentum across analyst recommendations (% over past three years).
Source: DrKW Macro research.

So, do analysts factor this into their decision-making process? Figure 10.7 shows the breakdown of long-term momentum (defined as the past 3-year price returns) across the deciles of analyst recommendations (so 1 in the chart is the decile the analysts like best, 10 the one they like least). If anything, analysts seem to prefer long-term winners to long-term losers – exactly the opposite of the strategy outlined above. Analysts appear to generally prefer stocks that have done well in the last few years; effectively they fall in love with the long-term performers – attracted, no doubt, to the glitz and glamour of the market's star performers.

Not only do many analysts not seem to use a sound valuation technique, but in coming up with their recommendations the evidence suggests that they pay scant attention to any valuation considerations. Instead they seem to favour stocks that have done well in recent years (ignoring the evidence on long-term reversal). All of this seems very strange to me, but perhaps the bigger question (to quote Obi Wan Kenobi in the original *Star Wars*) is "Who is more foolish, the fool, or the fool who follows him?"

SIN 2

The Illusion of Knowledge (Gluttony)

11
The Illusion of Knowledge or Is More Information Better Information?*

The amount of information that assails us on a daily basis is truly staggering. Unfortunately, we tend to equate information with knowledge. Sadly the two are often very different beasts. We also tend to labour under the misapprehension that more information is the same as better information. Experimental evidence suggests that often where information is concerned, less is more!

- The traditional view holds that more information is always preferable to less. After all, the argument goes, if the information is useless it will be ignored. However, implicit within this viewpoint is an assumption that we are all supercomputers who can deal with the seemingly endless torrent of informational deluge.
- However, we aren't idealized supercomputers. Instead we have only a limited capacity to process information. Despite our obvious cognitive constraints, many investors persist in believing that in order to outperform they need to know more than everyone else. Hence they get caught up trying to know absolutely everything there is to know about a stock before investing.
- Numerous studies have shown that increasing information leads to increased overconfidence rather than increased accuracy. For instance, Slovic (1973) asked bookmakers to select information they would like to know in order to work out the odds on a horse race. They were then given an increasing amount of information and asked for their prediction and their confidence in those predictions. While accuracy was pretty much a flat line regardless of information, confidence was strongly increased with the amount of information. So all that happened was that the extra information made the bookies more and more overconfident without improving their performance.
- Information can actually be detrimental to decision-making. Handzic (2001) set participants a challenge to estimate the demand for ice cream the next day, given either one useful signal or three useful signals. The group with three signals were less efficient in processing the information, and made the worst forecasts!
- Davis *et al.* (1994) asked people to forecast fourth-quarter earnings based on the last three quarters' EPS, net sales and stock prices (the base line), or the baseline plus some extra information (which in some cases was useful, and in others was irrelevant/redundant). Just the presence of extra information (be it useful or not) was enough to significantly increase the error rate of forecasts. As with many of the other studies discussed here, more information led to increased confidence; with redundant information increasing confidence above the

*This article appeared in *Global Equity Strategy* on 18 November 2005. The material discussed was accurate at the time of publication.

baseline, and relevant information leading to a marked increase in confidence over irrelevant information. In all cases, subjects displayed massive overconfidence.

- All these studies suggest that rather than obsessing with the bewildering informational fusion of news and noise, we should concentrate on a few key elements in stock in which selection, i.e. what are the five most important things we should know about any stock in which we are about to invest? Of course, if I knew the answer I would have retired long ago!

I have a penchant for quoting ancient Asian seers, and some words of wisdom come from Confucius, who stated "To know that we know what we know, and that to know we do not know what we do not know, that is true knowledge". For those who prefer more modern quotations, Daniel J. Boorstin's view that "The greatest obstacle to discovery is not ignorance – it is the illusion of knowledge" will suffice.

Some time ago I observed that the behaviour of many investors is consistent with a belief in the efficient market hypothesis (EMH). That is to say, many investors seem to believe that they need to know more than everyone else in order to outperform the market. This is related to EMH because under EMH the only way to beat the market is to know something that isn't embodied in prices. So they spend their days in what I have previously described as the futile quest for 'edge' – that is, reading, learning and researching absolutely everything there is to know about the firm in which they intend to invest, in the belief that an information edge will lead to outperformance.

This is generally part of a larger body of thinking that has its roots in economics, which is that more is always preferred to less (for a normal good). To most who have trained in economics, more choice is always preferable to less choice, and more information is always better than less information. After all, the economists argue, if the information is useless then people will simply ignore it.

At first glance this may well seem like a reasonable proposition. However, the key question must surely be: Is it true empirically? Is more information equivalent to better information? Are the cognitive constraints inherent in our brains binding?

The first person to study this conundrum was Oskamp in 1965. Oskamp set up a profile of a young man (Joseph Kidd) who was seeking clinical psychological help. In the first stage the psychologists were given just a very brief demographic-based analysis of Kidd. They were told he was 29 years old, white, unmarried, and a veteran of World War II. They were also informed that he was a college graduate who now works as a business assistant in a floral decorating studio.

At the end of each presentation of material the psychologists had to answer questions on Kidd's behavioural patterns, attitudes, interests and typical reactions to real-life events. Stage I was deliberately minimal to establish a base rate with which to compare later stages.

Stage II added $1\frac{1}{2}$ pages of information about Kidd's childhood through to the age of 12. Stage III was 2 pages on his high school and college experiences. The final stage of information covered his army service and later life up to the present day.

Figure 11.1 shows the impact of increasing information on accuracy and self-reported confidence among the psychologists. As Oskamp notes, "No judge ever reached 50% accuracy and the average final accuracy was less than 28%, where chance was 20%." Despite the fact that accuracy only increases marginally as the information increases, look what happens to the confidence measures. They explode from an average 33% in Stage I to an average 53% in Stage IV.

Oskamp also monitored the number of psychologists who changed their minds at each stage. He found that as the amount of information increased, so the number of participants changing their minds dropped from 40% in Stage II to just 25% in Stage IV Figure 11.2. As Oskamp notes, the psychologists 'may frequently have formed stereotype conclusions rather firmly from their first fragmentary information and then been reluctant to change their conclusions as they received new information'.

Oskamp's findings were confirmed in a very different setting by work by Paul Slovic (1973). Eight experienced bookmakers were shown a list of 88 variables found on a typical

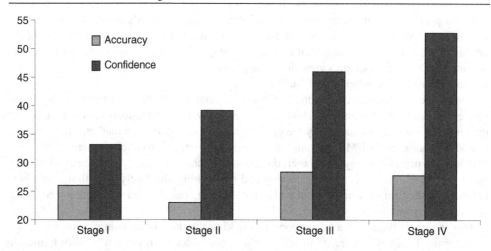

Figure 11.1   Accuracy and confidence (%).
Source: Adapted from Oskamp (1965).

past performance chart on a horse, e.g. the weight to be carried, the number of races won, the performance in different conditions, etc. Each bookmaker was then asked to rank the pieces of information by importance.

Having done this, the bookmakers were then given data for 40 past races and asked to rank the top five horses in each race. Each bookmaker was given the past data in increments of the 5, 10, 20 and 40 variables he had selected as most important. Hence each bookmaker predicted the outcome of each race four times – once for each of the information sets. For each prediction the bookmakers were asked to give a degree of confidence ranking in their forecast.

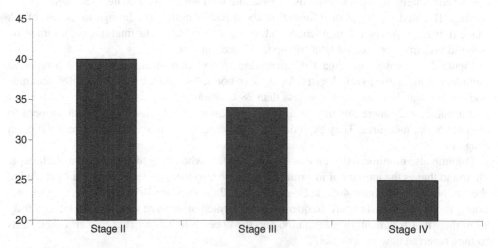

Figure 11.2   Percentage of participants changing their minds each round.
Source: Adapted from Oskamp (1965).

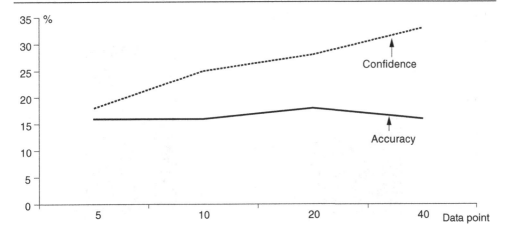

Figure 11.3   Accuracy vs confidence for bookmakers as a function of the information set.
Source: Slovic (1973).

Figure 11.3 shows how both accuracy and confidence change as the information set grows over time. Accuracy is almost a flat line regardless of the amount of information the bookmakers had at their disposal!

However, look what happened to the bookmakers' confidence. It soared as the information set increased. With five pieces of information, accuracy and confidence were quite closely related. However, by the time 40 pieces of information were being used, accuracy was still exactly the same, but confidence has soared to over 30%! *So more information isn't better information, it is what you do with it rather than how much you can get that truly matters.*

Two other experiments are worth bringing in at this stage. The first comes from work by Meliha Handzic (2001). She set an experimental task in which the objective was to make optimal production targets. She created an imaginary dairy firm supplying ice cream to an outlet at Bondi Beach. Participants took on the role of production manager at the dairy firm. They were told that underestimating and overestimating demand incurred equal costs (through loss of market to other outlets, or though spoilt product respectively). The goal was to try to minimize the costs incurred by incorrect production decisions.

At the end of each day, participants were asked to set production quotas for ice cream to be sold the next day. In order to help them with their decisions they were given either one piece of information or three pieces of information. After discussing with actual ice cream vendors on Bondi Beach, the factors identified as critical were the ambient air temperature, the amount of sunshine and the number of visitors. All these cues were deemed to be equally reliable in predicting the daily product demand. Participants were split into two groups; the only difference between the groups was the amount of information they received.

Handzic constructed two measures of performance. Firstly, processing efficiency (ROE) which was measured as an individual's error relative to the optimal error, where the optimal error was the result of a regression equation using the three informational cues. A ROE of 1 indicated an individual behaved in exactly the same way as the optimal regression model; a score above 1 indicates suboptimal information processing efficiency.

Figure 11.4 shows the ROE scores for the two groups. The group that received more information actually performed far worse than the group who received only one item of

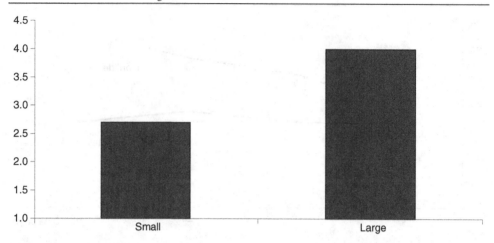

Figure 11.4   Processing efficiency (ROE) 1 = optimal, >1 suboptimal.
Source: Adapted from Handzic (2001).

information. So in terms of information processing, more information certainly hampered decision-making.

The other performance measure that Handzic used was decision accuracy (RNE), defined as the ratio of the absolute error in an individual's decision relative to the corresponding error from a simple naïve (random walk) prediction that the best guess of today's quota was yesterday's actual sales outturn. Because such models ignore all contextual information they usually perform poorly.

A RNE score of 1 indicates that individuals match the performance of the naïve model, indicating no improvement, while scores lower than 1 indicate an improvement relative to the naïve model. Figure 11.5 shows the average RNE scores for each group.

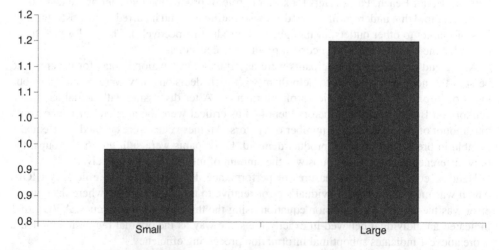

Figure 11.5   Decision accuracy (RNE, 1 indicates random walk, <1 improvement on random walk).
Source: Adapted from Handzic (2001).

The group with only one informational cue managed to produce a marginal improvement on a simple random walk. However, the group with all the information actually managed to significantly underperform the random walk, and the group with less information!

The final study I would like to draw to your attention is from Davis *et al.* (1994). This study is particularly relevant to finance as it concerns the impact of information on earnings forecasts. Davis *et al.*'s guinea pigs were students on an MBA course on advanced financial statement analysis, and most had worked in the industry prior to taking their MBAs. The task they were given was to forecast fourth-quarter earnings for various different firms. In fact, there were 15 firms, but each firm was presented in one of three different information formats. The information formats were (i) baseline data consisting of the past three quarters of EPS, net sales and stock price; (ii) baseline data plus redundant or irrelevant information, i.e. information that was already embodied in the baseline data such as the PE ratio; and (iii) baseline data plus non-redundant information that should have improved forecasting ability, such as the dividend was increased. None of the participants realized that they had all seen the same company in three different formats, perhaps because each presentation was separated by at least seven other profiles.

Each respondent was not only asked for their forecast but also for their confidence in their forecast. Figure 11.6 shows the mean square error [(forecast − actual)^2/actual] as a measure of accuracy. *Both redundant and non-redundant information significantly increased the forecast error!*

Figure 11.7 shows the self-reported confidence ratings for each of the conditions. Davis *et al.* found that redundant information led to a significant increase in confidence over and above the baseline information, and non-redundant information led to a marked increase over redundant information.

The amount of information that assails us on a daily basis is truly staggering. Noise and news have fused together in a bewildering deluge of data. Rather than obsessing about every piece of information that crosses our screens, we should attempt to avoid being sucked into the mire of emails, voicemails and other wild goose chases. Instead we should devote time to working out what we should really be looking at. What are the five most important things

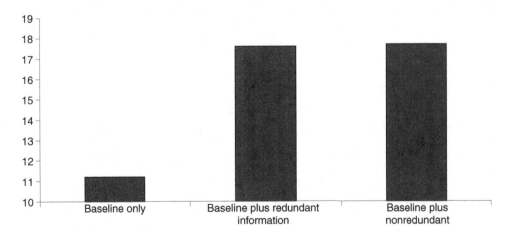

Figure 11.6 Mean square error of forecast.
Source: Adapted from Davis *et al.* (1994).

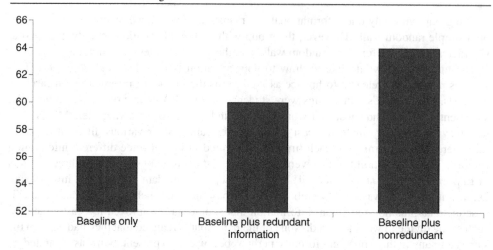

Figure 11.7   Confidence as a function of information (%).
Source: Adapted from Davis *et al.* (1994).

we should know about any stock we are about to invest in? Of course, as I said above, if I knew the answer I would have retired a long time ago! A hint might be that spending hours in meeting companies to gather information, may not be the best use of your time!

SIN 3

Meeting Companies (Lust)

12
Why Waste Your Time Listening to Company Management?*

> Why does meeting companies hold such an important place in the investment process of many fund managers? Is it because they provide deep insights into why we should invest in them? Or is it because we need to fill our time with something that makes us look busy? We outline five psychological reasons why meeting company management could well be a complete waste of time.

- The first of the reasons is simply that much of the information provided by companies is noise. We are already suffering informational deluge, so why add to the burden? As we have noted, more information isn't equivalent to better information. Yet the primary reason for seeing companies seems to be to collect more of it! All too often more information simply translates into increased confidence rather than better investment performance, but, of course, this won't stop people trying to gain what they mistakenly think is an informational edge.

- Secondly, corporate managers are just as likely as the rest of us to suffer from cognitive illusions. Corporate managers display just as much overoptimism and overconfidence as anyone else. For instance, the Duke University CFO survey reveals that managers are always more optimistic about the outlook for their firm than they are about the economy as a whole.

- Thirdly, we tend to suffer from confirmatory bias – that is, a habit of only looking for information that agrees with us, and interpreting all information as supportive of our base case, even if it clearly isn't. So rather than ask probing questions that look to disconfirm the base case, we tend to end up asking leading questions that support our original viewpoint. This tendency is exacerbated by the fact that company management tend to tell you what you want to hear. When was the last time a company turned up at your office and said they were a disaster and you should stay well clear?

- The fourth hurdle is our innate tendency to obey figures of authority. Stanley Milgram has clearly shown that we will obey orders if they come from someone who has the slightest pretence of power, even if those orders involve hurting someone else. Company managers are often seen as being at the pinnacle of their profession, hence it is easy to imagine situations in which analysts and fund managers find themselves effectively overawed.

- The final psychological barrier to making company meetings useful is that we are simply lousy at telling deception from truth. We perform roughly in line with pure chance; despite the fact that we all think we are excellent at spotting deception. For instance, if you are

---

*This article appeared in *Global Equity Strategy* on 18 November 2005. The material discussed was accurate at the time of publication.

talking to a manager who couldn't look you in the eye, and fidgeted throughout the meeting and kept correcting himself, you might well think he was hiding something. Unfortunately, none of these signs is a useful cue in spotting liars.

- Given the large number of psychological hurdles and the difficulties entailed in overcoming most of them, it would seem improbable that company meetings really add the value that so many investors seem to think they do. Indeed, one top performing European fund manager of our acquaintance actively eschews company meetings! A lesson for us all perhaps?

I have written a series of notes as assaults or a behaviouralist critique (if you prefer) on the way in which the 'average' fund management house goes about its business. Some others cover the lunacy of short time horizons, the folly of forecasting, the obsession with noise, the difficulty of being just one step ahead of everyone else, and the dangers of running decision-making by groups (see *Global Equity Strategy*, 7 June 2005, 24 August 2005, 31 August 2005, 17 February 2004, and 9 September 2004 respectively).

This chapter turns on another aspect of the standard approach to fund management that strikes me as largely a waste of time. The subject of my vitriolic diatribe is obvious from the title above, but why do investors spend so long meeting and talking to companies? (Let alone actually paying investment banks to bring companies around to see them!)

The most obvious answer is that companies provide information to investors. There are two issues here. Firstly, as we explored last week, more information is often not an aid to better decision-making, very often it just results in overload. Secondly, are the managers of companies any better than the rest of us when we consider behavioural biases?

MANAGERS ARE JUST AS BIASED AS THE REST OF US

The data shows that corporate managers are just as likely as the rest of us to display behavioural biases. A great source of information on management views is the Duke Survey of CFOs (see www.cfosurvey.org for details). This survey is carried out every quarter and covers around 500 of Americas major companies. The average firm in the sample has sales revenue of $2309 million, and roughly half of the companies are listed.

Each quarter these CFOs are asked a variety of questions, many of which are pertinent to our discussion here. For instance, they have regularly been asked to say how optimistic they were on both the economy and their own firms (with 100% being maximum bullish). Figure 12.1 shows the percentage optimism that was expressed. *In every case, managers were*

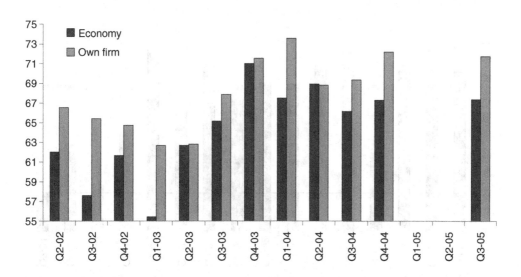

Figure 12.1   Optimism over the economy and own firm (%).
Source: Duke survey.

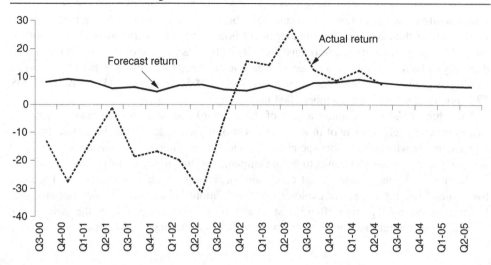

Figure 12.2 Corporate managers' market expectations and outturns – overoptimistic.
Source: Duke survey.

more optimistic about their own company than they were about the economy as a whole! This
is a classic case of illusion of control driving overconfidence.

An alternative measure of managers' overoptimism is provided in a paper by Graham and
Harvey (2005). They use the Duke survey but focus on corporate managers one-year ahead
forecasts of equity returns and track how their forecasts stack up against actual outturns
(Figure 12.2). Just like everyone else, corporate managers turn out to be overoptimistic. At a
one-year time horizon they are around about 10% too optimistic.

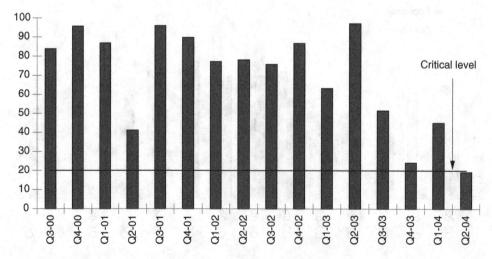

Figure 12.3 Percentage of returns outside the 80% confidence intervals.
Source: Duke survey.

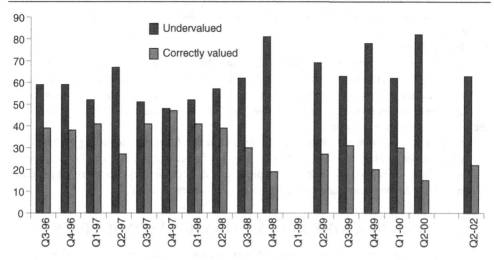

Figure 12.4 Percentage of CFOs who think their stock is undervalued or correctly valued. *Source:* Duke survey.

Table 12.1 Guidance is useless! – recurring profits vs outcomes

Date of estimate	Year to	Estimated profits A	Outcome B	Reality gap B − A
Mar-91	Mar-92	3.2	−20.3	−23.5
Mar-92	Mar-93	−0.1	−23.9	−23.8
Mar-93	Mar-94	11.6	−20.7	−32.3
Mar-94	Mar-95	0.5	17.1	16.6
Mar-95	Mar-96	17.4	25.5	8.1
Feb-96	Mar-97	17.3	25.1	7.8
Mar-97	Mar-98	13.6	−7.9	−21.5
Feb-98	Mar-99	6.6	−32.0	−38.6
Mar-99	Mar-00	25.6	18.4	−7.2
Mar-00	Mar-01	29.2	48.3	19.1
Mar-01	Mar-02	5.8	−56.9	−62.7
Mar-02	Mar-03	101.7	102.4	0.7
Mar-03	Mar-04	16.8	31.3	14.5
Mar-04	Mar-05	15.3	24.5	9.2

Source: Nikkei, DrKW Macro research.

Graham and Harvey also use the survey to investigate managers' overconfidence with regard to their estimates, because not only are the managers asked to provide forecasts, they are also asked to provide 80% confidence intervals. Figure 12.3 shows the percentage of time that the actual outturn was outside the intervals provided. Only a mere 30.5% of the time were the actual returns within the managers 80% confidence intervals. So just like everyone else, corporate managers are also overconfident.

An alternative perspective on overconfidence is also provided in the Duke survey. In the early days of the survey CFOs were asked if they thought their stock was undervalued by the market. On average 63% of CFOs thought their stock was undervalued, and 32% thought the in stocks were correctly valued!

Most amusing of all was Graham and Harvey's examination of tech CFOs views of their stock. At the peak of the bubble nearly 90% of tech CFOs thought their stock was undervalued (see Figure 12.4).

Of course, you may retort that you don't care what the CFOs say about the market, you care what they say about the firm. Fair enough, but here too there are problems. Table 12.1 was constructed a few years ago by our Japanese consultant, Peter Tasker. It shows the management forecasts for earnings growth of their firms against the actual outturn. As Peter so aptly called the exhibit – guidance is useless!

Let's now assume that you took my comments on the folly of forecasting to heart, and that you promise to eschew listening to and using any forecasts, and that you are prepared to take everything managers say with a large pinch of salt because they are overoptimistic and overconfident. Are you then safe to meet with company management?

CONFIRMATORY BIAS AND BIASED ASSIMILATION

Sadly the answer is 'probably not'. There are several more hurdles to overcome. Firstly, there is *confirmatory bias*. This is the unfortunate habit we have of only looking for information that happens to agree with our current view. Time after time, people have been shown to commit biased assimilation – that is, not only looking for information that agrees with them, but also seeing all information as being consistent with their prior beliefs.

The classic example of biased assimilation comes form Leeper *et al.* (1979). They asked 151 undergraduates to complete a questionnaire dealing with capital punishment. Of these students, 48 were then selected for a further experiment: 24 of the group were pro capital punishment, and 24 anti the death sentence. Subjects were then asked to read randomly selected studies on the deterrent efficacy of the death sentence (and criticisms of those studies). Subjects were also asked to rate the studies in terms of the impact they had had on their views on capital punishment and deterrence.

Figure 12.5 shows that all those who started with a pro death sentence stance thought the studies that supported capital punishment were well argued, sound and important. They also

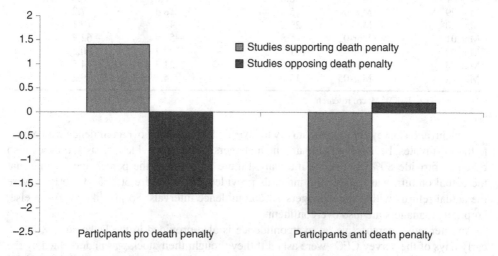

Figure 12.5   Biased assimilation: ratings of capital punishment studies (scale −5 to +5).
Source: Leeper *et al.* (1979).

thought that the studies that argued against the death penalty were all deeply flawed. Those who held the opposite point of view at the outset reached exactly the opposite conclusion.

As Lord *et al.* concluded, "Asked for their final attitudes relative to the experiments start, proponents reported they were more in favour of capital punishment, whereas opponents reported that they were less in favour of capital punishment."

Westen *et al.* (2004) conducted a series of investigations into biased assimilation in the context of political viewpoints. For instance, in an experiment completed just ahead of the presidential election, the participants were told a soldier at Abu Ghraib prison was charged with torturing prisoners. He wanted the right to subpoena senior administration officials. He claimed he'd been informed that the administration had suspended the Geneva Convention.

Westen *et al.* gave different people different amounts of evidence supporting his claims. For some, the evidence was minimal; for others, it was overwhelming. Westen *et al.* found that the evidence barely mattered at all. For 84% of the time, they could predict whether people believed the evidence was sufficient to subpoena Donald Rumsfeld based on just three things: the extent to which they liked Republicans, the extent to which they liked the US military, and the extent to which they liked human rights groups like Amnesty International. Adding the evidence into the equation allowed them to increase the prediction from 84% to 85%.

Westen *et al.* also use several real-time, real situation examinations. For instance, at the time of the Clinton–Lewinsky scandal just after the point at which Lewinsky had testified before a grand jury, Westen *et al.* asked people whether they thought the President had obstructed justice. The only two significant predictors of their judgements were whether they liked Clinton, and whether they were Democrats!

Of course, both the death sentence and politics are emotionally charged events. Has such behaviour been documented in less emotionally fraught situations? Strangely enough the answer is yes.

For example, Carlson and Russo (2001) investigated whether jurors' suffer biased assimilation in mock trial situations. They explored what they called predecisional distortion – which is the biased interpretation and evaluation of new information to support whichever alternative is currently leading during a decision process.

They ran two sets of tests: one using students, the other using real jurors. Both groups were asked to assess both a civil case and a criminal case. They were given seven sections of information. The first was a background statement concerning the nature of the case.

In the civil case test, the lawsuit was brought by the grandmother of a teenage accident victim against the owner of the company that had built the porch on which the accident occurred. In the criminal version, the case was a pre-trial hearing on the admissibility of cocaine seized during the search of a car.

Following the background information participants were given six witness affidavits to evaluate. After each piece of information had been presented, people were asked three questions. The first was to rate on a 9-point scale how much the information supported the plaintiff. The second question asked which party was in the lead. The third question recorded the participant's confidence that the current leader would eventually win the race.

Before they were given any of the information, all participants were shown a video designed to introduce jurors to the legal process. It explicitly mentioned that forming conclusions before hearing all the evidence was to be avoided at least three times.

Each affidavit was presented in each possible ordering sequence an equal number of times across the experiments. This allowed Carlson and Russo to construct a simple measure of information distortion. For each witness statement they found someone who favoured each

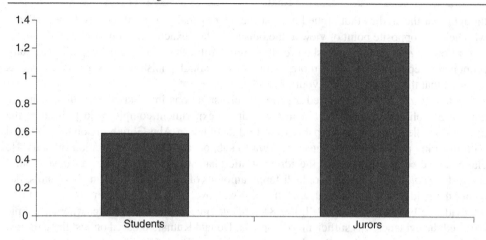

Figure 12.6 Mean level of information distortion measures.
Source: Adapted from Carlson and Russo (2001).

side in the case and averaged their score to give a so-called leader-free value on the 9-point scale mentioned earlier. Then each individual's response was evaluated as a deviation from this leader-free value. If the score deviated in a way that favoured the individual's belief in the leading verdict, then it was scored as +1, and if it favoured the trailing verdict, it was scored as −1.

Figure 12.6 shows the mean level of information distortion among the students and the mock jurors. Both are statistically significantly different from zero, so both groups were *guilty of distorting the information presented so that it favoured the current leading view*. In fact the jurors exhibited about twice the magnitude of the students distortion!

Carlson and Russo also tracked the confidence levels at the start of each case, and compared them with the final confidence reported. Figure 12.7 shows yet another example of

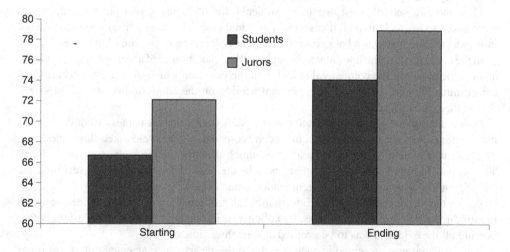

Figure 12.7 Starting and ending confidence ratings (%).
Source: Adapted from Carlson and Russo (2001).

information driving confidence. In fact the researchers found information distortion increased with confidence. *That is, the more sure people were that they had the correct verdict, the more they distorted new evidence to suit their existing preference.* Russo and others have found similar effects in a wide range of domains, including consumers, auditors and salespeople.

Just think about this in the context of our current topic. The chances are that you already have a view on a company when you go to meet them (which might well coincide with whether you hold the stock or not). On the basis of the evidence presented here it is highly likely that you will fail to be objective when you do see them. Rather than searching out all the disconfirming evidence, you are likely to interpret all the information you gather in the light of your previous view. If all you are doing is reconfirming what you already believe, there seems little point in meeting with the company.

This tendency to biased assimilation will be made all the worse by the fact that company managements always tell you what you want to hear. When was the last time a company arrived at your office and started to confess that they were a dreadful company with disastrous management, and little or nor hope of ever actually improving? Of course, it never happens. Instead, companies turn up and tell you that they have had a rough time, but whatever the problem was (be it unexpected inventory build, or gross margin pressure), it has now been solved and everything will now be going forward.

OBEDIENCE TO AUTHORITY

Not only do we have to contend with this tendency to look for information that agrees with us and our bad habits of biased assimilation, but we also have to be aware of our marked tendency to believe what we are told by people in positions of authority. I have previously explored this issue in the context of corporate governance (see *Global Equity Strategy*, 31 January 2005).

Stanley Milgram's work (1974) was triggered in the wake of World War II. He wanted to investigate why it was that so many ordinary people either simply said nothing about their leader's clearly abhorrent policies, or even worse chose to follow their example.

Milgram devised a simple but stunningly effective experiment in which subjects were asked to assist. They were told they would be administering electric shocks to a 'learner' at the instruction of a 'teacher'. The subjects were told that they were involved in a study on punishment effects on learning and memory.

The subjects sat in front of a box with electric switches on it. The switches displayed the level of volts that was being delivered, and a text description of the level of pain ranging from 'slight' through to 'very strong' and up to 'danger severe', culminating in 'XXX'. When the buttons were depressed, a buzzing sound could be heard. The 'teacher' was a confederate of the experimenters, and wore a white coat and carried a clipboard. They would instruct the subjects when to press the button.

In the classic variant of the experiment, the subject couldn't see the person they were shocking, but could hear him. At 75 volts, the 'learner' grunts, at 120 volts he starts to complain verbally, at 150 volts he demands to be released, at 285 volts the 'learner' makes a response that Milgram said could only be described as 'an agonized scream'. At 425 volts, a grim and deathly silence greeted the participants.

Before conducting the experiment, Milgram's prior belief was that very few people would administer high levels of shock. Indeed 40 psychiatrists canvassed by Milgram thought that less than 1% would give the full 450-volt shock. After all, they reasoned, Americans just

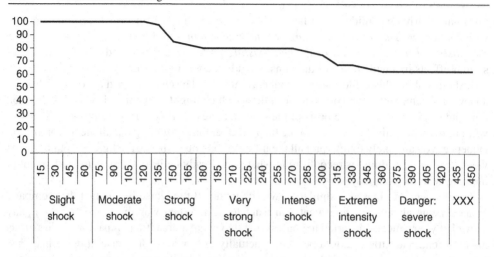

Figure 12.8 Percentage of participants reaching each level of voltage.
Source: Milgram (1974).

didn't engage in such behaviour. (Sounds like a classic case of the fundamental attribution error doesn't it!)

Figure 12.8 shows the percentage of respondents who progressed to each level of voltage. One hundred percent of ordinary Americans were willing to send up to 135 volts (at which point the 'learner' is asking to be released) through someone they didn't know. Eighty percent were willing to go up to 285 volts (at which point they are hearing agonising screams). Over 62% were willing to administer the full 450 volts, despite the screams and the labels on the machine stating 'severe danger' and 'XXX'!

Nor are Milgram's results unique. Table 12.2 shows the average compliance level to the maximum voltage from a number of studies. Incidentally, spoil sport university ethics boards outlawed Milgram style experiments in the late 1980s, therefore no other modern studies are available, although we have little reason to believe they would show anything different from the majority of findings in the table.

Table 12.2 International 'Milgram' studies

Study	Country	Percentage obedient to the highest level of shock
Milgram	USA	62.5
Rosenham	USA	85
Ancona and Pareyson	Italy	85
Mantell	Germany	85
Kilham and Mann	Australia	40
Burley and McGuiness	UK	50
Shanab and Yahya	Jordan	62
Miranda *et al.*	Spain	90
Schurz	Austria	80
Meeus and Raaijmakers	Holland	92

Source: Smith and Bond (1994).

So simply because we are told do something by a man in a white coat and carrying a clipboard, we appear willing to obey his instructions. This is the power of authority. Company managements are, of course, in a position of authority. They have generally reached the top of their field. As such it is all too easy for analysts and fund managers to think of them as authority figures, and hence believe whatever they are told.

The more god-like the management, the easier it will be for them to influence analysts who cover the stock. CEOs are generally successful people who have made it. As such we tend to interpret their success as the result of their disposition (the fundamental attribution error). We are in awe of such individuals. Few, if any, analysts were willing to ask critical questions of Bernie Ebbers at the height of the TMT boom, when he and his ilk were regarded as the new masters of the universe.[1] We need to train people not only to search for disconfirming evidence, but to be critical of company managements.

TRUTH OR LIE?

Let's assume that so far you are sitting reading this and feeling quite pleased with yourself because you know that managers are overoptimistic and overconfident, and you never listen to their forecasts. You always ask lots of difficult disconfirming questions and you certainly aren't in awe of company CEOs. So surely you have nothing to worry about!

There is one final psychological hurdle for you to pass. *Can you tell the truth from a lie?* Do you know when someone is trying to deceive you? Of course, like so many areas of behavioural biases we tend to answer that each and every one of us can tell truth from lies. However, the reality is very different.

Kassin *et al.* (2005) have explored people's abilities to tell truth from lies. They asked serving prisoners to videotape and audiotape confessions to their true crimes and to a crime they did not commit. They asked 61 students and 57 federal, state and local investigators to watch/listen to the tapes and asked them who was telling the truth and who was making a false confession. The professionals were all experienced with an average of nearly 11 years' service, and no less than 58% had received special training in deception detection training.

Across all participants (professionals and students) and all conditions (video and audio) the average overall accuracy rating was 53.9%, statistically indifferent from a pure chance performance! Table 12.3 details the main findings by Kassin *et al.* Students significantly outperformed the trained professionals with higher accuracy and lower confidence.

It is worth noting that the investigators thought almost everyone was guilty (Figure 12.9). That is to say, they had a much higher rate of false alarms (that is false confessions perceived as true) than the students did. This has become known as investigator bias.

Intriguingly both groups performed better on the audio versions of the test rather than the videotape evidence. That is an area to which we will return shortly.

Those with a touching faith in law and order may well suggest that the test was biased because investigators may well come across more true confessions than false confessions in their jobs, and so may have started the experiment with very different base rate expectations than the students. To counteract such claims, Kassin *et al.* ran a variant of the experiment

---

[1] Intriguingly, Malmendier and Tate (2004) Superstar CEOs, show that award winning CEOs extract more compensation from their companies following awards. They spend more time writing books and lecturing and gaining board seats. Most importantly, firms with Superstar CEOs have stocks that underperform the market on a 1-; 3- and 5-year horizon!

Table 12.3 Can we tell the truth from lies?

	Students		Investigators	
	Video	Audio	Video	Audio
Judgement accuracy (%)	53.4	64.1	42.1	54.5
Hit rates (%)	55.9	70	57.9	69.7
False alarms (%)	50.3	41.9	73.6	60.7
Confidence	6.18	6.25	7.65	6.7

Source: Kassin *et al.* (2005).

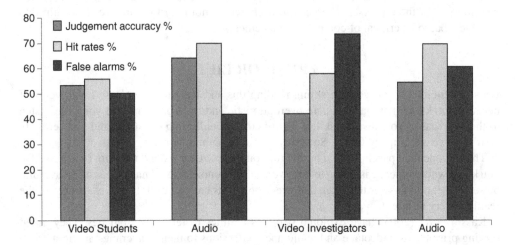

Figure 12.9 Judgement accuracy, hit rates and false alarms.
Source: Kassin *et al.* (2005).

in which the students and investigators were told that half of the confessions they would see would be true and half would be false. Table 12.4 details the results.

Once again the students performed better than the professionals. They had higher accuracy and lower confidence (see Figure 12.10). However, note that both groups did little better than by simply guessing.

In another pair of papers, Kassin and Fong (1999) and Meissner and Kassin (2002) explore the impact of training on deception training. They took three groups – students, students who had been trained in the most common methods of deception detection, and professional

Table 12.4 Rates when told that half are true

	Students	Investigators
Judgement accuracy (%)	53.8	48.5
Hit rates (%)	53.3	50
False alarms (%)	45.7	53
Confidence	5.74	7.03

Source: Kassin *et al.* (2005).

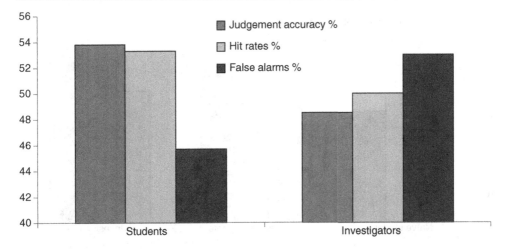

Figure 12.10   Judgement accuracy, hit rates and false alarms when told 50% will be true.
Source: Kassin *et al.* (2005).

investigators. To provide their confessions they recruited students from a different university, some of whom were asked to commit one of four criminal acts: vandalism, shoplifting, breaking and entering, and computer break-in. Those selected to be guilty actually carried out the crimes (under controlled conditions), while those who were innocent were placed in the vicinity of the crime.

For instance, in the case of shoplifting, the guilty participants were instructed to enter a local shop and steal an item of jewellery. They were not told how to commit the crime, only that they mustn't get caught. The cooperating storeowner pretended not to notice the crime. They were arrested on exiting the shop. The innocents in this case were told to enter, browse and exit the shop. They were told they would find a paper bag outside the shop upon their exit and they should pick it up. When they did this, they were arrested.

The guilty and innocent were then taken to a police station and interviewed. The guilty were told to maintain their innocence and make up any excuses to avoid admitting to the crime. These interactions were taped, and it was these tapes that the participants were then allowed to review.

Table 12.5 below shows the results from their experiments. The trained students and the investigators underperformed the naïve students (see Figure 12.11). Once again they seemed

Table 12.5   Training is a disadvantage

	Naïve students	Trained students	Investigators
Judgement accuracy (%)	56	46	50
Hit rates (%)	56	45	62
False alarms (%)	42	60	67
Confidence	5.91	6.55	7.05

Source: Kassin *et al.* (1999, 2002).

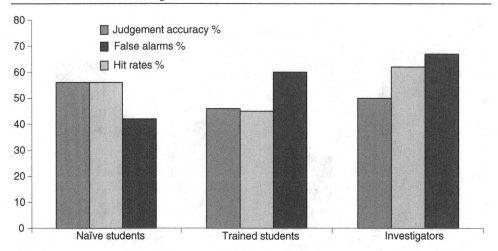

Figure 12.11   Training hampers performance!
Source: Kassin *et al.* (1999, 2002).

to think that everyone was guilty! It is also interesting to note that *confidence increased with training and experience but accuracy didn't!*

So how good are you at spotting when someone is not telling the truth? Which of the following is more likely to be lying: (i) someone who avoids eye contact, doesn't smile, and shifts his posture a lot, or (ii) someone who answers with short replies, tells you lots of irrelevant information and whose pupils dilate when answering questions?

The majority of people pick the first candidate. This is because lay psychology tells us that these are traits associated with those who are lying. This perception is then enhanced whenever we watch television and someone who lies is portrayed as a shifty character with wandering eyes, etc.

However, the second person above is actually more likely to be lying than the first. The first three traits have no correlation with whether people are telling the truth or not. The second three are relatively highly correlated.

DePaulo *et al.* (2003) have completed a massive meta-analysis (study of other studies) to discern the most likely cues to deception. They took 1338 estimates of 158 different cues and looked for items that showed up as significant.

They found that liars tended to fit the profile outlined in Table 12.6. Intriguingly they found that very few physical signs were of use in spotting deception. This accords with the finding from Kassin *et al.* above that people generally were better at spotting deception when they were listening rather than watching.

Given that we all appear to be so bad at spotting deception from truth, it might perhaps be better if we avoided putting tremendous faith in our ability to judge elements such as company management in the context of meetings with them.

For fans of US imports to our screen, this general message should be familiar. In CSI Gil Grissom spends his entire time reminding anyone who will listen that the evidence doesn't lie, with the implicit statement that people do. Or if your tastes run to medical dramas then House provides a weekly reminder that patients lie, but symptoms don't.

Table 12.6   Spotting liars

Category	Primary characteristics
(I) Liars are less forthcoming	Take less time in responses Provide fewer details Press their lips together
(II) Liars tell less convincing stories	Less plausible Lack logic Internally inconsistent Sound more evasive, unclear and impersonal Sound more uncertain Often had raised chin/direct eye contact Repetition of words and phrases
(III) Liars are less positive and pleasant	Less cooperative More negative statements Faces are less pleasant (don't smile)
(IV) Liars are more tense	More nervous and tense Vocally tense Higher pitch Dilated pupils
(V) Liars have fewer imperfections/content corrections	Lack of spontaneous corrections No memory failures More non-significant events

Source: Adapted from DePaulo *et al.* (2003).

CONCLUSIONS

It would seem that there are numerous psychological hurdles (listed below) to be passed before we can classify meeting with company managements as a key part of the investment process. It is also difficult to debias away from these problems. Given that we can't easily correct these biases, perhaps company meetings are best avoided! Indeed one of the best performing European fund managers of our acquaintance eschews meeting companies altogether. A lesson for us all perhaps?

The psychological barriers to the usefulness of company meetings are:

1. Managers are just as likely to suffer the same biases as the rest of us.
2. Information overload.
3. Confirmatory bias, biased assimilation, predecisional distortion.
4. Obedience to authority.
5. We aren't good at telling deception from the truth.

SIN 4
Thinking You Can Outsmart Everyone Else (Envy)

13
Who's a Pretty Boy Then? Or Beauty Contests, Rationality and Greater Fools*

> We have played a "Keynes's beauty contest" with our clients. The results show that most investors are gaming the market, using on average two steps of strategic thinking. The game demonstrates the difficulty of 'beating the gun', and highlights the extreme risk that investors run in momentum-oriented markets.

- Keynes likened professional investment to a newspaper beauty contest in which the aim was to pick the face that the average respondent would deem to be the prettiest. We have played a version of this game with our clients. The game was to pick a number between 0 and 100, and the winner would be the player who picked the number closest to two-thirds of the average number chosen.
- In fact, we had over 1000 respondents (my thanks to everyone who participated), making this the fourth largest such game ever played, and the first played purely among professional investors on such a scale. The average number picked was 26, giving a two-thirds average of 17.4.
- Many clients suffered a curse of knowledge – that is, once the solution is known, it is hard to imagine that others can't see it. Hence 8.5% of the players in our game ended up at the "rational" solution of zero. The largest spike occurred at 22, with nearly 9% of the players picking this number. On average, our market is characterized by those doing between one and two steps of strategic thinking.
- Hence, in order to escape the market before the mass exodus, you would need to be using three-step thinking. In our sample, that represents very few players. Perhaps this lends some support to our oft-voiced scepticism over the ability of the majority to 'beat the gun'.

*This article appeared in *Global Equity Strategy* on 18 November 2005. The material discussed was accurate at the time of publication.

BACKGROUND

In what must be the second most common quotation from Keynes (the first presumably being 'In the long run, we are all dead') the great man opines:

> The actual, private object of the most skilled investment to-day is 'to beat the gun', to outwit the crowd, and to pass the bad, or depreciating, half-crown to the other fellow.
>
> This battle of wits to anticipate the basis of conventional valuation a few months hence, rather than the prospective yield of an investment over a long term of years, does not even require gulls among the public to feed the maws of the professional – it can be played by professionals among themselves. Nor is it necessary that anyone should keep his simple faith in the conventional basis of valuation having any genuine long-term validity. For it is, so to speak, a game of Snap, of Old Maid, of Musical Chairs – a pastime in which he is victor who says Snap neither too soon nor too late, who passes the Old Maid to his neighbour before the game is over, who secures a chair for himself when the music stops. These games can be played with zest and enjoyment, though all the players know that it is the Old Maid which is circulating, or that when the music stops some of the players will find themselves unseated.
>
> Or, to change the metaphor slightly, professional investment may be likened to those newspaper competitions in which the competitors have to pick out the six prettiest faces from a hundred photographs, the prize being awarded to the competitor whose choice most nearly corresponds to the average preferences of the competitors as a whole; so that each competitor has to pick, not those faces which he himself finds prettiest, but those which he thinks likeliest to catch the fancy of the other competitors, all of whom are looking at the problem from the same point of view. It is not a case of choosing those which, to the best of one's judgement, are really the prettiest, nor even those which average opinion genuinely thinks the prettiest. We have reached the third degree where we devote our intelligences to anticipating what average opinion expects the average opinion to be. And there are some, I believe, who practise the fourth, fifth and higher degrees.
>
> If the reader interjects that there must surely be large profits to be gained from the other players in the long run by a skilled individual who, unperturbed by the prevailing pastime, continues to purchase investments on the best genuine long-term expectations he can frame, he must be answered, first of all, that there are, indeed, such serious-minded individuals and that it makes a vast difference to an investment market whether or not they predominate in their influence over the game-players. But we must also add that there are several factors which jeopardize the predominance of such individuals in modern investment markets. Investment based on genuine long-term expectation is so difficult today as to be scarcely practicable.

John Maynard Keynes, Chapter 12, *General Theory of Employment, Interest, and Money* (1935) pp. 155–156.

THE GAME

I fear that some of you think I have finally flipped. Two weeks ago I sent out an e-mail to the e-readers of our strategy product to ask them to participate in a guessing game. The e-mail is reproduced below:

> Dear all,
>
> We would like to ask your help. Please consider the following question and e-mail your reply to me. The overall results will be written up in a forthcoming weekly. However, as ever, none of your individual responses will be disclosed. As an incentive, we are offering a bottle of champagne to the winner.

> You are taking part in a competition with the other readers of our strategy products. The aim of the game is to pick a (real) number between 0 and 100 ([0, 100]). The winner will be the respondent who chooses the number closest to two-thirds of the average number chosen.
>
> Many thanks in advance for your input.

If you weren't on the e-mail list, to get the most out of the rest of this chapter consider your answer before you go any further. Having just read the quotation from Keynes it is presumably obvious that the game outlined in the e-mail is a version of Keynes's beauty contest.[1] So why are we playing a beauty contest game with you? We will show a little later that it has applications in understanding the dynamics of gaming the market, but for now please bear with us.

THE SOLUTION

The game itself should be a simple one under the standard assumptions of economics. i.e. rationality *and* common knowledge. Since all players want to choose two-thirds of the average, there is only one number that satisfies the equation $x = 2/3 \times x$, and that number is 0. So the only equilibrium[2] answer to this question is 0 (as many of you pointed out).

The game can be solved by a process known as "iterated dominance". A dominated strategy is one that yields a lower payoff than another, regardless of what other players are doing. For example, choosing a number greater than 67 is a dominated strategy because the highest possible solution to the game is 67 (i.e. if everyone else picks the maximum number 100). However, if no one violates dominance by choosing a number above 67, then the highest outcome is two-thirds of 67 and so on. Deleting dominated strategies in this fashion will eventually lead you to 0.[3] This fact was explicitly identified by some 14.5% of our sample (and probably many more who didn't bother to state the "rational" answer as it wasn't required).

Of course, this only works under the assumption that everyone you are playing against is rational, and they know that you are rational as well. As one client put it, "the whole thing gets much more difficult when you can't assume that everybody is a perfect logician trying to maximize his or her own best interest". As soon as we start to see that at least some of the market is not fully rational, then the problem becomes more and more complex.

Before looking at the results, I'll try to link this work back to our work on rational bubbles. In *Global Equity Strategy*, 12 January 2004, we outlined the conditions for various kinds of bubbles. One of these was the near rational bubble driven by myopia (short time horizons) and overconfidence. We concluded that this kind of bubble most closely matched the current market conditions.

A lack of backward induction is also part of this process. Even if all investors foresee a crash, they don't backward induct all the way to today – otherwise there would be no bubbles and no busts. They guess that other investors will try to sell a couple of steps before the crash. Hence everyone expects and plans to sell just before the mass exodus. This failure of backward induction helps to explain why bubbles can persist even when everyone knows that they must eventually burst.

---

[1] This game was first played by Nagel (1995).
[2] Technically, zero is the only fixed point Nash equilibrium.
[3] This process is also known as backward induction.

Another failure of backward induction – The paradox of the unexpected hanging

A man was sentenced on Saturday. "The hanging will take place at noon on one of the seven days of next week," said the judge. He continued "But, you will not know which day it is, until you are informed on the morning of the day of the hanging."

Can the judge's sentence be carried out?

It would seem not. If the man has not been hanged by next Friday, he will then know that he must be hanged the next day. However, this violates the judge's ruling that he won't know until the day itself. Thus we can rule out next Saturday as the execution day. Then by the same logic, if the man has not been hanged by next Thursday, then he knows he must be hanged on Friday (since we have just ruled out Saturday). This, of course, contradicts the judge's orders that he mustn't know the day until the morning of the day itself. And so we end up ruling out all the days. Hence it appears that the judge's sentence can't be carried out.

Actually, the man was hanged on Monday, and he did not know in advance that Monday would be the day of his death, just as the judge had ordered!

THE RESULTS

The beauty contest provides a simple way of roughly measuring the number of steps of strategic thinking that players are doing. As one client response noted,

> I am curious how this little game will end... So, let's see how inefficient this market is. Isn't that the dilemma/contradiction we are all in? We know the efficient (right) answer should be 0, however as a rational investor our estimates have to include our guesstimates on how rational our competitors are!

Since our e-mail list consists of professional investors alone, we can take our results as a proxy for the market as a whole. In fact, we had a truly impressive 1002 replies – making this the fourth largest such contest ever played! Thank you to everyone who took part.

The average number selected was 26, giving a two-thirds average of 17.4. Figure 13.1 shows the relative frequency of the choices in our game.[4] This reveals some interesting features about the level of strategic thinking that market participants are using.

Only 5% of the sample chose numbers above 67, implying that they didn't understand the question or that they are clearly irrational. As one player wrote "100... I'm not a rational investor, my favourite stocks are Amazon and EBAY". (US$46.38, US$68.60).

However, such responses don't really have market power because of the size of our sample. Technically we can define market power as the number of additional votes of "100" that would be necessary to change the result by "1", given that sample size. This comes down to $1002/(99 - 26) = 13.7$. So we would require a considerable number of "100" picks in order to affect our market (Figure 13.2).

Even if we exclude all those who chose numbers greater than 67, we still end up with an average number of 23, and hence a two-thirds average of 15.2 – still massively above the Nash equilibrium.

---

[4] For pedagogical, expositional, and graphical ease I've transformed the answers into integers. However, rest assured that the average was calculated on the true answers.

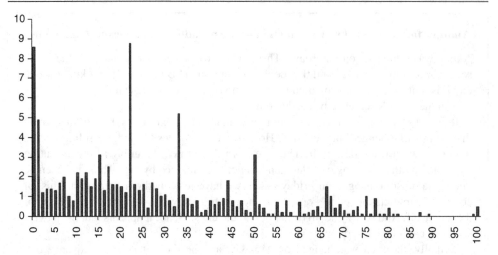

Figure 13.1   Relative frequency of choices in our game (%).
Source: DrKW Macro research.

Rather than using the iterated dominance strategies outlined earlier, most players assume (perfectly rationally) that the starting point should be 50, i.e. the mean from a random draw. Hence level-0 players chose 50 (3% of our total sample). Level-1 players chose the best reaction to the level-0 players i.e. they picked two-thirds of 50, providing a spike at 33 (5% of our sample). Level-2 players "best react" to a 33, yielding the massive spike at 22 (nearly 9% of our sample – the highest single selection). Level-3 players end up with 15 as their pick (3% of the sample). Once past level-2 or 3 reasoning, players frequently slide down the slippery slope towards the infinite iterations that produce 0 (8.5% of our sample).

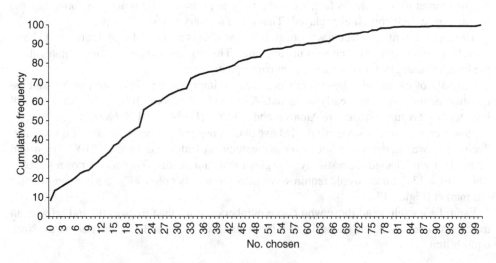

Figure 13.2   Cumulative frequency of choices in our game (%).
Source: DrKW Macro research.

It is easy to measure the number of steps of strategic thinking that are being carried out by the following formula (for choices less than 50) $\ln(x/50)/\ln(2/3)$. So with an average of 26, the average level of thinking comes out at 1.6. The most common level of thinking (the mode) was two steps of thinking (corresponding to 22).

This pattern of behaviour fits well with other studies of such contests. For instance, Nagel *et al.* (1999) actually called their paper "One, Two, (Three), Infinity" because the pattern of thinking seems to follow exactly the same behaviour as that outlined above.

As noted earlier, some 14% of our players identified 0 as the "rational" equilibrium. A majority identifying the "rational" answer ended up with that as their final answer. The following answers help to identify this sentiment:

> "If we were 100% logical, then everyone should enter 0. Since people seldom are, I should therefore, (also logically!), choose another, higher, number, reflecting human nature. However, I cannot bring myself to believe people are so irrational. I therefore stick with 0."

> "My guess is 0. But if I am right, nobody should win: It does not pay to be rational!"

This group was effectively suffering from the curse of knowledge. One particular form of the curse of knowledge is once we know something, we can't ever imagine thinking otherwise. This makes it hard for us to realize that what we know may be less than obvious to others who are less informed. Better informed players are unable to ignore private information even when it would be in their interest to do so, more information isn't better information![5]

Some 41% of those identifying the 0 equilibrium chose a number other than 0 as their estimate of the likely outcome. Effectively they are taking a rational view on the degree of irrationality or the amount of bounded rationality that governs the market. This kind of thinking was typified by responses such as:

> "If I remember correctly, that's a question about rational expectations and game theory and a rational answer should tend towards 0, but let's go for 10 to account for frictions and rigidities in real life."

> "Theoretically, the answer should be 0, if all participants were rational. Since I do not assume all participants to be rational, my pick is 6."

> "If all contestants are rational, the answer should be 0. However as I suspect that your recipients spend their time in the market for stocks, rationality is an irrational assumption, and I will therefore select the number 12 (!!!)"

> "I would like to choose 5.852. I know this is theoretically too high, but I'm relying on a lot of people picking randomly."

> "If everyone is rational and everyone knows that everyone else is rational and everyone knows that everyone knows that everyone is rational, then everyone will guess 0. So everyone gets half a thimble of champagne. So I'm guessing 1 in the hope that some people guess a random number."

This group also suffered from a curse of knowledge. In effect, they were suffering a false consensus effect – that is, the tendency to think that others are just like us. Ask a group of mixed smokers and non-smokers how common smoking is in the population and the chances are you will find that the smokers think more people smoke, and the non-smokers will think that smoking is a minority pastime.

---

[5] For evidence that such biases can affect market prices and behaviour, see Camerer *et al.* (1989).

Players who identified 0 as the "rational" solution seemed to anchor on that figure. That is to say, although they picked a number higher than 0, they generally stayed too close to 0, i.e. underestimating the degree of irrationality within the market.

The classic experiment in this field was conducted by Tversky and Kahneman (1974) (weren't they all!). In this experiment, people were asked a general knowledge question such as "What percentage of the UN is made up of African nations?" A wheel of fortune with numbers 1 to 100 was spun in front of the participants before they answered. Being psychologists, Tversky and Kahneman had rigged the wheel so that it gave either 10 or 65 as the result of a spin. The subjects were then asked if their answer was higher or lower than the number on the wheel, and also asked their actual answer. The median response from the group that saw the wheel present 10 was 25, while the median response from the group that saw 65 was 45! Effectively people were grabbing at irrelevant anchors when forming their expectations.

Of course, 0 isn't irrelevant in our contest, but it may be that players were fixating on 0 as too much of an anchor in forming their expectations of the overall game. However this shouldn't be taken as proof that all non-zero choices are a "rational" comment on the degree of irrationality within the market.

In an intriguing paper, Grosskopf and Nagel (2001) use two-player beauty contest games to assess whether players are boundedly rational or whether they are making a "rational" comment on the irrationality of others. The two-player game is a special case of the beauty contest because 0 is always a first best choice regardless of the number picked by your opponent (assuming a 'two-thirds' type of game). For instance, say one player picks 15 and the other picks 0, then two-thirds of the average will be 5, and the 0 player wins. This holds true for all numbers.

Thus, if players were truly rational one would expect them to pick 0 in two-player games. Grosskopf and Nagel used participants who were in general quite familiar with the beauty contest game (many of whom used the game in teaching). Yet despite this experience, in the first round a mere 12% of participants chose 0! Grosskopf and Nagel go on to show how information feedback can improve performance. However, their conclusion is that very few players are independently rational; instead, players seem to grope almost blindly, using imitation and adaptation, towards equilibrium.

So our market can be characterized by the following facts:

• Most players use one, two (three) or infinity levels of thinking.
• A significant number who reach 0 choose a number greater than 0 because they believe that others are boundedly rational. However, virtually all such players still ended up choosing too low a number.
• A significant proportion of players do choose either 0 or 1 – doomed by their own rationality, or the curse of knowledge.

A SIMPLE MODEL OF OUR CONTEST

Camerer *et al.* (2003) argue that a simple model can characterize many strategic games, including the kind we have played. The model assumes bounded rationality and overconfidence on the part of the players.

The model is based on the fact that players do not realize that other players are using more than a certain level of steps – that is to say, players have limited cognitive abilities (bounded rationality). The model also assumes that people are overconfident, in as much as they don't realize that others are using as many steps of thinking as they are.

Based on their model, Camerer *et al.* have found that most games are characterized by one or two steps of thinking. They recommend using a 1.6 average level of reasoning for a one-shot game. This would generate a mean number of 33, and a two-thirds average of 22.

However, in games with those trained in logic (as one would generally hope market participants are!) a higher level of reasoning should probably be expected. Hence I ran their model based on an average two steps of reasoning before the results of our game were known. Using this model resulted in a prediction of a mean number of 29.8, with a two-thirds average of 20. Not bad, compared to the actual outcome, and certainly a massive improvement on the standard game theory prediction of Nash equilibrium – 0.

In fact one client came very close to using a very similar methodology without even knowing about the cognitive hierarchy model:

> I believe that most people are going to go for 50 as the mean response and two-thirds of that is clearly 33.3. However I am anticipating that most of the people on your distribution list are going to anticipate that the average answer is 33.3 and will therefore go for two-thirds of that which is 22.2. The quandary now is to determine how many iterations the average person in your survey will assume that the other participants go through. On the assumption that 25% of the respondents are naive and say 33, and that 50% are more sophisticated and say 20, with the remaining 25% going to the logical extreme and saying 0, then I'm left with a weighted average of 19.4.

In actual fact, it transpires that our market is best characterized by an average of 2.8 steps in the thinking process (if we model up to level-6 players). Level-0 players essentially pick a random number (i.e. 50). Level-1 players assume that everyone else is a level-0 player, and hence pick two-thirds of 50. Level-2 players assume that they are the only level-2 players (overconfidence) and so normalize the true distribution to give the relevant weights, i.e. they assume that there are 30% level-0 players, and 70% level-1 players (8/28 level-0, and 20/28 level-1). Hence they "best react" to the combined mixture of level 0 and level 1, an average of 38.7, and pick a two-thirds figure of 25.1. This process continues at each level of thinking. The cognitive hierarchy model suggests that our game consists of a population as shown in Table 13.1.

Note that something interesting happens in this model. All players using two or more steps of strategic thinking end up selecting the same number. Effectively no one in this contest would need to think beyond two steps of reasoning, so even if players can, they are better off not doing so (i.e. avoiding the curse of knowledge). This occurs because the size of the distribution is so large at groups 1, 2 and 3.

Table 13.1   Cognitive hierarchy model of our game

No of steps	% of population	Number selected
0	7.9	50
1	20	33.3
2	25.4	25.1
3	21.5	25.1
4	13.7	25.1
5	6.9	25.1

Source: DrKW Macro research.

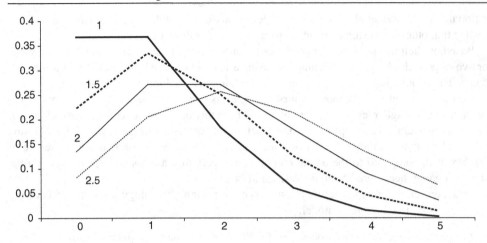

Figure 13.3   Population of the universe as a function of average number of thinking steps.
Source: DrKW Macro research.

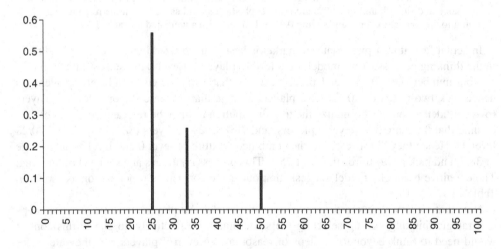

Figure 13.4   Cognitive hierarchy model prediction of the distribution of players in our contest.
Source: DrKW Macro research.

COMPARISON WITH OTHER EXPERIMENTS

So how do our results stack up against other beauty contests? Table 13.2 below shows a summary of beauty contests that have been played with a wide variety of participants. We have also estimated the average level of thinking from the cognitive hierarchy model outlined earlier. In general, the results we have obtained are very similar to those found by other researchers.

The closest games in terms of size have been those played in newspapers. The results of aggregation of all three papers (FT, *Expansion* and *Spektrum*) are shown in Figure 13.5.

Table 13.2   Summary of beauty contests

	Average	2/3rds	No of players	Experimenter	Average level of thinking
Caltech Board	42.6	28.4	73	Camerer	0.5
CEOs	37.9	25.3	20	Camerer	1
German students	37.2	24.8	14–16	Nagel	1.1
70 year olds	37	24.7	33	Kovalchik	1.1
US high school	32.5	21.7	20–32	Camerer	1.6
Econ Phds	27.4	18.3	16	Camerer	2.6
Portfolio Managers	24.3	16.2	26	Camerer	3.2
CalTech Students	23	15.3	17–25	Camerer	3.5
FT	18.9	12.6	1476	Thaler	4.3
Expansion	25.5	17	3696	Nagel	3
Spektrum	22.1	14.7	2728	Nagel	3.7
Game theorists	19.1	12.7	136	Nagel	4.3
CalTech students	30.2	20.1	10–12	Weber	2.1
Portfolio managers (single firm)	29.3	19.6	22	Montier	2.3
Harvard Econ students	18.3	12.2	124	Laibson	4.4
DrKW Strategists/Economists	12.3	8.2	6	Montier	5.7
BF Group	24.2	16.1	22	Montier	3.3
German institutions (Sentix)	40.5	27	61	Hüber	0.8
German private clients (Sentix)	44.3	29.6	185	Hüber	0.4
Global Investors	26	17.3	1002	Montier	2.8

Source: DrKW Macro research, Camerer *et al.* (2003).

I've also included four other new games. The first was played over Christmas 2001 by some of my colleagues in the macro team at DrKW. As you might expect from the game theorists examined by Nagel, the average number chosen was markedly lower, when economists were playing among themselves (Figure 13.6).

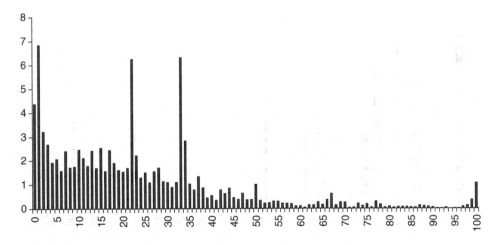

Figure 13.5   Newspaper beauty contests.
Source: DrKW Macro research.

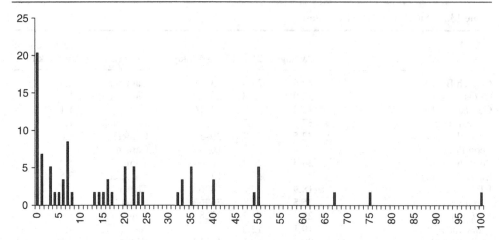

Figure 13.6 Game theorists and Experimenters contest.
Source: Nagel (1995).

The other three games were played simultaneously with the contest amongst our clients. I played the game with the Yahoo Behavioural Finance group (Figure 13.7). They showed a very similar performance to the newspaper readers in Table 13.2.

The final two games were played by a survey organization based in Germany (www.sentix.de). Manfred Hüber, founder of the site, offered to run the beauty contest as part of their weekly poll of sentiment. Always greedy for information I eagerly accepted Manfred's kind offer. Sentix separated the responses into private investors and institutional investors (Figures 13.8 and 13.9).

Perhaps because the question was written in English, the average answers were noticeably higher in both the Sentix polls, and hence characterized by much lower average levels of strategic thinking than our other experiments. For comparison I've also shown in Figure 13.10 the average results from student games played by Nagel (1995).

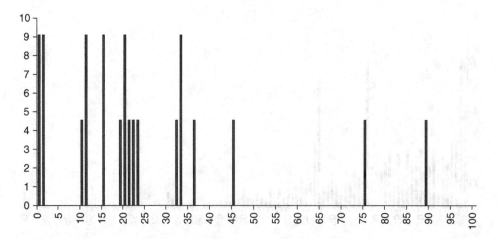

Figure 13.7 Yahoo Behavioural Finance group.
Source: DrKW Macro research.

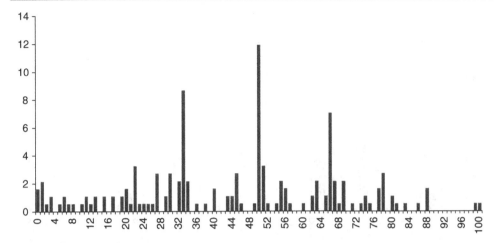

Figure 13.8   Sentix private investors contest.
Source: DrKW Macro research, Sentix.

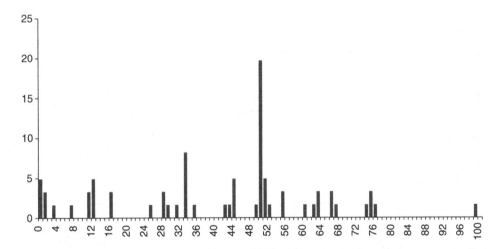

Figure 13.9   Sentix institutional investors contest.
Source: DrKW Macro research, Sentix.

LEARNING

Just in case you are assuming that everything I've discussed here is a function of this being a one-shot game, cast your eyes over Figure 13.11 which shows two typical multi-round game averages. In each case, the contest was played by several groups over many rounds. The average mean number across groups in each round is shown in the figure. Learning seems to occur only very slowly over time, a finding which sits very comfortably with the vast swathes of psychological research which suggest that learning is generally far more difficult than most of us tend to blithely assume!

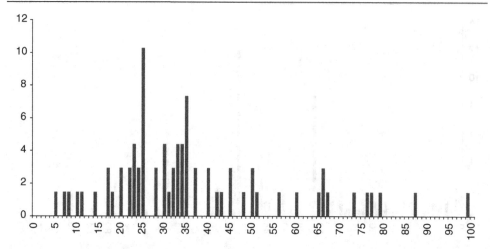

Figure 13.10   Student contest.
Source: Nagel (1995).

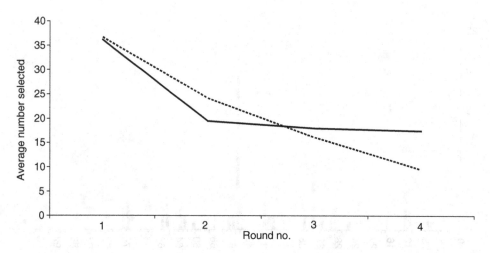

Figure 13.11   Typical learning time paths – average choice in each period.
Source: Camerer *et al.* (2003).

CONCLUSIONS

We have recently argued that the equity markets are currently experiencing a near rational bubble. This is being driven by increasingly short time horizons and investors' overconfidence. This combination gives birth to the momentum culture that we have all witnessed in recent years.

The pressure to perform on a month-by-month basis is driving professional investors to prolong their exposure to a risky situation. As Keynes noted, "It makes a vast difference to an investment market whether or not they predominate in their influence." Because of this pressure to perform on all time horizons, they are being forced to rely on their ability to time this market to perfection. However, not everyone can get out at the top. Inevitably, some will be crushed under foot in the rush for the exit. It was to assess this risk that we have used the classic 'Keynes's beauty contest'.

If our beauty contest is a proxy for market behaviour, then most investors seem to practise two steps of strategic thinking. In Keynes's parlance, most investors seem to be concerned with 'The third degree where we devote our intelligences to anticipating what average opinion expects average opinion to be'.

Our market seems to be best characterized by investors using between one and two degrees of strategic thinking. Hence, if you are to beat the exodus, then you need to be thinking in terms of three steps, but no more. In terms of our sample that represents just 4% of the players! Perhaps this lends some support to our oft-voiced scepticism over the ability of the majority of investors to 'beat the gun'.

SIN 5

Short Time Horizons and Overtrading

(Avarice)

14
ADHD, Time Horizons and Underperformance*

ADHD seems to plague financial markets at all levels. Performance is measured on increasingly short time horizons. Such myopia is often self-fulfilling, the more an investment is checked the more likely you are to find a loss. Even in an artifical universe of skilled investors we found that 3-year runs of back-to-back underperformance were common place. We need to extend our time horizons.

- Attention deficit hyperactivity disorder (ADHD) seems to be pervasive in our industry. Trustees, consultants and internal managers seem to want to evaluate fund managers as frequently as possible. Indeed recent evidence suggests that the average holding period of mutual fund investors has fallen from over 10 years in the 1950s to around 4 years currently.
- Short time horizon performance measurement leads to closet indexing. Fund managers are often rewarded with respect to assets under management. Hence they will try to maximize those assets and retention is usually, therefore, the end objective. The easiest way of losing funds under management is to underperform. The easiest way of avoiding underperformance is to track your benchmark.
- Professional investors have also seen their time horizons contract. The average holding period of a stock on the NYSE is just 11 months, compared to 8 years in the mid-1950s. Such short holding spans have nothing to do with investment, they are pure speculation. Corporate managers have also been caught up in this ADHD epidemic. Loaded up as they are with stock options, they too seem willing to sacrifice long-term value for short-term gain, all of which has led to a situation where, as Keynes put it, "*Investment based on genuine long-term expectation is so difficult to-day as to be scarcely practicable.*"
- To show how ridiculous this obsession with the short term is, we created an artificial universe of 100 fund managers. Each had a true alpha of 3% and a tracking error of 6% (such performance would put them in the top quartile of investors). We then subjected them to random shocks. After 50 years, the 'best' fund manager had an alpha of 5%, the 'worst' 1%.
- In every year roughly one in three of our fund managers underperformed. Over a 50-year time span, a skilled investor should expect to underperform in about 15 of these years. Perhaps most revealing was the risk of back-to-back years of underperformance. Almost half our universe experienced a run of 3 years of back-to-back underperformance, and runs of 4 or 5 years were not uncommon! Of our make-believe managers, 70% suffered 3 or

---

*This article appeared in *Global Equity Strategy* on 18 November 2005. The material discussed was accurate at the time of publication.

more years of underperformance. They would most likely have been fired many times over, despite their underlying true (by construction) value added.

- We need to extend time horizons. That means being honest with clients about the risk of underperformance, and admitting limited skill when it comes to picking investments for the short term. Of course, this will come as anathema to most investors.

Our industry seems bedevilled by myopic time horizons. Almost everywhere you look you seem to encounter an obsession with the short term. Trustees, consultants and internal managers seem to want to evaluate fund mangers as frequently as possible. Not only do people want to measure performance on increasingly short time horizons, but they also seem to wish to act more often. Indeed, John Bogle (2005) (of Vanguard legend) has recently noted that the average holding period for mutual fund investors has fallen from more than 10 years in the 1950s to around 4 years currently (see Figure 14.1).

The increasingly short time horizons that are used to evaluate fund mangers are likely to push them into closet index-tracking behaviour. In a world in which fund managers are motivated by being paid a fixed percentage of assets under management, they will, of course, aim to maximize assets under management rather than the returns from the assets. The easiest way of losing funds under management is to underperform. The easiest way of avoiding underperforming is to track your benchmark and thus we arrive at closet indexing.

The contraction of the ultimate investors' time horizons has driven/coincided with a collapse in the time horizon of institutional fund managers. Figure 14.2 shows the average holding period of stocks on the NYSE. In the mid-1950s, investors used to hold stocks for 7–8 years. The average holding period today is just 11 months! Nor is this decline merely the result of the rise of hedge funds. Bogle presents findings on the average holding period of professional investors from an entirely different source. Yet his data maps closely to the general trends of the NYSE series we use (see Figure 14.2).

Of course, corporate managers also feel the pressure. They have become obsessed with short-term earnings announcements motivated by their overload of stock options. Indeed a recent survey from Harvey *et al.* (2005) found that nearly half of the CFOs they interviewed would be willing to sacrifice a long-term valuable investment project if it meant missing earnings by $0.20!

Figure 14.3 highlights the results they found. The question the CFOs were asked was

Your company's cost of capital is 12%. Near the end of the quarter, a new opportunity arises that offers a 16% internal rate of return and the same risk as the firm. What is the probability that your

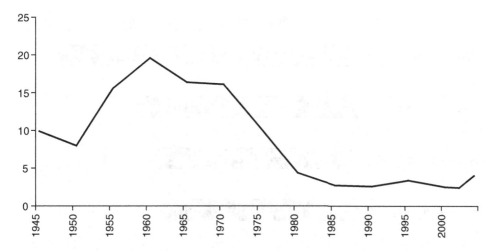

Figure 14.1   Average holding period of US mutual fund investors (years).
Source: Bogle (2005).

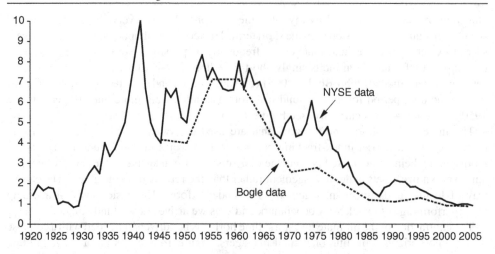

Figure 14.2 The average holding period of NYSE listed stocks (years).
Source: DrKW Macro research and Bogle (2005).

company will pursue this project in each of the following scenarios: If you take the project you will (i) exactly hit consensus earnings, (ii) miss consensus by $0.10, (iii) miss consensus by $0.20 and (iv) miss consensus by $0.50.

The Harvey *et al.* study also uncovered why so many CFOs aimed to meet expectations. The two most popular reasons given were, "to build credibility with the capital market" and "to maintain or increase our stock price". When asked why they preferred smooth earnings paths, the two top answers were, "It is perceived as less risky by investors" and "It makes it easier for analysts/investors to predict future earnings"!

All of which has led to a situation where, as Keynes put it,

Investment based on genuine long-term expectation is so difficult today as to be scarcely practicable. He who attempts it must surely lead much more laborious days and run greater risks than he

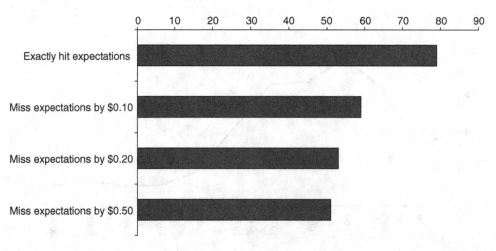

Figure 14.3 Percentage accepting positive NPV project.
Source: Harvey *et al.* (2005).

who tries to guess better than the crowd how the crowd will behave; and, given equal intelligence, he may make more disastrous mistakes. . . It needs more intelligence to defeat the forces of time and our ignorance of the future than to beat the gun. Moreover, life is not long enough; — human nature desires quick results, there is a peculiar zest in making money quickly, and remoter gains are discounted by the average man at a very high rate. The game of professional investment is intolerably boring and over-exacting to anyone who is entirely exempt from the gambling instinct; whilst he who has it must pay to this propensity the appropriate toll. Furthermore, an investor who proposes to ignore near-term market fluctuations needs greater resources for safety and must not operate on so large a scale, if at all, with borrowed money — a further reason for the higher return from the pastime to a given stock of intelligence and resources. Finally it is the long-term investor, he who most promotes the public interest, who will in practice come in for most criticism, wherever investment funds are managed by committees or boards or banks. For it is in the essence of his behaviour that he should be eccentric, unconventional and rash in the eyes of average opinion. If he is successful, that will only confirm the general belief in his rashness; and if in the short run he is unsuccessful, which is very likely, he will not receive much mercy. Worldly wisdom teaches that it is better for reputation to fail conventionally than to succeed unconventionally.

(Chapter 12, *General Theory of Employment, Interest and Money*, 1936)

If we are ever to hope of actually meeting the aims of the ultimate investors we will need to rethink incentives and investment approaches. I will postpone the discussion of changing the incentive structure of our industry for another time. Here I want to concentrate on just how ridiculous the obsession with the short term actually is. In order to illustrate the problem I decided to imagine a universe of 100 fund managers each with a 3% alpha and 6% tracking error or a population of 0.5 information ratio investors if you prefer. An information ratio of 0.5 is pretty good. According to Grinold and Kahn (2000) an information ratio of 0.5 would put these investors in or close to the top quartile (Table 14.1).

I set up a little universe of quite good investors and hit them with random shocks. Remember that, by set up each of these fund managers has a true alpha of 3%. In my little artificial universe I allowed these managers run money for 50 years and tracked their performance over time. The results were telling.

In terms of the range of returns the best fund manager displayed an alpha of 5.2%, while the worst showed an alpha of 1%. Figure 14.4 demonstrates just how hard it is to tell the 'good' from the 'bad' on the basis of annual returns. However, of more interest to me was the various statistics we collected on underperformance.

For instance, when looking at the cross-section, almost one in three of our fund managers underperformed the benchmark each and every year (Figure 14.5).

An alternative perspective is given in Figure 14.6. This shows the total number of years in which each of our fund managers encountered a negative return – that is, they underperformed

Table 14.1   US active equity information ratios

Percentile	Mutual Funds		Institutional Portfolios	
	Before Fees	After Fees	Before Fees	After Fees
90	1.33	1.08	1.25	1.01
75	0.78	0.58	0.63	0.48
50	0.32	0.12	−0.01	−0.15
25	−0.08	−0.33	−0.56	−0.72
10	−0.47	−0.72	−1.03	−1.25

Source: Grinold and Kahn (2000).

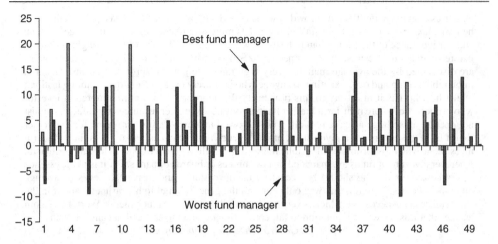

Figure 14.4   The best and worst fund managers in our universe (% return).
Source: DrKW Macro research.

their benchmark. On average, each of our managers spent about 15 years of our 50-year sample underperforming; the minimum was 9 years and the maximum was 24 years!

Figure 14.7 shows the histogram of consecutive years of underperformance. On average, even with an information ratio of 0.5, runs of 3 years of back-to-back underperformance were very normal. Indeed 4 or 5 years of continuous underperformance are far from unheard of.

Remember that each of these managers has 3% alpha by design, yet that doesn't stop them encountering bouts of up to 8 years of back-to-back underperformance. Despite the fund managers having a high alpha and a high information ratio, it wouldn't have been enough to prevent almost every one of the fund managers from being fired by their clients at some point over the 50 years of our data run.

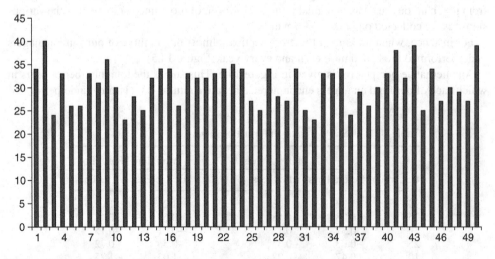

Figure 14.5   Percentage of our 100 fund managers underperforming each year.
Source: DrKW Macro research.

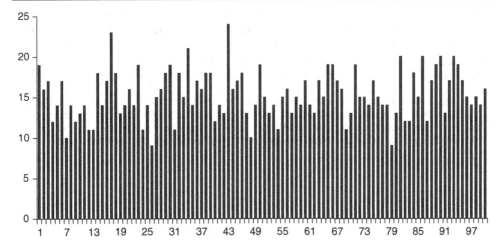

Figure 14.6   Number of years of underperformance per manager.
Source: DrKW Macro research.

Of course, when investors are myopic they tend to check their performance frequently. The more frequently they examine their portfolio performance, the more likely they are to encounter a loss. Such myopic behaviour almost becomes self-fulfilling.

We need to extend investors' time horizons, and that means being honest with the ultimate investors about the risk of loss in the short term (very high). It also means encouraging longer holding periods and better-structured contracts between the ultimate investors and their chosen agents. It requires dispelling the illusion of control and the illusion of knowledge such that fund managers admit to the truth that they can't pick stocks or markets over the short run.

It also requires that investors try to stop 'beating the gun': instead of focusing on *speculation* (Keynes's term for the activity of forecasting the psychology of the market), we need to refocus our industry on *enterprise* (Keynes's term for the activity of forecasting the prospective yield

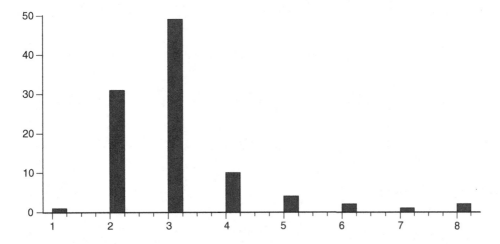

Figure 14.7   Frequency of cumulative years of underperformance.
Source: DrKW Macro research.

of assets over their whole life). This in turn means that analysts need to stop obsessing about the next quarterly set of results, and corporate managers can get back to running their business for the benefit of shareholders, rather than pampering to the investment equivalent of those suffering attention deficit hyperactivity disorder (ADHD).

Keynes, too, was exasperated by the obsession with short-term performance. He opined:

> The spectacle of modern investment markets has sometimes moved me towards the conclusion that to make the purchase of an investment permanent and indissoluble, like marriage, except by reason of death or other grave cause, might be a useful remedy for our contemporary evils. For this would force the investor to direct his mind to the long-term prospects and to those only.

If only!

SIN 6
Believing Everything You Read
(Sloth)

15

The Story is the Thing
(or The Allure of Growth)*

Shakespeare wrote "The play's the thing". For investors it appears that the story is the thing. In a rational world, we gather evidence, weight it and then decide. However, people rely on stories instead. We gather the evidence (in a biased fashion), construct a story to explain the evidence, and then match the story to a decision. This reliance on stories helps to drive investors into the growth trap.

- A former colleague of mine once wrote that 'stockbrokers exist to sell dreams'. I have long held that the corollary to this statement should be 'but they deliver nightmares'. Despite my scepticism, investors seem to love to listen to the siren songs of stockbrokers. Why?
- In a rational world, we would all go around gathering the evidence, and then evaluate it and weigh it before reaching our decision. However, real-world behaviour is a long way from the rational viewpoint. We collect evidence (usually in a biased fashion), then we construct a story to explain the evidence. This story (not the original evidence) is then used to reach a decision. Psychologists call this explanation-based decision-making.
- Experiments have shown that stories can have a massive impact upon decision-making. For instance, in a mock trial situation when the prosecution presented the evidence in a story order, but the defence presented evidence in witness order, 78% of jurors found the suspect guilty. However, when the formats were reversed only 31% of jurors found the suspect guilty!
- Other experiments have found that in simulation markets, participants trade on rumours (and lose money) but say that they don't believe the rumour and that it didn't impact their decision-making. The researchers found that to persuade participants to trade, the rumour merely needed to 'explain' current share price moves!
- New research shows that investors behave just like jurors. They map information into a story, and then use the story as a basis for making decisions. All too often investors are sucked into plausible sounding stories. For instance, the story that the internet would alter the way the world did business was probably true, but it doesn't necessarily translate into profits for investors.
- The current market obsession with China is another potential example of investors being sucked into a growth story. Those piling into commodities on the back of the fact that China is the largest consumer of just about everything are likely to end up ruing their decision.
- Indeed, trying to invest in the fastest growing emerging equity markets has been a very poor strategy in the past. Those economies with the highest GDP growth have delivered

*This article appeared in *Global Equity Strategy* on 18 November 2005. The material discussed was accurate at the time of publication.

the lowest returns, while those economies with the lowest GDP growth have delivered the highest returns. Why? Because investors end up overpaying for the hope of growth. Beware the growth trap.

Way back in the dim and distant past, I studied English Literature (not that any of the literary genius I studied rubbed off on me!). However, one of the few things I remember from those long ago studies was a quote from Shakespeare that could be wheeled out whenever one was discussing his plays. In order to stress the importance of seeing a play in production rather than simply reading it, a quotation from Hamlet was most useful: "The play's the thing wherein I'll catch the conscience of the king."

With profound apologies to the bard, the investment equivalent would seem to be 'the story's the thing wherein I'll capture the conscience of the investor'. A former colleague of mine once wrote that 'stockbrokers exist to sell dreams', I have long held that the corollary to this statement should be 'but they deliver nightmares'. The only snag is that people love to listen to the siren songs of the stockbrokers. Why?

We appear to use stories to help us to reach decisions. In the 'rational' view of the world we observe the evidence, we then weigh the evidence, and finally we come to our decision. Of course, in the rational view we all collect the evidence in a well-behaved unbiased fashion. Readers will know that this isn't a good description of the way in which most evidence is gathered. Usually we are prone to only look for the information that happens to agree with us (confirmatory bias), etc.

However, the real world of behaviour is a long way from the rational viewpoint, and not just in the realm of information gathering. The second stage of the rational decision is weighing the evidence. However, as the diagram below shows, a more commonly encountered approach is to construct a narrative to explain the evidence that has been gathered (the story model of thinking).

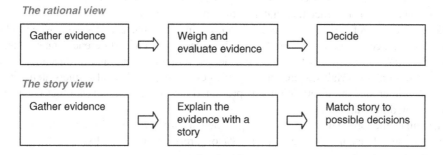

Hastie and Pennington (2000) are the leading advocates of the story view (also known as explanation-based decision-making).[1] The central hypothesis of the explanation-based view is that the decision maker constructs a summary story of the evidence and then uses this story, rather than the original raw evidence, to make their final decision.

Hastie and Pennington note

> This intermediate mental model of the decision facilitates evidence comprehension, directs inferencing, enables the decision maker to reach a decision, and determines the confidence assigned to the accuracy or expected success of the decision.

Much of the original work on the importance of stories has been investigated in the realm of jurors. However, the same mental processes are likely to be at work when it comes to investment decisions.

---

[1] See Hastie and Pennington (2000) for an up to date summary of the field.

Table 15.1 Percentage of jurors returning a guilty verdict

		Defence	
		Story order	Witness order
Prosecution	Story order	59%	78%
	Witness order	31%	63%

Source: Pennington and Hastie (1988).

Consider Hastie and Pennington's description of the juror's decisions task:

> First, a massive 'database' of evidence is presented at trial, frequently comprising of several days of testimony, exhibits, and arguments. Second, the evidence comes in a scrambled sequence, usually many witnesses and exhibits convey pieces of the historical puzzle in a jumbled temporal sequence. Third, the evidence is piecemeal and gappy in its depiction of the historical events that are the focus of reconstruction: event descriptions are incomplete, usually some critical events were not observed by the available witnesses, and information about personal reactions and motivations is not presented ... Finally, subparts of the evidence are interdependent in their probative implications for the verdict. The meaning of one statement cannot be assessed in isolation because it depends on the meanings of several other related statements.

In several empirical tests, Pennington and Hastie (1986, 1988) have investigated the decision making process of jurors. They discovered that jurors who had reached different verdicts had constructed different stories with distinctly different configurations of events. Their study also revealed that people found it easier to construct a story when the evidence was ordered in a temporal and causal sequence that matched the original events.

Table 15.1 shows the results of a mock juror test in which participants were asked to listen to a 100-sentence summary of a trial, with 50 prosecution and 50 defence statements, and a judge's charge to choose between a First degree murder verdict and a not guilty verdict. Exactly the same material was presented in each case, only the format of the statements was changed. Sometimes the information was presented in story order, and on other occasions it was presented in witness order.

The impact the format had was staggering. When the prosecution presented evidence in story order, and the defence used witness order, 78% of jurors returned a guilty verdict. Conversely, when the roles were reversed only 31% of jurors returned a guilty verdict!

Hastie *et al.* (1997) also investigated explanation-based decision-making in civil cases. They asked people to 'think aloud as you make your decisions about the verdict'. They noted that the first step was again the construction of a story to explain the evidence. This summary 'included the major events from evidence that the juror believed occurred, ordered in a temporal sequence. This narrative included causal linkages, many of them inferred, that serve as "glue" holding the story... together.'

If you are anything like me then the parallels between the juror and the investor are likely to leap out to you. Before giving you an example of one instance of explanation-based decision-making in real-world financial markets, I want to talk about two other studies.

The first is by DiFonzo and Bordia (1997). They tested the impact of rumours on financial markets. Having set up two experimental stock markets, they subjected one to news and the other to rumours. They found that when they introduced rumours, investors started to trade on them (but didn't make any money from them!). Participants claimed that the rumour sources weren't credible, and didn't impact upon their decision to trade. However, in a world in which

Table 15.2   The elements of the story

Stage	Type of information
Context	Company's past success
Problem	Criticism or praise recently received
Reaction	Company's intention to work harder or continue as usual
Plan	Hiring or firing of employees
Outcome	Stated whether the new product was successful or not

Source: Mulligan and Hastie (2005).

actions speak louder than words, the participants were found to trade as if the rumours were news! In order to persuade participants to trade, the rumour merely needed to 'explain' current share price moves. This fits with the importance of the explanation-based view of the world.

The other study is a paper by Mulligan and Hastie (2005). They aim to test if 'qualitative information in the financial investment arena is mentally organized in a story structure, analogous to the stories jurors rely on to "find the facts"'.

Participants were given stories about firms working in the medical sector. Each story contained five elements (listed out in Table 15.2). The aim of the task was to pick investments over the next 2–5 years. After each line of text was revealed, participants were asked whether or not they would purchase the stock for a long time horizon, and how confident they were (on a scale of 1 to 5).

In one format the story was given in order, in the other the elements of the story were scrambled. Figure 15.1 shows the mean regression weights for each story component as a function of the presentation format. Note the spike upwards in the regression weight assigned to the outcome when the story is told in the correct order.

Mulligan and Hastie conclude

Participants in the story order condition still relied primarily on the outcome piece when making decisions … Once a coherent mental representation of a story has been constructed, people do not break down the story into its component pieces and use them independently, even when it

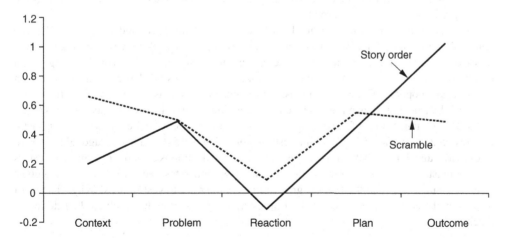

Figure 15.1   Mean regression weights for each story component.
Source: Mulligan and Hastie (2005).

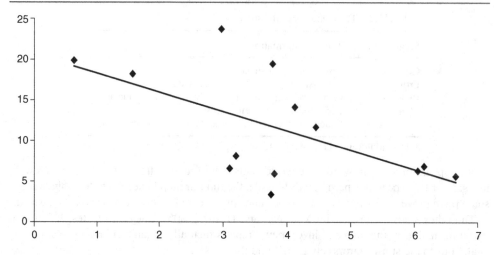

Figure 15.2   Average GDP growth vs average dollar stock returns (1988–2004).
Source: MSCI, DrKW Macro research.

might be sensible, even rational, to do so ... These order-of-information effects make sense in
the context of an explanation-based theory of judgement, but they are patently irrational in the
context of traditional theories of investment finance.

Just like jurors, investors seem to frame their worlds in terms of stories rather than facts.
It is exactly this trait that makes stories so dangerous. All too often investors are sucked into
plausible sounding stories. Indeed, underlying some of the most noted bubbles in history are
kernels of truth. For instance, the story that the internet would alter the way the world did
business is probably true, but it doesn't necessarily translate into profits for investors.

Indeed, we recently wrote on the dangers of growth investing based around the risks
involved in listening to the stories at the stock level (see *Global Equity Strategy*, 16 March
2005). However, investors' love affair with China stands out as another great example of the
seemingly insatiable thirst for growth.

Investors seem to be able to effortlessly trot out amazing facts and figures on Chinese
demand for raw materials. One of my favourite examples is a well-known fund management
house quoted in the FT as saying: "Chinese demand for commodities is revolutionizing global
commodity markets. China has already overtaken the USA as the largest consumer of iron
ore, steel and copper." The FT concludes, 'The China effect seems unstoppable'.[2] All of these
may well be true, but does it make sense to base an investment decision on such stories?

Indeed, in the realm of emerging markets investors seem to be addicted to growth.
Figures 15.2, 15.3 and 15.4 tell an interesting story. Figure 15.2 relates average GDP growth
rates to average dollar stock returns. The relationship is the opposite of the one many investors
believe exists. Those economies with the *lowest* growth rates seem to deliver the highest
returns, while those with the highest growth rates deliver the lowest returns! Why? The most
logical explanation is that investors end up overpaying for growth (much as they do at the
stock level).

---

[2] China effect convulses commodity markets, *Financial Times*, 15 November 2003.

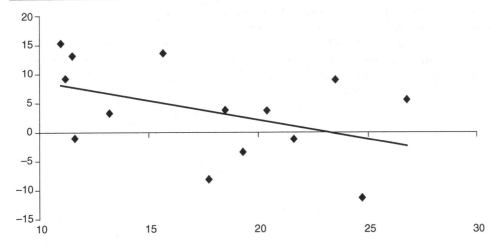

Figure 15.3   1995 PEs vs 10-year dollar stock market returns.
Source: MSCI, DrKW Macro research.

Figure 15.3 suggests that investors would be better off buying cheap emerging markets rather than being sucked into investing in fast-growing economies. The figure shows the relationship between PEs and subsequent returns over the next 10 years. The cheapest emerging markets have the highest returns, while the most expensive tend to have the lowest returns. This is the long-run counterpart of work we have previously done showing that cheap emerging markets outperform expensive ones [even in the relatively short term (see *Global Equity Strategy*, 12 January 2005, for details)].

Figure 15.4 is aimed at seeing if it is indeed fast growth that tempts investors to overpay. It shows the relationship between the GDP growth rates from 1990 to 1995 and the PEs at the

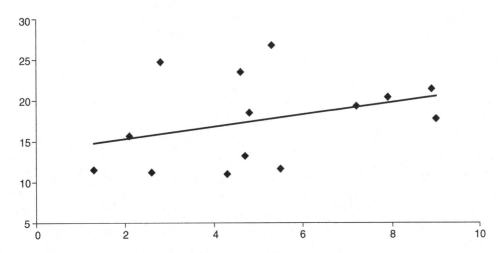

Figure 15.4   GDP growth rates 1990–1995 and 1995 PEs.
Source: MSCI, DrKW Macro research.

end of 1995. While there is not a very strong relationship, there is nonetheless a relationship which suggests that investors do indeed end up paying too much for growth.

Investors enamoured with China, and its growth potential, would perhaps be well advised to study history and understand that growth is often not the panacea that it seems to be. Dependency upon stories for decision-making is one reason why investors keep stumbling into the growth trap year after year.

16
Scepticism is Rare
(or Descartes vs Spinoza)*

In the blue corner, Descartes. In the red corner, Spinoza. Two great seventeenth-century philosophers; two very different views on the human mind. Descartes thought that understanding and belief were separate acts. Spinoza argued that they were one and the same. The evidence supports Spinoza. In order to understand something we seem to need to believe it. We seem to be hard-wired to 'believe'!

- Why is it that we end up believing such strange ideas? For instance, supposedly smart people buy into myths such as stocks for the long run and ideas such as dividends don't matter. In order to investigate why we end up holding such beliefs we need to understand how we handle ideas in our minds.
- Daniel Gilbert, a Harvard psychologist, has explored this issue in depth. He suggests that there are two visions of the way our minds work when presented with new ideas. According to the work of Descartes, we hold the idea in a sort of mental limbo, proceed to evaluate it, and then reach a conclusion as to its veracity. This sits well with folk psychology in as much as it sounds like the way we would like to think we work.
- However, Spinoza had an alternative take on the process. He believed that our minds had to hold an idea as true in order to actually understand it. Then, if we are lucky, we might engage in an evaluative process. Once this is completed, we then form a corrected belief.
- Gilbert and his co-authors have run many ingenious experiments designed to show which of these processes is the closest description of the way in which our minds work. The evidence they have uncovered strongly supports the Spinozan view of the world. For instance, people were asked to read statements on a crime. They were told some of the sentences they would read were false and written in red ink. However, when people were distracted from this task (by asking them to hunt for numbers at the same time as reading) they ended up believing the false statements to be true. This had a very material impact on the recommended jail term for the crime. When the false statements exacerbated the crime, and the readers were distracted, they recommended a jail time that was 60% longer than when they weren't distracted!
- The thought that we seem to believe everything in order to understand it, is more than a little disconcerting. It would seem to render us powerless to control our beliefs. However, don't despair just yet, two potential strategies are available to us. Firstly, what Gilbert calls 'unbelieving' effectively requires us to analytically assess our beliefs and confront them with reality. However, cognitive load, pressure and time constraints all sap our ability to follow

*This article appeared in *Global Equity Strategy* on 18 November 2005. The material discussed was accurate at the time of publication.

this path. Secondly, we can follow an exclusion strategy, simply avoiding the generators of false beliefs, just as dieters may choose to avoid doughnut shops.

- A combination of these strategies is likely to be optimal. When you are really trying to assess the validity of an argument do your best to avoid distraction. Turn off your screens and blackberries, put your phones on call forward, ignore your colleagues!

Some time ago a client asked us to compile a list of myths that the markets seemed to hold dear. We came up with 12 potential myths ranging from 'stocks for the long run' to 'dividends don't matter' via such topics as commodities for the future and bond supply matters. However, this exercise also made me wonder why it was that supposedly smart people ended up believing such strange things.

This pondering sent me (as is usually the case) to the annals of psychology. To some extent these errant beliefs seem to stem from bounded awareness/inattentional blindness and framing. We have explored such elements elsewhere (see *Global Equity Strategy*, 16 September 2004, What you see isn't what you get). However, there may well be another factor at work. We seem to be hard-wired to 'believe'.

Daniel Gilbert, a professor of psychology at Harvard, has explored how we go about believing and understanding information. In a series of truly insightful papers, Gilbert and co-authors (Gilbert *et al.*, 1990; Gilbert, 1991; Gilbert *et al.*, 1993; Gilbert, 1993) have explored the belief process using two alternative philosophical viewpoints.

CARTESIAN SYSTEMS

The first view is associated with the work of Rene Descartes. When it came to belief, Descartes suggested that the mind performs two separate mental acts. Firstly, it understands the idea. Secondly, the mind assesses the validity of the idea that has been presented. This two-stage process seems intuitively correct. After all, we can all imagine being presented with some novel idea, holding it in our minds and then pondering the truth or otherwise associated with the idea. The Cartesian approach fits well with folk psychology.

Descartes was educated by Jesuits and, like many seventeenth-century philosophers, generally deployed psychology and philosophy in the aid of theology. Like anyone of any sense Descartes was well aware that people were capable of believing things that weren't true. In order to protect the Church, Descartes argued that God had given Man the power to assess ideas. So it clearly wasn't God's fault when people believed things that weren't true.

As Gilbert (1993) notes, Descartes' approach consisted of two axioms. Firstly, the mental separation and sequencing of understanding and believing, and, secondly, that people have no control over how or what they understand, but are totally free to believe or disbelieve ideas as they please.

SPINOZAN SYSTEMS

Spinoza's background and thinking could not be much more different than that of Descartes. Born a Jew, Barauch de Espinoza (later to become Benedict Spinoza) outraged his community and synagogue. The tensions finally resulted in Spinoza being excommunicated, accused of abominable heresies and monstrous deeds. The order of excommunication prohibited other members of the synagogue from having any contact with him.

Freed of the need to conform to his past, Spinoza was able to explore anything he chose. One of the areas to which he turned his considerable mental prowess was the faults contained in the Cartesian approach. Spinoza argued that all ideas were first represented as true and only later (with effort) evaluated for veracity. Effectively Spinoza denied the parsing that Descartes put at the heart of his two-step approach. Spinoza argued that comprehension and belief were a single step – that is to say, in order for somebody to understand something, belief is a necessary precondition. Effectively all information or ideas are first accepted as true, and then only sometimes evaluated as to their truth, once this process is completed a 'corrected belief' is constructed if necessary.

LIBRARIES

Gilbert *et al.* (1990) use the example of a library to draw out the differences between these two approaches. Imagine a library with several million volumes, of which only a few are works of fiction. The Cartesian approach to filing books would be to put a red tag on each volume of fiction and blue tag on each volume of non-fiction. Any new book that appeared in the library would be read, and then tagged as either fiction or non-fiction. Any book that is unread is simply present in the library until it is read.

In contrast, a Spinozan library would work in a very different fashion. Under this approach a tag would be added to each volume of fiction but the non-fiction would be left unmarked. The ease of this system should be clear; it requires a lot less effort to run this system than the Cartesian approach. However, the risk is that if a new book arrives it will be seen as non-fiction.

Gilbert *et al.* note that under ideal conditions both systems produce the same outcome if allowed to run to conclusion. So if you pick up a copy of Darwin's *The Expression of Emotions in Man and Animals* and asked the Cartesian librarian what he knew about the book, he would glance at the tag and say non-fiction. The Spinozan librarian would do much the same thing, concluding that the book was non-fiction because of the absence of a tag.

However, imagine sneaking a new book into the library, say the latest Patricia Cornwell thriller. If you took the book to the librarian and asked what was known about the book, the response would reveal a lot about the underlying process governing the library's approach to filing. For instance, the Cartesian librarian would say 'I don't know what sort of book that is. Come back later when it has been read and tagged appropriately.' The Spinozan librarian would glance up and see the absence of a tag and say 'it doesn't have a tag so it must be non-fiction' — an obviously incorrect assessment.

A TESTING STRUCTURE

Figure 16.1, taken from Gilbert (1993), shows the essential differences between the two approaches, and also suggests a clever way of testing which of the two approaches has more empirical support.

Assume that an idea is presented to the brain,[1] and the person considering the idea is interrupted in some fashion. Under a Cartesian system, the person is left merely with an understanding of a false idea, but no belief in it. However, if people are better described by a Spinozan approach then interrupting the process should lead to a belief in the false idea. So giving people ideas or propositions and then interrupting them with another task should help to reveal whether people are Cartesian or Spinozan systems when it comes to beliefs.

THE EMPIRICAL EVIDENCE

It has long been known that distracting people can impact the belief they attach to arguments. For instance, in their review, Petty *et al.* report an experiment from 1976 which clearly demonstrated the impact of distraction techniques (see Petty *et al.*, 1976 and 1994).

---

[1] This hints that we support a Spinozan view of the human mind. Descartes was famous for arguing the difference between the brain and the mind, Spinoza in contrast saw the two as impossible to separate, they are two sides of the same coin from a Spinozan viewpoint. For more on this see Antonio Damasio's first and third books, *Descartes' Error* and *Looking for Spinoza* respectively.

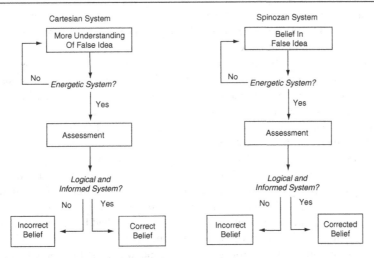

Figure 16.1   Descartes vs Spinoza: a question of belief.
Source: Gilbert (1993).

To test the impact of distraction, students were exposed to a message arguing that tuition at their university should be cut in half. Students listened to the ideas that were presented over headphones. Some heard strong arguments, others heard relatively weak arguments. At the same time, the students were subjected to a distraction task which consisted of tracking the positions of Xs that were flashed on a screen in front of them. In the high distraction version of the task, the Xs flashed up at a fast pace, in the low distraction task the rate was reduced heavily.

The results Petty *et al.* found are shown in Figure 16.2. When the message was weak, people who were highly distracted showed much more agreement with the message than did the people who only suffered mild distraction. When the message was strong and distraction

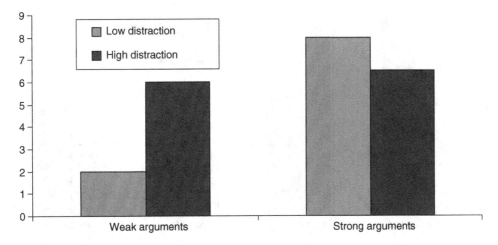

Figure 16.2   Post-message attitudes as a function of distraction and argument quality.
Source: Petty *et al.* (1976).

was high, the students showed less agreement than when the message was strong and the distraction was low. Distraction did exactly what it was meant to do . . . prevented people from concentrating on the important issue.

Petty *et al.* conclude, 'Distraction, then, is an especially useful technique when a person's arguments are poor because even though people might be aware that some arguments were presented, they might be unaware that the arguments were not very compelling.' Something to bear in mind at your next meeting with brokers perhaps? The next time an analyst comes around and starts showing you pictures of the next generation of mobile phones, just stop and think about the quality of their investment arguments.

Is there more direct evidence of our minds housing a Spinozan system when it comes to belief? Gilbert *et al.* (1990) decided to investigate. They asked people to help them with an experiment concerning language acquisition in a natural environment. Participants were shown ostensibly Hopi words with an explanation (such as a *monishna* is a bat). They had to wait until the experimenter told them whether the word they had been given was actually the correct word in Hopi or whether it was a false statement.

Subjects also had to listen out for a specific sound which, if they heard, required them to press a button. The tone sounded very shortly after the participant had been told whether the statement was true or false. This was aimed at interrupting the natural processing of information. Once they responded to the tone, the next Hopi word appeared preventing them from going back and reconsidering the previous item.

If subjects worked in a Spinozan way, then when later asked about their beliefs they should recall false propositions as true more often after an interrupt than the rest of the time. As Figure 16.3 shows, this is exactly what Gilbert *et al.* uncovered.

Interruption had no effect on the correction identification of a true proposition (55% when uninterrupted vs 58% when interrupted). However, interruption did significantly reduce the correct identification of false propositions (55% when uninterrupted vs 35% when interrupted). Similarly one could look at the number of true–false reversals (the right side of Figure 16.3) When false propositions were uninterrupted, they were misidentified as the true 21% of the

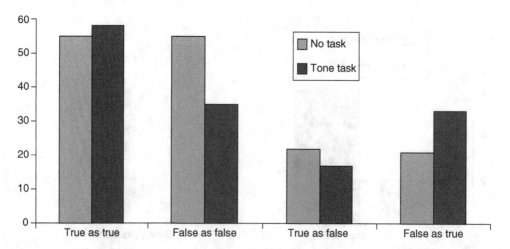

Figure 16.3   Percentage of words recognized by category.
Source: Gilbert *et al.* (1990).

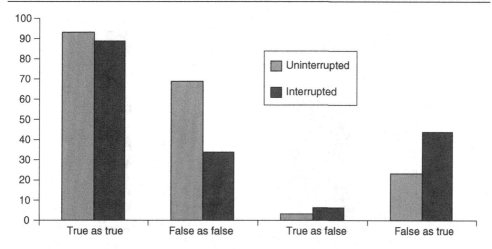

Figure 16.4   Percentage of statements recognized by category.
Source: Gilbert *et al.* (1993).

time, which was roughly the same rate as the true propositions were identified as false. However, when interrupted the situation changes, false propositions were identified as true some 33%, which was significantly higher than the number of true propositions that were identified as false (17%).

In another test Gilbert *et al.* (1993) showed that this habit of needing to believe in order to understand could have some disturbing consequences. They set up a study in which participants read crime reports with the goal of sentencing the perpetrators to prison. The subjects were told some of the statements they would read would be false and would appear on screen as red text, the true statements would be in black text.

By design, the false statements in one case happened to exacerbate the crime in question; in the other case they attenuated the crimes. The statements were also shown crawling across the screen — much like the tickers and prices on bubble vision. Below the text was a second row of crawling numbers. Some of the subjects were asked to scan the second row for the number 5 and when they saw it, they were asked to press a button.

At the end of experiment, subjects were asked to state what they thought represented a fair sentence for the crimes they had read about. Figure 16.4 shows that, just like the previous example, interruption significantly reduced the recognition of false statements (69% vs 34%), and increased the recognition of false statements as being true (23% vs 44%).

Figure 16.5 shows the average recommended sentence depending on the degree of interruption. When the false statements were attenuating and processing was interrupted, there was no a huge difference in the recommended jail term. The interrupted sentences were around 4% lower than those uninterrupted. However, when the false statements were exacerbating and interruption occurred, the recommended jail term was on average nearly 60% higher than in the uninterrupted case!

STRATEGIES TO COUNTERACT NAÏVE BELIEF

The thought that we seem to believe everything in order to understand it, is more than a little disconcerting. It would seem to render us powerless to control our beliefs. However,

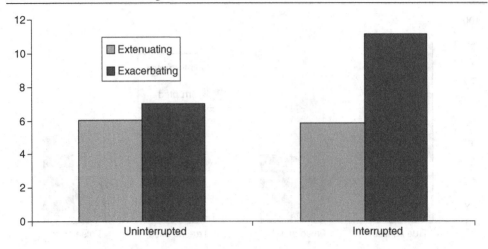

Figure 16.5 Recommended jail terms (years).
Source: Gilbert *et al.* (1993).

the absence of direct control over our beliefs doesn't necessarily imply that we are at their mercy.

Two potential strategies for countering our innate tendency to believe can be imagined. The first is what Gilbert (1993) calls 'unbelieving'. That is, we can try to carry out the required analytic work to truly assess the veracity of an idea. This certainly appeals to the empiricist in me. My own personal viewpoint is that we should accept very little at face value and use evidence to assess how likely the proposition actually is.

For example, we are often told that stock market earnings can grow faster than nominal GDP over extended periods. Of course, in year-to-year terms there isn't a close linkage between the two. However, in the long run, earnings (and dividends) have grown substantially below the rate of nominal GDP growth (on average earnings have grown 1–2% below the rate of nominal GDP. (See *Global Equity Strategy*, 16 August 2002, Return of the Robber Barrons, for more on this.)

Growth investing is another example. I don't doubt that some growth investors are very successful. However, the empirical evidence shows that picking winners in terms of growth is exceptionally difficult and fraught with danger (in that buying expensive stocks with high embodied expectations obviously opens up considerable downside risk if reality falls short of expectations). In contrast, buying cheap stocks offers a margin of safety against disappointment. (See *Global Equity Strategy*, 16 March 2005, Bargain Hunter, for more details).

Therefore, regularly confronting beliefs with empirical reality is one way of trying to beat the Spinozan system. However, 'unbelieving' is a risky strategy since it relies on you having the cognitive wherewithal to be on your guard. Gilbert *et al.* have shown that cognitive load, pressure and time constraints all undermine our ability to reject false beliefs.

The second potential belief control mechanism is called 'exposure control'. This is a far more draconian approach than 'unbelieving'. False beliefs can be avoided by avoiding all beliefs. Just as a dieter who loves doughnuts may choose to avoid shops that sell doughnuts, we can try to avoid sources of information that lead us to hold false beliefs. This is a conservative strategy that errs on the side of exclusion; it excludes false beliefs, but it may also exclude some true beliefs. However, it doesn't suffer from the problems of overload, pressure or time constraints, unlike the 'unbelieving' strategy.

All of this suggests that a combination of these strategies is likely to be optimal. When you are really trying to assess the validity of an argument do your best to avoid distraction. Turn off your screens, put your phone on call forward, and try to cut yourself off from all the sources of noise. Of course, management and colleagues may well think you have taken leave of your sense as you sit there with your screens off, but try to ignore them too. If you are likely to be distracted then either wait until later, when you can give the assessment the time and effort it requires, or simply follow an exclusion strategy.

SIN 7

Group Decisions (Wrath)

17

Are Two Heads Better Than One?*

Do you set your asset allocation by committee? Or perhaps sit on a stock selection team? If so, then read on. Psychologists have documented that group decisions are often among the worst decisions made. We explore why groups are prone to make mistakes, and offer some solutions for mitigating these errors.

- The eternal hope is that groups come together, exchange ideas, and reach sensible conclusions. The reality of group behaviour is frequently very different. Psychologists have documented that, on average, groups are more likely to amplify rather than alleviate decision-making biases.
- Groups tend to reduce the variance of opinions, and lead members to have more confidence in their decisions after group discussions (without improving accuracy). They also tend to be very bad at uncovering hidden information. Indeed, members of groups frequently enjoy enhanced competency and credibility in the eyes of their peers if they provide information that agrees with the group view!
- Groups also have a tendency to suffer cascades. Under cascades members abandon their individual information, choosing to agree with others, because they think they know more.
- Groups are also at risk of suffering polarization and possibly groupthink. Polarization occurs when members of a group end up in a more extreme position in line with their original beliefs after discussion with the group. Groupthink is an extreme version of polarization leading to all sorts of problems.
- Beating the biases of group behaviour is every bit as difficult as overcoming individual biases. However, secret ballots may help to reduce social pressures to conform. The use of devil's advocates may help (but they must believe the case they are arguing, and run the risk of being ostracized). Having respect for the other group members can help, but we all know how difficult that can be!

*This article appeared in *Global Equity Strategy* on 18 November 2005. The material discussed was accurate at the time of publication.

Do you conduct your asset allocation via committee? Or perhaps you sit on a stock selection committee? If so perhaps you should read on. Psychologists have spent many years documenting the fact that group decisions are among the worst decisions ever made, effectively endorsing the view that committees are groups of people who keep minutes but waste hours! The key reason for this appears to be that when we come together as a group we not only have to deal with our own biases, but also with everyone else's biases.

The well-informed reader might point out that James Surowiecki (2004) has recently published a book entitled *The Wisdom of Crowds*.[1] The book purports to show that "the many are smarter than the few". The basic idea of the book is that groups outperform individuals in decision-making. Surely this is in direct contradiction of my opening paragraph?

However, Surowiecki is correct that groups outperform individuals, but only under a very strict set of circumstances. Psychologists have shown that statistical groups can outperform individuals and deliberative groups. A statistical group effectively involves asking a large number of people what they think the answer is and taking the mean. Such groups have a good track record when it comes to forecasting.

For instance, when judging the number of beans in a jar, the group average is almost always better than the vast majority of the individual members. In one such experiment, a group of 56 students was asked about a jar containing 850 beans; the group estimate was 871, a better guess than all but one of the students (see Surowiecki, 2004).

In another experiment, a group was asked to rank 10 piles of buckshot, which were only minimally different in size from each other. The group's guess was 94.5% accurate, far more so than that of almost all the group members (Bruce, 1935).

However, for a statistical group to be a useful device, three conditions must be met:

1. People must be unaffected by others' decisions (effectively their errors must be uncorrelated).
2. The probability of being correct must be independent of the probability of everyone else being correct.
3. The participants must be unaffected by their own vote possibly being decisive.

If these conditions are broken the group's advantage is quickly lost. This is a particular cause for concern from a behavioural point of view. Critics of behavioural finance argue that if one person is overoptimistic and one is pessimistic, then their mistakes cancel out. One of the foundations of behavioural finance is that people, generally, err in a similar fashion. Hence, the mistakes they make are highly unlikely to be uncorrelated.

In addition, groups can be subject to anchors just like individuals (see *Global Equity Strategy*, 27 August). An anecdotal story may help to illustrate this point. Recently, my colleagues and I went to the Oval to watch England vs the West Indies. At about 5 pm, we decided to run a book on the total score for England's first innings. The run total was around 250 at that point. I went first and chose 350; the subsequent bets were surprisingly tightly clustered around the initial estimate. The group was at risk of anchoring. The eventual outturn was an England first innings of 470!

The other weak spot of statistical groups appears to be when the members have no idea of the answer to the question. For instance, Professor Sunstein (Sunstein, 2004) asked his fellow faculty the weight, in pounds, of the fuel cell that powers the space shuttle. The actual answer

---

[1] A client and friend sent me a signed copy of this book. Thank you Rob.

is 4 million pounds. The median response was 200,000; the mean was 55,790,555 (driven by a single outlier). Both answers are wildly inaccurate.

However, statistical groups are not a good description of the way in which the average asset allocation committee reaches decisions. Instead, the stereotypical asset allocation committee is formed of the regional heads of equity (i.e. Europe, USA, Japan and perhaps Global), the head of fixed income, the CIO and an economist/strategist. This group then sits down and debates the issues before arriving at a conclusion. This is the prototypical set up for what psychologists call deliberative groups.

The eternal hope is that such groups will come together, exchange ideas, each bringing something different to the discussion. The aim is of course to uncover all the information the group has. If one member has an irrelevant anchor, then the hope is that the group will expose this anchor, hence beating the bias.

However, the reality of group behaviour is very different. As MacCoun (2002) notes, "Groups generally can be expected to amplify rather than correcting individual bias" (sic). For instance, psychologists have shown that, in general, deliberation tends to reduce variance. After talking together, the members of a group will tend to reach a consensus; hence the variance of views is diminished.

Additionally, group discussion tends to lead to group members having more confidence in their decisions after the group deliberations (Heath and Gonzalez, 1995). However, sadly, this increased confidence is not matched by increased accuracy. People simply become more sure about the views they hold rather than enjoying an improvement in performance.

This confidence seems to be driven by the simple repetition of the view. The more you hear a view, the more you tend to have confidence that the view is correct!

Sunstein (2004) – see also Stasson et al. (1988) and Sniezek and Henry (1989) – notes,

> Groups have been found to amplify, rather than to attenuate, reliance on the representativeness heuristic; to reflect even larger framing effects; to show more confidence than individuals; ... In addition, groups demonstrate essentially the same level of reliance on the availability heuristic.

Deliberative groups also show an alarming inability to uncover information that isn't common knowledge, and instead end up centred on the knowledge that is easily available to all the group members. Sunstein cites a wonderful example from Hightower and Sayeed (1995):

> The purpose of the study was to see how groups might collaborate to make a personnel decision. Resumes for three candidates, applying for a marketing manager position, were placed before group members. The attributes of the candidates were rigged by the experimenters so that one applicant was clearly the best for the job described. Packets of information were given to subjects, each containing a subset of information from the resumes, so that each group member had only part of the relevant information. The groups consisted of three people, some operating face-to-face, some operating on-line. Almost none of the deliberating groups made what was conspicuously the right choice. The reason is simple: They failed to share information in a way that would permit the group to make that choice. Members tended to share positive information about the winning candidate and negative information about the losers. They suppressed negative information about the winner and positive information about the losers. Hence their statements served to 'reinforce the market toward group consensus rather than add complications and fuel debate'.

The general finding from a wide variety of such experiments is that unshared information is highly likely to be omitted from the discussion. Instead, members of the group will tend to concentrate on shared information leading to a hardening of view, creating an anchor for the subsequent discussions.

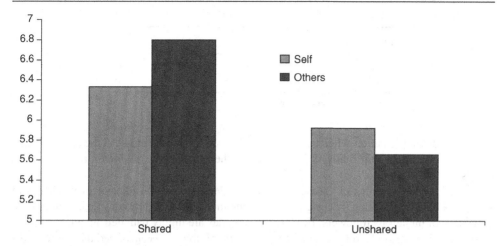

Figure 17.1 Communication bias: Evaluation ratings as a function of the type of information. *Source:* Wittenbaum *et al.* (1999).

Why are groups so bad at uncovering unshared information? In part it is a function of the statistical fact that shared information is more likely to be discussed and repeated. Of course, this will tend to influence the individuals in the group, and hence influence the group's eventual outcome.

The other factor that helps to explain why groups are so bad at sharing information concerns social pressure. Those who perceive themselves to be of a relatively low status (admittedly not a major problem for many in our industry!) are particularly likely to refrain from sharing unique information (Wittenbaum and Park, 2001; Stasser and Titus, 2003). They are scared of looking stupid in front of their colleagues. The reputational risk is simply too high for low-status members to chance sharing information if it doesn't conform to the group.[2]

Wittenbaum *et al.* (1999) have also shown that those who share information that confirms the group's views are seen as competent and more credible by their peers and by themselves! A situation Wittenbaum *et al.* call mutual enhancement.

Figure 17.1 shows the result of one of Wittenbaum *et al.*'s experiments. Once again information over candidates for a job was the topic. After hearing from the various members of the group, people were asked to rate the other members and themselves using a 0–9 scale (strongly disagree to strongly agree) on the following two questions (i) I feel competent at determining the better job candidate, (ii) the others are competent at determining the better job candidate.

Evidence of mutual enhancement would arise if participants evaluated themselves and the others more favourably when the information was common/shared by the group (i.e they don't reveal unique information). And, when people relied on unique information, they rate themselves lower and the group would also rate them lower rather than on unique information. That was exactly what was uncovered.

The third major problem that groups encounter is the tendency to suffer cascades. We have previously discussed cascades in the context of markets in *Global Equity Strategy*, 13 January 2004 and 19 May 2004. However, cascades can also affect group decision processes.

---

[2] We will explore a related issue on obedience to authority in a future weekly.

Table 17.1   Cascade creation: Actual pot used B

Player	1	2	3	4	5	6
Private signal	a	a	b	b	b	b
Decision	A	A	A	A	A	A

Source: Anderson and Holt (2004).

A cascade is a situation whereby an individual's action is potentially independent of his private information, and totally dependent upon the observation of other's actions and/or words.

One of the key features of cascades is their tendency to exhibit idiosyncrasy. That is to say, the behaviour resulting from signals of just the first few individuals drastically affects the behaviour of numerous followers. Effectively, cascades are highly path dependent.

Within the context of group discussions, once an opinion has been voiced then it becomes increasingly unlikely that others will argue against it. This is not only for the social reasons outlined above, but because they might assume that the person voicing the belief has more information than they do.

Cascades have proved to be easy to create in laboratory environments.[3] Players are told that one of two pots containing three balls is being used. One pot contains two red and one white ball (pot A), the other, two white and one red ball (pot B). Players are selected in a random order to announce which pot is being used after having received a private signal in the form of a draw from the pot.

The results from one of their experiments are shown in Table 17.1. The pot used was B. However, players 3 onwards decided that the other players knew more than they did and hence ignored their private signal, despite the fact that going with the private signal would be correct on two-thirds of occasions!

The fourth hurdle that deliberative groups must attempt to overcome is the risk of group polarization and possibly groupthink. Group polarization is the tendency for members of a group to end up in a more extreme position in line with their original beliefs after talking to one another. The increased confidence in view mentioned earlier, begins to create feedback into the extremity of view, generally creating a loop of increased confidence in more and more extreme views.

Even more extreme than group polarization is groupthink. The term was coined by Irving Janis in 1972. In his original work Janis cited the Vietnam War and the Bay of Pigs invasion as prime examples of the groupthink mentality. However modern examples are all too prevalent. The recent Senate report on the intelligence gathering by the CIA over the war in Iraq explicitly accused the CIA of displaying many of the elements of groupthink.

Groupthink is often characterized by:

- A tendency to examine too few alternatives
- A lack of critical assessment of each other's ideas
- A high degree of selectivity in information gathering
- A lack of contingency plans
- Rationalizing poor decisions

---

[3] For a very up to date survey see Anderson and Holt (2004).

- An illusion of invulnerability and shared morality by the group
- Suppressing true feelings and beliefs
- Maintaining an illusion of unanimity
- Appointing mind guards (essentially information sentinels) to protect the group from negative information.

BEATING THE BIASES

Can these various problems be overcome? As with all biases the solutions are never easy to implement. However, three possible routes to reducing group biases are given below:

Secret Ballots

The use of secret ballots obviously reduces the risk of group members coming under social pressure. So perhaps before the meeting starts members should write down their views and their preference for asset allocation, then count the votes, and debate the outcome if it is really necessary – bearing in mind the dangers inherent in this process.

Devil's Advocates

Appointing a devil's advocate[4] may help. However, all too often the person selected may not truly believe the role he is asked to play, and hence does not really try too hard to prevent the group reaching its consensus decision. Selecting prickly disagreeable individuals with a strong contrarian view and the ability and desire to argue on almost anything would be perfect. But such individuals are hard to find, and don't fit easily into most corporate cultures.

Respect for Other Group Members

The other factor that can help to reduce the dangers of group decisions is when the group members are acknowledged to be experts in their field, and hence disparate viewpoints are easier to deal with and unshared information may be easier to uncover. However, all too often people tend to believe that they know best on almost every subject and hence tend not to display respect for the views of others.

---

[4] The term comes from the process of canonization. When the Pope considers conferring sainthood, a devil's advocate is appointed unofficially to argue against the decision.

SECTION IV
Investment Process as Behavioural
Defence

18

The Tao of Investing

> **If the previous section outlined the major failings of the average institutional investment process, this section attempts to outline an investment process that is at least partially robust to behavioural biases. It focuses on a contrarian or value-oriented approach to investing. Topics covered include the traits of best fund managers, the evidence in support of value, and why risk is a four-letter word.**

- The evidence from over three decades of behavioural decision-making research contains a rather unpleasant findings that simply being aware of our biases is not enough (although obviously an important first step). Rather than relying upon self-insight to change behaviour, a better solution would appear to codify behavioural rules into an investment process.
- The chapters contained in this section aim to explore how we might pursue investment strategies that are at least partially robust to some of the behavioural problems identified in the earlier chapters. The papers collected here can be broken into three distinct (but related) areas.
- Part A deals with what it takes to be a successful investor. The chapters collected here cover areas as diverse as the traits shared by long-term successful value investors, the need to be prepared to take off-index positions, the investment advice of Ben Graham and John Maynard Keynes, and advantages offered by the use of quant models in investing. The final chapter in this part deals with why a value-oriented approach is likely to be a logical one going forward. It deals with the behavioural stumbling blocks that prevent otherwise sensible investors from doing what is right.
- Part B takes the perspective of an empirical sceptic. One of the key behavioural mistakes covered in the seven sins was believing stories. In order to avoid this pitfall, this part subjects the value approach to an empirical assessment. The chapters included here cover such topics as why value works (in terms of the margin of safety), improvements to basic value strategies such as using Joel Greenblatt's little book strategy, incorporating information from external finance, and using Graham and Dodd style PEs. We also explore the critical role that time horizon plays in investing. Patience is a virtue for value investors but an absolute nightmare for growth investors.
- Part C tackles the nature of risk. Risk is an integral part of the investment process, but probably a badly understood one. According to classical finance, risk is defined as price volatility. However, never yet have we met a long-only fund manager who cares about upside risk, strangely enough this gets lumped into return and is lauded. The chapters in this part explore the failure of price volatility and beta as measures of risk, and indeed the failures of risk managers (who would be better labelled as risk maniacs).

The seven sins of fund management (November 2005) represented a psychological critique of a 'typical' large fund management organizations investment process. As such it largely constituted a list of don'ts. This collection aims to be a list of do's.

As all investors are aware, we can't control return (would that we could). Instead we have to concentrate on the investment process. Our aim in this volume is to collect together some of the various notes we have written on how to invest.

An interesting article in the *Journal of Investing* by John Minahan (2006) helps to frame the debate that this collection aims to address. Minahan argues that a sound investment philosophy is vital in distinguishing alpha[1] from noise. He argues that managers are more likely to outperform if they:

1. *Have a clear thesis of how they generate alpha.* Managers are not likely to generate ex-ante alpha without having a very clear idea of what they do that generates alpha, what it is about the markets they invest in that provides the opportunity to generate alpha, and what their competitive advantage is in exploiting that opportunity.
2. *Put significant effort into understanding where their performance comes from.* Good managers recognize that they have as much stake as anybody in understanding whether their performance is due to the successful execution of the alpha thesis, benchmark misfit, or luck, and are therefore very thoughtful about evaluating their own performance.
3. *Have thought about whether their alpha-generation process will need to change over time.* In competitive capital markets, alpha-generation sources tend to be arbitraged away. Good managers understand this, and therefore monitor whether or not it is happening, and have a process for seeking out new alpha sources which lever the manager's competitive advantage.

These three questions frame the selection of chapters we have chosen here. Part A deals with why it is vital to do something different from the vast majority of investors. As Sir John Templeton said, "It is impossible to produce a superior performance unless you do something different from the majority."

The chapters in Part A cover areas as diverse as the traits shared by long-term successful value investors, the need to be prepared to take off-index positions, the investment advice of Ben Graham and John Maynard Keynes, and advantages offered by the use of quant models in investing. The final chapter in this part deals with why a value-oriented approach is likely to be a logical one going forward. It deals with the behavioural stumbling blocks which prevent otherwise sensible investors from doing what is right. This, of course, speaks directly to the third of Minahan's requirements listed above.

Part B takes the perspective of an empirical sceptic. One of the key behavioural mistakes covered in the seven sins was believing stories. In order to avoid this pitfall, this part subjects the value approach to an empirical assessment.

The chapters included in Part B cover the such topics as why value works (in terms of the margin of safety), improvements to basic value strategies such as using Joel Greenblatt's little book strategy, incorporating information from external finance, and using Graham and Dodd style PEs. We also explore the critical role that time horizon plays in investing. Patience is a virtue for value investors but an absolute nightmare for growth investors.

We then turn to look at varieties of value in terms of whether it is best defined at the stock or sector level. We also show the evidence that value works best when considered relative to

---

[1] I am not totally comfortable with alpha as a concept since it stems from CAPM — a fraudulent model (see CAPM is CRAP chapter). However, for the sake of argument I will use it here in its generally recognized sense of value added by fund managers.

industry (so-called sector neutral strategies). We also show that value and momentum can be used to aid country selection – so a value spin on GTAA if you like.

Part C tackles the nature of risk. Risk is an integral part of the investment process, but probably a badly understood one. According to classical finance, risk is defined as price volatility. However, never yet have we met a long-only fund manager who cares about upside risk; but strangely enough this gets lumped into return and is lauded. The chapters in this part explore the failure of price volatility and beta as measures of risk, and indeed the failures of risk managers (who would be better labelled as risk maniacs).

We hope that these chapters at least provide some response to Minahan's criteria for assessment, as well as providing an outline for a psychologically robust investment process that seeks to avoid many of the pitfalls detailed in the seven sins of fund management.

PART A

The Behavioural Investor

19

Come Out of the Closet
(or, Show Me the Alpha)*

Occasionally, the underperformance of fund managers vs the index is trotted out as evidence of the efficiency of the market. However, this confuses the absence of evidence with evidence of the absence. A new study suggests that closet indexing accounts for nearly one-third of the US mutual fund industry. Stock pickers account for less than 30% of the market, yet they have real investment skill.

- The fact that most fund managers fail to beat the index is not proof that the market is efficient. The managers might fail for a whole host of reasons, from institutional constraints to behavioural biases, none of which would imply efficient markets.
- A new paper by two US academics (Cremers and Petajisto, 2006) throws some light on these debates. They construct a new measure called active share. It measures the degree of overlap with the benchmark. For example, an active share of 100% would mean zero overlap with the index.
- By combining active share and tracking error, we can map out various groups of investors. For instance, those with high active share and low tracking error are diversified stock pickers. Those with low active share and low tracking error are closet indexers.
- Cremers and Petajisto show that closet indexing has become a very real problem in the last 10 years, rising from 10% of the total mutual fund market to over 30%. At the same time, stock-picking has declined from 60% in the 1980s to under 30% today. Similar numbers from an independent study using a very different methodology show this pattern to be fairly common in developed equity markets.
- This is all the more bizarre when one considers the alphas that these various groups of investors generate. Both diversified and concentrated stock-pickers seem to have genuine alpha (in both net and gross terms). However, those placing sector bets (i.e. those with low active share but high tracking error) and the closet indexers seem to have negative alpha. This helps to explain why so many fund managers underperform the index: they are doing the wrong thing! For every $100 invested in US domestic mutual funds, some $68 ends up in the hands of those with negative alpha.
- In terms of investment styles, the diversified stock-pickers tend to be large-cap value players. Concentrated stock pickers tend to be more small-cap oriented, but inhabit both value and growth universes. The closet indexers turn out to be momentum players, just like the index they hug.

---

*This article appeared in *Global Equity Strategy* on 19 July 2006. The material discussed was accurate at the time of publication.

- The good news is that active share is relatively persistent, so funds with high active share today are likely to have high active share next year and beyond. Cremers and Petajisto also found that past performance was a useful indicator – suggesting that there are a subgroup of managers who really do have investment skill. So the ideal fund would appear to have high active share and high past performance.
- The failure of active managers to beat the index is not proof of market efficiency, but rather testament to the rise of the closet indexer. It is about time they came out!

Every so often an academic economist will argue that markets are efficient. The "proof" offered for this ludicrous statement is the fact that the vast majority of active fund managers underperform the index.

The most recent example comes from Greg Mankiw, a professor at Harvard and former chair of the Council of Economic Advisors.[1] He recently wrote,

> According to Morningstar, over the past 10 years, Vangard's S&P 500 fund beat 74 percent of comparable funds on a before-tax basis and 86 percent on an after-tax basis. Even better is Vangard's tax managed capital appreciation fund, which is essentially an index fund that keeps one eye on the tax system. It beat 90 percent of comparable funds on an after-tax basis.

He concludes in another entry, "The efficient-market hypothesis is not strictly true, but it is close enough to true that most investors are better off believing in it nonetheless."

It has always struck me that taking the idea that most managers fall short of the index as proof of the efficiency of the stock market is confabulating what Taleb calls the absence of evidence with the evidence of absence.[2] The two are, of course, very different beasts. Most fund managers might fail to beat the index[3] because they are trapped in some institutional constraint or bedevilled by behavioural biases.[4]

A new paper that crossed my desk may help to explain the underperformance of most fund managers and also help to identify ex-ante those who are likely to succeed. Written by Martijn Cremers and Antti Petajisto from the ICF at Yale, it is one of the best papers I've read in recent times (Cremers and Petajisto, 2006).

They have come up with a new measure – active share. They argue that any portfolio can be decomposed into a 100% position in the benchmark plus a zero-net-investment long/short portfolio. The long/short portfolio represents all the active bets that the fund is running. Active share is calculated as:

$$\text{ActiveShare} = \frac{1}{2} \sum_{i=1}^{N} |w_{\text{fund},i} - w_{\text{index},i}|$$

where $w_{\text{fund},i}$ and $w_{\text{index},i}$ are the portfolio weights of the asset, i, in the fund and in the index, and the sum is taken over the universe of assets.

This has the neat interpretation of being the degree of non-overlap with the benchmark index. So an active share of 100% would mean no overlap at all with the benchmark index.

Cremers and Petajisto (2006) give the following example:

> Imagine that the manager starts by investing $100 million in the index (S&P 500), thus having a pure index fund. Assume the manager only liked half the stocks, so he eliminates the other half from his portfolio, generating $50 million in cash, and then he invests that $50 million in those stocks he likes. This produces an active share of 50%. If he invests in only 50 stocks out of 500... his active share will be 90% (i.e. a 10% overlap with the index).

By combining their measure of active share with the familiar tracking error, Cremers and Petajisto suggest they can identify various groups of investors. Table 19.1 shows the interaction

---

[1] http://gregmankiw.blogspot.com/, Greg is generally quite a sensible chap. He has done a lot of work trying to incorporate some behavioural traits into the macro economic arena.

[2] For more on this, see Taleb (2005).

[3] Why benchmarks are of such importance remains beyond me. I have long argued that it is absolute return that should matter to investors, not relative performance against an arbitrary benchmark but that is a debate for another day.

[4] See 'The seven sins of fund management' for more on this (*Global Equity Strategy*, November 2005).

Table 19.1   Types of managers

		Tracking error		
		High	Low	Zero
Active share	High	Concentrated stock-pickers (Active share >80%, tracking error >8%)	Diversified stock-pickers (Active share >80%, tracking error <8%)	–
	Low	Sector bets (Active share <80%, tracking error >6%)	Closet index funds (Active share <60%, tracking error <6%)	–
	Zero	–	–	Index funds

Source: Cremers and Petajisto (2006) and DrKW Macro research.

of active share and tracking error. I've also included the various criteria that Cremers and Petajisto use to define the groups.

Those with high active share and low tracking errors are diversified stock-pickers. Their active share is a testament to their taking lots of bets but a low tracking error suggests that they are running a portfolio which is large enough to diversify specific sector positions.

In the opposite corner of the matrix, are those with low active share but high tracking error. These fund managers are placing concentrated sector-like bets. They seem to be relatively passive in terms of stock selection.

Of course, some investors try to combine the best of both worlds, running concentrated stock portfolios. They have both a high active share and a large tracking error (inhabiting the top left of our matrix).

Those funds with low active share and low tracking error are closet indexers. Finally, very low (effectively zero) active share and very low tracking error are the hallmarks of the index funds.

Being good empiricists, Cremers and Petajisto submit their ideas to the data. Using a database of US domestic equity-only funds since 1980, they examine the behaviour of various groups. In order to assign benchmarks to the funds, various indices are used including the S&P 500, the Barra value and growth indices, the Russell 2000, and the Wiltshire 5000. Funds are measured against each index, and the one generating the lowest active share (i.e. the highest overlap with the index) is then selected as the appropriate benchmark. I've used their definitions (outlined above) to examine various aspects of the different groups they identified.[5]

THE ALPHA

Figure 19.1 shows the gross and net levels of alpha across the four key groups of funds. The diversified stock-pickers seem to have the edge in terms of gross alpha, and manage to maintain that edge when it comes to net alpha. The concentrated stock-pickers come in the second slot (although they seem to have slightly higher fees than the diversified stock-pickers).

---

[5] They themselves don't do this. Cremers and Petajisto use decile sorts to examine performance. I've taken the liberty of combining deciles in accordance with the criteria listed in Table 19.1 in order to preserve the groups outlined.

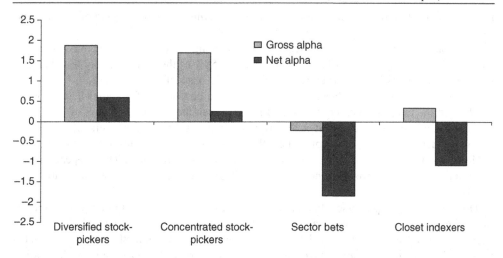

Figure 19.1   Gross and net alphas (% p.a.).
Source: Cremers and Petajisto (2006) and DrKW Macro research.

Those funds making sector bets with relatively passive stock selection are the worst performers. They have a negative gross alpha, and therefore a truly appalling net alpha of nearly −2%! The closet indexers also manage to destroy value at the net alpha level.

THE EVOLUTION OF THE MUTUAL FUND INDUSTRY

How can we reconcile the findings on those with active share having alpha, and Mankiw's comments on the underperformance of most fund managers? The answer lies in Figure 19.2.

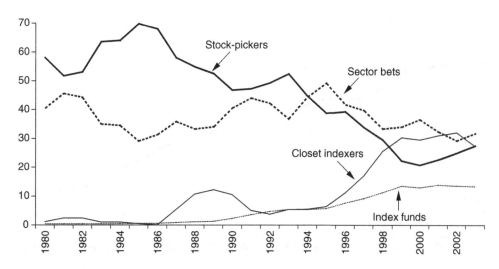

Figure 19.2   The evolution of the mutual fund industry — % of all equity assets.
Source: Cremers and Petajisto (2006) and DrKW Macro research.

It shows the evolution of the mutual fund industry in terms of the percentage of mutual fund equity assets.

Stock-picking (high active share – regardless of tracking error) has declined massively over the last 20 years. In the early 1980s, it accounted for 58% of the market; today less than one in every three dollars in mutual funds is invested on the basis of stock-picking.

The sector bet guys have been roughly constant in accounting for somewhere between 30–40% of the total assets in equity mutual funds. Given the disastrous nature of the alphas they have achieved on average, it isn't any wonder that so many funds underperform the index – evidence, perhaps, of misplaced confidence in their own abilities to time the market.

However, it is the rise of the closet indexers that is most noticeable. They appear to have risen in market share terms from nothing in the 1980s to around 30% in the latter part of the 1990s.

This has led to the perverse situation where, for every $100 invested in actively managed funds (i.e. non-passive), no less than $68 is given to those with negative net alpha!

Interestingly, Bhattacharya and Galpin (2005) use a very different methodology, but reach a very similar conclusion. They use a clever twist that if everyone is a passive investor, holding a portfolio that mirrors the market, the volume of trade in any single stock would reflect the company's weight in the index – pure and simple. For instance, if the market consisted of just two stocks, one large firm with a market capitalization of $75 million and a small stock with a cap of $25 million, and an investor had $1000 to invest, they would spend $750 on the large stock and $250 on the small stock.

They then go on to estimate how much of the volume of trade in a share is explained by the company's size. 1 minus the R^2 from this regression provides a limit on the amount of trade that can be accounted for by stock-picking. The numbers they arrive at are very similar to Cremers and Petajisto's estimates.

Figure 19.3 shows their measure of the volume in the market that can be explained by stock-picking for the MSCI developed markets. According to this measure, stock-picking only account for around 36% of total volumes, down from 55% in 1995.

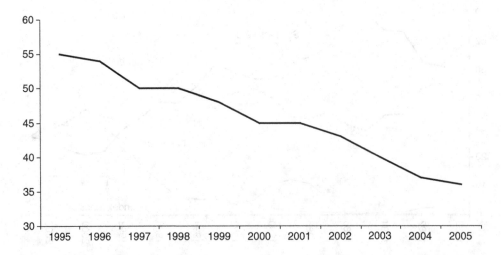

Figure 19.3 The maximum % of volume explained by stock-picking – MSCI developed markets.
Source: Bhattacharya and Galpin (2005).

Table 19.2   Factor betas by fund management group

	SMB	HML	UMD
Diversified stock-pickers	**−0.18**	**1.33**	0.05
Concentrated stock-pickers	**1.67**	−0.23	0.15
Sector bets	**0.92**	0.14	0.12
Closet indexers	**0.17**	0.02	**0.07**

Source: Cremers and Petajisto (2006) and DrKW Macro research.

CHARACTERISTICS OF THE FUNDS

Table 19.2 shows the factor loadings when the funds from the Cremers and Petajisto study are regressed on a Fama French four-factor model (market, size (SMB – small minus big), style (HML – high book to price minus low book to price), and momentum (UMD – up minus down). The results in bold are statistically significant.

A cursory glance at the table reveals that the diversified stock-pickers tend to be large cap value investors. The concentrated stock-pickers tend to inhabit the small cap arena (with a slight growth bias – although not statistically meaningful). The closet index funds are really just momentum players (reflecting the dominance of capitalization-weighted index construction).

The Average and Aggregate Active Share

Cremers and Petajisto also compute the average (value-weighted) active share. Given the findings on the evolution of the mutual fund industry above, it isn't surprising to see this measure decline over the sample, from 80% in the 1980s to 60% today.

They also compute an aggregate active share. This is constructed by taking all the funds that benchmark against the S&P 500 and adding all their individual holdings together to form one overall portfolio.

If funds never take positions against one another, the average should equal the aggregate. To the extent that these measures diverge, funds are trading among themselves. Figure 19.4 reveals that around half of the active share is taken against other mutual funds. So holding a portfolio of funds may actually reduce your overall active share. This certainly raises questions over the popular core-satellite view.

Persistence and Performance

Figure 19.5 shows that active share is highly persistent. If a fund has a high active share this year, it is likely to continue to have a high active share next year, and beyond.

Of course, over time funds will change. Petajisto[6] shows Figure 19.6 tracking the active share of the Fidelity Magellan fund over time. It has clearly moved from being a high active share fund to a closet index fund.

The Magellan example serves to highlight how important managers are. If some managers have skill, we would expect to see persistence across their performance. On the basis of the

---

[6] http://www.som.yale.edu/Faculty/petajisto/research.html.

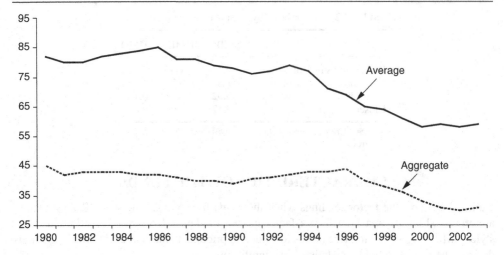

Figure 19.4   Average and aggregate active share.
Source: Cremers and Petajisto (2006).

evidence provided above, this persistence should be greatest among those with the highest active shares.

This is exactly what Cremers and Petajisto uncovered. So, past performance might just be a guide to future performance! Figure 19.7 shows the average alpha over time for the funds with highest and lowest active share, and good and poor past performance. Those funds with very high active share and good past performance have much higher future alphas than those with high active share and poor past performance. This disparity is far greater in the high active share groups than in the low active share groups. All of this suggests that there are a group of managers who do have skill when it comes to stock-picking, and this skill is persistent.

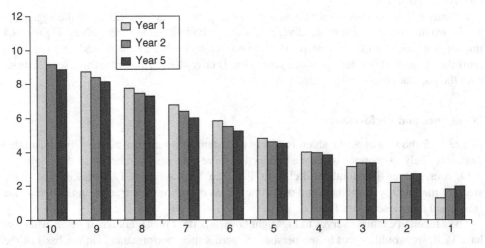

Figure 19.5   Active share decile rank over time.
Source: Cremers and Petajisto (2006).

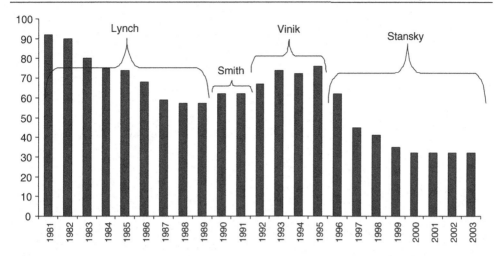

Figure 19.6   The active share of the Fidelity Magellan fund: managers matter.
Source: Petajisto.

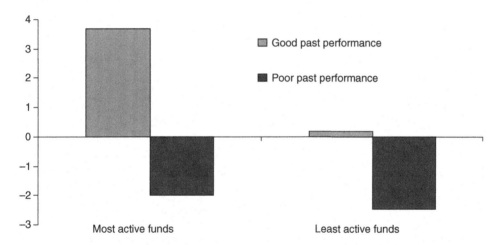

Figure 19.7   Future average alpha based on active share and past performance.
Source: Cremers and Petajisto (2006).

CONCLUSIONS

The confabulation of the absence of evidence with the evidence of absence is perhaps the weakest defence of the efficient markets hypothesis that I have come across. It may still be right to argue that the majority of investors are best off in index funds, but not because the market is efficient, but rather because it is full of passive funds masquerading as active funds.

Cremers and Petajisto provide us with a new measure which seems to make intuitive sense, and also have predictive power. Paying for active management is fine, but make sure that is what you are actually getting.

20

Strange Brew*

> **If the fund management industry is to stand any chance of hitting the return assumptions set by pension funds, it must change. In part it will be a revolution – abandoning indexing, a focus on absolute alpha, and a willingness to short. In part, the changes will need to be reactionary, with a return to balanced funds and wide mandates.**

- The death of passive investing is perhaps one of the most obvious implications of our work on long-run returns being dominated by valuations. As US equities are priced to deliver 3% real over the long term, why should any investor pay even 50 bps to track an index? A collary of this observation is that the core/satellite approach should also disappear.
- Active investors need to see a return to balanced funds. In order to get the long run right, fund managers should follow a strategic asset allocation based on long-term valuation. This currently suggests a mere 30% allocation to equities.
- Low returns are not the same as stable markets. Both the Japanese experience, and the recent behaviour of the US market, serve as reminders that secular bear markets contain heady rallies. Short-term moves can be captured through a more active TAA process.
- Equity only managers should concentrate on absolute alpha. In order to maximize insights, managers need to fully utilize their information set – that is, they need to be able to go short. The other way of enhancing alpha is to increase the opportunities to apply your insights. Broad-based mandates are likely to be optimal.

---

*This article appeared in *Global Equity Strategy* on 22 May 2003. The material discussed was accurate at the time of publication.

This chapter was inspired by an email from a client (yes, I do sometimes read and respond to emails!) The client posed a question along the following lines: 'A fund needs a 6% real return. I know this fund actually needs to adjust to lower expectations and save more, but the adjustment of expectations from plan sponsors moves at glacial speed. So how do I try to meet this return assumption?'

It struck me that at various times over the last 2 years we had explored issues that might shed some light on this question and indeed the shape of fund management in the years to come. I've combined these with some fresh thoughts to offer a few hints as to how the fund management industry may change over the coming years.

THE LONG RUN

We have shown many times before that long-run returns are dominated by valuation (see, for instance, *Global Equity Strategy*, 27 November 2002 and 12 December 2002). The essence of the argument is simplicity itself. Long-run returns can be decomposed into three component parts: dividend yield, real dividend growth and any change in valuations that occur during the holding period.

The importance of valuation should be obvious. Dividend yield is just another valuation ratio (D/P), so the purchase point should clearly impact your total returns. If you start with a high dividend yield you should expect a high return, and if you start with a low dividend yield you should expect a low return.

We have previously demonstrated the relationship between valuations and returns using a table of the form of Table 20.1. This shows real returns achieved dependent upon the valuation of the market at the time of purchase. Unsurprisingly, in the USA when the trailing 12-month as-reported PE is in its highest quartile, the median real return over the next 10 years is just 0.1% p.a!

The trailing 12-month as-reported PE on the S&P 500 is 30 times. So the US market remains firmly in the top quartile of Table 20.1, implying that if history is any guide then returns over the next 10 years will be minimal. So even if Plan B (the Fed moves to unconventional policy) is implemented from current levels of the market, any announcement rally is likely to be a final selling opportunity for those who are still seriously overweight equities (more on this later).

The fact that valuations are the long-run determinant of returns has two key implications for the future of fund management. The first is dependent upon the current state of the market. It is unrealistic to anticipate any further multiple expansion in the long term. Therefore, the

Table 20.1   US 10-year real returns by PE range (% p.a)

PE Range	Mean	Median	Standard Deviation
32–20	2.3	0.1	5.4
20–16	7.3	7.3	5.0
16–13.5	10.4	10.8	4.0
13.5–4	9.7	10.0	3.0

Source: DrKW Macro research.

total real return a rational investor can expect from the market is only 3% (the dividend yield of 1.7%, plus long-term real dividend growth of 1.5%).[1]

Death of Indexing

Index or passive funds have arisen for two key reasons. Firstly, they are an effective way of playing momentum. After all, indices are frequently little more than momentum measures, as the best performing stocks get added, and the worse performing stocks are deleted.

During the momentum inspired markets of the late 1990s, the management fee on index tracking funds was easily forgotten when equities were delivering 20% p.a. However, in a world where equities are priced to deliver a real return on only 3% p.a., why would an investor pay even 50 bps to track an index? After all even 50 bps represent 10% of the total return that investors are likely to receive (assuming 2% inflation). It seems unlikely that index funds will be able to justify their existence in such a low-return environment.

The second argument for indexing that is widely put forward is that a staggeringly large percentage of active managers underperform the broad market. However, in a world of low returns the historical underperformance of active managers is *not* an argument for indexing, rather it is an argument for careful manager selection. Later we will explore what plan sponsors should be looking for when considering active fund managers.

Getting the Long Run Right

The second key implication of valuations determining long-run returns is that investors need to have a sliding scale of strategic asset allocation. Traditionally, strategic asset allocation has been the long-run view set by the trustees and embodied in the mandate given to the fund manager. However, traditional views towards strategic asset allocation need to be challenged.[2]

We explored strategic asset allocation in *Global Equity Strategy*, 13 February 2003. To save you rummaging through your bins, the basic idea is that if valuations contain useful information about long-run returns, then we can use this information in forming our long-term allocations to asset classes.

In order to demonstrate the possibility of such an approach we examined the risk minimizing portfolio weights in a two-asset optimization. We ran four cases based around the data contained in Table 20.1 – that is to say, we looked at the optimal allocation to equities given the valuation level at purchase point. In order to do this we needed to know the risk and return of the alternative asset class, and, of course, the correlation and covariance between the alternative and equities.

In *Global Equity Strategy*, 13 February 2003, we used real bonds as the alternative. We have used the current yield on TIIPS as our proxy for the expected real return on bonds. In order to estimate the standard deviation of the real bond returns we used the historical record which reveals a 4% standard deviation. The correlation between 10-year real bond and 10-year real equity returns was 0.34.

In each case we found the risk minimizing weight to equities given by the efficient frontier. The results will make uncomfortable reading for many pension consultants. When the market is in the top quartile on the basis of simple trailing PE then the equity weight should be a mere

---

[1] This may seem low, but is clearly what the historical record shows. See Arnott and Bernstein (2002) and *Global Equity Strategy*, 16 August 2002.

[2] An excellent example of this can be found in Peter Bernstein's interview with Kate Welling. See Welling@weedon, 28 February 2003.

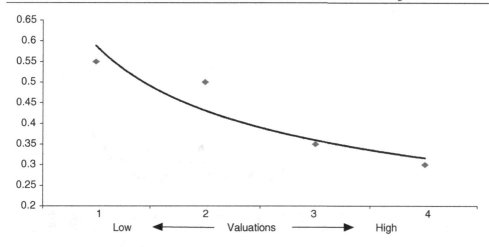

Figure 20.1   Optimal equity allocation dependent upon valuation range (%).
Source: DrKW Macro research.

30%. In contrast, when the market is at levels associated with its lowest quartile of valuation, the optimal equity weighting rises to 55% (Figure 20.1).

When we have been marketing and met bond managers most of them seem to be very worried about the current level of bond yields. Now, I'm certainly not a bond strategist; however, two things about the current level of yields occur to me. The first is that I wonder if bond managers are in danger of anchoring (the psychology tendency to grab onto irrelevant crutches). I worked in Japan in the mid-1990s, and the easiest thing in the world to convince yourself of was to be short JGBs; however, that hasn't stopped yields from falling massively from these low levels. Nor does the historical record suggest that the current yield is as low as it can go.

Secondly, in a recent article in the *Journal of Portfolio Management*, Hunt and Hoisington (2003) point out that the best 20-year period for bonds relative to equities was 1874–1894, when bonds outperformed by almost 1% p.a. The best 10-year period of bonds was 1928–1938 when bonds outperformed equities by 5.5% p.a. It may be surprising to know that in both cases, the bonds yield at the starting point of their outperformance was below the current 10-year yield (see Figure 20.2). In our own research (see *Global Equity Strategy*, 13 February 2003) we showed that real bonds had outperformed real equities on a 10-year time horizon around 18% of the time. Therefore, suggesting a 30% weight in equities over the long term, given the current state of valuations, doesn't strike us as radical.

THE SHORT RUN

Tactical Asset Allocation

While strategic asset allocation as outlined above should help to avoid the worst excesses of the kind seen during the bubble years, it suffers from a problem. Just because returns are likely to be low on average over a prolonged period (a secular bear market in the common parlance), it doesn't follow that markets will be stable.

So far the secular US bear market in equities has resulted in five rallies of over 20%. In a world in which your long-run return is likely to be around 3%, 20% represents over $6\frac{1}{2}$ years'

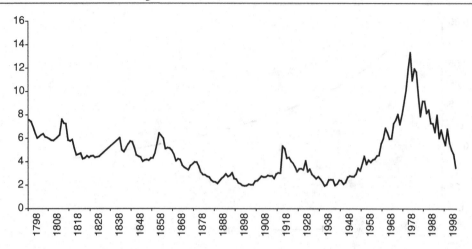

Figure 20.2 A long-term look at US government bond yields.
Source: Homer and Sylla.

worth of returns. So capturing those short-term bounces in markets becomes increasingly important.

A similar picture can be found by examining the period Albert Edwards refers to as the dismal years (see Table 20.2 and Figure 20.3) — the US market between 1964 and 1982. If you had used a buy and hold strategy, you would have seen barely 1% p.a. in real total returns. However, if we had been following the signals generated by our tactical asset allocation model (see *Global Equity Strategy*, 23 April 2003), we would have seen real returns of 4.5% p.a. with substantially less volatility than the equity market in general.

So investors will need to be much flightier of foot in order to maximize returns.

Equity Managers

Death of Benchmarking and the Rise of Absolute Alpha

Hand in hand with the death of indexing should go the death of benchmarking. The whole concept of relative return leaves me somewhat confused. It strikes me that the only people

Table 20.2 Performance during the dismal years

Strategy	Conditions to Buy Equities	Geometric Return	Arithmetic Return	Standard Deviation	Sharpe Ratio	Information Coefficient	Information Ratio
Value and momentum	I,II,III	10.9	10.1	12.6	0.20	0.07	0.24
Value only	I,II	10.0	9.4	12.8	0.14	−0.02	−0.07
Momentum only	I,III	12.2	11.4	5.5	0.69	0.21	0.73
Buy and hold	I,II,III,IV	7.5	7.4	14.7	−0.01		

Source: DrKW Macro research.

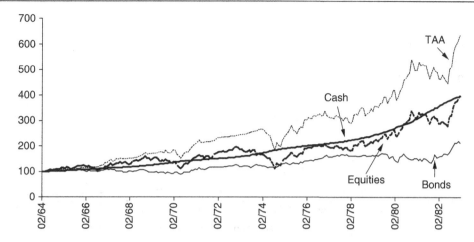

Figure 20.3   Our tactical asset allocation model in the dismal years.
Source: DrKW Macro research.

who can retire on relative performance are a fortunate few fund managers. After all it does me no good whatsoever to know that my pension fund has fallen 40% against a market that has fallen 50%. The only thing that matters to me is absolute returns.

A focus on absolute returns might be thought to be a natural reaction to the prolonged bear market in which we find ourselves. This may well be true. However, there is nothing in the rules about us not using the current situation to improve the future. So if plan sponsors are interested in absolute returns, let's give them what they want. The client's email that opened this chapter was quite rightly already expressed in absolute return levels. So we should educate and encourage plan sponsors to set absolute return targets, rather than some arbitrary benchmark.

This focus on absolute returns should also help to alleviate the problems of index hugging or closet indexing by fund managers. This in turn should help to reduce the risk of a bubble arising again – just as the death of passive management should. As Charles Ellis noted in the preface to *Winning the Loser's Game*,

> Successful investing does not depend on beating the market. Attempting to beat the market will distract you from the fairly simple but quite interesting and productive task of designing a long-term program of investing that will succeed at providing the best feasible results for you.

Absolute Alpha

Have I gone mad? First I say that benchmarking should die, and then I talk about alpha. Use of a benchmark from a performance measurement standpoint still makes sense, after all we may want to know if our managers' returns are skill or just loading up on market risk.

So how can equity fund managers add value in terms of absolute alpha generation? Of course, adding alpha by definition is a zero sum game, your gains are directly the result of someone else's losses. However, there are some things we can explore to improve our likelihood of adding alpha.

In an insightful paper, Kahn (2002) suggested that what plan sponsors need (as opposed to desire) is consistent outperformance. This might seem like a prime example of stating the blindingly obvious. However, Kahn goes on to define exactly how to measure outperformance.

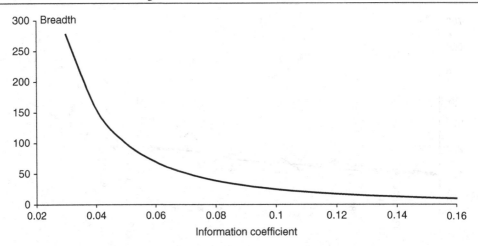

Figure 20.4 Combinations of information coefficient and breadth that generate IR = 0.5.
Source: DrKW Macro research.

He uses the information ratio as a measure of performance consistency. The information ratio has many representations. However, we will draw on two here. Firstly, the (ex-post) information ratio can be defined as the ratio of annualized residual return to annualized residual risk. Or the ratio of alpha over its standard error (the *t* stat) to the square root of the period over which we observe the returns:

$$IR = [alpha/SE(alpha)]/[\text{square root } (T)]$$

Grinold (1989) proposed that the information ratio can be defined as the information coefficient times the square root of breadth. This relationship is called the fundamental law of active management.

The information coefficient (IC) measures the correlation between the forecasts that a fund manager makes and the actual outcomes. It can be defined as $2 \times (f - 0.5)$ where f is the percentage of calls the manager got right.

However, correct calls are but one part of an active manager's role. The other key element is the breadth of his call. Breadth itself has two dimensions because it is the product of the number of assets covered plus the number of independent decisions made.

A relatively small amount of insight applied across a wide universe and with reasonable frequency translates into a high IR. Figure 20.4 shows a range of combinations of IC and breadth that give an IR = 0.5, which is equivalent to a top quartile fund manager.

Kahn offers the following example:

> Suppose a manager has an IC of 0.035 which corresponds to being right about 51 percent of the time. This manager follows 200 stocks and makes new informed decisions about the stocks roughly once a quarter. This means, in effect, that the manager has a total of 800 new views on these stocks each year. The IR for this manager is 0.99, a top decile investment manager.

BREAK THE LONG-ONLY CONSTRAINT

Now that we have defined our terms, we can begin to explore how we can improve our value added. The first and perhaps most obvious way of adding value is to use the full information set available to managers. If an investment process creates insights into which stocks to go long, it presumably also offers advice on which stocks to go short.

Shorting still has an ill-deserved bad reputation. Many see it as immoral to short a stock. In *Reminiscences of a stock operator*, Jesse Livermore recounts receiving death threats because he shorted stock! Although death threats are mercifully rare these days, some people still see red when discussing shorting. Yet all the experimental evidence shows that shorting in general improves the efficiency of the market.[3]

Not only does shorting improve the efficiency of the market, but it potentially improves the information ratio of those following such a strategy. The tightness of the long-only constraint will depend crucially on the size of the tracking error that the manager is allowed. If a manager has a 3% tracking error, he will be unable to take large bets in either direction – hence the need for the death of the benchmark discussed above.

An example of using the full information set can be provided from our recent study of country level value effects in *Global Equity Strategy*, 30 April 2003, in which we showed that cheap countries (defined as the six highest dividend yielding countries within the MSCI universe) outperformed both the MSCI World index, and six lowest dividend yielding countries. When compared with the World Index, our strategy showed a 6% p.a. annual outperformance (1975–2003). However, when compared to the bottom tritile, the annual outperformance came to 7% (1975–2003).

Thus breaking the long-only constraint makes good sense if the costs of shorting are less than the 1% performance enhancement that we receive from being able to go short the six lowest yielding countries. So we should break the long-only constraint. If fund mangers start showing an interest in the short side, then perhaps, just perhaps, it might have the added benefit of forcing analysts to come up with a few more sell recommendations

As an aside, this example can also be used to highlight the differences between ex-post and ex-ante versions of the IR. For instance, the ex-ante IR is the percentage of correct calls times the square root of breadth. Over the sample we tested, the model of cheap countries outperforming generated an IC of around 0.17 regardless of whether the bottom tritile or the market was used as the base for comparison. However, the ex-post IRs were substantially higher. For the long-only portfolio the ex-post IR was 1.05, and for the long/short portfolio the ex-post IR was 0.8 – both much higher than the ex-ante measures. A similar finding holds for our TAA model referred to earlier – the ex-ante IR for that model is 0.42, however, the realized IR is a much higher 1.1!

The information ratio also has an added advantage of having a representation in the time domain. That is to say, we can use it to show clients the *risks* involved in any particular strategy.

For instance, the US market is widely held to be a safer investment for the long run, regularly beating other asset classes. However, given the volatility of excess returns, the IR for US stocks over cash is 0.37, which equates to a 14-year holding period before clients could be 90% sure of actually seeing US stocks generate excess returns over cash. This seems to stretch the tolerance of even the most accepting of pension funds.

Our cheap country strategy does somewhat better with a 6-year holding period (based on the ex-ante IR), and our TAA model implies a 7-year holding period to be 90% sure of beating the benchmark (again based on ex-ante IRs). Note that even on our relatively high performing strategies the time horizon is still quite long (see Figure 20.5). So patience will be rewarded, and quarterly performance measurement remains a complete nonsense.

---

[3] See for example, Caginalp *et al.* (2000).

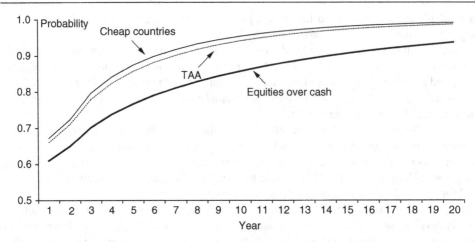

Figure 20.5   Time horizons and probabilities for various strategies.
Source: DrKW Macro research.

ADD BREADTH

The second key way of adding alpha relates to increasing the degree of breadth to which insights are applied. Plan sponsors should provide managers with wide-ranging mandates. If managers have value added they should be encouraged to use it wherever the opportunity arises. It is highly ironic that many pension consultants pushed for core/satellite structures and speeded the demise of the "balanced" fund approach which used a combination of SAA and TAA. If this hadn't occurred in such a widespread fashion, then perhaps balanced funds could have helped to mitigate some of the worst of the bubbles feedback mechanisms – a reactionary viewpoint, but one that I hope is not without merit.

If managers are to be allowed breadth to exploit their alpha, then the coresatellite approach to investing from plan sponsors must be brought to an end. Rather than having endless numbers of specialist managers, each charging a fee, surely it would be better to have one manager and pay one fee, but allow that manager freedom to invest wherever the opportunities lie.[4]

However, there is an important aspect to breadth that needs to be noted. Applying one strategy in many different markets can be very profitable but it is not the same thing as diversification. To see this, remember LTCM and the strategies they employed. Virtually all the strategies were based on convergence; no matter whether the market was US treasuries or Danish Mortgage Backed Securities, the strategies were replicated over and over again. However, LTCM was essentially applying one insight time and time again, geographic diversification was achieved, but strategic diversification wasn't.

Imagine managers who ranks US stocks on the basis of book to price, and buy "cheap" stocks and sell "expensive" ones. Let's say they cover some 800 stocks and rebalance once a quarter. However, they are really only applying one insight, so the breadth of the portfolio is not 800 stocks since the views on each stock are not independent, but it is greater than four, which is the number of rebalances per year.

---

[4] For more on this see Ennis (2002).

Table 20.3 Do hedge funds hedge? 1994–2000

Portfolio	Alpha (Annualized, %)	Sum All Beta
Aggregate hedge fund index	−4.45	0.84
Convertible arbitrage	−0.98	0.43
Event driven	−2.12	0.61
Equity market neutral	3.36	0.2
Fixed income arbitrage	−3.78	0.36
Long/short equity	−2.83	0.99
Emerging markets	−16.2	1.25
Global macro	−6.64	0.98
Managed futures	1.72	−0.19
Dedicated short bias	11.59	−1.27

Source: Adopted from Asness *et al.* (2001).

NOT JUST AN EXCUSE FOR HEDGE FUNDS

My obsession with absolute returns is not just a sop to hedge funds. In fact, I suspect that a large number of hedge funds are little more than leveraged long funds run by ex-traders who are punting the market. This doesn't strike me as fitting well with the idea of a carefully constructed equal long/short fund. However, we haven't been able to prove that this was the case. Asness *et al.* (2001)[5] examine the risk and value added characteristics of a large hedge fund universe. Their results are enlightening to say the least.

Table 20.3 shows that far too many hedge funds actually seem to have negative alpha, and have just been loading up on beta risk. They are effectively momentum players.

Hedge funds properly executed should be capable of generating the kind of alpha that we set out to identify in response to our client's question. However, beware of the existing funds, too many of which are leveraged long funds, and many of which are likely to explode in investors' faces.

TRULY ALTERNATIVE INVESTMENTS

The final area where it may still be possible to create alpha is in the realm of truly alternative assets. Having already professed a very limited knowledge of bonds, I can honestly claim to know even less about truly alternative asset classes, let alone how to go about investing in them. However, an interesting article in the *Journal of Alternative Investments* seems to make a good starting place for learning more about at least one of these alternative assets – timber.

Akers and Staub (2003) show that the total return to timber investment may be around 8%. Admittedly this obviously includes an illiquidity risk premium, and no pension fund is ever likely to invest a highly significant proportion of its funds into a highly illiquid asset. However, at 8% return this may yet be an attractive opportunity.

---

[5] Asness *et al.* (2001) point out that many funds hold difficult to price OTC securities or illquid assets. In order to account for these, they suggest using a lagged beta approach. So instead of using just the current market return, previous months' market returns are also included, and the beta summed over all its current and lagged values.

CONCLUSIONS

The future of fund management is changing. In part this will be reactionary, returning to the old days of balanced funds and wide-ranging mandates; and in part it will be revolutionary, with the death of passive investing and its poisonous cousin the benchmark. Absolute returns are likely to be the target, and fund managers will have to seek to create absolute alpha with the help of breaking the long-only constraint and being allowed to invest where they see the greatest opportunity.

21

Contrarian or Conformist?[*]

> Sir John Templeton once observed: "It is impossible to produce a superior per-
> formance unless you do something different from the majority." These wise words
> are often forgotten in a world obsessed with tracking-error, and where comfort is
> found in the herd. The biggest consensus portfolio bets seem to be small cap and
> low quality. So large cap, high quality looks like the better bet to us.

- Keynes opined, 'The central principle of investment is to go contrary to the general opinion, on the grounds that if everyone agreed about its merit, the investment is inevitably too dear and therefore unattractive.' This has always made excellent sense to us. However, today's investment market is better characterized by investors desperately trying not to underperform every quarter and fearing to go against the crowd.
- A recent paper by Dasgupta *et al.* (2006) shows that the stocks which institutional fund managers are busy buying are outperformed by the stocks they are busy selling! Over a two-year time horizon Dasgupta *et al.* found that, on average, the stocks that fund managers had bought most over the last five quarters underperformed the stocks they had sold most, by 17%! They found that this strategy worked for large and small caps, and value and growth stocks, so regardless of your universe, being a contrarian seems to make sense.
- So which are the big consensus trades at the moment? The most obvious is the love of risky assets. Our own fear and greed index is once again in the irrational exuberance territory. In the equity arena there has been a fascination with the lowest quality, junk equity. That has left high-quality stocks relatively cheap, which suggests that long high quality may be a good contrarian call.
- The fact that almost everyone seems bullish makes us nervous. All 12 strategists at the top US investment banks are bullish, and the Investors Intelligence survey shows nearly 60% bullish (a good contrarian indicator). Margin debt is back to the levels seen in 1990. Only the insiders seem cautious. They are selling out at near-record pace; in fact, according to a Bloomberg story, their "sales of stocks . . . exceeded purchases by the widest margin since 1987". This suggests that cash might well be the contrarian asset of choice.
- Baker and Wurgler (2006) showed in a classic paper that buying large, old, low-risk, highly profitable, dividend payers was generally a good idea when optimism was exceedingly high. This leads to our next contrarian view of long large caps, short small caps. The liquidity premium is negative, so by holding small caps you are paying for the pleasure of illiquidity.
- Our cheap country screen throws up Belgium, the UK, Netherlands, Spain, Norway and France as looking good value in the developed arena. Within the emerging market universe,

[*]This article appeared in *Global Equity Strategy* on 10 January 2007. The material discussed was accurate at the time of publication.

Thailand, Pakistan, Peru, Hungary, Korea and Turkey all look attractive. Among the sells, Japan, Hong Kong, Chile and China stand out.

- Of course, as Sir John Templeton noted, "To buy when others are despondently selling and to sell when others are greedily buying requires the greatest fortitude and pays the greatest rewards", but few will find this easy.

For the last couple of years, every January I have written a piece on the importance of being a contrarian – this year will be no exception. As Keynes opined, "The central principle of investment is to go contrary to the general opinion, on the grounds that if everyone agreed about its merit, the investment is inevitably too dear and therefore unattractive" or, as Sir John Templeton said, "It is impossible to produce a superior performance unless you do something different from the majority."

My view is very simple – an asset price reflects the sum of the market participants' views; as such, the consensus view is in the price. Now if the consensus is correct (and I don't think this occurs very often) then the investor gets the return embodied in the price (a 'fair' return, if you like). Of course, if markets were efficient then this would be the case for all investors all the time.

However, if markets aren't efficient, and investors are driven by fear and greed as much as by mean and variance, other approaches can add value. For instance, if we see a marked tendency to overreact to news, then one could either try to go with the flow (momentum) or bet on an eventual return to normality (contrarian strategies).

Moreover, in a world in which everyone is desperately trying to outperform each other, doing what everyone else is doing is unlikely to generate outperformance. This is brought home in a recent paper by Dasgupta *et al.* (2006). *They showed that the stocks institutional fund managers are busy buying are outperformed by the stocks they are busy selling!*

They examine US fund managers' filings from 1983 to 2004. Each quarter, stocks are assigned to different portfolios, conditional upon the persistence of institutional net trade (that is the number of consecutive quarters for which a net buy or a net sell is recorded). A persistence measure of −5 includes all stocks that have been sold for at least five quarters, and a persistence measure of 0 shows stocks that have been bought or sold in the current period.

Figure 21.1 shows the market-adjusted future returns for each persistence portfolio on a two-year time horizon. Even a cursory glance reveals the negative relationship between returns and institutional buying and selling. Over a two-year time horizon there is a 17% return difference – the stock that the institutions sold the most, outperforming the market by around 11%, and the stocks they purchased the most, underperforming by 6%!

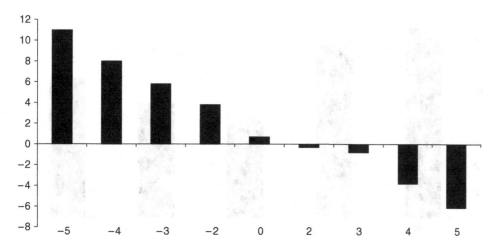

Figure 21.1   Abnormal returns over two years by buying persistence category (%).
Source: Dasgupta *et al.* (2006), DrKW Macro research.

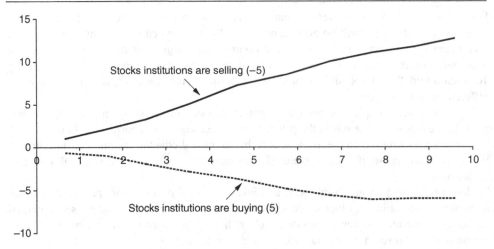

Figure 21.2 Abnormal returns by buying persistence category over time.
Source: Dasgupta *et al.* (2006), DrKW Macro research.

If 2 years is too long a horizon then Figure 21.2 shows the returns over time for the highest (−5) selling stocks and the highest bought stocks (5). On a one-year horizon the return differential is around 9%.

Interestingly, Dasgupta *et al.* found that this strategy works for large and small caps, and for value and growth stocks, so regardless of your universe, being a contrarian seems to pay dividends. (see Figures 21.3 and 21.4).

Dasgupta *et al.* also noted several characteristics of the stocks that fund managers seem to buy with high persistence. Such stocks tend to be liquid growth (low book to market) stocks with high momentum. Conversely, those that inhabit the selling portfolio are generally less liquid value stocks with poor past returns.

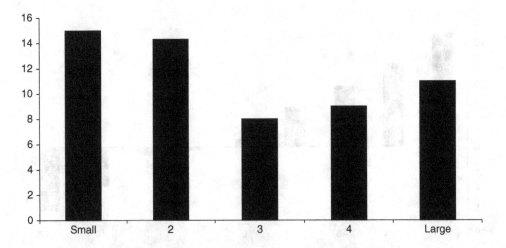

Figure 21.3 Abnormal returns over two years (long −5, short 5) by size category.
Source: Dasgupta *et al.* (2006), DrKW Macro research.

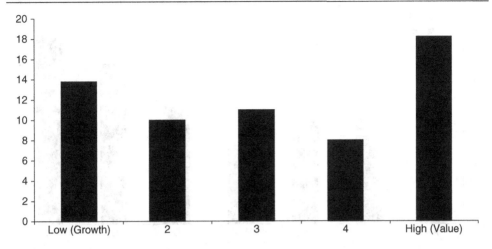

Figure 21.4 Abnormal returns over two years (long −5, short 5) by book to price category.
Source: Dasgupta *et al.* (2006), DrKW Macro research.

One final aspect of Dasgupta *et al.*'s work is noteworthy. They estimated a measure of how likely each manager is to herd (or conform, if you prefer). They called this measure the sheep index. They concluded, "We find that about three-quarters of institutions display conformist patterns when faced with high-persistence stocks . . . our measure of conformism is pervasive . . . with the majority of managers displaying a positive sheep value."

So it would appear that, as Keynes noted long ago, most fund managers accept that "worldly wisdom teaches us that it is better for reputation to fail conventionally than to succeed unconventionally."

At a more anecdotal level, how did our contrarian views from the beginning of last year pan out? As somebody witty once observed, "I'd rather be lucky than good". Last year was a lucky one from a contrarian perspective. Table 21.1 shows the positions suggested in last year's contrarian note (see *Global Equity Strategy*, 12 January 2006).

So where are the big consensus trades at the moment? The most obvious is the love of risky assets. In the equity arena there has been a fascination with the lowest quality, junk-like stocks. Figure 21.5 shows the performance of the US market, broken down and based around the Standard and Poor's quality rankings (on earnings and dividends) for the last quarter of 2006.

Table 21.1 Contrarian profits

Position	Return in 2006 (%)
Long value, short growth	9
Long large cap, short small cap	2
Long Europe, short US	19
Long World, Short Japan	9
Long cheap developed, short expensive developed	7
Long cheap emerging, short expensive emerging	38

Source: DrKW research.

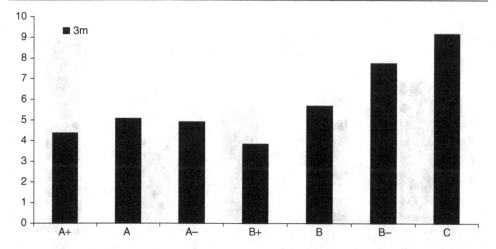

Figure 21.5   Last quarter 2006 US stock performance by quality ranking.
Source: DrKW Macro research.

As we have argued repeatedly, there is a relative value anomaly in the quality space. The highest quality stocks are the cheapest ones relative to their usual range, and the lowest quality stocks are most expensive relative to their historical averages. *This all suggests that long high quality is a good contrarian call.* Some of our clients and colleagues have questioned if this is truly a contrarian call, since it is a common theme among strategists. However, strategists don't control funds; prices and actions speak louder than words, and the price evidence shown above suggests that those who allocate funds are still enamoured with junk equity.

This is further supported by the overwhelming bullishness that is evident almost everywhere. For instance, Table 21.2 shows that all the strategists at top US banks appear to be bullish; on average, they are expecting a 10% rise in the S&P 500. Even the perennially bearish Richard Bernstein of Merrill Lynch appears to have turned bullish!

Table 21.2   US strategist's forecasts For S&P 500 (End Dec 06 = 1418)

Firm	Strategist	Target End 07
Bank of America	Thomas McManus	1465
Bear Stearns	Francois Trahan	1550
Citigroup	Tobias Levkovich	1600
Deutsche Bank	Binky Chadha	1540
Goldman Sachs	Abby Cohen	1550
JP Morgan Chase	A. Chakrabortti	1440
Merrill Lynch	R. Bernstein	1570
Morgan Stanley	Henry McVey	1525
Prudential	Edward Keon	1630
Strategas	Jason Trennert	1600
UBS	David Bianco	1500
Wachovia	Rod Smyth	1500
Average		1539

Source: DrKW Macro research.

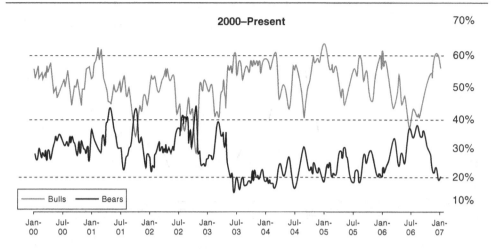

Figure 21.6 *Investors Intelligence* bulls and bears.
Source: Investors Intelligence, Market Harmonics, DrKW Macro research.

The *Investors Intelligence* measure of sentiment also shows a remarkably high level of bulls relative to bears. The current reading of around 57% bulls and 20% bears is a potential warning sign (see Figure 21.6).

Our own fear and greed index is once again in the irrational exuberance territory, suggesting that investors are pricing assets without any regard to the risk inherent within them (see Figure 21.7).

Margin debt levels are also extraordinarily high. In fact, it has now reached the same level as it did in 2000 (see Figure 21.8). However, insiders are selling out at an amazing pace. Through most of last year the ratio of insider sales to purchases was nearly 11-to-1. In November

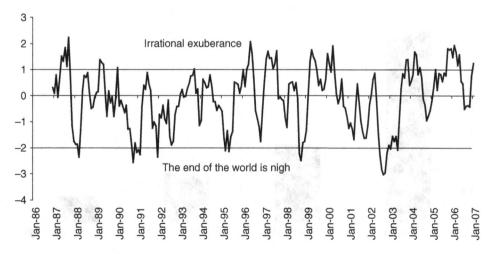

Figure 21.7 Our fear and greed index.
Source: DrKW Macro research.

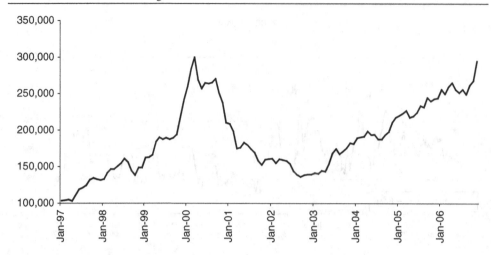

Figure 21.8   Net margin debt ($million).
Source: DrKW Macro research.

last year this soared to 35-to-1. Indeed according to one Bloomberg story, "Stock sales by America's corporate chieftains exceeded purchases by the widest margin since 1987"!

This all stacks up to a disturbing picture of general enthusiasm for equities, and leads us to our second contrarian call: *overweight cash*. As Sir John Templeton said, "The time of maximum pessimism is the best time to buy, and time of maximum optimism is the best time to sell."

Figure 21.9 looks at 12-month ahead excess returns over cash by sentiment reading from our fear and greed index. When sentiment is very low (below −2) the excess returns over the next 12 months are around 13%. When sentiment is very high (above 0.9) the excess return

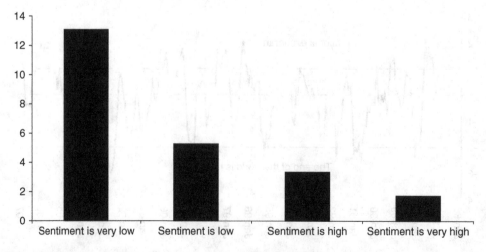

Figure 21.9   Excess returns over next 12 months by sentiment category (%).
Source: DrKW Macro research.

Table 21.3 Sorts based on characteristics and sentiment (% return over the next 12 months)

Characteristic	Sentiment is High			Sentiment is Low		
	Decile 10	Decile 1	Difference (10-1)	Decile 10	Decile 1	Difference (10-1)
Size	11.8	8.8	3.0	11.0	28.4	−17.4
Age	13.3	3.0	10.3	14.9	21.2	−6.4
Variance of returns	3.6	17.3	−13.7	28.9	12.1	16.8
Profitability	11.2	4.2	7.0	18.8	31.1	−12.2
Dividend payers	13.8	5.3	8.5	14.2	27.8	−13.7

Source: Baker and Wurgler (2006). DrKW Macro research.

Table 21.4 Guide to equity characteristics

	Decile 10	Decile 1
Size	Large	Small
Age	Old	Young
Variance of returns	Risky	Low risk
Profitability	Highly profitable	Unprofitable
Dividend payers	Dividend payers	Non-dividend payers

Source: DrKW Macro research.

is a mere 1.7% – well below any reasonable measure of the equity risk premium. So it would appear that when sentiment is high you are simpy not compensated for the risk of holding equities.

Sentiment is also useful when it comes to stock selection. In the past we have referred to a study by Baker and Wurgler (2006) who investigated stock performance when sentiment was high and low. Their results are summarized in Tables 21.3 and 21.4.

They concluded that when sentiment is high (i.e. optimistic) then investors should concentrate on old, low-risk, profitable, dividend-paying stocks (i.e. the quality stocks). Whereas when sentiment is low (pessimistic) then investors should buy small cap, youthful, low-profitability, non-dividend-paying equities (i.e. the junk stocks). Given the above, this again suggests that now is the time to be buying high-quality stocks.

This work also leads us onto our next contrarian viewpoint (a roll-over from one of our positions last year): *long large caps, short small caps.* The liquidity premium is still negative; that is to say, small caps are still trading at a significant premium to large caps, so effectively investors are paying for the pleasure of holding illiquid stocks. This doesn't seem to be very sensible.

Figure 21.10 shows the Graham and Dodd PE (5-year moving average for earnings) for the US large and small caps. It clearly shows the madness of the current juncture, with the small caps trading at 29× and the large caps trading at 25×.

Andy Lapthorne has recently provided another way of looking at this. He breaks the market down into deciles, each one containing an equal amount of market cap, so the top decile contains the top 10% of the market (around six stocks), while the bottom decile contains around 295 stocks. Figure 21.11 makes it transparently obvious that it is the largest stocks that are on the lowest forward PEs, while the smallest stocks are considerably more expensive, so the real value seems to lie in the mega caps.

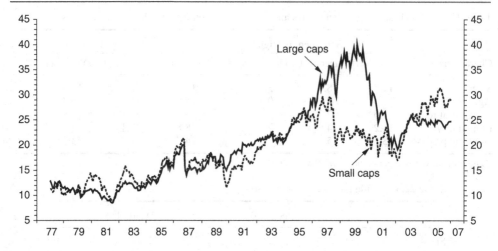

Figure 21.10   US large and small cap Graham and Dodd PEs.
Source: DrKW Macro research.

In terms of styles, we continue to favour value. Last year, many were itching to rotate into growth. We suspect that this urge remains unquenched. However, the empirical work we have done shows that style rotation is not often profitable without perfect foresight (sadly lacking among all investors). As such *maintaining a value bias* seems better placed to provide a sensible margin of safety.

There is little that stands out in terms of country selection. Often we find a large consensus over country selection; however, there are few obvious areas of agreement at the current juncture. The surveys show that Japan and Europe are the most favoured, with emerging markets and the UK as the least favoured. We ran a long emerging market position last year;

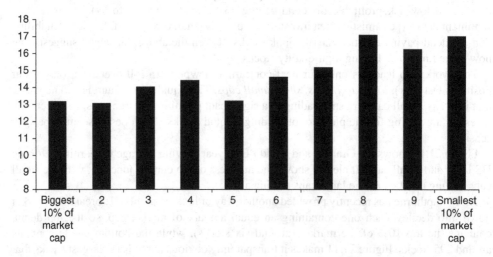

Figure 21.11   Global market: 12m forward PE by size decile.
Source: DrKW Macro research.

however, the valuation gap has been rapidly narrowing. In general, we see no particularly significant country opportunities from a contrarian perspective.

Instead we will rely on value-oriented country screen to aid with global equity market selection (see *Global Equity Strategy*, 30 April 2003 and 12 January 2005). Based on this simple value screen, Belgium, the UK, the Netherlands, Spain, Norway and France all look attractive, while Japan, New Zealand, Switzerland, Hong Kong, Denmark and Austria look relatively expensive.

Among the emerging markets, Thailand, Pakistan, Peru, Hungary, Korea and Turkey look relatively cheap. On the expensive side we find Chile, India, Morocco, Sri Lanka, China and the Czech Republic.

Looking at this list of potential buys I have no doubt that many investors will recoil, arguing that such markets are cheap for a myriad of perfectly sensible reasons. Norway, for instance, will be dismissed as an oil play – which no doubt it is, but a cheap play nonetheless.

When considering contrarian positions, investors might do well to remember one final piece of advice from Sir John Templeton: "To buy when others are despondently selling and to sell when others are greedily buying requires the greatest fortitude and pays the greatest rewards." But, of course, as Keynes noted, it isn't easy "for it is the essence of his behaviour that he should be eccentric, unconventional and rash in the eyes of average opinion. If he is successful, that will only confirm the general belief in his rashness; and if in the short run he is unsuccessful, which is very likely, he will not receive much mercy."

22

Painting by Numbers: An Ode to Quant*

What could baseball, wine-pricing, medical diagnosis, university admissions, criminal recidivism and I have in common? They are examples of simple quant models consistently outperforming so-called experts. Why should financial markets be any different? So why aren't there more quant funds? Hubristic self-belief, self-serving bias and inertia combine to maintain the status quo.

- There is now an overwhelming amount of data to suggest that in many environments, simple quant models significantly outperform human (expert) judgements. For instance, in their study of over 130 different papers, covering decision-making contexts as wide-ranging as occupational choice to the diagnosis of heart attacks, Grove *et al.* located a mere eight studies that found in favour of human judgements over the quant models.
- All eight of these studies had one thing in common. The humans participants had access to information not available to the quant models. Where quant models and humans had the same information set, the models performed much better. Across the full range of papers that Grove *et al.* examined, the average human participant had a 66.5% accuracy rating, whereas the quant models had an average hit ratio of 73.2%.
- Even when the human participants were given access to the quant models' results as an input for them to use if they chose, they still managed to underperform the models. This is an important point. One of the most common responses to quant superiority is that surely this could be a base for qualitative improvements by skilled users. However, the evidence is clear: quant models usually provide a ceiling (from which we detract performance) rather than a floor (on which we can build performance). We tend to overweight our own opinions relative to those of the models.
- The good news is that, in some fields, quant models have become relatively accepted. For instance, over half the states in the USA use a quant model when considering parole for convicts. However, in finance a quant approach is far from common. Those that do pursue a quant path tend to be rocket scientist uber-geeks. Once in a while a fairly normal 'quant' fund comes to light. Two explicitly behavioural-based funds stand out in my mind – LSV and Fuller & Thaler. Both have admirable track records in terms of outperformance. While this is far from conclusive proof of the superiority of quant, it is a step in the right direction.
- So why don't we see more quant funds in the market? The first reason is overconfidence. We all think we can add something to a quant model. However, the quant model has the advantage of a known error rate, while our own error rate remains unknown. Secondly, self-serving bias kicks in – after all, what kind of mess would our industry be in if 18 out of

*This article appeared in *Global Equity Strategy* on 2 August 2006. The material discussed was accurate at the time of publication.

every 20 of us were replaced by computers. Thirdly, inertia plays a part. It is hard to imagine a large fund management firm turning around and scrapping most of the process they have used for the last 20 years. Finally, quant is often a much harder sell, terms like 'black box' get bandied around, and consultants may question why they are employing you at all, if 'all' you do is turn up and crank the handle of the model. It is for reasons like these that quant investing will remain a fringe activity, no matter how successful it may appear.

Don't worry dear reader, there will be no gratuitous use of poetry in this missive, despite the title – I promise. However, pause for a moment and consider what baseball, wine, medical diagnosis, university admissions, criminal recidivism and I might have in common.

The answer is that they all represent realms where simple statistical models have outperformed so-called experts. Long-time readers of *Global Equity Strategy* may recall that a few years ago I designed a tactical asset allocation tool based on a combination of valuation and momentum. At first this model worked just fine, generating signals in line with my own bearish disposition. However, after a few months, the model started to output bullish signals. I chose to override the model, assuming that I knew much better than it did (despite the fact that I had both designed it and back-tested it to prove it worked). Of course, much to my chagrin and to the amusement of many readers, I spent about 18 months being thrashed in performance terms by my own model. This is only anecdotal (and economist George Stigler once opined "The plural of anecdote is data"), but it sets the scene for the studies to which I now turn.

NEUROSIS OR PSYCHOSIS?

The first study I want to discuss is a classic in the field. It centres on the diagnosis of whether someone is neurotic or psychotic. A patient suffering psychosis has lost touch with the external world; whereas someone suffering neurosis is in touch with the external world but suffering from internal emotional distress, which may be immobilizing. The treatments for the two conditions are very different, so the diagnosis is not one to be taken lightly.

The standard test to distinguish the two is the Minnesota Multiphasic Personality Inventory (MMPI). This consists of around 600 statements with which the patient must express either agreement or disagreement. The statements range from "At times I think I am no good at all" to "I like mechanics magazines". Fairly obviously, those feeling depressed are much more likely to agree with the first statement than those in an upbeat mood. More bizarrely, those suffering paranoia are more likely to enjoy mechanics magazines than the rest of us!

Lewis Goldberg (1968) obtained access to more than 1000 patients' MMPI test responses and final diagnoses as neurotic or psychotic. He developed a simple statistical formula, based on 10 MMPI scores, to predict the final diagnosis. His model was roughly 70% accurate when applied out of sample.

Goldberg then gave MMPI scores to experienced and inexperienced clinical psychologists and asked them to diagnose the patient. As Figure 22.1 shows, the simple quant rule significantly outperformed even the best of the psychologists.

Even when the results of the rules' predictions were made available to the psychologists, they still underperformed the model. This is a very important point: much as we all like to think we can add something to the quant model output, the truth is that very often quant models represent a ceiling in performance (from which we detract) rather than a floor (to which we can add).

Every so often, and always with the aid of a member of the quant team, I publish a quant note in *Global Equity Strategy*. The last one was based on the little book that beats the market (see *Global Equity Strategy*, 9 March 2006). When we produce such a note, the standard response from fund managers is to ask for a list of stocks that the model would suggest. I cannot help but wonder if the findings above apply here as well. Do the fund managers who receive the lists then pick the ones they prefer, much like the psychologists above selectively using the Goldberg rule as an input?

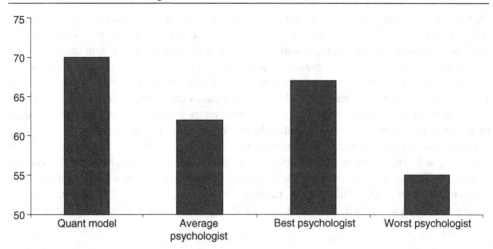

Figure 22.1   Hit rate for diagnosis (%).
Source: DrKW Macro research.

BRAIN DAMAGE DETECTION

Similar findings were reported by Leli and Filskov (1981) in the realm of assessing intellectual deficit due to brain damage. They studied progressive brain dysfunction and derived a simple rule based on standard tests of intellectual functioning. This model correctly identified 83% of new (out of sample) cases.

However, groups of inexperienced and experienced professionals working from the same data underperformed the model with only 63% and 58% accuracy respectively (that isn't a typo; the inexperienced did better than the experienced!). When given the output from the model the scores improved to 68% and 75% respectively – still both significantly below the accuracy rate of the model. Intriguingly, the improvement appeared to depend on the extent of the use of the model (see Figure 22.2).

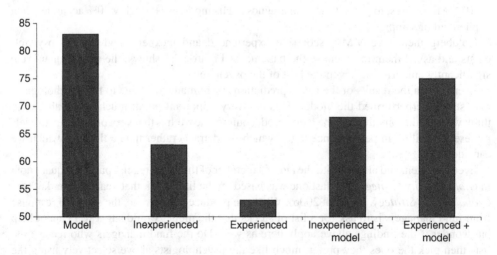

Figure 22.2   Hit rate for diagnosis (%).
Source: DrKW Macro research.

UNIVERSITY ADMISSIONS

Dawes (1989) gives a great example of the impotence of interviews (further bolstering our arguments as to the pointlessness of meeting company managements: see 'The seven sins of fund management,' *Global Equity Strategy*, November 2005).

In 1979, the Texas legislature required the University of Texas to increase its intake of medical students from 150 to 200. The prior 150 had been selected by first examining the academic credentials of approximately 2200 students, and then selecting the highest 800. These 800 were called for an interview by the admissions committee and one other faculty member. At the conclusion of the interview, each member of the committee ranked the interviewee on a scale of 0 (unacceptable) to 7 (excellent). These rankings were then averaged to give each applicant a score.

The 150 applicants who went to Texas were all in the top 350, as ranked by the interview procedure. When the school was told to add another 50 students, all that were available were those ranked between 700 and 800, and 86% of this sample had failed to get into any medical school at all.

No one within the academic staff was told which students had come from the first selection or which had come from the second. Robert DeVaul and colleagues (1957) decided to track the performance of the two groups at various stages – i.e. the end of the second year, the end of the clinical rotation (fourth year) and after their first year of residency.

The results they obtained showed no difference between the two groups at any point in time; they were exactly equal at all stages. For instance, 82% of each group were granted the MD degree, and the proportion granted honours was constant, etc. The obvious conclusion: the interview served absolutely no useful function at all.

CRIMINAL RECIDIVISM

Between October 1977 and May 1987, 1035 convicts became eligible for parole in Pennsylvania. They were interviewed by a parole specialist who assigned them a score on a 5-point scale based on the prognosis for supervision, risk of future crime, etc. Of these cases, 743 were then put before a parole board; and 85% of those appearing before the board were granted parole, the decisions (bar one) following the recommendation of the parole specialist.

Of the parolees, 25% were recommitted to prison, absconded, or arrested for another crime within the year. The parole board had predicted none of these. Carroll *et al.* (1988) compared the accuracy of prediction from the parole board's ranking, with that of a prediction based on a three-factor model driven by the type of offence, the number of past convictions and the number of violations of prison rules. The parole board's ranking was correlated 6% with recidivism. The three-factor model had a correlation of 22%.

BORDEAUX WINE

So far we have tackled some fairly heavy areas of social importance. Now for something lighter. In 1995, a classic quant model was revealed to the world: a pricing equation for Bordeaux wine!

Ashenfelter *et al.* (1995) computed a simple equation based on just four factors: the age of the vintage, the average temperature over the growing season (April–September), rain in September and August, and the rain during the months preceding the vintage (October–March). This model could explain 83% of the variation of the prices of Bordeaux wines.

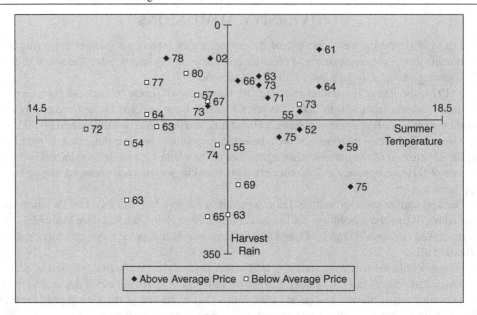

Figure 22.3 Bordeaux 1952–1980, summer temperature and harvest rain related to price.
Source: Ashenfelter *et al.* (1995).

Ashenfelter *et al.* also uncovered that young wines are usually overpriced relative to what one would expect based on the weather and the price of old wines (Figure 22.3). As the wine matures, prices converge to the predictions of the equation. This implies that "bad" vintages are overpriced when they are young, and "good" vintages may be underpriced.

Table 22.1 shows the basic pattern. It shows the price of a portfolio of wines from each vintage relative to the (simple average) price of the portfolio of wines from the 1961, 62, 64 and 66 vintages. The second column gives the value of the benchmark portfolio in GBP. The entries for each of the vintages in the remaining columns are simply the ratios of the prices of the wines in each vintage to the benchmark portfolio. The predicted price from the equation is also shown. Incidentally, this data is from a different sample than the original estimation of the equation, so it amounts to an out of sample test.[1]

PURCHASING MANAGERS

Professor Chris Snijders has been examining the behaviour of models versus purchasing managers.[2] He has examined purchasing managers at 300 different organizations and concludes

> We find that (a) judgments of professional managers are meagre at best, and (b) certainly not better than the judgments by less experienced managers or even amateurs. Furthermore, (c) neither general nor specific human capital of managers has an impact on their performance, and (d) a simple formula outperforms the average (and the above average) manager even when the formula only has half of the information as compared to the manager.

---

[1] For those with an interest, Ashenfelter publishes a newsletter called liquid asset.
[2] http://www.tue-tm.org/snijders/home/.

Table 22.1 Price per case of a portfolio of Bordeaux relative to benchmark portfolio

Year of Sale	Bench-mark Portfolio (£)	Vintage											
		1961	1962	1963	1964	1965	1966	1967	1968	1969	1970	1971	1972
1971	54	1.66	0.79	0.41	0.76	0.27	0.79	0.77					
1972	97	1.58	0.76	0.26	0.70	0.24	0.96	0.62		0.75			
1973	119	1.62	0.71	0.28	0.74		0.93	0.78	0.28	0.70	0.83		
1974	85	1.31	0.77	0.39	0.84		1.08	0.57	0.30	0.70	0.88		0.30
1975	76	1.65	0.77	0.29	0.78	0.35	0.80	0.51	0.31	0.41	0.84		0.44
1976	109	1.67	0.83	0.30	0.65	0.29	0.85	0.50	0.23	0.36	0.69	0.61	
1977	165	1.67	0.83	0.26	0.63	0.26	0.87	0.45	0.23	0.36	0.70	0.54	0.32
1978	215	1.67	0.76	0.26	0.65	0.18	0.91	0.49	0.25	0.31	0.70	0.51	0.25
1979	274	1.61	0.73	0.20	0.66	0.23	1.00	0.47	0.24	0.29	0.71	0.53	0.23
1981	296	1.75	0.62	0.22	0.70	0.04	0.93	0.39	0.25	0.29	0.82	0.50	0.22
1982	420	1.80	0.71	0.15	0.60	0.18	0.89	0.36	0.17	0.24	0.77	0.52	0.19
1983	586	1.77	0.53	0.10	0.59	0.18	1.11	0.30	0.18	0.21	0.91	0.55	0.20
1985	952	2.19	0.53	0.12	0.50	0.21	0.78	0.30	0.11	0.14	0.68	0.48	0.13
1986	888	2.10	0.56	0.25	0.54	0.17	0.80	0.32	0.15	0.19	0.65	0.46	0.14
1987	901	2.11	0.56		0.53		0.80	0.34	0.19	0.20	0.64	0.49	0.18
1988	854	2.01	0.56	0.21	0.61	0.14	0.82	0.27	0.23	0.20	0.67	0.58	0.17
1989	1048	2.09	0.61	0.28	0.53	0.19	0.77		0.24	0.18	0.66	0.43	0.15
Predicted price		**1.74**	**0.72**	**0.29**	**0.76**	**0.16**	**0.78**	**0.49**	**0.21**	**0.29**	**0.60**	**0.53**	**0.14**

Source: Ashenfelter *et al.* (1995).

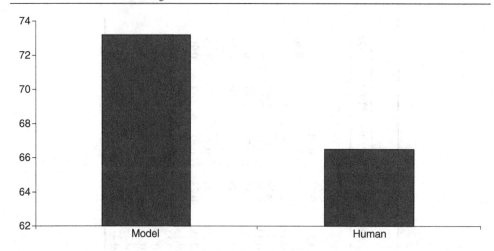

Figure 22.4   Hit rate across studies (%).
Source: DrKW Macro research.

META-ANALYSIS

Enough already, you may cry.[3] I agree. But, to conclude, let me show you that the range of evidence I've presented here is not somehow a biased selection designed to prove my point.

Grove *et al.* (2000) considered an impressive 136 studies of simple quant models versus human judgements. The range of studies covered areas as diverse as criminal recidivism to occupational choice, diagnosis of heart attacks to academic performance. Across these studies, 64 clearly favoured the model, 64 showed approximately the same result between the model and human judgement, and a mere eight studies found in favour of human judgements. All of these eight shared one trait in common: the humans had more information than the quant models. If the quant models had had the same information it is highly likely they would have outperformed.

Figure 22.4 shows the aggregate average 'hit' rate across the 136 studies that Grove *et al.* examined. The average person in the study (remember they were all specialists in their respective fields) were correct in 66.5% of the cases with which they were presented. However, the quant models did significantly better with an average hit ratio of 73.2%.

As Paul Meehl (one of the founding fathers of the importance of quant models versus human judgements) wrote:

> There is no controversy in social science which shows such a large body of qualitatively diverse studies coming out so uniformly in the same direction as this one ... predicting everything from the outcomes of football games to the diagnosis of liver disease and when you can hardly come up with a half a dozen studies showing even a weak tendency in favour of the clinician, it is time to draw a practical conclusion.

---

[3] For those wondering about the mention baseball at the beginning this wasn't a red herring ... Michael Lewis' book Moneyball is a great example of the triumph of statistics over judgement.

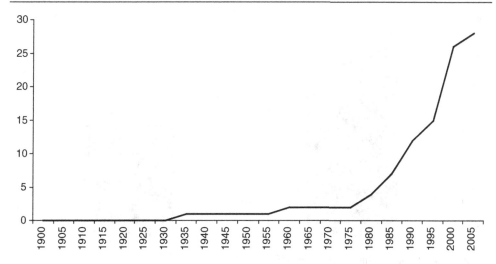

Figure 22.5   Number of states using a quant parole input.
Source: Harcourt (2006).

THE GOOD NEWS

The good news is that in some fields quant models have become far more accepted. For instance, Figure 22.5 shows the number of states in which the decision to parole has a quant prediction instrument involved.

However, in the field of finance most still shy away from an explicit quant process. A few brave souls have gone down this road, and two explicitly behavioural finance groups stand out as using an explicitly quantitative process – LSV and Fuller & Thaler. Figure 22.6 shows the performance of their funds relative to benchmark since inception. With only one exception all of these funds have delivered very significant positive alpha. Now, of course, this doesn't

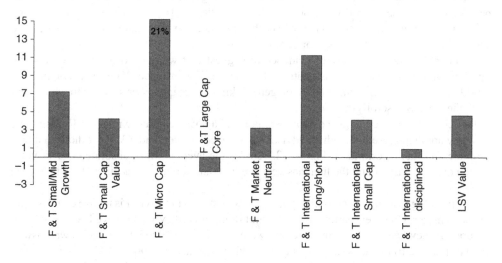

Figure 22.6   Performance versus benchmark since inception (% p.a.).
Source: DrKW Macro research.

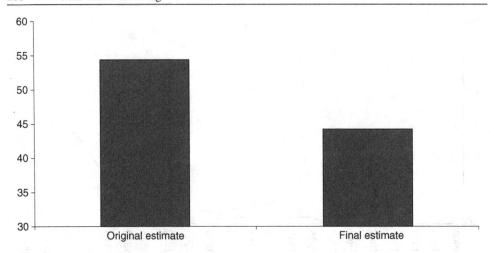

Figure 22.7   Mean absolute error (in years).
Source: DrKW Macro research.

prove that quant investing is superior; I would need a much larger sample to draw any valid conclusions. But it is a nice illustration of the point I suspect is true.

SO WHY NOT QUANT?

The most likely answer is overconfidence. We all think that we know better than simple models. My own confession at the start of this chapter is a prime example of such hubris. The key to the quant model's performance is that it has a known error rate, whereas our error rates are unknown.

The most common response to these findings is to argue that surely a fund manager should be able to use quant as an input, but still have the flexibility to override the model when appropriate. However, as mentioned above, the evidence suggests that quant models tend to act as a ceiling rather than a floor for our behaviour.

Additionally, there is plenty of evidence to suggest that we tend to overweight our own opinions and experiences against statistical evidence. For instance, Yaniv and Kleinberger (2000) have a clever experiment based on general knowledge questions such as: In which year were the Dead Sea scrolls discovered?

Participants are asked to give a point estimate and a 95% confidence interval. Having done this they are then presented with an adviser's suggested answer, and asked for their final best estimate and rate of estimates. Figure 22.7 shows the average mean absolute error in years for the original answer and the final answer. The final answer is more accurate than the initial guess.

The most logical way of combining your view with that of the adviser is to give equal weight to each answer. However, participants were not doing this (they would have been even more accurate if they had done so). Instead they were putting a 71% weight on their own answer. In over half the trials the weight on their own view was actually 90–100%! This represents egocentric discounting – the weighing of one's own opinions is much more important than another's view.

Similarly, Simonsohn *et al.* (2004) showed that, in a series of experiments, direct experience is frequently much more heavily weighted than general experience, even if the information is equally relevant and objective. They note, "If people use their direct experience to assess the likelihood of events, they are likely to overweight the importance of unlikely events that have occurred to them, and to underestimate the importance of these that have not." In fact, in one of their experiments, Simonsohn *et al.* found that personal experience was weighted twice as heavily as vicarious experience! This is an uncannily close estimate to that obtained by Yaniv and Kleinberger in an entirely different setting.

Grove and Meehl (1996) suggest many possible reasons for ignoring the evidence presented in this chapter; two in particular stand out as relevant to our discussion. Firstly, the fear of technological unemployment. This is obviously an example of a self-serving bias. If, say, 18 out of every 20 analysts and fund managers could be replaced by a computer, the results are unlikely to be welcomed by the industry at large.

Secondly, the industry has a large dose of inertia contained within it. It is pretty inconceivable that a large fund management house would say they are scrapping most of the processes they had used for the last 20 years, in order to implement a quant model.

Another consideration may be the ease of selling. We find it 'easy' to understand the idea of analysts searching for value, and fund managers rooting out hidden opportunities. However, selling a quant model will be much harder. The term 'black box' will be bandied around in a highly pejorative way. Consultants may question why they are employing you at all, if 'all' you do is turn up and run the model, then walk away again.

It is for reasons like these that quant investing is likely to remain a fringe activity, no matter how successful it may be.

23

The Perfect Value Investor[*]

> Once in a while, someone will ask me how I would structure an investment process (mad fools, I know). I'm still thinking about the answer, but can provide a partial solution by examining the behavioural characteristics of some of the world's best value managers. We find they appear to share six key traits, all of which stem from their investment philosophy.

- What is it that distinguishes the best value investors from the rest? Most obviously it is an undying adherence to their deeply-held value principles: an unwillingness to stray from the path set down by Ben Graham. These principles give rise to six traits that the best value managers seem to share.
- Firstly, they all hold highly concentrated portfolios. Across the 10 funds we examine, the average number of companies in the portfolio is around 35 (and this is bloated by the inclusion of a couple of international value funds – among the domestic funds the average holding is closer to 20 companies). In contrast, the average US domestic mutual fund holds around 160 stocks!
- Secondly, they are not obsessed with noise and do not worry about trying to know everything about everything. The funds examined do not employ legions of analysts to waste time forecasting next quarter's EPS. Instead, they try to focus on understanding the valuation and its associated risks. By risks, these managers mean concerns surrounding the outlook for profit margins and balance sheets, not the price volatility of the market.
- Thirdly, on average they display a willingness to hold cash in the face of a lack of investment opportunities. Much like the concentrated portfolios, this decision stems from the core philosophy. If they cannot find bottom-up bargains, they are happy to hold cash until they can. Right now, across the 10 funds we examine, their average cash level is 11%, nearly three times greater than the average mutual fund.
- Fourthly, our value investor groups have long time horizons. Their average holding period is 5 years. The maximum is 17 years, the shortest 3 years. In contrast, the average US mutual fund has a holding period of just one year. At such a time horizon, investing becomes speculation, purely a punt on a stock price rising.
- Penultimately, these managers accept that they will have bad years. Tweedy Browne published a study showing that a group of value managers with excellent track records underperformed the index some 30–40% of the time. One manager went as far as to say, "I would rather lose half my shareholders than half my shareholders' money".

---

*This article appeared in *Global Equity Strategy* on 8 June 2006. The material discussed was accurate at the time of publication.

- Finally, unusually in a world where asset managers are often paid with respect to assets under management, these managers are not afraid to close their funds to new money. The managers in our group are highly cognisant that there are limits to the size of funds they are capable of running without hitting problems. These managers still have a sense of fiduciary responsibility.

Table 23.1   Goldfarb's tried and tested value fund
selection

Clipper	Oakmark Select
FPA Capital	Longleaf Partners
First Eagle Gold	Legg Mason Value
Oak Value	Tweedy Browne American Value
Mutual Beacon	

Source: Lowenstein (2004).

Occasionally when I present on the seven sins of fund management, someone at the end (obviously a valiant soul who has managed to stay awake) will ask me how I would structure an investment process. In the spirit of good politicians everywhere, I am going to save my answer to that question for another time. However, I recently read a paper along similar lines that I thought was worth sharing.

Louis Lowenstein (2004) of Columbia University examined 10 value managers selected by Bob Goldfarb, CEO of Sequoia Fund. Lowenstein asked him to select 10 dyed-in-the-wool value investors who all followed the essential edicts of Graham and Dodd; obligingly, Goldfarb selected the list presented in Table 23.1.[1] To this list we have added a second Tweedy Browne fund, Tweedy Browne Global Value.

This may not be the most scientific of approaches, but nonetheless should allow us to draw out some of the characteristic behaviours of some of the best value investors. We have updated and extended Lowenstein's work. Table 23.2 shows the funds and some of their key characteristics.

TRAIT I: HIGH CONCENTRATION IN PORTFOLIOS

Contrary to the proclamations of classical finance, these investors tend to run highly concentrated portfolios. No portfolio diversification for these guys. Tracking error has little or no meaning to this group of investors.

Across these funds, on average, nearly 40% of the assets are in the top 10 holdings. Across a wide universe of funds, the top 10 holdings account for only around 10% of assets. The average number of stocks held is around 35 (and this is raised by the presence of three international funds, it would be closer to 20 for the domestic-only funds). In contrast, the average US domestic mutual fund holds around 160 stocks!

This seems to reflect a different philosophy on two counts. Firstly, these value managers seem to need a reason to invest – not investing is their default, so in order to actually go out and buy a stock, these investors need to be convinced of the merits. Presumably in accordance with Graham and Dodd's guiding principles, this is represented by a margin of safety. As Graham wrote,

> The margin of safety is the central concept of investment. A true margin of safety is one that can be demonstrated by figures, by persuasive reasoning and by reference to a body of actual experience.

Secondly, the average fund management outfit appears to be run either by the risk management department or the marketing department. I've come across several examples of this in the

---

[1] Yes I know there are only nine in the list, the other fund was a closed end mutual fund rather than a mutual fund.

Table 23.2 Characteristic traits of the best value managers

	Turnover Rate (%)	% of Assets in the Top Ten Holdings	Cash Level (%)	10-year Performance (% pa)	Relative to Benchmark
Clipper	13	56.48	4.5	11.75	5.0
FPA Capital	26	37.18	38.6	13.71	7.0
First Eagle Global	12	21.53	16.6	13.81	9.2
Mutual Beacon	35	21.37	10.0	–	–
Oak Value	29	57.6	2	8.98	2.3
Oakmark Select	16	25.12	5	13.0	6.3
Longleaf Partners	17	58.06	2.8	12.7	6.0
Legg Mason Value	13	43	1.1	13.2	6.5
Tweedy Browne American Value	9	42.07	12.6	8.73	2.0
Tweedy Browne Global Value	6	25.53	19.5	11.99	7.4
Average	**17.6**	**38.8**	**11.3**	**12.0**	**5.7**

Source: DrKW Macro research.

last few years. One client was relaying to me the joys of his risk managers telling him that he had to deploy more risk, because he was under his risk budget! Of course, when markets fall, those very same risk managers with their trailing correlation and volatility, will be the first in line to tell you to sell your positions. Risk managers are the financial equivalent of those who give out umbrellas on dry days, but snatch them back as soon as it starts to rain.

Another informed me that they were setting up a commodity fund, because the marketing department said there was an appetite for such a product. Does this not strike anyone as vaguely (and perhaps alarmingly) like the TMT bubble?

The result of these bizarre dynamics is that the average fund manager is more worried about tracking error and benchmark risk, than about finding the best investment for his clients. So their default is likely to be ownership. Hence they need a good reason *not* to invest in a stock. The fiduciary responsibility to the client is forced to take a back seat. Perhaps investment managers should take an equivalent of the Hippocratic Oath to do no harm.

As is often the case, Maynard Keynes sided with the value investors. In a letter to F.C. Scott, 6 February 1942 (*The collected writings of John Maynard Keynes*), he wrote:

> To suppose that safety-first consists in having a small gamble in a large number of different companies where I have no information to reach a good judgement, as compared with a substantial stake in a company where one's information is adequate, strikes me as a travesty of investment policy.

This was a view shared by Loeb in his classic, *The Battle for Investment Survival*. He opined, 'Diversification is an admission of not knowing what to do, and an effort to strike an average.'

It should be noted that concentrated portfolios are not, in and of themselves, a deliberate choice on the part of these funds, but rather stem from their investment discipline. There simply aren't very many good value opportunities to be found. The Brandes Institute (2004) published a paper exploring the use of concentrated portfolios. They concluded, 'In aggregate, and across peer groups, we find that concentrated portfolios, in and of themselves, do not provide improved returns, nor do they provide improved volatility-adjusted returns'. This

Table 23.3   Fortune 10: A buy-and-forget
portfolio

Broadcom ($30)	Nokia ($20.52)
Charles Schwab ($16.18)	Nortel Networks ($2.17)
Enron	Oracle ($13.54)
Genentech ($78.09)	Univision ($35.75)
Morgan Stanley ($59.14)	Viacom ($37.04)

Source: Fortune.

emphasizes the fact that the concentration among our group of value investors is the result of a process rather than a deliberate decision in its own right.

A graphic illustration of this point can be seen by examining the performance of a basket of stocks that Fortune assembled in the year 2000. The basket was labelled "10 stocks to last the decade – here's a buy-and-forget portfolio". The aim of the stocks was to allow you to "retire when ready", according to Lowenstein. The list of companies is shown in Table 23.3. Only one of these stocks had a PE of less than 50-fold!

The performance of this basket is shown in Figure 23.1. At least Fortune got one thing right – it was a portfolio to forget! It is still down around 40% from the time at which Fortune suggested its purchase. A prime example of what Ben Graham would have described as a permanent loss of capital.

The investors in our value group focus themselves upon business risk (Will profit margins shrink? Are there risks on the balance sheet?) rather than market risk (stock volatility), which these investors seem to treat with the scorn it deserves. They know that the market as a whole is best characterized as suffering bipolar disorder (the proper name for manic depression). As Ben Graham wrote:

> One of your partners, named Mr Market, is very obliging, indeed. Everyday he tells you what he thinks your interest is worth and furthermore offers either to buy you out or sell you an additional

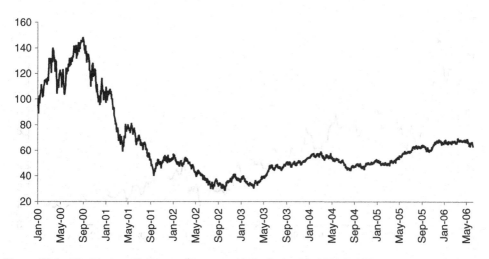

Figure 23.1   The Fortune 10: Buy and forget portfolio (Index Jan 2000 = 100).
Source: DrKW Macro research.

interest on that basis. Sometimes his idea of value appears plausible and justified by business developments and prospects as you know them. Often, on the other hand, Mr Market lets his enthusiasm or fears run away with him, and the value he proposes seems to you a little short of silly.

TRAIT II: THEY DON'T NEED TO KNOW EVERYTHING, AND DON'T GET CAUGHT IN THE NOISE

The investors in this group seem to be aware of the need to focus on a few key items of information, rather than attempting to try to overload themselves with noise. Lowenstein quotes Marty Whitman of the Third Avenue Value Fund as saying, 'the fund doesn't have superior information; "the trick" is to use publicly available information in a superior manner'. To this end, these funds don't employ legions of analysts wasting time forecasting next quarter's EPS; instead, they spend their time trying to understand the valuation and associated risks.

TRAIT III: A WILLINGNESS TO HOLD CASH

Their willingness to hold cash is clearly visible from a cursory glance at Table 23.2. Currently they hold around 11% cash, nearly 3 times the level held in the average US mutual fund. The average hides a wide range of current cash levels. For instance, FPA Capital is holding nearly 39% cash while Legg Mason Value holds a mere 1.1% cash.

Most of the traits displayed stem from the underlying philosophy of the funds in question. The generalized willingness to hold cash is the result of a lack of investment opportunities. In his year-end letter to shareholders of 2003, Seth Klarman wrote that his large cash position was the "result of a bottom-up [and failed] search for bargains". The guiding principle among our group of value gurus is, to borrow Buffett's expression, "holding cash is uncomfortable, but not as uncomfortable as doing something stupid".

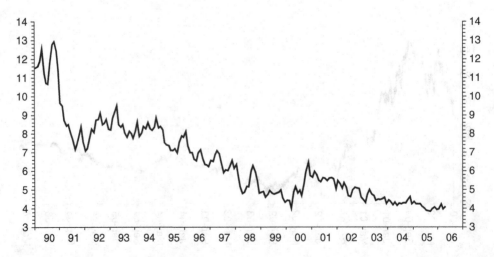

Figure 23.2   Average cash levels in US equity mutual funds (%).
Source: DrKW Macro research.

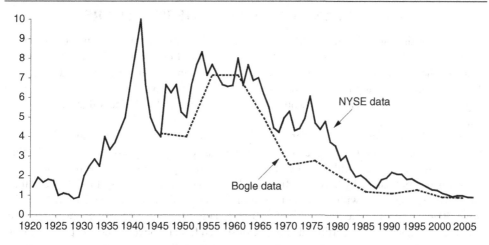

Figure 23.3   Average holding period for stocks on the NYSE.
Source: DrKW Macro research.

TRAIT IV: LONG TIME HORIZONS

I have often remarked that inherent within a value approach is the acceptance of long time horizons. You never know when a stock will reflect a sensible value. A good example was provided by the UK market in early 2003. The dividend yield on the UK market was higher than the 10-year government bond yield, suggesting that dividends were expected to decline on a decade view. This struck me as just plain wrong. A plethora of valuation work showed the UK to be unambiguously cheap (for details see *Global Equity Strategy*, 30 January 2003). The presence of forced sellers was making the UK market a bargain.

However, as with all bargains, they can repay you in one of two ways. Firstly, prices could correct. Secondly, they could just generate a high return via paying out high dividends for a long period of time. You never know which path will be taken. Hence the need for long time horizons.

Our selection of value managers all display long horizons. The average stock-holding period among these funds is over 5 years. The maximum is 17 years, the shortest 3 years. All compare favourably with the mutual fund industry's average stock-holding period of just 1 year (according to Morningstar).

This is supported by Figure 23.3 showing that average holding period for stocks on the NYSE. Back in the 1950s/1960s, investors used to do exactly that: invest. The average holding period was 7–8 years. However, today it appears as if everyone has become a speculator, with an average holding period of just 11 months.

When I present these findings, investors often dismiss the picture as yet further evidence of the way in which hedge funds have altered the investment landscape. However, the Morningstar data above, and the data from John Bogle below (Figure 23.3), show that long-only fund managers are just as much to blame for the time horizon shrinkage as the hedge funds. This may be because they feel the need to compete with the hedge funds but, regardless, they are certainly complicit in the shift from investment to speculation.

As Munger and Buffett have noted on many occasions, "If the job has been correctly done when a common stock is purchased, the time to sell it is – almost never."

TRAIT V: AN ACCEPTANCE OF BAD YEARS

Nearly all of the funds in our list have witnessed periods of negative returns, and/or under-performance relative to a benchmark (although note Trait I on the disregard for such items). Many of them saw large redemptions during the TMT bubble, but were prepared to stick to their tried and tested approach to investing. Lowenstein cites Eveillard (manager of the First Eagle Global Fund) as saying, "I would rather lose half my shareholders than lose half my shareholders' money."

Despite the very impressive performance data contained in Table 23.2, many of the funds examined have underperformed the index in as many as seven years out of the last 10! Absolute losses are relatively rare, with only two or three years seeing negative returns in the last 10.

In a paper published by Tweedy Browne (1998), they report a study that showed, for a group of value investors with excellent long-term track records, that underperforming an index some 30–40% of the time was perfectly normal. This fits well with our previous study of underperformance using an artificial universe of skilled fund managers who, despite having an information ratio of 0.5, saw 70% of their numbers witness three or more years of consecutive underperformance (see *Global Equity Strategy*, 7 June 2005).

TRAIT VI: PREPARED TO CLOSE FUNDS

In a world where asset managers are often rewarded with reference to funds under management, the quotation from Eveillard above is, sadly, an unusually ethical approach. Indeed, many of these funds display unusually high ethical behaviour and high levels of self control, in as far as many of these funds are closed to new investment. The managers are highly cognisant that there are limits to the size of funds that they are capable of running without hitting problems.

24

A Blast from the Past*

Regular readers of *Global Equity Strategy* will be acutely aware that I'm interested in the works of two legendary investors – John Maynard Keynes and Ben Graham. This chapter explores some of their shared views on the nature of investment. You may be surprised by the degree of overlap in their perspectives. The timelessness of their views is striking, and some of their analysis is very applicable to the current market.

- Distilling the massive amount of writing of two great investors into a readable length chapter is a trial worthy of Hercules himself. I have done my best to extract the areas of shared investment philosophy from Keynes and Graham. For instance, both thought it was important to distinguish between investment and speculation. They shared a faith in value-based investing, but recognized the dangers posed by excessive volatility. Interestingly, although not the subject of this chapter, they also both had somewhat complicated love lives!

- Not only do Keynes and Graham provide a useful reminder of the tenets of investing, and suggestions as to the nature of sensible investment process, but they also offer up advice on matters that seem to characterize the current market juncture amazingly well.

- For instance, given the obsession with junk equity that we have documented repeatedly over the last year or so, it may be worth remembering Graham's observation that "many years has taught us that the chief losses to investors come from the purchase of low-quality securities at time of favourable business conditions".

- As we have pointed out, sentiment is very high on a wide range of measures (from our own fear and greed index through to the Investors Intelligence bull bear measure), perhaps investors would do well to bear in mind Keynes's words of warnings that 'when disillusion falls upon an overoptimistic and overbought market, it should fall with sudden and even catastrophic force'.

- Some readers may recall our last article in *Global Equity Strategy* 2006, in which we applied a set of criteria for finding value derived from Ben Graham's work. To say there was a scarcity of value opportunities uncovered by that screen would be an understatement. Graham argued that this kind of exercise was useful as when

> True bargain issues have repeatedly become scarce in bull markets... one could even have determined whether the market level was getting too high or too low by counting the number of issues selling below working capital value. When such opportunities have virtually disappeared,

---

*This article appeared in *Global Equity Strategy* on 23 January 2007. The material discussed was accurate at the time of publication.

past experience indicates that investors should have taken themselves out of the stock market and plunged up to their necks in US Treasury bills.

- It is, of course, humbling to be reminded that almost everything worth saying about investment has been written before. However, much evidence suggests that Keynes's and Graham's words of advice have largely gone unheeded. While they extolled a patient, value-oriented stock selection process, many investors continue to chase after illusory growth stories, while investing on ever-shrinking time horizons. For those who have the discipline to follow Graham/Keynes, the opportunities still seem significant.

The roots of behavioural economics have been traced all the way back to Adam Smith. Much as economists hark on about Smith's *Wealth of Nations*, the companion volume, *The Theory of Moral Sentiments* (written in 1759), contains many of the same traits as now found in modern behavioural economics (Ashraf *et al.*, 2005). For instance, Smith discusses dual process theories with the system X (Smith calls this system the passions) vs system C (impartial spectator in Smith's terminology), loss aversion and overconfidence among others.

Rather than go all the way back to Smith I have decided to see what two of my favourite authors from the 1930s have to say about the art of investment, behavioural finance and, indeed, the current situation. The two authors I have chosen won't surprise regular readers of *Global Equity Strategy* – John Maynard Keynes and Ben Graham.

Both were skilled investors who lost and made fortunes. I have drawn on many sources but primarily used their writings from the 1930s. I have used Chapter 12 of the *General Theory* and the collected writings, volume XII, for Keynes's views. Graham's views are largely drawn from the 1934 version of *Security Analysis, and the Rediscovered Ben Graham* (ed. by Janet Lowe), with a complete range of insights from the *Intelligent Investor*. Distilling the insights of two such great men into a readable length chapter was a true challenge. I can only hope that I have been at least partially successful. Their words of wisdom should not be forgotten or ignored.

THE UNHEEDED WORDS OF KEYNES AND GRAHAM

On the Separation of Speculation and Investment

Both Keynes and Graham went to great lengths to remind investors of the differences between speculation and investment. Both would probably agree that our industry today would be better labelled 'speculation management' rather than 'investment management'.

Keynes wrote:

> The term *speculation* for the activity of forecasting the psychology of the market, and the term *enterprise* for the activity of forecasting the prospective yield of assets over their whole life... As the organization of investment markets improves, the risk of the predominance of speculation does increase... Speculators may do harm as bubbles on a steady stream of enterprise. But the position is serious when enterprise becomes the bubble on the whirlpool of speculation.

Graham opined:

> We doubt, however, whether many individuals are qualified by nature to follow consistently such an investment policy without deviating into the primrose path of market speculation. The chief reason for this hazard is that the distinctions between common-stock investment and common-stock speculation are too intangible to hold human nature in check ... But when the investor employs the same medium as the speculator, the line of demarcation between one approach and the other is one of mental attitude only, and hence is relatively insecure.

He also wrote:

> The most realistic distinction between the investor and speculator is found in their attitude toward stock-market movements. The speculator's primary interest lies in anticipating and profiting from market fluctuations. The investor's primary interest lies in acquiring and holding suitable securities at suitable prices.

And noted that:

> Speculators often prosper through ignorance... in a roaring bull market knowledge is superfluous and experience is a handicap.

On the nature of excess volatility

Both Keynes and Graham were painfully aware of the excessive volatility[1] that bedevils markets and causes investors such pain (as well as the fact that this price volatility was the very source of outperformance).

Keynes noted:

> Day-to-day fluctuations in the profits of existing investments, which are obviously of an ephemeral and non-significant character, tend to have an altogether excessive, and even an absurd, influence on the market.

Graham wrote:

> One of your partners, named Mr Market, is very obliging indeed. Every day he tells you what he thinks your interest is worth and furthermore offers to buy you out or to sell you an additional interest on that basis. Sometimes his idea of value appears plausible and justified by business developments and prospects as you know them. Often, on the other hand, Mr Market lets his enthusiasm or his fears run away with him, and the value he proposes seems to you little short of silly.

Keynes understood the dangers of such market volatility:

> A conventional valuation which is established as the outcome of the mass psychology of a large number of ignorant individuals is liable to change violently as the result of a sudden fluctuation of opinion due to factors which do not really make much difference to the prospective yield.

Graham advised investors:

> If you are a prudent investor or a sensible businessman, will you let Mr Market's daily communication determine your view of the value of a $1000 interest in the enterprise?... You may be happy to sell out to him when he quotes you a ridiculously high price, and equally happy to buy from him when his price is low. But the rest of the time you will be wiser to form your own ideas of the value of your holdings.

Keynes shared this viewpoint.

> One must not allow one's attitude to securities which have a daily market quotation to be disturbed by this fact or lose one's sense of proportion.

Or as Graham put it:

> The investor with a portfolio of sound stocks should expect their prices to fluctuate and should neither be concerned by sizeable declines nor become excited by sizeable advances. He should always remember that market quotations are there for his convenience, either to be taken advantage of or to be ignored.

---

[1] This theme of excessive volatility was later picked up in some of the early behavioural finance work from Robert Shiller. See Shiller (1992).

Keynes summed it up perfectly by saying:

> It is largely the fluctuations which throw up the bargains and the uncertainty due to the fluctuations which prevents other people from taking advantage of them.

However, Keynes also realized that most professional 'investors' won't be able to resist falling into an obsession with the short-term market outlook:

> The energies and skill of the professional investor and speculator are mainly occupied. . ., not with making superior long-term forecasts of the probable yield of an investment over its whole life, but with forecasting changes. . . a short time ahead of the general public.

He continued:

> This battle of wits to anticipate the basis of conventional valuation a few months hence, rather than prospective yield of an investment over a long term of years, does not even require gulls among the public to feed the maws of the professional; it can be played among the professionals themselves.

Graham observed the difficulties of remaining true to the principles of investment when facing sustained periods of poor performance:

> The wider the fluctuations of the market, and the longer they persist in one direction, the more difficult it is to preserve the investment viewpoint in dealing with common stocks. The attention is bound to be diverted from the investment question, which is price is attractive or unattractive in relation to value, to the speculative question, whether the market is near its low or its high point.

Keynes noted:

> The notion of us all selling out to the other fellow in good time is not, of course, a practicable policy for the community as a whole; yet the attempt to do so may deflect prices substantially from a reasonable estimate of their intrinsic value, and become a serious impediment to constructive investment.

On the folly of forecasting

As regular readers of *Global Equity Strategy* will know, I am deeply sceptical of our ability to forecast almost anything at all (see this issue for 24 August 2005). Both Keynes and Graham shared this distrust.

Keynes:

> It would be foolish, in forming our expectations, to attach great weight to matters which are very uncertain. It is reasonable, therefore, to be guided to a considerable degree by the facts.

Graham:

> In the pre-war period (WWI) it was the well-considered view that when prime emphasis was laid upon what was expected of the future, instead of what had been accomplished in the past, a speculative attitude was thereby taken. Speculation in its etymology, meant looking forward. . . The future was uncertain, therefore speculative; the past was known, therefore the source of safety.

This should not be taken as a green light to extrapolate the current situation indefinitely into the future.

Keynes:

> No one is so wise he can foresee the future far ahead.

Keynes:

Our usual practice being to take the existing situation and to project into the future

However, both men were well aware of the dangers of simple extrapolation of past events.[2]

Keynes:

The existing situation enters, in a sense disproportionately, into the formation of our long-term expectations; our usual practice being to take the existing situation and to project it into the future.

Graham warned:

There are several reasons why we cannot be sure that a trend in profits shown in the past will continue in the future. In the broad economic sense, there is the law of diminishing returns and of increasing competition which must finally flatten out any sharply upward curve of growth. There is the flow and ebb of the business cycle, from which the particular danger that arises that the earnings curve will look most impressive on the very eve of a serious setback.

Keynes also noted the very limited power of economic analysis when it comes to investing:

I can only say that I was the principal inventor of credit cycle investment and have seen it tried by five different parties acting in detail on distinctly different lines over a period of nearly 20 years, which has been full of ups and downs; and I have not seen a single case of success having been made of it.

On the Role of Governance and Agency Problems

Both Maynard Keynes and Ben Graham were also mindful of the dangers posed by principal–agent problems in a market environment.

Keynes:

With the separation between ownership and management which prevails today and with the development of organized investment markets, a new factor of great importance has entered in, which sometimes facilitates investment but sometimes adds greatly to the instability of the system.

Graham:

In our view much of the harm may be traced to the forgetting ... that corporations are the mere creatures and property of the stockholders who own them; that officers are only the paid employees of the stockholders; and that the directors ... are virtually trustees, whose legal duty it is to act solely on behalf of the owners of the business.

Graham also had sound advice for shareholders when it came to cash distributions. Graham was sceptical of what he called the 'profitable reinvestment theory' of firms retaining cash. He argued:

It has been gaining ground. The better the past record of growth, the readier investors and speculators have become to accept a low-payout policy. So much is this true that in many cases of growth favourites, the dividend rate – or even the absence of any dividend – has seemed to have virtually no effect on the market price.

---

[2] So both men were aware of what we behaviouralists now call representativeness – the tendency to extrapolate the immediate past into the indefinite future.

He went on to suggest:

It is our belief that shareholders should demand of their management either a normal payout of earnings – on the order, say, of two-thirds – or else a clear-cut demonstration that the reinvested profits have produced a satisfactory increase in per-share earnings.

Graham argued:

A successful company is one which can pay dividends regularly and presumably increase the rate as time goes on.

On the importance (and pain) of being a contrarian

Keynes:

The central principle of investment is to go contrary to the general opinion, on the grounds that if everyone agreed about its merit, the investment is inevitably too dear and therefore unattractive

Graham:

The fact that other people agree or disagree with you makes you neither right nor wrong. You will be right if your facts and reasoning are correct.

Keynes:

It is the long-term investor, he who most promotes the public interest, who will in practice come in for the most criticism ... For it is the essence of his behaviour that he should be eccentric, unconventional and rash in the eyes of average opinion. If he is successful, that will only confirm the general belief in his rashness; and if in the short run he is unsuccessful, which is very likely, he will not receive much mercy.

Keynes:

It needs more intelligence to defeat the forces of time and our ignorance of the future than to beat the gun.

Keynes:

The wise investor must now doubt all things

Graham:

If you believe ... that the value approach is inherently sound ... then devote yourself to that principle. Stick to it, and don't be led astray by Wall Street's fashions, illusions, and its constant chase after the fast dollar. Let me emphasize that it does not take genius ... to be a successful value analyst. What it needs is, first, reasonably good intelligence; second, sound principles of operation; and third, and most important, firmness of character.

Keynes:

It is the one sphere of life and activity where victory, security and success are always to the minority and never to the majority. When you find any one agreeing with you, change your mind.

Keynes:

There is nothing so disastrous as the pursuit of a rational investment policy in an irrational world (attributed).

On the flaws of professional investors

Graham:

> It was understood that managers of investment funds were to buy in times of depression and low prices, and to sell in times of prosperity and high prices. However ... the investment process consisted merely of finding prominent companies with a rising trend of earnings, and then buying the shares regardless of price ... The original idea of searching for the undervalued and neglected issues dropped completely out of sight.

Keynes:

> Worldly wisdom teaches that it is better for reputation to fail conventionally than to succeed unconventionally.

Graham:

> An investment operation is one which, upon thorough analysis, promises safety of principal and a satisfactory return. Operations not meeting these requirements are speculative.

Keynes:

> It is a leading fault of all institutional investors that their portfolio gradually tends to contain a long list of forgotten holdings originally purchased for reasons which no longer exist.[3]

Ben Graham was also disturbed by the focus on relative performance. At a conference one money manager stated 'Relative performance is all that matters to me. If the market collapses and my funds collapse less that's okay with me. I've done my job.'
Graham responded:

> That concerns me, doesn't it concern you?... I was shocked by what I heard at this meeting. I could not comprehend how the management of money by institutions had degenerated from the standpoint of sound investment to this rat race of trying to get the highest possible return in the shortest period of time. Those men gave me the impression of being prisoners to their own operations rather than controlling them ... They are promising performance on the upside and the downside that is not practical to achieve.

On the limits to arbitrage

Limited arbitrage is one of the key elements of behavioural finance (see Shleifer, 2000). Keynes and Graham were also obviously aware of these issues.

Keynes:

> The market can remain irrational longer than you or I can remain solvent (attributed).

Graham:

> Investment theory should recognize that the merits of an issue reflect themselves in the market price not by any automatic response ... but through the minds and decisions of buyers and sellers.

Keynes:

> An investor who proposes to ignore near-term market fluctuations needs greater resources for safety and must not operate on so large a scale, if at all, with borrowed money.

---

[3] Here Keynes clearly foresaw what we would now call the endowment effect.

Keynes:

If the reader interjects that there must surely be large profits to be gained from the other players in the long run by a skilled individual who, unperturbed by the prevailing pastime, continues to purchase investment on the best genuine long-term expectations he can frame, he must be answered, first of all, that there are, indeed, such serious-minded individuals and that it makes a vast difference to an investment market whether or not they predominate in their influence over the game players. But we must also add that there are several factors which jeopardize the predominance of such individuals in modern investment markets.

On the Importance of the Long Time Horizon

Keynes:

The spectacle of modern investment markets has sometimes moved me towards the conclusion that to make the purchase of an investment permanent and indissoluble, like marriage, except by reason of death or other grave cause, might be a useful remedy for our contemporary evils. For this would force the investor to direct his mind to the long-term prospects and to those only.

Keynes:

Human nature desires quick results, there is a peculiar zest in making money quickly, and remoter gains are discounted by the average man at a very high rate.[4]

Keynes:

An investor is aiming, or should be aiming, primarily at long-period returns, and should be solely judged by these.

Graham:

Undervaluations caused by neglect or prejudice may persist for an inconveniently long time, and the same applies to inflated prices caused by overenthusiasm or artificial stimulants.

Keynes was clearly cognisant of the short-term obsession among professional investors:

Compared with their predecessors, modern investors concentrate too much on annual, quarterly, or even monthly valuations of what they hold, and on capital appreciation . . . . and too little on immediate yield . . . and intrinsic worth.

Keynes:

Results must be judged by what one does on the round journey.

Keynes:

It is indeed awfully bad for all of us to be constantly revaluing over investments according to market movements.

Keynes:

Investment based on genuine long-term expectation is so difficult today as to be scarcely practicable. He who attempts it must surely lead much more laborious days and run greater risks than he who tries to guess better than the crowd how the crowd will behave.

---

[4] Here Keynes pre-empts today's notion of hyperbolic discounting, and some of the latest findings from neuroeconomics that show that we do indeed appear to be hard-wired to go for the short term.

On the Difficulty of Defining Value

Graham:

> Intrinsic value is an elusive concept. In general terms it is understood to be that value which is justified by the facts ... as distinct, let us say, from market quotations established by... psychological excesses. But it is a great mistake to imagine that intrinsic value is as definite and as determinable as is the market price.

Keynes:

> The outstanding fact is the extreme precariousness of the basis of knowledge on which our estimates of prospective yield have to be made. Our knowledge of the factors which will govern the yield of an investment some years hence is usually very slight and often negligible.

Graham:

> A conservative valuation of a stock issue must bear a reasonable relation to the average earnings... which should cover a period of not less than five years, and preferably seven to 10 years... We would suggest that about 16 times average earnings is as high a price as can be paid in an investment purchase of a common stock.

Graham also favoured dividends as the basis of valuation:

> Since the idea of investment is closely bound up with that of dependable income, it follows that investment in common-stocks would ordinarily be confined to those with a well-established dividend. It would follow also that the price paid for an investment common stock would be determined chiefly by the amount of the dividend.

On the Need to Understand Price Relative to Value

Graham clearly notes that value is not limited to a certain style of stock or sector, but instead is a function of the price:

> It is unsound to think always of investment character as inhering in an issue *per se*. The price is frequently an essential element, so that a stock may have investment merit at one price level but not at another.

Keynes:

> I believe now that successful investment depends on ... a careful selection of a few investments having regard to their cheapness in relation to their probable actual and potential intrinsic value over a period of years ahead ... a steadfast holding of these in fairly large units through thick and thin, perhaps for several years.

Graham:

> A stock may have investment merit at one price level but not at another.

Keynes:

> My purpose is to buy securities where I am satisfied as to assets and ultimate earning power and where the market price seems cheap in relation to these.

Graham appears here to be aware of the dangers of anchoring and argued that too many investors were subject to using market price as an anchor:

All my experience goes to show that most investment advisers take their opinions and measures of stock values from stock prices. In the stock market, value standards don't determine prices; prices determine value standards.

Keynes:

Prices bear very little relationship to ultimate values

On Why Behavioural Errors don't Cancel Out

On the criticisms that Gene Fama (1998) levels at behavioural finance is that the biases will cancel each other out. Keynes didn't share this view. Instead he argued:

Nor can we rationalize our behaviour by arguing that to a man in a state of ignorance errors in either direction are equally probable, so that there remains a mean actuarial expectation based on equi-probabilities. For it can easily be shown that the assumption of arithmetically equal probabilities based on a state of ignorance leads to absurdities.

On Diversification

On this topic we encounter a superficial difference of opinion between our two gurus. Our study of the traits that the best value investors seemed to share revealed one of them was concentrated portfolios. Keynes appears to agree with them.

To suppose that safety-first consists in having a small gamble in a large number of different companies where I have no information to reach a good judgement, as compared to a substantial stake in a company where one's information is adequate, strikes me as a travesty of investment policy.

Graham argued:

An investment might be justified in a group of issues, which would not be sufficiently safe if made in any of them singly. In other words, diversification might be necessary to reduce risk involved in the separate issues to the minimum consonant with the requirements of investment.

Graham:

Our formulation... holds diversification to be an integral part of all standard common-stock-investment operations.

However, I suspect that the two probably won't have disagreed in practice. While Graham obviously believed in diversification, I suspect he would have little truck with those holding positions in large stocks about which they knew nothing.

Keynes also noted that a concentrated portfolio didn't necessarily equate to an undiversified position. When discussing the perfect strategy Keynes noted:

A balanced position, i.e. a variety of risks in spite of individual holdings being large, and if possible opposed risk.

On the Current Juncture

While reading through the collected wisdom of Keynes and Graham, many of their ruminations struck me as highly apposite to the current market environment.

Given the obsession with junk equity that we have documented repeatedly over the last year or so (see *Global Equity Strategy*, 10 January 2007), it may be worth remembering Graham's view.

> Observation over many years has taught us that the chief losses to investors come from the purchase of low-quality securities at time of favourable business conditions.

With sentiment at a markedly high level of a wide variety of measures (see *Global Equity Strategy*, 10 January 2007), investors may be well advised to heed Keynes's words of warning:

> When disillusion falls upon an overoptimistic and overbought market, it should fall with sudden and even catastrophic force.

Given all the loose talk over liquidity that Albert Edwards discussed in his note in *Global Strategy Weekly*, 16 January 2007, Keynes's view of liquidity is noteworthy:

> Of the maxims of orthodox finance, none, surely, is more anti-social than the fetish of liquidity.

Corporates are sitting on large piles of cash, as was documented in *Global Equity Strategy*, 13 November 2006. Graham suggested:

> Let corporations return to their shareholders the surplus cash holdings not needed for the normal conduct of their business.

Regular readers of *Global Equity Strategy*, may remember the last note on 6 December 2006 where we searched largely in vane for bottom-up value opportunities. Graham argued that this kind of exercise was a useful timing tool.

> True bargain issues have repeatedly become scarce in bull markets. . . Perhaps one could even have determined whether the market level was getting too high or too low by counting the number of issues selling below working capital value. When such opportunities have virtually disappeared, past experience indicates that investors should have taken themselves out of the stock market and plunged up to their necks in US Treasury bills.

On the Margin of Safety

The margin of safety was at the very heart of Graham's approach to investing.

> The margin of safety idea becomes much more evident when we apply it to the field of undervalued or bargain securities. We have here, by definition, a favourable difference between price on the one hand and indicated or appraised value on the other. That difference is the safety margin. It is available for absorbing the effect of miscalculations or worse then average luck.

The growth-stock approach may supply as dependable a margin of safety. . . provided the calculation of the future is conservatively made, and provided it shows a satisfactory margin in relation to the price paid. . . The danger in a growth-stock program lies precisely here. For such favoured issues the market has a tendency to set prices that will not be adequately protected by a conservative projection of future earnings.

Keynes also understood the essence of value investing.

Keynes:

> All stocks and shares go up and down so violently that a safety-first policy is practically certain, if it is successful, to result in capital profits. For when the safety, excellence and cheapness of a share are generally realized, its price is bound to go up.

Graham:

> Another useful approach ... is from the standpoint of taking an interest in a private business. The typical [pre-World War I] common-stock investor was a businessman, and it seemed sensible to him to value any corporate enterprise in much the same manner as he would his own business.

Keynes:

> I am still convinced that one is doing a fundamentally sound thing, that is to say, backing intrinsic values, enormously in excess of the market price, which at some utterly unpredictable date will in due course bring the ship home.

Keynes:

> It is a much safer and easier way in the long run by which to make investment profits to buy £1 notes at 15s. than to sell £1 for 15s. in the hope of repurchasing them at 12s. 6d.

On Beta

Graham:

> Beta is a more or less useful measure of past price fluctuations of common stocks. What bothers me is that authorities now equate the beta idea with the concept of risk. Price variability, yes; risk no. Real investment risk is measured not by the percent that a stock may decline in price in relation to the general market in a given period, but by the danger of a loss of quality and earning power through economic changes or deterioration in management.

On the Dangers of Overcomplicating

Graham warned of the dangers of hindsight bias and ex-post justifications:

> In 44 years of Wall Street experience and study, I have never seen dependable calculations made about... stock values... that went beyond simple arithmetic or the most elementary algebra. Whenever excalculus is bought in... you could take it as a warning signal that the operator was trying to substitute theory for experience, and usually also to give speculation the deceptive guise of investment.

On the Use of History

Graham clearly understood hindsight bias and the meaninglessness of ex-post justifications:

> The applicability of history almost always appears after the event. When it is all over, we can quote chapter and verse to demonstrate why what happened was bound to happen because it had happened before.

There was a general tendency for security analysts to assume that a new level of value had been established for stock prices which was quite different from those we had previously been accustomed to. It may very well be that individual stocks as a whole are worth more than they used to be. But the thing that doesn't seem true is that they are worth so much more than they used to be that past experience – i.e. past levels and patterns of behaviour – can be discarded.

Graham also understood that human behaviour is pretty constant:

> It can hardly be said that the past six years have taught us anything about speculation that was not known before.

It is, of course, very humbling to once again be reminded that also everything that is worth saying about investing has been said before. But, as seems only fitting, the last words of this chapter should belong to one of Keynes's best-known quotations:

> The ideas of economists and political philosophers, both when they are right and when they are wrong, are more powerful than is commonly understood. Indeed the world is ruled by little else. Practical men, who believe themselves to be quite exempt from any intellectual influence, are usually the slaves of some defunct economist. Madmen in authority, who hear voices in the air, are distilling their frenzy from some academic scribbler of a few years back.

25

Why Not Value? The Behavioural Stumbling Blocks[*]

The fact that value outperforms over the long term is not new news. Yet despite this, there are relatively few 'true' value managers. This chapter seeks to explore the behavioural stumbling blocks that conspire to prevent us doing what we know to be right. Loss aversion, present bias, herding, availability and overconfidence are just a few of the hurdles that must be overcome to exploit value opportunities.

- Psychologists argue that knowledge and behaviour are not one and the same thing. That is to say, we sometimes do what we know to be wrong. For instance, the knowledge that safe sex can reduce the risk of HIV/AIDS doesn't always translate into the use of a condom. The same is true in other fields; simply knowing that value outperforms over the long term isn't enough to persuade everyone to be a value investor.

- Numerous other behavioural stumbling blocks help to explain why value investing is likely to remain a minority sport. Everyone is after the holy grail of investing, a strategy that never loses money! But it doesn't exist. Investing is probabilistic, so losses will occur. However, given our tendency to be loss averse (we dislike losses, more than we like gains) strategies that sometimes see short-term losses will be shunned.

- Long time horizons are integral to value investing. However, they are not natural to humans. Our brains appear to be designed to favour the short term. When faced with the possibility of a short-term gain, we get carried away and forget about the long term. So perhaps Keynes was correct when he wrote: "Investment based on genuine long-term expectation is so difficult to-day as to be scarcely practicable."

- Neuroscientists have found that social pain is felt in exactly the same parts of the brain as real physical pain. Value investing often involves going against the crowd, and hence involves social pain. So value investors are the financial equivalent of masochists.

- The stories associated with value stocks are generally going to be poor. There will be myriad reasons why any given stock is currently out of favour. It is exceptionally difficult to resist these stories, and instead focus on whether the bad news story is already in the price.

- As is ever the case, overconfidence also rears its ugly head. It is difficult to admit to ourselves (let alone to anyone else) that actually a simple rule can easily outperform us. We all like to think that we can pick stocks, or call asset classes, better than a rule or a model, but the evidence is not supportive of this misplaced, self-aggrandizing view.

*This article appeared in *Global Equity Strategy* on 29 August 2006. The material discussed was accurate at the time of publication.

- One final word of warning: we all set out with good intentions. However, psychologists have found that we massively overweight our current intentions in the prediction of our future behaviour. Thus, as much as we might say, "OK, now I'm going to be a good value investor", the likelihood of us actually doing so is far, far less than we would like to believe.

I have previously explored why people don't want to follow simple quant models even though they have been shown to outperform (*Global Equity Strategy*, 2 August 2006). This is a companion to that paper which seeks to explore why it is that not everyone is a value investor. In *Global Equity Strategy*, 8 June 2006, I explored the habits of the 'perfect value investor' by examining a selection of proven value investors. Six key traits stemming from their investment philosophy were identified:

1. Concentrated portfolios
2. Concerned with business risk not price volatility
3. Willingness to hold cash in the face of a lack of investment opportunities
4. Long time horizons
5. Acceptance of bad years
6. Willingness to limit the size of their funds.

So what is it that stops investors from being value investors, despite the long-run record of value outperforming?

KNOWLEDGE ≠ BEHAVIOUR

Knowing something to be true isn't always enough to promote changes in behaviour. So simply because we can show that value outperforms over the long term, it isn't easy to actually persuade everyone to adopt a value strategy.[1]

A recent paper by Dinkelman *et al.* (2006) makes the difference between knowledge and behaviour all too clear. They examined the difference between knowledge of HIV/AIDS and its prevention, and actual sexual behaviour (Figure 25.1). For example, 91% of men said they knew that the use of a condom could help to prevent the spread of HIV/AIDS, yet only 70% of them used a condom. Among women the situation was even worse: 92% reported that they knew condoms were useful in preventing HIV/AIDS transmission, but only 63% used them!

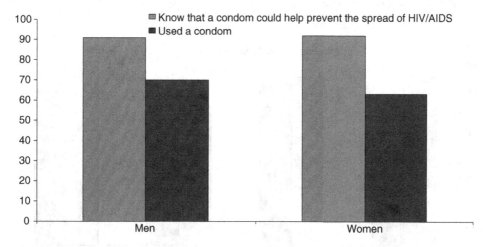

Figure 25.1   Percentage of respondents.
Source: Dinkelman *et al.* (2006). DrKW Macro research.

---

[1] Just as well, of course, otherwise value investing won't work.

If knowledge can't change behaviour in these tragic circumstances, why on earth would we expect it to do so in the trivial world of investing?

LOSS AVERSION

Everyone is after the holy grail of investing: a strategy that works all the time. It doesn't exist, so you might as well stop looking, or, even worse, pretending that you have one. The nature of markets is highly probabilistic; uncertainty is central to the act of investing. So nothing is likely to work continuously.

Figure 25.2 shows the percentage of time that value returns are positive on an annual basis (and the percentage of time that they exceed the broad market return). On an annual basis you could reasonably expect value strategies to generate positive absolute returns around 70% of the time (based on MSCI value 1975–2006).

In 3 years out of every 10, you would see a negative return, and this negative return certainly dissuades many from following such an approach. We all dislike losses much more than we enjoy gains – a phenomenon known as loss aversion.

In many studies, people have been found to dislike losses at least twice as much as they enjoy gains. Consider the following bet: On the toss of a fair coin, if you lose you must pay me £100. What is the minimum you need to win in order to make this bet acceptable to you?

In our survey of over 450 fund managers (see *Global Equity Strategy*, 2 February 2006) we found that the average response was £190! So professional fund managers are just as loss averse as the rest of us (see Figure 25.3).

Joel Greenblatt, in his wonderful *Little Book that Beats the Market* details the role that loss aversion plays in deterring investors from following his 'magic formula'. He notes,

> Imagine diligently watching those stocks each day as they do worse than the market average over the course of many months or even years... The magic formula portfolio fared poorly relative to the market average in 5 out of every 12 months tested. For full-year period... failed to beat the market average once every four years.

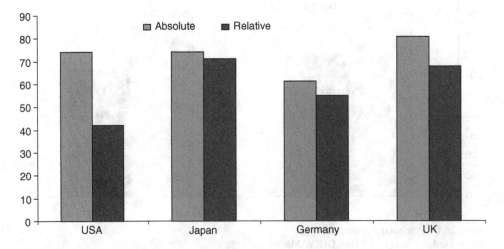

Figure 25.2 Percentage of time value strategies generate positive returns (absolute and relative). *Source:* DrKW Macro research.

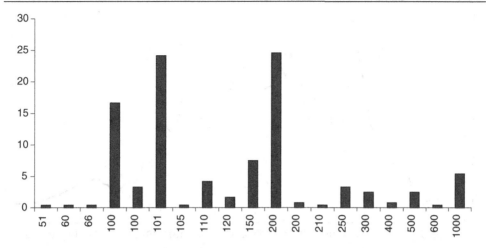

Figure 25.3   Fund managers are just as loss averse as everyone else (frequency %).
Source: DrKW Macro research.

So loss aversion certainly plays a pivotal role in dissuading people from becoming value investors.

DELAYED GRATIFICATION AND HARD-WIRING FOR THE SHORT TERM

Not only can value strategies go wrong but they can take time to work. When a value opportunity is exploited there are two ways for it to pay off. For instance, if I buy a significantly undervalued stock, it is possible that everyone else might realize that this is indeed a cheap stock and the price might correct. However, it is also possible that the stock remains undervalued and generates its higher long-run return by continuing to pay a high dividend yield. Both paths are possible, but when a value position is implemented, it is impossible to know *ex-ante* which mechanism will deliver the returns.

This means that value investors must have long time horizons. In our study of value investors we found they had an average holding period of 5 years, whereas the average holding period for a stock on the New York Stock Exchange is only 11 months (see Figures 25.4 and 25.5).

However, long time horizons don't come naturally to us humans. When we are faced with the possibility of a reward, our brains release dopamine. Dopamine makes people feel good about themselves, confident and stimulated. The majority of dopamine receptors are located in areas of the brain that are generally associated with the X-system (our fast and dirty mental system). The possibility of monetary reward seems to trigger the release of dopamine in the same way as enjoying food, or taking pleasure-inducing drugs (see Knutson and Peterson, 2005).

McClure *et al.* (2004) have recently investigated the neural systems that underlie decisions surrounding delayed gratification. Much research has suggested that people tend to behave impatiently today but plan to act patiently in the future. For instance, when offered a choice between £10 today and £11 tomorrow, many people choose the immediate option. However,

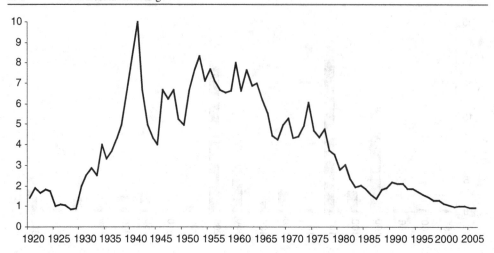

Figure 25.4 Average holding period for a stock on the NYSE (years).
Source: DrKW Macro research.

if you asked people today to choose between £10 in a year, and £11 in a year and a day, many of those who went for the immediate option in the first case now go for the second option.

In order to see what happens in the brain when faced with such choices, McClure *et al.* measured the brain activity of participants as they made a series of intertemporal choices between early and delayed monetary rewards. Some of the choice pairs included an immediate option; others were choices between two delayed options.

They found that when the choice involved an immediate gain, the ventral stratum (part of the basal ganglia), the medial orbitofrontal cortex, and the medial prefrontal cortex were all disproportionally used. All these elements are associated with the X-system. McClure

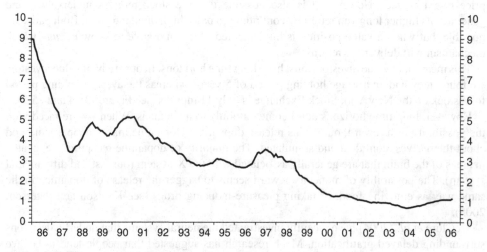

Figure 25.5 Average holding period for a stock on the LSE (years).
Source: DrKW Macro research.

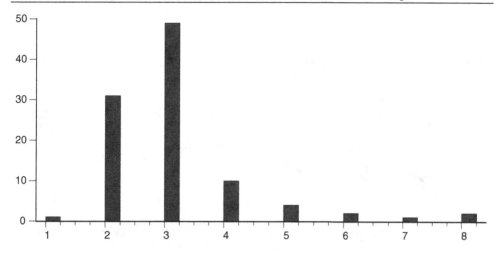

Figure 25.6 Frequency of cumulative years of underperformance.
Source: DrKW Macro research.

et al. point out that these areas are also riddled by the mid-brain dopamine system. They note, "These structures have consistently been implicated in impulsive behaviour".

When the choice involved two delayed rewards, the prefrontal and parietal cortex were engaged (correlates of the C-system). The more difficult the choice, the more these areas seemed to be used. It is very hard for us to override the X-system. Frequently, the X-system reacts before the C-system has even had a chance to consider the problem. All too often, it looks as if we are likely to end up being hard-wired for the short term. So perhaps Keynes was right when he wrote, "Investment based on genuine long-term expectation is so difficult to-day as to be scarcely practicable". Patience really is a virtue.

In investment, loss aversion and time horizon are not independent issues. The more frequently you check a portfolio, the more likely it is that you will witness a loss. In the past I have shown how it is perfectly possible for a skilled fund manager to display three years of back-to-back declines (see *Global Equity Strategy*, 7 June 2005). Figure 25.6 uses a constructed universe where all the fund managers have 3% alpha and a 6% tracking error. I then let the make-believe managers run money for 50 years. The chart illustrates the frequency of years of back-to-back underperformance. Around 70% of the make-believe fund managers displayed 3 or more years of underperformance!

A study by Goyal and Wahal (2005) shows why we need to explain the risks of investing to the end client far better than we currently do (Figure 25.7). It should be required reading by all pension plans and trustees. They review some 4000-plus decisions regarding the hiring and firing of investment manager by pension plan sponsors and trustees between 1993 and 2003. The results they uncover show the classic hallmarks of returns-chasing behaviour. The funds the sponsors tend to hire have an average outperformance of nearly 14% in the 3 years before hiring, but they have statistically insignificant returns after the hiring. In contrast, those fired for performance reasons tend to have underperformed by around 6% in the 3 years leading up to the dismissal. However, in the 3 years after the firing, they tend to outperform by nearly 5%. A powerful lesson in the need to extend time horizons.

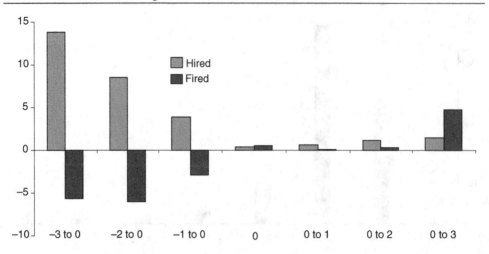

Figure 25.7 Performance around hiring and firing decisions (%).
Source: Goyal and Wahal (2005). DrKW Macro research.

SOCIAL PAIN AND THE HERDING HABIT

In the past, we have mentioned that there is strong evidence from neuroscience to suggest that real pain and social pain are felt in exactly the same places in the brain. Eisenberger and Lieberman (2004) asked participants to play a computer game. Players thought they were playing in a three-way game with two other players, throwing a ball back and forth.

In fact, the two other players were computer controlled. After a period of three-way play, the two other 'players' began to exclude the participant by throwing the ball back and forth between themselves. This social exclusion generates brain activity in the anterior cingulate cortex and the insula. Both of which are also activated by real physical pain.

Contrarian strategies are the investment equivalent of seeking out social pain. In order to implement such a strategy, you will buy the things that everyone else is selling, and sell the stocks that everyone else is buying. This is social pain. Eisenberger and Lieberman's results suggest that following such a strategy is like having your arm broken on a regular basis – not fun!

> To buy when others are despondently selling and sell when others are greedily buying requires the greatest fortitude and pays the greatest reward
>
> Sir John Templeton

> It is the long-term investor, he who most promotes the public interest, who will in practice come in for the most criticism... For it is in the essence of his behaviour that he should be eccentric, unconventional and rash in the eyes of average opinion.
>
> John Maynard Keynes

> Worldly wisdom teaches that it is better for reputation to fail conventionally than to succeed unconventionally.
>
> John Maynard Keynes

POOR STORIES

I have written elsewhere on the importance of stories in driving our behaviour (see *Global Equity Strategy*, 27 April 2005). When a value screen is performed (or any other screen for that matter), a list of stocks is generated. Upon production of this list, the first thing everyone does is look down the list and start to analyse the elements. For instance, 'I can't buy that stock, it's a basket case'. The preconceived stories associated with stocks begin to interfere. Just as glamour stocks have seductive stories of incredible future growth, so value stocks have myriad reasons for their cheapness. All of which conspire to prevent the investor from actually following the screen's suggestions. So perhaps ignorance really is bliss in this context.

Stories are powerful because they trigger availability. Our minds are not limitless super-computers; they are bounded by cognitive resource constraints. Very often people think of memory as functioning like a picture postcard or a photo. Unfortunately, this isn't the way memory works. Memory is a process, into which the truth is but one input. For instance, if you ask people, "Which is a more likely cause of death in the US, shark attacks or lightning strikes?", a bizarrely large number of people seem to think that shark attacks are more common, despite the fact that 30 times more people are killed each year by lightning strikes than by shark attacks. The reason for this error in people's reasoning is that shark attacks are salient (easy to recall – largely thanks to Jaws) and available (every time someone gets nibbled off the coast of Florida or Hawaii, we all hear about it).

The same thing happens when we hear other stories. For instance, when an IPO is launched you can bet it will have a great story attached, full of the promise of growth. This makes the 'growth' salient and available, and all too often these thoughts then crowd out other considerations such as the valuation – just as the vivid shark attack crowds out the more likely lightning strike.

The reverse happens with value stocks. The stocks will generally appear to be cheap, but investors will be able to find any number of arguments as to why they are likely to stay cheap. So the story will crowd out the fact of cheapness.

OVERCONFIDENCE

I have noticed in the past that, one of the key reasons that people don't follow quant models is their amazing overconfidence in their own abilities. The same is true when it comes to value investing. Rather than follow a simple rule like, say, buying the bottom 20% of the MSCI universe ranked by PE, investors often prefer to rely on their stock selection skills (however dubious these may be).

Both the illusion of control and the illusion of knowledge conspire to generate this over-confidence. The illusion of knowledge fosters the idea that because we know more, we must be able to make superior decisions. Intuitively, it is easy to see why having more information should enable you to make better decisions. However, much evidence has been collected to show flaws in this idea (see *Global Equity Strategy*, 31 August 2005). The empirical reality appears to be that more information isn't the same as better information. All too often investors suffer a signal extraction problem, that is to say they struggle to extract the meaningful elements among the deluge of noise.

The illusion of control also plays a part. We are experts in magical thinking – that is, believing we can influence things that we clearly can't. An article by Pronin et al. (2006) explores several aspects of this behaviour. In one of their experiments, they told people they were investigating voodoo. Participants were paired (one of each pair actually worked for the experimenter and was either a pleasant person or a real pain in the neck). The stooge was always selected to be the 'victim', while the real participant was selected to stick pins into a voodoo doll ('witch doctor').

However, before they were asked to do this, they spent a little time with their partner in the experiment (who, remember, is either pleasant or exceedingly irritating). Then the 'witch doctor' was told to go into a room and generate "vivid and concrete thoughts about the victim but not to say them aloud". Then they were allowed to stick pins into a voodoo doll. After this, the experimenter asked the 'victim' if he had suffered any pains. Because he was a confederate of the experimenter he said "yes, I have a bit of a headache". The participant playing the witch doctor was then asked to complete a questionnaire including a question on the degree of culpability they felt for the 'victim's' pain. Amazingly, when dealing with the annoying 'victim', the 'witch doctors' felt much more responsible than they did with the normal 'victim', presumably because they had done more visualization of being angry at this person.

Several follow-up experiments were also conducted. One involved watching someone who was blindfolded throw a basketball. Participants were asked to either imagine the player making the shot, or imagine the player doing something else, like stretching. Those primed to think about the player making the shot thought they were much more responsible for the success or failure than those given the alternative scenario.

Finally, at a real basketball match, attendees were asked either to state how important a potential player was and why, or simply asked to describe the physical appearance of the player. After the match they were then asked to rate how responsible they felt for their team's performance. Once again, those primed to describe the players' importance felt much more responsible than those simply asked to describe the players (Figure 25.8).

In all three cases, those primed to think about the issues displayed significantly more 'magical thinking' than the controls. Investors are certainly likely to have thought about the stocks they are selecting, and as such will feel 'responsible' for the outcomes even if they can't possibly influence them.

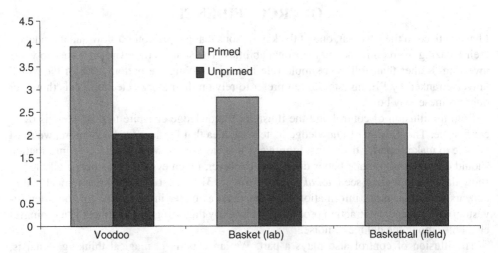

Figure 25.8   Degree of responsibility (1= not responsible at all, 7 = totally responsible).
Source: Goyal and Wahal (2005). DrKW Macro research.

FUN

The final stumbling block which I want to cover here is, simply, fun. As Keynes opined, "The game of professional investment is intolerably boring and over-exacting to anyone who is entirely exempt from the gambling instinct; whilst he who has it must pay this propensity the appropriate toll."

Following simple rules and procedures isn't exactly great fun. Whereas filling your day by meeting companies and talking with sell-side analysts may be (although, personally, if this is your definition of fun, I suspect you need more help than I can offer you).

As Paul Samuelson said, "Investing should be dull. It shouldn't be exciting. Investing should be more like watching paint dry or watching grass grow. If you want excitement, take $800 and go to Las Vegas."

NO, HONESTLY I WILL BE GOOD

Let me end with one final word of warning: we all start out with the best of intentions but, as the saying goes, the road to hell is paved with good intentions. A recent paper by Koehler and Poon (2006) demonstrates the point perfectly. They asked participants to complete a questionnaire about giving blood at an upcoming donation clinic. People were asked to rate how likely they were to give blood, and also rate on a scale of 1 (strongly disagree) to 9 (strong agree) a series of statements concerning their attitudes on the subject, including a final question which read, "Right now, as I think about it, I strongly intend to donate blood at the July 14–22 blood donation clinic." This was used to gauge participants' current intention strength.

Figure 25.9 shows the predicted probability of blood donation and actual outcome of blood donation by the strength of current intentions. In general, people were massively too optimistic about their blood donation. On average, they were around 30 percentage points too optimistic. The predicted probability of blood donation rose much faster across the strength of current intentions, than the actual outcome. This implies that current intentions have an overly strong effect on prediction of behaviour, but not on behaviour itself.

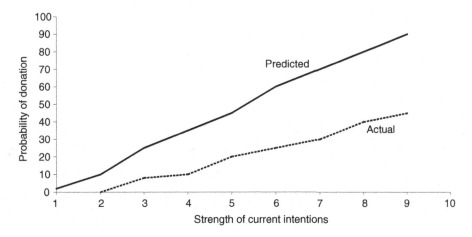

Figure 25.9   Predicted and actual probability of blood donation.
Source: Koehler and Poon (2006). DrKW Macro research.

So as easy as it might be to say, "From now on I'm going to be a value investor", the likelihood of it actually occurring is highly remote.

PART B
The Empirical Evidence: Value in
All its Forms

26
Bargain Hunter (or It Offers Me Protection)*

Written with Rui Antunes

Theoretically growth is a good investment. But identifying growth ex-ante is very difficult. We are all too confident and too optimistic about our ability to pick winners. Often growth investing ends up as buying expensive stocks. Value investing is an admission of our limitations. It offers protection against mistakes, and it outperforms!

- If we could pick the firms with the highest growth in earnings over the next 12 months, we could have beaten the market by around 7.5% p.a. since 1975. Combine this potential performance with our behavioural gullibility/vulnerability over 'stories' and the allure of growth investing is clear.
- However, we are generally overconfident and overoptimistic about our abilities to pick growth stocks ex-ante. For instance, following the forecasts of consensus, analysts would capture less than one-quarter of the potential returns to a perfect foresight strategy at the global level.
- If you persist in following a growth strategy, value considerations should not be ignored. Over one-half of the total outperformance of a perfect foresight growth strategy was delivered by the 'cheap' growth stocks.
- All too often, growth investing ends up as simply buying expensive (momentum?) stocks. Such a strategy is doomed to failure. Since 1975, a strategy of buying the top 20% of the MSCI world index in terms of simple trailing PE would have delivered nearly 6% p.a underperformance.
- Value investing is an admission of our limitations. By buying 'cheap' stocks, we allow ourselves a 'margin of safety' as Ben Graham put it. It also avoids relying on the vagaries of analysts' forecasts. In our sample, we find that a value strategy (defined as buying the 20% of the market with the lowest PEs) would have delivered 6% p.a. outperformance of the market at the global level.

---

*This article appeared in *Global Equity Strategy* on 16 March 2005. The material discussed was accurate at the time of publication.

I am an unabashed value investor. I like to buy cheap stocks. If you don't share this viewpoint, or aren't open to be persuaded of the merits of such an approach, stop reading now, for what follows will only distress you. I am also an empiricist at heart. Theories are all well and good, but sadly almost anything is possible in theory. The only way to resolve theoretical impasses is to examine the evidence. I am fond of quoting the words of Conan Doyle's Sherlock Holmes, "It is a capital mistake to theorize before one has data. Insensibly one begins to twist facts to suit theories, instead of theories to suit facts" or "The temptation to form premature theories based upon insufficient data is the bane of our profession".

So is there an empirical basis to my obsession with value? The short answer is 'yes'. The long answer takes up the rest of this chapter. My usual accomplice and compatriot in adventures involving large amounts of data is Rui Antunes, of our global quantitative team. It was with Rui's able help that I embarked upon an investigation of value strategies.

THE METHODOLOGY

We chose the MSCI indices as our universe. The stocks were ranked first by trailing PE and then by actual reported earnings growth over the next 12 months (as if we could perfectly predict the future). Each sort resulted in the formation of quintiles (with 20% of the universe in each quintile). Given that we sorted on two variables, we ended up with 25 portfolios of various combinations of PEs and delivered earnings growth. The performance of these portfolios was then tracked over the next 12 months. A sample of our results can be seen in Table 26.1.

In this particular case, we are examining the global market and measuring total returns[1] relative to the average of the stocks in our universe. The tables for each of the regions we examined are, for reference, provided in full at the end of this chapter. Portfolio (5, 5) represents the cheapest of the value stocks with the lowest achieved earnings growth. Portfolio (1, 1) is the most expensive stocks with the highest delivered earnings growth. Portfolio (1, 5) is the cheapest basket of stocks with the highest earnings growth, and so forth.[2]

Table 26.1 Global, returns relative to market %
(1975–2004)

		Earnings Growth					
		Low				High	
Global		5	4	3	2	1	Average
Low	5	−3.0	2.3	9.0	14.1	26.2	9.7
	4	−3.9	−5.7	−1.8	3.1	11.9	0.7
PE	3	−5.0	−6.4	−4.1	1.0	8.4	−1.2
	2	−3.1	−5.8	−3.0	−2.6	9.0	−1.1
High	1	−11.9	−9.0	−10.4	−9.0	1.0	−7.8
Average		**−5.4**	**−4.9**	**−2.1**	**1.3**	**11.3**	

Source: DrKW Macro research.

---

[1] The analysis was done in terms of both price and total returns. The results were invariant to the specification used.

[2] The portfolio labels always go across the table (columns) and then down the rows.

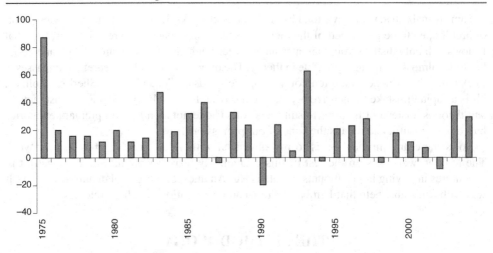

Figure 26.1 Raw returns to the global value strategy (%).
Source: DrKW Macro research.

DOES VALUE WORK?

Several findings are apparent from examining the table. First (and of foremost importance to me) is that *buying cheap stocks did indeed outperform*. Simply buying an equal weighted basket (assuming equal distribution of stocks across portfolios) of the lowest 20% of PEs within the MSCI World Index generated significant outperformance (9.7% p.a. on average). Such a strategy would have only resulted in absolute losses in only 5 out of the 30 years in our sample.

However, such analysis ignores the fact that firms are not equally distributed across all portfolios. Figure 26.1 shows the returns to a low PE strategy in which the returns have

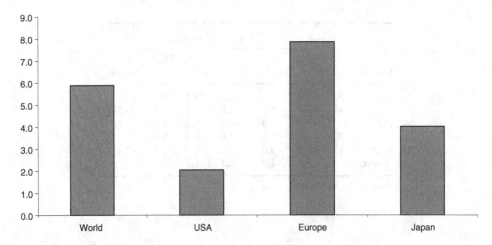

Figure 26.2 The value premium across regions (%, outperformance).
Source: DrKW Macro research.

been weighted by the actual distribution of earnings in each of the categories. The results of the previous analysis hold. The annual average raw return from a strategy of buying the lowest 20% of the MSCI World index ranked by PE was 20%. This represents a low PE stock outperformance of the market of nearly 6% p.a.!

Similar patterns were found when we examined the regional breakdowns. Figure 26.2 shows the outperformance of buying the bottom 20% by trailing PE in the various markets we examined. There is a *strongly consistent value premium across countries/regions.*

THE ANATOMY OF VALUE

It is also noteworthy that only one of the value portfolios resulted in underperformance (portfolio (5, 5)). Table 26.2 shows the distribution of firms across the portfolios. At the global level, 31% of the bottom 20% of the MSCI World index end up in the portfolio that generates value underperformance; 6.2% of all stocks ended up in portfolio (5, 5). Since, by design, the low PE stocks (portfolios $(x, 5)$) are 20% of the universe, we end up with 31% of the value universe in the underperforming portfolio. So the majority of value stocks outperform.

Table 26.3 shows the results for all the regions (see also Figure 26.3). None of the value portfolios generates a negative absolute return (supporting our hypothesis that value offers protection). However, in general, around 30–35% of the lowest PE stocks seem to generate underperformance. The most extreme case is the USA, where the value premium comes from a minority of stocks.[3] *This distribution suggests that value investing can be improved by avoiding losers.*

Table 26.2   Distribution of firms across portfolio (%) – Global

		Earnings Growth				
		Low				High
		5	4	3	2	1
Low	5	6.2	5.1	4.0	3.2	1.7
	4	3.9	4.4	4.6	4.6	2.6
PE	3	3.9	3.7	4.1	4.9	3.4
	2	3.4	3.8	3.9	4.3	4.6
High	1	2.7	3.1	3.4	3.1	7.4

Source: DrKW Macro research.

Table 26.3   The anatomy of value

Region	Underperforming (%)	Negative returns (%)
Global	30	0
USA	57	0
Europe	32	0
Japan	35	0

Source: DrKW Macro research.

---

[3] Consistent with the findings of Piotroski (2000).

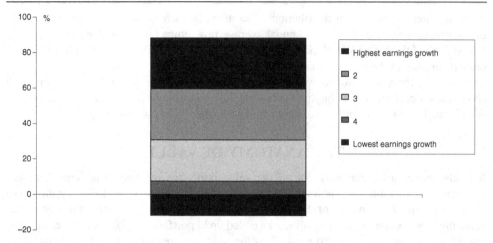

Figure 26.3 The anatomy of value (contribution to outperformance by delivered earnings growth quintile, %).
Source: DrKW Macro research.

If the underperforming 30% could be identified *ex-ante*, then the returns to value investing could be further enhanced. In previous work, we have highlighted the findings of Piotroski (2000), who uses a simple accounting screen on financial stability to help to avoid the value traps (see *Global Equity Strategy*, 20 October 2003 for more details). An alternative to this might be to use some measure of quality, as our quant team has developed in a series of notes (see *Quant Quickie*, 20 October 2004).

THE SIREN OF GROWTH

If you had perfect foresight and knew exactly what earnings growth would be achieved, and you bought the highest growth stocks regardless of valuation, you would have outperformed by

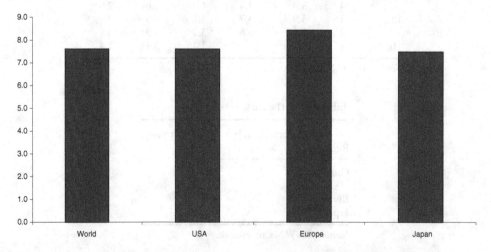

Figure 26.4 The lure of growth investing (perfect foresight returns, % outperformance).
Source: DrKW Macro research.

11.3% p.a on average. It is perhaps the hope or belief that investors can identify such equities that sucks investors into growth investing, like sailors to the calls of the sirens. However, the two most common behavioural biases are overoptimism and overconfidence. We are all massively too sure about our ability to predict the future.

Figure 26.4 shows the distribution weighted average returns if you had had perfect foresight across the markets. This weighting drops the return from 11.3% to a still very healthy 7.6% p.a. The eternal hope of growth investing is clear. If only the winners could be picked ex-ante! Combine this hope of major outperformance with the mental vulnerability to stories that we have outlined elsewhere (*see Global Equity Strategy*, 20 October 2004) and the lure of growth (Figure 26.4) is obvious for all to see.

GROWTH DOESN'T MEAN IGNORING VALUATION

The near monotonically declining performance of the delivered high-growth portfolios (column 1 in Table 26.1) should also be noted. That is to say growth investors shouldn't ignore value. The cheaper the stocks they buy, the better the performance achieved (Figure 26.5). Indeed the two lowest PE bands provide over 50% of the total outperformance of the perfect foresight growth premium.

All too often, growth-investing amounts to little more than buying highly valued equities. Table 26.1 reveals that buying the high PE stocks would have resulted in significant underperformance.

It is also interesting to note that to generate any outperformance from buying high PE stocks would require you to pick those stocks that delivered the very highest growth rates (portfolio 5, 1). Even if you could do this, you would only manage to beat the very worst of the value stock baskets. That is to say portfolio (1, 1) only manages to beat portfolio (5, 5). It fails to beat all the other value portfolios (*x*, 5).

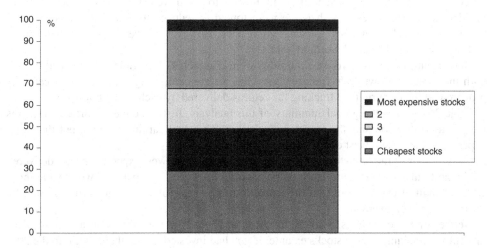

Figure 26.5 The anatomy of growth (contribution to growth outperformance by PE quintile, %).
Source: DrKW Macro research.

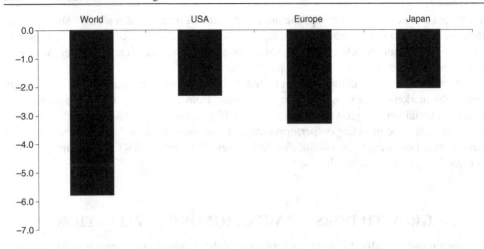

Figure 26.6 High PE strategy: doomed to disaster (%).
Source: DrKW Macro research.

Table 26.2 also shows that within the high PE universe only 37% of the stocks fall into portfolio (1, 5). *Therefore, growth stock investing as proxied by buying expensive stocks is all about picking a minority of winners.*

It is also worth noting that buying highly valued stocks also carries an enormous 'torpedo' risk. The worst returns were seen in the high PE stocks with the lowest delivered earnings growth (underperforming by 11.9% p.a. on average!).

THE DISAPPOINTING REALITY OF GROWTH

Of course, the natural response to these findings is to ask if we can forecast growth, and we decided to investigate exactly that. We were forced to reduce the time span of our sample because of the lack of analysts' forecasts going back. However, we were able to start this work in 1988, giving us 17 years' worth of data.

Once again, two-way sorts into quintiles were conducted. This time we replaced the PE with the forecast growth rate from analysts. So, we are comparing the forecast of earnings growth with the outturn, then tracking the returns delivered by each of the portfolios.

Table 26.4 shows the global summary of this analysis. Just to be clear, portfolio (1, 5) is the portfolio that contains the stocks with the highest actual earnings growth but that were expected to have the lowest earnings growth, and so forth.

Unsurprisingly, the best stocks were the ones that had the lowest expectations but delivered the highest outcome (portfolio 1, 5), outperforming by nearly 11% p.a. The worst were those with the highest expectations and the lowest outturns (portfolio 5, 1), underperforming by nearly 12% p.a on average.

Neither of these findings is likely to shock anyone. However, the table also shows the difficulty of picking growth stocks ex ante. If you had invested an equal amount into the 20% of stocks with the highest forecast earnings growth, then you would have underperformed by 2.5% p.a. on average!

Table 26.4   Global, total returns relative to market % (1988–2004)

		Earnings Growth					
		Low				High	
		5	4	3	2	1	Average
Low	5	−0.6	3.5	6.4	3.7	10.8	4.8
	4	−8.3	−2.1	2.7	9.2	16.9	3.2
EPS growth forecasts	3	−12.3	−4.7	−1.5	4.0	5.8	−1.8
	2	−9.8	−11.4	−5.9	1.6	4.9	−4.1
High	1	−11.7	2.3	−3.6	−4.5	2.6	−2.5
Average		**−8.8**	**−2.5**	**−0.4**	**2.8**	**8.2**	

Source: DrKW Macro research.

Table 26.5   Distribution of firms across portfolio, %

		Earnings Growth				
		Low				High
		5	4	3	2	1
Low	5	14.0	4.5	0.7	0.4	0.4
	4	3.0	10.3	5.0	1.1	0.6
EPS growth forecasts	3	1.3	3.0	10.3	4.5	0.9
	2	0.8	1.4	3.3	11.4	3.0
High	1	0.9	0.8	0.6	2.6	15.1

Source: DrKW Macro research.

In contrast, if you had invested in the 20% of stocks with the lowest growth expectations, then you would have outperformed by 4% p.a. on average. The role of expectations in this process couldn't be much clearer. *It is far easier to surprise on the upside if the expectations are low in the first place.*

ANALYST ACCURACY?

Of course, using these simple averages assumes an equal distribution of stocks within each portfolio-which is akin to saying that analysts are completely useless at forecasting the earnings growth. That strikes even me as slightly harsh (and I am certainly not known as an apologist for analysts, as those who have seen one of my behavioural finance presentations can attest).

But, we can also use our data to get some insight into the forecast accuracy of analysts. Table 26.5 shows the distribution of forecasts and outturns for the MSCI World index. Effectively the diagonals represent the points where analysts were correct. The good news for analysts is that the majority of forecasts are in the same quintile as the outturn. For instance, there is a 75% overlap between those firms that analysts forecast to have the highest earnings growth, and those that actually do have the highest earnings growth.

Sounds impressive doesn't it? But it still means that one in four of their forecasts is off the mark. More importantly, Table 26.2 shows that the outperformance generated by those firms with high expected and delivered growth is relatively small at 2.6% p.a. Whereas the 25% of firms the analysts say are going to have the highest earnings growth, but don't deliver have an

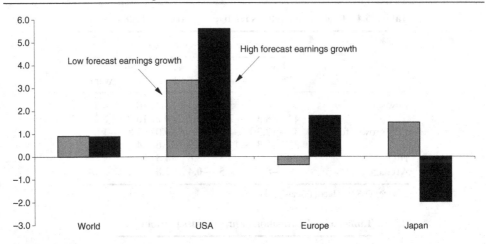

Figure 26.7 The performance of forecast based strategies (%, outperformance).
Source: DrKW Macro research.

average return of −3.7% p.a. The combined effect is that the weighted average return on the high growth forecast portfolio is an outperformance of 0.9%.

What about the low growth realm? There is a 70% overlap between those firms that the analysts think will have the lowest earnings growth, and those that do indeed have the lowest earnings growth. Indeed if we weight the returns by the distribution accuracy of analysts, those with low forecasts generate an outperformance of 0.9%. This is not statistically different from the high-growth result. So effectively *analyst forecasts can't tell us very much at all*! They certainly can't help us identify growth stocks as a source of significant outperformance.

Figure 26.7 shows the regional breakdowns of the weighted performance of forecast growth portfolios. In Japan you could have made money by shorting the stocks with high forecast earnings growth! Elsewhere, following the forecasts of analysts would have generated positive returns on average.

An alternative way to evaluate the power of following the forecasts is to ask how much the forecast strategy would have managed to capture if the idealized strategy of knowing exactly what growth was actually going to be delivered. Table 26.6 shows the percentage of the maximum attainable return that was actually achieved if one had bought the 20% of stocks with the highest growth forecasts from analysts.

Table 26.6 Percentage of possible growth captured by following the high growth forecasts

	%
World	24
USA	70
Europe	41
Japan	−220

Source: DrKW Macro research.

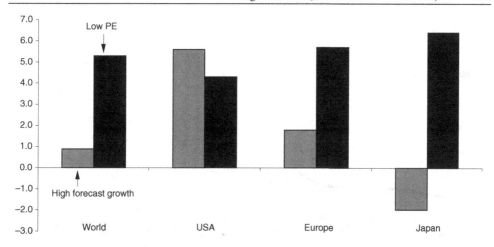

Figure 26.8   Value vs Growth (total return outperformance, %, 1988–2004).
Source: DrKW Macro research.

With the exception of the USA, the results are sobering. At the global level, following the analysts' forecasts of growth would have captured just 24% of the total growth premium available. In Europe this improves to 40%, still not an impressive performance. In Japan, the forecasts are actually a better contrarian indicator than having any value in their own right! In the USA, the strategy of following the analysts did much better, delivering 70% of the total possible return to the perfect foresight premium.

VALUE VERSUS GROWTH

Now, to the crucial question: value or growth? Figure 26.8 shows the weighted total return outperformance figures for the value and growth forecast strategies for the regions since 1988.

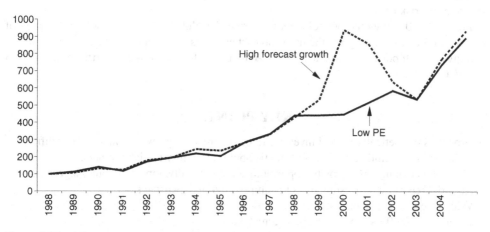

Figure 26.9   US value and growth portfolios (1987=100).
Source: DrKW Macro research.

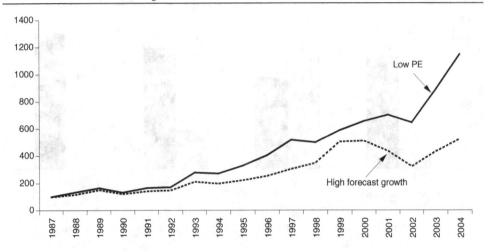

Figure 26.10   Global value and growth portfolios (1987=100).
Source: DrKW Macro research.

In general the results show the massive superiority of being a 'bargain hunter'. Ben Graham's concept of a margin of safety is still sound today. Buying cheap stocks offers significant protection against any potential bad news.

Only in the USA does the return on following the analyst's growth forecasts exceed the return from buying cheap stocks. However, Figure 26.9 shows the time path of the two portfolios. The impact of the bubble years becomes immediately obvious.

The US value and growth portfolios have actually generated very similar returns. The value portfolio has a CAGR of 13.7%, and the high forecast growth portfolio has a CAGR of 14.0% since 1988. Effectively there has been little to choose between the two strategies, although it should be noted that the value portfolio has a markedly lower standard deviation of returns (17.7% for the value portfolio, against 25.1% from the growth portfolio). Thus, on a risk-adjusted measure, value would have significantly outperformed growth. So much for value stocks being riskier!

Figure 26.10 shows the portfolio returns from the global portfolios, the performance of the low PE portfolio alongside the high forecast earnings growth portfolio. The high forecast earnings growth portfolio earns a 10.2% CAGR p.a., while the low PE portfolio generates a 15.4% CAGR p.a.

KEY POINTS

- Growth is theoretically a good investment, but identifying growth ex ante is very difficult.
- We are all too confident and too optimistic about our ability to pick winners.
- The stories that underlie growth opportunities are generally appealing, but dangerous.
- All too often growth investing ends up simply buying expensive stocks.
- Value investing is an admission of our limitations.
- Buying cheap offers protection against mistakes.
- Value generally outperforms.

REGIONAL TABLES

Global

Table 26.7   Raw returns (%) 1975–2004

		Low				High
		5	4	3	2	1
Low	5	11.8	17.1	23.8	28.9	41.0
	4	10.9	9.1	13.0	17.9	26.7
PE	3	9.8	8.4	10.7	15.8	23.2
	2	11.7	9.0	11.8	12.2	23.8
High	1	2.9	5.8	4.4	5.8	15.8

Source: DrKW Macro research.

Table 26.8   Relative to market (%)

		Low				High	
		5	4	3	2	1	Average
Low	5	−3.0	2.3	9.0	14.1	26.2	9.7
	4	−3.9	−5.7	−1.8	3.1	11.9	0.7
PE	3	−5.0	−6.4	−4.1	1.0	8.4	−1.2
	2	−3.1	−5.8	−3.0	−2.6	9.0	−1.1
High	1	−11.9	−9.0	−10.4	−9.0	1.0	−7.8
Average		**−5.4**	**−4.9**	**−2.1**	**1.3**	**11.3**	

Source: DrKW Macro research.

Table 26.9   Median return (%)

		Low				High
		5	4	3	2	1
Low	5	8.8	16.2	22.1	28.1	32.6
	4	12.4	8.0	11.5	20.7	25.7
PE	3	11.4	9.6	14.4	17.4	21.1
	2	10.6	7.3	7.0	14.0	23.5
High	1	6.5	5.4	5.3	7.8	13.9

Source: DrKW Macro research.

Table 26.10 Distribution of firms across portfolio (%)

		Earnings Growth				
		Low				High
		5	4	3	2	1
Low	5	6.2	5.1	4.0	3.2	1.7
	4	3.9	4.4	4.6	4.6	2.6
PE	3	3.9	3.7	4.1	4.9	3.4
	2	3.4	3.8	3.9	4.3	4.6
High	1	2.7	3.1	3.4	3.1	7.4

Source: DrKW Macro research.

Table 26.11 Raw returns (%) 1988–2004

		Earnings Growth				
		Low				High
		5	4	3	2	1
Low	5	11.0	15.1	18.0	15.3	22.4
	4	3.3	9.5	14.3	20.8	28.5
EPS growth forecasts	3	−0.7	6.9	10.1	15.6	17.4
	2	1.8	0.2	5.7	13.2	16.5
High	1	2.1	13.9	8.0	7.1	14.2

Source: DrKW Macro research.

Table 26.12 Relative to market (%)

		Earnings Growth					
		Low				High	
		5	4	3	2	1	Average
Low	5	−0.6	3.5	6.4	3.7	10.8	4.8
	4	−8.3	−2.1	2.7	9.2	16.9	3.7
EPS growth forecasts	3	−12.3	−4.7	−1.5	4.0	5.8	−1.8
	2	−9.8	−11.4	−5.9	1.6	4.9	−4.1
High	1	−9.5	2.3	−3.6	−4.5	2.6	−2.5
Average		**−8.1**	**−2.5**	**−0.4**	**2.8**	**8.2**	

Source: DrKW Macro research.

Table 26.13   Relative to market (%)

		Earnings Growth				
		Low				High
		5	4	3	2	1
Low		5	10.2	13.4	18.1	19.8	19.4
		4	4.6	15.0	18.2	16.2	8.4
EPS growth forecasts		3	−0.2	9.6	14.8	19.7	17.2
		2	3.2	2.9	9.3	14.6	22.3
High		1	1.4	1.5	0.3	12.5	15.3

Source: DrKW Macro research.

Table 26.14   Distribution of firms across portfolio (%)

		Earnings Growth				
		Low				High
		5	4	3	2	1
Low		5	14.0	4.5	0.7	0.4	0.4
		4	3.0	10.3	5.0	1.1	0.6
EPS growth forecasts		3	1.3	3.0	10.3	4.5	0.9
		2	0.8	1.4	3.3	11.4	3.0
High		1	0.9	0.8	0.6	2.6	15.1

Source: DrKW Macro research.

USA

Table 26.15   Raw returns (%) 1975–2004

		Earnings Growth				
		Low				High
		5	4	3	2	1
Low	5	8.7	13.4	15.4	23.7	57.1
	4	5.3	9.5	11.3	17.7	27.8
PE	3	13.9	7.0	10.2	17.2	19.1
	2	20.3	8.0	5.4	14.7	22.6
High	1	10.6	13.4	7.9	11.2	16.7

Source: DrKW Macro research.

Table 26.16   Relative to market (%)

		Low				High	
		5	4	3	2	1	Average
Low	5	−6.8	−2.1	−0.1	8.2	41.6	8.2
	4	−10.2	−6.0	−4.2	2.2	12.3	−1.2
PE	3	−1.6	−8.5	−5.3	1.7	3.6	−2.0
	2	4.8	−7.5	−10.1	−0.8	7.1	−1.3
High	1	− 4.9	−2.1	− 7.6	−4.3	1.2	−3.5
Average		**−3.7**	**−5.2**	**−5.5**	**1.4**	**13.2**	

Source: DrKW Macro research.

Table 26.17   Median return (%)

		Low				High
		5	4	3	2	1
Low	5	9.7	13.6	15.3	21.2	29.7
	4	6.6	9.8	7.2	15.8	25.3
PE	3	19.4	7.6	14.5	22.4	13.4
	2	14.0	10.2	8.9	14.3	22.4
High	1	9.5	11.0	6.6	12.5	19.2

Source: DrKW Macro research.

Table 26.18   Distribution of firms across portfolio (%)

		Low				High
		5	4	3	2	1
Low	5	6.2	5.2	4.0	2.8	1.7
	4	3.9	5.3	4.4	3.9	2.4
PE	3	3.5	3.9	4.8	4.3	3.5
	2	3.5	3.0	3.8	5.6	4.1
High	1	2.8	2.5	2.9	3.4	8.3

Source: DrKW Macro research.

Table 26.19   Raw returns (1988–2004) %

		Earnings Growth				
		Low				High
		5	4	3	2	1
Low	5	13.7	17.2	6.8	6.8	12.6
	4	8.2	12.5	13.7	14.1	16.2
EPS growth forecasts	3	1.8	6.8	11.1	19.5	21.6
	2	1.9	0.0	1.2	14.0	20.9
High	1	1.0	4.6	15.0	12.2	18.5

Source: DrKW Macro research.

Table 26.20   Relative to market (%)

		Earnings Growth					
		Low				High	
		5	4	3	2	1	Average
Low	5	2.9	6.4	−4.1	−4.1	1.8	0.6
	4	−2.7	1.6	2.8	3.2	5.3	2.0
EPS growth forecasts	3	−9.1	−4.1	0.3	8.6	10.7	1.3
	2	−9.0	−10.9	−9.7	3.2	10.0	−3.3
High	1	−9.9	−6.2	4.1	1.4	7.6	−0.6
Average		**−5.5**	**−2.6**	**−1.3**	**2.4**	**7.1**	

Source: DrKW Macro research.

Table 26.21   Median return (%)

		Earnings Growth				
		Low				High
		5	4	3	2	1
Low	5	14.6	18.6	0.0	0.0	0.0
	4	9.3	10.7	13.5	16.1	0.0
EPS growth forecasts	3	0.0	7.9	10.6	15.8	10.8
	2	0.0	0.0	4.7	11.9	18.5
High	1	0.0	0.0	0.0	9.6	20.8

Source: DrKW Macro research.

Table 26.22   Distribution of firms across portfolio (%)

		Earnings Growth				
		Low				High
		5	4	3	2	1
Low	5	16.15	3.40	0.23	0.08	0.15
	4	2.04	13.03	4.06	0.65	0.21
EPS growth forecasts	3	0.51	2.16	13.20	3.63	0.53
	2	0.64	0.93	2.37	13.81	2.23
High	1	0.65	0.46	0.17	1.83	16.88

Source: DrKW Macro research.

Europe

Table 26.23   Raw returns (%) 1975–2004

		Earnings Growth				
		Low				High
		5	4	3	2	1
Low	5	14.4	21.7	32.4	36.0	36.5
	4	10.2	11.9	17.7	21.7	30.2
PE	3	12.2	7.2	12.4	18.3	22.5
	2	12.2	9.0	10.1	11.2	24.5
High	1	4.1	8.5	7.3	9.6	22.4

Source: DrKW Macro research.

Table 26.24   Relative to market (%)

		Earnings Growth					
		Low				High	
		5	4	3	2	1	Average
Low	5	−2.2	5.1	15.8	19.4	19.9	11.6
	4	−6.4	−4.7	1.1	5.1	13.6	1.7
PE	3	−4.4	−9.4	−4.2	1.7	5.9	−2.1
	2	−4.4	−7.6	−6.5	−5.4	7.9	−3.2
High	1	−12.5	−8.1	−9.3	−7.0	5.8	−6.2
Average		**−6.0**	**−4.9**	**−0.6**	**2.8**	**10.6**	

Source: DrKW Macro research.

Table 26.25   Median return (%)

		Earnings Growth				
		Low				High
		5	4	3	2	1
Low	5	4.4	14.9	27.7	24.7	17.5
	4	5.4	12.5	13.2	25.6	26.7
PE	3	3.7	8.3	12.8	11.5	20.7
	2	13.4	9.3	5.5	12.9	24.1
High	1	5.6	9.1	4.2	8.5	19.7

Source: DrKW Macro research.

Table 26.26   Distribution of firms
across portfolio (%)

		Earnings Growth				
		Low				High
		5	4	3	2	1
Low	5	6.6	5.3	3.7	2.8	1.6
	4	4.0	4.7	4.5	4.1	2.7
PE	3	3.6	3.8	4.7	4.8	3.1
	2	3.2	3.4	3.8	4.7	5.0
High	1	2.5	2.8	3.3	3.6	7.8

Source: DrKW Macro research.

Table 26.27   Raw returns (1988 – 2004) %

		Earnings Growth				
		Low				High
		5	4	3	2	1
Low	5	9.8	13.5	22.2	8.2	23.0
	4	4.6	11.1	16.7	23.4	19.3
EPS growth forecasts	3	−1.4	9.0	11.6	16.2	10.8
	2	11.4	−1.4	9.5	14.1	18.3
High	1	5.9	9.3	11.0	7.4	15.9

Source: DrKW Macro research.

Table 26.28   Relative to market (%)

		Earnings Growth					
		Low				High	
		5	4	3	2	1	Average
Low	5	−2.1	1.6	10.3	−3.7	11.1	3.4
	4	−7.3	−0.8	4.8	11.5	7.4	3.1
EPS growth forecasts	3	−13.3	−2.9	−0.3	4.3	−1.1	−2.7
	2	−0.5	−13.3	−2.4	2.2	6.4	−1.5
High	1	−6.0	−2.6	−0.9	−4.5	4.0	−2.0
Average		**−5.8**	**−3.6**	**2.3**	**2.0**	**5.6**	**0**

Source: DrKW Macro research.

Table 26.29   Median return (%)

		Low				High
		5	4	3	2	1
Low	5	1.9	14.9	19.9	0.0	13.8
	4	1.3	12.7	18.5	17.6	3.8
EPS growth forecasts	3	0.3	13.9	11.3	17.7	5.1
	2	11.7	−4.6	16.8	15.0	19.3
High	1	2.4	0.0	10.1	8.1	22.6

Source: DrKW Macro research.

Table 26.30   Distribution of firms across portfolios (%)

		Low				High
		5	4	3	2	1
Low	5	13.7	4.3	0.9	0.5	0.6
	4	3.4	9.7	4.7	1.5	0.7
EPS growth forecasts	3	1.2	3.6	9.5	4.6	1.0
	2	0.8	1.6	4.0	10.5	3.1
High	1	0.9	0.8	0.8	2.9	14.5

Source: DrKW Macro research.

Japan

Table 26.31   Raw returns (1975–2004) %

		Low				High
		5	4	3	2	1
Low	5	9.1	10.8	17.2	19.6	30.4
	4	8.5	12.5	13.0	16.6	38.3
PE	3	0.6	7.7	7.3	9.9	20.9
	2	−3.5	4.3	3.2	5.7	14.0
High	1	1.0	18.9	−1.8	2.4	11.4

Source: DrKW Macro research.

Table 26.32   Relative to market (%)

		Earnings Growth					
		Low				High	
		5	4	3	2	1	Average
Low	5	−0.5	1.2	7.6	10.0	20.8	7.8
	4	−1.1	2.9	3.4	7.0	28.7	8.2
PE	3	−9.0	−1.9	−2.3	0.3	11.3	−0.3
	2	−13.1	−5.3	−6.4	−3.9	4.4	−4.8
High	1	−8.6	9.3	−11.4	−7.2	1.8	−3.2
Average		**−6.5**	**1.2**	**−1.8**	**1.3**	**13.4**	**0**

Source: DrKW Macro research.

Table 26.33   Median return (%)

		Earnings Growth				
		Low				High
		5	4	3	2	1
Low	5	11.1	9.8	16.9	17.2	10.9
	4	8.1	11.1	9.3	16.7	18.1
PE	3	−4.0	−2.4	1.6	−2.4	13.3
	2	−2.4	6.5	5.2	4.8	11.3
High	1	−1.3	2.6	−2.8	2.3	11.6

Source: DrKW Macro research.

Table 26.34   Distribution of firms across portfolios (%)

		Earnings Growth				
		Low				High
		5	4	3	2	1
Low	5	7.2	5.0	4.3	2.7	0.9
	4	3.8	5.1	5.1	3.9	2.1
PE	3	3.3	4.3	4.4	4.9	3.0
	2	3.2	3.7	3.4	5.1	4.6
High	1	2.5	2.0	2.7	3.4	9.4

Source: DrKW Macro research.

Table 26.35   Raw returns (1988–2004) %

		Earnings Growth				
		Low				High
		5	4	3	2	1
Low		5	5.2	6.9	9.9	6.0	3.6
	4	−0.9	1.9	8.1	10.9	20.0
EPS growth forecasts	3	−3.2	3.5	4.6	9.2	4.7
	2	−6.4	15.7	−3.1	−2.5	12.7
High	1	−5.0	−0.6	11.9	1.2	2.8

Source: DrKW Macro research.

Table 26.36   Relative to market (%)

		Earnings Growth					
		Low				High	
		5	4	3	2	1	Average
Low	5	0.7	2.4	5.4	1.5	−0.9	1.8
	4	−5.4	−2.6	3.6	6.4	15.5	3.5
EPS growth forecasts	3	−7.7	−1.0	0.1	4.7	0.2	−0.7
	2	−10.9	11.2	−7.6	−7.0	8.2	−1.2
High	1	−9.5	−5.1	7.4	−3.3	−1.7	−2.4
Average		**−6.6**	**1.0**	**1.8**	**0.5**	**4.3**	

Source: DrKW Macro research.

Table 26.37   Median return (%)

		Earnings Growth				
		Low				High
		5	4	3	2	1
Low	5	2.2	6.3	0.9	0.0	0.0
	4	−0.7	7.2	11.0	12.1	0.0
EPS growth forecasts	3	−5.4	4.1	1.4	5.1	0.0
	2	−2.2	0.0	−2.9	−1.1	7.2
High	1	0.0	0.0	0.0	−3.1	2.9

Source: DrKW Macro research.

Table 26.38   Distribution of firms across portfolios (%)

		Earnings Growth				
		Low				High
		5	4	3	2	1
Low	5	11.8	5.6	1.5	0.5	0.6
	4	3.8	7.8	6.0	1.8	0.5
EPS growth forecasts	3	2.4	3.9	8.2	5.2	0.7
	2	1.0	1.7	3.4	9.5	4.2
High	1	1.0	0.9	1.1	3.0	14.0

Source: DrKW Macro research.

27

Better Value (or The Dean Was Right!)[*]

Written with Rui Antunes

In 1934, Graham and Dodd argued that one should cyclically adjust PE ratios by using a moving average of earnings of "not less than 5 years and preferably 7 or 10 years". Despite the age of this advice, it doesn't appear that anyone has heeded it. We find evidence that using a Graham and Dodd PE can massively enhance stock selection relative to a simple trailing PE.

- In their bible, *Security Analysis* (1934), Ben Graham and David Dodd urged investors and analysts to use a cyclically adjusted PE to avoid being whipsawed around by the shifting sands of the economic cycle. If investors extrapolate the past, then during boom times they will be too optimistic and during downturns they will become too pessimistic. Thus the use of a moving average of earnings at a greater duration than the business cycle should help investors to focus on the true earning ability of a stock.

- We have long argued for the use of Graham and Dodd PEs when conducting country level valuation work. However, it struck me the other day that I had never seen Graham and Dodd PEs tested as a stock selection aid. So with the ever-indispensable aid of Rui Antunes of our Global Quant team, I set out to test whether using cyclically adjusted PEs could improve on a simple value strategy.

- A straightforward strategy of buying low one year trailing earnings PE and selling high PE stocks applied to the MSCI World Index generated a return of 11% p.a. over our sample period of 1980–2005 (with a one-year holding period and annual rebalancing). However, we found that extending the time horizon for the calculation of earnings could improve performance significantly.

- For instance, using a 5-year moving average of earnings the differential between high and low priced stocks rises to 18% p.a. on average. By the time we extend the time horizon all the way out to Graham and Dodd's maximum suggested 10-year moving average, the gap between low PE and high PE stocks is an average 25% p.a.!

- The gains to such a strategy appear on both sides of the equation. When using simple one-year trailing PEs high-priced stocks returned an average of 9% p.a. However, when a 10-year moving average of earnings is used the return from the highest PE stocks drops to −4% p.a.! A lesson here for growth managers perhaps?

- Of course, equal long/short portfolios are not available to everybody. If we focus on relative performance, we find that concentrating on low Graham and Dodd PEs outperforms the

[*]This article appeared in *Global Equity Strategy* on 28 June 2005. The material discussed was accurate at the time of publication.

market by 13% p.a. on average over our sample, compared to 5.5% outperformance using a simple one-year trailing PE.

- To our knowledge, this is the first time that anyone has tested the idea of stock selection using Graham and Dodd PEs. Not only are the potential returns impressive, it serves as a reminder of the persistence of bad habits in markets. Graham and Dodd suggested cyclically adjusting PEs way back in 1934, and yet investors still obsess and insist on trying to forecast the cycle as the best way of adding value!

Long time readers of *Global Equity Strategy* will know that we often refer to Graham and Dodd PEs. These are PEs based on current prices divided by the 10-year moving average of as reported earnings. The rationale for the use of such a method comes from Graham and Dodd's classic 1934 *Security Analysis*, in which they wrote that if one was to use price earnings ratios, then the earnings behind that calculation should be an average of *"not less than 5 years, preferably 7 or 10 years"*. The reason for such an average is simply to abstract from the business cycle. Graham recognized that the market was capable of getting carried away with the cycle: "The market is fond of making mountains of molehills and exaggerating ordinary vicissitudes into major setbacks. Even a mere lack of interest or enthusiasm may impel a price decline to absurdly low levels."

Many object to the notion of moving averages of past earnings since they obviously ignore future growth. However, forecasts of earnings growth seem to be notoriously unreliable. Indeed, as we have shown many times in the past, earnings forecasts are usually little more than extrapolations of past growth rates.

Graham (also known as the Dean of Wall Street) noted that this was a bad idea in the context of a prior investment mania "Why did the investing public turn its attention from dividends, from asset values, and from earnings, to transfer it almost exclusively to the earnings trend?" He urged analysts to base "the projection of future earnings and dividends. . . (on) some past average as the best measure of the future." Note that this statement is in *levels* not *growth rates*!

Some will object that using a simple trailing moving average is not good enough, and that we should use some fancy estimate of the trend of earnings to remove the cycle. But, as the Dean opined, he had never seen "dependable calculations made about common-stock values. . . that went beyond simple arithmetic or the most elementary algebra".

On a marketing trip to Paris, it suddenly struck me that I had never seen any work testing a value strategy based on Graham and Dodd PEs. Could it be that simply using cyclically adjusted PE could be useful as a stock selection tool?

With the ever able and indispensable aid of Rui Antunes of our Global Quant team I set out to test this hypothesis. The results we uncovered amazed even us. We used the MSCI World Index as our universe and our data runs from 1980 to 2005. At the start of each year deciles are formed and their performance measured over the next 12 months. Negative PEs were excluded, and Graham and Dodd PEs below 1 were excluded, as it is highly likely that such a pricing indicates that the stock is about to go bust. It would seem unlikely that any value-driven investors would have taken a risk on a stock trading at less than 1 times 5-year average earnings, say. We could have added them to the highest PE decile but chose to simply exclude them for a cleaner set of results. If a company did not have a full set of earnings, we computed the PE based on the maximum amount of data that was available.[1]

The potential gains that arise from moving from a simple trailing PE to a Graham and Dodd PE are exceptionally large. Table 27.1 highlights the pattern we uncovered. The value premium (the spread between the low PE and high PE deciles) increases monotonically as we extend the time horizon for the calculation of the earnings variable.

A one-year time horizon (i.e simple trailing earnings PE) generates an 11% differential between low and high PE stocks. However, as we increase the moving average on the earnings, so our returns begin to rise. Using a 5-year moving average of earnings, the differential between high and low priced stocks rises to 18% p.a. The extra performance comes from both sides of

---

[1] As usual we have ignored costs in our calculation but we suspect that they should be low given the annual nature of rebalancing.

Table 27.1   Returns to using G&D PEs (1980–2005)

Earnings time average (years)	Return from high PE stocks % p.a.	Return from Low PE stocks % p.a.	Differential % p.a.
1	9	20	11
3	8	23	15
5	5	23	18
7	0	22	22
10	−4	21	25

Source: DrKW Macro research.

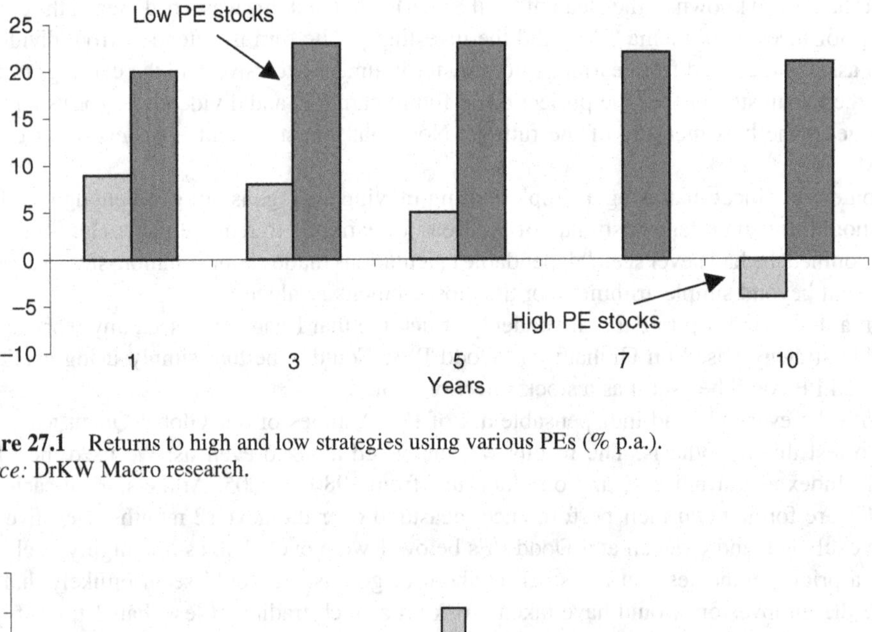

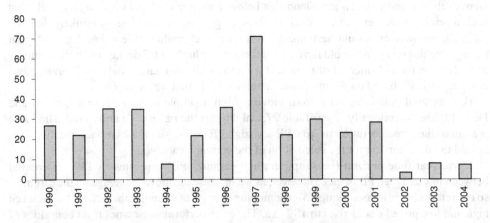

Figure 27.1   Returns to high and low strategies using various PEs (% p.a.).
Source: DrKW Macro research.

Figure 27.2   Annual returns to G&D 10-year PE equal long/short strategy (%).
Source: DrKW Macro research.

Table 27.2 Analysis of the G&D equal long/short portfolio
(1980–2005)

	vs. market	vs. value index
Beta	0.1	0.1
Alpha	24.3	24.3
t-stat	4.9	4.7
IR	1.4	1.3

Source: DrKW Macro research.

the equation. The return on expensive stocks drops to 5%, and that on cheap stocks rises to 23%.

By the time we get up to Graham and Dodd's favourite measure, 10-year moving average earnings, the return differential increase to 25% p.a.! The return on the most expensive stocks is now negative (−4% p.a.), while the cheapest stocks generate a 21% p.a. return. The advantages of removing the cycle from PEs should be clear for all to see (Figure 27.1).

Figure 27.2 shows the annual return for the equal long/short (zero net investment) portfolio going long the lowest Graham and Dodd PE decile and short the highest Graham and Dodd PE decile on the basis on 10-year moving average years. The absence of a single negative year even during the tech bubble is startling.

Table 27.2 shows the alpha, beta and information ratio of such a strategy. Given the equal long/short nature of the strategy, it isn't a surprise that the beta is close to zero. The alpha is very high, and very significantly positive. The information ratios would put this strategy into the top decile of active managers!

Of course, long/short strategies are not everyone's cup of tea. So could the use of Graham and Dodd PEs aid long-only fund managers in their stock selection? Table 27.3 shows the under- and overperformance relative to the World Index. It shows that long-only managers should be able to add value by using cyclically adjusted PEs.

Following a simple strategy of buying cheap trailing PEs has resulted in a 5.5% p.a. outperformance relative to the market (see Figure 27.3). However, if you had used a Graham and Dodd PE your results would have been markedly better. A 3-year moving average of earnings would have nearly doubled your outperformance to 10% p.a. At the longest horizon for our moving averages, a 13% p.a. outperformance would have been achieved historically!

Table 27.3 Returns to using G&D PEs (relative performance % p.a.)
(1980–2005)

Earnings time average (year)	Return from high PE stocks % p.a.	Return from Low PE stocks % p.a.
1	−5.5	5.5
3	−5	10
5	−7	11
7	−10	12
10	−12	13

Source: DrKW Macro research.

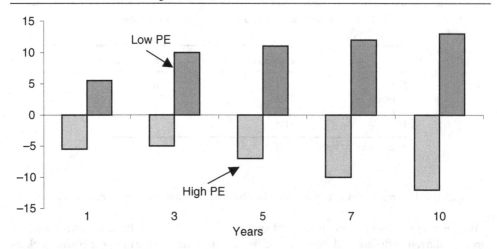

Figure 27.3   Returns to high and low strategies using various PEs (relative performance % p.a.).
Source: DrKW Macro research.

Table 27.4 shows the alpha, beta and information ratios for a long-only strategy using the Graham and Dodd 10-year moving average earnings measure. Given the long-only nature of the strategy, it isn't surprising to see a beta of one against both the market and the MSCI World Value index (Figure 27.4). However, the alpha is significant against both indices, around 10–12% p.a! The ex-post information ratios would put these strategies into the top quartile of active equity managers.

The difference between the long-only and the long/short strategies helps to support the idea that, to maximize returns, investors should be allowed to short equities. Figure 27.5 shows what the returns to $100 invested in one of four strategies since 1990 would have been.

A simple buy-and-hold strategy would have generated a 6.6% p.a. return. Buying the MSCI World Value index raised this return to 7.8% p.a. (see Table 27.5). However, our Graham and Dodd PE strategies did significantly better, the long-only portfolio generated a 17.8% p.a. return. It should be noted that the long-only G&D strategy did have higher risk than the buy-and-hold strategies. However, if we equalized the risk then the return on the G&D portfolio would still have been 13.2% p.a.

The star performer was, of course, the Graham and Dodd equal long/short portfolio. This strategy generated a 22.4% p.a. return over the period 1990–2004. Not only did it deliver stunning outperformance but it did so with less risk than the buy-and-hold strategies!

Table 27.4   Analysis of the G&D long-only portfolio (1980–2005)

	vs market	vs value index
Beta	1.0	1.1
Alpha	12.6	10.8
t-stat	2.9	2.5
IR	0.8	0.7

Source: DrKW Macro research.

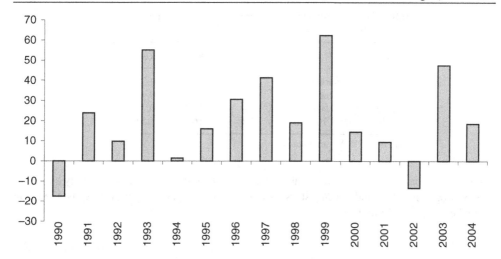

Figure 27.4   Annual returns to G&D 10-year PE equal long-only strategy (%).
Source: DrKW Macro research.

Investors would be well served to remember Ben Graham's advice on a wide variety of issues, including such sagely words as

> Buying a neglected and therefore undervalued issue for profit, generally proves to be a protracted and patience-trying experience. And selling (short) a too popular and therefore overvalued issue is apt to be a test not only of one's courage and stamina but also of the depth of one's pocketbooks.

To our knowledge this is the first time that anyone has tested the idea of stock selection using Graham and Dodd style PEs. The returns to such a strategy look to certainly be worthy of deeper investigation. It also serves as a testament to the nature of under reaction and the

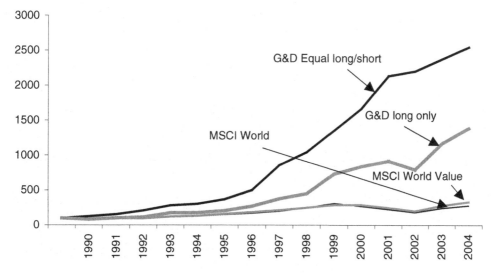

Figure 27.5 $100 invested in G&D PE strategies, MSCI World, and MSCI World Value.
Source: DrKW Macro Research.

Table 27.5   Return and risk of various strategies (% p.a.)
(1980–2005)

Strategy	CAGR	Risk	Return/Risk
Buy-and-hold market	6.6	17.9	0.37
Buy-and-hold value index	7.8	17.2	0.45
Long-only G&D 10 year	17.8	23.1	0.77
Long/short G&D 10 year	22.4	16.7	1.34

Source: DrKW Macro research.

persistence of bad habits in markets that Graham and Dodd first suggested cyclically adjusting PEs way back in 1934, and yet investors still obsess and insist on trying to forecast the cycle as the best way of adding value!

28

The Little Note that Beats the Markets[*]

Written with Sebastian Lancetti

In his best-selling *Little Book* Joel Greenblatt shows that buying good companies at cheap prices is a great idea. We have backtested his recommended approach in the USA, Europe ex UK, UK and Japan. On average we found that the *Little Book* strategy beat the markets by around 7% p.a. between 1993 and 2005, and with lower risk than the market! Value plus quality seems to make sense.

- Joel Greenblatt has done the world a service. He has distilled the essence of value investing into a mere 155 pages. Some 615 pages shorter than Graham and Dodd's *Security Analysis* and 471 pages shorter than Graham's *Intelligent Investor*, *The Little Book That Beats the Market* is a powerful guide to the ideas of value investing.
- In the *Little Book*, Greenblatt uses a simple screening technique combining value and quality. The basic idea is to rank the universe on return on capital and by earnings yield, and then to buy the 30 stocks with the best combined score, i.e. good companies at bargain prices.
- The results of our backtest suggest that Greenblatt's strategy isn't unique to the USA. We tested the *Little Book* strategy on US, European, UK and Japanese markets between 1993 and 2005. The results are impressive. The *Little Book* strategy beat the market (an equally weighted stock index) by 3.6%, 8.8%, 7.3% and 10.8% in the various regions respectively. And in all cases with lower volatility than the market! The outperformance was even better against the cap-weighted indices.
- Greenblatt argues that EBIT/EV is a better measure of value than the simple earnings yield since it explicitly incorporates the amount of debt deployed in the creation of operational leverage. We find that in all regions using EBIT/EV beats the simple earnings yield (except Japan where it has effectively equal honours).
- In general we find that the EBIT/EV value strategy is very powerful. For instance, in the UK, it outperforms the equally weighted market by nearly 13% p.a. over our sample! Performing even better than the *Little Book* strategy! A pure value strategy based on this modified earnings yield seems to perform particularly strongly in the USA and the UK.
- However, pure value strategies may have added career risk for professional investors. We show that a pure value strategy suffered far worse during the bubble years, than the *Little Book* strategy. So a fund manager following the *Little Book* strategy was unlikely to have been fired, while pure value fund managers would have found their life very uncomfortable.
- Greenblatt suggests two reasons why investors will struggle to follow the *Little Book* strategy. Firstly, following a quant model is relatively boring, not meeting company management or

---

[*]This article appeared in *Global Equity Strategy* on 9 March 2006. The material discussed was accurate at the time of publication.

brokers takes some of the fun out of investing! Secondly, because this is a value strategy it requires patience. There will be years when the strategy doesn't work (although it rarely results in absolute losses). Warren Buffet may well have been right when he said "Investing is simple but not easy".

On a recent trip to the USA I was afforded the rare luxury of perusing a book store. I didn't even have to venture to the business section to be accosted by Joel Greenblatt's best-seller – *The Little Book That Beats the Market*. Being a sucker for value stories I couldn't help but buy a copy (after all, the book was a value play in its own right costing a mere $20).

I wasn't disappointed. Greenblatt has captured the essence of value investing perfectly. Some 615 pages shorter than Graham and Dodd's *Security Analysis*, and 471 pages shorter than Graham's *Intelligent Investor*, the *Little Book* represents one of the shortest but wisest books I have ever had the good fortune to stumble across. As Greenblatt writes, "You must understand only two basic concepts. First, buying good companies at bargain prices makes sense... Second, it can take Mr Market several years to recognize a bargain."

Yes, the book is written so that an 11-year-old can understand it; yes, it does have a habit of repeating itself, but are either of these traits really so appalling? Certainly aiming for as wide an audience as possible is surely only sensible. As a behaviouralist, I am well aware of people's very limited capacity to learn, so repetition is no bad thing either.

Now I must confess to a degree of confirmatory bias while reading the book. I am known as an investor who places value above all else, so it is little wonder that I found Greenblatt's book comforting. I also regularly expound the virtues of quantitative analysis as a partial remedy to behavioural ills, so a book with a quant-driven screen at its heart was bound to find favour with me.

However, being a sceptic by nature I also wanted to check Greenblatt's findings, and more importantly to see if the same approach worked in other markets as a check on the robustness of the screen. So upon my return from the USA I began to pressure Sebastian Lancetti of the Quant team to run the numbers. Now poor Sebastian has the misfortune to have to sit next to me – a situation that resulted in my near constant nagging of the poor lad. Eventually my persistence paid dividends, Sebastian decided the only way to shut me up was to run the numbers.

Sebastian did, however, manage to extract a revenge fitting for a quant. He gave me an enormous amount of very exciting data/results, which left me in a quandary as to how best summarize it. So here is my best shot.

THE METHODOLOGY AND THE DATA

We decided to examine the USA, Europe ex UK, the UK and Japan. The universe utilized was a combination of the FTSE and MSCI indices. This gave us the largest sample of data. We analysed the data from 1993 until the end of 2005. All returns and prices were measured in dollars. Utilities and financials were both excluded from the test, for reasons that will become obvious very shortly. We only rebalance yearly.

In the *Little Book*, Greenblatt uses a simple screening technique combining value and quality. This is something we have written about in the past (see *Global Equity Strategy*, 16 March 2005). The basic idea is to rank the universe on return on capital (where 1 is the company with the highest ROC), and by earnings yield (where 1 is the company with the highest earnings yield), and then sum the two ranks to give a combined score. Greenblatt then recommends buying the 30 highest ranked stocks.

Return on capital is defined as EBIT/(Net working capital + Net fixed assets). EBIT is used to level the playing field across companies using different levels of debt and facing differing tax rates. Net working capital and net fixed assets are combined to give tangible capital employed. As Greenblatt notes, "Net working capital was used because a company has

Table 28.1 The *Little Book* strategy (1993–2005)

Global Summary	Top 30	Market	Outperformance	Relative Risk vs Market
USA	17.1	13.5	3.6	0.92
Europe ex UK	22.0	13.3	8.8	0.95
UK	17.0	9.7	7.3	0.91
Japan	18.1	7.3	10.8	0.87

Source: DrKW Macro research.

to fund its receivables and inventory ... but does not have to lay out money for its payables...
In addition ... a company must also fund the purchase of fixed assets necessary to conduct
its business." Together these two give an estimate of how much capital a company is using to
generate its business.

The earnings yield that Greenblatt deploys is not the standard upside down PE. Instead he
prefers to use EBIT/Enterprise value. Again this, he argues, takes account of the amount of
debt a company is using to generate its earnings. Effectively, Greenblatt takes almost a private
equity view of a company.

To test the importance of particular definitions, we also ran a more common earnings yield
(referred to as PE in the text below) and return on asset (ROA) version of the model. We also
ran separate tests on all the variables to see if, say, the earnings yield was really driving the
results or if ROA had an important role to play.

THE RESULTS

The *Little Book* Works

Table 28.1 shows the results from buying the top 30 ranked stocks versus an equal weighted
'market' index for each of the regions we investigated. The results certainly support the
notions put forward in the *Little Book*. In all the regions, the *Little Book* strategy substantially
outperformed the market, and with lower risk! The range of outperformance went from just
over 3.5% in the USA to an astounding 10% in Japan. Those eager to know which stocks the
Little Book strategy currently recommends should see the stock lists in Table 28.12.

However, as a value investor I have always believed that buying bad companies at very low
prices is also a perfectly viable strategy, provided, of course, they don't go bankrupt. So how
does the *Little Book* strategy stack up against a straight value strategy of buying the highest
earnings yield stocks using Greenblatt's definition of yield?

Table 28.2 EBIT/EV value strategy (1993–2005)

Global Summary	Top 30	Market	Outperformance	Relative Risk
USA	19.7	13.5	6.3	0.66
Europe ex UK	22.2	13.3	8.9	1.12
UK	22.6	9.7	12.9	0.78
Japan	14.5	7.3	7.2	0.70

Source: DrKW Macro research.

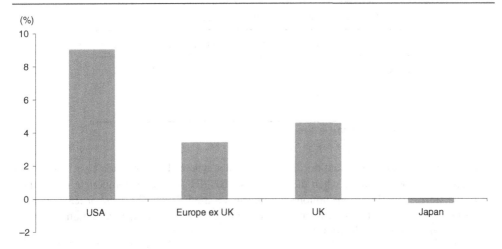

Figure 28.1 Highest decile EBIT/EV minus highest decile E/P return (1993–2005, average, %).
Source: DrKW Macro research.

Value works

The answer is shown in Table 28.2. In general, the return on capital seems to bring little to the party in the UK or the USA. In all the regions except Japan, the returns are higher from simply using a pure EY filter than they are from using the *Little Book* strategy. In the USA and the UK, the gains from a pure EY strategy are very sizeable. In Europe, a pure EY strategy doesn't alter the results from the *Little Book* strategy very much, but it is more volatile than the *Little Book* strategy. In Japan, the returns are lower than the *Little Book* strategy, but so is the relative volatility.

EBIT/EV better than simple PE

How does the Greenblatt modified earnings compare to a standard inverted PE? Is there extra information contained in the EBIT/EV calculation that is of use to investors relative to a simple trailing E/P?

The answer would generally appear to be a resounding yes. Figure 28.1 shows that the EBIT/EV earnings yield significantly outperformed the standard earnings yield strategy everywhere except Japan – where it made essentially no difference. The extra return was delivered with very little extra risk (indeed in the USA, the modified EY was actually lower risk than the normal E/P!). So EBIT/EV would seem to be a better indicator of value that the simple E/P.

QUALITY MATTERS FOR VALUE

At the end of the *Little Book*, Greenblatt suggests that a strategy using a standard earnings yield and return on assets should give results that relatively closely mimic those of his own preferred methodology. Table 28.3 shows the results of our backtest of this hypothesis. In general the returns are lower than the *Little Book* strategy, but of a similar magnitude. This again suggests the findings of the *Little Book* to be robust.

Table 28.3   PE and ROA strategy (1993–2005)

Global Summary	Top 30	Market	Outperformance	Relative Risk
USA	17.2	13.5	3.8	0.80
Europe ex UK	18.8	13.3	5.5	0.90
UK	16.2	9.7	6.5	0.90
Japan	16.6	7.3	9.3	0.60

Source: DrKW Macro research.

Interestingly, unlike the situation discussed earlier where the ROC didn't seem to add a huge amount to performance when the base was EBIT/EV, the ROA component does add a lot to the simple E/P. In all our regions the returns on the E/P + ROA were at least equal to (and often higher than) the returns on the E/P approach on its own (see the region reports at the end of the chapter for details).

CAREER DEFENCE AS AN INVESTMENT STRATEGY

The figures below suggest a reason why one might want to have some form of quality input into the basic value screen. Figure 28.2 shows the top and bottom ranked deciles by EBIT/EV for the USA (although other countries tell a similar story). It clearly shows the impact of the bubble. For a number of years, during the bubble, stocks that were simply cheap were shunned as we all know.

However, Figure 28.3 shows the top and bottom deciles using the combined *Little Book* strategy again for the USA. The bubble is again visible, but the ROC component of the screen prevented the massive underperformance that was seen with the pure value strategy. Of course, the resulting returns are lower, but a fund manager following this strategy is unlikely to have lost his job.

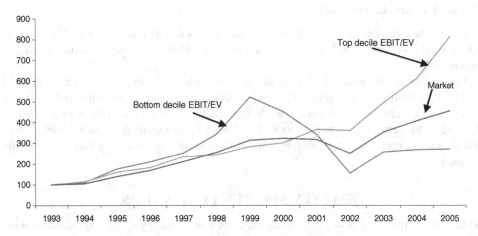

Figure 28.2   Top and bottom value decile performance using EBIT/EV.
Source: DrKW Macro research.

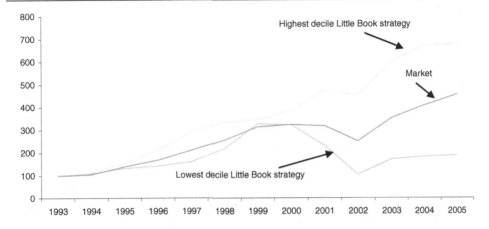

Figure 28.3   Top and bottom value decile performance using EBIT/EV plus ROC.
Source: DrKW Macro research.

WHAT ABOUT THE LONG/SHORT VIEW?

So far we have really only concerned ourselves with the long-only strategies – buying the top 30 ranked companies by the various criteria, although in the previous section we did highlight the performance of the bottom deciles. Could this strategy be deployed by those in hedge fund land?

In theory, yes. Figure 28.4 shows the spread in performance between the highest and lowest deciles for the various criteria we have tested. All show very high potential alpha. None is clearly any better than the rest across all regions but most suggest that a value plus quality strategy should be a viable option for those of the long/short persuasion. However, it should be noted that we only computed annual returns. The monthly profile may be less attractive for a hedge fund perspective (more on this below).

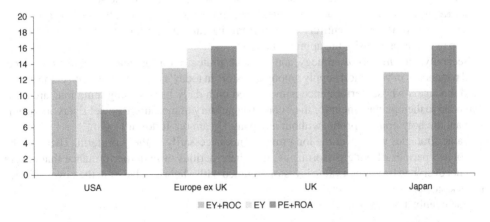

Figure 28.4   Spreads between the highest and lowest deciles across strategies (1993–2005).
Source: DrKW Macro research.

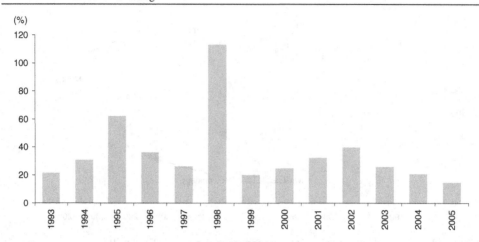

Figure 28.5 European EBIT/EV spread – high vs low decile (1993–2005).
Source: DrKW Macro research.

THE FUTURE FOR THE *LITTLE BOOK*

What does the future hold for the *Little Book* strategy and its related ilk? Well, as Greenblatt points out, the ranking tool is obviously a call on relative performance so in theory it should continue to generate returns over fairly long periods of time (Figure 28.5). As we have pointed out before, as the spread between the extremes in terms of value narrows so do the likely returns from such a strategy, but as long as the spread is positive, then in general it pays to continue to have a value tilt (see *Global Equity Strategy*,19 July 2005).

Greenblatt suggests two reasons why investors will struggle to follow the *Little Book* strategy. Both ring true with us from our meeting with investors over the years. The first is "investing by using a magic formula may take away some of the fun". Following a quant model or even a set of rules takes a lot of the excitement out of stock investing. What would you do all day if you didn't have to meet companies or sit down with the sell side?

As Keynes noted, "The game of professional investment is intolerably boring and over-exacting to anyone who is entirely exempt from the gambling instinct; whilst he who has it must pay to this propensity the appropriate toll."

Secondly, the *Little Book* strategy, and all value strategies for that matter, requires patience. And patience is in very short supply among investors in today's markets. I've even come across fund managers whose performance is monitored on a daily basis – congratulations are to be extended to their management for their complete mastery of measuring noise! Everyone seems to want the holy grail of profits without any pain. Dream on. It doesn't exist.

Value strategies work over the long run, but not necessarily in the short term. There can be prolonged periods of underperformance. It is these periods of underperformance that ensure that not everyone becomes a value investor (coupled with a hubristic belief in their own abilities to pick stocks).

As Greenblatt notes,

> Imagine diligently watching those stocks each day as they do worse than the market averages over the course of many months or even years. . . The magic formula portfolio fared poorly relative to

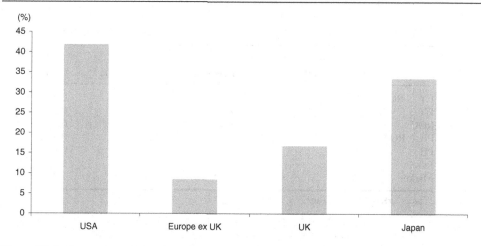

Figure 28.6   Percentage of years in which the *Little Book* strategy failed to beat the market average.
Source: DrKW Macro research.

the market average in 5 out of every 12 months tested. For full-year periods. . . failed to beat the market averages once every four years.

Figure 28.6 shows the percentage of years within our sample where the *Little Book* strategy failed to beat the market average in each of the respective regions. Both Europe and the UK show surprisingly few years of historic market underperformance. However, investors should bear in mind the lessons from the USA and Japan, where underperformance has been seen on a considerably more frequent basis.

It is this periodic underperformance that really helps to ensure the survival of such strategies. As long as investors continue to be overconfident in their abilities to consistently pick winners, and myopic enough that even a year of underperformance can send them running, then strategies such as the *Little Book* are likely to continue to do well over the long run. Thankfully for those of us with faith in such models, the traits just described seem to be immutable characteristics of most people. As Warren Buffet said, "Investing is simple but not easy".

TABLES AND FIGURES

Regional Results

The tables and charts below present the summary details on the various strategies tested.

EY + ROC = The *Little Book* strategy

EY = EBIT/EV

ROC = Return on capital as defined above

PE + ROA = simple trailing earnings yield plus return on assets

PE = simple trailing earnings yield

ROA = return on assets

USA

Table 28.4   Summary of tested strategies – top decile characteristics (1993–2005)

	Average Annual Return (%)	Risk (%)	Return/Risk	Beta
EY + ROC	18.1	15.2	1.2	0.6
EY	19.8	13.4	1.5	0.3
ROC	17.0	19.7	0.9	0.4
PE + ROA	18.8	14.0	1.3	0.7
PE	12.1	17.4	0.7	0.8
ROA	19.7	27.3	0.7	1.2
Market	14.7	16.9	0.9	1.0

Source: DrKW Macro research.

Table 28.5   The long/short view (CAGR,%) (1993–2005)

	High Decile	Low Decile	Spread
EY + ROC	17.2	5.3	11.9
EY	19.1	8.7	10.4
ROC	15.5	10.4	5.1
PE + ROA	18.0	9.8	8.1
PE	10.8	10.0	0.8
ROA	16.7	8.2	8.5

Source: DrKW Macro research.

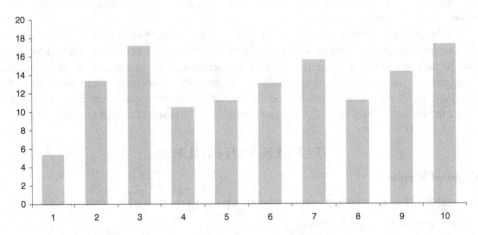

Figure 28.7   The *Little Book* strategy by decile – CAGR (1993–2005).
Source: DrKW Macro research.

Figure 28.7 shows the return by decile for the *Little Book* strategy. For those who have read Greenblatt's book, our deciles don't look as even. His show a monotonically increasing relationship. However, this results from his choice of the Russell 3000 as a universe. We have a much smaller universe of around 750 stocks, so in our equally weighted portfolios each stock matters more. Hence the very strong performance of decile 2 and 3 is actually down to only a couple of stocks in a single year.

Europe ex UK

Table 28.6   Summary of tested strategies – top decile characteristics (1993–2005)

	Average Annual Return (%)	Risk (%)	Return/Risk	Beta
EY + ROC	21.8	20.3	1.1	0.9
EY	24.3	21.6	1.1	0.8
ROC	18.4	23.3	0.8	0.7
PE + ROA	22.7	19.0	1.2	0.8
PE	22.5	24.3	0.9	1.1
ROA	21.8	25.8	0.8	1.1
Market	15.0	20.8	0.7	1.0

Source: DrKW Macro research.

Table 28.7   The long short view – CAGR returns % (1993–2005)

CAGR	High Decile	Low Decile	Spread
EY + ROC	20.2	6.9	13.3
EY	22.7	6.9	15.9
ROC	16.0	6.8	9.2
PE + ROA	21.3	5.2	16.2
PE	20.4	4.9	15.5
ROA	19.0	7.9	11.1

Source: DrKW Macro research.

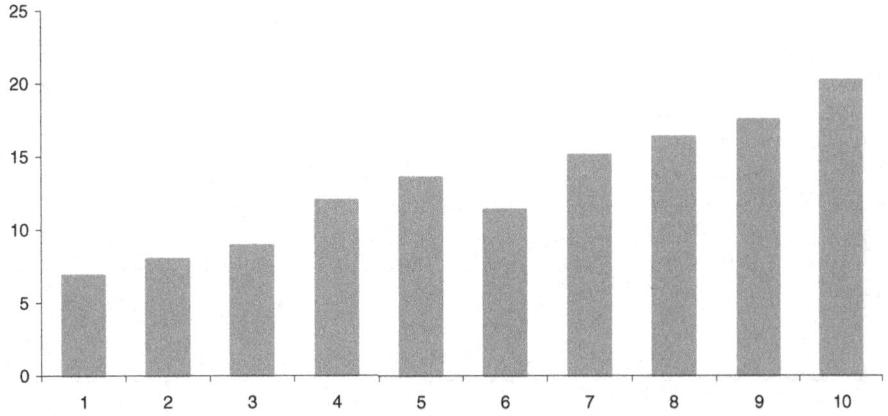

Figure 28.8   The *Little Book* strategy by decile – CAGR (1993–2005).
Source: DrKW Macro research.

UK

Table 28.8 Summary of tested strategies – top decile characteristics (1993–2005)

	Annual Average Return (%)	Risk (%)	Return/Risk	Beta
EY + ROC	18.7	21.5	0.9	0.8
EY	23.3	21.1	1.1	0.5
ROC	15.3	27.8	0.6	0.6
PE + ROA	18.2	21.6	0.8	0.8
PE	18.9	21.5	0.9	0.8
ROA	16.4	30.9	0.5	1.2
Market	12.0	24.3	0.5	1.0

Source: DrKW Macro research.

Table 28.9 The long short view – CAGR % (1993–2005)

	Highest Decile	Lowest Decile	Spread
EY + ROC	17.0	1.9	15.1
EY	21.8	3.8	17.9
ROC	12.4	5.4	7.0
PE + ROA	16.5	0.5	16.0
PE	17.5	4.1	13.3
ROA	12.7	−2.6	15.3

Source: DrKW Macro research.

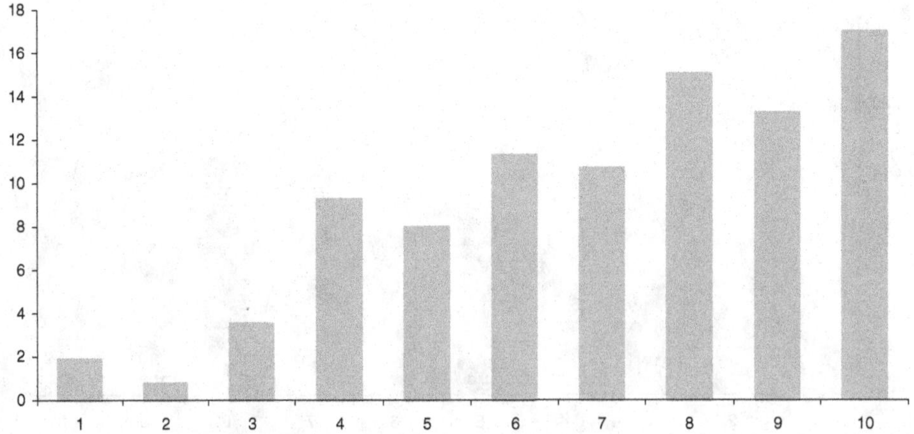

Figure 28.9 The *Little Book* strategy by decile – CAGR (1993–2005).
Source: DrKW Macro research.

Japan

Table 28.10   Summary of tested strategies – top decile characteristics (1993–2005)

	Annual Average Return (%)	Risk (%)	Return/Risk	Beta
EY + ROC	17.6	17.8	1.0	0.6
EY	15.6	18.2	0.9	0.6
ROC	10.2	19.0	0.5	0.3
PE + ROA	17.1	13.3	1.3	0.4
PE	15.4	18.1	0.9	0.6
ROA	14.2	22.6	0.6	0.7
Market	9.9	24.8	0.4	1.0

Source: DrKW Macro research.

Table 28.11   The long short view – CAGR % (1993–2005)

	High Decile	Low Decile	Spread
EY + ROC	16.5	3.7	12.7
EY	14.2	3.9	10.3
ROC	8.8	4.6	4.1
PE + ROA	16.4	0.4	16.1
PE	14.1	−2.8	16.9
ROA	12.2	3.9	8.3

Source: DrKW Macro research.

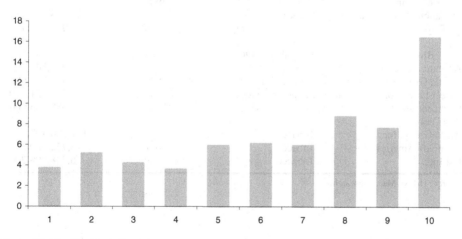

Figure 28.10   The *Little Book* strategy by decile – CAGR (1993–2005).
Source: DrKW Macro research.

US Little Book Strategy stock list

Table 28.12   Stock selection for *Little Book* strategy

Name	Sector (FTSE)	Price (local)	Market Capitalization (US$)
Brown-Forman Corporation	Beverages	44.59	2,876,768,440
Sherwin-Williams Company (The)	Construction & Building Materials	43.56	5,963,625,360
3M Company	Diversified Industrials	72.38	54,646,103,820
Ingersoll-Rand Company Limited	Engineering & Machinery	41.3	13,524,841,400
Paccar Inc	Engineering & Machinery	69.07	11,692,929,370
General Mills, Inc.	Food Producers & Processors	48.96	17,438,621,760
Abercrombie & Fitch Co	General Retailers	57.5	5,038,897,500
Coventry Health Care, Inc.	Health	58.1	9,439,158,400
IMS Health Incorporated	Health	24.69	4,919,309,670
Black & Decker Corporation (The)	Household Goods & Textiles	87.3	6,755,710,500
Jones Apparel Group, Inc.	Household Goods & Textiles	29.49	3,367,875,960
Mattel, Inc.	Household Goods & Textiles	17.04	6,624,129,600
V. V. Corporation	Household Goods & Textiles	53.79	5,980,210,830
Gannett Co., Inc	Media & Entertainment	60.77	14,467,878,520
News Corporation Limited (The)	Media & Entertainment	17.55	18,069,076,350
Tribune Company	Media & Entertainment	30.4	9,190,892,800
Westwood One, Inc.	Media & Entertainment	11.69	1,008,449,540
Freeport-Mcmoran Copper & Gold Incorporated	Mining	48.49	8,924,342,050
Ashland Inc.	Oil & Gas	64.1	4,568,086,500
ConocoPhillips	Oil & Gas	59.55	82,091,282,850
Marathon Oil Corporation	Oil & Gas	69.53	25,504,229,770
DST Systems Inc.	Software & Computer Services	56.92	4,076,553,480
H&R Block, Inc.	Speciality & Other Finance	22.15	7,257,181,700
Accenture Limited	Support Services	31.53	17,947,506,600
Apollo Group Incorporated	Support Services	49.8	8,621,226,600
Career Education Corporation	Support Services	34.07	3,345,231,090
Servicemaster Company (The)	Support Services	12.6	3,688,965,000
Altria Group, Inc.	Tobacco	72.65	151,284,107,850
Reynolds American Inc.	Tobacco	106.6	15,722,220,800
Ust Inc.	Tobacco	41.26	6,748,898,200

Source: DrKW Macro research.

Europe ex UK Little Book Strategy stock list

Table 28.13   Stock selection for *Little Book* strategy

Name	Sector (FTSE)	Price (local)	Market Capitalization (euro)
Aktieselskabet Dampskibsselskabet Torm		289.5	1,413,147,214
Compagnie Maritime Belge		25.39	888,650,000
Ford Otomotiv Sanayi A.S.	Automobiles & Parts	11.3	2,453,180,145
Renault (Regie Nationale Des Usines) Sa	Automobiles & Parts	79.85	22,752,219,450
Trakya Cam Sanayii A.S.	Construction & Building Materials	5.25	739,242,308
Unilever N.V.	Food Producers & Processors	57.75	33,008,514,000
Mondi Packaging Paper Swiece S.A.	Forestry & Paper	59.7	767,205,312
PPR SA	General Retailers	95.6	11,502,974,400
Fresenius AG	Health	135.77	3,467,158,490
Puma Aktiengesellschaft Rudolf Dassler Sport	Household Goods & Textiles	295.4	4,923,431,800
Turkiye Sise Ve Cam Fabrikalari A.S.	Household Goods & Textiles	5.6	1,467,224,920
Vestel Elektronik Sanayi Ve Ticaret A.S.	Household Goods & Textiles	5.1	501,990,628
Hyatt Regency Hotels & Tourism (Thessaloniki)	Leisure & Hotels	11.2	940,800,000
Opap S.A.	Leisure & Hotels	31.3	9,984,700,000
Independent News & Media plc	Media & Entertainment	2.65	2,003,808,100
Mediaset	Media & Entertainment	9.814	11,592,571,592
Schibsted ASA	Media & Entertainment	181	1,563,073,709
Norsk Hydro ASA	Oil & Gas	796	25,566,765,313
Statoil ASA	Oil & Gas	174	47,510,780,317
Total SA	Oil & Gas	208.9	128,497,732,400
Turkish Petroleum Refineries Corp.	Oil & Gas	25	3,873,134,142
L'Oreal	Personal Care & Household Products	74	48,748,388,000
Orion OYJ	Pharmaceuticals & Biotechnology	18.39	1,515,372,780
sanofi-aventis	Pharmaceuticals & Biotechnology	72.65	98,316,736,450
Eregli Demir Ve Celik Fabrikalari T.A.S.	Steel & Other Metals	7.7	2,324,084,273
Ssab Svenskt Stal Aktiebolaget	Steel & Other Metals	326	817,912,728
TNT NV	Support Services	26.97	12,394,333,200
France Telecom	Telecommunication Services	18.41	47,882,679,460
Mobistar SA	Telecommunication Services	62.2	3,935,642,800
Philip Morris CR A.S.	Tobacco	16810	1,116,847,645

Source: DrKW Macro research.

UK Little Book Strategy stock list

Table 28.14   Stock selection for *Little Book* strategy

Name	Sector (FTSE)	Price (local)	Market Capitalization (£)
European Motor Holdings plc	Automobiles & Parts	4.0775	222,048,418
Imperial Chemical Industries plc	Chemicals	3.3	3,932,497,800
Balfour Beatty plc	Construction & Building Materials	3.7975	1,621,205,915
Costain Group plc	Construction & Building Materials	0.4975	177,748,790
McCarthy & Stone plc	Construction & Building Materials	7.45	764,682,900
Morgan Sindall plc	Construction & Building Materials	12.15	514,321,650
Foseco plc	Engineering & Machinery	1.74	294,321,000
Unilever plc	Food Producers & Processors	5.94	17,141,598,540
Alexon Group plc	General Retailers	2.5575	146,375,955
Carpetright plc	General Retailers	11.465	777,292,605
Clinton Cards plc	General Retailers	0.68	140,588,640
French Connection Group plc	General Retailers	2.4525	234,049,433
Halfords Group plc	General Retailers	3.19	727,406,130
Land of Leather Holdings plc	General Retailers	1.955	99,362,875
Next plc	General Retailers	16.54	4,070,494,000
SCS Upholstery plc	General Retailers	4.78	161,573,560
Amstrad plc	Household Goods & Textiles	1.965	162,623,400
Games Workshop Group plc	Household Goods & Textiles	2.97	92,453,130
Hornby plc	Household Goods & Textiles	2.135	79,654,715
Psion plc	Information Technology Hardware	1.9	264,485,700
Telent plc	Information Technology Hardware	4	838,828,000
Johnston Press plc	Media & Entertainment	4.67	1,340,612,230
Trinity Mirror plc	Media & Entertainment	5.71	1,672,624,590
Antofagasta plc	Mining	19.57	3,858,636,470
Hays plc	Support Services	1.4975	2,227,682,498
John Menzies plc	Support Services	5.715	333,378,810
Telecom Plus plc	Telecommunications Services	1.285	87,852,880
Braemar Seascope Group plc	Transport	4.0275	79,647,840
Clarkson plc	Transport	8.52	139,804,680
Go-Ahead Group plc (The)	Transport	18.21	904,709,220

Source: DrKW Macro research.

Japan Little Book Strategy stock list

Table 28.15   Stock selection for *Little Book* strategy

Name	Sector (FTSE)	Price (local)	Market Capitalization (JPYm)
Arisawa MFG. Co., Ltd.	Chemicals	2415	88,193
Bosch Corporation	Automobiles & Parts	536	240,375
Canon Incorporated	Electronic & Electrical Equipment	7320	6,505,650
Circle K Sunkus Company Limited	Food & Drug Retailers	2815	242,605
CSK Holdings Corporation	Software & Computer Services	5510	426,738
Daito Trust Construction Company Limited	Construction & Building Materials	5450	705,001
Familymart Co., Ltd	Food & Drug Retailers	3530	344,821
Funai Electric Co., Ltd.	Household Goods & Textiles	11850	427,714
Glory Limited		2455	182,249
Hisamitsu Pharmaceutical Co., Inc.	Pharmaceuticals & Biotechnology	2840	270,269
Inpex Corporation	Oil & Gas	1060000	2,035,200
Kawasaki Kisen Kaisha Ltd	Transport	719	426,940
Koei Co., Ltd.	Software & Computer Services	2420	166,135
Kubota Corporation	Engineering & Machinery	1120	1,475,229
Lawson Inc.	Food & Drug Retailers	4420	462,332
Mitsui O.S.K Lines Limited	Transport	793	955,890
Nidec Copal Corp	Electronic & Electrical Equipment	1416	89,144
NOK Corporation	Automobiles & Parts	3340	578,284
NS Solutions Corporation	Software & Computer Services	2880	152,637
NTT Docomo Incorporated	Telecommunication Services	169000	8,230,300
Ono Pharmaceutical Co., Ltd	Pharmaceuticals & Biotechnology	5690	699,409
Pasona Incorporated	Support Services	238000	103,054
Ryoshoku Limited	Food Producers & Processors	3030	124,321
Sankyo Co., Ltd. (6417)	Household Goods & Textiles	7670	748,577
Showa Shell Sekiyu Kabushiki Kaisha	Oil & Gas	1292	486,890
Square Enix	Software & Computer Services	3060	338,785
Takeda Pharmaceutical Company Limited	Pharmaceuticals & Biotechnology	6720	5,975,908
Tokyo Steel Manufacturing Co., Ltd	Steel & Other Metals	2220	344,242
Uniden Corporation	Information Technology Hardware	1704	107,591
Yamaha Motor Co., Ltd	Automobiles & Parts	2620	749,163

Source: DrKW Macro research.

29

Improving Returns Using Inside Information[*]

> **Watching what companies do rather than listening to what they say can markedly improve your returns. Net equity issuance appears to offer powerful insights for both value and growth investors. However, most investors seem to prefer to talk to management rather than observe their market actions. Tempting as these siren stories may be, investors would be better off focusing on the facts.**

- Every so often I come across an academic paper that appears to be destined to become a classic. I recently stumbled over one such paper by Bali, Demirtas and Hovakimian. They combine a simple value strategy with another well-known 'anomaly', net equity issuance. Many studies have found that companies time their equity issuance; that is they sell shares when it is cheap for them to do so (i.e. expensive for investors), and repurchase them when valuations are cheap.
- Bali *et al.* (2006) examine US data from 1972 to 2002. They find significant gains to both value and growth investors from including net equity issuance in their analysis. For instance, a simple value strategy of buying cheapest 20% of the market by P/B yields an average excess return of 2.6% p.a. over their sample. However, by concentrating on value stocks with negative net issuance (i.e. net repurchases) this rises to 5.5% p.a. If you extend the time horizon the returns continue to improve. Over four years, a simple value strategy generates an excess return of 13% on average. Using net equity issuance improves this to 24% on average.
- The usefulness of this signal is not restricted to value investors (although Bali *et al.* don't draw this out explicitly). Growth stocks that are net equity repurchasers do markedly better than the general growth universe. Over one year they generate an average excess return of 1.2%, whereas the growth universe underperforms the market by 1.8% in the first year.
- A hedge strategy of going long value repurchases (VP) and short growth issuers (GI) vastly improves a simple long value short growth strategy. The simple value/growth portfolio earned an average of 4% in year 1, rising to 28% in year 4. However, the VP–GI strategy generated 10% in year 1, rising to 47% in year 4.
- Bali *et al.* show that the risk explanations so beloved by efficient market believers simply don't hold water. Indeed beta has the wrong sign in their analysis. The VP portfolio has the lowest beta and the highest return, while the GI portfolio has the highest beta and the lowest return. They also show that VP stocks witness an operating turnaround such that their

---

*This article appeared in *Global Equity Strategy* on 30 November 2006. The material discussed was accurate at the time of publication.

earnings growth improves significantly, while GI stocks have great past earnings growth but lousy future earnings growth – exactly what behavioural finance would predict.

- Sebastian Lancetti and I find similar returns in Europe. Buying VP in Europe since 1995 has generated an excess return of 5% p.a. While GI has underperformed the market by 5% p.a. over our sample. All of this evidence suggests that investors would be much better off paying attention to companies' actions in the market place, instead of the listening to their siren-like stories.

Before the FSA and SEC (not to mention our own supervisory analysts) start jumping up and down, turning apoplectic and foaming at their mouths, I should make it clear that I am not talking about inside information in the sense of information that isn't publicly disclosed. Rather I am talking about using the financial market transactions of firms (a matter of public record) to improve returns.

I am relatively well known (perhaps even infamous) for arguing that investors waste much of their time in meeting with company managements (see *Global Equity Strategy*, 7 September 2005). I much prefer to watch what they are doing rather than listen to their all-too-pat stories. As my grandmother is fond of saying, actions speak louder than words.

I spend a fair amount of time trawling through academic papers in both finance and psychology. Every so often I come across a paper that strikes me as simply brilliant, perhaps even destined to become a classic. I recently had the good fortune to stumble on such a paper.

Every investor should take the time to read Bali *et al.*'s (2006) paper 'Corporate financing activities and contrarian investment'. It is an easy read, clear, logical and well structured and applied (in short, a real rarity among academic papers!).

The premise they have is simple. The evidence shows that value outperforms growth over the long term (see *Global Equity Strategy*, 16 March 2005). Other studies have shown that firms that issue equity tend to underperform.[1] Indeed those who have sat through one of my behavioural finance presentations will recall my diatribe on the evils of IPOs and my near constant bemusement that investors cue up to buy into expensive underperformers. Yet others have demonstrated that firms that repurchase equity tend to outperform the market (Chan *et al.*, 2003).

In the past I have argued that this equity issuance is a message from management. They issue equity when it is cheap for them to do so (effectively the equity is expensive to investors), and they purchase equity when it is cheap for them (i.e. the stock is undervalued by the market). Bali *et al.* argue that by combing the usual value strategy with one that exploits the insider's views, returns can be enhanced significantly.

PATIENCE IS A VIRTUE

Sebastian Lancetti and I recently explored the potential returns to extending your time horizon as an investor (see *Global Equity Strategy*, 17 October 2006). Bali *et al.* show a similar pattern to the one we uncovered. However, our results were for Europe, Bali *et al.* use the USA 1972–2002, suggesting our results were more than just statistical fluke. The methodology Bali *et al.* employ is to split their universe into quintiles based on price to book.[2] Figure 29.1 shows the excess returns over the market for the two extreme PB portfolios. Once again patience appears to be a virtue for a value investor, and a disaster for growth investors.

USING INSIDE INFORMATION

However, as noted above, the focus of Bali *et al.*'s work is not extending time horizons. Instead they are interested in enhancing value strategies by using signals from companies' market transactions (that said, there is much in the paper relevant to growth investors, although Bali *et al.* do not draw it out explicitly). Bali *et al.* use last years net equity issuance divided by total

---

[1] For example, see Ritter (2006).
[2] They also show the results for PE and PCF as well, none are materially different from those presented here.

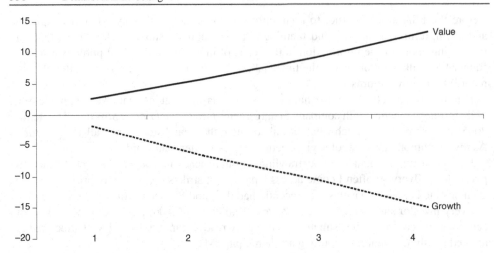

Figure 29.1 Patience is a virtue: cumulative excess returns to a simple value strategy (%).
Source: Adapted from Bali *et al.* (2006).

assets as their proxy for management's actions. This variable avoids the problem with some of the repurchase studies which confuse net and gross buybacks by ignoring options issuance. Within each P/B quintile a binary sort is conducted with each firm either being a net issuer or net repurchaser of equity. The impact for both growth and value investors is marked.

Figure 29.2 shows the picture from a value investor's perspective. By separating out the value repurchases (VP) from the value universe, excess returns over four years are raised from 13% to 24%! Even in year 1 there is a near doubling of the excess return from 2.6% to 5.5%.

The value issuers (VI) show a very different pattern. These stocks underperform the general market pretty much from the outset. So value investors would be well advised to avoid stocks within their universe that issue net equity, and concentrate firepower on those that repurchase.

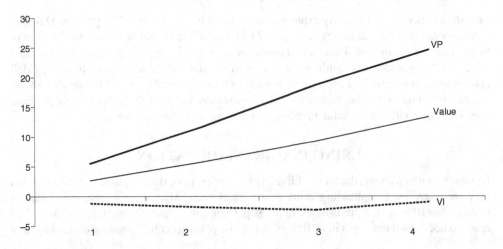

Figure 29.2 Using inside information – the value perspective (excess returns, %).
Source: Adapted from Bali *et al.* (2006).

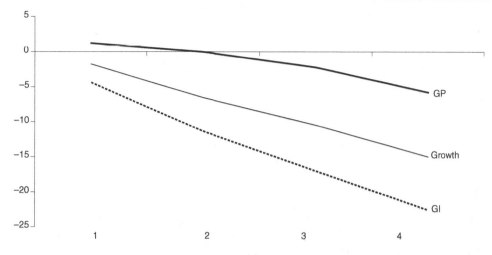

Figure 29.3 Using inside information – the growth perspective (excess returns, %).
Source: Adapted from Bali *et al.* (2006).

From a growth perspective, sorting by equity issuance can also pay dividends (not sure I should use that word since it is anathema to most growth investors). Figure 29.3 shows the picture for a growth investor.

Growth stocks that are net equity repurchasers (GP) do markedly better than the general growth universe. Over one year they generate an average excess return of 1.2%, whereas the growth universe underperforms the market by a 1.8% in the first year. Over four years, GP stocks underperform the market by nearly 6%, but growth stocks in general underperform by 15%.

Growth stocks that issue equity (GI) fare much worse than general growth stocks. They see a negative excess return of over 4% in year 1, rising to −22% over 4 years. So both value and growth managers can seek to use equity issuance as an effective way of improving their returns.

A HEDGE PERSPECTIVE

Of course the above analysis also suggests a strategy of going long VP and short GI. The improvement this offers over time is shown in Figure 29.4. The returns of long VP/short GI are almost twice those of simply going long value and short growth.

Figure 29.5 shows the year-by-year performance of long VP/short GI. It does remarkably well with only 6 out of 30 years showing negative returns. Also notable the strategy continued to generate positive returns even during the dot.com bubble in the late 1990s.

RISK OR MISPRICING?

There is an ongoing argument between those who believe in efficient markets (EMH) (yes, they still exist and still often dominate universities, more is the pity) and those who believe in behavioural finance. The efficient market zealots would have us believe that value's out-performance is the result of their higher risk. The behaviouralists think that people tend to

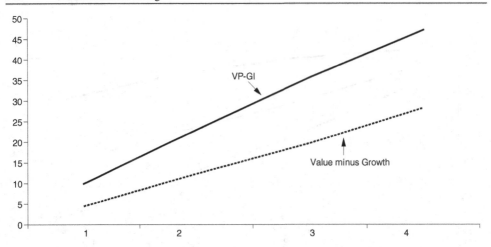

Figure 29.4   Long VP short GI (cumulative returns, %).
Source: Adapted from Bali *et al.* (2006).

overestimate the growth embodied within the pricing of growth stocks, and similarly get too depressed about the outlook for value stocks.

The efficient market believers won't like Bali *et al.*'s results, because it now behoves them to explain why it is that distress risk is much higher among value purchasers rather than value issuers. The only possible answer is that the value purchasers are increasing their degree of leverage and are thus more risky. However, it is hard to imagine a firm with high distress risk drawing down cash or raising debt to finance a buyback (more on this later).

EVIDENCE FOR BEHAVIOURAL ERRORS

The argument from behavioural finance is that investors seem to extrapolate past earnings/cash flow growth in a simplistic fashion (representativeness). That is to say, stocks with good past

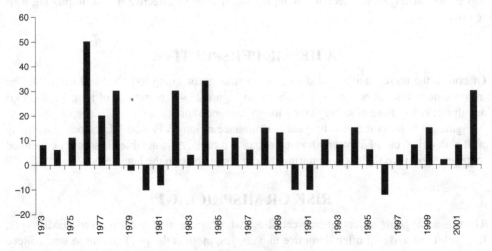

Figure 29.5   Long VP short GI annual return performance.
Source: Adapted from Bali *et al.* (2006).

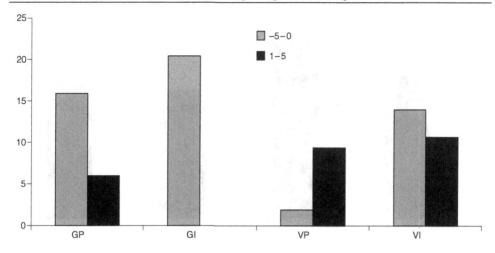

Figure 29.6   Earnings growth in the years before and after portfolio formation.
Source: Adapted from Bali *et al.* (2006).

earnings performance are expected to grow fast in the future, and those with poor track records are expected to do badly in the future.

Figure 29.6 shows the earnings growth rate in the 5 years before portfolio formation, and the growth rate in the 5 years after the portfolios are built. The picture certainly fits well with the behavioural story. Growth stocks (both GP and GI) have high historic growth, yet their future earnings growth is much lower. Indeed in the case of GI, the earnings growth after the formation of the portfolio is essentially zero. The GP portfolio also seems a dramatic tailing off of earnings growth but at least it still has some (around 6% p.a.). This helps to explain the underperformance of growth stocks in general and growth issuers in particular.

VP stocks have poor past performance, but the buyback seems to signal a turnaround in operating performance as earnings growth improves significantly. However, those stocks in VI show a different picture. The earnings growth slows from 14% p.a. to around 11% p.a. This helps to explain the performance of the VI stocks shown in Figure 29.2, their cheapness is offset by slowing earnings growth.

EVIDENCE AGAINST THE RISK VIEW

According to the believers in efficient markets, just one measure sums up the potential risk of a stock – its beta against the market. So Bali *et al.* map out the betas across the portfolios. Their results are shown in Figure 29.7. The findings are the inverse of those predicted by the risk based explanation so beloved by efficient marketers. Those stocks with the highest beta are the GI portfolio, which had the lowest return, whereas the stocks with the lowest beta, the stocks in the VP portfolio, had the highest return. So much for classical finance. This also suggests an important piece of advice when it comes to portfolio construction, for good long-run performance buy low beta stocks.[3] The tortoise beats the hare in the end.

---

[3] For more on this point interested readers should see Clarke *et al.* (2006).

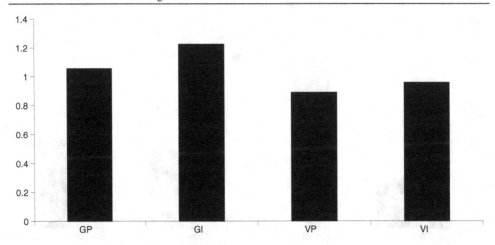

Figure 29.7   Average beta across portfolios.
Source: Dresdner Adapted from Bali *et al.* (2006).

Determined not to give up on their risk-based solutions, the EMH supporters say that value stocks do much worse in bad states of the world. Bali *et al.* use several measures to capture bad states of the world, we present just two here. Firstly, the default premium (the spread of low-grade corporate debt to government paper). When the default premium is high the economy is likely to be experiencing a downturn, so value should do much worse than growth. The second proxy we present here is the Chicago National Activity Index. When this is below zero the economy is growing below trend, again implying a poor outturn for value stocks.

Figure 29.8 shows the returns for VP–GI by states of the world. In all cases VP–GI is positive, that is to say value purchases outperform growth issuers regardless of the economic environment. This is yet another blow to the supporters of EMH.

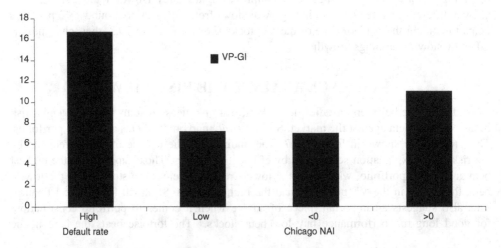

Figure 29.8   Returns in good and bad states of the world (%).
Source: Adapted from Bali *et al.* (2006).

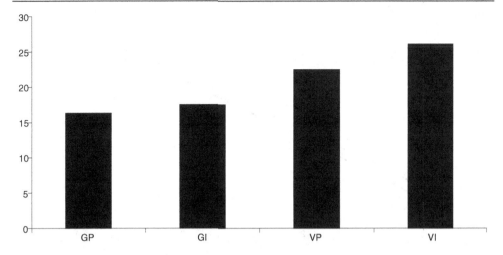

Figure 29.9   Leverage across portfolios.
Source: Adapted from Bali *et al.* (2006).

The final defence offered up by those desperate to cling to EMH is leverage. It has long been known that value stocks tend to have greater leverage (as measured by long-term debt to book value of assets). Bali *et al.* show this to be case (Figure 29.9). The VP and VI have a higher leverage (22.5% and 26.1%) than their growth counterparts (GP 16.3% and GI 17.5%).

However, note that VI portfolio leverage ratio is higher than the VP leverage ratio, and the same is true in the growth universe (GI/GP). Yet it is the lower leverage portfolios that offer better returns.

Additionally, the leverage ratio is only 5 percentage points higher for the VP portfolio than the GI portfolio; whereas it is double that between the VI portfolio and GP portfolio. Yet VP–GI generates very significant outperformance, whereas the difference between VI–GP is not significant.

Both of these issues raise major problems for the leverage as risk arguments propounded by the supporters of EMH. However, Bali *et al.* drive one final nail in the coffin for this argument by examining the performance of a sub-grouping of their sample, those firms with zero leverage. Figure 29.10 shows the zero leverage firm VP–GI against the all firm VP–GI. There is essentially no difference between these two portfolios. All of which shows the risk arguments to be rather hollow (not that I am biased, of course!).

EUROPEAN EVIDENCE

Having read the Bali *et al.* paper I was intrigued to know if similar patterns existed within Europe. So as usual I turned to our quant team for help. Sebastian Lancetti was working on his forthcoming magnum opus on earnings quality, but I managed to steal a little of his time to run the numbers for Europe. We used Worldscope data for net proceeds from equity issuance, and again used a binary sort as per Bali *et al.* Our data was over a much smaller sample, 1995 onwards, so we concentrated on one year ahead returns. The returns we found were still

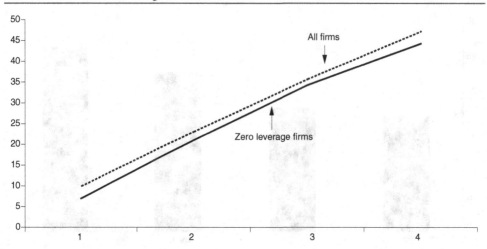

Figure 29.10 Zero leverage portfolio comparison.
Source: Adapted from Bali *et al.* (2006).

impressive. The VP portfolio earned excess returns of 5% p.a., the VI portfolio earned excess returns of 2% p.a. The GP portfolio underperformed the market by only 1% p.a., while the GI portfolio underperformed the market by 5% p.a. (Figure 29.11).

A portfolio that went long VP and short GI earned a total return of 6.4% p.a., whereas a simple long value short growth earned 2.6% p.a. So like the American data, the evidence from Europe shows significant improvement in returns by using a net equity issuance filter, in addition to a value screen (Figure 29.12).

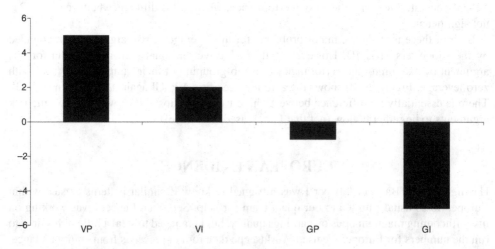

Figure 29.11 Average excess returns across European portfolios (% p.a.).
Source: Dresdner Kleinwort Macro research.

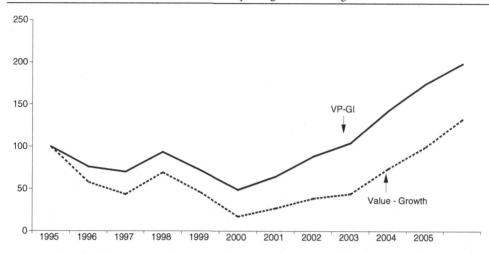

Figure 29.12 Portfolio improvement by using inside information – European evidence (1995 = 100). *Source:* DrKW Macro research.

CONCLUSIONS

The evidence collected here argues that the actions of corporates should be watched much more closely than their stories. Net equity issuance appears to offer powerful insights for both value and growth investors. However, most investors seem content to waste hours sitting down and talking to company managers. Perhaps it is believing the stories they are told at these meetings that leads investors to extrapolate past performance into the future. But a company's actions in the market place seem to offer a much better guide to their future performance (both operating and financial) than the siren calls of management.

30

Just a Little Patience: Part I*

> The average holding period for a stock on the NYSE is just 9 months! Investors
> have transformed into speculators. This must surely open up the opportunity for
> time arbitrage. However, the excessive volatility that creates the opportunity also
> makes it difficult to exploit. Perhaps investors might be well served to remember
> that short-term and long-term performance are pretty much uncorrelated beasts.

- The attention span of today's investors gives ADHD a bad name, but what has driven this obsession with the short term? Surely not all investors are tartrazine addicts! I suspect that three core reasons lie behind the massive increase in turnover.
- Firstly, the ease of information acquisition has improved massively. Whereas in the 1950s and 1960s, analysts were expected to dig out and analyse company information, today they are spoon-fed and seem little better than PR machines. Behaviourally speaking, more information (albeit noise not news) tends to increase confidence, which in turn, increases turnover.
- Secondly, the obsession with performance measurement on ever-decreasing time horizons has played a role. Internal managers want smooth returns, and even a few days of under-performance may bring them down from on high. End clients appear to share this passion for constant performance. The average holding period for a mutual fund has fallen from 16 years in the 1950s to 4 years today.
- However, a new study from the Brandes Institute shows that this obsession with the short term is a bad idea. They show that the best-performing long-run funds have all witnessed periods of major underperformance. For instance, those funds in the top decile by long-run performance, have an average worst 3-year performance of nearly −10% relative to benchmark!
- The third reason for the shrinkage in time horizons is the rise in hedge funds. However, I suspect that this reason is often overstated, as horizons were shrinking long before hedge funds became big business.
- Whatever the ultimate cause for the obsession with the short term, the fact that it exists strongly suggests that time arbitrage could well be a profitable strategy. If everyone else is busy dashing around placing bets on a 9-month time horizon, then assets will be pushed to inappropriate levels, setting up an opportunity for the patient investor (not an oxymoron, I hope!)
- Price volatility remains several orders of magnitude greater than fundamental volatility. Over the last 10 years, real prices have been 14 times more volatile than fundamentals! This

*This article appeared in *Global Equity Strategy* on 11 October 2006. The material discussed was accurate at the time of publication.

excessive volatility is both an opportunity and a problem. It obviously sets up mis-pricing, but simultaneously makes it painful to try to exploit the situation. However, until investors realize that short-term performance is an illusory veil, this situation is unlikely to change.

• In the next chapter we will discuss a portfolio perspective on time arbitrage.

One of the simplest and yet most difficult ways in which to add value is through time arbitrage. Markets have witnessed a massive shrinkage in time horizons. Figure 30.1 shows the average holding period for a stock on the NYSE. In the 1950s/1960s investors used to hold stocks for an average of 7–8 years. Today the average holding period is just 9 months!

Professional investors have transformed into speculators, obsessed with the shortterm. Why have we seen this shrinkage in horizons? I suspect there are three (not mutually exclusive) reasons why we have observed this pattern.

Firstly, the ease of information acquisition is now an order of magnitude 'better' than it was in the 1950s/1960s. Being a financial analyst then involved actually gathering data and performing analysis. Today analysts are spoon-fed information and seem little better than PR machines for the corporates. Quarterly earnings results see the analysts dashing off to their favourite companies to receive the word on pro forma earnings from company management, followed by a verbatim reproduction of results for immediate dissemination to all and sundry.

Why, you may ask, do analysts persist in this behaviour? The answer is that their clients require it (as hard as it is for me to comprehend, there really are fund managers that want such a service). Behaviourally speaking, more information seems to lead to increased confidence. In turn, this overconfidence translates into an increased turnover as everyone thinks they know more than everyone else, and hence trade more than everyone else (see Odean, 1998). Remember, more information isn't better information.

McKinsey recently published the results of a survey of CEO and CFOs on earnings guidance (*McKinsey Quarterly*, 2006). The single biggest reason (76% cited as in the top two) for issuing guidance is 'Satisfying requests from investors and analyst'. Half of the executives McKinsey surveyed said that sell-side analysts were the major group demanding earnings guidance; and 37% said that mutual/pension funds were the most insistent on earnings guidance.

Of course, one might ask why fund managers would want such a service? The answer to this conundrum is their clients' and managers' demands to perform on a quarter-by-quarter basis. The obsession with performance measurement on ever-decreasing time scales is the second reason for shrinking holding periods. I know of some fund managers who are aware of their

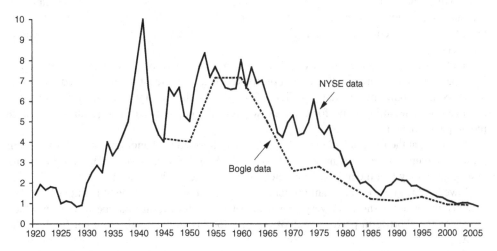

Figure 30.1   Average holding period for a stock on the NYSE (years).
Source: DrKW Macro research.

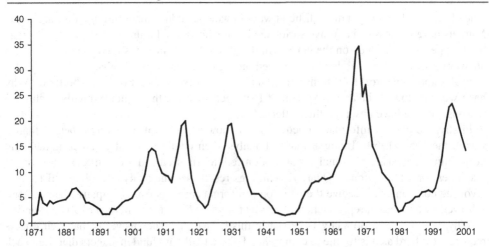

Figure 30.2 Excess volatility: ratio of price to fundamental volatility.
Source: DrKW Macro research.

portfolio performance intra-day. Unless this is scaled by the normal variance of the stocks you hold, you have simply mastered the art of measuring noise!

The effort to find informational edge on a daily, weekly, monthly or quarterly basis is the very aspect of the financial markets that makes time arbitrage a viable strategy. The obsessive preoccupation with the immediate means that assets are likely to be driven to extreme highs and extreme lows as investors struggle to decipher the signal/noise ratio. This volatility is the very thing I suspect long-term investors can seek to exploit, as well as, of course, the source of the pain in trying to follow a long-term strategy.

Figure 30.2 gives some idea of the potential scale of the problem of short-term obsession. It is based on the work of Robert Shiller, and shows the ratio of 10-year price volatility to underlying fundamental volatility. Price volatility is several orders of magnitude greater than fundamental volatility. Over the last 10 years, prices have been 14 times more volatile than the underlying fundamentals (dividends). So by focusing on the short term, investors are creating too much volatility.

The third (oft cited) reason for the shrinkage in time horizons is the rise of hedge funds. Personally, I am not sure that this aspect of markets is as significant in terms of reducing time horizons as is sometimes stated. As Figure 30.2 shows, the average holding period of stock has been on a declining trend for decades, whereas the popularity of hedge funds is a more recent phenomenon.

Of course, at the margin hedge funds are likely to have created another group of short-term focused players. Indeed, this may even have a knock-on effect on more traditional long-only managers as they feel the need to compete with the hedge funds on similar terms.

However, the quest for constant outperformance is futile. The Brandes Institute (2006) has recently produced a short but very powerful paper on short-term underperformance which examines the short-term performance of the best long-term performing mutual funds in the USA.

The top decile of funds by long-term performance has outperformed the S&P 500 by 3% p.a. over 10 years. However, they were all subject to periods of significant underperformance.

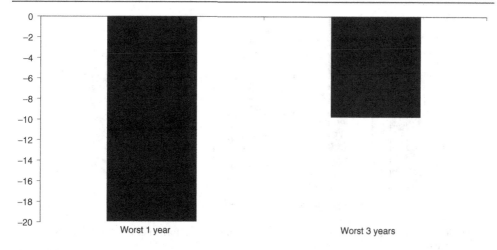

Figure 30.3   Percentage outperformance in ...
Source: Adapted from Brandes Institute (2006).

For instance, in their worst single years the top decile funds underperformed the S&P 500 by between 6.5% and 37.6%. The average was a worst single year of 19.9% underperformance.

A similar pattern is shown if we examine the worst 3-year period these funds suffered (Figure 30.3). The range was 1.2% to 20.4% underperformance. The average was just short of 10% underperformance in the worst 3 years.

A similar picture was painted if performance was peer-group based rather than measured against the index. Figure 30.4 shows the percentage of the top decile that can be found in the stated decile based on various time horizons.

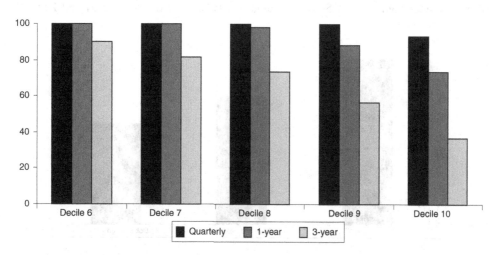

Figure 30.4   Percentage of long-term top performers in lower performance deciles – US evidence.
Source: Adapted from Brandes Institute (2006).

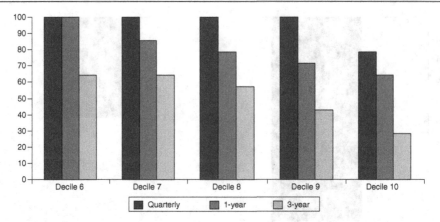

Figure 30.5 Percentage of long-term top performers in lower performance deciles (Non-US).
Source: Adapted from Brandes Institute (2006).

So using annual data, 73% of the top performing funds have found themselves in the lowest decile. Even on a 3-year basis, one in three of the best-performing long-term funds suffered a period in the lowest decile.

This performance isn't unique to US equity managers. The Brandes Institute also examined the performance of international mutual fund managers. As Figure 30.5 illustrates, they found a very similar picture to the US managers discussed above.

So even the best of fund managers witness sustained periods of underperformance. The reality of short-term underperformance and long-term outperformance needs to be fully communicated to the end investor.

There is a mass of evidence showing that investors tend to sell at just the wrong point. Retail investors are well known to chase returns. A new study by Frisen and Sapp (2006) investigates just how much returns-chasing behaviour costs mutual fund investors (Figure 30.6). They examined some 7125 US equity mutual funds between the years 1991 and 2004. For

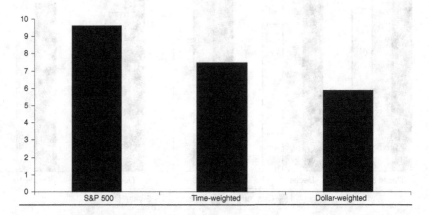

Figure 30.6 The impact of returns-chasing behaviour (p.a. %).
Source: Adapted from Frisen and Sapp (2006).

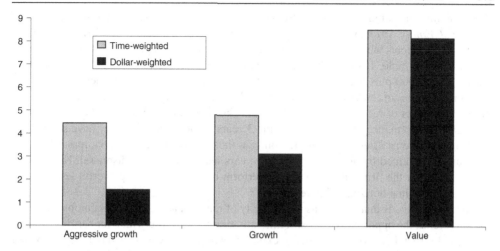

Figure 30.7   The impact of returns-chasing behaviour by style of fund purchased.
Source: Adapted from Frisen and Sapp (2006).

each fund they constructed a time-weighted return and a dollar-weighted return series. The average return to the time-weighted series was 0.62% p.m. (or 7.44% p.a.) some 2 percentage points below the index. This reflects the well-known general underperformance of active fund managers relative to the index. However, investors then manage to lose another 1.56% p.a. by trading their mutual funds very badly.

When Frisen and Sapp break down the returns by fund style, the results make interesting reading. The funds that seem to be the worst example of returns chasing are the aggressive growth funds; at the other extreme, the value fund buyers seem to do little to damage their fund returns (Figure 30.7).

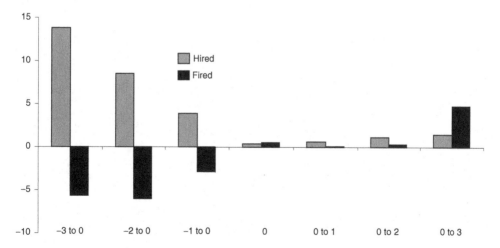

Figure 30.8   Performance around hiring and firing decisions (%).
Source: Goyal and Wahal (2005). DrKW Macro research.

Nor is this trait unique to the individuals who buy and sell mutual funds. For instance, in *Global Equity Strategy*, 28 August 2006, we discussed a paper by Goyal and Wahal (2005) which shows why we need to explain the risks of investing to the end client far better than we currently do. It should be required reading by all pension plans and trustees. They review some 4000-plus decisions regarding the hiring and firing of investment managers by pension plan sponsors and trustees between 1993 and 2003. The results they uncover show the classic hallmarks of returns-chasing behaviour. The funds the sponsors tend to hire have an average outperformance of nearly 14% in the 3 years before hiring, but they have statistically insignificant returns after the hiring. In contrast, those fired for performance reasons tend to have underperformed by around 6% in the 3 years leading up to the dismissal. However, in the 3 years after the firing, they tend to outperform by nearly 5% – a powerful lesson in the need to extend time horizons (Figure 30.8).

The bottom line is that as long as the majority of market participants remain obsessed with the short term, the opportunity for exploiting mis-pricing for those with a longer time horizon must surely exist. However, the ability to exploit this opportunity will need to be accompanied by re-education of the final investor and internal management. Until these two groups realize that short-term performance is an illusory veil and has almost nothing to do with long-term performance, the obsession with hitting short-term targets is likely to remain.

31

Just a Little Patience: Part II[*]

Written with Sebastian Lancetti

Patience is a virtue; well, at least for value investors. Evidence suggests that extending the time horizon leads to dramatically improved returns from value investing. However, patience seems to be a disaster for the growth universe. Instead, growth investors would be better off ensuring that price momentum is one of the factors in their stock selection process, and remembering that they shouldn't ignore value.

- Can value and growth investors exploit the excessive volatility of markets to add value? Does time arbitrage make sense for investors from a portfolio perspective? The evidence we uncover unambiguously shows that there are very clear benefits to value investors from extending their time horizons.

- For instance, a simple value strategy of buying the cheapest 20% of the MSCI Europe has generated around 3% outperformance in the first year relative to the market since 1991. However, if investors had continued to hold that portfolio the return would have risen dramatically, to an average 32% outperformance over 5 years!

- In previous work, we have shown that some of the best value investors have much longer time horizons than the average fund. We found that the average holding period for our group of 'perfect' value investors was 5 years, against only 1 year for the average US mutual fund currently.

- However, we also find that only around half of the stocks selected generate the outperformance in the first year, rising to nearly 60% of stocks at the 5-year time horizon. This means that value investors not only need to be patient, but also need to avoid narrow framing. If they start looking at the performance of the individual companies, the relatively high proportion of losses may dissuade them from following such a strategy.

- For growth investors we find a very different picture. Patience is not rewarded in the growth universe. A simple strategy of buying the top 20% of the market by PE generates worse and worse returns, as time goes by, with more and more stocks in the portfolio getting torpedoed. In the first year, only 38% of stocks within this universe outperform. At the 5-year time horizon this has fallen to 34% of stocks.

- However, all is not lost. By adding either price momentum or value filters into a growth universe, significant improvements in performance are possible. For instance, by buying high momentum growth stocks, a 400 bps improvement in performance is witnessed at a one-year time horizon. By buying the cheapest stocks within the growth universe a 300 bps improvement is recorded over one year.

---

[*]This article appeared in *Global Equity Strategy* on 17 October 2006. The material discussed was accurate at the time of publication.

- The benefits of adding momentum to a value strategy are more muted. Indeed, we present evidence that value managers seem generally to have a tougher time outperforming the value universe, than the growth managers have in outperforming the growth universe.
- However, above and beyond all else, we show that patience is *the* prerequisite for value investors. Meanwhile, growth investors would do well to add momentum and value considerations to their stock selection processes.

In chapter 30 we explored the 'big picture' case for time arbitrage. In this chapter we want to look at the benefits (and costs) of long-term investing from a portfolio point of view. Can value and growth managers exploit the noise to generate superior long-run returns?

In order to answer this question I enlisted the help of Sebastian Lancetti of our Global Quant team (I would be lost without them!). I asked Sebastian to form quintiles based on simple trailing PE.[1] The universe we used was MSCI Europe since 1991. We called the cheapest 20% of the universe 'value', and the most expensive 20% of the universe 'growth'. Of course you might argue that isn't a great definition of growth, and indeed it isn't, but the results don't look dramatically different if we use price to book, or any other valuation measure.

Each month, portfolios were formed and then let to run over various time horizons. Of course, this creates problems with overlapping sample periods, but the results don't alter materially if we try to avoid this.

VALUE PERSPECTIVE

As is my want, I am going to start from the value perspective. Is time arbitrage a profitable pursuit for value investors? Certainly *a priori* one would expect so. As Ben Graham said, "Undervaluations caused by neglect or prejudice may persist for an inconveniently long time." As I have written many times before, when a value position is established, one can never be sure which potential return pathway will be taken. Effectively, any value position falls into one of three categories:

(I) those that enjoy a re-rating as the market more generally recognizes that a mispricing has occurred (type I);
(II) those that generate a higher return via dividend yield, but are not immediately re-rated (type II);
(III) those that simply don't recover, the value traps (type III).

So patience really should be a virtue for value managers as long as we are dealing with a type I or type II value stock. Figure 31.1 confirms just how strongly this is true, and shows the cumulative returns to an incredibly simple value strategy (buying the lowest 20% of the MSCI Europe ranked by trailing PE). The figure provides very graphic evidence for the rewards to patience.

The strategy tends to generate around 3% outperformance relative to the market in the first 12 months. But if you hold for another year, this rises to 5.7% (a year-2 return of just over 2%). However, at 3-year time horizons and beyond, the excess return pick-up is much sharper, running at the rate of 8–10% p.a. for years 3, 4 and 5 (Figure 31.1)!

Also noteworthy is that the value strategy appears to start working from day 1. This surprised me as I expected to see a period of underperformance or non-performance, rather than an immediate return to the value approach.

This finding sits well with the fact that successful value investors seem to display patience. As we showed in *Global Equity Strategy*, 8 June 2006, the average holding period for our group of long-term outperforming value managers was 5 years, against the average holding period of just 11 months for stocks listed on the NYSE, and just over 1 year for the average US mutual fund.

---

[1] See *Global Equity Strategy*, 26 September 2006, for why it is cheaper and easier to use trailing rather than forecast earnings.

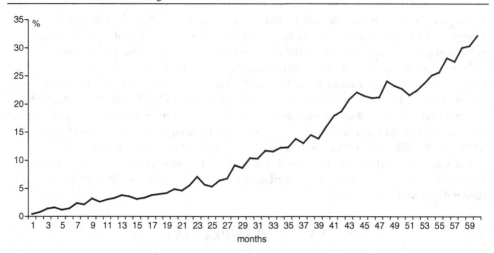

Figure 31.1   Patience is a virtue: cumulative excess returns to a simple value strategy (%).
Source: Dresdner Kleinwort Macro research.

A recent paper by Fama and French (2006) shines some light on the relative probability of each type of value situation occurring. They examine both the returns and the probabilities of transition among US value and growth stocks over the period 1926–2004.

They formed portfolios based around the interaction of price to book and size. In Table 31.1, V = value, G = growth, N = neutral, B = big and S = small. The columns give four possible outcomes; the column labelled 'Same' refers to the group of stocks that one year later are in the same style and size basket as they were in the original sort. The 'Plus' column covers stocks that have moved into a higher price to book category, i.e. value stocks that have moved back towards market average pricing (or been acquired). The 'Minus' column depicts the opposite: here we find stocks that have been growth stocks and are now returning to, say, more normal valuations. The final column heading is 'Change in size' and reflects stocks that switch between size groups from t to $t + 1$ – that is small stocks that become big, and big stocks that become small.

So let's take BV (big value) as an example. The upper part of the table shows the average p.a. excess return over the market that such stocks have generated since 1926. So stocks that started in BV and then moved back towards the market average pricing, generate 17.5% outperformance p.a. (type I value stocks from our earlier discussion). However, stocks that start in BV and are still in the BV universe one year later have, on average, generated 3.4% p.a. outperformance (type II stocks). Value traps return an average −34.5% p.a.

Of course, these statistics mean nothing on their own. We need to know the frequency with which they occur, in order to gauge how important they are. A 17.5% p.a. excess return sounds very impressive, but it doesn't mean a lot if there is essentially no chance of it actually occurring. The middle part of the table details the average transition probabilities. For instance, in the BV portfolio, some 75% of stocks remain in the BV portfolio after a year (type II value stocks). Around 23% move to a higher price to book ratio, which moves them out of the BV portfolio (type I value stocks). A mere 2.3% of stocks end up being very serious value traps (type III stocks).

Table 31.1 Returns and transition probabilities

Average excess return	Portfolio	Minus	Same	Plus	Change in Size
SG	2.5	−19.2	−2.8	17.1	61.7
SN	5.9	−14.9	0.6	21.9	50.1
SV	9.6	−15.1	−0.2	21.8	62.6
BG	−0.5	−11.7	1.2	16.4	−37
BN	1.5	−11.3	0.7	16.9	−30.9
BV	5.1	−37.1	3.4	17.5	−31.5
Average transition vector					
SG		25.9	59.6	2.7	11.8
SN		16.7	60.8	12.3	10.3
SV		1.1	70.5	19.9	8.5
BG		10.8	87.5	0.8	0.9
BN		8.7	74.9	15.2	1.3
BV		0.1	74.6	23	2.2
Average contribution to average excess return					
SG		−5.3	−1.4	0.6	8.6
SN		−2.6	0.6	2.8	5.1
SV		−0.2	−0.4	4.4	5.7
BG		−1.2	0.9	0.1	−0.4
BN		−0.9	0.5	2.3	−0.4
BV		0.0	2.3	3.5	−0.7

Source: Fama and French (2006).

In fact, Joseph Piotroski (2000) has gone even further. He found that a minority of value stocks created the US value premium. Piotroski uncovered the fact that only 42% of value stocks outperform the market on a one-year view. We now know from the Fama and French work that 23% of the value stocks re-rate towards a more normal multiple, and that this generates sizeable returns for the investor. This implies that only around 25% (or one in four) of the type II value stocks generate positive excess returns. This helps to explain why the type II value stocks only generate 3.4% p.a. excess returns: the category of type II value stocks is a broad spectrum that hides a multitude of sins.

In our own work we have found that 50% of the stocks in our simple value screen outperform over a one-year time horizon. This implies that investors who follow such strategies not only need to be patient, but also need to avoid narrow framing. If they look at the portfolio in totality, then such investors are likely to be all right, even in the short term. However, if they frame narrowly and start to look at the individual performance of stocks within the portfolio, then problems could arise. With a relatively high percentage of stocks underperforming, the pain of running the strategy would be psychologically hard to bear, and result in the abandonment of the process.

One potential solution is to combine a value selection with a stop-loss system. We leave the investigation of this for another time, but it certainly looks like value investing could be said to be about avoiding losers.

Figure 31.2 shows the improvement in the percentage of correct calls as we extend the time horizon. Interestingly, the percentage of stocks outperforming the market rises over time, but not massively. So a 50% hit ratio rises to a 57% hit ratio when a 5-year time horizon is used.

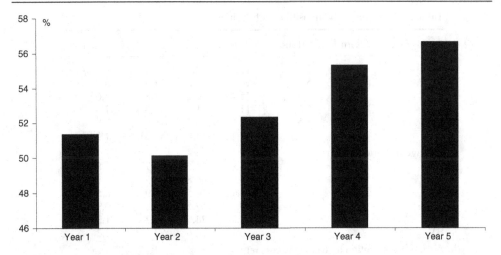

Figure 31.2   Value universe hit ratio as a function of time horizon.
Source: DrKW Macro research.

This improvement presumably stems from a greater proportion of value stocks managing to turn their businesses around as time goes by.

GROWTH PERSPECTIVE

So does time arbitrage pay for growth investors? The answer is a resounding 'no'. Patience just results in more and more stocks being torpedoed. Figure 31.3 makes the point graphically. Over our sample period, growth stocks have lost, on average, 6% p.a. in the first year of portfolio construction. Year 2 sees a further 3% loss. In year 3 a further 2% is lost, and then

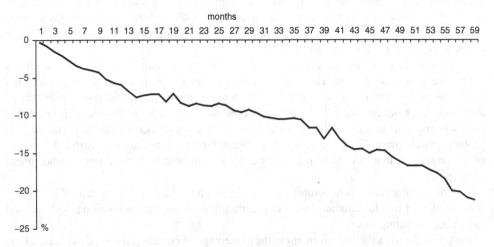

Figure 31.3   Patience is a killer: cumulative excess returns to a simple growth strategy.
Source: DrKW Macro research.

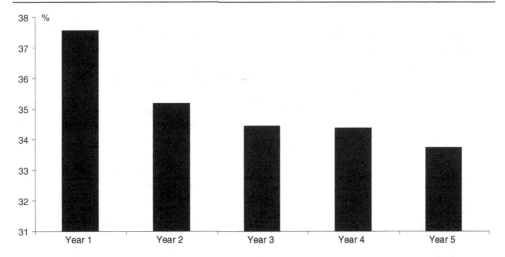

Figure 31.4   Growth universe hit ratio as a function of time horizon.
Source: DrKW Macro research.

things heat up with years 4 and 5 witnessing around 6% p.a. declines. As Peter Tasker might say, time is a killer, not a healer for growth stocks.

In terms of the percentage of stocks that outperform, the numbers don't make for good reading. Only around 38% of the stocks in the growth portfolio have an above-market return. So successful growth investing is all about picking winners, i.e. identifying the stocks that can generate positive returns.

When we extend the time horizon, the hit ratio declines – that is to say, the longer we wait, fewer and fewer stocks manage to outperform the index. Effectively, the risk of being hit by an earnings torpedo increases as time goes on (Figure 31.4).

GROWTH AND MOMENTUM

One obvious way in which we might be able to improve on growth portfolios is to introduce a momentum filter. To test this we take the top 20% of stocks by PE and then split the portfolio into three, based around the past 6 months' price momentum lagged by one month (see Sebastian Lancetti's note – *Winner and Losers*, 6 September 2006, for a lot more detail on the optimal momentum strategy).

The impact of this is dramatic. Figure 31.5 shows the high and low momentum portfolios for the growth universe. The benefits of using momentum are massive. The median p.a. performance improvement is over 400 bps.

Of course, the absolute returns are still negative, but the relative gains are massive. Now personally I've never been a great fan of the relative performance game but the potential value added by inclusion of momentum into a growth strategy can't be ignored (Figure 31.6). Moreover, the best benefits of the momentum input are achieved when the holding period is extended!

In terms of improving the hit rate of the screen, the inclusion of momentum improves the percentage of stocks outperforming from 38% to 41% at the one-year time horizon.

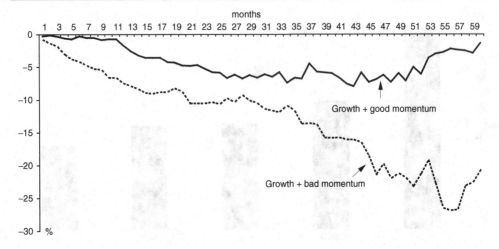

Figure 31.5   Growth plus momentum – a great improvement (cumulative excess returns %).
Source: DrKW Macro research.

VALUE FOR GROWTH INVESTORS

Of course, there is an alternative approach which growth investors might consider – use value. Figure 31.7 shows the excess 12-month returns to our various quintiles, with each quintile further broken down into three value baskets. It shows that the cheapest of the value stocks achieve relatively little outperformance, with the majority of the value premium being generated by the other two groups.

However, look at the growth stocks. The cheapest of the growth stock significantly outperforms both the growth category generally (by nearly 3% p.a.) and the most expensive of

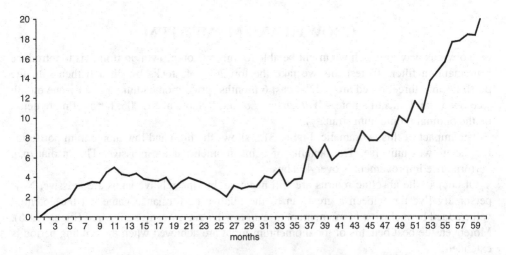

Figure 31.6   Improvement generated by including momentum in a growth universe (%).
Source: DrKW Macro research.

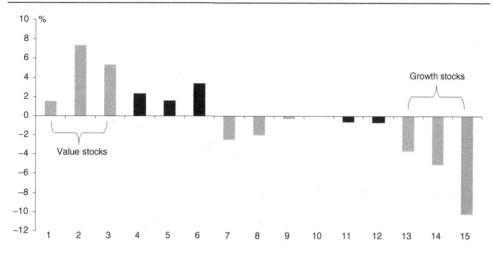

Figure 31.7   The importance of value across quintiles (% p.a. excess return).
Source: DrKW Macro research.

the growth stocks (by nearly 7% p.a.) So growth investors would be wise to remember that value matters – even for growth stocks. (We explored this issue once before, see *Global Equity Strategy*, 16 March 2005, for more details.)

So bizarrely, growth works within the value universe, and value works within the growth universe. Ah, the ironies of investment management.

VALUE AND MOMENTUM

If momentum is so useful in a growth context, what is its impact in a value universe? The results are less impressive than their growth cousins. The median value added is 130 bps p.a. Not inconsequential, but not in the same league as the growth results. Figure 31.8 shows the cumulative returns for the high- and low-momentum portfolios within the value universe.

It transpires that the improvement in the hit ratio is roughly similar to that seen in the growth arena. The 12-month hit rate rises from 50% to just over 55%.

This finding that momentum works better for growth stocks than for value stocks was first documented by Cliff Asness (1997) for US stocks. Figure 31.9, taken from Sebastian's magnum opus on momentum, provides a simple view of the conclusion for European stocks. Here each PE quintile has been split into three, based on price momentum. The difference between high- and low-momentum stocks in the value universe is around 4% p.a. However, the difference between the high- and low-momentum stocks in the growth universe is much higher, at around 12% p.a.!

IMPLICATIONS

The fact that momentum adds relatively little to performance of a value portfolio, but adds major benefits to a growth portfolio, has implications for the portable alpha addicts out there (you know who you are).

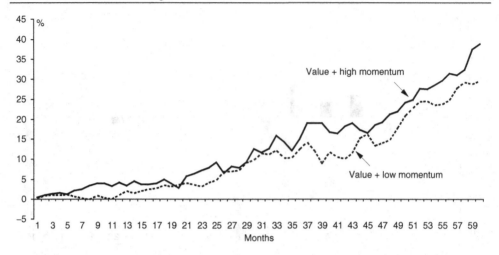

Figure 31.8   Improvement generated by including momentum in a value universe (cumulative excess return, %).
Source: DrKW Macro research.

If value managers find it hard to beat their benchmark (more on this below) but growth managers can do it far more easily, then a structure which is long value beta and then transports the alpha from a momentum using growth manager, should be fairly attractive.

Indeed, Chan *et al.* (2006) show that across a wide variety of benchmark measures, growth managers seem to be better able to generate abnormal returns relative to their universe than value managers do. Chan *et al.* found that the average alpha (from 1989 to 2001) for US growth managers is 2.6% p.a.; the corresponding number for value managers is 1.2% p.a. – entirely consistent with the finding outlined above (Figure 31.10).

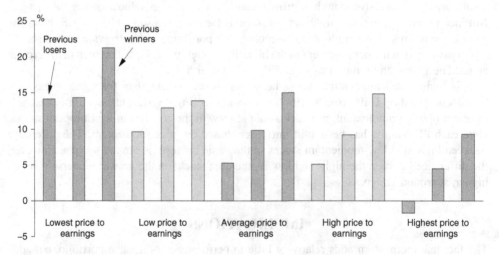

Figure 31.9   PE quintiles sorted by price momentum (% p.a.) 1990–2006.
Source: DrKW Macro research.

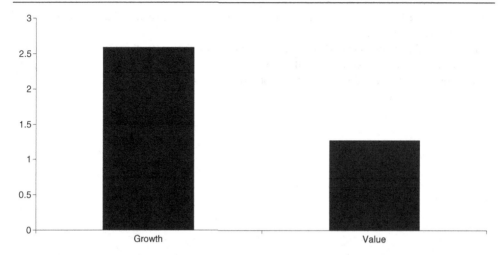

Figure 31.10 Average alpha from value and growth investors (1989–2001)% p.a.
Source: Chan *et al.* (2006).

A similar picture is painted by Figure 31.11. Here we have taken data from Houge and Loughran (2006) who formed two groups of US fund managers based around their factor loadings on the value premium. Those in the highest loading quartile are value investors, those in the lowest quartile are growth.

The figure compares the returns on the simple stock decile rankings from 1965 to 2002, against the returns from the two manager groups (net of fees) over the same sample period.

The value universe showed a 16% p.a. return over the period. Value managers (net of fees) showed only 11% p.a. return. The growth universe showed a 10% p.a. return, while growth

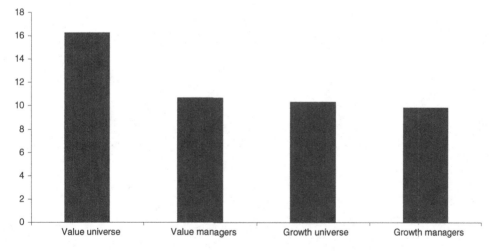

Figure 31.11 Failing to capture the value premium (1965–2002) % p.a.
Source: DrKW Macro research.

managers showed a 9.9% (net of fees) return. So value managers seem to have trouble actually capturing the value premium.

However, above and beyond all else, we have also shown that patience is certainly a prerequisite for value investors, while growth investors would be better off ensuring that momentum is one of the factors in their stock selection process, and remembering that they shouldn't ignore value.

32

Sectors, Value and Momentum[*]

While both value and momentum investing do work at a sector level, they are much more successful at a stock level. Investors should avoid the common preconception of certain sectors as value or growth. History shows that every sector has been value and growth at various points in time. However, to maximize returns, effort should be directed to stock selection not sector calls.

- We recently stumbled upon a dataset for US sector performance from 1926 onwards. This allowed us to test whether value and momentum make sense as sector strategies. The good news is that both strategies add value.

- Cheap sectors outperform expensive sectors by around 3% and beat the market by 2.5% p.a. over our sample period. High-momentum sectors outperformed low-momentum sectors and the market by around 2% p.a. However, none of these is massively statistically significant.

- In fact, the returns to a stock level value or momentum strategy are an order of magnitude greater than those at the sector level. For instance, a (zero net investment equal long short) value strategy at the stock level has generated returns of 4.4% p.a. since 1926, while a stock level momentum strategy has generated nearly 10% p.a. over the same period. This strongly argues that value and momentum are stock level concepts rather than sector level constructs.

- This makes intuitive sense as the 'buying' of a sector will result in the purchase of a mixture of stocks – some expensive and some cheap (or some with high momentum and some with low momentum, alternatively). This mixture will dilute the potency of the return strategy, so the finer the degree of gradation the better.

- However, occasionally an investor will say something along the lines of "I won't touch Tech" or bemoan the lack of value in 'traditional' value sectors. The long-term data shows that every sector has been a value sector and a growth sector at various points in time. So dismissing a sector as permanently growth or value is likely to lead to investors missing opportunities.

- The idea that value and momentum are stock level, rather than sector level, attributes ties in nicely with something we noted recently: the decline of stock-picking as an investment process. In *Global Equity Strategy*, 19 July 2006, we showed that the percentage of the market accounted for by stock-pickers had been declining consistently over the last 20 years. Whenever I see a declining line I become interested. The lack of stock-pickers could well mean that the best way of adding value is to do exactly that – exploit the neglected areas of the market.

---

[*]This article appeared in *Global Equity Strategy* on 19 September 2006. The material discussed was accurate at the time of publication.

- Additionally, if we are in a low return enviroment (Albert Edwards' Ice Age) then it is perfectly possible for the market in aggregate to go nowhere for a prolonged period (like '*the dismal years*' 1965–1982). If this is the case then stock selection may well be the best way of adding value for equity managers.

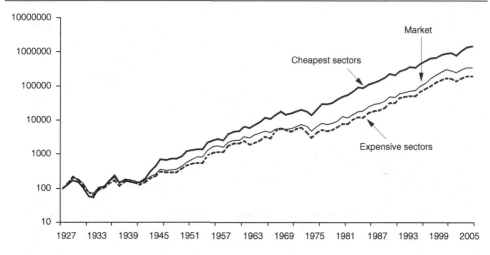

Figure 32.1   Performance of value based sectors (1926 = 100).
Source: DrKW Macro research.

In the past we have explored the performance of value and momentum strategies at the stock and country level (see *Global Equity Strategy*, 16 March 2005 and 30 April 2003 respectively). However we haven't been able to find a consistent series to allow us to test sector level value. This changed when we stumbled upon a long-term dataset on US sector performance from Professor Ken French.[1]

We chose to use the data set from 1926 onwards using annual data. The sectors are broken down into 30 categories based around four-digit SIC codes (Standard Industrial Classification). The tests we then ran were simple. The universe was sorted by the variable in question (say price to book), and then tritiles were formed based around the variable. The performance of the highest and lowest tritiles was then tracked for a year, and the process was repeated.

VALUE

The first factor we chose to investigate was value. We used the price to book ratio as the measure of value. Figure 32.1 shows the performance of the cheapest and dearest sectors and the market overall for comparison purposes. Not totally unsurprisingly, cheap sectors do outperform expensive sectors (by nearly 3% p.a.) and outperform the market (by 2.5% p.a.) over the full sample. It should be noted that neither of these results is massively statistically significant.

MOMENTUM

The second factor we tested was momentum. We used 12-month total return momentum to construct our baskets. Figure 32.2 shows the performance of the highest and lowest momentum tritiles, plus the market for comparison. Much like value, high-momentum sectors outperformed both the low-momentum sectors (by around 2% p.a.) and the market (by a

---

[1] See http://mba.tuck.dartmouth.edu/pages/faculty/ken.french/data_library.html.

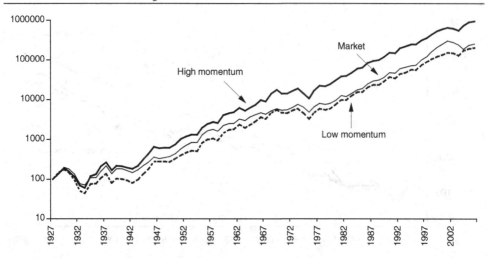

Figure 32.2   Performance of momentum ranked sectors (1926 = 100).
Source: DrKW Macro research.

similar margin). These are unusually low returns from a momentum-based strategy, and again are only borderline statistically significant at best.

SECTORS: VALUE OR GROWTH

One of the traps that investors occasionally fall into is thinking that certain sectors are permanently value sectors or growth sectors. So value investors may be unwilling to look at tech stocks, while growth investors may be unwilling to look at mining stocks.[2]

However, the long-run data reveals that just about all industries have been value and growth at differing points in their life cycles. Figure 32.3 shows the maximum and minimum absolute price to book ratios for each of the industries in our full sample.

The same picture holds if we transfer the data into relative valuation space. Figure 32.4 shows the maximum and minimum relative price to book for each sector. The same conclusion holds – most sectors have been both value and growth at different times.

Perhaps an explicit sector example will help make this point clear. Figure 32.5 shows the absolute and relative price to book for the Telecoms sector in the USA. You can clearly see that the Telecoms sector has moved from value to growth and perhaps back again on the absolute measure, and from a growth to a value sector on the relative basis.

So value and growth are not permanent attributes of a sector; rather sectors can be value or growth. So 'value' investors who swear they will never go near tech stocks are perhaps missing opportunities.

---

[2] Not that for one minute we would advise buying mining. We remain convinced that it has been a bubble; see *Global Equity Strategy*, 14 February 2006 for details.

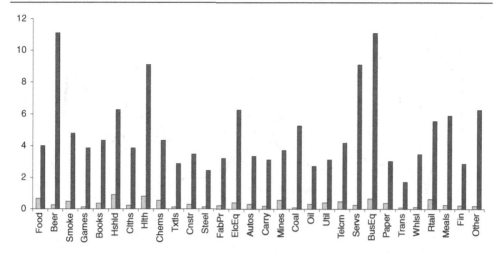

Figure 32.3   Maximum and minimum absolute price to book by sector.
Source: DrKW Macro research.

STOCKS OR SECTORS

The value and momentum premia for sectors were noticeably lower than those found at the stock level. Table 32.1 shows the premia available to value and momentum (measured using long/short zero net investment portfolios) over two time periods. In both cases the premia at the stock level are markedly bigger than those at the sector level (Figure 32.6). This strongly suggests that both value and momentum are stock level concepts.

As such, value and momentum will have both more meaning and higher returns when applied in the arena of stock selection. In many ways this makes sense as a sector may well

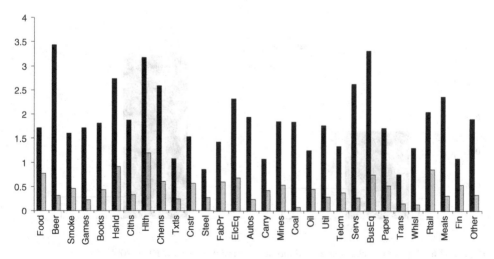

Figure 32.4   Maximum and minimum relative price to book by sector.
Source: DrKW Macro research.

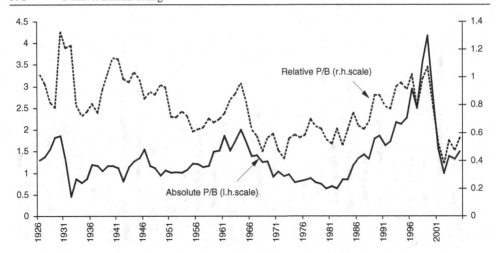

Figure 32.5   Absolute and relative price to book for US Telecoms.
Source: DrKW Macro research.

Table 32.1   US value and momentum premia (% p.a.)

Period	Value (%)	Momentum (%)
1926–2005		
Stocks	4.4	10.0
Sectors	2.9	2.2
1974–2005		
Stocks	5.2	9.9
Sectors	1.8	1.3

Source: DrKW Macro research.

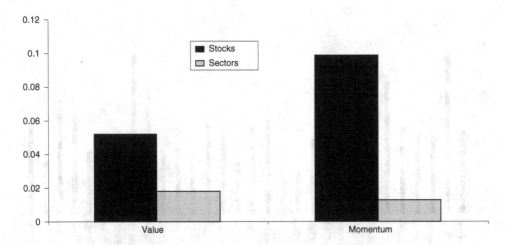

Figure 32.6   Stock and sector value and momentum premia (% p.a.) 1974–2005.
Source: DrKW Macro research.

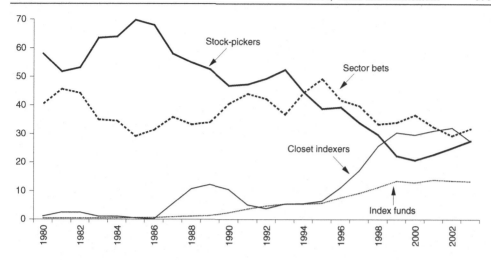

Figure 32.7 The evolution of the mutual fund industry – % of all equity assets.
Source: Cremers and Petajisto (2000) and DrKW Macro research.

contain a spread of firms enjoying very different multiples. Hence when you buy a sector you get a mixture of both cheap and expensive firms (or high- and low-momentum firms, alternatively) which dilutes the potential available premium (Figure 32.7).

This is intriguing given some ideas we developed in a recent article (see *Global Equity Strategy*, 16 July 2006) arguing that stock-picking has become a far less prevalent approach to investing. In part, this move must reflect the shift to a 'risk management' driven approach in which it would appear to be "Better for reputation to fail conventionally than to succeed unconventionally" as Keynes opined. Under such an approach fund managers appear to be rewarded for hugging a benchmark and not underperforming, rather than maximizing returns. I'd better stop before I deteriorate into a rant on the subject (which I will save for another time).

This all adds up to a situation where the returns are likely to be highest from bottom up stock selection for two reasons. Firstly, because stock level information offers a greater level of differentiation. Secondly because fewer than usual investors are pursuing such a strategy.

Additionally, if we are in a low return enviroment (Albert Edwards' Ice Age) then it is perfectly possible for the market in aggregate to go nowhere for a prolonged period (like '*the dismal years*' 1965–1982). If this is the case, then stock selection may well be the best way of adding value for equity managers.

Figure 22.7...

33

Sector-Relative Factors Work Best[*]

Written with Andrew Lapthorne

Value, size and momentum are well-documented providers of excess returns but can lead to some uncomfortably large sector bets. Using industry-relative factors reduces this problem, as well as getting around many problems associated with accounting regimes and capital structures. Our back-testing suggests that value and size work best on a sector-adjusted basis, while price momentum does not.

- Should we screen stocks on absolute levels of valuation, momentum and size or should we look at everything relative to a set of sector peers? Despite most research teams being organized along sector-lines, much quant work seems less enthusiastic about making stock-to-peer comparisons, preferring to select stocks using absolute valuation and to adjust sector bets afterwards, typically through some kind of optimization process.

- Perhaps the reason why sector-relative measures are not overly popular is that most back-tests, looking back over the last 10 or so years, would highlight how absolute levels of valuation (in particular), momentum and size would have worked better unadjusted to differing industry characteristics. We argue in this chapter that this period of factor performance, typified by big swings in sector rotation (courtesy of the TMT bubble) is not particularly representative and, as such, a sector-relative approach to factor selection is more appropriate going forward.

- Certainly the fundamental arguments for a sector-relative approach are compelling. Industries have different capital requirements and accounting regimes and, as such, a low price to book, for example, rather than representing a "value" opportunity, may simply be defining a type of business.

- Constructing portfolios based on absolute rather than sector-relative measures, reduces sector diversification (i.e. can result in some fairly large sector bets). While sector constraints can be imposed later, this would have the effect of diminishing the exposure to any given factor and possibly future returns. A sector-relative approach might allow for a more diversified portfolio from the offset and without diminishing the exposure to any given factor.

- We have back-tested four valuation metrics (PE, PC, PB and DY), size and a common (6-month) price momentum strategy. Our results confirm our prior comment, that over the last 10 years, a non-adjusted approach generally worked best, although not always.

- However, over a more extended 30-year period and in the 10 years prior to the bubble commencing, a sector-relative approach has generally outperformed a market-wide approach. Absolute and risk-adjusted returns were found to be higher for most valuation metrics and

---

[*]This article appeared in *Global Quantitative Strategy* on 23 November 2006. The material discussed was accurate at the time of publication.

in most regions with the exception of Japan (as ever!). Statistical significance of these returns also improved in most cases. Even small versus large size was found to have better returns on a sector-adjusted basis. The results for price momentum was more mixed with the industry-relative measure delivering results with greater statistical significance, but lower absolute returns. Given that price itself is not a function of industry make-up or accounting regime, this result is probably not too surprising.

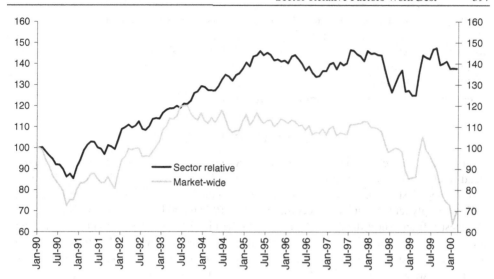

Figure 33.1   Sector-relative versus rather than absolute price to book strategies in the US during the 1990s (using long/short quintiles).
Source: DrKW Macro research.

There is a wide body of research recognizing that selecting stocks based on price momentum and/or a low valuation has generated excess returns over the long term. Most of this research concentrates on using absolute levels of such things as price to earnings, cashflow and so on. This research note asks if there is any benefit to looking at such measures on an industry-relative rather than a market-wide basis.

For a start, constructing portfolios based on absolute levels of valuation is likely to lead to large sectors bets, which, while perhaps profitable in the long-term, can result in sustained periods of underperformance. (Witness the suffering and asset losses incurred by value managers during the TMT bubble.) Building a portfolio based on sector-relative rather than market-wide measures should lead to a more diversified portfolio and, as such, perhaps offer better risk-adjusted returns. Figure 33.1 shows that during the 1990s the style rotation was not so much towards growth stocks but towards growth sectors.

In a research note published in June 1996,[1] we highlighted how style-returns were not simply a function of sector rotation. We found that the returns produced from constructing factor portfolios within sectors were equivalent to, and highly correlated with, market-wide factor portfolios. So we concluded that the excess returns from taking a value and/or momentum approach were still available even when constraining sector exposure.

Unfortunately building individual portfolios within sectors was not optimal. Many sectors did not have a sufficient number of liquid stocks and we were forced to create long/short baskets using tritiles rather than deciles or quintiles. As a consequence the resulting factor spread between the long and short portfolios was reduced, and subsequently the alpha generated was not as attractive as when executed market-wide.

Another way of minimizing sector risk is to use sector-adjusted factors rather than simply using market-wide variables. Research by Asness *et al.* (2000), for example, has highlighted how

---

[1] See *Global Quantitative Strategy*, Intra-sector style returns – its more than sector rotation (5 June 2006).

industry-relative factors appear to offer better returns than using a simple market-wide variable. Beyond reducing sector-risk within a portfolio, there are several compelling arguments for using industry-relative measures. Cohen and Polk (1998) argue along with Asness *et al.* that valuation measures such as price to book are highly dependent on accounting standards, and that capital requirements will vary greatly across industries. A low price to book, rather than representing a "value" opportunity, may simply be defining a type of business.

METHODOLOGY

Every month for each region we use a proprietary universe of stocks corrected (which includes dead stocks) to create long/short quintile portfolios based on two sets of factors. The first set of factors we test are simply the straightforward unadjusted values. So, for example, in testing P/E we simply rank the universe according to their P/E and go long the 20% of stocks with the cheapest P/E and short the 20% of stocks with the highest P/E.[2] The second set of variables we measure are all relative to the median value of the sector in which the stock resides. If a stock has a dividend yield of 4% and the median dividend yield of stocks in its sector is 3%, then the value we test is 1%, i.e. 4% − 3%. The valuation data is based on 'as reported' MSCI data. For each set of factors, we measure the average unweighted performance of each of these portfolios over the month, rebalancing every month for the last 30 years.

As ever, when performing sector work we encounter the problem that the GICS classification system we use did not exist for a considerable proportion of our back-testing period. Nonetheless as most of the sectors seen today represent similar descriptions of what existed previously, we are not overly concerned. Also we are reassured that our results are similar to those seen in other research where an entirely different classification system has been used.

Therefore, each month we have calculated the performance of long and short portfolios based on both an absolute and a sector relative factor. However, because we are only selecting stocks at the more extreme end of any given variable, if a sector's factors are all tightly clustered around a particular level, then the sector would probably see no representation in either the long or the short portfolio. So, although the sector-relative measure reduces sector skew, it does not fully diversify industry exposure. However, this method, compared to trying to represent all sectors, does allow a wider factor exposure and therefore hopefully better returns.

Figure 33.2 compares the difference in global sector weightings of the long and short price to book portfolios put together, based on either an absolute or a sector-relative price to book measure. For example, when building portfolios using an unadjusted price to book, there is almost a 7% difference between the weighting of the material sector in the long portfolio and the short portfolio (i.e. a 12% weighting in the long portfolio versus a 5% weighting in the short). When using a sector-relative price to book measure this difference is reduced down to almost nothing.

THE RESULTS

Despite the apparent attraction of such an intra-sector methodology and research suggesting that it improves returns, many seem unconvinced by such an approach. Back-testing results over the last 10 or so years suggest the reasons why. Just as being underweight the TMT sectors

---

[2] In practice we use earnings yield so as to include stocks with negative profits.

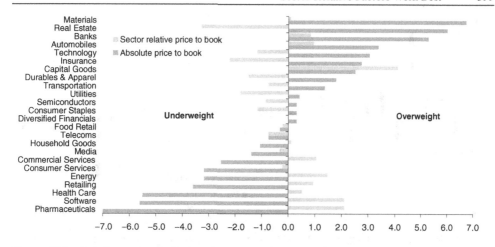

Figure 33.2 Relative sector weightings in an absolute and sector relative long/short price to book strategy (global universe, % difference).
Source: DrKW Macro research.

hurt investors during the inflating of the equity bubble, did it help them after the subsequent bust? Much of the value outperformance subsequent to the bust was down to being in cheap (i.e. non-TMT) sectors.

However, in the periods prior to the bubble-bursting, sector-relative valuation delivered the better returns. An exception to this was Japan where the non-adjusted valuation measures worked best. Looking forward, our argument would be that, with little in the way, extreme sector-valuations out there, i.e. cross-sectional sector valuation spreads, are very low rather than very high as they were in the latter part of the 1990s. So, as such, sector-relative measures may win out once again.

Figures 33.3–33.6 show the annual difference in returns between employing either sector-relative or absolute value strategies in four regions. They highlight how, for a long period of time prior to the bubble-bursting, making a sector adjustment improved returns to a long/short value strategy.

We realize that Table 33.1 doesn't look particularly friendly and needs some explanation. The figures quoted outside the brackets are the annualized returns for a zero net investment strategy based on our long/short baskets. The numbers inside the brackets are the *t*-stats, which is simply a measure of statistical significance. We are only really interested in those annualized returns with *t*-stats above 2.0. For each period, we have highlighted the better return (with a minimum *t*-stat of 2.0) in *italic* for each factor in each region.

On initial inspection, the results appear quite mixed. Most of the value strategies appear to benefit from a sector-relative approach, which makes sense given different accounting regimes, capital structures, and so on. The results for dividend yield are a bit more mixed. This perhaps highlights how the level of dividend yield is not so much a function of company's industry and more a decision by management on payout levels earnings to retain. It could also suggest that dividend yield is more related to sector rotation than the other value strategies we've looked at.

Perhaps somewhat surprisingly Smallcap versus Largecap also worked well on a sector relative basis and even though this must be viewed within the context of a universe that most

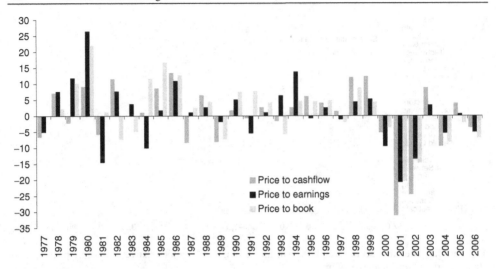

Figure 33.3 Europe ex-UK – sector-relative versus market-wide factor returns (annual returns, % difference between both approaches).
Source: DrKW Macro research.

academics would consider to be Largecap, it does suggest that the size effect is not about buying "small industries" but by buying smaller companies within Industries.

Price momentum, as we have noted in prior studies while still working on an industry-relative basis (the results were marginally more statistically significant), is not as effective as when employed on a market-wide basis.

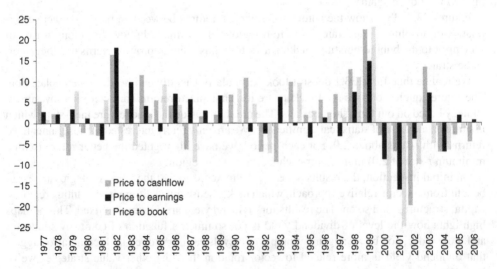

Figure 33.4 USA – sector-relative versus market-wide factor returns (annual returns, % difference between both approaches).
Source: DrKW Macro research.

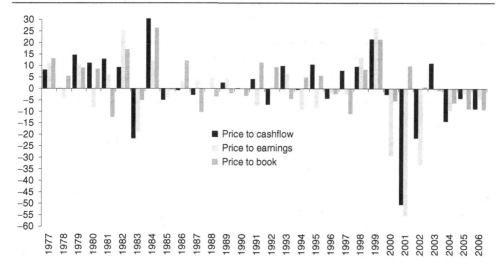

Figure 33.5 UK – sector-relative versus market-wide factor returns (annual returns, % difference between both approaches).
Source: DrKW Macro research.

The *t*-statistics in Table 33.1, a measure of significance, are generally higher for the sector-relative approach. This would suggest, and confirmed in Table 33.2, that risk-adjusted returns should be better for the industry adjusted measures. We have highlighted in italic the better measure of each factor for each region. We would point out that some risk-adjusted returns are fairly meagre and should simply be ignored. Again for price to cashflow, price to earnings, and price to book there have been clear benefits to using the sector-relative measures over

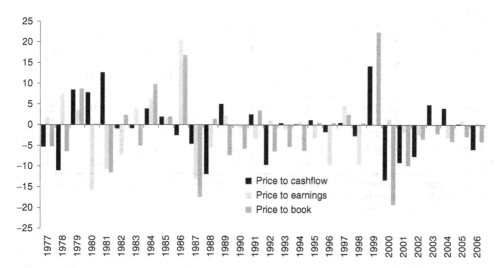

Figure 33.6 Japan – sector-relative versus market-wide factor returns (annual returns, % difference between both approaches).
Source: DrKW Macro research.

Table 33.1   Regional market-wide versus sector relative factor returns (annualized returns with *t*-stat* in brackets)

	Last 30 years		Last 10 years		Prior 10 years	
	Sector-relative	Market-wide	Sector-relative	Market-wide	Sector-relative	Market-wide
Price to Cashflow						
Europe ex-UK	6.3 (3.5)	5.6 (2.6)	8.6 (2.8)	10.6 (2.3)	6.4 (2.4)	5.7 (2.1)
US	7.9 (4.6)	6.8 (2.3)	10.2 (2.6)	8.7 (1.2)	1.8 (0.9)	0.5 (0.2)
UK	7.9 (4.1)	6.6 (2.4)	9.5 (2.4)	13.9 (2.0)	6.1 (2.1)	3.9 (1.2)
Japan	8.0 (4.8)	7.8 (3.6)	8.7 (3.4)	10.4 (2.8)	8.6 (3.1)	9.2 (2.6)
World	10.5 (5.9)	9.7 (4.7)	14.1 (5.5)	13.8 (3.3)	6.8 (1.9)	5.7 (1.5)
Price to Earnings						
Europe ex-UK	9.0 (5.3)	7.5 (3.4)	6.6 (2.1)	9.5 (2.2)	9.9 (3.9)	8.1 (3.1)
US	6.4 (4.0)	5.5 (2.0)	5.3 (1.3)	6.0 (0.9)	0.9 (0.5)	−0.6 (−0.2)
UK	8.1 (4.5)	9.7 (3.6)	11.4 (3.0)	18.2 (2.7)	4.4 (1.6)	4.3 (1.3)
Japan	5.9 (3.8)	7.2 (3.6)	4.1 (1.2)	6.0 (1.5)	8.0 (3.3)	9.7 (2.9)
World	9.7 (4.3)	9.4 (3.9)	9.3 (2.9)	10.5 (2.6)	7.7 (1.6)	7.3 (1.5)
Price to Book						
Europe ex-UK	6.5 (3.4)	5.7 (2.6)	7.0 (2.0)	11.4 (2.8)	7.0 (2.2)	4.1 (1.2)
US	5.0 (2.9)	5.9 (2.4)	4.6 (1.2)	7.2 (1.3)	2.9 (1.3)	2.1 (0.7)
UK	7.3 (3.8)	5.0 (2.0)	7.3 (2.2)	8.2 (1.6)	7.1 (2.4)	4.9 (1.4)
Japan	10.5 (5.2)	11.5 (4.0)	10.7 (2.2)	12.3 (1.9)	14.4 (6.4)	16.6 (4.0)
World	8.8 (4.1)	8.5 (3.7)	9.4 (2.2)	9.9 (2.0)	7.7 (2.1)	7.7 (2.1)
Dividend Yield						
Europe ex-UK	5.0 (3.0)	2.5 (1.3)	7.8 (2.8)	10.7 (3.0)	4.3 (1.8)	2.1 (0.9)
US	1.9 (1.3)	−2.4 (−1.0)	−0.1 (−0.1)	−4.3 (−1.0)	−1.1 (−0.6)	−4.8 (−1.4)
UK	−0.3 (−0.1)	2.4 (0.9)	5.7 (1.6)	10.2 (1.8)	−3.9 (−1.2)	−2.4 (−0.6)
Japan	8.9 (3.9)	8.7 (2.8)	9.6 (1.9)	9.8 (1.4)	15.4 (6.2)	16.7 (5.1)
World	8.7 (4.0)	8.5 (3.5)	9.9 (3.0)	11.1 (2.8)	9.1 (1.9)	10.8 (2.1)
Small versus large						
Europe ex-UK	7.2 (4.4)	5.2 (2.5)	5.2 (1.8)	0.2 (0.1)	6.5 (2.3)	7.4 (2.0)
US	3.9 (2.5)	7.4 (3.2)	2.8 (0.7)	8.3 (1.4)	1.9 (0.9)	2.6 (0.8)
UK	5.0 (2.9)	2.4 (0.9)	2.7 (0.8)	−2.9 (−0.5)	4.0 (1.4)	2.0 (0.4)
Japan	5.4 (2.4)	6.7 (2.1)	4.4 (0.9)	3.8 (0.6)	8.2 (2.3)	11.6 (2.2)
World	8.2 (5.3)	7.8 (3.9)	7.4 (2.7)	5.3 (1.3)	6.7 (2.4)	7.4 (2.3)
6-month price momentum (execution lagged by 1 month)						
Europe ex-UK	10.7 (5.2)	12.0 (4.8)	10.9 (2.7)	12.0 (2.3)	7.0 (1.9)	8.3 (2.0)
US	4.1 (2.8)	5.7 (2.5)	7.4 (2.6)	11.1 (2.5)	0.7 (0.3)	−0.7 (−0.2)
UK	7.7 (3.8)	9.9 (3.6)	7.5 (1.7)	11.5 (1.7)	7.2 (2.1)	8.0 (2.0)
Japan	0.5 (0.2)	1.1 (0.4)	3.6 (0.8)	4.4 (0.8)	−3.7 (−1.1)	−7.1 (−1.6)
World	8.0 (4.3)	9.3 (4.5)	10.5 (2.7)	11.6 (2.5)	5.9 (1.8)	5.6 (1.7)

* We are interested in those returns with a *t*-stat at 2.0 or above, then we highlight either the sector relative or market-wide factor with the best annualized returns.
Source: DrKW Macro research.

the market-wide number. For price momentum the results are marginally in favour of the sector-relative measure but only just, and in most cases the absolute level of achieved returns are the more interesting.

Table 33.2 Risk-adjusted returns by factor and by region

Region	Last 30 years Sector	Last 30 years Market	Last 10 years Sector	Last 10 years Market	Prior 10 years Sector	Prior 10 years Market
Price to Cashflow						
Europe ex-UK	0.61	0.46	0.88	0.71	0.76	0.67
US	0.81	0.42	0.83	0.37	0.29	0.05
UK	0.72	0.42	0.76	0.65	0.66	0.38
Japan	0.84	0.64	1.07	0.88	0.98	0.82
World	1.05	0.83	1.73	1.05	0.59	0.48
Price to Earnings						
Europe ex-UK	0.93	0.60	0.67	0.69	1.23	0.99
US	0.71	0.36	0.43	0.28	0.16	−0.06
UK	0.79	0.64	0.95	0.86	0.50	0.42
Japan	0.67	0.64	0.37	0.49	1.03	0.91
World	0.76	0.70	0.90	0.82	0.50	0.46
Price to Book						
Europe ex-UK	0.61	0.47	0.64	0.88	0.68	0.37
US	0.51	0.43	0.38	0.42	0.42	0.21
UK	0.67	0.35	0.69	0.50	0.75	0.44
Japan	0.92	0.72	0.69	0.59	2.03	1.27
World	0.73	0.66	0.71	0.64	0.65	0.67
Dividend Yield						
Europe ex-UK	0.53	0.22	0.89	0.95	0.57	0.30
US	0.23	−0.17	−0.02	−0.32	−0.19	−0.44
UK	−0.02	0.16	0.49	0.58	−0.38	−0.20
Japan	0.70	0.50	0.60	0.46	1.96	1.62
World	0.70	0.63	0.96	0.90	0.61	0.67
Small versus large cap						
Europe ex-UK	0.79	0.44	0.57	0.02	0.73	0.64
US	0.44	0.56	0.24	0.46	0.27	0.25
UK	0.51	0.16	0.26	−0.16	0.44	0.14
Japan	0.42	0.38	0.29	0.18	0.72	0.69
World	0.94	0.70	0.86	0.42	0.76	0.72
6-month price momentum (lagged by 1 month)						
Europe ex-UK	0.93	0.87	0.86	0.74	0.61	0.63
US	0.50	0.45	0.82	0.80	0.10	−0.06
UK	0.68	0.65	0.54	0.53	0.68	0.64
Japan	0.04	0.07	0.26	0.25	−0.36	−0.52
World	0.78	0.81	0.86	0.79	0.58	0.54

Source: DrKW Macro research.

CONCLUSION

So our back-tests seem to conclude that when building a stock screening or selection process, most valuation criteria benefit from being adjusted relative to their sector peers but price momentum doesn't. Size, while working sector-relative, presents a practical problem in that given the lower returns from a stand-alone size strategy it would need to be timed, and from our perspective small size tends to outperform from a low not high valuation base. As such size, while undoubtedly an important factor, can be ignored in favour, of sector-relative valuation, i.e. if Smallcaps were cheap the model should be highlighting them anyway.

34

Cheap Countries Outperform*

Cheap countries outperform their expensive counterparts by around 7% p.a. Instead of worrying too much about correlations, those with a global equity mandate should concentrate their portfolios in the cheapest markets. We also find a strong momentum effect within relative equity market selection.

- In this chapter we update and extend work originally done by Asness *et al.* (1997). They found strong parallels between the cross-sectional performance of stocks and countries; that is to say, cheap countries outperformed expensive countries (just as cheap stocks tend to outperform expensive stocks). And those countries that have done best over the last 12 months tend to continue to do well (just as happens with stocks).

- Our empirical findings show that cheap countries outperform expensive countries by around 7% p.a. The worst performing "value" strategy was simple PE which still showed a 5.5% outperformance by cheap countries! Dividend yield and price to book both showed higher "value" outperformance. The value effects we find are not just compensation for greater risk.

- Momentum effects are even stronger than value effects. The highest momentum countries outperform the lowest momentum countries by nearly 16% p.a.!

- We explore both long-only and long/short versions of these value and momentum-based strategies, and present various diagnostics on these baskets. In general, both value and momentum strategies add value to country selection.

*This article appeared in *Global Equity Strategy* on 30 April 2003. The material discussed was accurate at the time of publication.

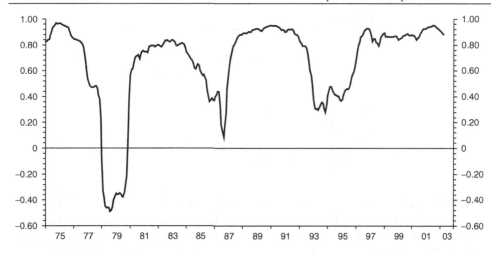

Figure 34.1 Problem or distraction? 36 month rolling correlation US and UK equity returns. *Source:* DrKW Macro research.

Several client meetings have uncovered much sympathy for our view on the UK market. However, one question keeps coming up time and time again: What about the correlation with the US market? The trouble with correlations is that they alter over time – for instance, according to Goetzmann *et al.* (00), the UK/US correlation has ranged from 0.08 to 0.51 at various times since the 1870s (see *Global Equity Strategy*, 22 July 2002, for more details). One client even suggested that my much beloved valuation framework might be as good as useless! I would refute this on the grounds that, in the long run, as we have shown many times before, valuations determine returns. However, this leads to the obvious question of the necessary time horizon in order to exploit such opportunities (Figure 34.1).

Now I have to make a confession. I am, at heart, a value investor, and as such I have pretty much taken on faith the idea that cheapness tends to outperform. However, upon further reflection it struck me that most of the studies I had read, or the empirical work I had done, was actually based on stock data – that is to say, within each country, value strategies tended to outperform over the long run. But I had seen very little work on whether this was true at the country level.

As I have noted in other contexts, Sherlock Holmes was fond of opining "It is a capital mistake to theorize before you have all the evidence. It biases the judgement." Could I have fallen foul of this advice?

Somewhere in the dim and distant past, I was sure I had seen someone writing on whether value strategies worked at the country level. A quick search of my study at home revealed that the article I had been thinking of was 'Parallels between the cross-sectional predictability of stock and country returns' by Asness *et al.* (1997). This insightful paper showed that value effects (as defined by high book to price outperforming low book to price), and momentum effects were both seen at the country level as well as the stock level.

I decided to update and extend their study, and with the invaluable aid of Rui Antunes from our Global Quantitative Strategy team, we embarked on doing so. The first runs weren't promising; we couldn't find the effects we had hoped. So I contacted Cliff Asness who kindly pointed out that there was an error in our data-downloading process which altered the lining

Table 34.1   Summary of performance

Strategy	Average Long/Short Return % p.a	Average Excess Return % p.a.
Dividend yield	6.8	6.0
Price to book	7.3	6.1
Price to earnings	5.5	4.6
Momentum	15.8	9.0

Source: DrKW Macro research.

up of the dates.[1] Once we had put this right, the splendid truth was revealed. *Cheap countries outperformed expensive countries* in the cross-section. My faith in value investing was restored.

In order to test the hypothesis we followed the methodology set out by Asness *et al.* The universe of countries is the MSCI World in local currency (excluding Finland, Ireland, New Zealand and Malaysia[2]). Each month we sorted the universe into tritiles on whichever criteria we were examining. We then formed equally weighted portfolios at the month end, and tracked total returns over the next month. We repeated this process monthly. The sample we used was 01/1975–03/2003.

Table 34.1 provides a summary of our findings. The first column shows the average annual return to a portfolio that goes long the top tritile (in terms of dividends and momentum) or long the bottom tritile (in terms of price to book and price to earnings) against a short position in the bottom tritile (in terms of dividends and momentum) or the top tritile (in terms of price to book and price to earnings). Regardless of how we choose to define 'value' the strategies show that an equal long short portfolio in favour of cheapness produces good returns. For instance, a strategy that is long the highest dividend yielding tritile of the MSCI World, and short the lowest yielding tritile, generates an average annual return of 6.8%.

As per Asness *et al.*, we also check to see if countries exhibit a momentum effect. In our sort, momentum is defined as the price change over the prior 12 months. *A very strong momentum effect is uncovered.* Countries that have risen the most over the last 12 months continue to do so in the following month; conversely, those that have seen the weakest momentum in the previous 12 months continue to be weak in the next month.

The second column shows the equivalent return for a long only fund manager, assuming a benchmark of the MSCI World. Thus the returns are expressed as the excess of the tritile relative to the benchmark. Once again we find a significant performance enhancement from concentrating on value and momentum. For instance, the highest dividend yielding tritile of the MSCI World outperforms the index by 6% p.a. The top tritile, in terms of the prior 12 months' price performance, outperforms the MSCI World by 9% p.a.

This value and momentum outperformance is not simply a function of taking on extra risk. The tables and figures on the following pages lay out the detailed information on each strategy. However, a summary is provided in Table 34.2. It shows the return per unit of risk differential between the high and low tritiles, and the high tritile against the market. In all cases, the

---

[1] Thanks to Cliff for sparing the time and effort to correct our oversight.

[2] The removal of these countries is not designed to fix our results. It is just that they enter the universe later than 1975. We tested to see if their exclusion significantly altered the results, and found it didn't.

Table 34.2   Return risk differentials across strategies

	Long/Short Return/Risk Differential	Long Only Return/Risk Differential
DY	0.13	0.10
PB	0.14	0.09
PE	0.12	0.07
MOM	0.26	0.12

Source: DrKW Macro research.

Table 34.3   Current basket contents

DY	PB	PE	MOM
Long	**Long**	**Long**	**Long**
Belgium	Germany	Japan	Austria
Netherlands	Hong Kong	Belgium	Canada
Italy	Norway	Hong Kong	Australia
Norway	Japan	UK	Hong Kong
France	Singapore	Netherlands	USA
Hong Kong	Belgium	Spain	Japan
Short	**Short**	**Short**	**Short**
Denmark	Canada	USA	Norway
Austria	Spain	Switzerland	France
Canada	Australia	Italy	Belgium
USA	Netherlands	Germany	Sweden
Switzerland	Switzerland	France	Netherlands
Japan	USA	Sweden	Germany

Source: DrKW Macro research.

strategies show a positive differential, suggesting that *their value added is not simply a result of higher risk.*

You may be wondering which countries are being suggested by this approach at the moment. Table 34.3 lists out the long and short basket contents for April 2003. Sadly from my point of view the UK only appears in the PE based selection!

STRATEGY BY STRATEGY INFORMATION

For each of the strategies we present a summary table and five graphs. The tables, like Table 34.4, show a variety of information, most of which is hopefully self-explanatory. However, some elements might benefit from a little expansion.

We present two *t*-tests. The first (labelled as T-test for difference in means) checks to see if the average value obtained from the high and low portfolios are statistically different – an absolute value greater than 1.6 is sufficient to say we are 95% sure that the means are different. Each of the strategies passes this test.

The second *t*-test we perform is to assess whether the average return from a long/short portfolio is statistically different from zero. Again a figure of greater than absolute 1.6 is

Table 34.4   Summary data on dividend yield baskets (1975–2003)

DY	Average Monthly Return	Average Monthly Risk	Return/risk
High	1.5	4.5	0.33
Medium	1.0	4.6	0.23
Low	0.9	4.4	0.20
Market	1.0	4.0	0.24
T-test for difference in means	1.83	long-only α 1.38 (5.6)	long-only β 0.11 (1.9)
T-test for long/short portfolio	3.69	long/short α 0.69 (4.0)	long/short β −0.1 (−1.7)
% of correct calls	0.59		
IC	0.17		
IR	0.60		

Source: DrKW Macro research.

enough for us to be sure that we can be 95% confident that such a portfolio doesn't have a zero average return. Once again all the portfolios pass this test.

The other pieces of information within Table 34.4 are the information coefficient (IC) and the information ratio (IR). The IC measures the correlation between the forecasts of the model and the outcomes. It can be defined as $2 \times (f - 0.5)$, where f is the percentage of calls the model predicted accurately.

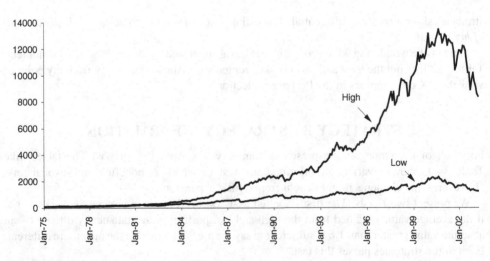

Figure 34.2   Portfolio performance 01/75=100.
Source: DrKW Macro research.

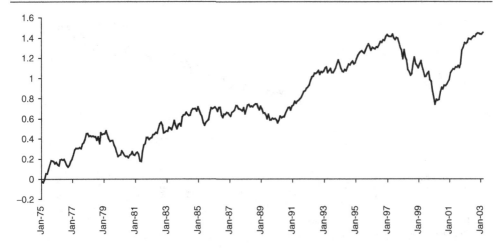

Figure 34.3   Cumulative returns on long/short portfolio.
Source: DrKW Macro research.

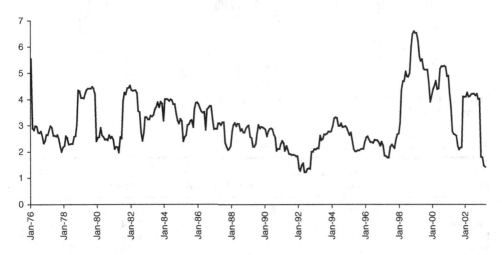

Figure 34.4   Standard deviation of long/short returns.
Source: DrKW Macro research.

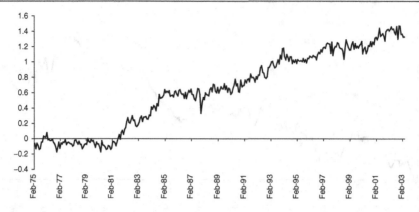

Figure 34.5   Cumulative excess returns – long-only portfolio.
Source: DrKW Macro research.

Figure 34.6   Standard deviation of long-only excess returns.
Source: DrKW Macro research.

Table 34.5   Summary data on price to book baskets (1975–2003)

PB	Average Monthly Return	Average Monthly Risk	Return/Risk
High	0.9	4.7	0.19
Medium	1.1	4.4	0.24
Low	1.5	4.4	0.33
Market	1.0	4.0	0.24
T-test for difference in means	−1.59	long only α 1.35 (5.5)	long only β 0.10 (1.7)
T-test for long/short portfolio	−3.06	long/short α 0.64 (3.4)	long/short β −0.1 (−1.9)
% of correct calls	0.56		
IC	0.13		
IR	0.44		

Source: DrKW Macro research.

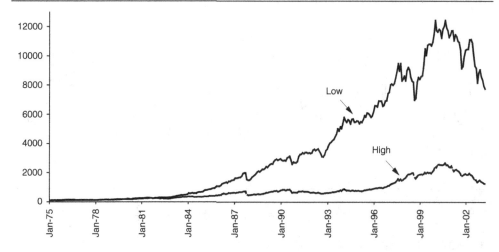

Figure 34.7   Portfolio performance 01/75 = 100.
Source: DrKW Macro research.

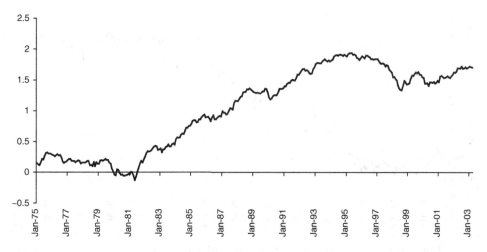

Figure 34.8   Cumulative returns on long/short portfolio.
Source: DrKW Macro research.

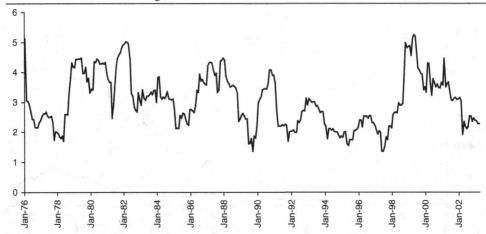

Figure 34.9   Standard deviation of long/short returns.
Source: DrKW Macro research.

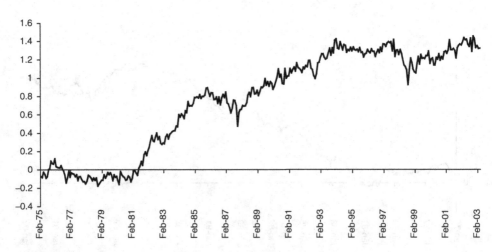

Figure 34.10   Cumulative excess returns – long-only portfolio.
Source: DrKW Macro research.

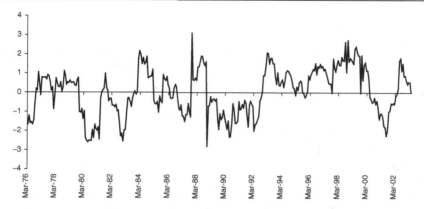

Figure 34.11   Standard deviation of long-only excess returns.
Source: DrKW Macro research.

Table 34.6   Summary data on price to earnings baskets (1975–2003)

PE	Average Monthly Return	Average Monthly Risk	Return/Risk
High	0.8	4.4	0.19
Medium	1.2	4.4	0.24
Low	1.4	4.6	0.33
Market	1.0	4.0	0.24
T-test for difference in means	−1.70	long only α 1.33 (5.2)	long only β 0.1 (1.4)
T-test for long/short portfolio	−3.31	long/short α 0.67 (3.7)	long/short β −0.1 (−2.0)
% of correct calls	0.57		
IC	0.13		
IR	0.46		

Source: DrKW Macro research.

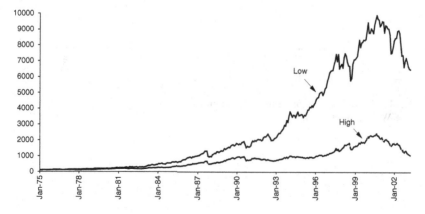

Figure 34.12   Portfolio performance 01/75 = 100.
Source: DrKW Macro research.

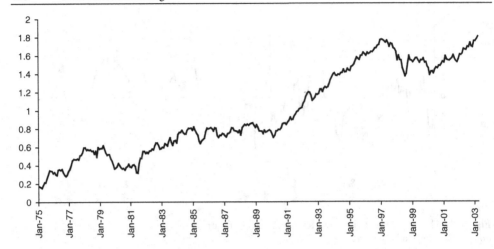

Figure 34.13   Cumulative returns on long/short portfolio.
Source: DrKW Macro research.

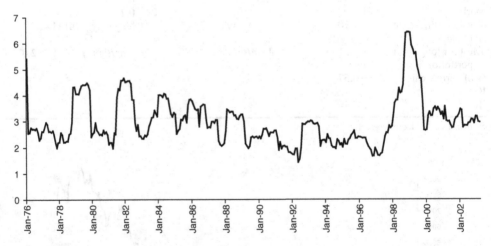

Figure 34.14   Standard deviation of long/short returns.
Source: DrKW Macro research.

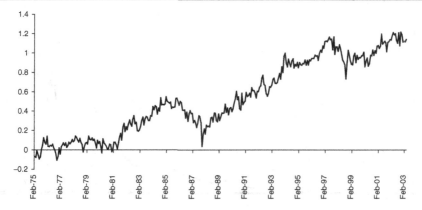

Figure 34.15   Cumulative excess returns – long-only portfolio.
Source: DrKW Macro research.

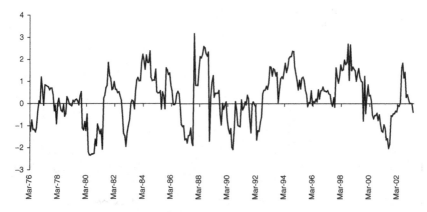

Figure 34.16   Standard deviation of long-only excess returns.
Source: DrKW Macro research.

Table 34.7   Summary data on momentum baskets (1976–2003)

MOM	Average Monthly Return	Average Monthly Risk	Return/Risk
High	1.7	4.9	0.34
Medium	1.1	4.0	0.27
Low	0.4	4.6	0.08
Market	0.9	4.2	0.23
T-test for difference in means	3.53	long only α 0.81 (4.8)	long only β 1.0 (24.1)
T-test for long/short portfolio	6.07	long/short α 1.2 (5.6)	long/short β 0.1 (2.0)
% of correct calls	0.67		
IC	0.34		
IR	1.19		

Source: DrKW Macro research.

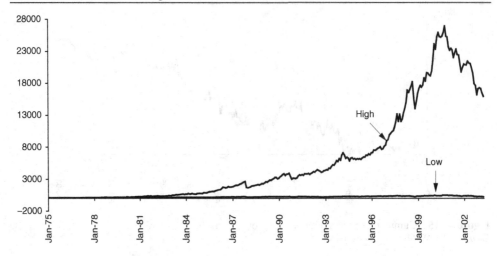

Figure 34.17   Portfolio performance 01/75=100.
Source: DrKW Macro research.

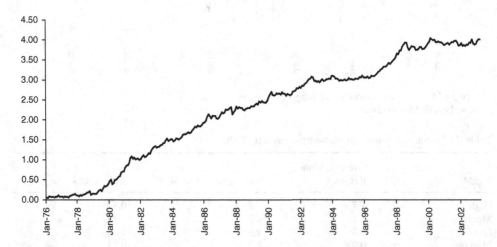

Figure 34.18   Cumulative returns on long/short portfolio.
Source: DrKW Macro research.

Table 34.8 Summary data on dividend yield baskets (1975–2003)

DY	Average Monthly Return	Average Monthly Risk	Return/Risk
High	1.5	4.5	0.33
Medium	1.0	4.6	0.23
Low	0.9	4.4	0.20
Market	1.0	4.0	0.24
T-test for difference in means	1.83	long-only α 1.38 (5.6)	long-only β 0.11 (1.9)
T-test for long/short portfolio	3.69	long/short α 0.69 (4.0)	long/short β −0.1 (−1.7)
% of correct calls	0.59		
IC	0.17		
IR	0.60		

Source: DrKW Macro research.

The information ratio combines the IC (which is essentially the model or fund manager's insight) with the number of opportunities that we have to apply the insights. Technically, the IR is the IC × Square root of breadth. All of our IRs are highly respectable. Kahn (2002) shows that an IR above 0.5 is in the top 25% of active managers. An IR above 1 is in the top 10% of active managers.

We also show the alphas and betas for both the long only and long/short versions of each strategy. The numbers in brackets are *t*-tests. In all cases they show strong statistical significance for the value added from our strategies. Interestingly, the betas on the long/short portfolios are in general negative, suggestive of potential diversification benefits. The graphs are hopefully clear. In each case, the first graph shows a portfolio with 100 units invested

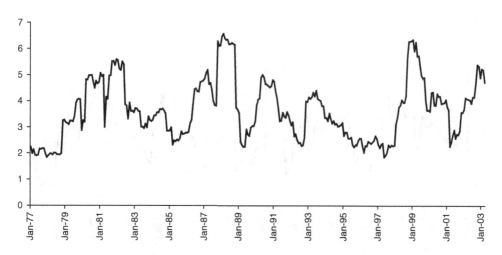

Figure 34.19 Standard deviation of long/short returns.
Source: DrKW Macro research.

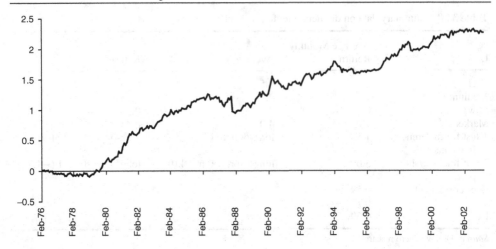

Figure 34.20   Cumulative excess returns – long-only portfolio.
Source: DrKW Macro research.

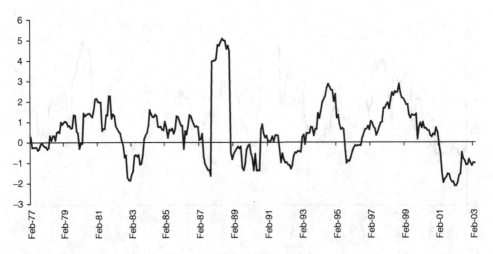

Figure 34.21   Standard deviation of long-only excess returns.
Source: DrKW Macro research.

in 1975 in the top and bottom tritiles and tracks the subsequent performance with monthly rebalancing. Then a graph of cumulative returns from an equal long/short portfolio, and the 12-month rolling standard deviation of the returns from a long/short portfolio. Finally, the cumulative excess return from the long-only strategy, and a rolling 12-month standard deviation from the long-only strategy are shown.

PART C

Risk, But Not As We Know It

35

CAPM is CRAP (or,
The Dead Parrot Lives!)*

> **The capital asset pricing model (CAPM) is insidious. It finds its way into all sorts to finance discussions. Every time you mention alpha and beta you are invoking the CAPM. Yet the model is empirically bogus. It doesn't work, in any way, shape or form. Instead of obsessing about alpha, beta and tracking error it is high time we concentrated on generating total returns with acceptable levels of risks.**

- The CAPM is the financial theory equivalent of the 'Monty Python Dead Parrot Sketch'. As many readers will know, an exceedingly annoyed customer who recently bought a parrot from a pet shop returns to the owner and berates:

  > He's passed on. This parrot is no more! He has ceased to be! He's expired and gone to meet his maker. He's a stiff! Bereft of Life, he rests in peace! If you hadn't nailed him to the perch he'd be pushing up daisies! His metabolic processes are now history! He's off the twig! He's kicked the bucket. He's shuffled off his mortal coil, run down the curtain and joined the bleedin' choir invisible!! This is an ex-parrot!!

- Despite the massive amount of evidence the shopkeeper persists in trying to argue that the parrot is merely resting. CAPM seems to have the same effect on those in finance. There is an overwhelming amount of evidence that CAPM simply doesn't work. Beta is not a good description of risk. No wonder analysts have such trouble forecasting stock prices when they routinely use beta as a key input.
- CAPM woefully underpredicts the returns to low beta stocks and massively overestimates the returns to high beta stocks. Sadly our industry seems to have a bad habit of accepting a theory as a fact. This is at odds with a scientific approach which likes to test theoretical models by subjecting them to empirical evaluation.
- The CAPM fails because its assumptions are clearly at odds with reality. Two of the critical assumptions in particular stand out. Firstly, that we can all take any position we please (long or short) in any stock with absolutely no price impact. Secondly, that everybody uses Markowitz Optimization (MO) to assign portfolios. Even Harry Markowitz himself doesn't use MO! The CAPM is, in actual fact, Completely Redundant Asset Pricing (CRAP).
- Instead professional fund managers seemed obsessed with tracking error. To a tracking error focused investor the risk-free asset isn't an interest rate (as in CAPM) but rather the market itself. No wonder that mutual fund cash levels seem to have undergone a structural decline – active management has become benchmark beta.

---

*This article appeared in *Global Equity Strategy* on 16 January 2007. The material discussed was accurate at the time of publication.

- An entire industry seems to have arisen dedicated to portable alpha. Yet if CAPM is bogus then the separation of alpha and beta is at best a distraction and, at worst, actually interfering with the true job of investors to generate returns. Our fixation with alpha and beta seems to stem from our desire to measure everything on ever-decreasing time scales. Instead of succumbing to this dark side of investment, we should refocus on delivering total (net) returns to investors at a level of acceptable risk. We got closer to this idea during the early 2000s. On that basis, roll on the next bear market!

The capital asset pricing model (CAPM) is insidious. It creeps into almost every discussion on finance. For instance, every time you mention alpha and beta you are tacitly invoking the CAPM, because the very separation of alpha and beta stems from the CAPM model.

A BRIEF HISTORY OF TIME

Let's take a step back and examine a brief history of the origins of CAPM. It all started in the 1950s when Harry Markowitz was working on his PhD. Markowitz created a wonderful tool which allows investors to calculate the weights to give each stock (given expected return, expected risk, and the correlation) in order to achieve the portfolio with the greatest return for a given level of risk. Effectively investors using the Markowitz methods will have mean-variance efficient portfolios; that is to say, they will minimize the variance of portfolio return, given expected return, and maximize expected return given the variance.

Markowitz gave the world a powerful tool that is much used and loved by quants everywhere. However, from there on in, the finance academics proceeded down a slippery slope. Somewhere around the mid-1950s Modigliani and Miller came up with the idea of dividend and capital structure irrelevance. They assumed that markets were efficient (before the efficient market hypothesis was even invented), and argued that investors didn't care whether earnings were retained by the firm or distributed as income (this will be important later).

In the early 1960s the final two parts of efficient markets school dawned to the unsuspecting world. The first of these was CAPM from Sharpe, Litner and Treynor. In the wonderful world of CAPM all investors use Markowitz Optimization. It then follows that a single factor will distinguish between stocks. This all-encompassing single factor is, of course, beta.

The second was the summation of all ideas, the birth of the efficient market hypothesis itself from Eugene Fama (another PhD thesis). I don't want to rant on about market efficiency as my views on this topic are well known.

CAPM IN PRACTICE

It is worth noting that all these developments were theoretical. It could have been very different. In a parallel world, David Hirshleifer (2001) describes:

> A school of sociologists at the University of Chicago proposing the Deficient Markets Hypothesis: that prices inaccurately reflect all information. A brilliant Stanford psychologist, call him Bill Blunte, invents the Deranged Anticipation and Perception Model (DAPM), in which proxies for market misevaluation are used to predict security returns. Imagine the euphoria when researchers discovered that these mispricing proxies (such book/market, earnings/price, and past returns), and mood indicators such as amount of sunlight, turned out to be strong predictors of future returns. At this point, it would seem that the deficient markets hypothesis was the best-confirmed theory in social sciences.
>
> To be sure, dissatisfied practitioners would have complained that it is harder to actually make money than ivory tower theorists claim. One can even imagine some academic heretics documenting rapid short-term stock market responses to new arrival in event studies, and arguing that security return predictability results from rational premia for bearing risk. Would the old guard surrender easily? Not when they could appeal to intertemporal versions of the DAPM, in which mispricing is only correct slowly. In such a setting, short window event studies cannot uncover the market's inefficient response to new information. More generally, given the strong theoretical underpinnings of market inefficiency, the rebels would have an uphill fight.

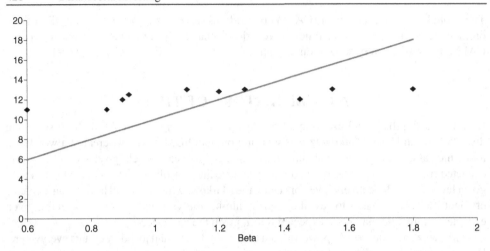

Figure 35.1 Portfolio returns by beta decile (1923–2003).
Source: Fama and French (2004). DrKW Macro research.

If only we lived in such a parallel reality! In general our industry seems to have a *bad habit of accepting theory as fact*. As an empirical sceptic my interest lies in whether CAPM works. The evidence from the offset has been appalling. Study after study found that beta wasn't a good measure of risk.

For instance, Figure 35.1 is taken from Fama and French's 2004 review of CAPM. Each December from 1923 to 2003 they estimate a beta for every stock on the NYSE, AMEX and NASDAQ using 2–5 years of prior monthly returns. Ten portfolios are then formed based on beta, and the returns are tracked over the next 12 months.

Figure 35.1 plots the average return for each decile against its average beta. The straight line shows the predictions from the CAPM. The model's predictions are clearly violated. *CAPM woefully underpredicts the returns to low beta stocks, and massively overestimates the returns to high beta stocks.* Over the long run there has been essentially no relationship between beta and return.

Of course, this suggests that investors might be well advised to consider a strategic tilt towards low beta and against high beta – a strategy first suggested by Fisher Black in 1993.

Nor is this simply another proxy for value. Table 35.1 (taken from some recent work by Vuolteenaho, 2006) shows that the beta arbitrage strategy holds across book to price

Table 35.1   Jensen's alpha across beta and b/p categories
(% p.a. 1927–2004)

	Low B/P	2	3	4	High B/P
High beta	−6.0	−3.0	−3.0	−3.0	−0.5
4	−3.0	−3.4	0.5	1.0	3.4
3	0.5	−0.2	−0.5	2.0	3.8
2	1.0	1.0	2.0	3.0	5.0
Low beta	−1.0	1.0	2.0	5.0	7.8

Source: Vuolteenaho (2006). Dresdner Kleinwort Macro research.

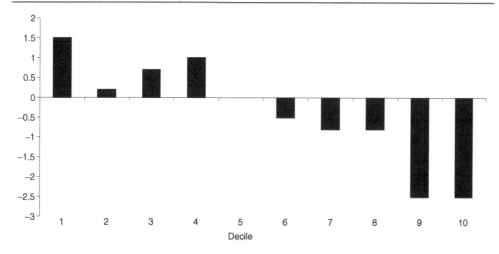

Figure 35.2 US portfolio relative returns by beta decile (1963–2006).
Source: Grantham (2006). DrKW Macro research.

(B/P) categories. For instance, within the growth universe (low B/P) there is an average 5% differential from being long low beta, and short high beta.

Within the value universe (high B/P), a long low beta, short high beta created an average difference of 8.3% p.a. over the sample. So growth investors and value investors can both exploit a strategic tilt against beta.

A 2006 paper from the ever-fascinating Jeremy Grantham of GMO reveals that among the largest 600 stocks in the USA; since 1963 those with the lowest beta have the highest return, and those with the highest beta have the lowest return – the complete inverse of the CAPM predictions. This is yet further evidence against the CAPM.

Nor is this purely a US problem. With the aid of Rui Antunes of our Quant team I tested the performance of beta with the European environment. Figure 35.3 shows that low beta on average has outperformed high beta! Yet another direct contradiction of the CAPM.

Another of CAPM's predictions states that the cap-weighted market index is efficient (in mean-variance terms). With everyone agreeing on the distributions of returns and all investors seeing the same opportunities, they all end up holding the same portfolio, which by construction must be the value-weighted market portfolio.

There is a large amount of evidence to suggest that CAPM is also wrong in this regard. For instance, in a recent issue of the *Journal of Portfolio Management*, Clarke *et al.* (2006) showed that a minimum variance portfolio generated higher returns with lower risk than the market index.

Rob Arnott and his colleagues at Research Affiliates have shown that fundamentally weighted indices (based on earnings and dividends, for example) can generate higher return and lower risk than a cap-weighted index.[1] Remember that the fundamentally weighted index is still a passive index (in as much as it has a set of transparent rules which are implemented in a formulaic fashion).

Figure 35.4 shows the return per unit of risk on selected Fundamental Indices vs the MSCI benchmark. It clearly shows that the cap-weighted indices are not mean variance efficient.

---

[1] See, for example, Hsu and Campollo (2006).

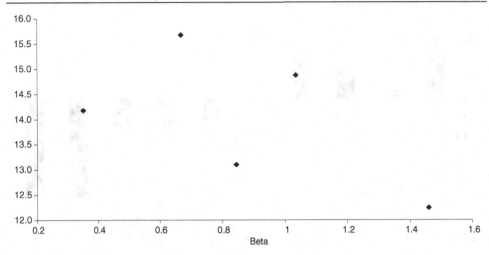

Figure 35.3 European portfolio returns by beta decile (1986–2006).
Source: DrKW Macro research.

On average the Fundamental Indices shown outperformed MSCI cap-weighted equivalents by an average 278 bps p.a. between 1984 and 2004. They delivered this outperformance with lower risk than the MSCI equivalents, and the Fundamental Indices had a volatility that was on average 53 bps lower than the MSCI measure. Something is very wrong with the CAPM.

Of course, those who believe in CAPM (and it is a matter of blind faith, given the evidence) either argue that CAPM can't really be tested (thanks for a really useless theory guys) or that a more advanced version known as ICAPM (intertemporal) holds. Unfortunately the factors of the ICAPM are undefined, so once again we are left with a hollow theory. Neither of these CAPM defences is of much use to a practioner.

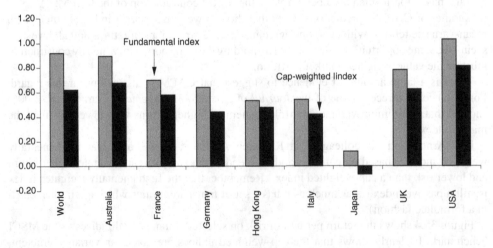

Figure 35.4 Risk-adjusted returns from selected Fundamental Indices vs MSCI (1984–2004).
Source: Hsu and Campollo (2006). DrKW Macro research.

Ben Graham once argued that

> Beta is a more or less useful measure of past price fluctuations of common stocks. What bothers me is that authorities now equate the beta idea with the concept of risk. Price variability, yes; risk no. Real investment risk is measured not by the percent that a stock may decline in price in relation to the general market in a given period, but by the danger of a loss of quality and earning power through economic changes or deterioration in management.

WHY DOES CAPM FAIL?

The evidence is clear: CAPM doesn't work. This now begs the question: Why? Like all good economists, when I was first taught the CAPM I was told to judge it by its empirical success rather than its assumptions. However, given the evidence above, perhaps a glance at its assumptions might just be worthwhile:

1. No transaction costs (no commission, no bid-ask spread).
2. Investors can take any position (long or short) in any stock in any size without affecting the market price.
3. No taxes (so investors are indifferent between dividends and capital gains).
4. Investors are risk averse.
5. Investors share a common time horizon.
6. Investors view stocks only in mean-variance space (so they all use the Markowitz Optimization model).
7. Investors control risk through diversification.
8. All assets, including human capital, can be bought and sold freely in the market.
9. Investors can lend and borrow at the risk-free rate.

Most of these assumptions are clearly ludicrous. The key assumptions are numbers 2 and 6. The idea of transacting in any size without leaving a market footprint is a large institution's wet dream . . . but that is all it is – a dream.

The idea that everybody uses the Markowitz Optimization is also massively wide of the mark. Even its own creator Harry Markowitz,[2] when asked how he allocated assets, said "My intention was to minimise my future regret. So I split my contributions 50–50 between bonds and equities." George Aklerof (another Nobel prize winner) said he kept a significant proportion of his wealth in money market funds; his defence was refreshingly honest, "I know it is utterly stupid." So even the brightest of the bright don't seem to follow the requirements of CAPM.

Nor is it likely that a few 'rational' market participants can move the market towards the CAPM solution. The assumption that must be strictly true is that we *all* use Markowitz Optimization.

Additionally, institutional money managers don't think in terms of variance as a description of risk. Never yet have I met a long only investor who cares about up-side standard deviation; this gets lumped into return.

Our industry is obsessed with tracking error as its measure of risk not the variance of returns. The two are very different beasts. Tracking error measures variability in the difference between the returns of fund managers' portfolios and the returns of the stock index. Low beta

---

[2] It is worth noting that Harry Markowitz recently wrote an article in the FAJ observing that if one broke the unlimited borrowing assumption of CAPM then the conclusions of the model change drastically, the cap-weighted market is no longer the optimal portfolio and beta is no longer lineally related to return. See Markowitz (2005).

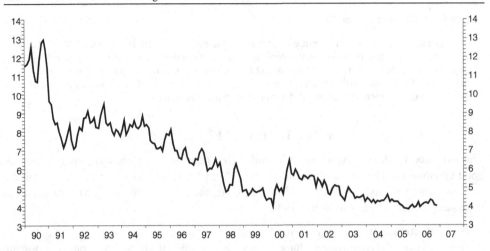

Figure 35.5 Cash levels of US mutual funds (% of total assets).
Source: DrKW Macro research.

stocks and high beta stocks don't have any meaning when the investment set is drawn in terms of tracking error.

To tracking error obsessed investors the risk-free asset isn't an interest rate, but rather the market index. If you buy the market then you are guaranteed to have zero tracking error (perhaps a reason why mutual fund cash levels seem to have been in structural decline – Figure 35.5).

CAPM TODAY AND IMPLICATIONS

Most universities still teach CAPM as the core asset pricing model (possibly teaching APT alongside). Fama and French (2004) wrote:

> The attraction of CAPM is that it offers powerful and intuitively pleasing predictions about how to measure risk and the relation between expected return and risk. *Unfortunately, the empirical record of the model is poor – poor enough to invalidate the way it is used in applications.*

Remember that this comes from the high priests of market efficiency.

Analysts regularly calculate betas as an input into their cost of capital analysis. Yet the evidence suggests that beta is a really, really bad measure of risk; no wonder analysts struggle to forecast share prices!

An entire industry appears to have arisen obsessed with alpha and beta. Portable alpha is one of the hot topics if the number of conferences being organized on the subject is any guide. Indeed Figure 35.6 shows the number of times portable alpha is mentioned in any 12 months. Even a cursory glance at the figure reveals an enormous growth in discussion on the subject.

However, every time you mention alpha or beta remember that this stems from CAPM. Without CAPM alpha and beta have no meaning. Of course, you might choose to compare your performance against a cap-weighted arbitrary index if you really wish, but it has nothing to do with the business of investing.

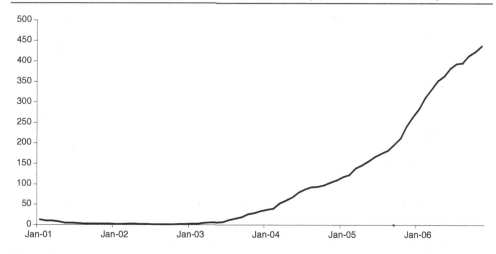

Figure 35.6   Word count on portable alpha (12m sum).
Source: DrKW Macro research.

The work from Rob Arnott mentioned above clearly shows the blurred line that exists between these concepts. The fact that Fundamental Indices outperform cap-weighted indices, yet are passive, shows how truly difficult it is to separate alpha from beta.

Portable alpha strategies may not make as much sense as their exponents would like to have us believe. For instance, let us assume that someone wants to make the alpha of a manager whose universe is the Russell 1000 and graft in onto the beta from the S&P 500. Given that these are both large-cap domestic indices, the overlap between the two could well be significant. The investor ends up being both potentially long and short exactly the same stock – a highly inefficient outcome as the cost of shorting is completely wasted.

Now the proponents of portable alpha will turn around and say that obviously the strategy works best when the alpha and the beta are uncorrelated, i.e. you are tacking a Japanese equity manager's alpha onto a S&P 500 beta. However, if the investor's already long Japanese equities within their overall portfolio, they are likely to have Japanese beta, hence they end up suffering the same problem outlined above they are both long and short the same thing. Only when the alpha is uncorrelated to all the elements of the existing portfolio can portable alpha strategies make any sense.

My colleague Sebastian Lancetti suggested another example to me. It is often argued that hedge funds are alpha engines; however, the so-called attack of the clones suggests that they are in large part beta betters (a point I have explored previously, see *Global Equity Strategy*, 11 August 2004, for details). If their performance can be replicated with a six-factor model, as it is claimed by the clone providers, then there isn't too much alpha here.

Alpha is also a somewhat ephemeral concept. A fund's alpha changes massively depending upon the benchmark it is being measured against. In a recent study, Chan *et al.* (2006) found that the alphas delivered on a variety of large cap growth funds ranged from 0.28% to 4.03%, depending upon the benchmark. For large cap value managers, the range was −0.64% to 1.09%.

The terms alpha and beta may be convenient shorthand for investors to express notions of value added by fund managers, and market volatility, but they run the risk of actually hampering the real job of investment – to generate total returns.

A simple check for all investors should be "Would I do this if this were my own money?" If the answer is no, then it shouldn't be done with a client's money. Would you care about the tracking error of your own portfolio? I suggest the answer is no. In a world without CAPM the concept of beta-adjusted return won't exist. In as much as this is a fairly standard measure of risk adjustment, it measures nothing at all, and potentially significantly distorts our view of performance.

Perhaps the obsession with alpha and beta comes from our desire to measure everything. This obsession with performance measurement isn't new. While researching another paper (on Keynes and Ben Graham) I came across a paper written by Bob Kirby (1976). In the 1970s Kirby was a leading fund manager at Capital group where he ran the Capital Guardian Fund. He opined:

> Performance measurement is one of those basically good ideas that somehow got totally out of control. In many, many cases, the intense application of performance measurement techniques has actually served to impede the purpose it is supposed to serve – namely, the achievement of a satisfactory rate of return on invested capital. Among the really negative side effects of the performance measurement movement as it has evolved over the past ten years are:
>
> 1. It has fostered the notion that it is possible to evaluate a money management organisation over a period of two or three years – whereas money management really takes at least five and probably ten years or more to appraise properly.
> 2. It has tried to quantify and formulize, in a manner acceptable to the almighty computer, a function that is only partially susceptible to quantitative evaluation and requires a substantial subjective appraisal to arrive at a meaningful conclusion.

It is reassuring to see that good ideas such as Kirby's can be as persistent as bad ideas such as the CAPM. Kirby also knew a thing or two about the pressures of performance. During 1973, Kirby refused to buy the rapidly growing high-multiple companies that were in vogue. One pension administrator said Capital Guardian was "like an airline pilot in a power dive, hands frozen on the stick; the name of the game is to be where it's at". Of course, had Kirby been "where it's at" he would have destroyed his client's money.

Ben Graham was also disturbed by the focus on relative performance. At a conference one money manager stated "Relative performance is all that matters to me. If the market collapses and my funds collapse less that's okay with me. I've done my job." Graham responded:

> That concerns me, doesn't it concern you?... I was shocked by what I heard at this meeting. I could not comprehend how the management of money by institutions had degenerated from the standpoint of sound investment to this rat race of trying to get the highest possible return in the shortest period of time. Those men gave me the impression of being prisoners to their own operations rather than controlling them... They are promising performance on the upside and the downside that is not practical to achieve.

So, in a world devoid of market index benchmarks, what should be we doing? The answer, I think, is to focus upon the total (net) return and acceptable risk. Keynes stated:

> The ideal policy ... is where it is earning a respectable rate of interest on its funds, while securing at the same time that its risk of really serious depreciation in capital value is at a minimum.

Sir John Templeton's first maxim was "For all long-term investors, there is only one objective – maximum total real returns after taxes." Clients should monitor the performance of fund managers relative to a stated required net rate of return and the level of variability of that return they are happy to accept.

We came closer to this idea during the bear market of the early 2000s. However, three years of a cyclical bull market have led once again to a total obsession with relative performance against a market index. On this basis, roll on the next bear market!

36

Risk Managers or Risk Maniacs?*

A one way round market being driven by momentum-based "cynical" investors
makes for a very risky environment. Even worse, the risk management systems
that are meant to act as a safeguard are doing anything but. Far from acting as a
rational break on behaviour, these systems seem to amplify the problems.

- Too many risk models are based on extrapolating recent market conditions. However, in times of market turbulence, historical volatility and correlation are likely to prove poor guides.
- The key failure of most risk models is that they assume that risk is exogenous (like a gambler playing roulette, where the actions of other players don't matter). The reality is that in overcrowded trades, risk is endogenous (like a gambler playing poker, the actions of others are of vital importance).
- Just how bad could it be? Simple (simplistic?) calculations suggest that VaR models could easily be understating the true risk by 20–30% just on the basis of inappropriate correlations. Add in a doubling or tripling of volatility and disaster awaits!
- The key risk is that there is no "fundamental" trigger to end the reflation trade, but rather that it simply fails because everyone has the same trade on. If and when the trade does fail, everyone will head for the exit at the same time. Just as they reach for the door, the collective risk management systems will go into overdrive. The result could be an exceptionally swift and brutal conclusion to a run in markets.

*This article appeared in *Global Equity Strategy* on 8 March 2004. The material discussed was accurate at the time of publication.

We have previously described the market as a fragile "near-rational" bubble echo (see *Global Equity Strategy*, 12 January 2004). Most investors we speak to don't seem to have any fundamental or long-term faith in the *rally that has occurred* over the last years. However, despite this lack of conviction many have played the market. Indeed, if current conversations with clients are anything to go by, most are still bubble riding, exploiting the global reflation trade.

We have repeatedly pointed out that such a position is highly dangerous, especially at the current juncture. Because of a lack of fundamental faith, this bubble echo is being driven by short horizons and overconfidence with respect to each individual investor's ability to get out before the peak. There is also a dominance of momentum or trend following strategies in this environment. The other feature of the current market that we have explored is the alarming degree of unanimity among investors – everyone seems to be one-way round (see *Global Equity Strategy*, 19 January 2004). Combine this widespread use of momentum investing with cynical investors, and a one-way round market, and the conclusion must surely be that when an unwinding of the trade begins, it will happen far faster than many currently expect.

However, there is another key risk hidden in the current market behaviour, which will only act to ensure that the end of the global reflation trade is a swift and brutal affair. In fact, it is a risk that we have all seen before, but one that appears to have been forgotten. Hence this chapter has become the second in the risk series. *This unspoken risk relates to the behaviour of risk models that are widely implemented across our industry, from investment banks' trading desks, and hedge funds to fund management houses.*

Value-at-risk (VaR) models are commonplace as measures of the degree of risk that investors are taking on. Indeed, a particularly astute client pointed out an article in an edition of the *Economist* which highlights the way in which investment banks have seen their VaR rise as they chase the diminishing returns available from asset markets. This point was further reinforced by an LEX column of the FT.

However, the widespread use of VaR models is in great danger of unleashing positive feedback trading, exacerbating market trends in both directions, and the reason is simple. Far too many VaR models are built on the basis of recent history continuing into the future. Under the Basle agreement, internal VaR models have a set of quantitative inputs defined as:

- A horizon of 10 trading days or two calendar weeks.
- A 99% confidence interval.
- An observation period based on at least one year of historical data and updated at least once a quarter.

It is the last of these factors that we fear generates the positive feedback situation. As risk measures (i.e. trailing volatility and trailing correlations) fall, so investors are left with spare risk budgets. The pressure is then to increase the positions to use up the risk budget. This is likely to be the situation in which many investors find themselves at the moment.

Figure 36.1 shows the historic volatility for the S&P 500. On all the measures shown, the volatility has been declining, and this will lead to low VaR readings. The *Economist* article on rising VaRs among investment banks within such an environment was all the more worrying for the fact that VaRs should have been falling!

Of course, the positive feedback can occur in the opposite direction as well, creating a vicious VaR circle (see Figure 36.2). Imagine that for some reason volatility and correlation rise, and some funds hit their risk limits; they are then forced to sell assets to reduce risk. This forced sale causes further rises in volatility and correlations, which in turn cause other funds to hit their limits, so they are also forced into selling, and so on. At the risk of mixing my

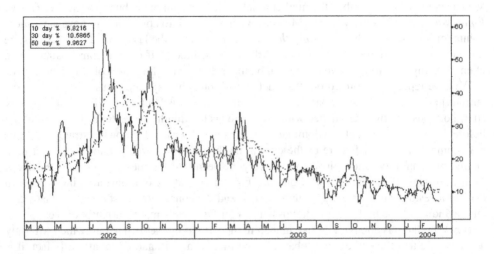

Figure 36.1   S&P 500 historical volatility.
Source: DrKW Macro research.

metaphors, the market begins to resemble swimmers in a shark-infested sea – the harder they kick to escape, the more the sharks are attracted!

Effectively, many risk models assume that risk is exogenous (like a gambler at a roulette wheel, where the actions of the other players are irrelevant). However, in reality, during periods of market turbulence, risk is effectively endogenous (like a gambler playing poker, where the interaction between the gambler and the other players is of prime importance). As we demonstrated with our Keynes's beauty contest (see *Global Equity Strategy*, 17 February 2004), strategic thinking (i.e. second guessing what others are doing) is exceptionally difficult.

Of course, the key determinants of how likely a vicious VaR circle is to occur are obviously leverage and the commonality of position. If everyone has different positions, then the circle is unlikely to develop because assets can simply be crossed, and hence the price feedback loop

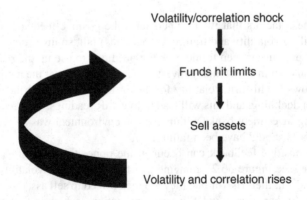

Figure 36.2   The vicious VaR circle.

is avoided. However, if everyone is running exactly the same positions, then the risk of a spike in volatility or correlation ripping through the system is that much greater.

In fact, the effect of herding into similar trades is likely to exacerbate the situation. Volatility and correlations measured over the time when the trade was being put on will almost certainly be too low. Hence, not only does the commonality of position increase the likelihood of a knock-on effect, but it also drags the risk measures lower.

How does this apply to today's markets? Previously, we have noted that the global reflation trade is amazingly popular, just about everyone we speak to seems to be running some variant or another of this approach. Everywhere we look we see evidence of a desire for reflation-trade-inspired risk assets. The sheer scale of conformity among investors doesn't bode well in the light of the above discussion.

One of the strongest implications of positive feedback systems is that a *moderate* move is exceptionally unlikely. Asset prices either don't move or they move very sharply. But all this seems strangely familiar, and indeed positive feedback trading has exacerbated market declines throughout time.

The most infamous example is probably the demise of LTCM in 1998. Indeed LTCM itself used a VaR methodology as its risk control process. However, LTCM style trades were widespread among the bond arbitrage desks at investment banks. Strangely enough, they too used VaR style risk controls. LTCM believed it was well diversified across markets. However, geographical diversification proved to be insufficient protection. Strategy diversification was needed. The intellectual dominance of so-called "convergence" trades meant that when the markets experienced a prolonged bout of divergence, LTCM haemorrhaged from all its trades. Of course, they were not alone; just as their VaR models flashed danger signals, so did the rest of Wall Street. A feedback loop, like the one outlined above, was unleashed. The end result: an asset fire sale of epic proportions. I can clearly remember the head of the firm I was working for at the time, appearing at our morning meeting to try to explain why the inability of our massive team of risk managers and credit officers to distinguish between a US T-bond and the Russian GKO, meant that the bank was under threat!

Another classic example of positive feedback trading can be found from examining the dollar/yen carry trade during October 1998 (very shortly after the bailout of LTCM). Since 1995, the dollar had been appreciating against the yen (with a brief hiatus in 1997), with a positive interest rate differential, leading to a "highly profitable" carry trade borrowing in yen, buying dollar assets, gaining on the appreciation of the currency and the interest rate differential. The long duration of the dollar's ascent sucked in all the trend following momentum players, and the yen carry trade was massively exploited by just about everyone (much like the global reflation trade now!).

The reversal of the trade began with the Russian default in August 1998. At first, the decline was relatively orderly, with the dollar falling less than 10% against the yen and the DM between mid-August and early October.

However, in the week beginning 5 October (Figure 36.3), *the dollar's decline exploded, closing down 15% on the week!* What evidence supports the suggestion that this was positive feedback trading caused by an overcrowded trade? Well, the dollar/mark fell less than 2% over the same week, plus there was a massive steepening of the yield curve (Figure 36.4) for almost all markets outside of Japan – the spread between 3-month money and long bonds rose nearly 100 bps in a week! All of this cumulatively points to the unwinding of the yen carry trade.

The stock market crash of 1987 also contains many elements of positive feedback trading. Portfolio insurance, dynamic hedging, and the informal use of stop-losses all played a major

Figure 36.3   Dollar/Yen in 1998.
Source: DrKW Macro research.

role in the 1987 crash (see Shiller, 1987, 1989). Indeed, for the real history junkies, Schnabel and Shin (2003) find parallels between the events of LTCM and those that swept European markets in 1763!

So just how bad could it be this time? A simple way of getting a feel for this, is to examine the shifts in correlation between good times and bad times. Tables 36.1 and 36.2 show the total pairwise correlation between equity markets, and the semi-correlation in markets where both are rising, both are falling or a mixed phase market. The data sample used was 1970–2004. In particular, look at the difference between the up–up semi-correlations and the down–down semi-correlations. Why look at this case? The up–up is a good proxy for the current market

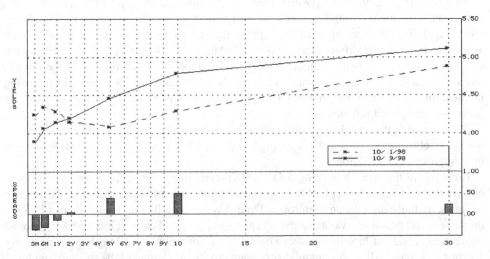

Figure 36.4   Yield curve gyrations over one week in October 1998.
Source: DrKW Macro research.

Table 36.1 Equity market return correlations

1970–2004	USA/Germany	USA/Japan	USA/UK	Germany/UK	Germany/JP	UK/Japan
Total	0.45	0.31	0.52	0.46	0.36	0.37
Down–down	0.55	0.32	0.51	0.36	0.17	0.39
Up–up	0.18	0.18	0.36	0.26	0.12	0.16
Mixed	−0.62	−0.59	−0.38	−0.61	−0.48	−0.49

Source: DrKW Macro research.

Table 36.2 Equity market return correlations

1995–2004	USA/Germany	USA/Japan	USA/UK	Germany/UK	Germany/JP	UK/Japan
Up–up	0.44	0.31	0.36	0.54	0.05	0.07
Down–down	0.67	0.24	0.58	0.71	0.06	0.35

Source: DrKW Macro research.

climate where all markets seem to have been rising together (see Figure 36.5). Should the reflation trade start to unwind as we envisage, then the down–down market environment is likely to be a more appropriate guide.

The average up–up semi-correlation is 0.21 across the markets we considered. The average down–down correlation is 0.38. To see how this might impact a VaR calculation, consider a large diversified portfolio, under which the risk is proportional to the square root of the correlation. To correct for the asymmetric correlation, the VaR estimate should be multiplied by the square root of (0.38/0.21), or 1.35. That is to say, simply *using an overly optimistic correlation can lead to a VaR that understates true risk by 35%!*

Just in case you think there is something funny about using the data from 1970 onwards, Table 36.2 uses the data from 1995 onwards. A similar conclusion is reached; downside correlations are always higher than upside correlations. The average up–up semi-correlation across the markets examined is 0.30; the average down–down correlation is 0.44. Using the

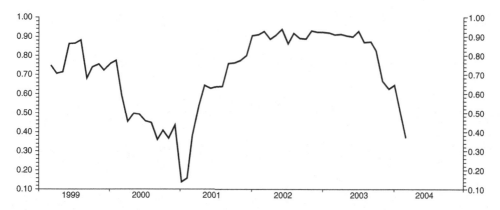

Figure 36.5 Rolling 12m correlation of 1m returns – US and German equities.
Source: DrKW Macro research.

same process as above, this leads to a potential 21% understatement of the true risk by a VaR model based on up–up correlations.

Remember that these statistics are just based on changing correlations. If volatilities change at the same time (as seems incredibly likely), then the understatement of VaR based on correlations is just the start. *The volatilities could easily triple from any current levels* (see Figure 36.1). The understatement of the degree of risk currently being taken in the equity market is potentially massive.

To us, *the lessons of effective risk management simply don't appear to have been learned.* In an already fragile market environment glued together by overconfidence and myopia and momentum trading, the last thing that is needed is yet another source of positive feedback trading. Yet, many risk management tools are effectively just that. They may go by exotic names such as dynamic hedging or VaR, but the reality is that such strategies simply exacerbate market trends. This poses extra danger at the current juncture. Almost everyone we meet seems to be running the global reflation trade. *The risk is that there is no "fundamental" trigger to the end of this trade*, that it simply fails because everyone has already put the trade on, and hence there are no marginal buyers. If and when the trade does fail, everyone will head for the exit at the same time. Just as they reach for the door, the collective risk management systems will go into overdrive. The result could be an exceptionally swift and brutal conclusion to the recent run in markets.

37

Risk: Finance's Favourite
Four-Letter Word*

Risk is perhaps the most misunderstood concept in finance. It is *not* relative price volatility (beta). Downside risk (i.e. loss) is what matters from a performance measurement perspective. From an investment viewpoint, risk is better broken into three interrelated elements – business, financial and valuation risk. Focusing on these elements should help investors to better understand the true nature of risk.

- Classical finance would have us believe that risk is defined as relative price volatility, or beta, if you prefer. However, this is not only empirically dubious (see *Global Equity Strategy*, 16 January 2006), but it also fails to capture the way in which people really see risk. I have never yet met a long only fund manager who worries about upside risk; it gets lumped into return.

- Real people worry about loss, what Ben Graham called "a permanent loss of capital". The psychological evidence supports this view. People worry about losses far more than they enjoy gains (a property known as loss aversion). Consider the following question: On the toss of a fair coin, if you lose you must pay me £100; how much do you need to win to make this bet attractive? The average amount required among our sample of over 500 professional investors was £200. So professional investors seem to dislike losses just like everyone else. Indeed, there is evidence that our dislike of losses is hard-wired into our brains, and is part of our automated thought process (system X).

- If it is negative returns that concern investors, then using standard deviation and volatility as a measure of risk is clearly wrong. Instead we should be using downside risk. This can be easily incorporated into performance measurement. Rather than using Sharpe ratios, Sortino ratios make more sense. These divide the excess return (over cash or the minimum required return) by the standard deviation of negative excess returns. Thus they don't penalize for upside volatility.

- However, performance measurement doesn't really interest me particularly. I am more interested in risk from an investment perspective. Here we find Frank Martin's trinity of risk analysis insightful. Martin (a dedicated value investor) argues that there are three sets of interrelated risk that investors should consider. Firstly, business risk – this is the possibility that the business you buy will go broke, or at least suffer in the future. Graham was well aware of this sort of risk when he wrote, "Real investment risk is ... the danger of a loss of quality and earning power through economic changes or deterioration in management."

*This article appeared in *Global Equity Strategy* on 1 February 2007. The material discussed was accurate at the time of publication.

- Secondly, there is financial risk. This is largely self-explanatory, and deals with the dangers of investing using leverage. The third element of Martin's trinity is valuation risk. This is probably the most important element, and is all about the margin of safety. In essence this is simplicity itself – if you buy something that is very cheap you have a reasonable degree of protection should things go wrong. For instance, cheap stocks in the USA that disappointed on earnings underperformed by 0.1% over the following 12 months. However, expensive stocks that disappointed underperformed by over 9%. This is valuation risk.

Risk is perhaps the most misunderstood of all the concepts in finance. According to the Oxford Concise Dictionary risk is "a chance or possibility of danger, loss, injury or other adverse consequences". Somewhere along the lines this idea was bastardized by classical finance which argues that risk is measured by relative price volatility (i.e. beta). However, as we wrote in *Global Equity Strategy*, 16 January 2007, this measure simply doesn't cut it, beta does not work.

For those who are not interested in CAPM and beta, let's put it this way, I have never yet met a long only fund manager who cares about upside risk – that gets lumped in with return and celebrated. It is downside risk that is the concern of real investors, what Ben Graham called "a permanent loss of capital".

THE PSYCHOLOGY OF RISK

Certainly the psychological evidence suggests that its very much the downside we fear. We have discussed some of the studies before, so a brief recap will suffice here. The key study in this area is Bechara *et al.* (2004) who play an investment game.

Each player was given $20. They had to make a decision each round of the game: invest $1 or not invest. If the decision was not to invest, the task advanced to the next round. If the decision was to invest, players would hand over $1 to the experimenter. The experimenter would then toss a coin in view of the player. If the outcome was heads, the player lost the dollar; if the coin landed tails up, then $2.50 was added to the player's account. The task would then move to the next round. Overall 20 rounds were played.

Bechara *et al.* played this game with three different groups: 'normals', a group of players with damage to the neural circuitry associated with fear[1] (target patients who can no longer feel fear), and a group of players with other lesions to the brain unassociated with the fear neural circuitry (patient controls).

The experimenters uncovered that the players with damage to the fear circuitry invested in 83.7% of rounds, the 'normals' invested in 62.7% of rounds, and the patient controls in 60.7% of rounds.

Was this result attributable to the brain's handling of loss and fear? Figure 37.1 shows the results broken down, based on the result in the previous round. It shows the proportions of the various groups that invested. It clearly demonstrates that 'normals' and patient controls were more likely to shrink away from risk-taking, both when they had lost in the previous round and when they had won!

Players with damaged fear circuitry invested in 85.2% of rounds following losses on previous rounds, while normal players invested in only 46.9% of rounds following such losses. So bad was the pain of losing even $1 that they refused to invest more than half the time following a loss.

It is noteworthy that this reaction is associated with part of the X-system (the brain's quick and dirty decision-making tool kit). Thus loss aversion would seem to be hard-wired into us.

RISK IN PERFORMANCE MEASUREMENT

This fits with our commonsense view of risk, and indeed Ben Graham's view. There is even a simple way of incorporating this downside risk into portfolio analysis. It goes by the name

---

[1] Technically speaking this group had suffered lesions to the amygdala, orbitofrontal and insular/somatosensory cortex

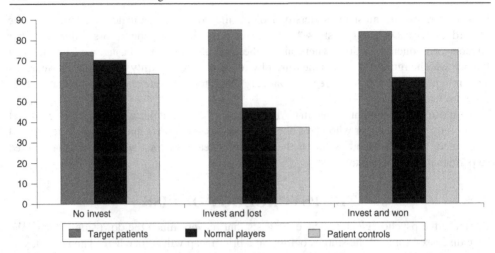

Figure 37.1 Percentage of players investing divided into the outcomes from the previous round. *Source:* Bechara *et al.* (2004).

of the Sortino ratio. It is very like a Sharpe ratio, but uses the downside semi-variance instead of the normal standard deviation. Downside semi-variance is simply the standard deviation calculated with only negative returns. This measure captures excess return per unit of downside risk. Given the findings above this surely makes considerably more sense than the Sharpe ratio that often gets trotted out.

The formula is simply $S = (R - Rf)/\text{Sigma d}$, where R is the return on the fund, Rf is the risk free rate, and Sigma d is the standard deviation using only the negative excess returns.

You can also calculate a Sortino ratio using minimum acceptable return (MAR). Simply replace the risk-free rate with the return you require, and calculate the risk as the shortfall against the required return. This makes excellent sense to us as a half decent measure of value added. Neither variant of the Sortino ratio is rocket science but it appears to be a measure that is not often used as far as I can tell.

To provide a numeric example, the Sharpe ratio for the US market since 1953 is around 0.34. The Sortino ratio is 0.46, showing that there is less chance of absolute loss relative to cash than the Sharpe ratio would suggest. Figure 37.2 shows the 5-year rolling Sharpe and Sortino ratios for the US equity market. It shows how at various times the Sortino ratio gives a higher reading than the Sharpe ratio for those who care about underperformance relative to cash. This seems to be a better measure of risk to us.

RISK FROM AN INVESTMENT PERSPECTIVE

However, performance measurement is not my primary interest. I am more interested in viewing risk from an investment perspective. In his wonderful book, *Speculative Contagion*, Frank Martin (a dedicated value investor) argues that real risk has three inter-related components – business risk, financial risk and valuation risk.

Business risk is defined as the possibility that the business you buy will go broke, or at least suffer rather than rebound. Note that this definition of business risk is very different from the most common one in our industry, which refers to the risk of losing funds under management

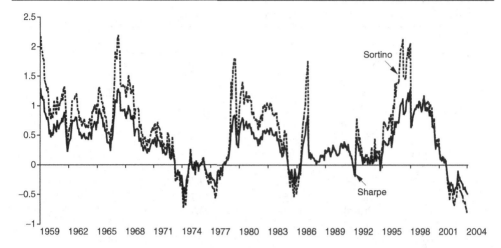

Figure 37.2   5-year rolling Sharpe and Sortino ratios for the S&P 500.
Source: DrKW Macro research.

(this is better described as career risk). Ben Graham was acutely aware of true business risk when he wrote, "Real investment risk is measured not by the percent that a stock may decline in price in relation to the general market in a given period, but by the danger of a loss of quality and earning power through economic changes or deterioration in management."

Table 37.1 provides some insight into the business risk faced by various types of investors. It is taken from a paper by Dreman and Lufkin (2000). They examined the operating performance of some 1500 US firms between 1973 and 1996, and the table presents a summary of their findings. For both value and growth portfolios they track several key profitability and growth measures for the 10 years before the formation of the portfolios, and then the 5 years post-formation.

The table shows that for three of the operating measures value stocks actually see ongoing declines in their performance. Two are particularly significant – sales growth and profit margins see marked deterioration in the post-formation period. For instance, in the 5 years before the formation of the portfolio, the value stocks recorded sales growth of 10.4% p.a. This drops to 6.8% p.a. in the 5 years after the portfolios were formed.

However, on two of the measures (earnings growth and cash flow growth) value stocks actually witness a rebound in the 5 years after portfolio formation. For example, in the 5 years before the portfolios are formed value stocks display an average earnings growth of 6.4% p.a. In the post-formation period this rises to 11.6% pa.

The very fact that, on a number of these measures, value stocks witness deterioration highlights the pivotal role played by the third element of risk – valuation risk (to which we will return shortly).

We have written previously on the use of such measures as Z-scores, Merton scores and the Piotroski screen as methods of avoiding business risk. They are all examples of ensuring that you don't buy stocks that are 'cheap for a reason' or effectively going bust. Some form of solvency screen seems to make a great deal of sense within a stock selection process.

Martin's second category of risk is **financial risk**, which he describes as "the often catastrophic downside of the excessive use of borrowed money to fund the purchase of assets".

Table 37.1   Operating developments (past and future, %) US firms

		−10 to −5 years	−5 to 0 years	0 years to +5 years
Cash flow growth	Value	11.5	9.9	12.2
	Growth	21.3	26.1	15.8
	Market	14.3	15.5	12.2
Sales growth	Value	12.4	10.4	6.8
	Growth	18.0	21.0	14.9
	Market	13.8	13.6	10.1
Earnings growth	Value	9.3	6.4	11.6
	Growth	18.6	24.6	12.1
	Market	12.2	14.2	10.6
ROE	Value	10.5	9.7	8.1
	Growth	15.3	17.9	17.4
	Market	12.4	13.0	12.3
Profit margin	Value	9.8	7.4	5.3
	Growth	12.2	13.6	12.8
	Market	11.1	10.2	8.7

Source: Dreman and Lufkin (2000).

Keynes also warned of the dangers posed by the use of leverage for long-term investors: "An investor who proposes to ignore near-term market fluctuations needs greater resources for safety and must not operate on so large a scale, if at all, with borrowed money." Little more needs to be said by us on this subject, as it is one that we suspect is widely understood by professional investors (although that is not to say that even the best and the brightest don't occasionally forget – witness LTCM).

This leaves us with **valuation risk**. Valuation risk is intimately tied in with Ben Graham's margin of safety concept. The essence of the margin of safety is simplicity itself – if you buy something that is very cheap, you have a reasonable degree of protection should things go wrong. As Graham himself put it:

> The margin of safety idea becomes much more evident when we apply it to the field of undervalued or bargain securities. We have here, by definition, a favourable difference between price on the one hand and indicated or appraised value on the other. That difference is the safety margin. It is available for absorbing the effect of miscalculations or worse than average luck.
>
> The growth-stock approach may supply as dependable a margin of safety ... provided the calculation of the future is conservatively made, and provided it shows a satisfactory margin in relation to the price paid... The danger in a growth-stock program lies precisely here. For such favoured issues the market has a tendency to set prices that will not be adequately protected by a conservative projection of future earnings.

The truth of Graham's words are amply demonstrated by Figures 37.3 and 37.4, taken from Dreman's incredibly useful book *Contrarian Investment Strategies: The Next Generation* (1998).[2] Figure 37.3 shows the market-adjusted returns for value and growth stocks experiencing a negative earnings surprise. The abnormal return for both the quarter and over the next 12 months are shown.

---

[2] I understand that Dreman has a new version of his book due out later this year.

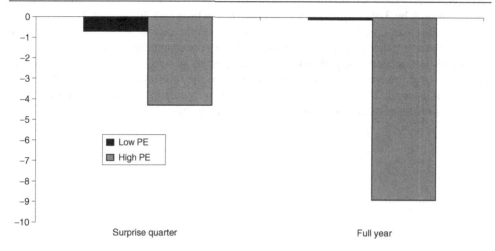

Figure 37.3 Abnormal returns by PE grouping – negative earnings surprise (%).
Source: Dreman (1998).

The benefit of a margin of safety becomes clear from even a cursory glance at this figure. When a low PE stock suffers a disappointment it tends to underperform 0.7% in the quarter and then recover to finish the year roughly in line with the overall market. However, when a high PE stock disappoints, the results aren't pretty. It, on average, underperforms by just over 4% in the quarter in which the disappointment occurs, and then continues to drag, ending the year with a 9% underperformance. Thus the concept of valuation risk becomes clear. Buying a stock without regard to its valuation is perhaps the biggest risk faced by any investor.

Figure 37.4 shows the reverse situation. Here Dreman shows the impact of positive earnings surprises upon performance. Low PE stocks react strongly to a positive earnings surprise

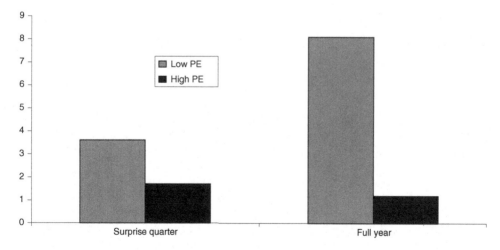

Figure 37.4 Abnormal returns by PE grouping – positive earnings surprise (%).
Source: Dreman (1998).

(outperforming by 3.6% in the quarter, and over 8% in the year). In contrast, high PE stocks with a positive earnings surprise outperform by 1.7% in the quarter, and 1.2% over the year. So even when they deliver a surprise, investors aren't very enamoured with them.

Martin's interrelated trinity of risk from an investment perspective seems to us to capture the aspects that investors should be considering when they are thinking about the risk of an investment position. They certainly seem to be a better guide to risk than the relative price volatility so beloved by risk managers and classical finance.

SECTION V

Bubbles and Behaviour

38
The Anatomy of a Bubble*

> **Despite the disparate nature of assets on which bubbles have formed, there is an uncanny similarity about the phases through which each moves. We identify five stages of bubbles. In 2002 the USA was only at the start of the fourth period and further downside was expected. Volumes may be a key indicator of the final stages.**

- Each bubble tends to move through five stages: displacement, credit creation, euphoria, financial distress and finally revulsion. Each stage is outlined inside. The experience of the US between 1991 and 2002 is mapped against our theoretical bubble pattern. During that period the US was at the early part of the financial distress stage.
- The financial distress/critical stage is the point where a set of insiders decide to take their profits and cash out. Significant selling by insiders had been a hallmark of 2000/1. The fact that insiders were still selling four times the amount of stock they were buying should tell you something about how confident they were over the prospects for equity markets.
- Financial distress refers to an awareness on the part of a considerable segment of the speculating community that a rush for liquidity may develop. Kindleberger notes, "The specific signal that precipates the crisis may be . . . the revelation of a swindle." How prescient! We document how the USA compared with other past bubbles in this and other respects.
- We had yet to see capitulation or indeed revulsion. Trading volumes remained amazingly high. We took this as a sign that people had not yet fully adjusted to the post-bubble world. Valuations were far from supportive; if buyers of last resort emerged, we should have sold to them!

*This article appeared in *Global Equity Strategy* on 18 July 2002. The material discussed was accurate at the time of publication.

Despite the wide range of assets that have witnessed bouts of irrational exuberance (tulips, sugar, coins, bonds, cotton, wheat, land and, of course, equities to name but a few), bubbles seem to follow a similar pattern. As Marx noted, history repeats itself, first as tragedy, second as farce. This chapter attempts to outline the anatomy of an asset price bubble, and then assesses where we currently are along this path.

The model of bubbles that we wish to present is one promoted in Kindleberger's truly superb "Manias, panics and crashes". It is largely the result of work carried out by the economist Hyman Minsky. Hence we will refer to the framework as the Kindleberger/Minsky model. A diagrammatic outline of the bubble stages is presented below:

Displacement
↓
Credit creation
↓
Euphoria
↓
Critical stage/financial distress
↓
Revulsion

DISPLACEMENT

Displacement is generally an exogenous shock that triggers the creation of profit opportunities in some sectors, while shutting down profit availability in other sectors. As long as the opportunities created are greater than those that get shut down, investment and production will pick up to exploit these new opportunities. Investment is likely to occur in both financial and physical assets. Essentially a boom is engendered.

In the most recent bubble in the US equity market, the exogenous shock was clearly the arrival of the internet. Here was something capable of revolutionizing the way in which so many of us conducted our businesses (and lives more generally).

CREDIT CREATION

The boom is then further exacerbated by monetary expansion and/or credit creation. Effectively the model holds money/credit as endogenous to the system, such that for any given banking system, monetary means of payment may be expanded not only within the existing system of banks, but also by the formation of new banks, the development of new credit instruments and the expansion of personal credit outside the banking system.

Sooner or later demand for the asset will outstrip supply, resulting in the perfectly natural response of price increases. These price increases give rise to yet more investment (both real and financial). A positive feedback loop ensues: new investment leads to increases in income which, in turn, stimulate further investment.

Monetary and credit creation in the US high tech bubble were largely the result of overly accommodative monetary policy on the part of the Fed in 1998 (Figure 38.1). In response to the emerging market/LTCM crisis (and later Y2K), the Fed cut rates to protect the soundness

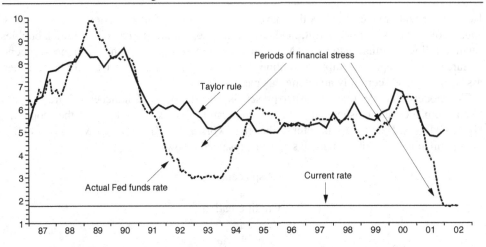

Figure 38.1   Fed funds and the Taylor rule (1987–2002).
Source: DrKW.

of the financial system. However, we suspect (admittedly with the benefit of hindsight) that the Fed kept monetary policy too easy, resulting in a massive liquidity surge into financial assets.

This official monetary creation spurred on massive levels of private sector credit creation. Figure 38.2 shows the scale of margin buying as a percentage of household disposable income.

The prominent role that investment played in driving the US boom is immediately obvious from even a cursory glance at Figure 38.3, which shows that investment as a percentage of GDP soared from around 14% in the late 1980s to nearly 19% at the peak in 2000.

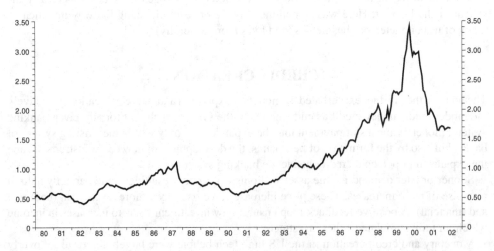

Figure 38.2   Buying on margin – margin debt as percentage of personal income (1980–2002).
Source: Thomson Financial Datastream.

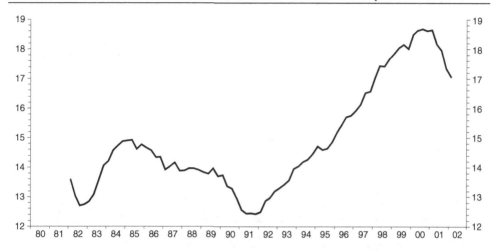

Figure 38.3 Investment as a % of GDP (1980–2002).
Source: DrKW.

EUPHORIA

'Euphoria' is the term given when speculation for price increase is added to investment for production and sales. Effectively this is momentum trading or the "greater-fool-theory" of investment. Adam Smith referred to such developments as "overtrading". Kindleberger correctly notes that overtrading is a nebulous concept. However, he notes that overtrading may involve pure speculation, an overestimate of prospective returns or excessive gearing.

The US experience between 1991 and 2002 certainly fits all three of these elements. The massive popularity of such creations as aggressive growth funds testifies to the large purely speculative elements at work within the US equity market. Analysts clearly had excessive overestimates of the prospective returns at least in terms of the long-term earnings potential of US corporates (see Figure 38.4).

Given that analysts and corporates tend to work so closely, these estimates essentially receive sign off from the companies as well. As such, they reflect the ridiculous levels of overoptimism that infected corporate managers during the late 1990s.

Further reflections of overoptimism among corporate managers can be witnessed by the scale of recent goodwill write-downs. After all, a goodwill write-down is nothing more than an admission that a company overpaid for its acquisitions.

Overgearing is also a prominent feature of the recent US experience. Driven by a desire to meet or beat analysts' forecasts of ever-growing EPS (largely reflecting the dominance of option grants as a form of compensation), firms increased their gearing to truly awe-inspiring levels. Figure 38.5 shows the level of total liabilities to corporate GDP soaring in the late 1990s.

CRITICAL STAGE/FINANCIAL DISTRESS

The fourth stage of the bubble process is labelled the critical stage or the financial distress stage. The critical stage is the point where a set of insiders decide to take their profits and cash

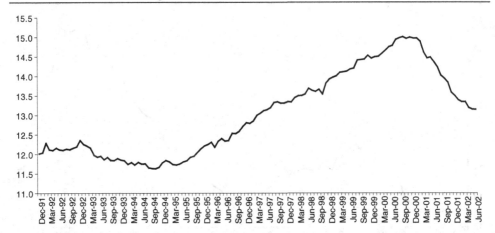

Figure 38.4 Bottom up consensus expectations of long term earnings growth (%).
Source: DrKW.

out. Significant selling by insiders has been a hallmark of 2000/1 (Figure 38.6). The fact that, by 2002, insiders were still selling four times the amount of stock they were buying should tell you something about how confident they were over the prospect for equity appreciation over the following 12 months!

Financial distress usually follows straight on from the critical stage (indeed the two can be hard to separate, hence we have tacked them together). The term 'financial distress' is borrowed from the finance literature where it refers to a situation in which a firm must contemplate the possibility that it may not be able to meet its liabilities. For an economy as a whole, the equivalent condition is an awareness on the part of a considerable segment of the speculating community that a rush for liquidity (out of assets into cash) may develop.

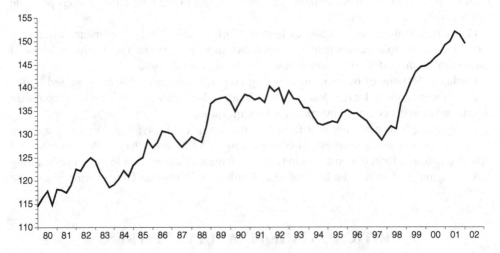

Figure 38.5 Liabilities to Corporate GDP.
Source: Thomson Financial Datastream.

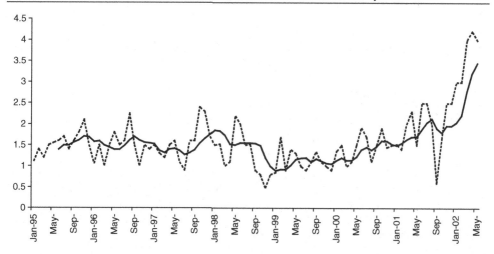

Figure 38.6 Insider sales to purchases ratio (and 6mma).
Source: Thomson Financial Datastream.

As the distress persists, so the perception of crisis increases. Kindleberger notes, "The specific signal that precipates the crisis may be a failure of a bank, or a firm stretched too tight, the revelation of a swindle." His words, not mine, but oh so appropriate in the prevailing conditions.

The occurrence of swindling/fraud seems highly procyclical. Fraud follows Keynes's law that demand creates its own supply (rather than Say's law that supply creates it own demand). We will return to fraud and its role in bringing down bubbles later.

The USA was clearly in financial distress in both the finance and bubble interpretations of the word. Figure 38.7 shows Altman's Z-score for the S&P 500 (and the percentage of firms

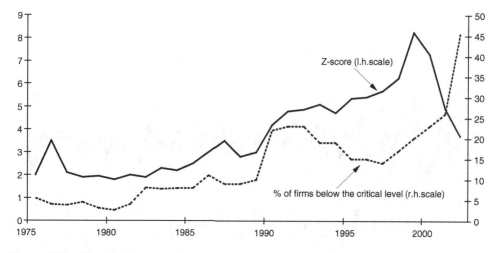

Figure 38.7 Altman's Z-score and the percentage of firms below the critical level.
Source: Thomson Financial Datastream.

Figure 38.8 Relative performance: US asset classes.
Source: Thomson Financial Datastream.

within the universe that are currently below the critical 1.8 level). It clearly shows the scale of financial distress that was being observed in the equity market.

The preference for liquidity is easily observable from the performance of the various asset classes shown in Figure 38.8. Government bonds outperformed corporate bonds which in turn outperformed equities.

The longer-term picture (Figure 38.9) shows the relative annual performance of equities vs bonds going back to 1926. It shows the scale of liquidity preference that had occurred. Bonds had delivered one of their best performances relative to equities since the 1930s!

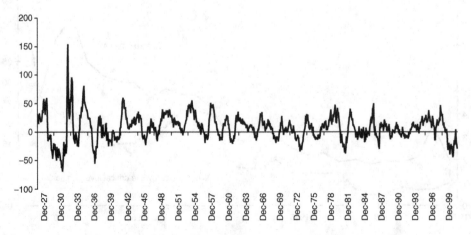

Figure 38.9 Long-term relative annual performance: US equities vs bonds.
Source: Ibbotson, DRKW.

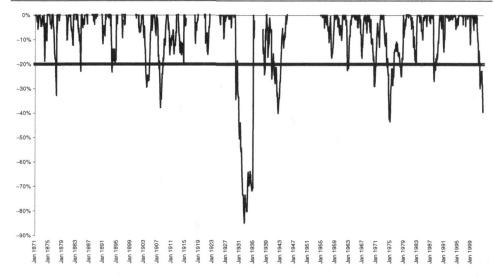

Figure 38.10   S&P 500 – percent from peak.
Source: DrKW.

An alternative perspective is given by Figure 38.10. This shows the peak to trough performance of the S&P 500. Surely no one can deny the severity of this bear market. No wonder people had a liquidity preference!

The role of swindles in bursting bubbles is intriguing. Later in this book we will illustrate just how prevalent swindles and wrong-doing have been at the peak of prolonged bull markets.

This is the stage the US post bubble was going through. The wrong-doers were being exposed for all to see, and a strong liquidity preference existed.

REVULSION

Revulsion is the final stage of the bubble cycle. Revulsion refers to the fact that people are so badly scarred by the events in which they were embroiled that they can no longer bring themselves to participate in the market at all. It is clearly related to that most dreadful of current buzz words – capitulation. Capitulation is generally used to describe the point when the final bull admits defeat and throws in the towel. In the language of the Kindleberger/Minsky model, capitulation is described as degenerate panic. Revulsion is obviously not exactly the same thing, since it can (and frequently does) occur post-capitulation.

In terms of the 2002 market we saw no signs of capitulation. Most strategists were still amazingly bullish. Perhaps more significantly volumes remained very high. We have written before on the use of volumes as a sentiment indicator (see *Global Strategy Weekly*, 29 November 2001). Figures 38.11 and 38.12 show some further evidence that capitulation remained some way off.

Figure 38.11 shows our measure of volumes. It is the detrended turnover on the NYSE (reported volume to average number of shares listed). Usually the end of bear markets is coincident with collapses in volume. No such sign emerged from Figure 38.12. Turnover remained massively high.

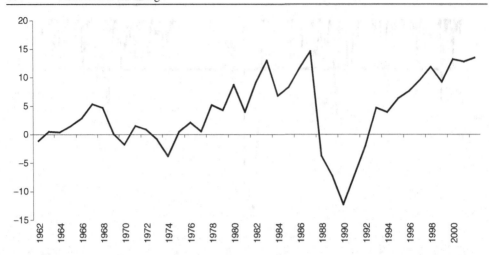

Figure 38.11   Detrended turnover on the NYSE.
Source: DRKW.

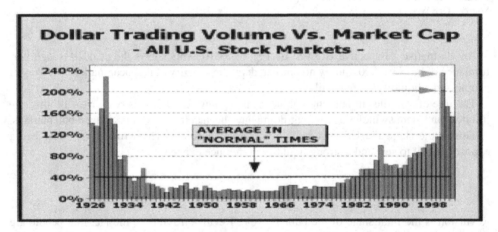

Figure 38.12   Dollar trading volume vs market cap.
Source: cross-currents.net.

Figure 38.13 confirms this view of volumes, and shows volumes relative to market capitalization. Once again the extreme nature of optimism was plain for all to see. Volumes remained
at amazingly high levels – comparable to the late 1920s!

The degenerate panic ends when one of three events occur:

• Prices fall so low that investors are tempted to move back in to the asset.
• Trade is cut off by setting limits on price declines.
• Lender of the last resort steps in.

So let's assume we get a degenerate panic. Which, if any, of these options will present itself as
a potential escape route from the markets' declines? Well, equity prices have a considerable

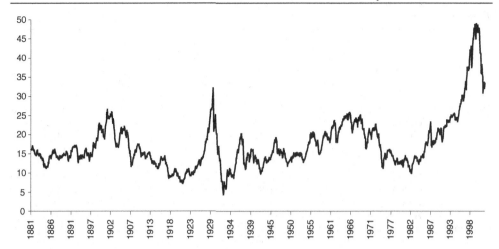

Figure 38.13 Graham and Dodd PE – based on 10-year moving average of as reported earnings.
Source: Shiller, DrKW.

downside before we can start to claim valuation support. At the very least, 30% declines in prices are likely to be required before valuations look tempting to us.

The second route provides only temporary release from panic. A halt on trading may allow people to reassess, however, it may simply result in the market dropping in stages in the face of persistent panic.

The third route is perhaps the most appealing – a lender (or rather buyer) of the last resort emerges. This is a favourite of the current market rumours that the US authorities are buying equities. It seems unlikely to us that the Fed is actively seeking to perform a Japanese style PKO.

It is very unlikely that the Fed itself is involved in the purchase of equities. They have no mandate to do so. Table 38.1 shows the private sector assets that the Fed is and isn't allowed to purchase.

There is some room for discretion under the provision that if the Board of Governors found that there were "unusual and exigent circumstances" and at least five governors voted to authorize a broadish range of "notes, drafts and bills of exchange . . . indorsed or otherwise

Table 38.1 Private sector assets the Fed may, and may not, purchase

No express authority	May purchase
Corporate bonds	Gold
Commercial paper	Foreign Exchange
Mortgages	Bankers' Acceptances
Equity	Bills of Exchange
Land	

Source: Clouse *et al.* (2000).

Table 38.2 Bubble paths

	South Sea bubble	First British railway boom	1920s US equity bubble	1960s Conglomerate mergers boom	1980s Japanese land and equity bubble	1990s US equity bubble
Displacement	Profits from conversion of government debt, supposed monopoly on trade with Spanish Americas	End of depression, new means of transport	Decade of fast growth, end of fears of WWI deflation, rapid expansion of mass production	Two decades of rising stock markets, the joys of growth investing	Financial liberalization. Monetary easing	Widespread acceptance of the internet, strong growth, and monetary easing
Smart money response	Insiders buy up debt in advance of the conversion scheme	Build a railroad	Expansion of supply of new shares, creation of new closed end funds	Emergence of professional conglomerates	Zaitech	Aggressive growth funds, stock options, start a dot.com
Sustaining the bubble	Development of coffee house network for speculation	?	Regional exchanges, growth of margin accounts and brokers loans	Stock swaps to create apparent earnings growth	Cross share-holdings, buybacks (tokkin funds), latent asset value, Q ratio, PKO in 1987 crash	Pro forma earnings, New valuation metrics, buybacks
Authoritive blessing	Government approval, royal involvement	Government approval for each railroad	Blessing from Coolidge, Hoover, Mellon and Irving Fisher	McGeorge Bundy	Nomura calls for 80,000 by 1995	Greenspan joins the New Era
Swindle/ Fraud	Ponzi scheme	George Hudson paying dividends out of capital (Ponzi scheme)	Harold Russell Snyder, Samuel Insull buying binge and debt mountain	?	Recruit Cosmos, Bubble lady	Accounting fraud – Enron, WorldCom *et al.*
Political reaction	Ex post facto punishing of directors, restrictions on the use of corporate form	Reform of accounting standards, rules passed so that dividends must be paid out of earnings not capital	Glass-Steagall Act, creation of the SEC, holding company act	Reform of accounting practices, Williams Act	?	Sarbanes & Oxley Bills, voluntary option expensing as corporates seek moral high ground

Source: Shleifer, DrKW.

secured to the satisfaction of the Federal Reserve Bank". However, it is far from clear how broadly the Fed would interpret this ruling. In *extremis*, anything is possible.

Perhaps official inspired intervention *à la* Japan is more likely. Edward Chancellor in "Devil take the hindmost" points out that in 1987, "The day after the October crash, representatives of Japan's largest brokerages . . . were summoned to the Ministry of Finance. They were ordered to keep the Nikkei average above 21,000." Indeed similar intervention was attempted during the US crash of 1929, when bankers met at the offices of J.P. Morgan to supply funds and stabilize the market (their attempts failed dismally, by the way). In the context of the US this, of course, is idle speculation that can neither be proved nor disproved. Either way, our view is that should buyers of the last resort emerge, investors should be happy to sell to them!

Table 38.2 takes some of the major bubbles in history and maps them to the model we have outlined here. Our essential finding is that the Kindleberger/Minksy model fits the empirical evidence well.

39

De-bubbling: Alpha Generation[*]

We map out our view of the de-bubbling process and tease out its implications for alpha generation. Old relationships between bonds and equities will be shown as illusory. Absolute returns are the way forward. Stock selection should focus on balance sheet strength, earnings quality, low capex and avoiding previous bubble winners.

- Bursting bubbles pose a special danger to investors. Few will have ever experienced anything similar before. In order to understand survival strategies a reasonable knowledge of the causes and consequences of bubbles is required.
- Bubbles contain the seeds of their own destruction. The excessive optimism and overconfidence that help to sustain bubbles form the Achilles' heel when it comes to bust time. Excessive expectations lead firms to gear up in order to overinvest. This can unleash a deflationary debt spiral during the bust.
- The key lesson for asset allocators is that established relationships between bonds and equities break down. The illusory correlation of bull markets is exposed as the product of investors confusing real and nominal variables. Trading on the basis of old relationships is likely to be hazardous to your wealth.
- Where possible, investors should focus on absolute returns via true equal long/short portfolios. Portfolios based around balance sheet strength, earnings quality, and low capex stand out as obvious winners. Use this rally to position. Bubble winners do not usually lead us out of the bust, yet each of the major US rallies has been tech dominated. Until investors give up this hope, the bear market won't end.

---

[*]This article appeared in *Global Equity Strategy* on 6 November 2002. The material discussed was accurate at the time of publication.

Bursting bubbles pose special problems for investors. They alter the investment landscape massively. This note takes our previously proposed framework for analysing bubbles and busts and tries to draw out advice for both stock selection and asset allocation. In order to understand the optimal strategies in a post-bubble world, we need to understand bubbles in the first place. Let's start our journey in the laboratory.

BUBBLES IN THE LABORATORY

It strikes us as slightly evening up the scales when, following Alan Greenspan's knighthood for services to bubble blowing, that Daniel Kahneman and Vernon Smith won the Nobel prize for economics. Kahneman helped to catalogue many of the psychological traits that underlie the bubble process. While Smith was the first economist to find a bubble in an experimental market.

Figure 39.1 shows the results from one of Smith's latest papers (see Caginalp *et al.*, 2000). The idea is simply to create a clean market in which a financial asset can be traded. The payoffs (dividends) on the asset are uncertain, but the distribution of the payoffs is known, and shown in Table 39.1.

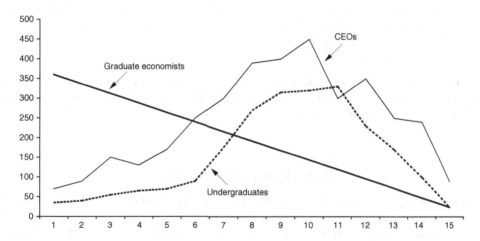

Figure 39.1   Bubbles in the laboratory.
Source: Caginalp *et al.* (2000).

Table 39.1   Dividend distribution

Probability	Payoff
0.25	0
0.25	8
0.25	28
0.25	60

Source: Caginalp *et al.* (2000).

We know that if investors followed the laws of classical finance then they would work out the expected value of the asset, which is 24. Since the experiment lasted for 15 periods, the price should have been 360, decreasing by 24 per period until the end of the game.

However, the results show the alarming ease with which bubbles can be created. When the game was played by graduate economists, the results were predictably dull. They managed to trade at the correct right price, although volumes were much higher than theory would have suggested.

Thankfully for the rest of us, the world isn't populated by graduate economists. When the game was played by undergraduates, a bubble was quickly created. The undergraduates started with a price that was just 10% of fundamental value, and at the height of the bubble, the disparity between price and value, was a staggering 270%!

However, they weren't the worst players. When business executives were the traders, a truly awe-inspiring bubble was created. Price started off at 20% of fundamental value. At the peak of the bubble prices represented a breathtaking 570% of value! And remember this was in the simplest, cleanest possible market.

Experimentalists have uncovered many traits that make the creation of a bubble more likely. A bubble is more likely to be found when:

- The ratio of inexperienced to experienced traders is high.
- The greater the uncertainty over fundamental value.
- The lottery characteristics of the security are high (effectively a small chance of a big payoff increase the likelihood that people will overpay for an asset – growth stocks?).
- Buying on margin is possible.
- Short selling is difficult.

The last of these strikes us as particularly interesting given the recent debate over short selling in the UK. The experimental evidence shows that far from being an "evil", short selling helps to move the market towards efficiency.

BUBBLES IN THE FIELD

However, enough of artificial bubbles; what of bubbles in the real world of financial markets (surely an oxymoron?) We have previously presented a framework for analysing bubbles (see *Global Equity Strategy*, 18 July, The anatomy of a bubble). In that note we explored bubbles in a very general way, drawing our examples from a wide range of historical events.

In this chapter, we will examine the US and Japanese bubbles in order to see what lessons we can derive from them. The framework we use to characterize the bubble process is drawn from the work of Irvine Fisher and Hyman Minsky, popularized by Charles Kindleberger in his *tour de force – Manias, Panics and Crashes*.

Fisher was among the leading economists in the USA at the time of the 1929 crash. Indeed, he is perhaps best remembered for his proclamation that stocks had reached a permanently high plateau in 1929! Steve Keen, in this entertaining book (Keen, 2001) notes that Fisher provided four key reasons why stock valuations were justified:

- Changed expectations of future earnings.
- The higher retained earnings of corporates (allowing for faster future growth).
- A change in risk premiums.

• Longer time horizons for investors.

It is a list that will seem uncannily familiar to modern-day investors. I can clearly recall having seen each of these arguments during the bubble (indeed I fear I even used one or two of them myself!).

However, Fisher's faith in the rationality of the market was cruelly stripped away by the crash of 1929. In the wake of such overwhelming evidence against his belief, Fisher turned his attentions to explaining how collapsing bubbles could cause deflation. He concluded that two factors stood out above all others in the creation of a depression: "over-indebtedness to start with and the deflation following soon after". As Keen notes, Fisher "has the dubious distinction of fathering both the conventional theory of finance – which, like his 1929 self, reassures finance markets that they are rational – and an unconventional theory that argues speculative bubbles can cause economic depressions".

Sadly, Fisher was largely ignored and treated as a leper, the economist's equivalent of a fallen angel. Thankfully, however, Minsky breathed new life into Fisher's work, and it is this work that provides us with a framework for analysing bubbles and their busts.

The Minsky/Kindleberger model can be simplified to five stages through which a bubble passes:

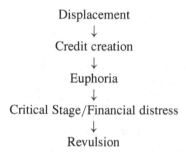

Displacement
↓
Credit creation
↓
Euphoria
↓
Critical Stage/Financial distress
↓
Revulsion

Let us examine each of these in turn.

DISPLACEMENT: THE BIRTH OF A BOOM

Displacement is generally an exogenous shock that triggers the creation of profit opportunities in some sectors, while closing down profit availability in other sectors. As long as the opportunities created are greater than those that get shut down, investment and production will pick up to exploit these new opportunities. Investment in both financial and physical assets is likely to occur. Effectively, we are witnessing the birth of a boom.

In Japan's case, massive liberalization of the financial system seems to have been the exogenous shock. In the USA, the widespread adoption of the internet was certainly a good candidate for a proximate displacement event.

CREDIT CREATION: NURTURING THE BOOM

Just as fire can't grow without oxygen, so a boom needs liquidity to feed on. Minsky argued that monetary expansion and credit creation are largely endogenous to the system. Effectively,

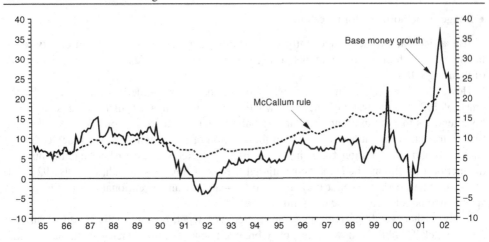

Figure 39.2 Base money growth in Japan and the McCallum rule.
Source: Thomson Financial Datastream, DrKW.

not only can money be created by the existing banking system, but also by the formation of new banks, the development of new credit instruments and the expansion of personal credit outside the banking system.

Sooner or later demand for assets will outstrip supply, resulting in the perfectly natural response of price increases (*à la* Economics 101). These price increases give rise to yet more investment (both real and financial). A positive feedback loop ensues: new investment leads to an increase in income which in turn stimulates yet further investment.

Figure 39.2 shows the role of monetary expansion in the creation of the Japanese bubble. It shows the McCallum rule for base money growth[1] against the actual rate of growth in base money. Even a cursory glance reveals the massive over creation of liquidity during the mid and late 1980s.

Looking at the US experience shows that the bubble gained two liquidity injections. Figure 39.3 shows the Fed funds rate against a Taylor rule. It is certainly possible to argue that in the wake of the S&L debacle in the early 1990s, the Fed kept interest rates too low for too long, and began to engender a boom. An additional flood of credit creation occurred in response to the emerging markets/LTCM crisis (and later Y2K). Of course, both of these are far easier to spot with the benefit of hindsight. At the time they may well have appeared totally rational, indeed even admirable responses by the central bank.

This official deluge of monetary creation spurred on massive levels of private sector credit creation (just as the model outlined). Figure 39.4 shows the scale of margin buying as a percentage of household disposable income.

Of course, this liquidity has to find a home. It usually ends up in a mixture of real and financial assets. The real proportion usually creates a massive investment boom – bubbles are rarely purely financial, but are all too often economic as well.

---

[1] The McCallum rule relates growth rate of base money to the growth rate of nominal GDP adjusted for changes in technology (via the velocity of circulation). Technically: Change in base money growth = Potential nominal output growth rate – (4-year moving average in velocity of circulation) +0.5× Nominal output gap.

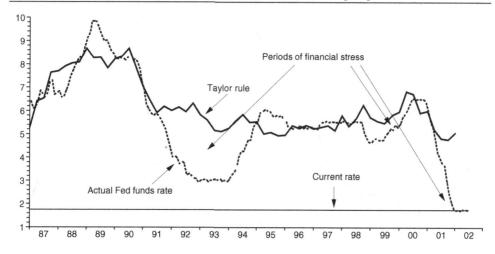

Figure 39.3 Fed funds and the Taylor rule.
Source: Thomson Financial Datastream.

Figures 39.5 and 39.6 show the scale of the investment booms that were part of the bubbles in both Japan and the US. In Japan's case, investment as a percentage of GDP rose from 26% in the mid 1980s to a peak of just under 32% at the height of the bubble.

The US case shows investment rising from somewhere around 13/14% "normally" to a peak of nearly 19% at the zenith of the bubble.

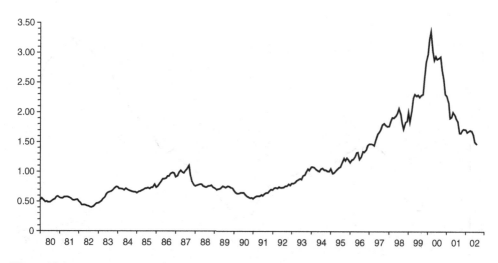

Figure 39.4 US margin buying (% of disposable income).
Source: Thomson Financial Datastream.

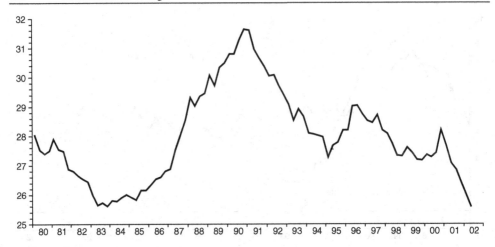

Figure 39.5   Japan: Investment to GDP ratio.
Source: Thomson Financial Datastream.

EUPHORIA

Everybody begins to buy into the "new era". During the Japanese bubble countless books were written on why Japanese management techniques were going to dominate the world, and why it would be a case of 'imitate or perish' for corporate managers around the rest of the world. Indeed, Peter Tasker, our consultant Japanese strategist, recalls that inside Japan there was much talk of Japan moving from being a production-driven economy to a new era of consumption-based economic development!

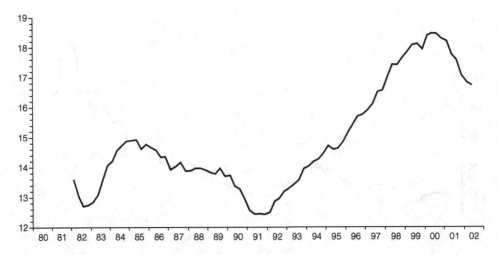

Figure 39.6   US Investment to GDP ratio.
Source: Thomson Financial Datastream.

The other example of new era thinking is the creation of new valuation techniques in order to justify the soaring asset prices. In the USA, analysts moved up the income statement in order to justify stratospheric stock prices. When PEs based on net income were looking too stretched, analysts drifted up the statement reaching for price to sales. Then came along pro forma earnings – leaving out ad hoc elements of the income statement. Eventually, eyeballs, clicks and ARPU were all introduced!

In Japan, Tobin's Q was regularly wheeled out to justify stock prices, as were latent asset valuations techniques. Who can forget the time when the grounds of the Imperial Palace in Tokyo were worth more than the entire state of California.

The quotations below, taken from John Rothchild's book (1998), all show that previous bubbles in the USA have been accompanied by discussion over the arrival of a new age.

It seemed to be taken for granted in speculative circles that this is a market of "manifest destiny" and that destiny is to go continuously forward. (*New York Times*, September 1929)

At least two members of the Federal Reserve Board now are saying that prosperity can go on and on. (*US News & World Reports*, 15 November 1965)

Is the market crazy? Hardly. Underlying the equity boom is the emergence of a New Economy, built on the foundation of global markets and the Information Revolution. (*Business Week*, 30 December 1996)
  Source: Jim Stack

These developments spur a dangerous psychology into force. The seemingly invincible growth of the economy, and the inexorable rise in stock prices, leads to a marked increase in feelings of overoptimism and overconfidence. These traits are ever present, and largely a part of the human condition, but receive an extra boost during bubble periods.

Overoptimism and overconfidence are a potent combination. We have shown elsewhere (see Montier, 2002) that this combination leads people to overestimate their knowledge, understate the risks, and overestimate their ability to control the situation.

These traits lead to three developments in terms of the bubble framework. The greater fool theory kicks in. Investors begin to speculate for the sake of speculation. Indeed, one could see the rise in popularity of aggressive growth funds in the USA as a sign of such behaviour.

Because of the overconfidence and overoptimism, long-term growth expectations and long-term return expectations get ratcheted higher and higher. Unfortunately, investors and corporates believe these new expectations. Investors set themselves up to be disappointed. The corporate managers engage in excessive gearing. Because of their blind faith in the new era, firms take on debt in the belief that faster growth will generate the necessary payback with ease (see Figures 39.7 and 39.8).

CRITICAL STAGE/FINANCIAL DISTRESS

Eventually the euphoria gives way to the critical stage. This is the point at which the insiders sell out. One good proxy for this is the number of firms conducting initial public offerings; after all this is a prime example of insiders selling out! Figures 39.9 and 39.10 suggest that tracking equity issuance can be a valuable tool in tracking bubble progress.

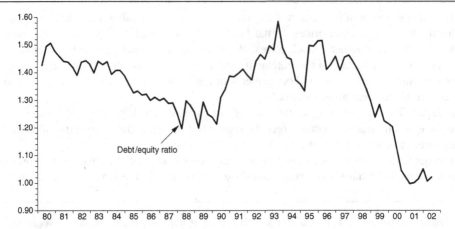

Figure 39.7   Debt/Equity ratio of corporate Japan.
Source: Thomson Financial Datastream.

My favourite measure of insiders' behaviour during the previous US bubble is provided in a paper by Rau *et al.* (2001), who track the number of firms adding or deleting dot.com to or from their name (Figure 39.11).

Financial distress results when the over-leveraging of euphoria receives an economic reality check. It can be a cruel and painful experience for the overenthusiastic debt accumulators. In Figure 39.12 we show our work from 1975 to 2000 on one measure of balance sheet strain. We have used Altman's Z-score to track the degree of financial distress in the USA. The chart shows not only the absolute level of Z for the S&P 500 (ex. financials) but also the percentage of firms that register a score below 1.8 (the critical level). This stands at a terrifying 33%!

Figure 39.8   US corporate debt to GDP ratio.
Source: Thomson Financial Datastream.

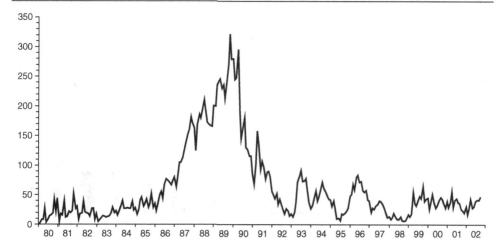

Figure 39.9 No. of IPOs per month – Japan.
Source: Thomson Financial Datastream.

It is this build-up in debt that poses the most critical danger in the bursting of the bubble. If deflation arrives while the overhang of debt is still massive, then a nightmare is created. Indeed, if inflation is low at the time the bubble bursts, that act alone can force the economy into deflation.

Cash flows will be inadequate to service the debt. Firms whose cash flows are exceeded by their interest payments will be forced to undertake extreme measures. They will be forced to attempt to create cash flows by capturing market share, effectively buying in volume. The most likely path to capturing market share is to lower prices – which of course only exacerbates the deflationary pressures.

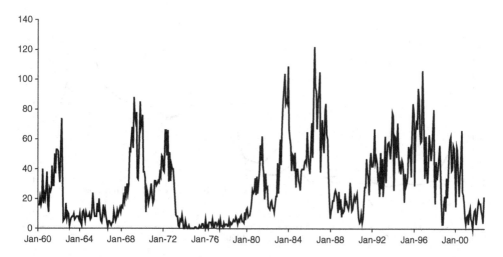

Figure 39.10 No. of IPOs per month – US.
Source: Thomson Financial Datastream.

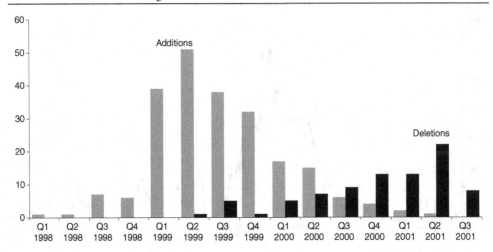

Figure 39.11   No. of firms changing their names to/from dot.com.
Source: Rau *et al.* (2001).

The alternative route to raise cash flow is to seek to sell assets. Of course, if whole industries have created massive excess capacity, buyers of such assets will be few and far between. A fire sale results in a decline in asset prices as well. And, any assets that are purchased are likely to be used to produce low cost output, again undermining the already fragile pricing structure in the real economy, and in the markets.

The only other way out is to default and go bankrupt. Once again this results in asset fire sales, and more asset price depreciation. So all three paths to debt reduction are deflationary in the extreme.

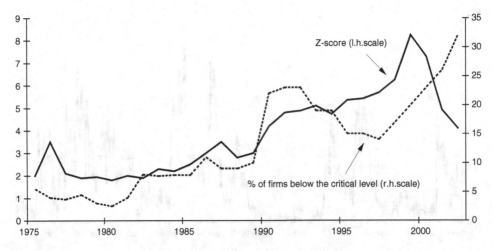

Figure 39.12   Z-score for the S&P 500 and number of firms in distress.
Source: DrKW.

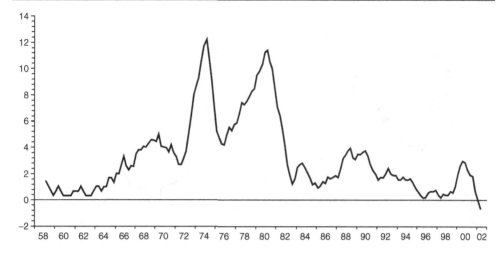

Figure 39.13   US corporate sector deflator YoY shows deflation.
Source: Thomson Financial Datastream.

Here we hit a fallacy of composition. In the immortal words of Inspector Clouseau "er, what?" A fallacy of composition is simply what may be true at the micro level does not hold at the macro level. For instance, every analyst thinks the firms he covers are capable of generating 15% long-term growth; however, we know that in aggregate this can't possibly be true. Hence, while it may be perfectly rational for each firm to pursue such cash flow generation policies, it can't possibly be true for the economy as a whole.

Of course, the saliency of this analysis depends entirely upon the starting level of inflation. In a portentous weekly, our colleague, Dylan Grice, noted that deflation is much closer than many currently believe (see *Global Economics for Investors*, 18 October 2002). He estimates that some 50% of the US CPI components are already showing deflation (Figure 39.13) and the US corporate sector deflator is already in deflation, as is the core PPI measure (Figure 39.14).

Those arguing that the headline series remains well above deflation are running the risk of focusing too much upon the headline data. At our recent conference, Peter Tasker, noted that the headline CPI (Figure 39.14) was one of the last measures to slip into deflation. By which time, it was too late for the BoJ (Figure 39.15) to do anything about it!

Keynes noted that deflation left firms with the unenviable situation of being long real assets and short nominal assets, exactly the wrong way round for a deflationary environment. The only way of closing this position is to shut down production. This is a hard reality for firms to face.

Figure 39.16 shows that it has taken almost a decade for Japan Inc. to realize that they need to shut down production, and remove capacity (destroy the capital stock) in order to make any progress.

The USA may just be learning a little quicker than Japan. As Dylan Grice noted (*Global Economics for Investors*, 1 November 2002) the USA has been reducing its capital stock (at least in the non-financial sector). Although, it should be noted that the capacity reduction occurring in the early 1990s was much larger than reduction we have so far witnessed. Given the scale of the over-investment boom, a very large cut back in the capital stock would seem to be warranted (Figure 39.17).

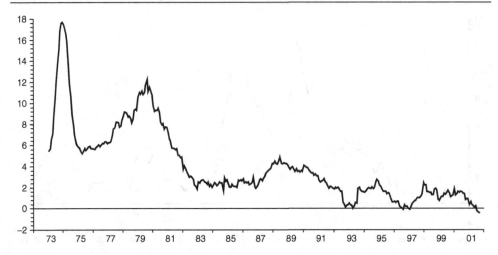

Figure 39.14 Core PPI inflation in the US at lowest reading on record.
Source: Thomson Financial Datastream.

Fraud also tends to emerge at this stage of the bubble process. Fraud follows Keynes's law that demand creates its own supply – that is to say, investors are so keen for growth that firms will deliberately seek to manufacture growth. In Japan, Recruit Cosmos was a scandal that embroiled several very high-profile Japanese ministers. My favourite tale is that of the bubble lady, a restaurant owner who managed with the help of a crooked bank manager to secure massive funds from one of Japan's leading banks. These funds were then invested on the basis of advice from a ceramic toad! The memories of recent US frauds are still fresh in investor's minds, from Enron to WorldCom and Tyco (and this time around a ceramic poodle umbrella stand!)

Figure 39.15 Japanese service sector inflation is the last to go negative.
Source: Thomson Financial Datastream.

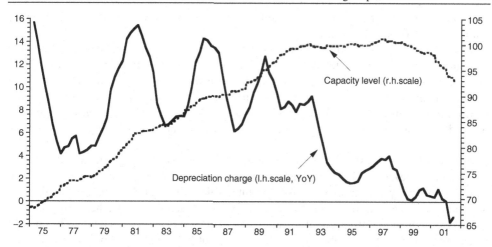

Figure 39.16 Japanese capacity level, and depreciation charge (YoY).
Source: Thomson Financial Datastream.

REVULSION

The final stage of a bubble is revulsion. Investors are so scarred by the events in which they participated that they can no longer bring themselves to participate in the market at all.

Revulsion usually follows in the wake of a degenerate panic. However, this has been absent so far. Equity weightings remain extraordinarily high, both in terms of actual fund allocations and indeed in most strategists' recommendations.

It has become clear that institutional investors are all waiting for their fair value targets to be reached in order to buy stocks. However, as we noted in *Global Equity Strategy*, 18 October

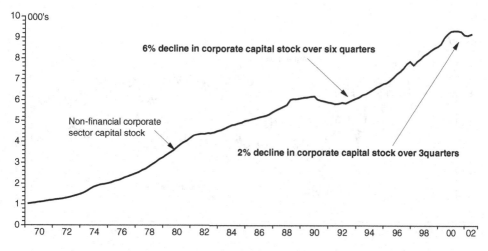

Figure 39.17 Flow of funds data suggests decline in non-financial corporate capital stock.
Source: Thomson Financial Datastream.

2002, markets should be cheap rather than fair value. Clients know this too, so why are they opting to get back in at fair value?

Psychology and peer group benchmarking may help to explain this bizarre behaviour. There is a human tendency to feel the pain of regret at having made small errors, without putting those errors into any context. In common parlance, it is the same thing as kicking yourself for doing something foolish. If you wish to avoid the pain of regret, then you may act in ways that appear irrational unless the pain of regret is taken into account. Effectively, investors are more worried about the risk of missing the next move up, than about waiting for equities to become cheap.

Another group of investors have been arguing that bear markets only tend to last "X" number of months. However, that is like saying that simply because stocks have fallen a lot they must be cheap. It simply isn't true. There is no statute of limitations on bear market duration. As Tasker noted at the conference, in a world with deflation time is a killer rather than a healer!

Tasker also made an insightful observation that in the wake of previous bubbles it is not the stocks that led you into the bubble that will lead you out (Figure 39.18). For instance, the star performers in Japan post-bubble were the electricals and autos (Figure 39.19), however during the bubble these were laggards and considered to be an irrelevance to the changing economy.

This provides yet more evidence that the current rally in the USA is just another example of a bull snap in the overall bear market. Figure 39.20 shows the way in which technology has been leading each of the attempted rallies since the US bubble burst. The bear market won't end until investors finally give up hope on the tech stocks!

One of the hallmarks of the end of the bubble will be a collapse in volumes, a sign that investors have truly lost their faith in the equity culture. However, current volumes remain at massive levels. In order to track volumes we use a measure of turnover (reported volume relative to the average number of shares listed), then we detrend that series in order to remove the effect of an increasing habit of traders to trade with each other (Figure 39.21). Yet even after making this adjustment we find that volumes remain at record levels!

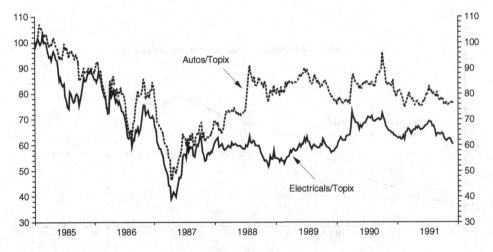

Figure 39.18   Laggards of the bubble years . . ..
Source: Thomson Financial Datastream.

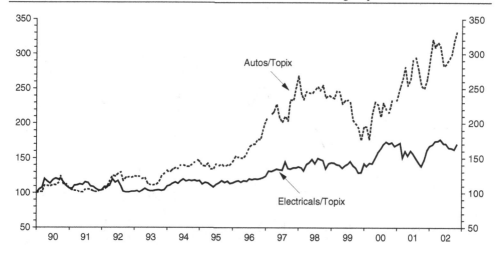

Figure 39.19 But winners in the post-bubble era.
Source: Thomson Financial Datastream.

Let's assume that we eventually get to a degenerate panic. What will pull us out? We have recently explored two potential endgames that can be mapped out. Firstly, just as valuations get stretched beyond all reasonable levels in the bubble, so valuations should likewise fall too truly cheap levels during the burst.

We examined markets on both a top-down and bottom-up perspective in terms of valuation in our *Global Strategy Weekly*, 18 October 2002. The conclusion was that markets simply weren't cheap. Figure 39.22 shows our much loved Graham and Dodd PE (using a 10-year moving average of reported earnings) for the US market. It still stands at a lofty 25 times, against bear market bottoms of around 10 times.

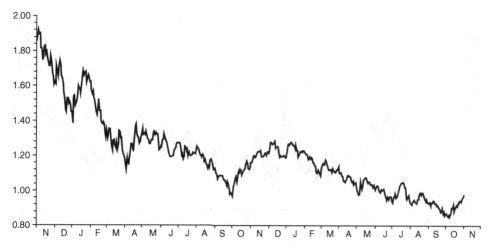

Figure 39.20 Tech driven rallies will not end the bear market.
Source: Thomson Financial Datastream.

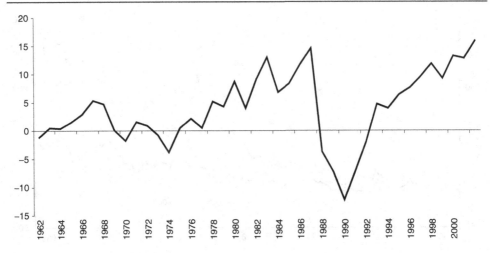

Figure 39.21 US detrended turnover still at manic levels.
Source: NYSE, DrKW.

The other mechanism was explored by Albert Edwards in *Global Strategy Weekly*, 1 November 2002, which was the path of unconventional policy response. Effectively a lender of the last resort steps in to provide a floor to the market. As Albert writes, "It may be a move to money targeting (base or broad). It may involve T-bond purchases. It has to be something different and to be credible." However, before we see such a response "things will get much, much worse first".

Figure 39.22 US Graham and Dodd PE.
Source: DrKW.

APPLICATIONS

The above lays out the framework and provides some hints to the asset allocation and stock selection ideas that we will now seek to draw out more fully.

Asset Allocation

Japan offers asset allocators one simple lesson – forget everything you think you know about the nature of the relationship between bonds and equities. The arrival of deflation wreaks havoc upon prior relationships.

Too many investors have grown up only experiencing bull market conditions, and disinflationary bull market conditions at that. There is a lost generation of analysts because they spent so long preparing rather than analysing income statements, let alone balance sheets. Similarly, there is a lost generation of asset allocators who have only experienced bonds driving equities.

We have written many times before that this supposed relationship between bonds and equities is an illusory correlation. It results from equity investors trying to have their cake and eat it. Think of it this way, prices should be determined by discounted cash flow models. Such valuation models will have inflation factored into both their numerator and denominator; that is to say, cash flows projections will be in nominal terms, and the discount rate will be in nominal terms. Hence inflation should cancel out to leave the resulting value in "real terms".

However, investors have been willing to drop their discount rates as bond yields declined owing to low inflation. Of course, as inflation declines so should cash flow projections in nominal terms. But investors haven't done this, resulting in seriously overvalued equities, and an illusory correlation between nominal bonds and equities!

Figure 39.23 shows the relationship between bond and equity returns in Japan. We have overlaid inflation on the chart, and it is no coincidence that the correlation drops negative at the same time that deflation arrives on quite a permanent basis.

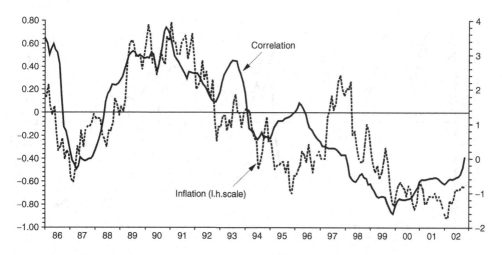

Figure 39.23   Japanese bond/equity return correlation and inflation.
Source: Thomson Financial Datastream.

Figure 39.24   Japanese BEER.
Source: Thomson Financial Datastream.

Of course, when the correlation between bonds and equities shifts so dramatically, it should be obvious that models based on positive correlations between bonds and equities will "break down". Figure 39.24 shows the Japanese bond equity earnings yield ratio. Unsurprisingly it breaks down when deflation arrives and the illusory correlation between bonds and equities is revealed for all to see.

Lest those of us who live in the Western world assume that the lessons from Japan are somehow irrelevant, take a look at the evidence presented below (Figure 39.25). In both Germany and the USA, the correlation between bond and equity returns is negative. Yet still

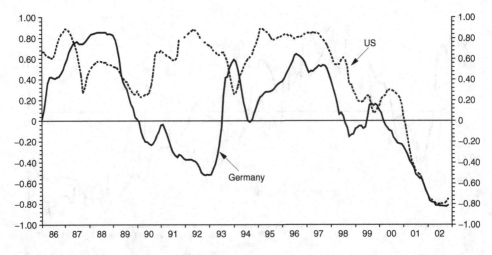

Figure 39.25   US and German bond/equity return correlations.
Source: Thomson Financial Datastream.

bullish strategists insist on producing bond equity earnings yield charts to illustrate that equities are cheap! Don't be fooled into relying on old valuation ranges. They simply aren't valid.

ALPHA GENERATION

Unlike the long bull market, investors won't simply make money by being long equities. Effectively, investors will be forced to focus more and more on absolute returns rather than relative performance. This in turn should cause a shift from the time series to the cross-section of returns. Investors will need to exploit differences between firms more and more. The focus should be on true long/short portfolios. Too many of the so-called hedge funds set up over recent years are really nothing more than leveraged long funds. Active management should become more valuable, and index funds could find themselves out in the cold.

We can identify three such cross-section strategies that should be among the vanguard of those benefiting in a debubbling/deflationary period.

Balance Sheets

Given all we have said about the risks of firms taking on too much debt during the euphoria stage, it should come as little surprise that we feel that balance sheet strength should be a key component of any stock selection process in the post-bubble world.

As an example of the cross-section strategies mentioned earlier, Dichev (1998) shows that the lowest 10% of Z-scores underperform the market by 33% over 3 years. Investors only incorporate the information contained in a low Z-score slowly over time. Hence we see a pattern of prolonged adjustment. In terms of an equal long/short portfolio, Dichev shows that the annual average return to such a trade is around 7% p.a.

An alternative screen was created by Piotroski (2000). He set out to examine whether using a simple accounting screen could help with stock selection in a value universe. He found that a minority of value stocks created the long run outperformance of value stocks relative to growth stocks. In fact just 44% of the value universe created the entire value premium. He then asked if using historical accounting information could help find that minority. He found that it could indeed.

Piotroski then formed an equal long/short portfolio based around going long those with a score greater than 5 (the financially sound value stocks), and short those with a score of less than 5 (the financially vulnerable value stocks). Such a strategy yielded annual average returns of 9% p.a. for zero cost! Equally impressive, and highly relevant for absolute return funds, the trade only generated 2 years of negative returns between 1976 and 1996.

Earnings Quality

This should really be in the forefront of investors' minds at all times. However, the reality of overoptimism is that quality tends to take second place to quantity. However, with fraud rife once again, it would seem that a strategy designed to exploit high-quality earnings should merit investigation.

Of course, it is easy to talk of high-quality earnings but exactly how do we define such a concept? Well, one obvious way is to think about what earnings really represent. Earnings can be seen as the summation of two components, cash flows (about which we should care) and accruals (accountants' tricks).

Table 39.2 Cash flows vs accruals – raw returns (% pa)

Low accruals	18.4%	High accruals	10.2%
Low cash flows	10.4%	High cash flows	18.6%

Source: Houge and Loughran (2000).

It has long been known that accruals tend to be reversed, and that firms that use accruals tend to have high earnings at the time, naturally enough. However, they can't keep hiding the truth forever, and sooner or later the accruals are reversed to reveal a poor underlying earnings situation.

Table 39.2 shows the returns based on portfolios formed by the degree of accruals contained in the earnings numbers (and conversely, the same thing based on cash flows).

Houge and Loughran (2000) point out that this suggests a natural earnings quality trade. Investors should find firms with low earnings but a high cash flow percentage (or a low percentage of accruals) to those earnings. Conversely, firms with high earnings but low cash flows (or high accruals) should be shorted. They show that an equal long/short portfolio based on this generated returns of 16% p.a. (Table 39.3).

Capital Expenditure

The final alpha generation strategy that we wish to explore as relevant to a post-bubble world relates to the overinvestment hypothesis outlined above. Just as overinvestment is a major problem for the economy, so it can be for firms. We have witnessed countless examples of firms wasting shareholders' cash on massively expensive purchases of other firms, and a plethora of bizarre investment projects in general.

Titman *et al.* (2001) show that firms that carry out high levels of cap ex relative to their sales (or total assets) underperform firms that resist the temptation to splurge on pointless expenditures. The variable they use is cap ex over sales in year 0 relative to the average of the same variable over the last 3 years. Although their results are remarkably robust to altering the definitions.

They find strong evidence that firms that carried out high levels of investment tend to underperform those that didn't. Being good academics they measure returns as the excess return after adjusting for style, size and momentum. Even then they show a 2% p.a. difference between the two groups. Now excess returns generally don't mean much to investors, but roughly speaking this is equivalent to an equal long/short portfolio generating 6–8% p.a. Again, in a world of low numbers, hardly a return to be sniffed at.

Table 39.3 Earnings quality trade construction

	Low earnings	High earnings
Low cash flows	—	Earnings largely composed of accruals, implies poor earnings quality SELL
High cash flows	Earnings dominated by cash flows, implies high earnings quality BUY	—

Source: Houge and Loughran (2000).

Table 39.4   Long only portfolio returns

Strategy	Return	Market Return
Z-scores	16%	14.4
Earnings quality	18%	15.4
Cap Ex	4%	16.2

Source: DrKW.

LONG-ONLY FUNDS

While we believe that absolute returns are the way forward, we acknowledge that many clients are concerned largely with peer group relative performance, and many more are constrained to long-only positions. However, the same stock selection criteria can add value to such managers as well. Table 39.4 shows the annual percentage returns from the long-only side of the strategies outlined above, proving that the gains aren't all on the short side!

SUMMARY

This is an unusually long chapter by our standards; in general we prefer to follow Keynes's advice and "fling pamphlets to the wind". However, this is a complex topic, and a basic understanding of the causes of bubbles is necessary in order to understand the ways in which we can exploit the debubbling process.

The key points are:

• Starting from a point of low inflation, a bursting bubble can easily unleash debt deflation.
• Bear markets don't have time limits.
• Don't rely on the soundness of prior relationships.
• Deflation alters the investment landscape radically.
• Previous winners won't lead you out.
• Where possible concentrate on absolute returns.
• Balance sheets, earnings quality, and low cap ex are key stock selection criteria.

40
Running with the Devil: A Cynical Bubble*

Not all bubbles are born equal. To us, the current market environment is largely a greater fool market. Because such markets lack fundamental support, they are liable to precipitous declines. This is exacerbated when everyone seems to be watching the same indicator (earnings optimism). The risk of a crash is rising fast.

- The specific behavioural foundations of various bubble types determine the market dynamics of the debubbling process. In this chapter, we analyse four different types of bubble in order to try to work out which is relevant to the current market situation.
- The 1990s bubble was best characterized as a fad (or a bubble of belief). Many investors really did believe in the "new paradigm". However, the current bubble echo is a very different beast. It has all the hallmarks of a near rational bubble. As such, too many investors are confident that they can get out before the peak. This must surely risk a stampede with the unlucky getting crushed in the dash for the exit.
- Moreover, the continued use of short-term performance measurement creates a myopic element within the market. That is to say, it is "rational" for investors to participate in the market, if they have time horizons less than those at which the bubble is expected to burst.
- Myopia also causes herding around a single piece of information. If our meetings are anything to go by, earnings optimism seems to be the key signal chosen by many. However, an equally significant risk is that the market simply falls under its own weight. As Keynes noted "When disillusion falls upon an overoptimistic and overbought market, it should fall with sudden and catastrophic force."

*This article appeared in *Global Equity Strategy* on 12 January 2004. The material discussed was accurate at the time of publication.

Figure 40.1   Hussman PE – S&P 500.
Source: DrKW Macro research.

The bubble is reborn. Some are declaring the birth of a new bull market. To us, nothing could be further from the truth. In fact, the terms bull and bear markets are not very helpful, since it is only with the benefit of hindsight that we know whether we are in a bull or a bear market. However, one thing remains clear to us, bull markets have never begun from such obscenely high levels of valuation.

For instance, Figure 40.1 shows a Hussman PE (current price relative to past cycle peak earnings). A cursory glance at the graphic reveals that the current reading of 21 times is unprecedented with the exception of the dot.com bubble years. Major bear markets have usually ended with this measure of valuation around 5–6 times. That would imply the S&P 500 around 300-400!

Further evidence of a continuing bubble in equity markets can be found by looking at the work of Robert Shiller. Shiller (1981) used a dividend discount model with perfect foresight. That is to say, he assumed that investors knew exactly what dividends were going to be in the future, and priced the equity market appropriately.[1] Figure 40.2 shows how far (and indeed for how long) real stock prices have deviated from this measure of fundamental value.

In order to gain some perspective, Figure 40.2 is plotted using a log scale, so the situation looks far better than it would do if we plotted the relationship on a linear scale. In fact, using this approach, real stock prices are actually 2.7 times higher than the intrinsic fundamental value! This analysis supports the Hussman valuation work shown above, which suggested similar levels of overvaluation.

---

[1] Astute readers may wonder how this is done. The answer lies in a clever trick that allows us to guess the solution and then use backwards induction (see either the original paper or Montier (2002) for details).

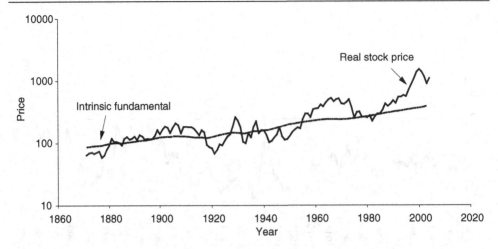

Figure 40.2   S&P 500 in real terms, and intrinsic fundamental value (log scale).
Source: DrKW Macro research, Shiller.

THE MAJOR TYPES OF BUBBLE

Although the issue of overvaluation may be relatively simple, and may be indicative of a bubble, it is important to understand the nature of the beast, because not all bubbles are the same. In fact, a review of the academic literature throws up four major types of bubble[2]:

- Rational/near rational bubbles
- Intrinsic bubbles
- Fads
- Informational bubbles.

Because of the differing psychological causes behind these bubble varieties, understanding which bubble is appropriate is key to understanding the dynamics of the market during the de-bubbling phase. So let's examine each of these types of bubble in turn.

Rational/Near Rational Bubbles

Under rational expectations (see Blanchard and Watson, 1982), the price of an asset is a function of the expected fundamentals, plus the expected value of whatever you can sell that asset for in the next period based on all available information or

$$P(t) = E(D(t+1)|I(t)) + a(E(P(t+1)|I(t)), \quad \text{if you prefer!}$$

where $P(t)$ is the current price; $E(D(t+1)|I(t))$ is the expected value of the fundamentals dependent upon all the information available in time t; and $E(P(t+1)|I(t)$ is the price in period $t+1$ dependent upon all the information available at time t.

---

[2] Camerer (1989) is an excellent early summary covering three of these bubble types (intrinsics weren't covered, because they hadn't been written about!). I am grateful to Prof Camerer for making his paper available to me.

This expression can be rearranged to generate an equilibrium condition. However, because we have one equation and two unknowns, the equilibrium has an infinite number of solutions (technically, the solution is indeterminate).

One potential solution to the equilibrium condition is an arbitrary bubble, as long as the value of the bubble in period t equals the expected discounted value of the bubble in $t + 1$. That is the same as saying that the bubble must grow at the rate of the discount rate, i.e. *for a bubble to survive in this paradigm it must keep rising at a given rate.*

A more sensible formulation of this kind of bubble goes by the name of *rational stochastic bubbles*. These have a probability of bursting each period. However, although investors can be sure that eventually the bubble will collapse, they are uncertain as to the timing of that crash. Hence, in each period investors must decide whether to sell or continue to ride the bubble. if they ride the bubble, then they will demand compensation for the risk of doing so. Therefore, if the probability of a crash increases, prices must rise even faster to compensate for the increased risk of the crash (witness the exponential price explosions that characterize many bubbles as evidence of this kind of pattern).

A more common (and probably more accurate) name for rational bubbles is greater fool markets. Investors are buying purely and simply because they think they can sell to others at higher prices. Because of the lack of fundamental faith displayed in these bubbles, I have termed it a *cynical bubble*.

As Bagehot (1873) observed insightfully:

> Every great crisis reveals the excessive speculation ... which commonly had not begun, or had not carried very far those speculators till they were tempted by the daily rise in prices and the surrounding fever.

Or as Keynes (1936) opined:

> The actual, private object of most skilled investment today is to 'beat the gun...' This battle of wits to anticipate the basis of conventional valuation a few months hence, rather than the prospective yield of an investment over the long term, does not even require gulls amongst the public to feed the maws of the professional; it can be played by professionals amongst themselves.

Economists have spent a long time trying to rule out rational bubbles, because frankly they aren't pretty! Tirole (1982, 1985) worked out the conditions under which rational bubbles cannot be seen. The most important condition preventing rational bubbles that Tirole unearthed was that *an asset with a finite life couldn't suffer a rational bubble.* If the asset has a finite life then its terminal value can be calculated. For instance, rational bubbles shouldn't occur in bond markets because they are clearly finite life assets. In the final period (T), no rational trader will pay more than the bond's terminal worth for the asset. So in period $T - 1$, no rational trader will pay more than the discounted terminal value in $T - 1$, and so on. Hence the bubble can never arise.

However, if investors are overoptimistic, or overconfident, then near rational bubbles can occur because people will think they can get out before other investors. Alternatively, if investors are myopic (i.e. they have short time horizons) and hence have a time horizon shorter than the time period when the bubble is expected to burst, then near rational bubbles can exist in asset markets with finite lives.

These two conditions strike us as particularly relevant to the current environment. Many of our client meetings over the last six to eight months have been characterized by two features. The first is investors' attitude to being able to time their exit from the market (a classic case of

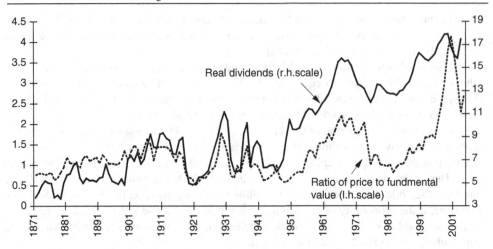

Figure 40.3   Ratio of prices to intrinsic value, and real dividend levels.
Source: DrKW Macro research, Shiller.

overconfidence?). The second is the massive shrinkage of time horizons on which professional investors are operating.

Intrinsic Bubbles

Unlike rational bubbles, where the bubble is independent and exogenous to the fundamentals, intrinsic bubbles (Froot and Obstfeld, 1991) are those in which the bubble depends upon the fundamentals (albeit in a non-linear deterministic fashion). As the fundamentals increase ("improve"), the bubble grows.

Intrinsic bubbles exhibit several features that fit the empirical evidence. For instance, departures from fundamental value are highly persistent, and have quite long durations (see Figure 40.2 on Shiller's work to see the empirical plausibility of this).

Intrinsic bubbles tend to be characterized by overreaction to "news" about the fundamentals. Figure 40.3 shows the ratio of the bubble to fundamental value against the real dividend level (as a proxy for the fundamentals). There appears to be an uncanny relationship between the bubble and the fundamentals, as predicted by the intrinsic bubble viewpoint.

This kind of bubble characterizes those where investors start to extrapolate past high rates of growth into the future. Hence, from a behavioural perspective they are likely to be driven by representativeness (the judging of things by how they appear, rather than by their statistical probability).

A possible example of an intrinsic bubble is the commodities markets. In 2004 the newspapers were rife with stories over China's demand for raw inputs. There was certainly some truth to China's role in creating world demand. But speculative interest in commodities had been running at record levels suggesting that China alone was not the full story. In fact, it seemed that hedge funds had been highly active in the commodity markets as part of a global reflation trade.

Fads

Shiller (1984) starts with the following quotation by Henry Fielding (1745):

> Fashion is the great governor of this world: it presides not only in matters of dress and amusement, but in law, physics, politics, religion, and all other things of the gravest kind: indeed, the wisest of men would be puzzled to give any better reason why particular forms in all these have been at certain times universally received, and at others universally rejected, than that they were in or out of fashion.

It would seem, therefore, fad bubbles are those caused by social psychological factors. We have previously analysed such bubble processes using the Minsky/Kindleberger framework (see *Global Equity Strategy*, 18 July 2002, and *Global Equity Strategy*, 6 November 2002 for details).

It is the psychology of the euphoria stage that is of relevance to us in the present context. The euphoria stage might, for example, be characterized by a general belief in the "new era". *Groupthink* is an important contributor in such environments. People come under immense pressure to conform to the majority's view, frequently suppressing their own views in the process.

The "new era" seemed invincible and was supported by rapid expansion of the economy and a seemingly inexorable rise in stock prices. This process leads to feelings of overoptimism and overconfidence. These two traits are a potent combination leading people to overestimate returns, understate the risk, and be far too sure about their knowledge and ability to control the situation. Hand in hand with this goes the extrapolation of the recent past as representativeness rears its head (that is, judging things by how they appear, rather than how statistically likely they are, presuming that companies with good recent track records are "obviously" great companies, and therefore the belief that they will always be great companies).

The combined outcome of these psychological biases is that long-term growth expectations and long-term return expectations are ratcheted higher and higher, while all comprehension of risk is reduced to truly minuscule levels. The prime example of this was arguments advanced at the height of the dot.com bubble, that equities were less risky than bonds for long-term investors and therefore a buy-and-hold strategy regardless of purchase price was the optimal strategy!

Unfortunately, when investors and corporates believe these new expectations, they set themselves up to be disappointed. Corporate managers engage in excessive gearing, and M&A binges. Because of their blind faith in the new era, firms take on debt in the belief that faster growth will generate the necessary payback with ease. This, of course, makes the ensuing adjustment all the more painful.

Informational Bubbles

Fundamental value is the value based upon *all* the information available to *all* traders. If prices fail to reveal all the information (called an information aggregation failure), then prices deviate from fundamental value, and an informational bubble exists.

Grossman and Stiglitz (1980) pointed out the impossibility of an informationally efficient market if information is costly. If prices were informationally efficient, then there wouldn't be any incentive to collect the information because there would be no advantage. Of course, if no one collects the information then how can markets aggregate it, and hence make prices informationally efficient? Thus the impossibility of informationally efficient markets.

Table 40.1   Behavioural and market foundations of bubbles

	Bubble type			
	Near Rational	Intrinsic	Fads	Information
Behaviour/ market inefficiency	Myopia Overconfidence Illusion of control Illusion of knowledge	Representativeness Overoptimism	Groupthink Wishful/magical thinking Framing Overoptimism Representativeness Salience effects	Lack of aggregation

Source: DrKW Macro research.

Lee (1998) presented a model where information is dispersed as private signals throughout the market. Each investor must make a decision based on their own private signal and the history of previous investors' decisions (i.e. current market prices). Information aggregation failure occurs because investors place too much emphasis on past price history in an attempt to utilize public information. Lee described these momentum style situations as *information cascades*.

Such cascades are inherently fragile. They develop on the basis of very little information, being based on others' behaviour rather than information. During these phases hidden information accumulates. Because of all this hidden information, a small trigger (perhaps a well-known stock missing its expectations) can engender a major change in behaviour. Lee referred to these sudden switches as informational avalanches.

PSYCHOLOGY OF BUBBLES

Each of the above bubble types has drawn on differing psychological foundations and market imperfections. Table 40.1 simply summarizes some of the major traits to be expected in differing bubble environments. These will be important when we discuss the market dynamics of the de-bubbling phase below.

COMPOSITE BUBBLES AND THE DE-BUBBLING PROCESS

The real world of financial bubbles (if that isn't too much of an oxymoron!) is rarely characterized purely and simply by one type of bubble. In general, real stock market bubbles are combination events. For instance, in the late 1990s the majority of investors both institutional and individual believed in the new era. It was effectively a *bubble of beliefs* (or a *fad* in the terminology used above). With some intrinsic support, as investors focused on earnings growth, albeit on pro forma earnings!

Of course, some investors were deeply sceptical of the bubble, but nevertheless rode it anyway. Brunnermeier and Nagel (2003) document that many hedge funds were effectively bubble riders rather than the stabilizing arbitrageurs so beloved by the high priests of efficient markets theory. They also show that hedge funds reduced their holding in tech stocks before prices collapsed.

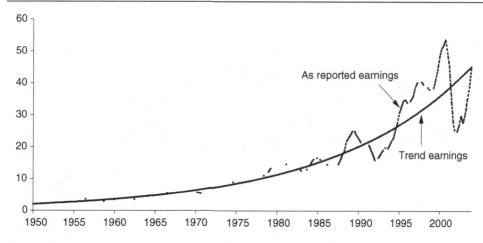

Figure 40.4   Trend earnings and as reported earnings (1950–2000).
Source: DrKW Macro research.

However, the current situation within equity markets is very different. If our client meetings are anything to go by, then most institutional investors are highly sceptical of the current rally. They don't feel it has fundamental drivers on a sustainable basis (in contrast to the belief witnessed in the dot.com bubble). Of course, some may be confusing cycle and trend, i.e. the rapid bounce back in earnings from very depressed levels (see Figure 40.4). If this particular form of myopia is at work, then, to some extent, the current situation may have some intrinsic element to it. However, effectively the majority of professional investors are playing the greater fool market, riding the bubble, and hoping to get off before it bursts!

Of course, there are some elements within the market who do undoubtedly think that this is a new bull market. Indeed, surveys of individual investors show that they are still hopelessly deluded over the likely returns from equity investment. For instance, the latest SIA survey reported individuals expecting equities to generate around 10% p.a. (see *Global Equity Strategy*, 12 November 2003 for details).

Our own model of individuals' irrational expectations supports these kinds of numbers. Figure 40.5 shows the irrational expectation and the rational expectation (as proxied by our generous return model). The gulf between the two remains massive.

In addition to the current near-rational bubble, perhaps with intrinsic elements, some (behavioural) individual investors are also suffering *"get-even-itis"* (or dynamic loss aversion for the technically oriented). Berkelaar and Kouwenberg (2000) find that, if they embed loss aversion[3] in a standard economic model, then the loss averse investors are momentum traders in good states of the world. In moderately bad states of the world, they become contrarians, buying as prices fall (in effect doubling up). Only in *extremely* bad states of the world do these loss averse investors become outright sellers.

These theoretical findings support our analysis of how the average individual investor might feel about equities. In order to model this we assume that an investor has been dollar cost averaging into an S&P 500 tracker since 1995 at the rate of $100 per month (Figure 40.6). We

---

[3] Loss aversion is the fact that people dislike losses far more than they enjoy gains. Empirically, it transpires that people dislike losses between 2 and 2.5 times as much as they enjoy gains.

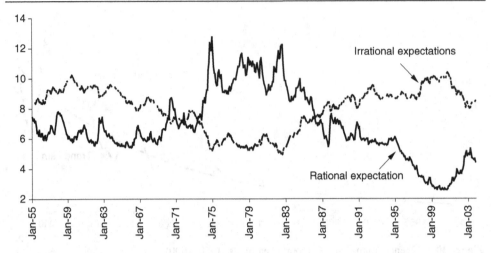

Figure 40.5   Rational pessimism vs irrational exuberance?
Source: DrKW Macro research.

then monitor the gains or losses on the principal invested (for full details and explanations of why we chose to do this, see *Global Equity Strategy*, 20 February 2003).

Despite the bear market, our "typical" dollar cost averaging investor never suffered prolonged exposure to capital losses. Currently such an investor would be sitting on around $3000 worth of gains, and presumably would be feeling quite good about life, the universe and everything.

We would argue that the bubble of the late 1990s was *mainly* a bubble of belief (*fad*), spurred on by some intrinsic elements, and with some investors following a near-rational bubble-riding approach. However, the current bubble is basically a near rational (cynical) greater fool market

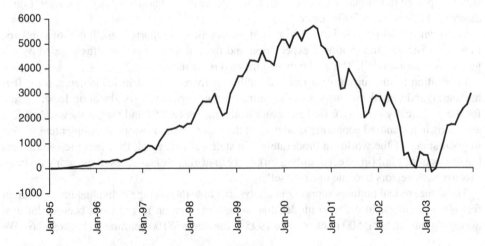

Figure 40.6   Capital gains from dollar cost averaging since 1995.
Source: DrKW Macro research.

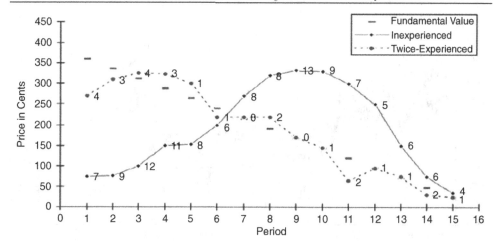

Figure 40.7   Evidence from experimental markets.
Source: Caginalp *et al.* (2000).

perhaps with some myopic intrinsic behaviour thrown in. The risks that investors run are very different in this environment.

EXPERIMENTAL EVIDENCE: BUBBLE ECHOES

We have written previously about the bubble echo feature of markets, and the fact that experimental markets exhibit very similar patterns. But it bears repeating in the current context. Vernon Smith (joint winner of the 2002 Nobel economics prize) is the major authority within this sphere. His work has shown that inexperienced traders take time to learn the errors of their ways – helping to explain the echo bubble pattern observed in so many data series (Figure 40.7). In Caginalp *et al.* (2000), Smith writes "once a group experiences a bubble and crash over two experiments, and then returns for a third experiment, trading departs little from fundamental value."

That is to say, having created a bubble and crash in the first experiment, they managed to do so again the second time they played! It was only on the third attempt that participants finally realized the error of their ways and moved the market towards a rational pricing structure.

Intriguingly, *Smith finds that the bubbles created in the first and second round of trading are very different in nature.* The first is a bubble in beliefs or a *fad*. But the second time traders played the game, the bubble were the result of overconfidence (a classic *near rational bubble*). Traders knew that the bubble was a long way from fundamental value, but were sure they could get out before it burst! The parallels with the current market are uncanny.

MARKET DYNAMICS AND THE INVESTMENT DANGERS OF NEAR RATIONAL BUBBLES

One of the most regular questions we are asked is when will this bubble burst? Of course, if we knew the answer to that we would have retired long ago, and be enjoying life on a Pacific island. However, we can at least speculate over possible triggers.

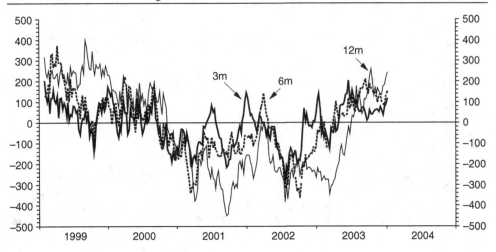

Figure 40.8 Simple price momentum for the S&P 500.
Source: DrKW Macro research.

Abreu and Brunnermeier (2002, 2003), note that the dispersion of information is vital to the duration of the bubble. They argue that rational arbitrageurs will watch a bubble, but they don't know if other investors see the same thing they do. This is called a synchronization problem. No one investor can burst the bubble and "coordinating" the attack is difficult. This view allows small pieces of news to have a disproportionate effect on prices if they act as a synchronizing event.

Of course, prices themselves could act as a synchronizing event. If prices start to decline, investors may take this to be other investors selling out, and hence believe there is an "attack" on the bubble, and thus join in. Abreu and Brunnermeier also show that thanks to asymmetric holding costs (i.e. it is more costly to short, rather than to go long) overpricing persists longer than underpricing or bad news travels slowly, if you prefer.

Abreu and Brunnermeier also find that if an "attack" fails, then the bubble is temporarily strengthened. The ability of prices to act as a synchronizing event is determined by the degree of dispersion of opinion. If the dispersion of views/information is very high then bursts via an endogenous mechanism (i.e. prices) will be very unlikely. However, if the dispersion of views is narrow (as we believe it is at the moment) then an endogenous trigger is increasingly likely! *This highlights the fact that any failure in price momentum could unleash a self-fulfilling downswing in equity markets.* However, as Figure 40.8 shows (and indeed our tactical asset allocation model keeps reminding us) price momentum has been strong of late.

If investors also have short time horizons they will tend to herd to collect the same piece of information. Froot *et al.* (1992) note that if investors are myopic, then they may "choose to focus on very poor quality data ... even on completely extraneous variables that bear no relation at all to fundamentals".

Effectively a positive feedback loop exists in the process of acquiring information – the more attention paid to a particular variable, the more value new information about that variable becomes, and hence the focus on it will intensify, and so on.

We have reported before that an alarmingly high proportion of the client base seems to be focused upon earnings optimism (Figure 40.9) as the key trigger for timing their exit strategy

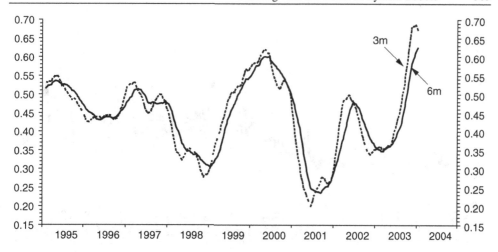

Figure 40.9   Earnings optimism for the S&P 500.
Source: DrKW Macro research.

from the current market. As Albert Edwards has noted elsewhere (see *Global Strategy Weekly*, 4 December 2003) this is now clearly beginning to turn down. Given the widespread obsession with this series, the risks of a substantial market decline increase with every release.

If the rational investors are to be successful in "attacking" a bubble then they must exceed the behavioural (get-even-itis) investors. With individuals pushing around $20bn a month into equity mutual funds, overcoming the behavioural investors is no mean feat. The critical breakeven level of the S&P 500 is now 1008, based on this price cost averaging behaviour.

CONCLUSIONS

Perhaps, a better title for this chapter would have been "Everything you ever wanted to know about bubbles but were afraid to ask". I guess I owe an apology to any reader who has managed to make it this far through the chapter. We are known for our short discussions, and this one has managed to be both dense and long. We should take Keynes's advice: "Leave to Adam Smith alone the glory of the quarto ... pluck the day, fling pamphlets into the wind, write always *sub specie temporis*."

We believe the current market has all the hallmarks of a bubble echo. The majority of professional investors don't seem to have very much faith in this upswing yet they are busy investing in it. This is a near rational bubble/greater fool market. To us, too many investors seem overconfident in their ability to exit before the peak in the market. They also seem to be herding around one piece of information – earnings optimism.

This exacerbates the risk of a crash, especially given the extreme overconfidence, over-optimism and overboughtness of the market. If everyone observes earnings optimism fading at the same time, they will presumably all try to head for the exit at the same time. While a fortunate few may skip out of the door without damage, the risk must surely be that other investors get caught in the stampede, and be effectively crushed in the rush for the exit (see Figures 40.10 and 40.11).

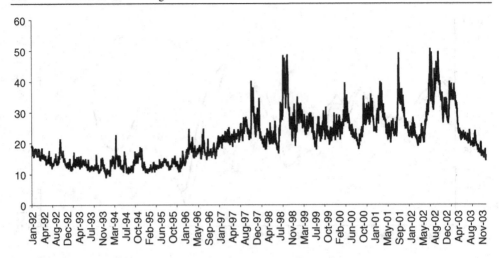

Figure 40.10   Implied option volatility for the S&P 100 (VXO).
Source: DrKW Macro research.

It seems appropriate to leave the last word to John Maynard Keynes (1936, Ch. 22):

> It is the nature of organised investment markets, under the influence of purchasers largely ignorant of what they are buying and speculators who are more concerned with forecasting the next shift of market sentiment than with a reasonable estimate of future yield of capital-assets, that, when disillusion falls upon an over-optimistic and over-bought market, it should fall with sudden and catastrophic force.

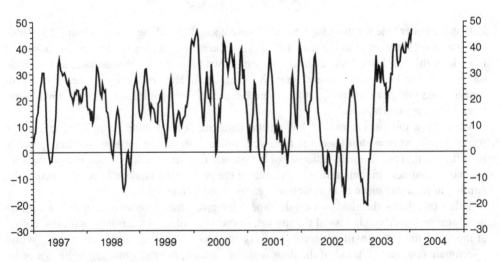

Figure 40.11   AAII survey of bulls–bears (4 wk ma).
Source: DrKW Macro research.

41

Bubble Echoes: The Empirical Evidence[*]

Bubbles appear to share common features during both the inflation stage and the de-bubbling phase. Most of the bubbles we have found exhibit a bubble echo – a relatively short-lived rebound in markets. This seems to be driven by conservatism bias. Only when the bubble echo finally fails, do investors lose their illusions.

- Bubble echoes appear to be commonplace in the range of historical experiences ranging from the South Sea Bubble to the UK railroads of the 1840s, right through to Japan in the 1990s.
- We believe these patterns are driven by the immutable nature of human psychology. Investors suffer conservatism bias – an unwillingness to give up previous beliefs. Psychologists have found that it takes "anywhere between two and five observations to do one observation's worth of work in inducing a subject to change his opinion".
- Examining the relationship between the current US experience and that from past bubbles reveals that this is almost exactly the right time for the bubble echo to start to deflate.
- We are not alone in finding a commonality within the bubbles and busts of history. Experimental economics also shows that bubble echoes are commonplace, as investors take time to learn the errors of their ways. Technical analyses such as Dow theory and Elliot Wave theory also identify the bubble echo scenario, and the mistake investors make of confusing a bull rally in bear market with the hope of a new bull market.
- The simple truth is that new bull markets are usually born from exceptionally cheap valuations, not the excessively expensive ones that we see now. When the psychology of the long bull market finally breaks, the resulting reality check will be all the more painful for investors. The loss of illusion is a necessary step on the road to revulsion.

*This article appeared in *Global Equity Strategy* on 23 March 2004. The material discussed was accurate at the time of publication.

Karl Marx once stated:

> Men make their own history, but they do not make it just as they please; they do not make it under circumstances chosen by themselves, but under circumstances directly found, given and transmitted from the past. The tradition of all the dead generations weighs like a nightmare on the brain of the living.

We have argued that what we have been witnessing in equity markets is a bubble echo. We suspect that bubbles and the de-bubbling process have an underlying dynamic all of their own. In previous research we have laid out the broad outline of the de-bubbling process which eventually culminates in revulsion (the point at which everyone has given up hope, (see *Global Equity Strategy*, 18 July 2002, for more details).

The bubble echo we have witnessed in 2004 is a normal part of that process. The psychology of investors takes time to shift from that that was prevalent during the bubble years. Psychologists have found that people tend to cling tenaciously to a view or a forecast. The proper term for this tendency is 'conservatism bias'. In his classic paper on the subject, Ward Edwards (1968) notes

> ...An abundance of research has shown that human beings are conservative processors of fallible information. Such experiments compare human behaviour with the outputs of Bayes's theorem, the formally optimal rile about how opinions ... should be revised on the basis of new information. It turns out that opinion change is very orderly, and usually proportional to numbers calculated from Bayes's theorem – but it is insufficient in amount. A convenient first approximation to the data would say that it takes anywhere from two to five observations to do one observation's worth of work in inducing a subject to change his opinions.

This very limited ability to recognize and deal with change leads to anchoring and slow adjustment. Once a position has been stated, most people find it very hard to move away from that view. When movement does occur it does so only very slowly – that is to say, people hold their prior beliefs too long and only change their views when there is irrefutable proof that they were wrong. During the last market rally, investors have been effectively anchored in the bubble environment, still applying "bubble" standards to valuations and behaviour. It is likely to take more than one downturn to shake the faith that investors have built up over the long bull market.

Have we any evidence of the normalcy of bubble echoes? Well, we examined a wide range of past historical bubbles and their aftermaths to see if they exhibited similar patterns. In fact we selected nine previous bubbles (see Table 41.1). Of course, there is always a risk of hindsight bias in dealing with selective episodes from history. There is also the risk of representativeness – judging things by how they appear or how similar they are, rather than how statistically likely they actually are.

However, the markets we selected were based on two criteria, they must be a freely traded asset in which there was a clear case of irrational exuberance, and we must have reasonable data (Figures 41.1–41.4).[1] The first of these criteria ruled out the housing markets, since these don't trade in the same fashion as financial assets in general. The second ruled out some of the most famous bubbles such as tulipmania.

Having identified our sample of bubbles, we can proceed along two lines. The first, and most obvious, approach is to run a regression of the current situation on our sample of bubbles. This regression can then be used to forecast the likely path of the equity market over future

---

[1] I am particularly grateful to Sandy Nairn, author of the excellent *Engines that Move Markets*, for making his data on the UK railroad share prices in the 1800s onwards, available to me.

Table 41.1   Our sample of previous bubbles

	Peak
South Sea Bubble	1720
UK 1840s mini	1837
UK 1840s maxi	1845
US 1929	1929
Silver	1980
Gold	1980
Japan	1990
Thailand	1996
Chinese Red Chips	1997

Source: DrKW Macro research.

years. This yields the chart that Albert Edwards used in one of his articles (see *Global Strategy Weekly*, 10 March 2004). The chart generated a considerable interest, and hence I decided that it is was time that I wrote up the work behind it (having put it off for weeks!).

Figure 41.5 reveals that, on the basis of past bubbles, the future outlook for the US equity market is unpleasant. The time scale measures months, with the peak of the bubble occurring at month 60. The R^2 of the regression is 0.93, even the adjusted R^2 (which adjusts for the number of variables used) is 0.926! Effectively, the US equity bubble so far has conformed incredibly closely to the pattern observed from previous bubbles.

However, this regression is not without econometric issues (which have no place here). The essence of the problem is that we have lots of bubbles that all look very similar, and this creates some problems when running regressions (technically, we have multicollinearity problems).

A common way of avoiding this problem is to extract the principle components from the series. Sounds horrific, I know, but it isn't that bad really. All principle components analysis does is split the series into $(x-1)$ new series, each of which is uncorrelated with the others (x is the number of series). So instead of nine bubbles that all look similar, we can extract 8 principle components that are unrelated to each other. In fact, it is even easier than that, since

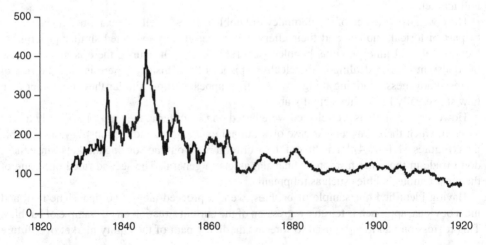

Figure 41.1   The UK railway share price index (1820–1920).
Source: Nairn (2002).

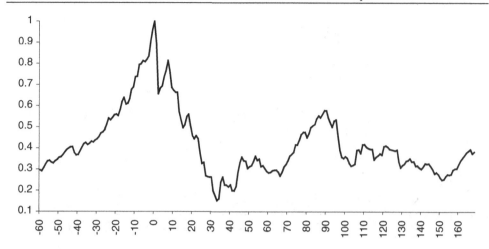

Figure 41.2 US equities in the 1920/30s.
Source: DrKW Macro research.

we are actually only really interested in the first principle component (i.e. the major pattern that our nine bubbles share in common).

Figure 41.6 shows the first principle component shared by our nine bubbles. It effectively shows the core features that all our bubble processes have displayed.

We can now use this archetypical bubble to examine how the US experience compares. As in the first case we have run a regression of the S&P 500 on the core bubble series, and then generated forecasts (Figure 41.7). The results are very supportive of our first attempt to model the bubble process above.

We are not alone in finding a commonality within the bubbles and bursts of history. One source of support that we have regularly referred to is the realm of experimental economics. This is an area of economics that uses laboratories to study the nature of economic interactions.

Figure 41.3 Japanese equities in 1990s.
Source: DrKW Macro research.

Figure 41.4   Gold in the 1980s.
Source: DrKW Macro research.

The advantage of laboratories is, of course, that information can be fully controlled in a way that just isn't possible in the real world.

The major authority within this sphere is Vernon Smith (joint winner for the Nobel economics prize in 2002). His work has shown that inexperienced traders take time to learn the errors of their ways – helping to explain the echo bubble pattern observed above. In Caginalp *et al.* (2000), Smith writes, "once a group experiences, trading a bubble and crash over two experiments, and then returns for a third experiment, trading departs little from fundamental value".

That is to say, having created a bubble and crash in the first experiment, they managed to do so again the second time they played! It was only on the third attempt that participants finally realized the errors of their ways and moved the market closer to a rational pricing structure.

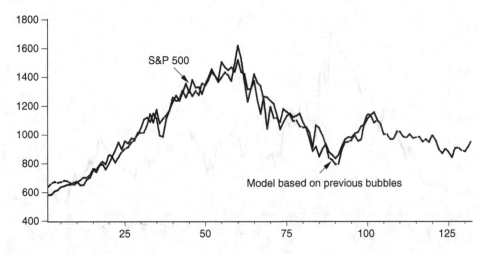

Figure 41.5   Bubble echo – S&P 500 and previous bubbles.
Source: DrKW Macro research.

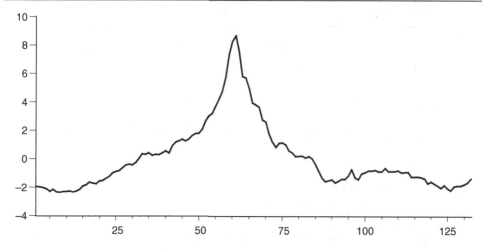

Figure 41.6 The core bubble – the first principle component of our nine bubbles (index).
Source: DrKW Macro research.

In fact, study after study of experimental markets has shown that the only reliable way of eliminating bubbles is via experience. A typical study is shown in Table 41.2 and Figure 41.8. It is based on work by Ackert and Church (2001). The set up in the experiment is a typical one with a given payoff structure and given probabilities. The expected value should then easily be calculable (in this case $0.48 per period, so in period 15, the expected value is 15 × 0.48 = $7.20, and it declines by $0.48 per period).

In fact, Ackert and Church alter the payoffs in each round of the market; however, we have standardized them to enable us to show the patterns on one chart. The line labelled 'Novices' is the results from first time that players took part in the market. Then we have shown the 'Once experienced' players – this is the bubble echo. The final game played by Ackert and Church

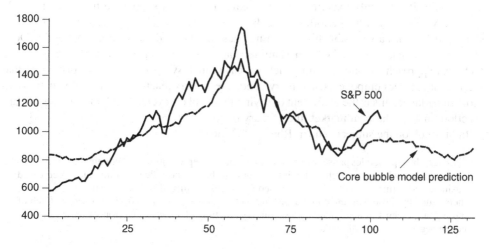

Figure 41.7 S&P 500 and forecasts based on the core bubble.
Source: DrKW Macro research.

Table 41.2 Payoffs and probabilities in the Ackert and Church experiment

Payoff	Probability	Expected value
0.00	0.25	0.00
0.16	0.25	0.04
0.56	0.25	0.14
1.20	0.25	0.30
		0.48

Source: DrKW Macro research.

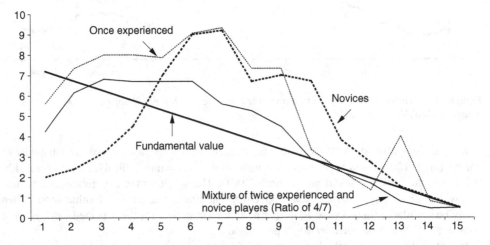

Figure 41.8 A typical laboratory bubble experiment.
Source: DrKW Macro research, adapted from Ackert and Church (2001).

shows that even twice experienced players can't quite manage to hold the 'Fundamental value' line when novices are involved in the market.

However, it isn't only experimental economics that offers support to the idea of bubble echoes. At least two of the important schools of technical analysis also suggest such patterns.

Dow theory has a venerable history dating back to 1900 and the writings of Charles Dow. His work was taken up by William Hamilton, and later by Rupert Rhea. Dow theory is a technical approach to market, with which we have much sympathy.[2] Dow theory posits that markets have three components: a primary trend, a secondary reaction and daily fluctuations. In modern parlance, this is the equivalent of saying things like a cyclical bull rally (the secondary reaction) in a secular bear market (the primary trend).

In his book on the subject, Rupert Rhea (1932) notes:

> There are three principles phases of a bear market: the first represents the abandonment of the hopes upon which stocks were purchased at inflated prices; the second reflects selling due to decreased business and earnings, and the third is caused by distress selling of sound securities, regardless of their value, by those who must find a cash market for at least a portion of their assets... Each of these phases seems to be divided by a secondary reaction which is often erroneously assumed to be the beginning of a bull market

---

[2] Indeed there is even academic support for Dow Theory. See Brown *et al.* (1998).

Figure 41.9   S&P 500 and Fibonacci lines.
Source: DrKW Macro research.

Hamilton notes "the secondary rallies in a bear market are sudden and rapid", which sounds very much like what we have been experiencing in equity markets over the last year or so. Rhea opines

> Any student of the averages knows that bull markets do not begin with violent rallies. Moreover, a reaction recovering from 25 per cent or even 100 per cent of the ground lost is not without precedent in the early stages of a primary bear movement.

Our final quotation from Rhea's masterpiece is taken from the chapter on secondary reactions:

> Hamilton frequently stated his belief that secondary reactions generally retraced from 40 to 60 per cent of the price change of the preceding primary movement, In checking this belief, it was found that all secondaries in bear markets averaged a retracement of 55.8 per cent of the preceding primary decline, with 72.5 per cent of all such secondaries rallying not less than one-third or more than two-thirds of the preceding primary decline. All rallies recovered an average of 49.5 per cent of the last preceding primary movement.

This is all the more interesting as the rally since March last year appears to have stalled out at the 50% Fibonacci retracement (Figure 41.9), and suggests that the rally has been nothing out of the ordinary, supporting our work on bubble echoes.

The second technical theory is also long established, tracing its roots back to R.N. Elliot, writing in the 1930s and 1940s. Today, Elliot Wave theory's best-known exponent is Robert Prechter. In his book (with Alfred Frost), *Elliot Wave Principle*, Prechter lays out in Figure 41.10 a stylized "corrective wave" (Frost and Prechter, 1980).

Frost and Prechter describe each phase of the wave as follows:

> During the A wave of a bear market, the investment world is generally convinced that this reaction is just a pullback pursuant to the next leg advance. The public surges to the buy side despite the first really technically damaging cracks in the individual stock patterns.
>
> B waves are phonies. They are sucker plays, bull traps, speculator's paradise, orgies of odd-lotter mentality or expressions of dumb institutional complacency (or both). They are often focused on a narrow range of stocks, are often 'unconfirmed' by other averages, are rarely technically strong, and are virtually always doomed to complete retracement by wave C.

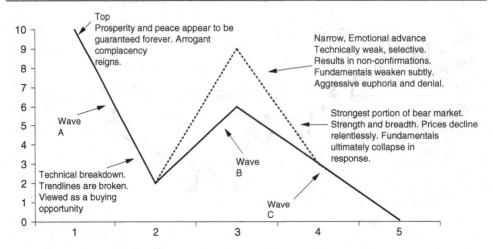

Figure 41.10 A stylized corrective wave.
Source: Frost and Prechter (1980).

> Declining C waves are usually devastating in their destruction. . . It is during these declines that there is virtually no place to hide except cash. The illusions held throughout waves A and B tend to evaporate, and fear takes over. C waves are persistent and broad.

The notion that illusions are maintained in waves A and B sounds very close to the conservatism bias that we outlined at the start of this chapter. So we suspect that Elliot Wave theory also adds some support to our notion of a bubble echo.

CONCLUSIONS

It seems to us that various bubbles from history share many characteristics in common. These similarities are not just inherent in the generation of the bubble, i.e. "new eras", but also in the de-bubbling process. The key reason for these parallels seems to lie in the immutable nature of human psychology. Conservatism bias, causing anchoring and slow adjustment, seems likely to be the core driver behind the bubble echo we have seen over the last 12 months. It is not often that we find ourselves able to agree with Sir Alan Greenspan, the bubble blower, but his statement in 1998 was one of those rare occasions!

> The same enthusiasms and fears that gripped our forebears, are, in every way, visible in the generations now actively participating in the American economy. Human actions are always rooted in a forecast of the consequences of those actions. . . . judging the way prices behave in today's markets compared with those of a century or more ago, one is hard pressed to find significant differences. The way we evaluate assets, and the way changes in those values affect our economy, do not appear to be coming out of a set of rules that is different from the one that governed the actions of our forebears.

Or, as Karl Marx put it, "History repeats itself, first as tragedy, second as farce."

All too often investors in post-bubble environments fail to recognize the new world in which they are forced to operate, confusing a bear market rally with the beginning of a new bull market. Bull markets usually begin from exceptionally low, not high, levels of valuation. In no way could today's US market be described as cheap (see *Global Equity Strategy*, 12 March 2004, for our latest rant on this subject). When the psychology of the long bull market finally breaks, the resulting reality check will be all the more painful for investors. The loss of illusion is a necessary step on the road to revulsion.

SECTION VI

Investment Myth Busters

42

Belief Bias and the Zen of Investing*

> When we believe something to be true, we tend to throw logic out of the window, preferring to judge by our belief rather than analysis. This habit seems to stem from part of the X-system, and hence is hard to beat. We also tend to confuse confidence with ability, believing those who sound most sure. Neither of these traits is likely to result in sensible investment behaviour.

- Consider the following syllogism: *No addictive things are inexpensive. Some cigarettes are inexpensive. Therefore, some addictive things are not cigarettes.*
- If you are like the vast majority of people, you have just accepted this as true. However, it isn't logically the case. The final conclusion does not follow in strict logical order from the two premises. But the conclusion is believable, and this is the criteria that people use to judge its validity.
- When presented with syllogisms that are both logically valid and believable, around 90% of people accept them as correct. However, when the conclusion is invalid, but believable nonetheless, around 60% of people will accept the conclusion as correct. Even when given clear instructions to only use logic, these findings hold. When told to take time to reflect, rather than reassessing their answers, people seem to spend time justifying their original conclusions.
- These habits are known collectively as *belief bias*. This is a tendency to evaluate the validity of an argument on the basis of whether or not one agrees with the conclusion, rather than whether it is logically true or not.
- So what has this to do with investing? Financial analysis should really be a logical process. The calculation of intrinsic value and its comparison to market prices should be a function of analysis. However, very often analysts and fund managers have strong beliefs about stocks. They love them or loathe them. This predisposition colours their ability to use logic. The evidence from psychology suggests that logic withers and dies when faced with belief.
- The answer? Adopt a Zen-like attitude to investing. If you can avoid holding beliefs, or at the very least test the beliefs you hold by checking their empirical validity, then you are developing the Zen of investing.
- One other lesson from the literature on logic and beliefs stands out. Those who answer problems like those above are equally confident regardless of their actual performance. This has dramatic consequences for circumstances where confidence is often used as a proxy for correctness. For instance, juries often believe eyewitnesses when they sound confident, even

*This article appeared in *Global Equity Strategy* on 26 July 2006. The material discussed was accurate at the time of publication.

if they are completely wrong. Fund managers may believe analysts who sound confident, regardless of their accuracy. We need to break the illusory correlation between ability and confidence.

Consider the four problems (syllogisms) below. Try to assess each according to whether the final line follows logically from the preceding statements.

(1) No police dogs are vicious
    Some highly trained dogs are vicious
    Therefore, some highly trained dogs are not police dogs
(2) No nutritional things are inexpensive
    Some vitamin pills are inexpensive
    Therefore, some vitamin pills are not nutritional
(3) No addictive things are inexpensive
    Some cigarettes are inexpensive
    Therefore, some addictive things are not cigarettes
(4) No millionaires are hard workers
    Some rich people are hard workers
    Therefore, some millionaires are not rich people

Each of these syllogisms can be mapped along two dimensions. The first, and most obvious, aspect is whether the conclusion is logically valid or invalid. The problems above take one of two forms, either:

No A are B; some C are B, therefore some C are not A (which is valid)

or

No A are B; some C are B, therefore some A are not C (which is invalid).

The second dimension is whether the conclusion is believable or unbelievable. Table 42.1 shows the mapping of the four problems outlined above along the two dimensions. Questions (1) and (2) logically follow from the premises outlined; the difference is the believability of the conclusion. In questions (3) and (4) the conclusion doesn't follow logically from the premises at all. However, question (3) seems to be true, i.e. it is believable.

The tendency to see problem (3) as logically true is belief bias.[1] Evans and Curtis-Holmes (2005) defined belief bias as "the tendency to evaluate the validity of an argument on the basis of whether or not one agrees with the conclusion, rather than on whether or not it follows logically from the premises".

The classic study is from Evans et al. (1983). They gave participants a list of problems like those above and asked them to evaluate whether the conclusion followed logically from the premises. Some were given prose texts with the statements embodied within them; others were given the problems in a format similar to those presented above. However, the presentation didn't alter the percentage of correct responses given.

Table 42.1   Validity and belief

		Belief	
		Believable	Unbelievable
Logic	Valid	Dogs (VB)	Vitamins (VU)
	Invalid	Cigarettes (IB)	Millionaires (IU)

Source: DrKW Macro research.

---

[1] I have long been interested in the role of beliefs. At least two previous articles have dealt with the subject (see *Global Equity Strategy*, 27 April 2005 and 26 October 2005).

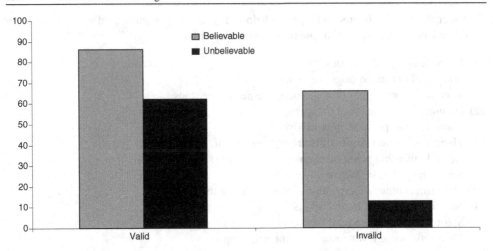

Figure 42.1 Percentage accepting conclusion as true.
Source: Evans *et al.* (1983).

Figure 42.1 shows the percentage of respondents accepting the conclusion as true in each of the four cases. When the logic was valid and the conclusion believable, 86% accepted the conclusion. When the logic was valid but the conclusion unbelievable, this dropped to 62%. When the logic was invalid but the conclusion believable, 66% incorrectly accepted the conclusion as true! The belief/logic conflict is clear to see. People accept things that aren't logically valid when they believe in them, and refuse to accept things that are valid but not believable. This is clear evidence of a belief bias: logic goes out of the window when beliefs are strong.

Evans and Curtis-Holmes (2005) suggest that three indices are constructed from this data. The logic index (VB+VU−IB−IU, in Table 42.1) measures the difference between acceptance of valid and invalid conclusions: the bigger the index, the more logical the response. The belief index (VB+IB−VU−IU) measures the difference in acceptance of believable and unbelievable conclusions: the bigger the index, the more belief bias is observed. Finally, the interaction index (VU+IB−VB−IU) measures the extent to which belief bias is greater on invalid than on valid syllogisms.

Figure 42.2 shows the scores for each of these indices.[2] The belief index stands out as much more important than the logic index − consistent with the idea of belief bias. The interaction index is relatively low, suggesting that the valid and believable syllogisms were probably accepted because of their believability rather than their logical validity.

BELIEF BIAS AND THE X-SYSTEM

I have often argued that a dual process theory is helpful in thinking about the way our brains work. The basic idea is that our minds contains two broad systems (see *Global Equity Strategy*, 20 January 2005, for more details). The X-system is automatic and effortless in the way it

---

[2] I've calculated them from the percentages across participants. Evans and Curtis-Holmes calculate them for each individual. However, the results are not significantly different.

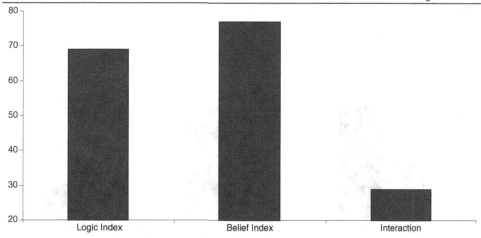

Figure 42.2   Indices analysis.
Source: DrKW Macro research.

processes information; it is also a fast system. In contrast, the C-system requires a deliberate effort to actually engage and operates a slow but logical process.

Could belief bias stem from the X-system? If this is the case then by applying time pressure we should observe a greater degree of belief bias. This idea was investigated by Evans and Curtis-Holmes (2005). Once again a similar set of syllogisms were used; but one group faced a time constraint of 10 seconds, and the other group could take as long as they needed.

Figure 42.3 shows the percentage of respondents accepting the various conclusions as true. Those under time pressure rejected a lot more valid but unbelievable questions, and accepted a lot more invalid but believable problems, than the group who could take their time.

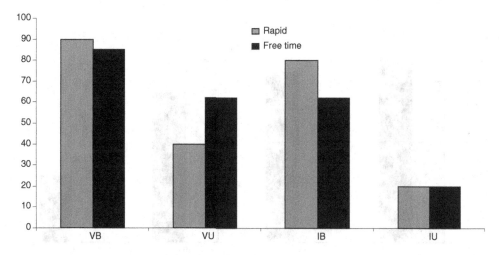

Figure 42.3   Percentage accepting conclusion as true.
Source: Evans and Curtis-Holmes (2005).

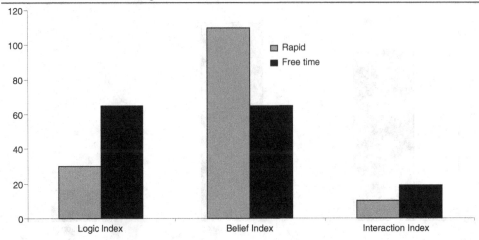

Figure 42.4   Indices analysis.
Source: DrKW Macro research.

As before, we have calculated the various indices. This reveals the impact of forcing people to answer before they can complete a full logical analysis. The belief index in Figure 42.4 is heading off the scale when people are placed under time pressure, and the logic index plummets.

This represents a between-subject experiment. Shynkaruk and Thompson (2006) perform a similar task but in a within-subject setting. In this case, participants were placed under pressure to respond within X seconds, and then given another minute to see if they wanted to change their minds.

Figures 42.5–42.7 show the by now familiar percentage of participants accepting the conclusion as true. One of the elements that stands out in Figure 42.5 is the very small differences despite the increase in time. That is to say, people didn't seem to change their minds very much, especially in the category of logically false but believable problems. The extra time

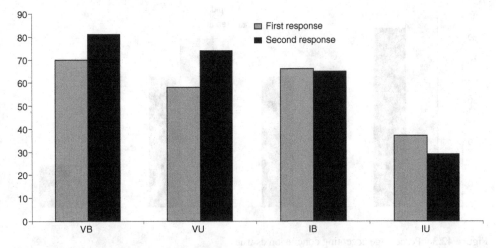

Figure 42.5   Percentage accepting conclusion as true.
Source: Shynkaruk and Thompson (2006).

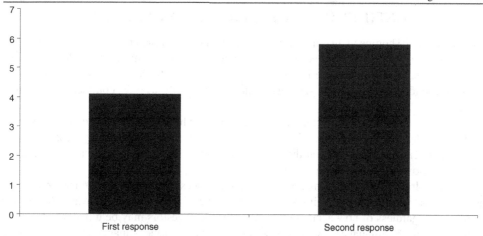

Figure 42.6   Average confidence ratings (scale: 1(not confident) – 7(very confident)).
Source: Shynkaruk and Thompson (2006).

seemed to be used for finding a rationale for the original answer rather than testing the truth of the answer.

More evidence of the X-system origin of belief bias comes from the work of Goel and Dolan (2003). They performed fMRI scans on subjects given syllogisms similar to those used above. They found that when subjects correctly identified a believable but invalid problem, the right lateral prefrontal cortex was highly activated (part of the C-system). In contrast, when participants succumbed to belief bias, the engagement of the ventral medial prefrontal cortex (VMPFC) was obvious. The VMPFC is a part of the brain that has been repeatedly found to be involved in emotional processing (part of the X-system).

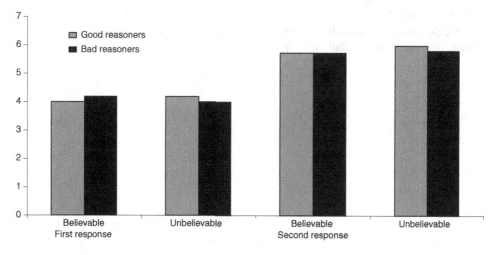

Figure 42.7   Confidence ratings (scale: 1(not confident) – 7(very confident)).
Source: Shynkaruk and Thompson (2006).

CONFIDENCE ISN'T A PROXY FOR ACCURACY

Shynkaruk and Thompson also investigated how confident people are in their reasoning abilities. On a scale of 1 (being not very confident at all) to 7 (very confident) people were asked to rate how confident they were in their answers (Figure 42.6). When pressed for time, the average confidence rating was 4. After a minute's reflection the average confidence rating rose to nearly 6!

Intriguingly, there was no difference between those who were actually good at reasoning and those who were poor. Figure 42.7 shows the average confidence rating across question domains. Even a cursory glance at the figure reveals that bad reasoners were just as confident as good reasoners! So they were confidently wrong.

This has dramatic implications for many circumstances in which we often use confidence as a proxy for correctness. For instance, juries often believe eyewitnesses when they sound confident, regardless of how accurate they actually are. Investors may be lulled into funds by confident sounding managers, without assessing the ability of the manager.

BELIEF BIAS AND THE ZEN OF INVESTING

So what does this have to do with investment? To my mind the lessons are clear. Financial analysis should really be a logical process, i.e. the calculation of intrinsic value and its relation to market price. However, very often analysts and fund managers have strong beliefs about stocks. They love them or loathe them, and this predisposition colours their ability to use logic. The evidence presented above clearly shows that logic withers and dies when faced with belief.

This implies that those who can master the Zen of investing might well have an advantage. What do I mean by the Zen of investing? This idea is meant to represent having the peace and tranquillity of mind to avoid one's own predispositions. If you can avoid holding beliefs, or at the very least test the beliefs you do hold by checking their empirical validity, then you are starting down the right path.

One other lesson from this research is not to confuse confidence with ability. All too often we work on the basis that confidence is a good proxy for ability. The more confident a presenter, the more the audience are likely to believe the message, even if it is logically flawed. We need to break this imagined correlation. It simply doesn't exist.

43

Dividends Do Matter[*]

> **Two great myths have sprung up from the US bull market of the late 1990s. Firstly, increased share repurchases have offset the declining dividend payments. The second myth is that granting share options to managers align their interests with those of the shareholders. In this chapter we reveal a very different truth.**

- Whenever we refer to dividends in the context of the USA, we are met with questions over the role of share repurchases. The consensus seems to be that increased use of repurchases has offset the decline in the dividend yield. The truth is that they haven't even come close!
- Too many investors focus on headline repurchase numbers without checking whether the announced repurchases are actually carried out. Actual buybacks by S&P 500 companies account for only around 55% of the oft-quoted headline figures. Even worse, many fail to adjust for equity issuance. Measuring net repurchases reveals a very different picture from the headline data.
- The total yield on the S&P 500 has fallen from over 5% in the late 1980s, to 2% in 2001! Why? Because shareholders have allowed managers to get away with blue murder. Giving management share options doesn't align their interests with equity holding investors. Rather, they have an incentive to seek to reduce dividends (since options aren't dividend protected), and increase the volatility of the firms' equity. They have exploited these incentives to the full.
- If investors are to protect their returns, these practices must be reversed.

---

*This article appeared in *Global Equity Strategy* on 12 April 2002. The material discussed was accurate at the time of publication.

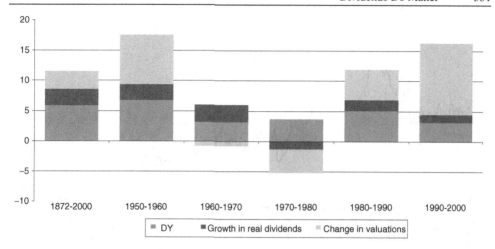

Figure 43.1   Decomposing returns (%).
Source: DKWR.

In the heady days of the bull market, dividends became a dirty word. When earnings growth was seemingly invincible, only the truly dull would concern themselves with the minuscule return embedded in the dividend yield. However, as earnings have started to disappoint, dividends started to gain more attention once more – witness the revival of value style investing.

In the past, we have opined that investors who choose to ignore dividend yield and dividend growth are making a mistake. In a world of small numbers, a far greater portion of investors' total return will stem from the dividend yield. Figure 43.1 is an example we have used before, but it bears repeating.

It shows the total nominal return to US equities (as proxied by the S&P 500) decomposed into its three components – dividend yield, real dividend growth and changes in valuation. *Over the long term, dividend yield has provided over 50% of the total return to equities!*

This bodes badly for the future. The S&P 500 dividend yield has fallen to a mere 1.6% (see Figure 43.2), and firms are paying out a paltry 32% of their earnings in dividends (see Figure 43.3). Scott McNealy, CEO of Sun Microsystems ($8.10), opined in a recent issue of *Business Week*:

> Two years ago we were selling at 10 times revenue . . . At 10 times revenue, to give you a 10-year payback, I have to pay you 100% of revenues for 10 straight years in dividends. That assumes I can get that by my shareholders. That assumes I have zero cost of goods sold, which is very hard for a computer company. That assumes zero expenses, which is really hard with 39,000 employees. That assumes I pay no taxes, which is very hard. And that assumes you pay no taxes on your dividends, which is kind of illegal. And that assumes with zero R&D for the next 10 years, I can maintain the current revenue rate. . . Do you realize how ridiculous those basic assumptions are? You don't need any transparency. You don't need any footnotes. What were you thinking?

'Ahh', say the optimists, smiling knowingly, dividends don't matter any more. Repurchases have replaced dividends. At long last the world has recognized the inherent truth of the Modigliani and Miller (M&M) irrelevance theorem.[1] Furthermore, the bulls point out that in

---

[1] M&M showed that under conditions of perfect markets, investors should be indifferent as to whether a firm pays dividends or retains the cash, since this should just translate directly into future dividends for the investor.

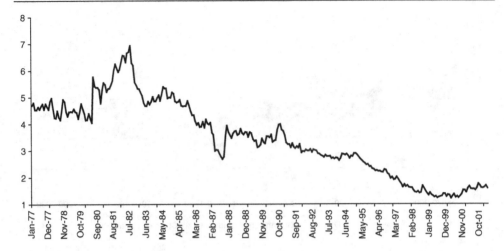

Figure 43.2   Dividend yield (%).
Source: Standard and Poor's.

a world in which income is taxed at higher rates than capital gains, people should actively prefer repurchases to dividends.

If only it were so simple! The first problem is measurement. It may seem that measuring repurchases would be a trivial exercise; however, it transpires it is far from easy. A firm can legally repurchase its own stock whenever it chooses without announcing its intention to do so.

However, by *announcing* a repurchase programme a firm can protect itself from the accusation of stock price manipulation (under rule 10b-18, SEC). Since *announcing* a repurchase

Figure 43.3   Dividend payout (%).
Source: Standard and Poor's.

Table 43.1   Repurchases: Announced vs Completed ($mn)

	Announced buybacks	Completed buybacks by top 100 firms	Estimated total completed buybacks	%
Q4 2000	58,185	27,498	45,647	78
Q1 2001	54,621	24,577	40,798	75
Q2 2001	44,195	23,360	38,778	87
Q3 2001	77,589	27,484	45,623	35

Source: TrimTabs, DKWR.

programme is essentially costless to the firm, we can assume that virtually all firms *do* announce their repurchases.

These announcements are usually made over wire services, and collected by bodies such as Securities Data Company (now part of Thomson Financial). However, data from sources such as SDC may seriously overstate the true level of buybacks.

Firstly, an announcement of a repurchase is simply a statement of the firm's intention to buy back stock, the firm is not obligated to do so. The estimates in Table 43.1 suggest that around 80% of announced buybacks are actually completed (an opinion supported by academic work – (see Sniezek, Stephens and Weisbach, 1998).

Secondly, the aggregate dollar value of announced repurchase programmes reported by firms such as SDC overstates the total value of repurchases due to the methodology employed. For instance, firms may announce their repurchase programmes to multiple sources, i.e. on the wires and the press. SDC tends to count both announcements. Also, any programmes that are withdrawn do not get removed from the data, and privately negotiated also get counted as a repurchase under the SDC approach.

Thankfully, we can gain a better insight into the *true* level of repurchases via the statement of cash flows issued by US listed companies once a quarter. *In their cash flow statements, firms are required to report the actual dollar amount of repurchases carried out.*

Thus by aggregating across firms we can see just how much corporates are really spending in returning cash to investors. Figure 43.4 shows three series, the Dealogic announced buybacks series for the total market, the *actual* S&P 500 repurchases, and a line we have labelled net repurchases. The differences between the three are marked. Actual buybacks by firms in the S&P 500 fall well short of those reported by Dealogic – on average, actual S&P 500 buybacks are only around 55% of those reported by Dealogic.

The most interesting line from our perspective, however, is the bottom line, which we have labelled Net S&P 500 buybacks. Looking purely at repurchases is a dangerous game. It is the sort of game played by people who want you to believe that firms have been switching dividends into repurchases.

However, this ignores the *issuance* of equity that firms carry out. The relevant measure (in terms of assessing the returns to equity holders) is net buybacks – that is repurchases minus issuance. Figure 43.4 presents a very different picture from the gross repurchase series. Net repurchases are far more cyclical, indeed in the early 1990s, net repurchases were negative!

This fits well with the idea that net repurchases are used to disburse excess cash of a *temporary nature*. It has long been known that dividend changes are relatively infrequent, and managers will not raise dividends only to cut them a year or two later. For economists, think of

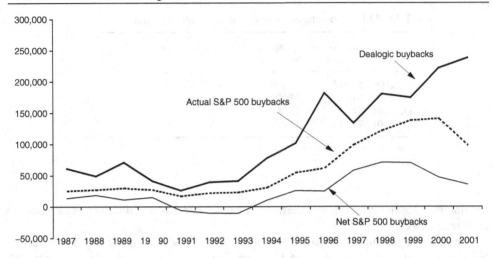

Figure 43.4   US buybacks – various measures.
Source: DKWR.

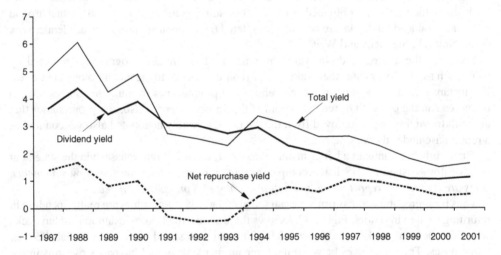

Figure 43.5   Total yield on the S&P 500.
Source: DKWR.

it as a corporate version of the permanent income hypothesis, permanent changes in cash flows are distributed via dividends, and temporary gyrations are dispersed via net repurchases.[2]

Figure 43.5 shows the very minor effect that net repurchases have had on the total yield return to investors in the S&P 500 – adding a mere 50 bps to the dividend yield in 2001. This is hardly massive recompense for the relentless decline in dividend yield over the last decade. Nor does it alter the downward trend.

So why have we seen such a massive surge in repurchases, and then an offsetting increase in issuance?

---

[2] A view confirmed by Lie (2001).

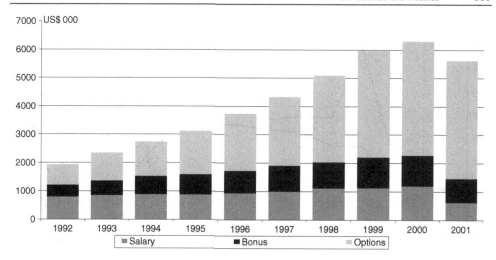

Figure 43.6 Median CEO compensation.
Source: DKWR.

The reason is not hard to find. The increased use of options must surely have a prima facie case to answer in this respect. One of the greatest myths of the bull market of the late 1990s was that options align the interests of shareholders and management. The idea that managers should have a financial stake in the business they are running is fine, otherwise we end up paying management like bureaucrats (to borrow an expression from Michael Jensen). However, this doesn't translate into loading them up with stock options (see Figure 43.6).

The value of an option depends upon six inputs (Capital budgeting and Finance 101): the riskless rate of interest, the price of the underlying security, the exercise price of the option, the time remaining until the option expires, the rate of dividend payment on the underlying security, and the volatility of the underlying equity.

Since executive options are call options, their value will increase with the underlying share price, and so having options supposedly ensures that managers will try to run the firm to increase the company's stock price.

However, managers also have some control over two other determinants of option values – dividend payments and the volatility of the underlying equity. Call option values are decreasing in the dividend level (dividend payments lower the stock price – share prices drop immediately after dividends are paid), and executive options are rarely dividend protected, hence the management's clear incentive is to reduce dividends as much as possible.

We don't believe in coincidence – the decline in dividends occurring simultaneously with the gearing up of management via stock options. Indeed, Jolls (1998) finds that the managers with the most stock options are much more likely to use repurchases rather than dividends.

Interestingly, she also finds that if managers are rewarded with restricted stock (which gives managers a share in the dividend distributions), the problem doesn't arise.

Secondly, managers can affect the volatility of a firm's equity. Remember that call option value increases in the level of underlying equity valuation. So managers loaded with options will seek to increase the volatility of the underlying equity. Two potential avenues for increasing volatility are to take on riskier projects (effectively increasing the left-hand side of the firm's

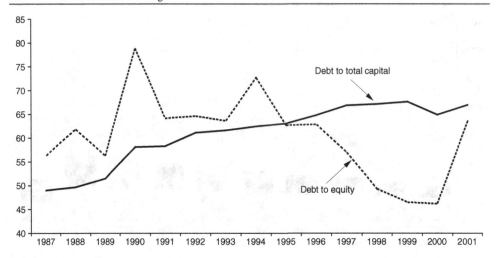

Figure 43.7   S&P 500 measures of leverage (%).
Source: DKWR.

balance sheet), and, secondly, to increase the leverage of the firm (increase the risk on the right-hand side of the balance sheet).

Let's deal with the second of these issues. If managers are seeking to increase the volatility of the firm's equity, we would expect to see evidence of increasing leverage. Figure 43.7 shows two regularly used measures of leverage – debt to equity, and debt to total capital employed. Of the two we prefer the latter measure simply because it removes the vagaries of equity market ups and downs (and not just that it fits our case – honest!). It clearly shows a trend towards higher leverage over the course of the option compensation explosion during the 1990s.

Option Impact on Earnings

Later, we will return to the issue of managers seeking to take on riskier investments, but first, indulge us in a little detour on the options impact on earnings. In the early 1990s, the FASB tried to force firms to expense their option grants, i.e. count them as a cost in the compensation figures. However, in the wake of protest from USA Inc. and a supportive legislature which threatened to remove the FASB's right to set accounting policy, the FASBs moves were relegated to footnotes in the annual reports.

However, for anyone desperate enough, the impact of option expensing can be uncovered by reading the small print – and believe me, having spent three days doing exactly that, it really is small print! Not everyone has filed their 10-ks for 2001 just yet, but with 62% of firms disclosed, we know that if options were fully expensed as per the FASBs recommendation, then GAAP reported earnings would be 17% lower than they are currently. Remember, that is GAAP reported, *not* pro forma! (See Figure 43.7).

Let us return to the issue of managers taking on "excessively" risky investments as a method of creating volatility. Certainly, the late 1990s can offer plenty of anecdotal examples of over

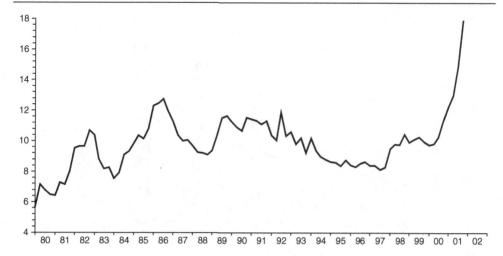

Figure 43.8 Whole economy – non-financial debt to profits ratio (×).
Source: Thomson Financial Datastream.

ambitious investment by corporate managers – witness the scale of the goodwill write downs that companies are now announcing.

Alternative evidence of inefficient investment can be found by looking at the relationship between earnings, dividends and retained earnings. It is often said that the earnings yield serves as a proxy for total returns from equities. The logic behind this statement is that the earnings yield implicitly consists of two elements – the dividend yield, and a "retained earnings yield". If investment is efficient then the future dividend growth should be equal to the retained earnings yield.

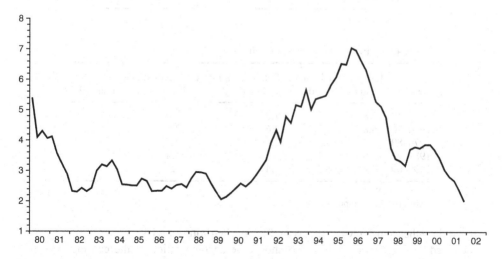

Figure 43.9 Whole economy – non-financial net interest cover (×).
Source: Thomson Financial Datastream.

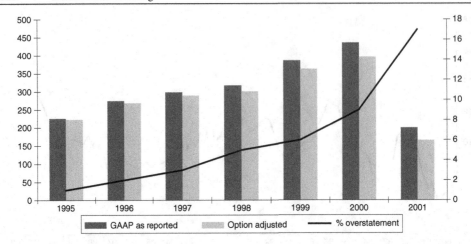

Figure 43.10   Option expensing impact on S&P 500 earnings.
Source: DKWR.

Table 43.2   Percentage earnings overstatement due to option
non-expensing – S&P 500

Sector	2001	2000
Basic	14	7
Consumer cyclicals	72	6
Consumer non-cyclicals	6	7
Communications	32	31
Energy	7	3
Financials	9	7
Industrials	8	6
Technology	96	16
Utilities	3	2

Source: DKWR.

Table 43.3   Efficient investment – sadly not

Decade	Earnings yield (%)	Dividend yield (%)	Retained earnings yield (%)	Delivered real dividend growth rate (%)
1950–60	13.8	6.8	7.0	2.6
1960–70	5.8	3.2	2.6	2.8
1970–80	6.3	3.5	2.8	−1.3
1980–90	13.5	5.1	8.4	1.8
1990–00	6.6	4.2*	2.4	1.3

Source: DKWR.
*Adjusted for net repurchases.

If, on the other hand, investment is inefficient then future dividend growth will be below
the retained earnings yield. Table 43.3 shows the decomposition of the earnings yield into
the dividend yield and the retained yield. We have also shown the growth in real dividends
achieved over the subsequent 10 years.

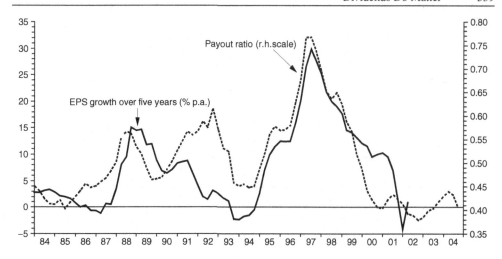

Figure 43.11   Inefficient investment?
Source: Thomson Financial Datastream.

The results don't make comfortable reading for those who believe that corporate managers know best. In general, corporate managers have consistently failed to deliver real dividend growth even close to the retained earnings yield. That is to say, investors would have been substantially better off if managers had returned the cash to the shareholders rather than investing for them!

Only the 1960s stand out as years where corporate managers' investments seem to have been efficient. We have adjusted the 1990s for the increased use of net repurchases, and still managers have failed to deliver reasonable real dividend growth to investors. Over the 1990s,

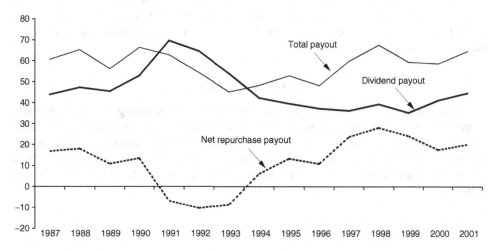

Figure 43.12   Total payout policy – using all firms (% of earnings).
Source: DKWR.

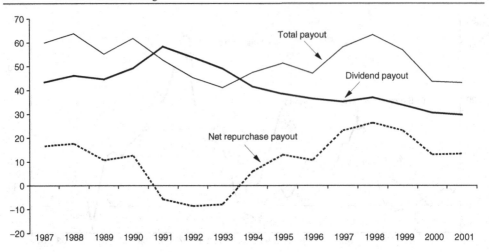

Figure 43.13   Total payout policy – positive earnings only (% of earnings).
Source: DKRW.

real dividends grew at a rate of just 1.3% CAGR, while the retained earnings yield required them to grow at 2.4%! This was still better than the 1980s, however!

So just how much money are firms returning to shareholders? Figure 43.12 shows the payout policy for the S&P 500, based on all firms, and using net repurchases. This figure makes the situation look good from a corporate point of view. The total payout ratio appears to be somewhere between 50% and 70%. So why am I criticising USA Inc. for its lack of cash distributions?

The answer is shown in Figure 43.13. This restates the payout policy using positive earnings only. Figure 43.12 uses *total* earnings, and hence lowers the denominator by including firms with negative earnings. If we strip out firms with negative earnings then the payout level is very different. Instead of paying out 64% of their earnings as Figure 43.12 shows, the rebased series shows corporates who created profits paid out a mere 43% of those earnings to investors in 2001. Given our comments above about the inefficient nature of investment by USA Inc., this doesn't bode well.

CONCLUSIONS

Investors should not be blindsided by two of the great myths stemming from the bull market of the late 1990s – firstly, repurchases *don't* offset reduced dividends, and, secondly, stock options *don't* give managers the same incentives as equity holders. Corporates should focus on returning cash to the owners and, failing that, they should concentrate on growing dividends – both have been sadly lacking from investors' experience in the US equity market over the 1990s.

44

Dividends, Repurchases, Earnings and the Coming Slowdown*

What is the US market yielding? That might sound like a simple question, but repurchases complicate the picture. If buybacks keep running at their current pace they will add 3 percentage points to the dividend yield in 2006! However, they appear to be used to distribute cyclical earnings. So high levels of buybacks could be an omen as to the extended nature of earnings and the risks ahead.

- In the past I have often noted that buybacks had not replaced dividends as a method of cash distribution. However, the latest data show an incredible pick-up in repurchases – even in net terms. If buybacks continue at the current pace, they could add 300 bps to the dividend yield of the US market. This would take the yield to just short of 5%, or approximately to its long-run average!

- Now, before you get all excited that I have written something vaguely bullish on the US, it is worth considering another point I have made in the past. That is, buybacks are used to distribute temporary (cyclical) earnings. Firms tend to only change their dividend policy when they believe it is sustainable. So buybacks are used to distribute earnings that deviate from trend. The trend rate of buybacks is probably closer to 50–100 bps in terms of dividend yield.

- As such, a very high repurchase level suggests that firms believe their earnings are at a cyclical peak. Our model shows that earnings are around 40% above their trend. This degree of extension usually marks peaks.

- Additionally, the payout ratio is soaring. According to our numbers, nearly 80% of earnings are being distributed to shareholders. The dividend payout ratio is only 30%, the rest comes from repurchases. It seems unlikely that firms will maintain this level of payout (much as I might approve of it).

- It is also worth considering whether repurchases are the best use of funds. For instance, 30% of firms in the S&P 500 have an earnings yield below the 10-year bond yield. Arguably, such firms could increase EPS more by investing in bonds than by buying back shares.

- Several indicators point to earnings peaking out. For instance, William Hester of Hussman Funds has pointed out that the Conference Boards CEO Confidence measure is a good lead indicator of profits growth. When CEO confidence is greater than 55, profits growth over the following 12 months averages 12%. When CEO confidence is below 45, profits growth averages 1%. CEO Confidence is rapidly heading towards 45.

---

*This article appeared in *Global Equity Strategy* on 31 August 2006. The material discussed was accurate at the time of publication.

- Of course, analysts are still expecting around 12% earnings growth over the next 12 months (and indeed 12% p.a. over the next 5 years). If they are right, then repurchases are likely to continue apace. However, personally I don't have much faith in their ability to forecast their way out of a paper bag, let alone earnings over the next 5 years!

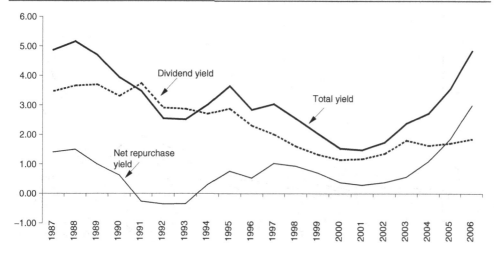

Figure 44.1 Dividends and repurchases in yield space (S&P 500, %).
Source: DrKW Macro research.

In the past I have often pointed out that, contrary to popular belief, buybacks have not exceeded dividends in terms of cash distribution mechanisms. However, the latest data show that I can no longer make this claim. In fact, if (net) repurchases continue at the rate seen in the first half of this year, they will add 3 percentage points to the dividend yield of the US market, leaving the market yielding just short of 5% (Figure 44.1).

To put this in perspective, Figure 44.2 shows the long run dividend yield with the buyback adjustment. In contrast to almost all our other valuation indictors, this suggests that the US market has repaired the damage done by the bubble years, and offers long-run fair value!

Figures 44.1 and 44.2 use the net repurchase yield which is the level of repurchases after all the issuance for share options has been deducted. However, US corporates continue to

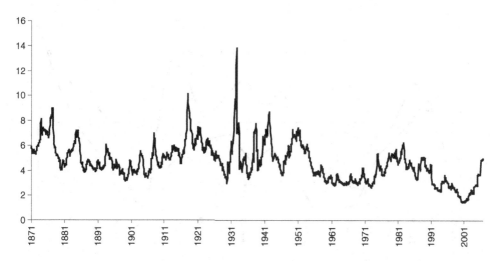

Figure 44.2 Buyback-adjusted dividend yield.
Source: DrKW Macro research.

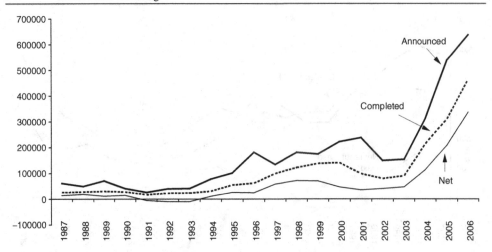

Figure 44.3   Announced, completed and net repurchases (US$ mn).
Source: DrKW Macro research.

announce far more buybacks than they actually manage to complete (let alone turn into net repurchases). On average since 1987, 57% of the announced level of repurchases are actually completed, and only 22% of announced buybacks actually translate into net repurchases.

In line with the surge in net repurchases shown in Figure 44.2, these numbers are significantly higher for H1 2006 (Figure 44.3): 73% of the announced repurchases have been completed, and 53% of announced buybacks have become net repurchases!

Before you all dash out and get very excited about the 'fair value' of the US market, it might be worth considering a point I have argued before – that is, repurchases are used to distribute temporary earnings.

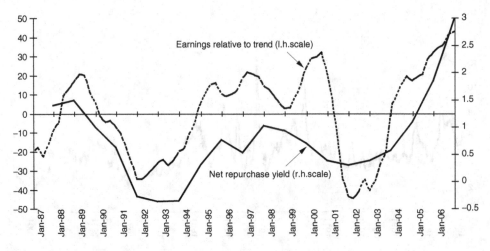

Figure 44.4   Deviation of US earnings from trend, and net repurchases (%).
Source: DrKW Macro research.

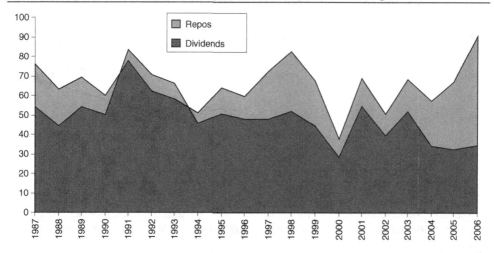

Figure 44.5 Buyback corrected payout ratio (%).
Source: DrKW Macro research.

If a firm increases its dividend, they are generally reluctant to then later cut the dividend as it sends a poor signal to investors. Hence dividend changes are not taken lightly by firms, resulting in a high degree of dividend stickiness.

However, repurchases are altogether more transitory in nature. Figure 44.4 shows the deviation of US earnings from their trend and the net repurchase series. The two are reasonably correlated. As earnings surge above their trend, so firms distribute cash via share buybacks. When earnings take a tumble, firms scale back on the level of the repurchases.

The willingness of firms to distribute cash has certainly surprised us. However there are limits on their ability to continue to do this. Firstly, firms' payouts are incredibly high. With

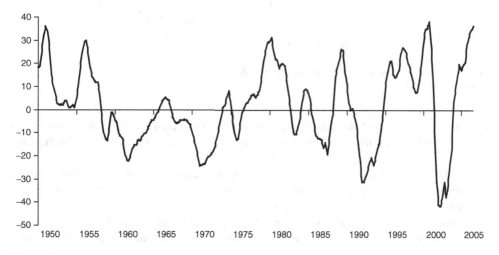

Figure 44.6 Deviation of US earnings from trend (%).
Source: DrKW Macro research.

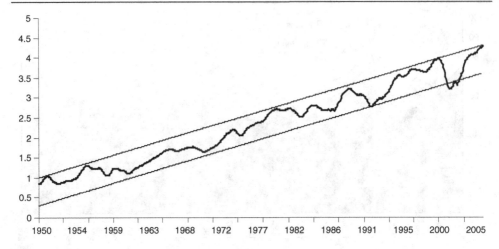

Figure 44.7   Log S&P 500 earnings and 6% channels.
Source: DrKW Macro research.

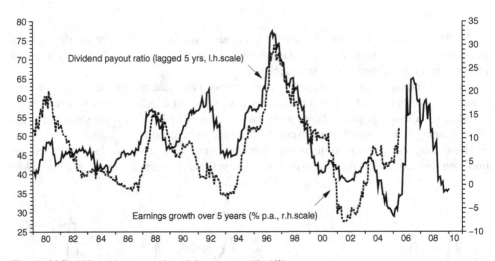

Figure 44.8   US earnings growth and the payout ratio (%).
Source: DrKW Macro research.

net repurchases included, firms are paying out nearly 80% of their earnings! (See Figure 44.5).
It seems unlikely that firms will continue to pay out at this rate (much as I would like them
to!).

Secondly, earnings are quite extended at the current juncture. Figure 44.6 shows the deviation
from trend for US as reported earnings since 1950. At nearly 40%, this represents the peak
levels seen in the post-war period.

A similar picture is revealed if one uses the approach suggested by John Hussman.[1] He
uses Figure 44.7. Which uses log earnings that, when measured peak to peak (or equivalently

---

[1] See www.hussmanfunds.net

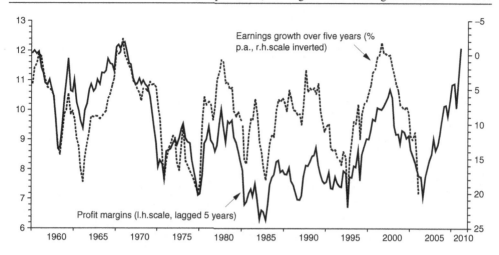

Figure 44.9   Profit margins and corporate earnings growth (%).
Source: DrKW Macro research.

trough to trough), show that US earnings have never ever grown by more than 6% p.a. Where are we right now? Right at the top of the channel – firmly in peak earnings territory.

There is also plenty of evidence to suggest that US earnings are likely to face cyclical pressure in the not too distant future. Much as I wish I could take credit for Figures 44.9 and 44.10, I can't. They come from John Hussman and William Hester. Both argue for a slowdown in US earnings.

Of course, you might prefer to believe the bottom-up analysts who are still predicting 12% earnings growth for both next year and over the next five years. In which case expect those repurchases to keep on rolling. Personally, somehow I doubt it.

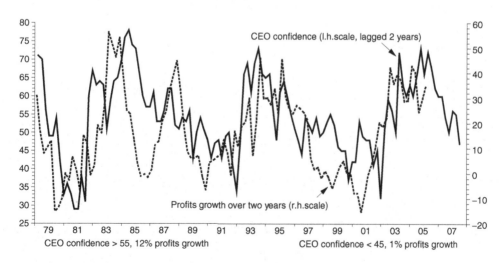

Figure 44.10   CEO confidence survey and corporate earnings growth.
Source: DrKW Macro research.

45

Return of the Robber Barons[*]

> As Sherlock Holmes said, "It is a capital mistake to theorize before you have all the evidence. It biases the judgement." However, investors, and analysts regularly assume that EPS growth can exceed GDP growth. The empirical evidence suggests that this is fallacious. Dilution is an unpleasant fact of life for investors.

- Investors regularly assume that EPS (and DPS) growth can exceed GDP growth. The reasons offered range from the dominance of buybacks, to sector differences in the composition of market indices versus the broader economy. While theoretically plausible, the empirics show these factors to be irrelevant.
- A stream of continuous buybacks will raise EPS growth into the future. However, buybacks in the USA have frequently been used to fund option plans. EPS growth remains unchanged, if a share is repurchased, only then to be reissued.
- Sector weights between the economy and the market are not vastly different (at least in the context of the USA). For instance, financials account for 21% of the S&P 500, 20% of the NIPA profits, and 18% of national income. Despite this closeness, EPS growth has consistently lagged both NIPA profits and GDP.
- The slippage is the result of the net creation of shares, as existing and new firms capitalize their businesses with equity. The robber barons are back, and diluting investors at the rate of 3% p.a. Nor is this purely a US phenomena. We present evidence to show similar patterns in the UK, Germany, France and Japan.

*This article appeared in *Global Equity Strategy* on 16 August 2002. The material discussed was accurate at the time of publication.

I have written an article on the equity risk premium (see *Global Equity Strategy*, 2 August 2002). Buried at the back of that article was a discussion on the way in which earnings growth was usually below GDP growth — in direct violation of the working assumption of most analysts. This chapter seeks to explore the issue in some more depth, and also assess whether the same relationship holds for a wide variety of countries.

Strategists frequently assert that EPS growth can exceed trend GDP growth for a variety of reasons. For instance, share buybacks may raise EPS growth for a given level of earnings (and GDP growth). Expansion into overseas markets may allow corporates to escape domestic growth straitjackets. The other fallback is that old chestnut, sectoral differences between the equity market and the economy. All these excuses sound plausible ... and indeed in theory some are plausible. But as the always insightful Sherlock Holmes noted, "It is a capital mistake to theorize before you have all the evidence. It biases the judgement."

Let's examine the empirical evidence on these claims. Firstly, share buybacks. In theory, a stream of continuous buybacks will raise future growth in per share terms. I can't think that too many people would object to that simple statement. However, as has been mentioned many times before, buybacks in the USA have frequently been used to fund option plans. EPS growth remains unchanged if a share is repurchased, only to be reissued.

Figure 45.1 shows the relationship between announced, completed gross, and net repurchases. From the point of view of improving future EPS it is the net repurchase series that matters. The figure exposes the cruel deception propagated during the bull market that repurchases were a major part of returns to investors. While announced repurchases were indeed significant, actual net repurchases were a drop in the ocean. In fact, in 2001, net repurchases were just 13% of announced repurchases, and 34% of gross repurchases. Anyone expecting EPS growth to be higher as a result of massive repurchases is likely to be sorely disappointed.

Especially noteworthy is a study on sector differences in repurchases by Andy Lapthorne and Rui Antunes (of our Global Quantitative Strategy team, see *Quant Quickie*, 8 August 2002). They find in terms of net repurchases that the traditional cash generative defensive sectors

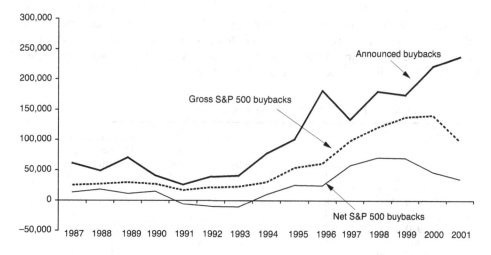

Figure 45.1   When is a buyback not a buyback?
Source: Thomson Financial Datastream.

Table 45.1 Highest and lowest net repurchase yields by sector since 1990 (%)

US Sector	Net Repurchase Yield	Dividend Yield	Total Distribution Yield
Top 5 sectors			
Tobacco	1.9	4.3	6.2
Chemicals	1.7	2.7	4.4
Food Producers	1.6	2.1	3.7
Beverages	1.3	1.5	2.8
Aerospace	1.2	2.1	3.3
Bottom 5 sectors			
Water	−2.9	3.9	0.8
Gas distribution	−2.3	3.9	1.6
Autos	−1.2	3.2	2.0
Telecommunications	−0.7	2.8	2.2
Electricity	−0.4	5.6	5.2

Source: DrKW Quant.

have done most to improve their EPS growth, while many of the glamour sectors purporting high growth have actually been issuing far more shares than they have been repurchasing (Table 45.1).

For the final nail in the repurchase coffin, see Table 45.2. I have used this many times before, and to those who are overly familiar with it, I apologise. However, it still bears repeating. The earnings yield on the market can be broken down into two components: the dividend yield and a retained earnings yield. Now, if investment is efficient and repurchases have boosted per share growth, then the delivered real dividend growth rate should be higher than the retained earnings yield. Some chance! The delivered real dividend growth rate has been massively behind the retained earnings yield.

What about sector differences between the market and the economy? Surely, the market can exceed GDP growth because it is full of dynamic growth firms – the lifeblood of the economy? Well, you might just be surprised at the relative closeness of the weights in the market and the economy. Table 45.3 compares the sector distributions for the S&P 500 with the weights in the NIPA profits series, and the NIPA national income data.

Table 45.2 Repurchases not raising growth rates

Decade	Earnings Yield (%)	Dividend Yield (%)	Retained Earnings Yield (%)	Delivered Real Dividend Growth Rate (%)
1950–1960	13.8	6.8	7.0	2.6
1960–1970	5.8	3.2	2.6	2.8
1970–1980	6.3	3.5	2.8	−1.3
1980–1990	13.5	5.1	8.4	1.8
1990–2000	6.6	1.5	5.1	1.3

Source: DrKW.

Table 45.3   Sector weights: Market vs economy

	S&P 500		NIPA Profits	Economy
Consumer discretionary	13.2	} 23.0	36.0	27.9
Consumer staples	9.8			
Financials	20.6		20.0	18.0
Health care	14.6			
Industrials	12.4		20.0	15.0
Information technology	13.9		1.0	2.5
Materials	2.8		4.8	2.2
Telecommuncation services	3.8		5.0	2.0
Utilies	2.9	} 8.9	8.0	9.0
Energy	6.0			
Total	100.0		94.8	76.6

Source: DrKW.

By and large, the sector distributions are relatively similar. For instance, the consumer sectors account for some 23% of the S&P 500, 36% of the NIPA profits, and 28% of national income. Financials account for 20.6% of the S&P 500, against 20% of the NIPA profits and 18% of national income. It can be seen that the S&P 500 is overweight information technology by a factor of 5.6 times the economy as a whole. Health care also stands out as a major sector of the S&P 500, but I have been unable to get data on its contribution to either NIPA profits or indeed the economy as a whole.

While on the subject of differences in sectors, let us dismiss the overseas exposure argument. The S&P 500 derives around 35% of its earnings from overseas markets (although post the removal of the seven international stocks, this is probably closer to 25–30%). With the NIPA profits, overseas earnings account for approximately 20% of the total, which, once again, is not compellingly different from the market.

Given the arguable similarity between the economy and the market, the disconnect shown in Figure 45.2 is all the more distressing. S&P 500 earnings have clearly grown at a significantly slower pace than both NIPA profits, and the economy as a whole.

Therefore, the arguments used by strategists to promote the idea that EPS growth can exceed GDP growth appear to be empirically fallacious. What, then, is driving a wedge between GDP growth and EPS growth?

One explanation is that when you buy the market at a point in time, you buy whatever the index consists of at that precise moment. Let's say you bought the index in 1970; you couldn't have purchased Microsoft ($49.71) since it didn't exist until 1986. So when Microsoft did come along, you would need to rebalance your portfolio, selling a little of each of the stocks within the portfolio in order to accommodate the new listing. This is, of course, exactly what S&P does when it includes new stocks in the index: one stock is deleted, another is added. Typically, the added stock is larger than the deleted one, which increases the divisor for constructing the index, i.e. dilution occurs.

Effectively, the slippage is the result of the net creation of shares, as existing and new companies capitalize their businesses with equity. Thinking of the problem in these terms

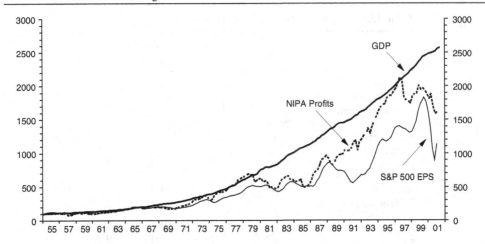

Figure 45.2   Lagging behind – nominal market earnings vs NIPA profits and GDP.
Source: Thomson Financial Datastream.

produces a simple measure for gauging the degree of dilution: the ratio of market capitalization to the price index. For example, if, over a given period, the market cap increases by a factor of 10, and the cap-weighted price index increases by a factor of 5, then there has been 100% net share issuance over the period.

Of course, this measure is really only appropriate for broad indices, since narrow measures such as the S&P 500 are effectively very highly managed and will show rapid growth in the ratio of market cap to price simply because they alter their composition frequently.

Figures 45.3 and 45.4 show the ratio of market cap to price for the Datastream total US universe and the S&P 500. The Datastream universe is relatively broad, and as such captures well the relentless dilution that investors have had to deal with over the past 30 years.

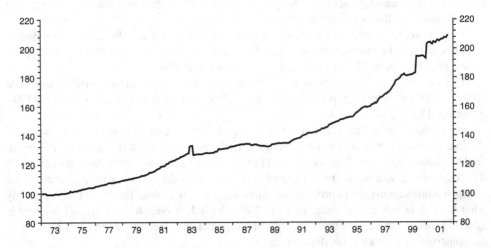

Figure 45.3   Total US market dilution – market cap to price.
Source: Thomson Financial Datastream.

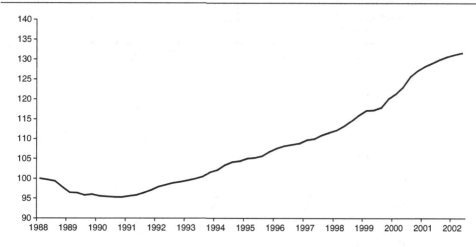

Figure 45.4   S&P 500 divisor index.
Source: Thomson Financial Datastream.

The interesting feature of the S&P 500 diagram is its early stages. In 1988–1991 the ratio has actually declined; that is to say, repurchases were actually doing their job! So like many good fallacies, the repurchase myth contains just a grain of truth. Sadly, this is now in the dim and distant past. Since 1975, market capitalization has grown at 13% CAGR, while the price index has grown at 10% CAGR. Investors in the USA have been suffering dilution to the tune of 3% per year. The robber barons are back with a vengeance. Edward Chancellor, in his entertaining history of financial speculation (*Devil Takes the Hindmost*), notes that investors

Table 45.4   The nominal evidence: EPS growth & DPS growth fail to live up to GDP growth (CAGR%)

	Earnings	Dividends	GDP
USA			
1970–2001	6.0	5.1	7.5
1970–1998	7.0	6.0	8.1
UK			
1970–2001	8.5	8.0	10.2
1970–1998	12.0	10.9	13.4
Germany			
1970–2001	5.8	6.0	6.1
1970–1998	5.3	6.0	8.0
France			
1972–2001	8.0	7.9	8.5
1972–1998	6.9	7.4	9.0
Japan			
1970–2001	3.2	1.4	6.5
1970–1998	−2.1	2.2	9.1

Source: DrKW.

Table 45.5   The real evidence: EPS growth, and DPS growth fail to
live up to GDP growth (CAGR%)

	Earnings	Dividends	GDP
USA			
1970–2001	1.0	0.2	3.1
1970–1998	1.5	0.6	3.2
UK			
1970–2001	0.9	0.4	2.5
1970–1998	1.7	0.7	3.0
Germany			
1970–2001	2.3	2.5	2.7
1970–1998	0.9	1.6	3.5
France			
1972–2001	2.0	1.9	2.5
1972–1998	0.5	0.9	2.5
Japan			
1970–2001	−0.6	−2.3	2.6
1970–1998	−7.0	−2.9	3.7

Source: DrKW.

in the 1920s were accustomed to the fact that management would often dilute shareholders if
a company was successful. It seems that little has changed.

Nor are these robber barons purely based in the USA. A similar pattern holds in other
countries. Table 45.4 shows the compound annual growth rates in nominal terms between
1970 and 2001. Because 2001 was clearly a bad year for earnings (the US suffering its worst
profits recession since the 1930s) we have also taken the sample such that it ends in 1998.
The choice of this more generous end point does little to alter the conclusions of the analysis.
Without exception, EPS growth and DPS growth are consistently below GDP growth by an
average of 1–2% p.a.

The evidence in real terms is equally depressing for investors (Table 45.5). Once again EPS
and DPS growth in real terms are in general 1–3% below the rate of growth in real GDP
(Table 45.6). For those interested in pictures, Figures 45.5 to 45.8 set out the graphs for each
situation. In each case the (a) graphs show the progress of nominal GDP, EPS and DPS; the
(b) graphs show exactly the same series but in real terms, and the (c) graphs show the ratio of
market cap to price over time.

Table 45.6   Index dilution measure – ratio of market
cap to price growth (1970–2002)

Country	Dilution
UK	4.7%
Germany	4.5%
France	8.7%
Japan	3.2%

Source: DrKW.

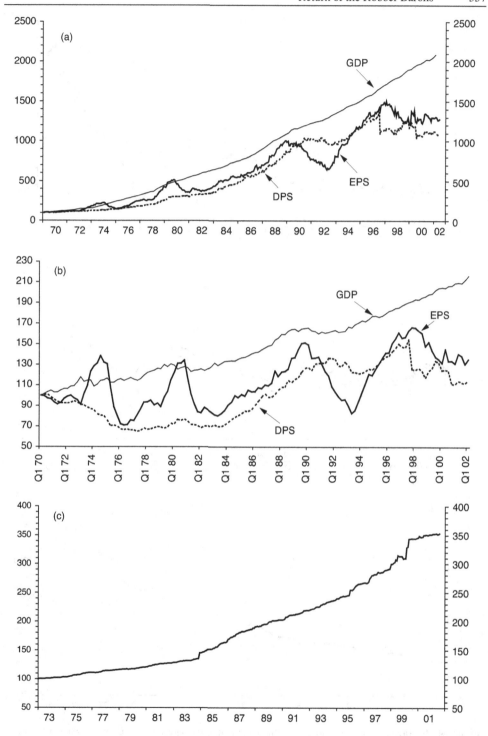

Figure 45.5 (a) UK dilution – nominal evidence, (b) UK dilution – real evidence and (c) UK dilution index – ratio market capitalization to price.
Source: (a) Thomson Financial Datastream, (b) Thomson Financial Datastream, (c) DrKW.

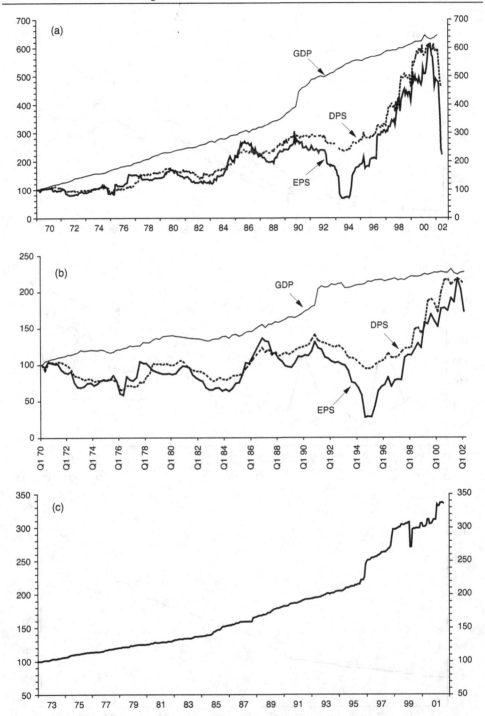

Figure 45.6   (a) Germany dilution – nominal evidence, (b) Germany dilution – real evidence and (c) German dilution index – ratio market capitalization to price.
Source: (a) Thomson Financial Datastream, (b) Thomson Financial Datastream and (c) DrKW.

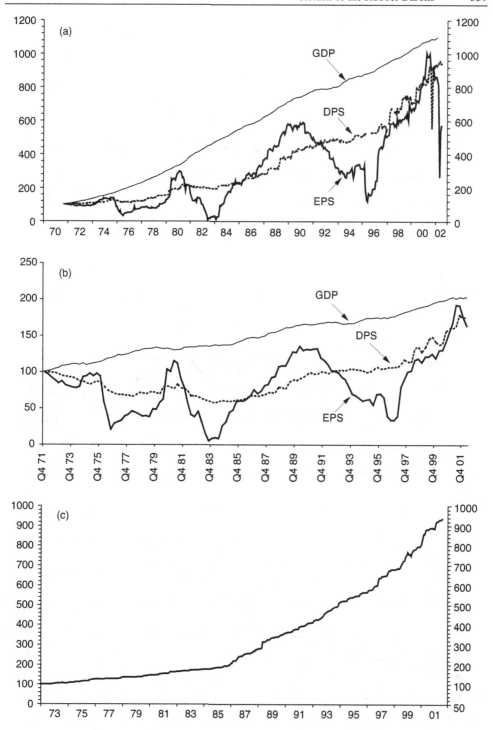

Figure 45.7   (a) French dilution – nominal evidence, (b) French dilution – real evidence and (c) France dilution index – ratio market capitalization to price.
Source: (a) Thomson Financial Datastream, (b) Thomson Financial Datastream and (c) DrKW.

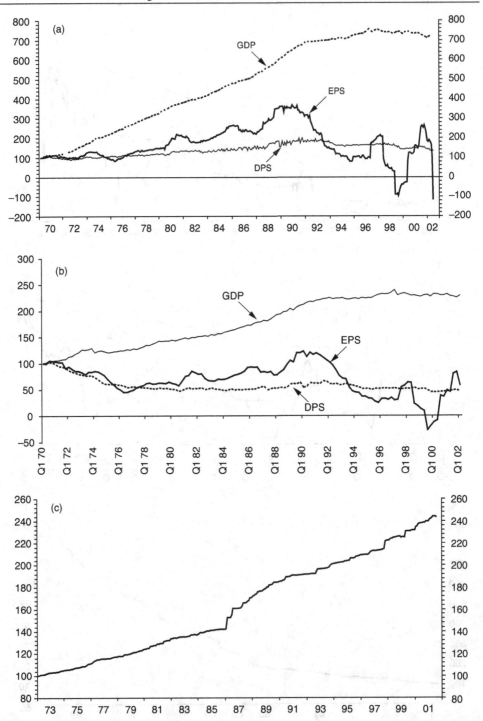

Figure 45.8 (a) Japanese dilution – nominal evidence, (b) Japanese dilution – real evidence and (c) Japan dilution index – ratio market capitalization to price.
Source: (a) Thomson Financial Datastream, (b) Thomson Financial Datastream and (c) DrKW.

The practical implications of these findings are significant. Virtually all valuation models are sensitive to the terminal growth rate assumed. For instance, I set up a simple DCF calculation using some Mickey Mouse numbers. I assumed that the DCF was conducted in nominal terms, and our profile of growth rates was similar to the forecasts currently being made by consensus analysts. I also assumed a 10% discount rate, and an initial terminal growth rate of 9%. This model yielded a price target in which 21% of the value was attributable to the terminal value.

I then cut the terminal growth rate to 7%; this yielded a price target in which only 8% was driven by terminal value. The target price was some 16% lower purely and simply because I dropped the terminal growth rate. Those stocks that are most susceptible to swings in terminal growth (i.e. long duration equities) should be examined particularly carefully in the light of the findings within this chapter.

While it is theoretically true that EPS is not constrained by GDP, the empirics offer a very different conclusion. Of course, investors may choose to place blind faith in the uncertain future without acknowledgement of the historical record. However, this sounds very like the mentality (or folly) that helped to create the bubble of recent years. Investors can ignore the historical record at their peril.

46

The Purgatory of Low Returns*

Buying the US market at current levels is likely to condemn you to the purgatory of low returns. Valuations are all important in long-run return determination. The US market is still in overvalued territory. Anyone buying in the market now is playing the greater fool theory, and we all know the mess that got us into last time around!

- Any investor with a long-term horizon can't afford to ignore valuations. They can radically alter the returns you expect. Simply put, your expected return is equal to your dividend yield, plus any dividend growth, plus any change in valuations that occurs. Hence valuations matter.
- Historically, the median 10-year nominal return from buying US equities when valuations are in the top quartile (as they are now) is 5.7% p.a. In contrast, buying when PEs are in the lowest quartile generates a median nominal return of 15% p.a. over 10 years.
- In real terms the 10-year median return in the highest quartile by valuation is a paltry 0.1% p.a. Based on the past empirics, investors have only around a one in three chance of achieving anything more than 5% in real terms when the market is so highly valued.
- Given that dividends have been dominant in return generation, and that the current dividend yield is so low, it may be more appropriate to use real price appreciation. On the basis of past overvalued markets, investors only have a 50/50 chance of seeing any positive price appreciation over the long term.
- The simple truth is that buying in the US market at current levels is likely to lead to investors wallowing in the purgatory of low returns.

*This article appeared in *Global Equity Strategy* on 27 November 2002. The material discussed was accurate at the time of publication.

Table 46.1   Valuation/Sentiment matrix

		Sentiment	
		Strong	Weak
Valuations	High	Investors will tend to ignore valuation	Valuation all important
	Low	Good gains from equities for all investors	Buying opportunities for the long-term investor

Source: DrKW.

While markets get blown around by sentiment and noise, in the long run it is valuations that determine returns. Some will argue that Keynes's view that, in the long run, we are all dead, makes valuations irrelevant. This viewpoint has merit, but as we will show below it doesn't hold if your time horizon is 10 years or so. There are times when valuations are all important, and times when they simply don't matter at all. The easiest way of thinking about this may be viewing it as a matrix (Table 46.1), with valuation against sentiment.

When sentiment is strong, the tendency is to ignore the valuations. This is fine if you are a short-term investor, and you know you are explicitly playing the greater fool theory. However, at some point in time, sentiment will shift and leave you looking like Wiley Coyote – running in thin air with nothing to prop you up. At this point, valuation tends to become all important.

Any investor with a long-term horizon can't afford to ignore valuations. They can radically alter the returns you expect. Simply put, your expected return is equal to your dividend yield, plus any dividend growth, plus any change in valuations that occurs. It should be obvious that dividend yield is nothing more than a valuation measure (D/P), hence the role of valuations in determining long-run returns is hopefully clear.

In a wonderfully insightful paper, Thomas K. Philips (1999) showed mathematically why valuation ratios should influence returns. Philips showed that this can also be expressed via the residual income model, or in terms of the earnings yield. All the representations are isomorphic.

We present a simplified version of Philips's approach below. We have used this kind of framework before (see *Global Equity Strategy*, 2 August 2002) to explore the equity risk premium. For those who can bear to trudge through the algebra, hopefully it should become clear why, mathematically, valuations are so important to long-run returns.

The algebra of the earnings yield as the expected real return on stocks

We will start with the constant Gordon growth model:

$$p = d/(k - g)$$

where p is the price, d is the dividend, k is the required return from equities, which is equal to the cost of capital, and g is the growth rate.

Now note that the growth rate of earnings is:

$$e(t + 1)/e(t) = 1 + b \times (\text{ROE})$$

where b is the retention ratio, and ROE is the return on equity

Now this is where we make our big assumption that the return on equity is equal to the required return on stocks and the cost of capital! This gives

$$g = b \times k$$

Hence we can substitute the retention ratio times the cost of capital for g, which gives

$$p = d/(k - b \times k)$$

We can substitute earnings and the payout ratio for d to give:

$$p = (1 - b) \times e/(1 - b) \times k$$

which cancels out to give

$$p = e/k \quad \text{or} \quad k = e/p$$

This isn't purely an ivory tower issue. Not only does the algebra suggest that valuations determine long-run returns but the empirics weigh in to offer their support for the proposition as well.

Table 46.2 shows the nominal returns achieved dependent upon the valuation of the market at the time of purchase. Unsurprisingly, when the simple PE is in its highest quartile (32–20 times as reported earnings) then the median geometric nominal return achieved over the subsequent 10 years is a mere 5.7% p.a. Conversely, when the PE is in the lowest quartile the median nominal return over the subsequent 10 years is 15% p.a., nearly three times the return achieved from investing in the highest quartile.

A similar picture is obtained when we examine the data in real terms (Table 46.3). When the simple PE is in its highest quartile, the median geometric real return over the subsequent 10 years is a truly paltry 0.1% p.a. Just as in the nominal case, the returns from investing in the lowest quartile are massively higher than the returns from investing when the market is in its highest quartile.

An alternative way of presenting this kind of data was suggested by Michael Alexander in his excellent book *Stock Cycles*. Alexander suggests using cumulative normal charts! Sounds horrible, but actually they can make vast amounts of data presentable and comprehensible. Our version of his chart is shown in Figure 46.1. The way to read these charts is to look at the level of real return on the vertical axis, say 5%, and then read across to the line, and follow down to the horizontal axis which gives you the empirical probability of achieving at least this level of real return.

Table 46.2   10-year nominal returns by PE range (1926–1992) (%)

PE range	Mean Nominal Returns	Median	Best Nominal	Worst Nominal
32.0–20.0	6.3	5.7	18.8	−4.9
20.0–16.0	10.9	10.5	19.5	−2.9
16.0–13.5	14.0	14.8	20.1	0.8
13.5–4.0	13.7	15.2	21.4	1.5

Source: DrKW.

Table 46.3   10-year real returns by PE range (1926–1992) (%)

PE range	Mean Real Returns	Median	Best Real	Worst Real
32.0–20.0	2.3	0.1	15.5	−4.3
20.0–16.0	7.3	7.3	16.3	−2.0
16.0–13.5	10.4	10.8	17.9	1.6
13.5–4.0	9.7	10.0	19.0	1.9

Source: DrKW.

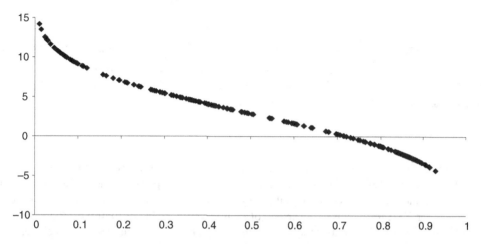

Figure 46.1   Probability of a given level of real total returns over ten years when market is overvalued. *Source:* DrKW.

The data used to compile Figure 46.1 is drawn from only those markets when the simple PE is in its top quartile.[1] It reveals an unpleasant truth for the market bulls, they are condemning themselves to achieve sub par returns. For instance, there is only around a one in three chance that buying the market at current levels will result in anything more than 5% real return p.a. over the next 10 years. Indeed, there is only a 50% chance that investors will achieve 3% p.a. in real terms over the next 10 years.

As we have shown many times before, in the long run over 50% of investors' total returns in US equities have been delivered via dividend yield. Given that dividend yields are still exceptionally low at a mere 1.7%, then the total return chart may overstate the returns that investors can expect (see Figures 46.2 and 46.3).

To allow for the lower dividend yield, Figure 46.4 shows the real price appreciation/ depreciation over 10 years, again drawn from the sample of the most overvalued markets. Once again the lessons for long-term returns are disconcerting from a bullish perspective. Based on the historical record, investors have only a 30% chance of seeing a 2.5% or greater p.a. price appreciation. Indeed investors only have a 50/50 chance of seeing positive price appreciation in real terms over 10 years!

---

[1] For the record we also measure the returns based around high market valuations assessed on the basis of Graham and Dodd PEs, the results were insensitive to the valuation measure used.

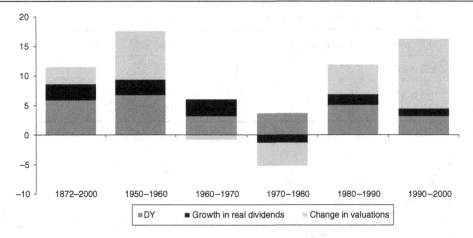

Figure 46.2 Long-run returns dominated by dividends.
Source: DrKW.

All of this begs the question: Where is market valuation right now? We have long argued that this bear market is unlikely to end until markets become cheap (or the authorities implement Plan B – some form of unconventional policy see Albert Edwards' *Global Strategy Weekly*, 1 November 2002 for details). The arrival of Plan B would enable us to turn off the valuation switch in the matrix laid out at the start of this chapter, at least temporarily. Of course, any announcement rally caused by Plan B may well just create another selling opportunity because, unless the market declines ahead of Plan B, there will still be a binding valuation constraint. However, absent Plan B, the bad news is quite simply that the US market is still in the top quartile in terms of valuation.

Figure 46.3 S&P 500 dividend yield still at very low levels.
Source: DrKW.

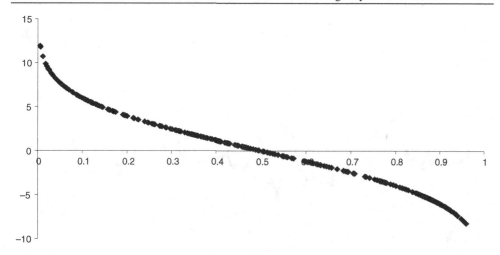

Figure 46.4 Probability of a given level of real price returns over 10 years when market is overvalued.
Source: DrKW.

The important thing to remember in terms of any valuation technique is to examine it relative to its own history. For instance, it is meaningless to compare a forward PE multiple based on operating earnings against a Graham and Dodd PE history. This should be obvious but this mis-comparison is all too common.

So let's look at four valuation measures, starting with the simple PE based on 12-month trailing as-reported earnings. Figure 46.5 shows that this measure remains exceptionally stretched relative to its own history. The latest data suggests that the PE measured on this basis is a stratospheric 27 times!

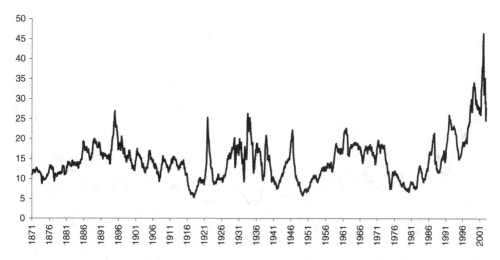

Figure 46.5 Simple PE – trailing 12-month as-reported earnings.
Source: DrKW.

Figure 46.6   Graham and Dodd PE – trailing 10-year moving average as-reported earnings.
Source: DrKW.

The second approach is the much-loved Graham and Dodd PE. This draws on the work of Graham and Dodd who in their magnum opus, *Security Valuation*, urged investors to use a moving average of earnings of not less than 5 years and preferably 7 or 10 years. We heed the advice of such skilled analysts and examine price relative to a 10-year moving average of as-reported earnings (Figure 46.6).

Once again we find that valuations are still stuck in the highest quartile. The current Graham and Dodd PE is 26.5 times! A far cry from the bargain basement levels of well below 10 times seen at the end of previous bear markets.

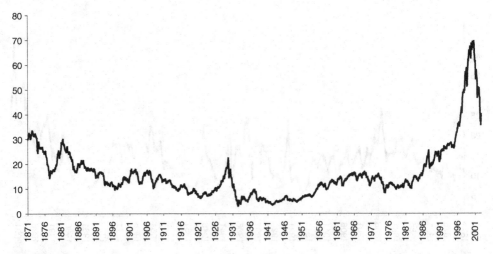

Figure 46.7   Trend E PE – trend estimated 1871–2002.
Source: DrKW.

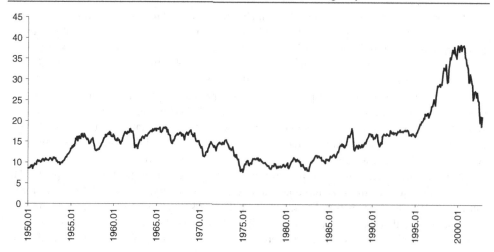

Figure 46.8   Trend E PE – trend estimated 1950–2002.
Source: DrKW.

Our third measure is for those who prefer to use a measure of trend earnings. Unfortunately trend earnings are generally sensitive to the estimation of the trend. For instance, in Figure 46.7 we estimate a trend for earnings that uses all the available data from 1871 to 2002. Calculating a PE on this basis reveals the S&P 500 currently trading on a 37 times multiple, the highest it has ever been bar the bubble of the last few years.

However, in order to show the sensitivity of this measure, in Figure 46.8 we show a PE based on trend earnings estimated over the much shorter period of 1950–2002. On this basis the current PE is 21 times, but once again this is still far higher than its average reading of 16 times (including the bubble years) or 14 times (excluding the bubble years).

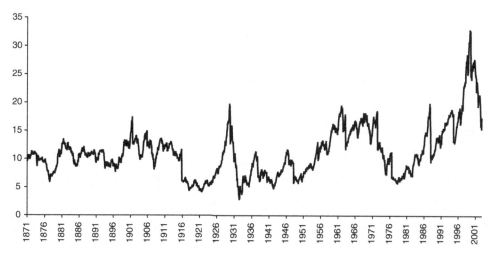

Figure 46.9   Hussman peak E PE.
Source: DrKW.

The final approach was suggested by John Hussman – a fund manager and former professor of finance.[2] Hussman has pioneered a good, clear method of valuation. He simply takes the peak level of earnings in each cycle and values the market relative to that peak potential. Figure 46.9 shows our version of Hussman's peak earnings PE. Just like all our other valuation measures it shows that the US market is still significantly overvalued. The current peak earnings PE is 17 times, this compares with an historical average of 11.2 times (including the bubble years) or 10.8 times excluding the bubble years. Add in the known fact that earnings were distinctly overstated during the last cycle (owing to a combination of fraud and dubious accounting habits such as ignoring the cost of share options) and the peak multiple measure would probably suggest a very serious continuing overvaluation of the US market.

Regardless of which valuation measure we adopted, the simple truth is inescapable. The US market remains in the very top quartile in terms of valuations. This should matter for all but the shortest-term investors. Those who buy the markets at these levels for the long term are condemning themselves to return oblivion. Even the short term players should remember that when sentiment changes (and let's remember that emotions especially with regard to the stock market are among the most fickle) they are likely to find themselves running in thin air with nothing below to support them.

---

[2] For more details see www.hussman.net

47

How Important is the Cycle?*

Historically, there has been no predictive relationship between the economic cycle and equity returns in the USA. However, we present evidence that in range-trading/low-inflation environments the cycle becomes markedly more important. Additionally, the real power of the cyclical analysis is as an aid to sector rotation strategies.

- Using a selection of cyclical indicators (both trailing and forecast) we can find scant evidence of any cyclical predictive influence on either absolute equity returns or the excess return of equities over bonds.
- Of course, just because something has or hasn't occurred in the past doesn't mean that it will not be important in the future. For instance, we have often talked of Japan in the Ice Age, ceasing to be a bond-driven market, and becoming an earnings-driven market instead.
- In Japan's post-bubble environment we find that cyclical indicators have reasonable predictive power over equity returns. For example, consensus GDP forecasts can explain over 20% of the variation in the one year ahead excess return of Japanese equities over bonds.
- If we are right, that the cycle matters far more in trading-range/low-inflation markets, then we should find reasonable predictive power for cyclical indicators during the 'dismal years' in the USA (1964–1981). This is exactly what we uncover.
- Finally, cyclical analysis really comes into its own in terms of sector rotation. Both the ISM and the DrKW MCI have shown strong predictive power over the timing of the cyclical/defensive switch.

---

*This article appeared in *Global Equity Strategy* on 17 September 2003. The material discussed was accurate at the time of publication.

Table 47.1 Predictive power of ISM (1984–2003)

Return	Variable	Time Horizon	t-statistic	Adjusted R^2
Equity	ISM	1 month	−1.1	0.00
	ISM	3 month	−0.93	0.00
	ISM	12 month	0.37	0.00
Excess return	ISM	1 month	−0.11	0.00
	ISM	3 month	−0.09	0.00
	ISM	12 month	−0.05	0.00

Source: DrKW Macro research.

In client meetings of late, one recurring topic has stood out – the role of the cycle in investing. Just how important is the duration and scale of any economic upswing in determining equity returns? The "theoretical" arguments in support of cyclical importance are straightforward and clear. The cycle influences earnings, and earnings matter for equities. However, does the empirical evidence support this kind of thinking?

In a wonderful book on the history of statistical concepts (*Statistics on the Table*, 1999) (yes, there really is such a thing), Stephen Stigler offers the following quotation from 1910:

> I am too familiar with the manner in which actual data are met with the suggestion that other data... might show something else, to believe it to have any value as an argument. "Statistics on the table, please", can be my sole reply
>
> (Karl Pearson, 1910. In a letter to *The Times*)

This struck me as a powerful antidote to much of the story-telling that goes on within our industry. It simply isn't good enough to assert that something is true, rather we must strive to present evidence that it is true[1] and some analysis as to the reliability of the evidence being presented.

So rather than boldly stating that the cycle is clearly important for equity returns, we need to look for evidence that this is the case. So let's start with the most naive case. Can we predict equity returns (or the excess return of equities over bonds) by looking at historical economic performance? *A priori*, we would expect to find little evidence of predictability based on past economic performance, after all we are forever hearing that the stock market is forward looking.

We choose the ISM as our proxy for economic growth, given the attention that the survey attracts in the market place. Table 47.1 shows the predictive power of the ISM over equity returns and the excess of equity over bonds at the 1-, 3-, and 12-month time horizons. A quick glance at the table reveals that the ISM has no predictive power over either of the return groups at any horizon.[2]

As an alternative, we tested historic earnings growth over the prior 12 months. Unlike the ISM, using trailing earnings growth revealed some predictability with respect to equity returns at all three time horizons. Of course, the predictive power is not high (Table 47.2). Only around 5% of the total variation in one year returns can be explained by historic earnings growth. However, the fact that past growth has any predictive power is a blow to those who think

---

[1] More correctly, we should seek to find evidence that the hypothesis is false, if we are following Popper's approach to science.
[2] For the anoraks, the t-stats are produced using the Newey-West correction for hetroskedasticity and autocorrelation where appropriate.

Table 47.2   Predictive power of trailing earnings growth (1984–2003)

Return	Variable	Time Horizon	t-statistic	Adjusted R^2
Equity	Historic earnings growth	**1 month**	**1.92**	**0.01**
	Historic earnings growth	**3 month**	**2.13**	**0.04**
	Historic earnings growth	**12 month**	**1.80**	**0.05**
Excess return	Historic earnings growth	1 month	1.64	0.01
	Historic earnings growth	3 month	1.47	0.02
	Historic earnings growth	12 month	1.31	0.03

Bold fonts indicate statistical significance.
Source: DrKW Macro research.

that the market is always forward looking! Essentially, the power that trailing growth has in predicting future returns suggests that expectations of earnings growth are highly adaptive. In contrast, no statistically significant relationship could be found for excess returns.

All well and good you might say. But history is history and markets are forward looking. So what about forward looking variables? Surely if we could find a good indicator of the future state of the cycle we would gain some insight into the likely returns to equities?

Well perhaps, but we couldn't find any evidence of predictive power from a wide variety of leading indicators. We tried the slope of the yield curve, the OECD's lead indicator, forecast GDP from the consensus, the DrKW monetary conditions indicator (MCI), forecast earnings growth from analysts, and earnings momentum – all to no avail.

Out of the 36 regressions we ran, only one showed a statistically significant outcome. The OECD lead indicator explained 2% of the 3-month variation in the excess return of equities over bonds. Given such a large-scale exercise in data mining, we suspect that this is a spurious result (full results are shown in Table 47.3).

The sad but unavoidable conclusion is that for the period we investigated, there is no evidence that the economic cycle or indeed expectations about that cycle have any predictive influence upon returns.[3] Those arguing for buying equities because of a cyclical upswing have nothing on which to base their arguments.

Of course, just because something has or hasn't occurred in the past doesn't mean that it will not be important in the future. For example, we have often talked about the Japanese market ceasing to be a bond-driven market, and becoming an earnings-driven market. Many of the equity market rallies in Japan's post-bubble environment have coincided with economic upswings.

Coincident indicators aren't much use, and when we run our predictive regressions we lag the returns so they can only reflect the information that was available at the time we had to make a forecast. When we tested various relationships in Japan over the full sample 1984–2003 we could find no evidence of cyclical influence (see Table 47.4).

However, when we tested the post-bubble period we found evidence that equity returns were influenced by cyclical factors. The highest explanatory power seen was 20% of one-year returns (Table 47.5). The predominance of negative coefficients (indicated here by negative *t*-stats) suggests that the variables we are using are serving as a proxy for mean reversion. That is to say, they suggest buying equities over bonds when growth is slumping. This fits

---

[3] For the record we did extend the sample period back to 1960 for some variables without altering the conclusions reported here.

Table 47.3 Predictive power of various cyclical indicators (1984–2003)

Return	Variable	Time Horizon	t-statistic	Adjusted R^2
Equity	Yield Curve	1 month	−0.64	0.00
	Yield Curve	3 month	−0.85	0.01
	Yield Curve	12 month	0.55	0.00
Excess return	Yield Curve	1 month	−1.03	0.00
	Yield Curve	3 month	−0.83	0.01
	Yield Curve	12 month	−0.79	0.01
Equity	MCI	1 month	1.07	0.00
	MCI	3 month	0.95	0.00
	MCI	12 month	−0.41	0.00
Excess return	MCI	1 month	0.48	0.00
	MCI	3 month	0.21	0.00
	MCI	12 month	0.28	0.00
Equity	Forecast earnings growth	1 month	−0.38	0.00
	Forecast earnings growth	3 month	−0.41	0.00
	Forecast earnings growth	12 month	−0.38	0.00
Excess return	Forecast earnings growth	1 month	−0.2	0.00
	Forecast earnings growth	3 month	−0.18	0.00
	Forecast earnings growth	12 month	−0.31	0.00
Equity	Forecast GDP growth	1 month	−1.19	0.00
	Forecast GDP growth	3 month	−1.01	0.00
	Forecast GDP growth	12 month	−1.3	0.03
Excess return	Forecast GDP growth	1 month	−1.06	0.00
	Forecast GDP growth	3 month	−0.7	0.00
	Forecast GDP growth	12 month	−0.88	0.01
Equity	Earnings momentum	1 month	−0.27	0.00
	Earnings momentum	3 month	−0.28	0.00
	Earnings momentum	12 month	−0.12	0.00
Excess return	Earnings momentum	1 month	−0.15	0.00
	Earnings momentum	3 month	−0.14	0.00
	Earnings momentum	12 month	−0.15	0.00
Equity	Lead Indicator	1 month	−0.01	0.00
	Lead Indicator	3 month	0.13	0.00
	Lead Indicator	12 month	−0.24	0.00
Excess return	Lead Indicator	1 month	1.5	0.00
	Lead Indicator	**3 month**	**1.7**	**0.02**
	Lead Indicator	12 month	0.15	0.00

Bold fonts indicate statistical significance.
Source: DrKW Macro research.

comfortably with our oft-stated view that it takes a crisis to trigger a policy response in Japan, hence you buy at the darkest hour.

I'm not suggesting that this is all you need to know in order to forecast the relative returns to equities versus bonds in Japan. Figure 47.1 shows the "forecasts" against the actual outturns. It can be clearly seen that the model fails dramatically to capture the full extent of the moves. However, bear in mind that we are just using a single variable (forecast GDP in this case) to forecast year ahead excess returns, and we have some success.

Perhaps when a market has been "bond driven", cyclical factors seem redundant. But in a trading range environment, where equities are no longer bond driven, then a stronger case exists for using the cycle to time equity returns.

Table 47.4   Predictive power of cyclical indicators for Japan (1984–2003)

Return	Variable	Time Horizon	*t*-statistic	Adjusted R^2
Equity	Industrial production	1 month	0.28	0.00
	Industrial production	3 month	0.44	0.00
	Industrial production	12 month	−0.33	0.00
Excess return	Industrial production	1 month	0.03	0.00
	Industrial production	3 month	0.18	0.00
	Industrial production	12 month	−0.59	0.00
Equity	Earnings momentum	1 month	0.11	0.00
	Earnings momentum	3 month	0.16	0.00
	Earnings momentum	12 month	−1.30	0.03
Excess return	Earnings momentum	1 month	0.30	0.00
	Earnings momentum	3 month	0.33	0.00
	Earnings momentum	12 Month	−0.77	0.01

Source: DrKW Macro research.

In order to test this hypothesis we looked at the US market between 1964 and 1982, the 'dismal years' where the market effectively went sideways for 17 years. Of course, we are limited by the availability of data but we have the ISM and the slope of the yield curve. We could find no evidence that the ISM was of any value in predicting returns during the dismal years (Table 47.6). However, the slope of the yield curve (as a proxy for market expectations of growth and inflation) was significant, with the potential to explain some 15% of the variation in one-year equity returns.

Table 47.5   Predictive power of cyclical indicators for post bubble Japan (1991–2003)

Return	Variable	Time Horizon	*t*-statistic	Adjusted R^2
Equity	Industrial production	1 month	−0.33	0.00
	Industrial production	3 month	−0.06	0.00
	Industrial production	12 month	**1.7**	**0.08**
Excess return	Industrial production	1 month	−0.54	0.00
	Industrial production	3 month	−0.31	0.00
	Industrial production	**12 month**	**−2.0**	**0.10**
Equity	Earnings momentum	1 month	−0.36	0.00
	Earnings momentum	3 month	−0.38	0.00
	Earnings momentum	**12 month**	**−1.85**	**0.06**
Excess return	Earnings momentum	1 month	−0.34	0.00
	Earnings momentum	3 month	−0.36	0.00
	Earnings momentum	**12 month**	**−1.80**	**0.05**
Equity	Forecast GDP	**1 month**	**−1.8**	**0.01**
	Forecast GDP	**3 month**	**−1.9**	**0.04**
	Forecast GDP	**12 month**	**−2.1**	**0.14**
Excess return	Forecast GDP	**1 month**	**−2.0**	**0.02**
	Forecast GDP	**3 month**	**−2.1**	**0.05**
	Forecast GDP	**12 month**	**−2.7**	**0.21**

Source: DrKW Macro research.

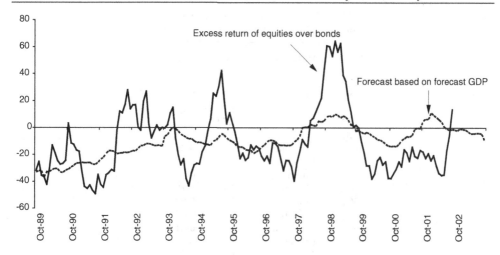

Figure 47.1   Japanese equity versus bond returns, forecast GDP based forecast.
Source: DrKW Macro research.

So, looking at the asset level data we can conclude that macro factors aren't as important as many would have us believe. There isn't an automatic case for favouring equities over bonds on the basis of the economic cycle alone. However, in a trading range environment there is some evidence to suggest that the cycle becomes more important.

For any economists who have made it this far through the chapter without relegating it to the rubbish bin, here is your reward. While cyclical analysis may not be very helpful from an asset class return point of view, it is still of major importance from a "within the equity market" perspective.

Stating the blindingly obvious: that is to say, *cyclical forces are vitally important to an analysis of sector rotation strategies.* As a test of this hypothesis we looked at the relative performance of US basic industries (as a proxy for cyclicals) against US utilities (as a proxy for defensives). As before we lag the variables of interest so that we can only use information that is available at the time we make the forecast.

Table 47.7 and Figure 47.2 show the importance of cyclical factors in our stylized sector rotation. The number of statistically significant relationships dwarfs those found at the asset class level. In particular, the ISM and the MCI stand out as having high power (bearing in mind we are using 12-month trailing data and single factor equations) to predict the relative

Table 47.6   Predictive power during the Dismal Years (USA, 1964–1981)

Variable	t-statistic	Adjusted R^2
ISM	−0.79	0.08
Yield curve	−3.01	0.15

Source: DrKW Macro research.

Table 47.7 Predictive power of cyclical indicators for US sector rotation (1984–2003)

Variable	Time horizon	t-statistic	Adjusted R^2
ISM	1 month	−1.1	0.00
ISM	3 month	0.79	0.00
ISM	12 month	**−4.1**	**0.22**
FGDP	1 month	**−1.79**	**0.02**
FGDP	3 month	0.82	0.00
FGDP	12 month	**−1.97**	**0.05**
EM	1 month	**−1.6**	**0.01**
EM	3 month	1.7	0.01
EM	12 month	**−2.4**	**0.10**
MCI	1 month	**2.5**	**0.02**
MCI	3 month	−0.46	0.00
MCI	12 month	**4.3**	**0.21**
LID	1 month	−0.06	0.00
LID	3 month	1.35	0.00
LID	**12 month**	**−2.22**	**0.06**

Bold fonts indicate statistical significance.
Source: DrKW Macro research.

returns to this cyclical trade. Both the MCI and the ISM can explain over 20% of the variation of relative returns. This is no mean feat.

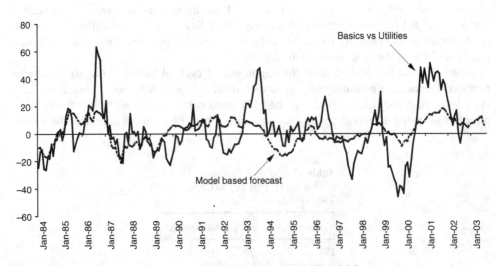

Figure 47.2   US basic industries vs utilities one-year returns and model forecasts.
Source: DrKW Macro research.

48

Have We Really Learned So Little?[*]

Many investors say they are using earnings optimism to time the market. However, it has now turned down, yet investors are still long equities. This is a case of cognitive dissonance. To combat this, Graham and Dodd argued that 16 times average earnings was as high a price as can be paid for an investment. The S&P 500 is on 31 times !

- When Graham and Dodd wrote *Security Analysis* in 1934, they talked of the folly shown in the late 1920s for investing on the basis of the "earnings trend, i.e. . . . the changes in earnings expected in the future". They continued, "Instead of judging the market price by established standards of value, the new era based its standards of value upon market price." Sounds a lot like momentum investing, doesn't it?
- Despite Graham and Dodd's advice, many fully invested participants have told us they are using earnings optimism to time their exit from the market. However, this "trend-of-earnings" measure has already turned down. Yet, investors are still long equities. This seems to be a classic example of *cognitive dissonance*.
- Cognitive dissonance is the discomfort caused by an inconsistency between a person's belief, attitudes and/or actions. This discomfort induces shifts in beliefs to remove the dissonance. We suspect that investors have been suffering dissonance with earnings optimism turning down, while remaining long equities. Hence, investors have been forced to adopt the Fed-driven global reflation trade as an excuse to justify long positions. The chances are that these shifts in cognition have happened without investors even realizing!
- Rather than being blown around by the economic cycle, or the mental gymnastics of dissonant minds, Graham and Dodd suggested using a 10-year moving average of earnings. They then argue "16× average earnings is as high a price as can be in an investment purchase of a common stock". Roughly speaking that would mean an S&P 500 of 600!

[*]This article appeared in *Global Equity Strategy* on 24 February 2004. The material discussed was accurate at the time of publication.

Contrary to popular belief I don't just read books from the 1930s. I recently finished *Eats, Shoots and Leaves*, a highly readable and entertaining guide to punctuation. A book, my proofreaders will attest, I sorely needed to read! However, having finished that, I needed a fix of classic investing advice. Having exploited Keynes's sagely works of late, I turned to Graham and Dodd's *Security Analysis*, the original 1934 edition, for a change.

As so often is the case, their tome provided both inspiration and depression. Inspiration because of the clarity and soundness of their advice; depression because I was once again reminded that virtually everything worth saying has been said before, and frequently said in a much more eloquent fashion than I could ever manage.

> Why did the investing public turn its attention from dividends, from asset values, and from earnings, to transfer it almost exclusively to the earnings trend, i.e., to the changes in earnings expected in the future? The answer was, first, that the records of the past were proving an undependable guide to investment; and secondly, that the rewards offered by the future had become irresistibly alluring... A continuous increase in profits proved that the company was on the upgrade and promised still better results in the future than had been accomplished to date... These statements sound innocent and plausible. Yet they concealed two theoretical weaknesses which could and did result in untold mischief. The first of these defects was that they abolished the fundamental distinctions between investment and speculation. The second was that they ignored the *price* of a stock in determining whether it was a desirable purchase... The notion that the desirability of a common stock was entirely independent of its price seems incredibly absurd... Instead of judging the market price by established standards of value, the new era based its standards of value upon market price...Since the trend-of-earnings theory was at bottom only a pretext to excuse rank speculation under the guise of 'investment', the profit-mad public was quite willing to accept the flimsiest evidence of the existence of a favourable trend. Rising earnings for a period of five, or four, or even three years only, were regarded as an assurance of uninterrupted future growth and a warrant for projecting the curve of profits indefinitely upward.
>
> (Graham and Dodd (1934), Part IV Ch. XXVII)

Graham and Dodd are effectively pointing out the folly of using a rebound in earnings as a justification for buying equities. Yet this same folly is seen by many as a "perfectly acceptable" approach to investment. Figure 48.1 shows the earnings recovery on which so many investors seem to have built their current portfolio positions.

The other thing this figure reveals is that the relationship between "operating" earnings and "as-reported" earnings is now back to normal levels. That is to say, firms are back to the "normal state" of affairs of announcing $1.10 of operating earnings, for every $1 of as-reported earnings. Of course, this fails to explain why it is that investors accept this ridiculous state of affairs, where one-off costs are anything but one-off – recurring year after year after year.

On many occasions recently, we have remarked on the faith being placed in earnings optimism as a key to timing markets. When we were marketing in the second half of last year, seemingly countless investors informed us that earnings optimism (the ratio of upgrades to estimate changes) was key to their enthusiasm for equities. This, of course, is just another reflection of investing on the basis of the trend-of-earnings. However, even those with faith in the power of earnings optimism are now faced with the cold hard reality that this has now topped out. (See Figure 48.2)

Despite this clear evidence that earnings optimism is turning down, investors are staying in equities. This strikes us as a classic case of *cognitive dissonance*. Cognitive dissonance is the psychological discomfort caused by an inconsistency between a person's belief, attitudes and/or actions.

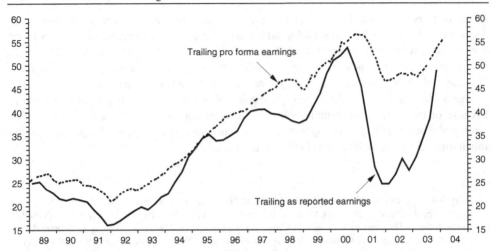

Figure 48.1   GAAP vs Pro Forma 12-month trailing earnings ($/share).
Source: DrKW Macro research.

The discomfort felt induces a "drive" state – a need to avoid or reduce dissonance by changing beliefs, attitudes or behaviours to enable them to be perceived as consistent. The prime example of dissonance is car purchase. Before buying a car, purchasers are generally open-minded and seek all information about various automobiles. However, post-purchase, people only look for good reports about the car they have bought, and cease to look objectively for information.

It seems to us that investors holding equities and using earnings optimism as the rationale would be experiencing acute cognitive dissonance at present. In order to reduce the dissonance, investors have been forced to adopt the Fed-driven global reflation trade as an excuse to justify

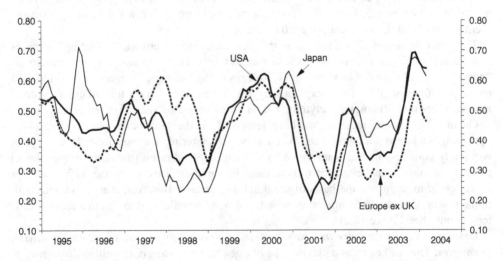

Figure 48.2   Earnings optimism topping out (upgrades/no. of estimate changes, sa 3 mma).
Source: DrKW Macro research.

Table 48.1 Average change in rank

Pair	Amnesics	Controls
Selected	+1.13	+0.86
Rejected	−1.20	−1.12
Spread (selected–rejected)	+2.33	+1.98

Source: Lieberman *et al.* (2001).

long positions in equities (see *Global Equity Strategy*, 19 January 2004, and 9 February 2004 for more on this trade).

Intriguingly, investors may not even be consciously aware of the shift in their thinking! We have previously explored the fact that the brain seems to play home to two distinct forms of thinking, one conscious (the C-system) and one unconscious (the X-system). (see *Global Equity Strategy*, 20 October 2003). Lieberman *et al.* (2001) have uncovered evidence that dissonance reduction seems to be a function of the X-system.

In the Lieberman *et al.* study, individuals ranked 15 small-sized art prints and were then asked to choose whether they would prefer full-sized copies of the prints they ranked 4th and 10th or the pair they ranked 6th and 12th. In either case, the decision involves rejecting one picture that was liked (4 or 6) and accepting one that was disliked (10 or 12). Then at the end of the experiment, participants were asked to re-rank the 15 prints based on their current feelings.

Normally, this exercise results in the chosen pairing of prints appearing higher in the rankings, and the rejected pair appearing lower in the rankings than they did on the first occasion. By exaggerating the differences between the two groups the choice made becomes more consonant/harmonious.

Amnesics can't form new conscious (or technically speaking, explicit) memories. So once the choice between 4/10 and 6/12 has been made, and they are distracted, they should have no recall on the choice. Hence on the re-ranking they should show no noticeable difference in the positioning of the prints.

Table 48.1 shows the average change in rank between the first ordering and the second. The controls show the usual pattern of dissonance reduction (i.e. increasing the rank of the chosen pair, and reducing the rank of the rejected pair). The amnesics (clinically defined) showed the exact same pattern! Remember, amnesics can't lay down new (explicit) memories. Hence, their dissonance reduction must be a function of unconscious (implicit) memory, part of the X-system. Hence we may well not be aware of when we are in dissonance-reducing mode.

Table 48.2 The maximum level of the S&P 500 consistent with 'investment' purchase

Years	Average earnings	16 times
5	37.70	603
7	38.72	620
10	36.90	590

Source: DrKW Macro research.

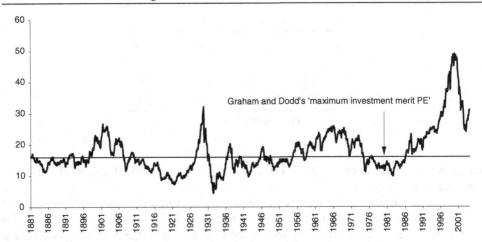

Figure 48.3   S&P 500 Graham and Dodd PE (×).
Source: DrKW Macro research.

Using the C-system to overcome cognitive dissonance is hard, especially when we don't even know we are suffering from it. However, as Graham and Dodd noted, 'The notion that the desirability of a common stock was entirely independent of its price seems incredibly absurd.' Rather than being blown around by the vagaries of the economic cycle, or the mental gymnastics of dissonant minds, Graham and Dodd suggested looking at average earnings, 'which should cover a period of not less than five years, and preferably 7 to 10 years'.

Graham and Dodd opine, "We would suggest that *about sixteen times average earnings* is as high a price as can be paid in an *investment* purchase of a common stock." Table 48.2 shows the level of the S&P 500 consistent with the Graham and Dodd definition of an investment purchase. Hardly comforting reading! The S&P 500 is trading on 31-fold 10-year moving average earnings – almost double the maximum investment purchase price that Graham and Dodd thought was reasonable (Figure 48.3).

49

Some Random Musings on Alternative Assets*

Alternative assets seem to have attracted much attention if the number of conference invites in my mailbox is anything to go by. However, investors need to think
carefully about the nature of the expected returns and risks embedded within such
investments. For instance, commodity futures returns may be more like 6% p.a.
going forward rather than the 12% they have generated historically!

- I am far from an expert on matters concerning alternative assets. However, several ideas
  have been fermenting in my brain for some time now. They are not necessarily complete
  and probably not correct, but I will leave it to brighter people than I to highlight my errors.
- Two types of so-called alternative assets have attracted a lot of attention. Firstly, **hedge
  funds**. My views on hedge funds being a bubble have been documented before. However,
  recently I've been struck by the way in which hedge fund returns seem to move together. I
  ran a quick correlation analysis, and found that the median correlation between hedge fund
  strategies (excluding the dedicated shorts) had exploded from 10% in the mid 1990s to 65%
  today! The highest on record.
- How can funds that purport to invest in as diverse markets as emerging market debt, equity
  long/short and global macro enjoy such high correlations? The only plausible answer is that
  all the various funds are doing exactly the same thing – either riding beta/momentum or
  selling volatility. This doesn't bode well for an exit from their positions, nor does it make
  sense for pension funds to pay such high fees if strategies such as selling volatility are the
  true drivers of hedge fund performance.
- The other alternative asset of popular appeal is **commodities**. Now, I struggle with commodities as an investment because they have no value anchor. Unlike a bond or an equity
  there is no cash flow associated with a commodity, making its valuation opaque.
- When investors talk of commodities they are usually discussing commodity futures. However, the choice of benchmarks makes an enormous difference to likely returns and diversification benefits. For instance, the widely used GSCI is 76% energy, while the CRB index
  is 18% energy!
- A commodity index future has three components to its return: the spot return, the roll return,
  and the collateral return.
- The spot return is obviously a gamble on what someone is willing to pay for the underlying
  asset.

---

*This article appeared in *Global Equity Strategy* on 29 November 2005. The material discussed was accurate at the time of
publication.

- The roll return is only positive if the commodity is in backwardation. As more and more investors enter the market, they are forcing contango to occur, which means that roll returns are likely to be negative.
- The collateral return is simply the yield on the cash saved from holding a future rather than a psychical. If inflation stays under control then interest rates are likely to be lower than they have been historically. Thus the collateral return will be lower than it has been in the past. *The total return could easily be half its historical level.*

This chapter covers some thoughts on hedge funds and commodities that have been fermenting in my excuse for a brain. Neither of the issues covered here is fully developed. However, in the interest of adding to the discussion I thought I would throw these half-baked ideas into the mêlée and let someone who knows far more than I do tell me what an idiot I am.

HEDGE FUNDS

Let's start with hedge funds. I have expressed my views on hedge funds as a bubble in *Global Equity Strategy*, 11 August 2004. One of my criticisms of hedge funds was that they were all doing the same thing. I decided to run a simple correlation to see just how similar the strategies across funds actually were. The results surprised even me.

As Figure 49.1 shows, the median correlation between hedge fund strategies is 0.56. Given the fact that a large number of hedge funds seem to be beta plays, I decided to exclude the dedicated short funds since they obviously should have a negative correlation to anyone betting on rising markets. Under these conditions the median correlation rises to 0.65!

This simply strikes me as absurdly high. How on earth can funds that purport to invest in as diverse markets as emerging market debt, equity long/short and global macro enjoy such high correlations?

The only plausible answer is that all the various funds are doing exactly the same thing! They are either riding beta/momentum or selling volatility. Every time the equity market goes down or volatility goes up, all hedge fund styles seem to lose money.

This provides evidence of an overcrowded trade. It also serves to suggest that fund of hedge funds are likely to be not only a massive cost trap, but also fail to deliver any kind of diversification benefits.

Figure 49.1   The median correlation between hedge fund strategies.
Source: DrKW Macro research.

COMMODITIES

The other idea that I have been mulling over for some time concerns commodities. Pension funds seem to be keen to buy into this asset class as a strategic investment, and I can't help wondering if they are simply extrapolating past returns into the future.

My biggest issue with commodities is that they have no fundamental cash flow attached to them, which makes valuation (almost?) impossible. A bond obviously has a cash flow associated with it, an equity should have a cash flow attached to it (although some investors forgot this during the bubble years), but a commodity has no stream of income. It is simply a price, the interaction of supply and demand, and as such it is only worth what someone is willing to pay for it.

In terms of this spot rate price, the forces of supply and demand are presumably generally industrial (i.e. non-speculative). However, many, many moons ago when I was studying economics, commodities were always used as a prime example of a cobweb model with unstable dynamics. Supply is generally inelastic in the short term, so prices are determined by demand in the short term. However, suppliers often determine future supply on the basis of the past price. So when prices have been historically high, the suppliers produce more the following year, and end up deluging the market, destroying the price structure they were so keen to exploit. However, this new lower price stimulates demand, but supply is cut back the year after, so prices soar. This pattern continues *ad infinitum*, the tracing out of the demand and supply interactions give rise to the name of the model.

Of course, this is a highly simplified view of the world. There are analysts who make a living analysing the interactions of supply and demand for each of the various commodities. And they will be able to offer a far more insightful analysis than my Microeconomics 101.

From a strategic viewpoint, what should we expect from commodity prices? Presumably, over the long term the marginal demand for a commodity will tend towards global economic growth. So perhaps we should expect price increases in line with economic activity as a long-run benchmark.

However, as noted above, physical commodities are usually the realm of the suppliers. It seems to me that most of the time when investors are talking about investing in commodities they are really talking about investing in commodity futures.

WHICH INDEX?

This opens up a whole can of worms. For instance, which benchmark do you use? Table 49.1 shows the vast differences between the indices. The widely used GSCI is 76% energy, while the CRB is just 18% energy. So the choice of index is quite an important strategic decision.

The returns you gain are going to be intimately related to the benchmark you choose. Erb and Harvey (2005) show that the GSCI managed to generate an excess return of 4.5% p.a. between December 1982 and May 2004. However an equally weighted index using the same commodities as those contained in the GSCI (with a buy and hold strategy) returns only 0.7% p.a.

Table 49.2 shows the wide range of returns and standard deviations that can be seen over a common time period across the three commodity indices discussed in this chapter. The GSCI has a much higher volatility than either of the other two indices. In risk-adjusted terms the CRB index is the best performer in our sample (although this is purely a function of the sample period).

Table 49.1   The composition of various commodity indices (weights %)

	GSCI	DJ-AIG	CRB
Energy	76	33	18
Industrial Metals	7	18	12
Precious Metals	2	8	16
Agriculture	10	18	18
Livestock	5	11	12
Softs	0	12	24

Source: DrKW Macro research.

Table 49.2   Risk and return across commodity indices (%, 1991–2005)

	Return	Risk
DJ-AIG	4.1	4.4
GSCI	5.7	6.3
CRB	3.1	2.9

Source: DrKW Macro research.

COMPOSITION OF COMMODITY FUTURES RETURNS

Let's leave the debate about indices, having noted that it is quite fundamental to your likely returns. Now let's turn to thinking about future returns. Commodity index futures have three components: the spot return, the roll return and the collateral return.

We have discussed the spot return above; it is simply the price of the commodity. The roll return is derived from rolling forward existing futures contracts. If the futures contract is negatively sloped, reflecting the fact that commodity producers are willing to accept a lower future returns to remove price uncertainty, and the price has not changed by the time the contract expires, the investor gains the difference between the actual price and futures price.

Of course, it only holds if the futures curve is negatively sloped (i.e. backwardation). If the curve is positively sloped (i.e. contango) then the contract is rolled forward at a loss to investors (Figure 49.2). This often gets overlooked, but will be discussed later.

The third component of the commodity index futures return is the collateral return. Since futures take up less cash than a position in physicals, the surplus cash can be invested into a cash instrument with an obvious yield return.

THE TIMES THEY ARE A-CHANGIN'

For the sake of argument we have taken the GSCI as this seems to be a popular index (albeit one that seems to be largely a bet on energy). Figure 49.3 shows the return breakdown over various time periods. Two patterns leap out immediately. Firstly, the enormous contribution that the spot return has made towards the total return in the last 5 years. This reflects the explosion in energy prices, of course. Over the longer run (i.e. since 1970), spot prices have contributed around 31% of the total return.

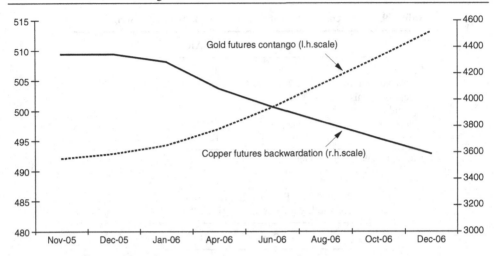

Figure 49.2 Examples of backwardation and contango markets (as of 25/11/05).
Source: DrKW Macro research.

Secondly, the roll return seems to be negative over the last two time ranges studied. That is to say, contango has become more common than backwardation. This could well reflect the increasing role of non-commercial investors in the market.

If commodity futures markets are increasingly dominated by speculators, then the insurance premium arguments that generate backwardation are likely to be eroded and even reversed. So, in a world where speculators are increasingly important it may not be wise to assume that the term 'structure of commodities' will always remain the same.

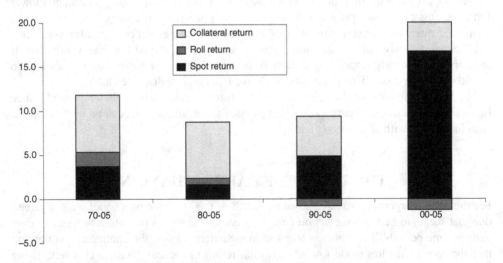

Figure 49.3 The breakdown of the GSCI into component elements.
Source: DrKW Macro research.

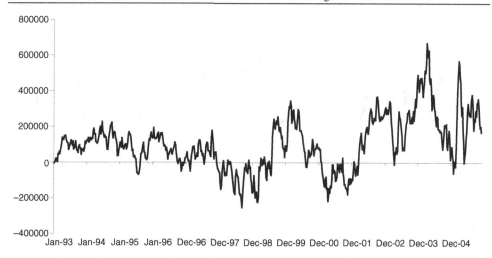

Figure 49.4   Net speculators positions.
Source: DrKW Macro research.

Figure 49.4 shows the overall net position across all the commodities in the CRB index, and represents how enthusiastically or otherwise speculators (i.e. non-commercial) view the outlook for commodities.

However, of more importance in the current context is Figure 49.5. This shows the percentage of the futures market that is accounted for by the speculators. It is calculated by summing the absolute value of their longs and shorts relative to the absolute number of contracts in the market. As even a cursory glance at the figure reveals, speculators have become increasing important in the market. In the early 1990s speculators accounted for around 25% of the total commodity futures market. However, over the last 15 years or so, this has doubled and

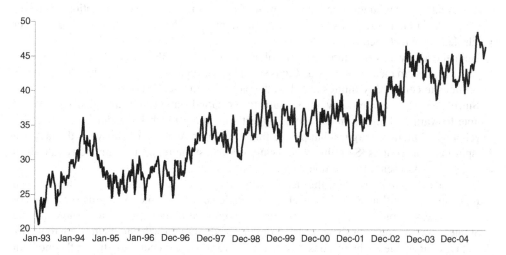

Figure 49.5   Percentage of the commodity futures market accounted for by speculators.
Source: DrKW Macro research.

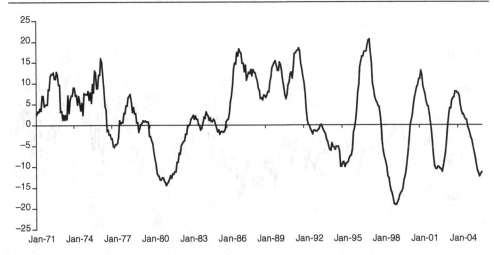

Figure 49.6   The GSCI roll return over time (% p.a).
Source: DrKW Macro research.

now stands at nearly 50%. So almost half the entire commodity futures market is a reflection of those without any commercial interest in the underlying good! No wonder that contango occurrences have become more frequent, and hence the roll return has become negative (Figure 49.6). Indeed, the negative roll return seems to be coincident with the rise in speculators' share of the market as per the above hypothesis.

However, the single biggest contribution over the long run has been the collateral return. It has accounted for 55% of the total return since 1970. Figure 49.7 shows the YoY collateral return for the GSCI. It is likely to be highly familiar to those with a worrying familiarity with economic series – it is the yield on the 3-month US T-bill, just as it should be.

However, the dominance of this component to commodity returns should perhaps give investors pause for thought. Interest rates have been on a trend decline as inflation has fallen since 1980. If inflation remains under control, then interest rates may well be capped at lower levels than have historically been the case.

Both the likely lower future rate of collateral return and the possibility of continuing negative roll return mean that pension funds should think very carefully about making strategic allocations to commodity futures based on the past performance of commodities.

Since 1970 the geometric average return to the GSCI has been 11.8% p.a. However, a simple forward-looking estimate would suggest something much lower for the future. The psychological literature argues that people find it easier to make forecasts when the task can be split into subsections. So rather than trying to forecast the return to commodity futures in one step, it makes sense to examine the three components.

The spot rate going forward is the element I find hardest to envisage. I am not a fundamental 'supply and demand' analyst. However, such people should be able to give us some idea of the likely pressure on spot prices. For the sake of argument I am just going to assume that the spot rate grows in line with some measure of real trend GDP growth and, being generous, say 3.5%. Of course, one of the reasons that investors are so keen on commodities at the moment is that they are implicitly replacing global growth with Chinese growth. Is this evidence of another simple story driving investor behaviour?

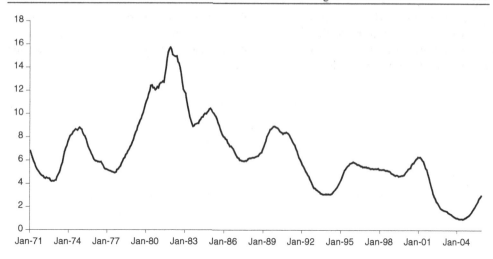

Figure 49.7   The GSCI collateral returns (% p.a.).
Source: DrKW Macro research.

If speculators continue to drive commodity futures markets into contango situations, then there is no reason to assume anything other than negative roll. However, to err on the side of generosity again, let's assume a zero roll return.

This leaves us with the collateral return. Since this is only an illustrative exercise I am going to steer well clear of the discussion that has raged over the neutral rate of interest. However, one of the most common estimates I have heard bandied about is 4.5%, so for the sake of argument I will use that.

Summing over the three components gives an expected return of 8% p.a. over the long run. Remember, this is our best case scenario. Using more cautious assumptions the expected return could easily drop to 6% p.a. Even our higher figure is noticeably below the historic average, and well below the rate seen in the last 5 years or so.

CONCLUSIONS

While pension funds seem to be enamoured of alternative assets, they may be failing to see the risks embodied in such areas. Personally I am not sure that hedge funds are an asset class, I prefer to see them as an investment vehicle. But more importantly, the average correlation between hedge fund strategies has been rising strongly. They all seem to be doing the same thing. This doesn't bode well for an exit to their positions, nor does it make sense for pension funds to pay such high fees if strategies such as selling volatility are the true drivers of hedge fund performance.

In terms of commodities, the challenges facing would-be investors are manifold. The most obvious issue is how to judge value, and, given the general advice to buy low and sell high, the absence of any value benchmark should give pause for thought. The choice of index seems to be all important. However, even ignoring this, investors chasing recent years' returns are likely to be severely disappointed. The components of commodity future's returns are likely to be far lower than those seen in the past. Investors should think carefully before jumping into the latest craze! But that has rarely stopped anyone.

SECTION VII

Corporate Governance and Ethics

Abu Ghraib: Lesson from Behavioural Finance and for Corporate Governance*

Bad apples or bad barrels? It is tempting to believe that bad behaviour is the result of a few rotten individuals. However, the overwhelming psychological evidence suggests that if you put good people into bad situations they usually turn bad. Corporate malfeasance and the events in Iraqi prisons are examined and the lessons explored.

- We all tend to assume that our own actions are the results of a careful analysis of the situation in which we find ourselves. However, we also assume that everybody else's actions are the result of their inherent attitudes. This is called the fundamental attribution error. It means that we shouldn't be so quick to judge others, since we can't be sure that we would act differently if we found ourselves in their situation.
- Back in 1971, Zimbardo (a psychology professor) put willing mentally and physically sound volunteers into a mock prison environment. People were randomly assigned to be guards or prisoners. Despite this random allocation of roles, the guards abused the prisoners, and the prisoners became zombie-like. The experiment was halted after just 6 days.
- Milgram (another psychology professor) was horrified to find that over 60% of people were willing to subject others to a potentially lethal electric shock merely at the instruction of a man in a white coat with a clipboard. Such is our obedience to authority.
- Both experiments are classic evidence for the importance of understanding context on predicting behaviour. The factors that lead to increased risk of turning bad are explored in this chapter.
- From a corporate governance point of view, the importance of situational factors should lead us to be on our guard for situations and incentives that could give rise to bad behaviour. If found guilty, the men now standing trial for misbehaviour during the bubble years are unlikely to be the last corporate wrong-doers. Investors should note that academic work has shown that good governance does pay.

---

*This article appeared in *Global Equity Strategy* on 31 January 2005. The material discussed was accurate at the time of publication.

This week will see the start of three trials in the USA all related to corporate malfeasance during the bubble years. Bernie Ebbers, formerly of WorldCom fame, goes on trial in New York. Dennis Kozlowski, formerly head of Tyco, will also enter the dock for his second trial, the first having ended with a hung jury. Down in Alabama, Richard Scrushy, former head honcho of HealthSouth, will also be appearing before the courts.

Also in court in the USA are some more of the soldiers accused of abusing prisoners in the Abu Ghraib prison. Our own press here in the UK are full of stories of prisoner abuse by UK soldiers.

What could connect these events? The answer is that human nature lies at the root of both sets of problems. In order to understand what drives this behaviour we need to outline two diametrically opposed views – the situational and dispositional perspectives. Those who subscribe to the situational viewpoint argue that if you put good people in bad places, they tend to become bad. That is, it is the situation that determines behaviour. Those who follow the dispositional school believe that people's actions reflect their attitudes, or that it is people's nature that determines their behaviour.

FUNDAMENTAL ATTRIBUTION ERROR

We all tend to believe that our own actions are the considered reflective outcome of our analysis of the situation. At the same time we believe that the actions of others are reflections of their underlying disposition. We see ourselves from a situational viewpoint, and others from a dispositional perspective. Psychologists call this the fundamental attribution error (also known as actor/observer bias).

Nisbett *et al.* (1973) were the first to observe this schism in beliefs. Nisbett and his co-authors asked male students to write four paragraphs on why they had liked the girl they had dated most regularly in the past year or so, and why they had chosen their particular major at university. They were then asked to repeat the process, but pretend to be their best friend (i.e. see the situation through their best friend's eyes). Finally, they were asked to repeat the process, but pretending to see themselves through their best friend's eyes.

The sentences they had written were then scored on the basis of the number of times situational remarks were made (i.e. she's a relaxing person – a comment about external factors) and the number of times dispositional remarks were recorded (i.e. I need someone I can relax with – a comment about internal factors or one's self).

Subjects gave more than twice as many situational reasons compared to dispositional reasons when talking about their girlfriends. Subjects gave four times as many dispositional reasons for their friend's choice of college course than situational reasons. When pretending to be their best friend commenting upon themselves, subjects duplicated the results for when they were commenting upon their best friend's choices.

Ross *et al.* (1977) offer an alternative example. They asked people to participate in a quiz game. The subjects were divided into three groups, questioners, contestants and observers. Questioners had to compose 10 difficult questions to ask the contestants. The contestants, of course, had to try to answer them. The final group watched the interaction.

The subjects were asked to rate the general knowledge of the questioners and the contestants. The results are shown in Figure 50.1. The contestants' ratings are consistent with the fundamental attribution error – that is to say, they rated the questioners as having higher levels of general knowledge than they themselves had. The observer's scores were even more pronounced in favour of the questioners. Behaviour was essentially ascribed to dispositional

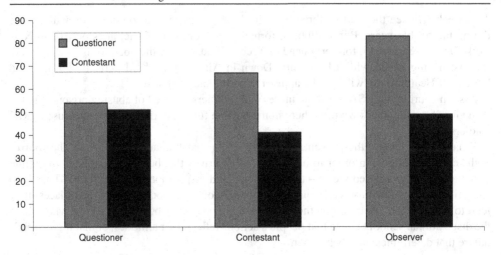

Figure 50.1   Rating by subject group.
Source: Ross *et al*. (1977).

qualities, rather than the subject's role in the study. That is, the participants who asked the questions were seen as having very good general knowledge, while those who answered them were seen as having limited general knowledge – their actions and behaviour were attributed to their underlying nature (dispositional view) – whereas in fact they reflected the random role assignment at the start of the experiment (situational factor).

The fundamental attribution error leads us to believe that the various heads of US corporates who are now on trial are essentially bad people. In a similar fashion, it is tempting to believe that the actions of the prison guards at Abu Ghraib are just the limited actions of a few 'bad apples'.

However, two classic experiments in social psychology argue strongly for a more situational perspective. That is, we shouldn't be so quick to judge the accused as bad or evil people. We simply cannot be sure that we wouldn't act in a similar fashion if placed in a similar circumstance.

ZIMBARDO'S PRISON EXPERIMENT

The events in Abu Ghraib and other prisons were actually sadly predictable (of course, all the more so with hindsight). In 1971, Philip Zimbardo (1973) designed an experiment[1] that has eerie parallels with events of late.

Zimbardo and his colleagues literally built a prison under the psychology department of Stanford University. The experimenters selected 22 subjects to participate in the prison environment. The 22 were selected from an initial pool of 75. The chosen 22 were judged to be the most stable, both mentally and physically, the most mature, and the least involved in antisocial behaviour. They were, to all intents and purposes, the most 'normal' of the potential candidates. The resulting group predominantly consisted of middle-class Caucasians. They were unknown to each other. All participants were paid $15 per day.

On a *random* basis, half the subjects were assigned to the role of guards, and half to the role of prisoners. The 'prisoners' were to remain in the prison for 24 hours a day for the duration

---
[1] See www.prisonexp.org for a slide show and further details on this experiment

of the experiment. The 'guards' worked on three-man, 8-hour shifts, going about their usual lives at other times.

The 'guards' were briefed on the day before the arrival of the 'prisoners'. Their instruction was simple: "maintain a reasonable degree of order within the prison necessary for its effective functioning". The specifics of how this was to be achieved were left to the discretion of the guards. An explicit prohibition against the use of physical punishment or aggression was given. The guards wore khaki shirts and trousers, carried a whistle and a nightstick, and were told to wear reflecting sunglasses.

The prisoners had a somewhat rougher time. The police 'arrested' each of the prisoners at their residences. They were charged with either armed robbery or burglary, read their rights and handcuffed, and taken to the police station. At the station, each was fingerprinted and photographed just like any other suspect. They were then blindfolded and taken to the mock prison.

On arrival, the prisoners were stripped, sprayed with a delousing liquid, left to stand naked alone for some time, then put into their new prison uniform. These consisted of a loose fitting smock, with an id number on the front and back. Underwear was not allowed, a light lock and chain was placed on the ankle.

The prisoners were to be served three bland meals per day, were allowed three supervised toilet visits, and given 2 hours of reading or letter writing per day. Work assignments were issued. Two visiting periods per week were scheduled. Three times a day the prisoners assembled for a roll call, during which they were tested on their id numbers and the rules of the prison.

At first such roll calls lasted only around 10 minutes. However, as the days progressed, these calls extended until some lasted several hours! Many of the pre-set features of the routine were modified or ignored by the guards, and many of the privileges (such as reading) were forgotten as time went on.

The results of this experiment were dramatic to say the least. Zimbardo *et al.* note that:

> guards and prisoners showed a marked tendency toward increased negativity of affect . . . prisoners expressed intentions to do harm to others more frequently . . . encounters became negative, hostile, and dehumanizing. Prisoners immediately adopted a generally passive response mode, while guards assumed a very active initiative role in all interactions.

The prisoners became zombie-like in obedience, even trying to side with the guards against each other. The guards became sadists who seemed to enjoy dominating and humiliating the prisoners.

Zimbardo (2005) recently noted disturbingly similar outcomes of his prison experiment and events in Abu Ghraib. The similarities even extend to the sorts of humiliation inflicted by the guards on the prisoners! Zimbardo notes that in his 'prison' the guards forced the prisoners to engage in mock sodomy, a feature repeated in Abu Ghraib.

The most dramatic evidence of the impact was seen in the extreme reactions of five prisoners. They had to be released because of extreme emotional depression, crying, rage and acute anxiety. The experiment was terminated after just 6 days!

As you read this, the chances are that you are sitting saying to yourself, I would behave differently. After all, there was nothing to stop the guards and prisoners interacting in a pleasant fashion. They were simply put into an environment, the rules of which were largely flexible and endogenously determined. But remember, these were ordinary young men, fit, healthy and generally well adjusted. Also remember, the fundamental attribution error outlined at the start of this chapter. Zimbardo's work seems to offer massive support for a situational view of the world.

MILGRAM: THE MAN THAT SHOCKED THE WORLD[2]

The second classic experiment from social psychology that is relevant here is the work of Stanley Milgram (1974). Intriguingly, Milgram was a classmate of Zimbardo. Milgram's work was triggered in the wake of World War II. He wanted to investigate why so many ordinary people either simply said nothing about their leaders' clearly abhorrent policies or, even worse, chose to follow their example.

Milgram devised a simple but stunningly effective experiment in which subjects were asked to participate. They were told they would be administering electric shocks to a 'learner' at the instruction of a 'teacher'. The subjects were told that they were involved in a study on punishment effects on learning and memory.

The subjects sat in front of a box with electric switches on it. The switches displayed the level of volts that was being delivered, and a text description of the level of pain ranging from 'slight' through to 'very strong' and up to 'danger severe', culminating in 'XXX'. When the buttons were depressed, a buzzing sound could be heard. The 'teacher' was a confederate of the experimenters, and wore a white coat and carried a clipboard. They would instruct the subjects when to press the button.

In the classic variant of the experiment, the subject couldn't see the person they were shocking, but they could hear him. At 75 volts, the 'learner' grunts, at 120 volts he starts to complain verbally, at 150 volts he demands to be released, at 285 volts the 'learner' makes a response that Milgram said could only be described as 'an agonized scream'.

Before conducting the experiment, Milgram's prior belief was that very few people would administer high levels of shock. Indeed 40 psychiatrists canvassed by Milgram thought that less than 1% would give the full 450-volt shock. After all, they reasoned, Americans just didn't engage in such behaviour. (Sounds like a classic case of the fundamental attribution error doesn't it!)

Figure 50.2 shows the percentage of respondents who progressed to each level of voltage: 100% of ordinary Americans were willing to send up to 135 volts (at which point the 'learner' is asking to be released) through someone they didn't know; 80% were willing to go up to 285 volts (at which point they are hearing agonizing screams); over 62% were willing to administer the full 450 volts, despite the screams and the labels on the machine stating 'severe danger' and 'XXX'!

Nor are Milgram's results unique. Table 50.1 shows the average compliance level to the maximum voltage from a number of studies. Incidentally, university ethics boards outlawed Milgram-style experiments in the late 1980s, so no more modern studies are available, although we have little reason to believe that they would show anything different from the majority of findings below.

Milgram tested many variations of his experiment. However, few seemed to have major impacts upon the level of obedience to authority. For instance, Figure 50.3 shows the effects of enabling the subject to now see (as well as hear) the 'learner', and when the subject had to force the 'learners' hand onto a metal plate to administer the shock. In the former condition, 40% of subjects still went to 450 volts. In the latter, 30% still went to the maximum level of shock!

Once again these were ordinary people, people like you and me; yet simply because a figure in authority instructed them to do so they became willing to make another person suffer. Another clear win for the situational perspective.

---

[2] This title is stolen from Thomas Blass's excellent biography of Stanley Milgram.

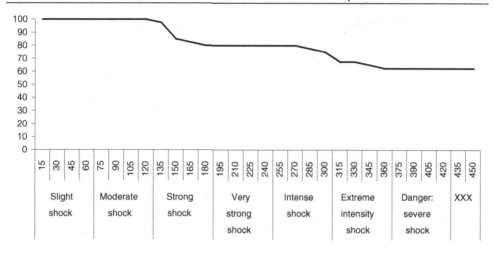

Figure 50.2 Percentage of participants reaching each level of voltage.
Source: Milgram (1974).

The Milgram experiment has some very clear implications for finance. Firstly, given people's tendency to obey, *a culture of corporate integrity must come from the very top down*. Simply stated, if the head of an organization orders an employee to do something, the evidence here suggests that the person will generally comply.

From a situational viewpoint the man at the top may not be intrinsically bad, but if put in the 'correct' environment may turn out that way. I have regularly berated the use of stock options to pay management. In our view, it tends to cause the holders of such options to be extremely myopic and take on excessive risk since they enjoy an asymmetric payoff due to the nature of zero downside inherent within options. However, once such devices are in place, the situational prediction is that management will behave in a manner consistent with the incentive. Often, share options are enough to turn otherwise good people bad.

Another application of Milgram's results is that we should train analysts to be critical of company management. The more god-like the management, the easier it will be for them to

Table 50.1 International 'Milgram' studies

Study	Country	Percentage obedient to the highest level of shock
Milgram	USA	62.5
Rosenham	USA	85
Ancona and Pareyson	Italy	85
Mantell	Germany	85
Kilham and Mann	Australia	40
Burley and McGuiness	UK	50
Shanab and Yahya	Jordan	62
Miranda *et al.*	Spain	90
Schurz	Austria	80
Meeus and Raaijmakers	Holland	92

Source: Smith and Bond (1994).

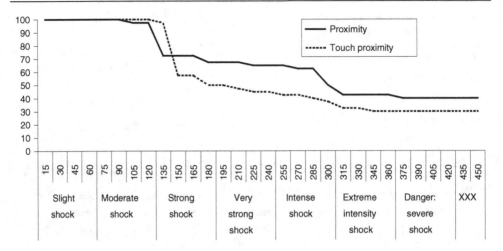

Figure 50.3   Percentage of participants reaching each level of voltage – proximity variants. *Source*: Milgram (1974).

influence analysts who cover the stock. CEOs are generally successful people. They have made it. As such we tend to interpret their success as the result of their disposition (the fundamental attribution error). We are in awe of such individuals. Few, if any, analysts were willing to ask questions of Bernie Ebbers at the height of the TMT boom, when he and his ilk were regarded as the new masters of the universe (see Malmendier and Tate, 2004).[3]

Dissent is key. We must learn to question those in authority. In the past, my managers have often reminded me that investment banking is not a democracy. Indeed it is not, but if we lose the will to dissent, the results can be disastrous (at least that is my defence for being a cantankerous pain to manage!).

The only thing Milgram found that consistently resulted in rapid dropoffs in compliance within his experiment was dissent. For instance, Milgram ran one variant of his experiment with one psychologist and three helpers (two of whom were confederates of the experimenters, and one genuine subject). One of the helpers asks the question, another says whether the answer is correct, the third (the real subject) throws the switch to administer the shock.

At 150 volts one of the helpers (one of the confederates) walks out of the experiment. At 210 volts, the other helper (confederate) also walks out. The psychologist goes on alone with the true subject. Figure 50.4 shows the percentage of compliance at various voltages.

Once the first helper leaves, the number of compliant subjects drops from 90% to around 35%. Following the second helper walking out, the compliance rate drops steadily, although 10% still go on to administer the maximum voltage.

The single best method of generating dissent among the subjects was to have conflicting authorities. In this version, two psychologists were present and one subject. At 150 volts, one of the psychologists began a prepared argument with the other over whether the experiment should be stopped. As Figure 50.5 shows, this argument resulted in the complete cessation of shocking.

---

[3] Intriguingly, Malmendier and Tate (2004) *Superstar CEOs*, show that award winning CEOs extract more compensation from their companies following awards. They spend more time writing books and lecturing and gaining board seats. Most importantly, firms with Superstar CEOs have stocks that underperform the market on a 1-, 3- and 5-year horizon!

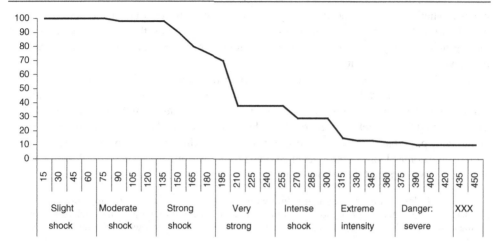

Figure 50.4 Percentage of participants reaching each level of voltage – dissenting peers.
Source: Milgram (1974).

Morck (2004) has used the Milgram experiments to argue that truly independent directors are our best hope of good governance. Too many boards are populated by cronies of the management. The Higgs report finds that almost half of the so-called independent directors on UK boards are recruited by the CEO through personal contacts or friendships! Morck argues that dissenting boards may help to "induce greater rationality and more considered ethics in corporate governance".

New support for good governance comes from a recent study by Bebchuk *et al.* (2004). They construct an entrenchment index, which attempts to measure the limits of shareholders to impose their will onto management. There are six inputs into their score – whether the company has a staggered board, whether it has limits to shareholders' amendments of the

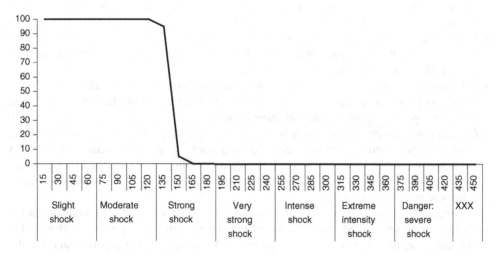

Figure 50.5 Percentage of participants reaching each level of voltage – dissenting authority.
Source: Milgram (1974).

bylaws, whether a supermajority is required for merger and charter amendments, whether poison pill and golden parachutes are used. Firms are ranked on the basis of the number of these provisions they have with 0 being a low entrenchment firm, and 6 being firms with very high levels of entrenchment.

Bebchuk *et al.* find that an equal weighted long/short portfolio which is long those stocks with a 0 score and short those stocks with a 6 score generates a 7.2% annual compound abnormal return (after correcting for market, size, style and momentum) in the sample 1990–2003. They also find that the return rises to 9.6% when value-weighted portfolios are used! So good governance pays, but it is much more than just a box-ticking exercise. Indeed, an email interview with Thomas Donaldson, a legal studies professor from Wharton, arrived in my inbox. The interview contained the following passage:

> We have followed a mythology that if you write an elaborate code of ethics, appoint people to distribute it, and get everybody to sign off on a fat rule book every year, this will somehow prevent major disasters. We have abundant evidence now that it simply doesn't work this way.

CONDITIONS THAT TURN GOOD PEOPLE BAD

In order to understand the factors that lead good people to behave in a bad way, we can turn to the work of Albert Bandura (1999), who has spent many years studying the factors that lead to moral disengagement. His major findings can be summarized as follows:

- *Moral justification* – Behaviour is reconstructed so that it is no longer deemed to be immoral. The clearest examples of such behaviour are wars in which the enemy is seen as a ruthless oppressor, and thus those fighting the war are morally justified.
- *Euphemistic labelling* – Language is very important as it shapes and frames our thoughts. Harmful conduct can be made seemingly respectable if it is given the right name: for instance, the euphemism of 'resettlement' for the mass murder; 'voluntary refugee camps' for concentration camps; and 'collateral damage' for civilians killed during military actions.
- *Advantageous comparison* – How behaviour is viewed is coloured by what it is compared against. Setting up off-balance sheet entities to hide transactions may seem perfectly reasonable when compared to the evils of murder.
- *Displacement of responsibility* – This is the key finding from Milgram's work. People seem able to suspend moral judgement if a 'legitimate' authority accepts responsibility for their actions. The 'I was only following orders' defence.
- *Diffusion of responsibility* – Moral disengagement is easier in groups. Bandura *et al.* (1975) found that people acted far more cruelly under group responsibility than when they held themselves personally accountable for their actions.
- *Disregard or distortion of consequences* – It is easier to do the wrong thing when the consequences are ignored or minimized. The shareholder is quite an abstract concept from a manager's point of view, so the consequences of harming the shareholder may be easily minimized. In the same way, smart bombs and surgical strikes enable us to wage war from a distance never before known.
- *Dehumanization* – It is far easier to hurt or harm someone we view as non-human. In the Bandura *et al.* study cited above, in one of the experiments a group of subjects were led to believe that they were overhearing the research assistant tell the experimenter that the students from another college were ready to start the study in which the listeners would be administering electric shocks to these students from another college.

The exact phrasing they overheard was randomly selected from one of three possible choices. The visiting students were either described as 'nice', 'animal-like' or without any descriptive label.

The shock intensity varied massively with the description the students overheard. When the visitors were described as 'animals', the shock level rose linearly over 10 rounds. Those labelled 'nice' were given the least shock. So, just overhearing a single word proved to be enough to dehumanize in this study.

It is also worth noting the limits to self-control. The more we use self-control, the less self-control we have ready to use for the next occasion.

CONCLUSIONS

People have a bad habit of believing that others act according to their disposition, while simultaneously believing that we act according to our circumstances. It is tempting to believe that bad behaviour is the result of a few bad apples. However, the bulk of evidence argues that, in general, a situational perspective is much closer to the truth. That is to say, good people will go bad in the wrong situation. It isn't a particularly comforting view of humanity.

From a corporate governance point of view, the situational perspective tells us that we must always be on our guard for situations that could give rise to bad behaviour. The men now standing trial for misbehaviour during the bubble years are unlikely to be the last corporate wrong-doers.

51

Doing the Right Thing or the Psychology of Ethics*

We all believe we behave in an ethical fashion. Unfortunately the evidence suggests this is just another in the long list of positive illusions we lumber under. Our moral judgements are often not the result of reflective logical thinking, instead they are driven by unconscious emotions. Being aware of our own implicit biases is an important step along the road to learning to be mindful about ethics.

- We all tend to suffer from an ethical blindspot. We have a good idea about how others will act in moral situations, but we are hopelessly optimistic about our own behaviour. We tend to think we will behave much better than we actually do. We also think we will be uninfluenced by biases or conflicts of interest – the illusion of objectivity. Sadly, the reality of our behaviour is very different.
- Historically, moral judgement has been held to be the result of logic. Ethical dilemmas are meant to be resolved by a process of reflective logic. However, recent evidence suggests that more often than not our moral judgements are made on the spur of the moment by emotion. Moral reasoning is often a post hoc justification for the decision we made, rather than a balanced review of the relevant information before we reach a conclusion.
- Bazerman *et al.* have referred to our behaviour as bounded ethicality (as a parallel to the bounded rationality of judgement and decision-making). Just as bounded rationality consists of a well-defined group of common biases and errors in thinking, so bounded ethicality covers some generalized traits of unethical behaviour.
- Four key ethical biases have been identified. Firstly, we have a tendency towards implicit attitudes or unconscious prejudices. We tend to think of ourselves as free from biases such as racism or sexism. However, implicit attitude tests reveal that while we think we are unbiased, many of us actually display stereotypical thinking.
- Secondly, we tend to display in-group bias – a tendency to favour those who are like us. For instance Van Knippenberg *et al.* created a mock crime, giving jurors information about the crime and witness statements. When they were placed under high cognitive strain, they fell back on stereotypes. When told the suspect was a banker only 44% of jurors said he was guilty, when told the suspect was a drug addict 80% of jurors said he was guilty.
- Thirdly, we all tend to overclaim credit. If you ask spouses to estimate their contribution to household chores, the sum is almost certainly greater than 100%. Similar findings hold for most groups.

*This article appeared in *Global Equity Strategy* on 8 July 2005. The material discussed was accurate at the time of publication.

- Finally, we underestimate the impact that conflicts of interest will have upon us. Experiments reveal that we fail to correct for the degree of influence that conflicts will have on our decisions. For instance, professional auditors were 31% more likely to accept dubious accounting if they worked for the company rather than an outside investor! Becoming mindful of our proneness to ethical failure is perhaps the only way of dealing with insidious bias. Legislation and disclosure simply won't work.

Are you ethical? Without a doubt you will have answered 'yes'. Sadly, this is yet another example of our long list of positive illusions. Just as we tend to see ourselves as better drivers than everyone else, so we tend to believe we will act in a more ethical fashion than everyone else.

THE ETHICAL BLINDSPOT

Epley and Dunning (2000) show that we are quite reasonable at predicting how others will act in the moral domain, but hopelessly overoptimistic about just how 'good' we will be. For instance, a group of students were asked to complete a set of questions taking about 20 minutes or so. At the end they get paid $5. Some of the participants were asked if they would like to donate some of their pay to a charity. Others were asked a hypothetical question as to how much they would donate, and how much others (a group of peers) would be willing to donate.

Figure 51.1 shows the outcomes that Epley and Dunning uncovered. The average predicted self-donation was $2.44. The average predicted others donation was $1.83. The average actual donation was $1.53! *Predicted self-donations were far more out of kilter with reality than the predicted behaviour of others.*

A second example of our self-deception also comes from Epley and Dunning. This time participants (college age students) were asked to assign two tasks, one to themselves and one to their partner. The partner's identity was manipulated via a photo. The participants were either shown a photo of someone very like themselves (a standard college student) or a 10-year-old girl. The tasks were watching videos of varying lengths and then answering a few questions. One of the tasks would last approximately 5 or 6 minutes, the other would last around 30 minutes.

Figure 51.2 shows the percentage of time that participants would take the longer video, dependent upon whether they faced someone like themselves or a young girl. As before some of the participants predicted their own behaviour, all predicted the behaviour of others, and the experimenters observed actual behaviour.

When participants thought they were playing a young girl, they predicted that they would take the longer task nearly 80% of the time. They predicted that others would take the long

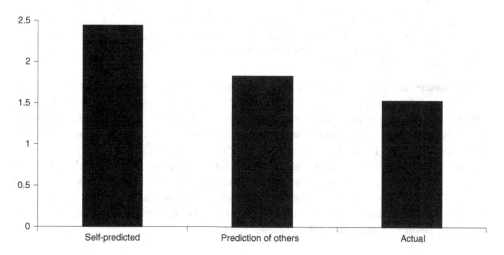

Figure 51.1   Dollar donations – actual and predicted.
Source: Epley and Dunning (2000).

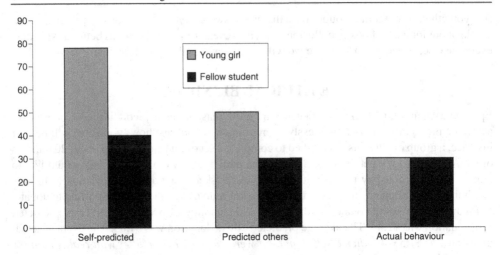

Figure 51.2 Percentage choosing long (moral) task.
Source: Epley and Dunning (2000).

task around 50% of the time. Actual behaviour once again revealed a very different picture: only 30% of the participants actually assigned themselves the longer task!

Once again this seems to confirm that we have a distinctly egocentric bias when it comes to ethical behaviour. *We generally have a good insight into the way others will act, but hold ridiculously overoptimistic views of our own tendency to do good.*

THE ORIGINS OF MORAL JUDGEMENTS

Now consider the following[1]:

> Julie and Mark are brother and sister. They are travelling together in France on summer vacation from college. One night they are staying alone in a cabin near the beach. They decide that it would be interesting and fun if they tried making love. At the very least it would be a new experience for each of them. Julie was already taking birth control pills, but Mark uses a condom too just to be safe. They both enjoy making love, but they decide not to do it again. They keep that night as a special secret, which makes them feel even closer to each other. What do you think about that? Was it OK for them to make love?

The chances are you have recoiled, shocked by the siblings wrong-doing, strenuously insisting that Julie and Mark are acting immorally. Now explain why you think this is the case.

People usually start with concerns over inbreeding. But the text clearly states that not one but two types of birth control were used. After several fumbled attempts most people end up with something like, "I don't know, I can't explain, it is just wrong".

Here we hit a snag. Moral judgement is often held to be the remit of rationalists (at least since the time of Kant, in 1780). According to the rationalists, moral judgements are reached via a reasoning process with scope for reflection. However, the question above exposes this to be a false belief. *More often than not our moral judgements are made on the spur of the moment by emotion, rather than reflected logic.*

---

[1] This example is taken from Haidt (2001).

As Haidt notes, "Moral reasoning is usually an ex post facto process" used to justify the decisions already taken by the emotional moral system. Or, as Haidt puts it, we are more akin to a lawyer building a case, rather than a judge seeking the truth.

Researchers in the field of decision-making long ago identified our tendency to engage in post hoc justification for actions. Nisbett and Wilson (1977) asked women to select from 12 pairs of stockings the pair that they liked most. Having selected a pair, the researchers then asked the women to explain their reasons for the choices. Colour, sheerness and denier featured among the selected reasons. Sadly, all the pairs of stockings were, in fact, identical. So the women were simply making up reasons for their judgements. The simple example above suggests that moral thought may involve a very similar process. Haidt refers to this post hoc reasoning as the illusion of objective reasoning.

Many of the biases of decision-making stem from an overreliance on intuitive thinking driven by the X-system (see *Global Equity Strategy*, 20 October 2003 for more on this). Readers will probably be familiar with the concept dual system theories of thought – that is a posh way of saying we have two different ways of thinking contained within our minds.

For the Trekkies, these two systems can, perhaps, be characterized as Dr McCoy and Mr Spock. McCoy was irrepressibly human, forever allowing his emotions to rule the day. In contrast, Spock (half human, half Vulcan) was determined to suppress his emotions, letting logic drive his decisions.

McCoy's approach would seem to be founded in system X. System X is essentially the emotional part of the brain. It is automatic and effortless in the way that it processes information. That is to say, the X-system prescreens information before we are consciously aware that it even made an impact on our minds. Hence, the X-system is effectively the default option. The X-system deals with information in an associative way. Its judgements tend to be based on similarity (of appearance) and closeness in time. Because of the way the X-system deals with information it can handle vast amounts of data simultaneously. To computer nerds it is a rapid parallel processing unit. In order for the X-system to believe something is valid, it may simply need to wish that it were so.

System C is the "Vulcan" part of the brain. To use it requires deliberate effort. It is logical and deductive in the way in which it handles information. Because it is logical, it can only follow one step at a time, and hence in computing terms it is a slow serial processing unit. In order to convince the C-system that something is true, logical argument and empirical evidence will be required. Table 51.1 provides a summary of the main differences between the two systems.

The X-system works as an unconscious system. We are not consciously aware of its actions or its processes. The automatic response to the brother/sister problem outlined earlier is classic trait on an X-system process. It codes things as good or bad, right or wrong and we are left trying to justify the X-system output.

Those working in the field of neuropsychology have provided support for the idea that moral judgements are an X-system process. For instance, the work of Moll *et al.* (2002) has shown that key emotional sites within the brain are activated when people are required to make a moral decision.

Greene *et al.* (2001) ask people the following:

A runaway trolley is headed for five people who will be killed if it proceeds on its present course. The only way to save them is to hit a switch that will turn the trolley onto an alternate set of tracks where it will kill one person instead of five. Is it permissible to switch tracks in order to save five people at the cost of one?

Table 51.1   Two systems of reasoning

System One/X-system/Reflexive/Intuitive	System Two/C-system/Reflective
Holistic	Analytic
Affective (what feels good)	Logical
Associative – judgements based on similarity and temporal contiguity	Deductive
Rapid parallel processing	Slow, serial processing
Concrete images	Abstract images
Slower to change	Changes with speed of thought
Crudely differentiated – broad generalization	More highly differentiated
Crudely integrated – context-specific processing	More highly integrated – cross context processing
Experienced passively and preconsciously	Experienced actively and consciously
Automatic and effortless	Controlled and effortful
Self-evidently valid: "Experiencing is believing" or perhaps wishing is believing	Requires justification via logic and evidence

Source: Modified from Epstein (1991).

Now consider the next question: Once again the trolley is heading for five people. You are standing next to a large stranger on a footbridge that spans the tracks, in between the oncoming trolley and the five people. The only way to save the people is to push the large stranger in front of the oncoming trolley. Is this permissible?

Most people answer 'yes' to the first question, but 'no' to the second question. Yet in theory these questions are almost identical, you end up killing one person in both cases, but saving five. However, the responses are very different.

Greene *et al.* monitor people's brain activity while they struggle over such questions. They find that in the second question a lot of the emotionally relevant areas of the brain light up like a Christmas tree. The act of pushing someone under a trolley seems to be emotionally more salient than hitting a switch.

The work of both Moll *et al.* and Greene *et al.* helps to demonstrate the role of emotion in moral debate. We frequently code moral problems/solutions as good/bad or right/wrong via how our gut feels rather than some mental reflective process.

Further support for the role of emotion in moral decisions comes from two very different sources. First, is the work of Antonio Damasio and colleagues (1994, 1995, 1999) who have spent a long time investigating people with damage to the areas of the brain that are integral to feeling emotion. These individuals still have higher order cognitive ability, but can no longer feel emotion.

The most famous of these studies concerns the strange story of Phineas Gage (Damasio *et al.*, 1994). Gage was a 25-year-old construction foreman working for a railroad company in New England in 1848. One of his many tasks was to push down the gunpowder into the blowhole. However, before this is done the hole must be filled with sand on top of the gunpowder. On this fateful day, Gage was distracted and failed to notice the hole had not been filled with sand. The disastrous consequence was that he ignited the powder, and three and a half foot rod that Gage was using was blown through his head.

Amazingly Gage survived this tragedy, but his personality was altered beyond belief. Prior to the accident he was a capable, efficient and industrious employee. Post the trauma Gage became a drifter, unable to maintain a job or his friends. He also showed a marked increase

Table 51.2   Key symptoms of psychopathy

Emotional/Intrapersonal	Social deviance
Glib and superficial	Impulsive
Egocentric and grandiose	Poor behavioural controls
Lack of remorse or guilt	Need for excitement
Lack of empathy	Lack of responsibility
Deceitful and manipulative	Early behavioural problems
Shallow emotions	Adult antisocial behaviour

Source: Hare (1999).

in antisocial (immoral) behaviour. Damasio *et al.* (1994) show that Gage suffered enormous damage to those parts of the brain that analyse emotion.

The final piece of evidence that we wish to present on the emotional basis of moral judgements comes from the work of Robert Hare (1999), who has spent his life working on the diagnosis of psychopaths. He generally finds that they can tell right from wrong (i.e. moral reasoning is intact), but they don't seem to have moral judgement (i.e. the emotional tagging of moral rights and wrongs fails).

Table 51.2 highlights the key symptoms of psychopathy. The lack of ability to understand and use emotions stands out as one of the key features. So the findings of Hare support the idea that moral judgements have their origins in the X-system.

Greene *et al.* (2004) show that many moral quandaries involve a battle between the X-system and the C-system. In the past, we have used the work of Gary Klein (1999) to show the conditions under which the X-system is likely to dominate our decision-making. Klein has identified that the X-system is more likely to dominate when:

• The problem is ill structured and complex
• Information is incomplete, ambiguous and changing
• Goals are ill defined, shifting or competing
• Stress is high
• Decisions involve multiple participants.

So if we are forced to make moral decisions when any, or all, of the above conditions apply, we are likely to make them without any C-system cognitive check. Think carefully about this, we are saying that *many moral decisions are made without our conscious awareness*. Bazerman, *et al.* (2005) refer to this as *bounded ethicality* (as a parallel to bounded rationality) – defined as good people engaging in unethical behaviour without their awareness, on a regular basis.

If bounded ethicality is to be as useful a concept as bounded rationality we need to identify a set of common traits, behaviours and biases much like overoptimism, overconfidence, and narrow framing.

EXAMPLES OF BOUNDED ETHICALITY AND UNCONSCIOUS BIASES

Implicit Attitudes (Unconscious Prejudices)

Implicit attitudes are biases towards groups of people of which we are not consciously aware. For example, most people reading this will likely consider themselves to be free of any bias over race. However, some may have an implicit attitude that favours whites over blacks, say. If you wish to test to see if you have an implicit attitudes visit https://implicit.harvard.edu/implicit/demo/selectatest.html. Here you will find a range of tests aimed at discovering whether or not you have any implicit biases on matters ranging from race and gender to sexuality and religion.

The implicit attitude tests (IAT) rely on using the speed of response time to represent the strength of unconscious association. For instance, if you take the IAT on race, you will be presented with pictures of either white of black faces and words such as good or bad. Each test has two subsections. In the first, you will be asked "compatible" pairs according to a stereotype, so good words and white faces, and bad words and black faces. In the second section the pairings are now stereotype "incompatible" so good words are now paired with black faces, and bad words with white faces. Implicit bias will show up as differential response time between the two versions.

In general, the creators of the tests have found that most white people respond more quickly in compatible pairing when black faces are paired with bad words, say, rather than good, demonstrating a stronger mental response to stereotype thinking. (Black people tend to have the reverse effect.)

Perhaps such findings help to explain the findings of Bertrand and Mullainathan (2004). In a superb experiment, Bertrand and Mullainathan submitted CVs to real employers who had advertised. They responded to more than 1300 employment ads and sent out close to 5000 resumés! Names were assigned to CVs on a random basis.

Figure 51.3 shows the call back rates received by the fictitious job applicants. Candidates with white-sounding names were 50% more likely to receive a callback than candidates with black-sounding names!

Bertrand and Mullainathan also find that the degree of discrimination increases with the quality of resumé. High-quality resumés sent by candidates with white-sounding names get nearly 30% more callbacks than low-quality resumé whites, but get a 60% higher callback rates than candidates with black-sounding names with high-quality resumés!

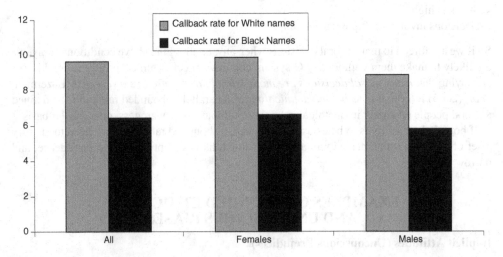

Figure 51.3   Callback rates (%).
Source: Bertrand and Mullainathan (2004).

Table 51.3 Judgements of guilt and proposed punishment

	Positive stereotype		Negative stereotype	
	Low load	High load	Low load	High load
% Responding guilty	62	44	21	80
Probability of guilt	57.1	50.4	44.6	64.4
Term of imprisonment (years)	1.89	2.3	1.83	3.12

Source: Van Knippenberg *et al.* (1999).

Evidence of the influence of time pressure on the reliance on X-system thinking can be found in a study by Van Knippenberg *et al.* (1999). Participants were asked to evaluate a criminal act and read a scenario concerned with the crime (in this case, burglary) including witness statements. They were told that the man accused either worked for a bank (positive stereotype) or was a hard drug addict (negative stereotype). Some of the group were subjected to a cognitive load (i.e. they were given only a very short time to absorb the information).

The results that Van Knippenberg *et al.* uncovered are shown in Table 51.3. The influence of stereotypes is clear. Under high load conditions people were much more likely to judge the drug addict guilty relative to the bank worker, and imprison him for significantly longer.

In-Group Bias (Bias that Favours Your Own Group)

A related issue is that while we may rely on negative stereotypes we also rely on positive ones (as the study above demonstrated). **We are likely to favour those who are like us.** So, when we are asked to do someone a favour, we are much more likely to agree if they are part of 'our circle'. Thus In-group bias is not a vote *against* those who are different from us, but rather a vote *for* those who are similar.

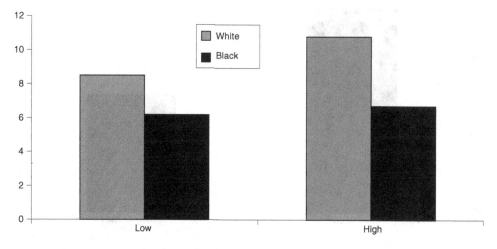

Figure 51.4 Callback rates by resumé quality (%).
Source: Bertrand and Mullainathan (2004).

When a positive stereotype is used by Van Knippenberg and the participants are under high load, they are much more likely to rely on that stereotype, so only 44% of participants thought that the banker was guilty under high load conditions.

At least being aware of implicit attitudes and in-group bias may help us to overcome their insidious nature. Awareness is no guarantee of being able to beat the biases but at least it is better than the illusion of objectivity that we all too frequently lumber under.

Overclaiming Credit (Bias that Favours You)

If you ask spouses what proportion of household chores they each do, their individual contributions will almost certainly sum to more than 100%. Caruso *et al.* (2005) have explored this tendency and ways of mitigating it.

In one experiment, Caruso *et al.* asked academic joint authors of papers to estimate their contribution to the paper. In one form they were asked, "Of the total work that your group did on the article, what percent of the work do you feel you personally contributed?". In the alternative presentation authors were asked, "For all authors of the paper, please take a few moments to think about the contributions that they made to the article. Go down the list of authors and consider the work that each person prepared and the contributions they made based on their area of expertise."

When asked to think about their own contributions the answers summed to an average of 140% (Figure 51.5). When asked to think explicitly about each of the authors' contributions, the degree of overclaiming dropped, but was still significant with a total sum of 123%!

A second study conducted by Caruso *et al.* concerned students working in study groups. This time the participants were split into three different formats. One group was asked to estimate their own contribution to the group's activities (self-focused), a second group was asked to think about everyone's contribution to the group but to report only their own (implicit others), and a third group was asked to actually estimate the percentage of work contributed by each member of the team (explicit others).

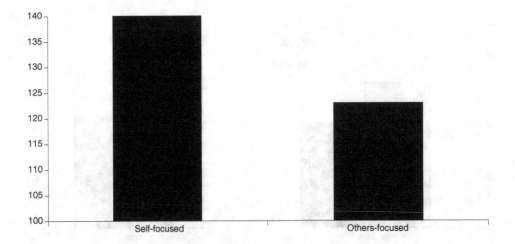

Figure 51.5   Academic co-authors overclaiming credit (%).
Source: Caruso *et al.* (2005).

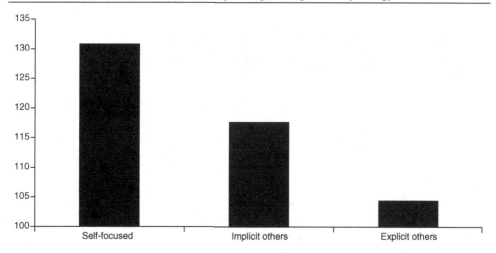

Figure 51.6 Student study groups overclaiming credit (%).
Source: Caruso *et al.* (2005).

When the self-focused groups were summed, the average was nearly 131% (Figure 51.6). Those in the implicit others format produced a less biased 118%. Those in the explicit others presentation reported a very impressive 104.4%.

So 'unpacking' can help to mitigate the tendency towards overclaiming credit. Unfortunately, Caruso *et al.* found that 'unpacking' also had a cost. They found that such 'unpacking' "reduces satisfaction and interest in future collaborations among those who contributed (or believed they contributed) more than other group members . . . Some members who look beyond their own perspective may not like what they see." Yet more evidence that we are happiest when deluded!

Conflicts of Interest (Bias that Favours Those Who Can Pay You)

Everyone is aware that conflicts of interest can lead to intentionally corrupt behaviour. But evidence from an increasingly large number of psychological experiments suggest that conflicts can easily skew our behaviour in ways we simply aren't conscious of.

Think about analysts' behaviour during the bubble years. At the peak of the bubble in 2000, some 98.4% of analyst recommendations were either strong buy, buy, or hold (see Figure 51.7). With the benefit of hindsight, we know now that many analysts were being driven by conflicts of interest spurred on by the fact that they were directly paid for by corporate finance.

However, even I, cynic that I am, don't believe that all the analysts were as deliberately two-faced as Henry Blodget. Many undoubtedly truly believed that the analysis they were undertaking was accurate, but they couldn't see that the clear conflict of interest they faced was blinding them to the implicit bias of their misguided views.

Our industry is riddled with conflicts of interest. For instance, some analysts are measured by the amount of revenue they generate in their sector. Hence, they have a strong bias towards trying to get investors to transact in their sector. Fund managers are often paid in relation to funds under management, rather than with relation to performance (for more on this see *Global Equity Strategy*, 7 June 2005). Corporate managers are loaded up with stock options

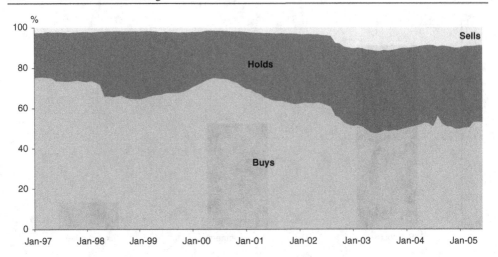

Figure 51.7   Distribution of US analysts' recommendations (%).
Source: DrKW Macro research.

and don't necessarily behave in a way that maximizes shareholder benefit, but rather in a way that maximizes option holders benefit.

Are we all corrupt? The honest answer is probably 'yes', but perhaps not deliberately so. Rather we fail to see that conflicts of interest will impact on our behaviour, it is the *illusion of objectivity raising its ugly head again*.

Moore *et al.* (2004) explore the issue of unconscious bias and auditors. They start their paper with a wonderful quotation:

> By certifying the public reports that collectively depict a corporation's financial status, the independent auditor assumes a public responsibility transcending any employment relationship with the client. The independent public accountant performing this special function owes ultimate allegiance to the corporation's creditors and stockholders, as well as to the investing public. This 'public watchdog' function demands that the accountant maintains total independence from the client at all times and requires complete fidelity to the public trust.
>
> Chief Justice Warren Burger (1984)

The behaviour of auditors has obviously been exposed as a million miles away from Burger's ideal. The provision of other services by auditors distorted their incentive pattern to such an extent that they 'forgot' their public watchdog role.

Moore *et al.* experimented with 139 professional auditors. Participants were given five different auditing cases to examine. They concerned a variety of controversial aspects of accounting: for instance, one covered the recognition of intangibles, one on revenue recognition, and one on capitalization vs expensing of expenditures. The auditors were told the cases were independent of each other. The auditors were randomly assigned to either work for the company or work for an outside investor considering investing in the company in question.

As Figure 51.8 shows, the auditors who were told they were working for the company were 31% more likely to accept the various dubious accounting moves than those who were told they worked for the outside investor!

The size of the discrepancy is all the more impressive given that Moore *et al.* were working with auditors in the post-Enron era. All the auditors concerned had all been hired away from Arthur Andersen!

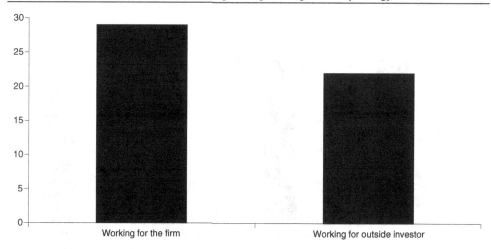

Figure 51.8 Percentage of auditors that allow various accounting measures.
Source: Moore *et al.* (2004).

In a second experiment, Moore *et al.* switched to using lay people for the study. This time all participants were assigned to one of four roles: sellers, buyers, buyer's auditor, or seller's auditor. All four participants were given exactly the same information concerning a company. After reading through the materials the two principals (seller and buyer) made public statements as to the value at which they would be willing to transact.

The auditors then viewed these reports and were asked if they endorsed their respective principal's views. They were also asked to state the highest purchase price they would agree for the buyer and the lowest sales price for the seller. Finally, they were asked to state their own private estimate of the true value, and to estimate the extent to which the private value estimate had been influenced by the role that had been played.

A panel of eight accounting and finance professors had estimated the value of the firm at $14mn. Figure 51.9 shows the average estimates given by each of the groups involved in the study. In general, the endowment effect (see *Global Equity Strategy*, 6 April 2005) was marked, with sellers asking nearly double the amount that the buyers wanted to pay. Intriguingly, the auditor's private estimates were vastly different dependent upon the role they played. Auditors working for the seller thought the company was worth 78% more than auditors working for the buyer!

When asked to what extent the role assigned had influenced their decisions, sellers' auditors said their price had only been on average $0.89mn higher than it would otherwise have been. However, their values averaged some $2.9mn above the experts valuation. Buyers' auditors reported their valuations were $1.3mn less than they would have otherwise been. In fact, their appraisals averaged $4.2mn below the experts' view! So although both sets of auditors were aware of the biasing influence of the roles they played, neither group understood just how powerful it was, and they were unable to correct for it (Figure 51.10).

Moore *et al.* also varied the incentives facing the auditors. Three possible pay options were available. Firstly, a fixed fee (auditors received a flat rate of $9); secondly, pay for performance (auditors received a base fee of $3 plus $0.50 per $1mn above $0 (for the seller) or below $30mn (for the buyer)); thirdly, a future business incentive (whereby the principal could choose to award the auditor anywhere between $0 and $10 after the transaction was completed).

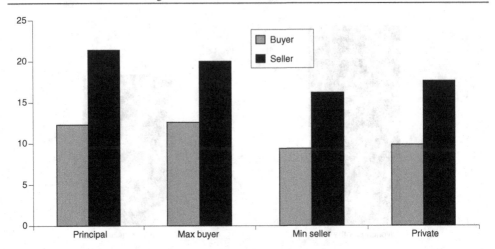

Figure 51.9 Prices for various roles (US$ mn).
Source: Moore *et al*. (2004).

Figure 51.11 shows auditors' pricing dependent upon the pay plan they were working under. Those working under the fixed payment condition had absolutely no financial incentive to offer valuations that supported the principals they were working for. Yet, despite this lack of incentive, there was still an enormous difference between those working for the buyer and those working for the seller. As Moore *et al*. note,

> It was accountability to the partisan, whose preferences were clear, that biased judgement. When they provided valuations that were biased in the directions of their principals' interests, they were acting as faithful agents of the buyer and the seller. When acting at the behest of someone else, people are more willing to engage in actions that they would otherwise find ethically problematic.

See *Global Equity Strategy*, 31 January 2005, for more on this.

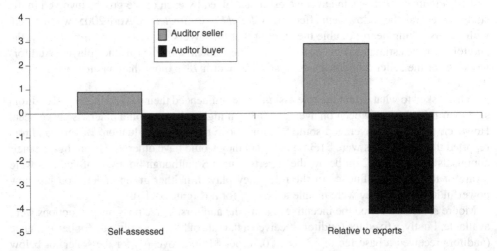

Figure 51.10 Auditors bias ($ mn).
Source: Moore *et al*. (2004).

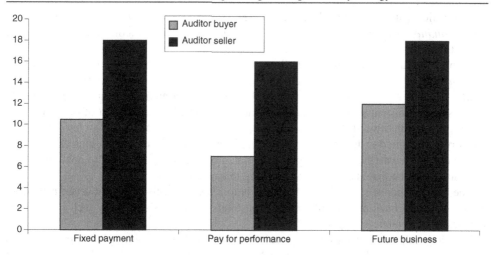

Figure 51.11   Auditors prices based around payment plan.
Source: Moore *et al.* (2004).

The final experiment conducted by Moore *et al.* was designed to see just how strong the accountability relationship actually was. In this experiment all auditors received a fixed payment of $9. This time, the degree of contact between the auditors and the principals was manipulated into three conditions. In the anonymous condition the principals and the auditors had no direct contact. In the impersonal condition, auditors and principals sat next to each other, but the interaction was limited to the exchange of paper. In the personal condition, auditors and principals spent a few minutes getting to know each other before they started work.

Figure 51.12 shows the auditors' private estimates of value under the three conditions. Intriguingly, there was relatively little difference between the auditors' views when there was

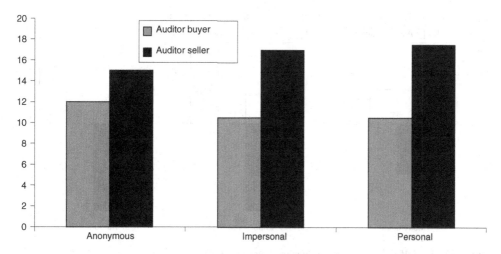

Figure 51.12   Auditors private valuations based around interaction.
Source: Moore *et al.* (2004).

no interaction with the principal. *However, even minimal interaction between the principals and the auditors increases the amount of bias shown.* Now think about the interaction between analysts and companies!

Moore *et al.* also found that *the auditors who thought of themselves as least biased in the personal condition, actually displayed the highest degree of bias!* (See Figure 51.13). Moore *et al.* conclude, "When they felt accountable to a partisan audience, participants came to conclusions consistent with the interests of their audience." In the context of our industry it is little wonder that we still have so few sell recommendations or indeed so few bears. Our industry is structured to do well when equity markets rise, and the dream-pushing cheerleaders that make up the vast ranks of analysts and strategists are only too happy to continue to tell their audience that that is exactly what is going to happen.

The usual response to conflicts of interest is to reach for legislation. However, if the root cause of such behaviour is mental and unconscious, then legislation may well prove to be hopelessly inadequate as a cure.

You can't help but notice for the new rules of research that disclaimers have got longer and larger. However, as is all too often the case, 'solutions' and 'policies' are implemented without reference to people's behaviour. This has always struck me as madness, how could policy be set without thinking about how people might respond. In order to understand response we need to understand how people think. Cain *et al.* (2005) explore the perverse effects that disclosing conflicts of interest can actually have.

They designed a clever experiment in which participants were either assigned to estimators or advisers. Six jars full of coins were shown to the participants. The advisers were allowed to examine the jars closely, and were given a range by the experimenters within which the true content value would fall. The estimators could only see the jar from a distance and for only a very short time, but did get the reports from the advisers, and were told that the advisers had better information.

The advisers were either given an incentive in line with the estimators, or given a payoff that encouraged them to give far too high an estimate. Estimators were paid on the basis of the

Figure 51.13 Self-reported vs actual bias by condition (US$ mn).
Source: Moore *et al.* (2004).

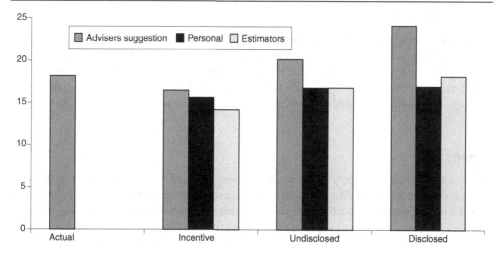

Figure 51.14   Value of coins in the jar ($).
Source: Cain *et al.* (2005).

accuracy of their forecasts. They were told when the adviser had the same incentives as they had, but weren't always told that when the advisers were paid to get them to generate a high estimate, the advisers knew if their pay scheme had been disclosed.

Figure 51.14 shows the average actual value of the coins contained in jar, the advisers' suggestion dependent upon the degree of disclosure, the advisers' personal estimate, and the estimators' guesses.

Have a look at the advisers' suggestion when they knew that the estimators knew they were giving biased advice. It was much more biased! In fact, when the bias was disclosed the advisers gave a suggestion that was 47% above the one given when incentives were aligned, and 20% higher than when the bias was undisclosed! It was also 42% above the level the advisers truly believed to be correct.

Estimators also fell into a classic anchoring situation (see *Global Equity Strategy*, 27 August 2004). They failed to discount the advisers' suggestion anywhere near enough. Despite being told the advisers were being paid more the higher they guessed, the estimators gave a forecast that was 27% higher than they did when incentives were matched.

MECHANISMS DRIVING POOR ETHICAL BEHAVIOUR

We have previously explored the list of factors and mechanisms that turn good people bad (see *Global Equity Strategy*, 31 January 2005). However, lapses in ethics often seem to revolve around our ability to believe we are acting in an honest and fair way while actually behaving totally differently. Tenbrunsel and Messick (2004) suggest that self-deception 'causes the moral implications of a decision to fade, allowing individuals to behave incomprehensibly and, at the same time, not realize that they are doing so'. They introduce the concept of ethical fading and define it as a process by which "moral colors of an ethical decision fade into bleached hues that are void of moral implications".

They argue that there are four enablers of self-deception that allow unethical behaviour to flourish:

Language euphemisms

We relabel things we find ethically challenging, until they no longer trouble us. Language is important because it frames and shapes our thoughts. Harmful conduct can be made seemingly respectable if it is given the right name. So we now refer to 'collateral damage' for civilians killed during military actions; 'friendly fire' to being shot by our own side; and 'pro forma' earnings for the made-up numbers that companies would like us to think they achieved.

Slippery slope

We also tend to use a slippery slope when it comes to moral wrong-doing. Rarely does behaviour undergo seismic shifts; instead it is much easier to present small changes in behaviour one at a time. Consider an accountant who is presented with a company he has been auditing, and they suddenly ask him to approve some seriously questionable accounting changes. Because of the sudden change of behaviour, the accountant is likely to refuse to sign off on these accounts.

Now consider what might well happen if the accountant agrees to stretch one element of the report. He says 'yes', because the company and he have a long-standing relationship and he generally trusts them. Next quarter the company again asks for a little more leeway in accounting. The accountant finds it hard to say 'no', because he has already agreed to something similar in the previous quarter. The slippery slope of moral decision-making is hard to get off once you are on it.

Errors in perceptual causation

Tenbrunsel and Messick note that 'Causation is complex and humans are self-interested and fallible. The end result: misconstrued judgements about moral responsibility.' This harks about to our tendency to interpret others actions as representative of their dispositions rather than their situations. We tend to assume that if a person behaves badly it is because he is intrinsically bad, rather than a good person caught in a bad situation.

Tenbrunsel and Messick cite a good example in which the presence of a monitoring system designed to decrease undesirable behaviour actually managed to produce an increase. The tempting conclusion is that the employers need to spend more on the monitoring system, as it is clear that the employees can't be trusted. However, this will spark off an arms race.

Another habit that falls into this category concerns acts of omission. These are misperceptions caused by failing to disclose the truth, rather than acts of omission where you have to deliberately lie. The failure to act is often easier to justify to others and oneself. For instance, if you are selling a car and you know it has a dodgy starter motor, do you tell the person you are about to sell it to. . . probably not, instead you fall back on caveat emptor. By shifting the onus onto the buyer, the moral responsibility of the seller seems to fade.

As Tenbrunsel and Messick write

Errors in perceptual causation allow us to distance ourselves from the ethical issues at hand. We erroneously believe that we cannot fix the problem, because it is a people, and not a system issue. We also falsely believe that it is someone else's problem, either because they are to blame or because the responsibility is someone else's, not ours.

Constraints Induced by Representations of the Self

The final point they examine is the simple but often overlooked insight that we always see the world from our own perspective. We can't help but see the world through our own eyes; we will never see ourselves in the way that others see us. Our views of the world are biased, a function of who we are, constructed by our brains. We simply can't be objective, it is a logical impossibility. Any belief that we are objective is itself a form of self-delusion. Our inability to have a truly objective view of the world means that we can't properly estimate the impact our behaviour has on others, yet this perfect unbounded objectivity is the basis of many ethical theories.

COMBATING UNETHICAL BEHAVIOUR

Formal training in ethics is unlikely to be highly effective in reducing unethical bias if, as we propose here, it is driven largely by unconscious processes. We need to learn to beat self-deception. This means that we need to learn to question ourselves, and that involves becoming mindful of the motivations that drive our actions, the way in which we leap to moral conclusions, and the ex-post justifications we create.

It might seem counter-intuitive to say we need to be mindful. After all, much of this chapter has been dedicated to trying to persuade you that many of the problems of unethical behaviour stem from unconscious systems. However, just as a car can be pulled back on track if it drifts by a mindful driver, so we can stop our unethical behaviour by being vigilant.

For instance, try wearing a veil of ignorance. Let's assume that you are considering increasing the amount of holiday available for directors of the firm. Before you make your decision, just imagine that you don't know whether you are a director or not, and that you won't find out until you've made the decision. What decision would you now make? Would you be willing to risk being in the disadvantaged group by your own decision? Of course, applying a veil of ignorance is likely to be an imperfect process but it might at least give you cause to question some decisions.

Take IAT to check to see if you have an implicit bias. Forewarned is forearmed, and the next time you face a moral dilemma, stop, pause and reflect on the role of the unconscious in your decision-making.

52
Unintended Consequences and Choking under Pressure: The Psychology of Incentives*

Economists and consultants would have us believe that incentives are the answer to almost everything. However, psychologists have documented that incentives can actually have perverse effects. Sometimes they fail because they don't lead to increased motivation; other times they fail because we get distracted by the incentive or its consequences and forget to focus on the task in hand.

- Incentives abound. Whenever a problem arises, you can count on a well-meaning economist to suggest that an incentive is required: CEOs aren't doing what shareholders want, then give them options; fund managers need to be paid with reference to funds under management, etc. Few things seem to be as commonly accepted as the power of incentives.
- However, a recent body of work has been putting this collective wisdom to the test. The findings don't make pleasant reading for those with a faith in incentives. Incentives don't always work and appear to fail for one of two reasons.
- Firstly, they may fail to increase motivation. For instance, if you send people out collecting for charity, studies show that they collect more if they *don't* get paid, rather than if they get a share of the donations.
- Secondly, incentives may fail because the increase in motivation doesn't lead to an increase in performance. That is to say, people choke under pressure. Choking appears to occur for one of two reasons. If the task involves a well-honed automatic skill like putting a golf ball, then it appears that large incentives trigger the logical part of the mind to get involved, and interfere with the natural flow.
- If the task requires logic and attention, then large incentives seem to soak up exactly the same spare mental capacity that we use to solve the problem in the first place. So instead of focusing on the task in hand, people end up thinking about the situation and the consequences.
- Ironically, it appears that those who are best placed to solve difficult logical problems in normal circumstances are exactly the ones who are most likely to choke under pressure. They have high 'working memory' capacity, but unfortunately the pressure/incentives steal this capacity, rendering them no better off than those with low 'working memory' capacity.

---

*This article appeared in *Global Equity Strategy* on 4 July 2006. The material discussed was accurate at the time of publication.

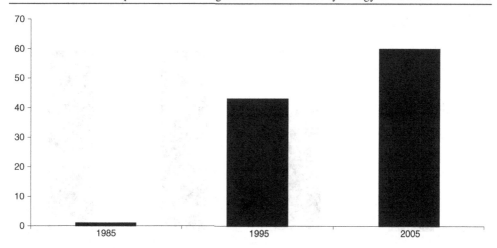

Figure 52.1   Percentage of CEO pay that is stock-related.
Source: DrKW Macro research.

Economists tend to blithely assume that people respond to incentives. The dominance of this view (and indeed of economics more generally) has permeated policy almost to the exclusion of all the other social sciences. For instance, it was economists who argued that options were a good way of paying CEOs.

I've been openly critical of this theory for a long time. Although options may now be taking a back seat in management pay, stock-related compensation has been an increasingly important element of executive remuneration. In 1985, just 1% of the total compensation of US CEOs was related to the stock market. A decade later, this had risen to 43%. By 2005, 60% of total pay was market related!

As the well-known saying goes, when you *assume* you make an *ass* out of *u* and *me*. As an empirical sceptic[1] I thought I would examine the behavioural literature on incentives and see what has been uncovered. The study of incentives is a young area of behavioural economics, probably because economists have been so adamant that they must be right in this context.

If performance contingent incentives are to work, a two-step process is required. Firstly, the incentive must lead to greater motivation and effort, and, secondly, this increased motivation and effort must improve performance.

Breaking down the incentive process into these two stages makes it clear that an incentive might fail at one or both of these junctions. For instance, incentives could fail to lead to results because they reduce the intrinsic motivation of a person but fail to provide a sufficient offset in terms of explicit motivation. This is a failure of the first stage of an incentive.

Gneezy and Rustichini (2000a) ran two experiments that illustrate this kind of failure. In the first, Israeli students were asked to take an IQ-style test. The candidates were split into four groups. Each member got a 60 NIS payment for taking part. However, the four groups faced very different incentives. The first group got no incentive; the second group was promised an additional 10 cents for each correct answer: the third group was promised 1 NIS per correct answer; and the fourth group was promised 3 NIS per correct response.

---

[1] One who needs proof before displaying any faith

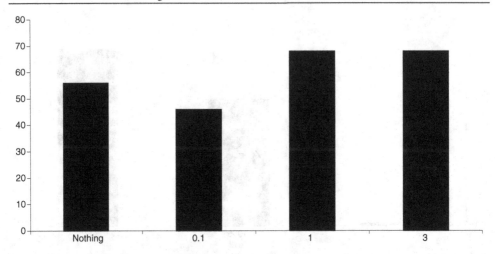

Figure 52.2 Percentage of correct answers given by incentive group.
Source: Gneezy and Rustichini (2000a).

Figure 52.2 shows the percentage of correct answers given by the incentive group. The group who received a very small incentive had the worst performance. This is consistent with the degradation of intrinsic motivation without sufficient monetary compensation.

In their second experiment, Gneezy and Rustichini asked high school students to go door-to-door and collect donations for a charity. Students were organized into groups facing three possible incentive schemes. Some were just asked to collect donations, some were offered 1% of everything they collected, and the third group were offered 10% of their total takings.

Again, Figure 52.3 reveals the detrimental effects of damaging intrinsic motivation without sufficient monetary compensation. The group without any incentive collected the largest amount of donations. The group with the 1% incentive collected the least. The group with the

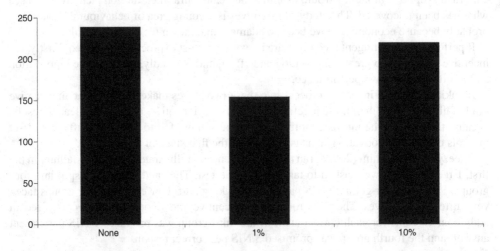

Figure 52.3 Total donations collected by incentive groups (NIS).
Source: Gneezy and Rustichini (2000a).

10% incentive collected less than the group with no incentive but more than the 1% incentive group.

Alternatively, incentives could fail because they lead to choking under pressure. That is, the objective is prized so highly that the mind focuses on it alone, and tends to forget about the task at hand. This is a failure of the second stage of the incentive process. (More on this later.)

EVIDENCE FROM THE LABORATORY

Let's turn to some laboratory experiments and see just how good incentives really are. A recent paper by Ariely *et al.* (2005) examines the performance of villagers living in rural India. This location was selected because it is possible to provide participants with meaningful incentives without breaking the budgetary constraints of academia.

Ariely *et al.* asked participants to take part in six games, which fell into three broad categories: creative games, concentration games, and motor skills games. However, as they found essentially no difference between the types of games and behaviour, we won't dwell on that here.

To give you an example of the games, one was called 'Recall last 3 digits'. The experimenters would read out a sequence of numbers, stopping at some unannounced point and ask the player to recall the last three digits. In each game, participants were told they should try to reach a 'good' or 'very good' standard. In the 'Recall the digits' game a 'good' standard was at least four correct trials. A 'very good' standard was at least six correct trials. Each player had 10 trials in total. Each was also assigned to one of three payment structures.

In the low-incentive group, participants received 4 Rupees if they reached the 'very good' standard, and half of that if they reached the 'good' standard. In the medium incentive group, the payment was 40 Rupees for a 'very good' standard. In the high-incentive group, it was 400 Rupees for the 'very good' standard.

The maximum possible payout of 400 Rupees is close to the all-India average monthly per capita consumption. Thus, if players in the high-incentive version of the game reached the 'very good' standard in all six games, they would win the equivalent of half a year's consumption – not an insignificant amount!

Figure 52.4 shows the percentage of maximum earnings that were achieved by each of the groups. Those who faced the lowest incentive captured around 35% of the maximum available to them. Those who faced the medium incentive achieved 37% of total amount available. However, those who faced the highest incentive managed to capture only 19.5% of the maximum earnings available to them!

A similar result is found by examining the percentage of players in each incentive category who managed to reach the 'very good' standard. In the low-incentive versions of the games, just over 25% of players reached the 'very good' standard. Of those facing the medium incentive, 22% reached the highest standard. However, only 6% of those facing the highest incentive managed to reach the 'very good' standard.

Two conclusions stand out from Ariely *et al.*'s experiments. Firstly, despite a significant increase in incentive size (the medium incentive was 10× the low incentive), there was no increase in performance. Secondly, and more importantly, the group with the highest incentive produced the worst performance.

Of course, the economists keen to maintain their orthodoxy of incentive dominance will object to the Ariely *et al.* experiments as using a non-representative sample. Surely, they will

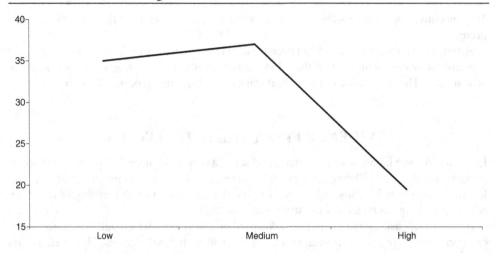

Figure 52.4   Percentage of maximum earnings obtained by incentive group.
Source: Ariely *et al.* (2006).

argue, rural India can't be compared to an advanced capitalist system (personally I find this argument rather pejorative, but nonetheless it is made).

To counter this objection, Ariely *et al.* ran a second experiment using MIT students at the term end. Strangely enough, students tend to be a little cash-strapped at term ends, so the incentives offered were probably quite meaningful. This time, all the students faced all the conditions (a within-subject design as opposed to a between-subject design). Two tasks were set. The first was a simple physical task: alternate pressing of the 'v' and 'n' keys on a keyboard for 4 minutes. The second task was more cognitive in nature. Students were asked to examine a 3×3 matrix containing numbers with two decimal places. The task was to find the number cells of the matrix that summed to 10.

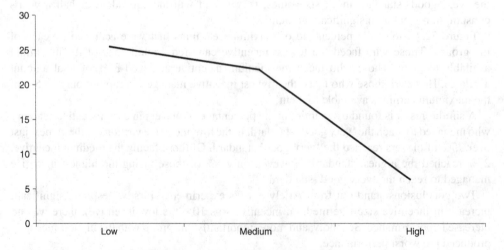

Figure 52.5   Percentage of players reaching the 'very good' standard.
Source: Ariely *et al.* (2006).

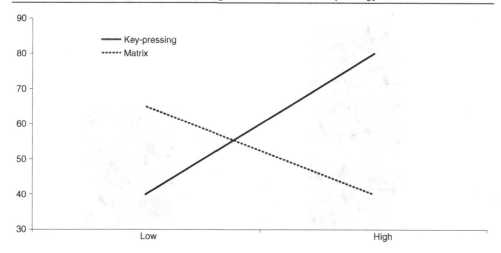

Figure 52.6   Percentage of maximum earnings obtained.
Source: Ariely *et al.* (2006).

A high- and low-incentive version of each game was played. In the key-pressing game, students were rewarded with $0 for 599 presses or less. In the low- (high-) incentive version, 600 presses earned $15 ($150) and an extra $0.10 ($10) was then offered for each additional correct pair of presses, up to a maximum of $30 ($300).

In the matrix challenge, students were offered nothing for getting 9 or less matrices correct. In the low- (high-) incentive version, $15 ($150) was paid for 10 correct, with an additional $1.50 ($15) for each correct matrix thereafter, up to a maximum of $30 ($300).

Figure 52.6 shows the percentage of maximum earnings that the students achieved on average. The incentives worked in the fashion that economists would have predicted in the key-pressing task. 40% of the total amount available was captured in the low-incentive version; this rose to 80% in the high-incentive game.

However, in the matrix task a very different result was uncovered. In the low-incentive condition, around 65% of the total payout was obtained. In the high-incentive version, only 40% of the total available payout was captured. This is consistent with the choking under pressure (distraction) explanation of the perverse effects of a high incentive.

This is our first important hint that incentives may have varying impacts depending upon the nature of the task in hand. For example, putting a 'piece rate' in a factory may be analogous to the key-pressing test above, in which case incentives may behave as one would expect. However, the use of incentives in cognitively demanding tasks (like the matrix game) may have perverse consequences.

The final experiment that Ariely *et al.* ran concerned social rather than financial pressure. This time the task was solving anagrams. The payment consisted of $5 for showing up, plus 33c for each correct anagram solved. However, in half the sessions the participants solved the anagrams in private, while in the other half they tried to solve the anagrams in front of an audience of other participants.

Figure 52.7 shows the average number of anagrams solved. Nearly twice as many anagrams were solved in private than in public. Once again this provides significant evidence of choking under pressure.

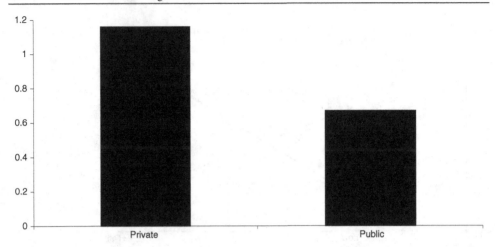

Figure 52.7   Average number of anagrams solved.
Source: Ariely *et al.* (2006).

EVIDENCE FROM THE FIELD

All well and good, you may say, but laboratories aren't the 'real world'. Fair enough, let's cast an eye over some studies that have examined the impact of incentives in the field.

Child Care Centres

The first study we'll examine comes from another paper by Gneezy and Rustichini (2000b). They examined the time at which parents picked up their children from a day care centre. They monitored 10 centres in Israel for 20 weeks. During the first four weeks, Gneezy and Rustichini simply observed the number of parents turning up late. In week 5, 6 of the 10 centres introduced a fine for the late collection of children. Parents were charged NIS 10 for every 10 minutes they were late per child. Parents were rarely more than 30 minutes late to collect their children. To put this into perspective, the fine for illegal parking is NIS 75.

Most economists would suggest that the introduction of a fine would decrease the incidence of the event. As a check, I even asked one of my best friends, who is an economist with a young child in day care, what she would predict the result of an introduction of a fine for late pick-up to be. She said the number of late pick-ups would decrease.

Now cast your eye over Figure 52.8. Far from decreasing the number of late pick-ups, the introduction of the fine actually managed to cause a very significant increase in the number of late pick-ups! In fact, parents facing the fine were nearly twice as likely to arrive late as those who faced no punishment.

In week 17 the fine was removed again. However, behaviour remained at existing levels: those who had become used to turning up late continued to do so.

Blood Donations

The next 'real world' example comes from blood donors in Sweden. Mellstrom and Johannessen (2006) examined the willingness to give blood under three different conditions.

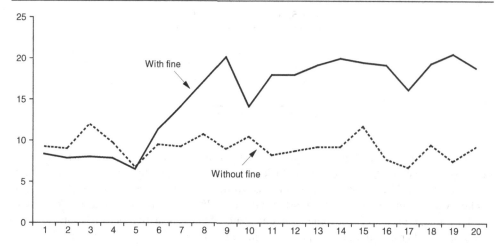

Figure 52.8 Number of parents arriving late to collect their child.
Source: Gneezy and Rustichini (2000b).

The first provided no financial incentive. The second offered a payment of SEK 50. The third offered a payment of SEK 50 but with an option to donate this payment to a children's cancer fund.

With no payment, around 43% of the participants chose to become blood donors. With a straight SEK 50 payment, this dropped to 33%. With the SEK 50 payment and a charity option, this rose to 44%.

Once again, the pure monetary incentive had a perverse effect upon participation.

Football Penalty Kicks

I have often confessed to an extraordinary disinterest in the game of football, yet it has featured in some of my previous writings. Is my subconscious telling me something?

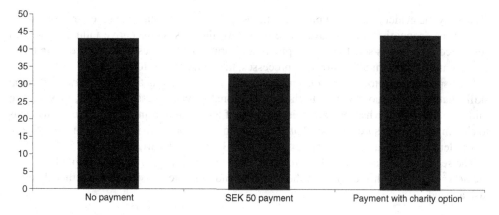

Figure 52.9 Percentage of blood donors.
Source: Mellstrom and Johannesson (2006).

Table 52.1   Penalty goals (%)

	Home	Away
Converted	73.59	75.83
Saved	18.87	18.6
Choked	7.54	5.57

Source: Dohmen (2005).

Dohmen (2005) looked at data from the German first division football league from 1963 to 2004, in which he examined penalty kicks. Over his sample there were some 3619 penalty kicks, of which 74.25% were successfully converted, 18.79% were saved and 6.96% were kicked wide of the goal, hit the crossbar, etc. This 7% is of interest because it represents choking under pressure. The other outcomes are effectively a two-person strategic game where the striker and the goalkeeper are competing. However, with misses it is purely the striker making an error.

Dohmen argues that the social pressure exerted by a home crowd will be greater than during an away match, and this one would expect to see more misses when it is a home match compared to an away match, and this is exactly what the data revealed (Table 52.1).

The percentage of goals saved was very similar. However, the home team tended to convert around 2.2 percentage points less than the away team. Nearly 90% of this 2.2 percentage point difference was accounted for by misses resulting from choking.

Basketball Players

Our final field evidence comes from an article by Dandy *et al.* (2001) who examined the performance of Australian basketball players in terms of free throws in training and in games. During practice some 75.4% of throws were successful. During games this dropped to 62%! This is yet more evidence of choking under pressure.

BACK TO THE LABORATORY

Hopefully the evidence we have presented helps to demonstrate that incentives are not always as clear as economists would have us believe. Two theories for incentive failure have been suggested. The first is self-focus or explicit monitoring. This argues that the harder we try to exert control over normally automatic processes, the worse we perform.

Sportspeople tend to suffer from this problem. They have practised for years to develop skills that become second nature to them. Occasionally, when pressure mounts, they start to think too hard about what they are doing instead of letting their training take over. This leads to choking under pressure. This kind of explicit monitoring problem has been found in golfers, footballers and baseball players, for example (see Beilock and Carr, 2001).

The second explanation is called *distraction theory*. This argues that our limited working memory[2] fills up with thoughts on the situation and possible consequences, rather than the task at hand.

---

[2] Working memory is the brains scratch pad. It is surprisingly small in size. In an oft-quoted paper Miller (1956) argues that we can generally only hold between 5 and 9 pieces of information in the working memory.

This kind of choking seems to appear when we are dealing with cognitive problems – that is, problems that we need to process logically rather than letting our automatic systems supply the answer.

These two kinds of choking may seem contradictory. The first argues that too much attention is bad news; the second argues that too little attention is the problem. However, while this may appear confusing, it really shouldn't be. The first kind of choking is an X-system problem, the second kind is a C-system problem – both of which have been defined previously.

To me, investing should be more like a maths problem than playing golf (I'm sure there are some who will disagree with me on this). As such, it is likely to be choking in the C-system that is more of a problem for investors. So let's examine this in a little more detail.

Beilock *et al.* (2004) asked people to perform modular arithmetic. For instance, to evaluate $51 \equiv 19 \pmod 4$. To test whether this statement is true you subtract $51 - 19 = 32$, and then divide by the mod, so $32 \div 4 = 8$. If the resulting number is whole, then the statement is true; if it is not a whole number, then the statement is false.

All participants performed three blocks of 24 modular arithmetic problems. Each block contained eight easy problems such as $7 \equiv 5 \pmod 2$ and eight difficult problems such as the one shown earlier. The remaining problems were pitched between the two extremes.

The first block of questions was simply used as a practice. The second block was introduced as further training, but in the third block pressure was applied. In the low-pressure version, participants were simply told that this was another set of questions for them to answer.

In the high-pressure situation, participants were told that the computer would be monitoring them for speed and accuracy (with equal weight), that they should try to improve performance by 20%, and that, if they managed to do that, they would be able to claim $5 because they had been paired with another (fictitious) student who had already improved by 20%. But, if they failed to improve, then neither student would get the $5. Finally, participants were told that their performance would be videotaped for review and teaching purposes. So, effectively, every form of pressure was piled onto these poor individuals.

Figure 52.10 shows the accuracy rates of each group. With the low-pressure group, performance was generally slightly higher in the test rather than the practice sessions (but not massively so). With the easy level questions, the high-pressure group was OK, showing little difference between the practice and the test. However, when it came to the difficult questions under high pressure, things went very badly wrong. There was a major deterioration in performance.

People appeared most likely to crack under pressure just when it was important that they shouldn't. Effectively, their working memory became flooded by thoughts of the situation rather than focusing on the task in hand.

WHO IS LIKELY TO CRACK UNDER PRESSURE?

The failure to perform can further increase anxiety, which itself eats up working memory, leading to yet worse performance. This creates a potentially vicious feedback loop of pressure and poor performance.

But who is most likely to suffer from this kind of choking under pressure? In tasks without pressure, those with high working memory capacity tend to outperform those with lower levels of working memory ability. However, under pressure, if working memory is key to choking then it may be those with high working memory capacity that suffer most. This may sound counter-intuitive but it isn't necessarily so.

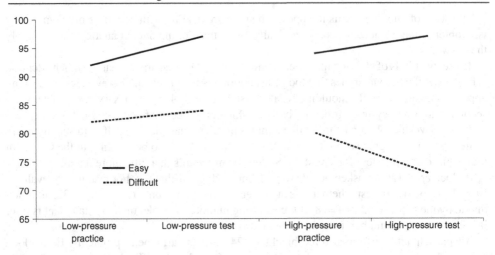

Figure 52.10   Percentage of correct answers by pressure grouping.
Source: Beilock *et al.* (2004).

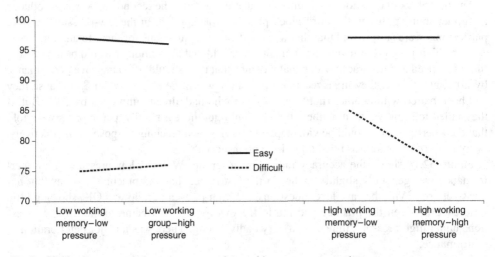

Figure 52.11   Percentage of correct answers by working memory capacity.
Source: Beilock and Carr (2005).

Beilock and Carr (2005) performed an experiment exactly like the one involving modular arithmetic above, but this time they separated participants into two groups based upon working memory capacity.[3] As before, there was an even split between easy and difficult questions, and the degree of pressure the participants faced was varied, as detailed previously.

Figure 52.11 shows the results that Beilock and Carr uncovered. The group with low working memory were not influenced by pressure. In contrast, the group with high working memory lost all of their edge over the low working memory group when they were placed under pressure.

---

[3] Assessing working memory capacity is based on Operation Span. Participants are presented with an equation and an unrelated word, i.e. $(5 \times 2) - 2 = 8$, Dog. They are asked to check the validity of the equation and then remember the word. At the end of the test, they are asked to write down as many as possible of the words they saw. The performance on the test plus the number of words remembered gives a good indication of working memory capacity.

As Beilock and Carr conclude,

"Under normal conditions, [those with] high working memory outperform [those with] low working memory because they have superior attentional allocation capacities. . . when such attentional capacity is comprised. . . [those with] high working memory [find their] advantage disappears. . . Ironically, the individuals most likely to fail under pressure are those who, in the absence of pressure, have the highest capacity for success.

CONCLUSIONS

Incentives don't always work in the way economists have assumed. This isn't to say that incentives always fail, but rather that we need to be aware that incentives require a two-step process to work. Firstly, they must increase motivation, and, secondly, this increased motivation must lead to improved performance.

Psychologists have documented that failures can occur at both junctures. Sometimes incentives fail because they are insufficient to improve motivation. Sometimes they fail because they are too large and we tend to become obsessed with the situation and its consequences rather than focusing on the task at hand.

Tasks where logical cognitive reflection is required seem particularly likely to suffer when participants are offered incentives. The evidence suggests that those who seem to be best prepared to deal with such problems are the worst hit by choking under pressure.

So the next time someone offers you an incentive to perform, or you see a CEO with 60% of his pay tied to the performance of his share price, just give pause to thought and remember this chapter.

SECTION VIII

Happiness

53

If It Makes You Happy[*]

If you are after specific investment advice, stop reading now. We seek to explore one of Adam Smith's obsessions: what it means to be happy. We also discuss why that's important to investors, and how we can seek to improve our own levels of happiness. The list below shows our Top 10 suggestions for improving happiness.

- *Don't equate happiness with money.* People adapt to income shifts relatively quickly, the long-lasting benefits are essentially zero.
- *Exercise regularly.* Taking regular exercise generates further energy, and stimulates the mind and the body.
- *Have sex (preferably with someone you love).* Sex is consistently rated as among the highest generators of happiness. So what are you waiting for?
- *Devote time and effort to close relationships.* Close relationships require work and effort, but pay vast rewards in terms of happiness.
- *Pause for reflection, meditate on the good things in life.* Simple reflection on the good aspects of life helps to prevent hedonic adaptation.
- *Seek work that engages your skills; try to enjoy your job.* It makes sense to do something you enjoy. This in turn is likely to allow you to flourish at your job, creating a pleasant feedback loop.
- *Give your body the sleep it needs.*
- *Don't pursue happiness for its own sake, enjoy the moment.* Faulty perceptions of what makes you happy may lead to the wrong pursuits. Additionally, activities may become a means to an end rather than something to be enjoyed, defeating the purpose in the first place.
- *Take control of your life, set yourself achievable goals.*
- *Remember to follow all the rules.*

[*]This article appeared in *Global Equity Strategy* on 17 June 2004. The material discussed was accurate at the time of publication.

With apologies to Monty Python, this chapter is perhaps best summed up as 'And now for something completely different'. We have a reputation (admittedly deservedly) for being bearish. Indeed, on occasions, we even manage to depress ourselves. However, as professional pessimists it behoves us to be happy in other aspects of our lives. Our colleague Albert Edwards has documented his own search for happiness with articles concerning his exploits at speed dating (see *Global Strategy Weekly*, 15 January 2004).

Albert's adventures have inspired me to, once again, drag the psychological literature. The psychological study of well-being and happiness is still a relatively new field. However, despite its relative youth, the field has already delivered some powerful insights and advice.

But before we get to these, let's start at the beginning. Why be happy? The psychological literature shows that effectively the benefits of happiness can be broken down into three areas. These may seem like a long list of the blindingly obvious, but all are based on careful scientific studies (rather than cheap self-help books!).[1]

1. *Social rewards*
   (a) Higher odds of marriage
   (b) Lower odds on divorce
   (c) More friends
   (d) Stronger social support
   (e) Richer social interactions

2. *Superior work outcomes*
   (a) Greater creativity
   (b) Increased productivity
   (c) Higher quality of work
   (d) Higher income
   (e) More activity, more energy

3. *Personal benefits*
   (a) Bolstered immune system
   (b) Greater longevity
   (c) Greater self-control and coping abilities.

So let's assume that you share the desire to enjoy this list of happiness-induced benefits (and I'd be surprised if anyone had issues with any of these benefits). How do you go about becoming happy (see Figure 53.1)?

In order to understand how we can improve our level of happiness we need to understand its components. The latest research suggests that happiness is composed of three sections (Sheldon *et al.*, 2003).

The largest contributor to happiness is the genetically determined set point (or, more accurately, set range). That is to say, people are predisposed to a certain level of happiness, which is determined by characteristics inherited from their parents! As Sheldon *et al.* note:

> The set point likely reflects immutable interpersonal, temperamental and affective personality traits, such as extraversion, arousability and negative affectivity, that are rooted in neurobiology, ...are highly heritable... and change little over the lifespan.

---

[1] Anyone wanting more on the benefits of happiness is referred to the massive volume of work carried out by Professor Lyubomirsky (http://faculty.ucr.edu/~sonja).

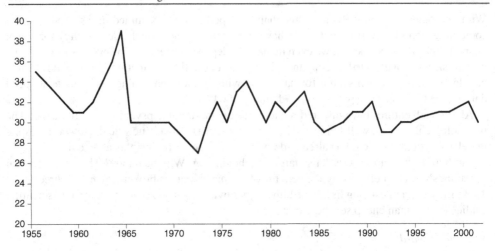

Figure 53.1 Percentage of Americans describing themselves as very happy.
Source: NOCR.

Adam Smith, author of *The Wealth of Nations*, also wrote the *Theory of Moral Sentiments*, a text far closer to understanding the nature of human beings than the better known favourite of economists.[2] Smith noted:

> The mind of every man, in a longer or shorter time, returns to its natural and usual state of tranquillity. In prosperity, after a certain time, it falls back to that state; in adversity, after a certain time, it rises up to it.

Current estimates suggest that this genetically determined set range accounts for around 50% of an individual's happiness. However, the set point is only the base line or default level of happiness that an individual enjoys. It is the level of happiness that an individual would have in the absence of other factors. Because the set point is generally fixed, it is not something we can alter in order to improve our happiness lot. This, of course, means that in order to increase our happiness we need to look elsewhere.

The second component of happiness is circumstances. Life circumstances include demographic factors, age, gender, ethnicity and geographic factors. It also includes personal history and life status. Frequently, people focus upon the last element of this feature.

Indeed, among the most commonly reported correlates of happiness are marital status, occupation, job security, income, health and religious affiliations. In general, married, well paid, secure, healthy and religious believers are more likely to report themselves as being happy than the rest of us.

That said, a vast array of individuals seriously overrate the importance of money in making themselves, and others, happy. Indeed, it seems to me that too many individuals within our industry tend to equate money with happiness.

However, study after study from psychology shows that money doesn't equal happiness. For instance, Loewenstein (1996) asked visitors to Pittsburgh International Airport to rank from 1 (most important) to 5 (least important) a list of "things that might be important when it comes

---

[2] Indeed a new paper by Ashraf *et al.* (2004) argues that Adam Smith was actually one of the first behavioural economists. They cite the *Theory of Moral Sentiments* as a good example of how insightful Smith really was.

Table 53.1 Rankings and ratings of happiness factors

Item	Mean rank	Mean points
Family life	1.7	37
Friends	2.4	22
Satisfying job	2.5	26
High income	3.6	15

Source: Loewenstein (1996).

to making people happy". They were then asked to assign percentages as to the importance of each factor in determining overall happiness. Table 53.1 shows the mean ranking and percentage weights that respondents assigned to each variable. High income received the lowest ranking and rating.

A similar finding is contained by Diener and Oishi (2000) who surveyed some 7167 students across 41 countries. Those who valued love more than money reported far higher life satisfaction scores than those who seemed to be money focused (see Figure 53.2).

However, for all the emphasis that gets put upon life circumstances as a generator of happiness, the correlations between such variables as money, job security, marriage etc., and happiness are relatively small. In fact, Sheldon *et al.* argue that in total all circumstances account for only around 10% of the variations in people's happiness.

There is an additional problem with changing life circumstances as a path to increasing happiness. It goes by the frightening name of hedonic adaptation (Frederick and Loewenstein, 1999). Simply put, hedonic adaptation means that we are very good at quickly assimilating our current position, and then judging it as normal; hence only changes from our "normal" level get noticed.

Gains in happiness quickly become the norm. So changing life circumstances seems to lead to only temporary improvement in people's happiness. This helps to explain Figure 53.1, which shows that since the 1950s people's happiness levels have been remarkably constant, despite a massive growth in income per head over the same time horizon.

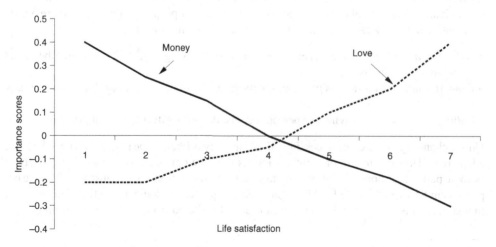

Figure 53.2 Money $\neq$ happiness.
Source: Diener and Oishi (2000).

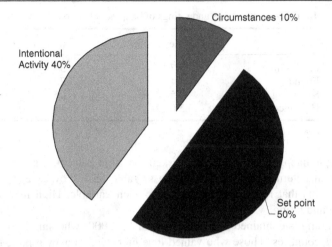

Figure 53.3 Contributions to happiness.
Source: Sheldon *et al*. (2003).

Schkade and Kahneman (1998) show that while "living in California" was an appealing idea for many Americans, it didn't actually boost long-run happiness. That is to say, people living in California were about as happy as other Americans on average. Therefore, while moving may provide a temporary increase in happiness, it is soon adapted into the perception of the "norm".

Hence hedonic adaptation severely limits the ability of changing life circumstances to improve long-run happiness; and neither life circumstances nor the set point seem to hold the key to creating sustainable increases in happiness.

All of which means that any hope for increasing happiness on a long-term basis must lie with the third and final component of happiness – intentional activity. Sheldon *et al*. define intentional activity as "discrete actions or practices that people can choose to do". By a process of elimination, intentional activity must account for 40% of people's happiness (Figure 53.3).

Intentional activity can be (somewhat artificially) broken down into three areas:

- *Behavioural activities* – such as exercising regularly, having sex,[3] being kind to others, and spending time socialising.
- *Cognitive activities* – such as trying to see the best, pausing to count how lucky one actually is.
- *Volitional activities* – striving for personal goals, devoting effort to meaningful causes.

Unlike changing life circumstances, intentional activity is likely to be more resistant to hedonic adaptation. The very nature of activities means they are episodic, and hence are unlikely to become part of the "norm" in the way alterations to circumstances do. Because activities are not permanent they can be varied, which again helps to prevent hedonic adaptation. For instance, in taking exercise the particular activity can easily be altered from cycling to swimming.

---

[3] In Kahneman *et al*. (2003) the authors found that, among a sample of 1000 employed women, sex was rated retrospectively as the activity that produces the largest amount of happiness. Commuting turns out to be the least pleasurable activity. Also Blanchflower and Oswald (2004) find that sexual activity enters strongly into happiness equations.

Cognitive activities, such as pausing to think about the good things in one's life, can also help to counteract the hedonic adaptation process directly. After all, counting one's blessing helps to prevent them from becoming part of the "norm".

Of course, just like New Year's resolutions, happiness-increasing strategies are relatively easy to devise, but much harder to implement on a consistent basis. A deliberate effort is required to pursue activities. However, an individual has much more chance of being able to start an activity than, say, change the set point or alter life circumstances. So just how can we seek to improve our intentional activities to enhance happiness? The list below is drawn from my reading of the literature, and all of these have withstood laboratory testing in a scientific environment.

TOP 10

This is the Top 10 list for improving happiness (in no particular order):

1. *Don't equate happiness with money.* People adapt to income shifts relatively quickly, the long-lasting benefits are essentially zero.
2. *Exercise regularly.* Regular exercise is an effective cure for mild depression and anxiety. It also stimulates more energy, and is good for the mind and body.
3. *Have sex* (preferably with someone you love). Need I say more?
4. *Devote time and effort to close relationships.* Confiding and discussing problems and issues is good for happiness, so work on these relationships.
5. *Pause for reflection; meditate on the good things in life.* Focusing on the good aspects of life helps to prevent hedonic adaptation.
6. *Seek work that engages your skills, try to enjoy your job.* Doing well at work creates happiness, and the easiest way of doing well at work, is doing a job you enjoy.
7. *Give your body the sleep it needs.* Too many people have a sleep deficit, resulting in fatigue, gloomy moods and lack of concentration.
8. *Don't pursue happiness for its own sake, enjoy the moment.* Because people don't understand what makes them happy, pursuing happiness can be self-defeating. Additionally, if people start to aim for happiness they are doing activities for happiness's sake rather than actually enjoying the activity itself.
9. *Take control of your life, set yourself achievable goals.* People are happiest when they achieve their aims, so set yourself goals that stretch you, but are achievable.
10. *Remember to follow rules 1–9.* Following these guidelines sounds easy, but actually requires willpower and effort.

Let's leave the last words to Adam Smith (quoted in Adam Smith, Behavioural Economist by Ashraf *et al.* (2004) from the *Theory of Moral Sentiments*):

> Through the whole of his life he pursues the idea of a certain artificial and elegant repose which he may never arrive at, for which he sacrifices a real tranquillity that is at all times in his power, and which, if in the extremity of old age he should at last attain to it, he will find to be in no respect preferable to that humble security and contentment which he had abandoned for it. It is then, in the last dregs of life, his body wasted with toil and disease, his mind galled and ruffled by the memory of a thousand injuries and disappointments which he imagines he has met with from the injustice of his enemies, or from the perfidy and ingratitude of his friends, that he begins at last to find that wealth and greatness are mere trinkets of frivolous utility, no more adapted for procuring ease of body or tranquillity of mind, than the tweezer-cases of the lover of toys.

54
Materialism and the Pursuit
of Happiness*

Materialistic pursuits are not a path to sustainable happiness. A mass of evidence shows that people who have more materialistic goals are less happy than those who focus on intrinsic aims such as relationships or personal growth. Spending on experiences rather than possessions seems to make people happier. Don't judge yourself against others; happiness should be an absolute not a relative concept.

- Over a year ago I wrote an article on the psychology of happiness. It proposed 10 rules to follow in order to try to attain sustainable happiness. The first of these was anathema to many in the financial world: Don't equate money and happiness. This chapter seeks to expand on that idea by examining the relationship between materialism and happiness.
- Tim Kasser, Richard Ryan, and Ken Sheldon *inter alia* have amassed a wealth of evidence which shows that those who value materialistic goals higher than intrinsic aims are less happy. For instance, Sheldon and Kasser asked students to write down their goals for the upcoming months, and then rate the degree to which achieving those goals would help towards materialistic and intrinsic outcomes. Two months later the degree of progress was checked, as was the participant's level of happiness. Those that had made little progress on intrinsic goals were less happy; those who had made good progress on such goals were much happier. *The degree of progress towards material goals made no difference towards people's assessment of their well-being.*
- According to research by Cohen and Cohen, those who pursue materialistic goals are much more likely to suffer a wide variety of mental disorders. They found that those pursuing material targets were 1.37 times more likely to have attention deficit disorder, 1.6 times more likely to be paranoid, 1.6 times more likely to be histrionic, 1.5 times more likely to be borderline, 1.5 times more likely to be narcissistic, and 1.8 times more likely to have dependency issues!
- The good news is that Van Boven and Gilovich have unearthed evidence that spending income on *experiences* makes people much happier than spending on material goods (beyond a threshold level of income). So to increase happiness, concentrate on experiences (diving, safari and concerts) rather than possessions (new house, fast cars or flash watches).
- Experiences are more significant than possessions for four reasons. Firstly, they seem to be open to positive review. We effectively create own our revisionist histories. Secondly, they appear to be far more immune to hedonic adaptation. We don't integrate relatively unique experiences into our normal everyday benchmark. Thirdly, experiences are more central to

---

*This article appeared in *Global Equity Strategy* on 3 November 2005. The material discussed was accurate at the time of publication.

our identity. We are the sum of our experiences, not the sum of our possessions. Finally, experiences are often more social, both in terms of actual real-time participation, and in terms of being able to share them after the fact. People seem to enjoy hearing about the experiences of others. The obsession with materialism is exacerbated by social comparisons. Happiness should be an absolute not relative concept.

As colleagues are well aware, my interests lie in the intersection of psychology and finance. However, once in a while I take a slightly broader perspective and explore aspects of human nature that intrigue me. Last year I wrote an article on the psychology of happiness, and some questioned what on earth an investment bank was doing publishing such research. However, it remains my most widely read piece by a wide margin. This chapter is a sequel to that original article.

Many in our industry still struggle to accept the very first rule I proposed for sustainable happiness, which was not equating money and happiness. There is a wealth of evidence on the fact that, beyond a certain threshold of basic requirements, increasing wealth doesn't equate to increasing happiness. Of course, to many in finance this seems like heresy.

I am fond of quoting Lao Tzu and it is he who wrote the lines below:

> Chase after money and security
> And your heart will never unclench.
> Care about people's approval
> And you will be their prisoner.
> Do your work, then step back.
> The only path to serenity.

Despite these ancient words of wisdom, I suspect that very few of us have really taken such an approach to heart.

ASPIRATION INDEX

This chapter seeks to explore a related issue, the link (or lack thereof) between materialism and happiness. To get the full benefit from this concept I suggest you spend a few minutes examining the Aspiration Index (http://www.psych.rochester.edu/SDT/measures/aspir_scl.html). This scale was devised by Kasser and Ryan (1996) and measures the importance of various factors in our lives. After answering the questions, the scores can be combined to analyse how important the six dimensions are to you.[1] My scores on these six dimensions are shown in Figure 54.1. In addition, I've aggregated them into two groups following Kasser and Ryan: wealth, fame and image combine to give the *extrinsic aspiration* score, while personal growth, relationships and community combine to give the *intrinsic aspiration* score.

As you can see, I score highly on the intrinsic motivation scores, and much lower on the extrinsic scales (especially image, which for those who know me and the way I dress won't come as a big surprise!). It should be noted that one's answers are not always constant. Had I taken this test when I first joined the City (many many moons ago), the findings would have more or less been reversed. Time is often a good if expensive teacher!

Extrinsic aspirations focus on the outside world and hence are often described as materialist goals. Intrinsic aspirations relate much more to the way we feel about ourselves and others, and hence are generally low in materialist attributes. Could these differing aspirations be linked to people's level of happiness?

---

[1] Actually the survey has three dimensions, the first is how important these factors are to you, the second is how well you have done in achieving these goals, and the third is how likely you are to achieve these goals in the future. For obvious reasons I chose to only disclose the first!

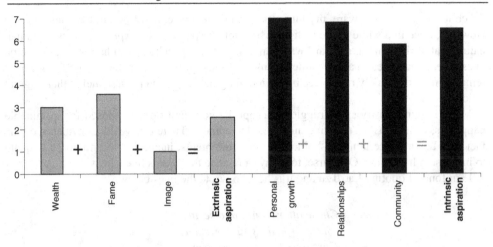

Figure 54.1 My scores for the importance sections of the Aspirations Index.
Source: DrKW Macro research.

MATERIALISM AND HAPPINESS: THE EVIDENCE

Kasser and Ryan (2001) present evidence that the nature of aspirations and happiness are closely related. They used the Aspiration Index but rather than focusing on the 'importance' questions they used the 'attainment' questions. That is, Kasser and Ryan asked people to rate how much they felt they had attained materialistic goals (money, fame, and image) and non-materialistic goals (personal growth, relationships, and community involvement).

After answering the questions, the participants were assigned to one of four categories: those high in both types of achievements; those high only in non-material goals but low in material achievements; the reverse group, that is, those high in material attainment but low in nonmaterial achievements; and finally those low in both sets of goals. Kasser and Ryan then compared the groups in terms of personal well-being, self-esteem, and other general measures of happiness.

Figure 54.2 shows the well-being (happiness) scores of the four different groups. Attaining materialistic goals was not very beneficial to people's feelings of happiness. For instance, the first two bars show equivalent levels of happiness for those who attained high levels of non-materialistic goals regardless of the degree of materialistic achievements. Conversely, those groups who reported low levels of non-material goal attainment showed below average levels of happiness regardless of the degree of material goals they may have achieved.

Vansteenkiste *et al.* (2005) investigate the aspirational values of two groups of students – those on a business course and those training to become teachers. As one might expect, the business studies students had significantly higher extrinsic aspirations, especially when it came to wealth, while the would-be teachers were much more interested in contributing to the community than the business studies students (Figure 54.3).

Vansteenkiste *et al.* found that intrinsic values were associated with higher levels of well-being and extrinsic values were related to low levels of happiness. They conclude

> The mean differences in self-reported well-being ... between business students and infant school teacher students could be fully explained by the type of values that each group was primarily

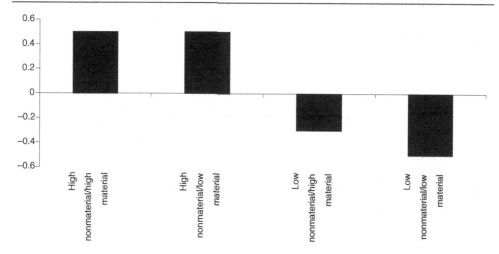

Figure 54.2 Subjective well-being of four groups sorted by aspiration attainment.
Source: Kasser and Ryan (2001).

concerned about. Business students are less satisfied with their present lives, feel less vital . . .
because they are more oriented towards wealth than towards helping people in need.

Sheldon and Kasser (1998) asked students to write down their goals for the upcoming months
and then rate the degree to which achieving those goals will help them towards materialistic
and intrinsic outcomes. Having done this the participants were asked to fill out a progress
report every 5 days for 2 months. They were also asked to complete a 'well-being' diary every
5 days to check the change in their happiness.

Figure 54.4 shows the changes in well-being that occurred over the 2- month study period.
As even a cursory glance at the graph reveals, making little progress in terms of intrinsic goals
(such as personal growth and relationships) decreased the level of happiness, whereas making

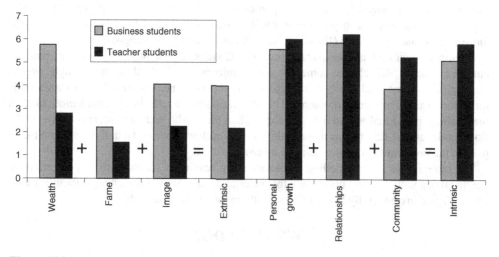

Figure 54.3 Aspiration Index scores for business studies and teacher training students.
Source: Vansteenkiste *et al.* (2005).

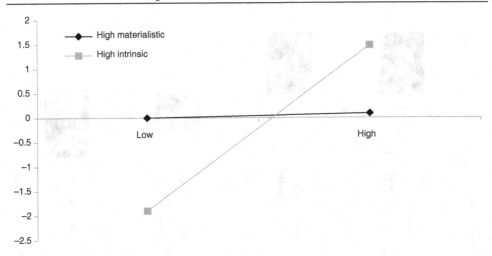

Figure 54.4   Changes in happiness as a function of progress towards goals.
Source: Sheldon and Kasser (1998).

progress towards such goals had a strongly positive effect on the level of well-being. However, those making little or lots of progress towards materialistic aims did nothing to alter the level of happiness.

PROBLEMS OF MATERIALISM

Not only are people who pursue materialistic goals setting themselves up for a generally unful-filling experience, but they are also considerably more prone to mental anguish and problems.

Cohen and Cohen (1996) studied a group of around 700 12–20 year olds living in New York. The participants were asked to rate how much they admired different traits, designed to either reflect materialistic desires or intrinsic goals. Having completed their analysis of goals, the Cohens then arranged for each of the participants to be interviewed by psychologists. The psychologists assessed each person for a wide range of problems from the *Diagnostic and Statistical Manual of Mental Disorders*, the clinical bible of psychologists.

Having interviewed all the participants, the Cohens investigated whether any patterns emerged. Table 54.1 shows some of their findings for both those with high overall materialistic scores, and those with high wealth subcomponent scores. It also shows odds ratios for a variety of mental problems. The odds ratio simply reflects how much more likely a materialistic individual was to have a disorder than those who were aiming at intrinsic goals. So an odds ratio of 1.50 means that a materialistic youth was one and a half times more likely to have the problem than an intrinsically motivated youth.

The table makes for compelling if disconcerting reading. Compared to non-materialistic youths, those with a strong preference for material desires are likely to have difficulties with attention, and are generally likely to be socially inept and overcontrolling!

WHAT TO DO?

So what is one to do? Obviously the first step is recognizing that materialism isn't the optimal route to happiness. Once this has been accepted, one can start to refocus on what really matters.

Table 54.1   Odds ratio of mental problems

	High materialistic scores	High "Being rich" scores
Conduct disorder	1.14	1.29
Attention deficit disorder	1.37	1.53
Paranoid	1.6	1.43
Histrionic	1.6	1.14
Borderline	1.48	1.33
Narcissistic	1.52	1.4
Dependent	1.8	1.34

Source: Cohen and Cohen (1996).

This doesn't mean that you have to give your worldly possessions away, although there may be a lot to say for this. But a more palatable suggestion may be to focus on spending your money on experiences rather than material goods.

Van Boven and Gilovich (2003) investigate whether material or experiential goods make people happier. Of course, there can be a fine line between the two categories. It is perfectly possible for the same object to be material for one person and experiential for another. For instance, owning a car that is bought because it can handle the kinds of roads you drive on better than any other, may be experiential. Buying another Ferrari for the collection is purely material.

While this duality of purpose can make classifying goods tricky, it doesn't invalidate the concept. As Van Boven and Gilovich note, at dusk it can be hard to tell whether it is day or night, but the existence of dusk doesn't result in day and night being meaningless concepts.

They set up a series of surveys and experiments to see how people treat experiences and material goods. In the first study 100 students were asked to think about either a material purchase or an experiential purchase that can cost more than $100. Participants were asked a variety of questions such as 'When you think about this purchase, how happy does it make you?', 'How much does this purchase contribute to your happiness in life?', 'To what extent would you say this purchase was money well spent?' and so forth.

As a check, a different group was given a selection of the various items purchased (half experiential, half material), but weren't told which was which. They had to state whether they thought the good was experiential or material, and were also asked to rate how happy each purchase would make them.

As Table 54.2 and Figure 54.5 clearly show, experiential purchases were rated higher on all the scales used. Experiential purchases rated as making people happier than material purchases, contributed more to people's overall happiness with life, were generally seen as money well spent, and had a lower score of alternative uses of the money spent. In most respects, people were much happier with experiential as opposed to material purchases.

The second study Van Boven and Gilovich undertook was an US nationwide survey covering some 1279 participants. The experiment was conducted over the telephone and was embedded in a broader survey. In contrast to the previous example, this time participants were asked to think of both an experiential purchase and a material purchase. As in the previous results, more people found that the experiential purchases made them happier than the material purchases (57% against 34%) reporting the reverse (Figure 54.6).

Table 54.2   Ratings of purchases (on a nine point scale, higher = better)

Evaluation	Type of purchase	
	Experiential	Material
How happy does thinking about it make you?	7.51	6.62
Contributed to our overall happiness in life?	6.4	5.42
Money well spent?	7.3	6.42
Better spent on something else?	3.77	4.52
Outsiders' evaluation of anticipated happiness	6.78	4.25

Source: Van Boven and Gilovich (2003).

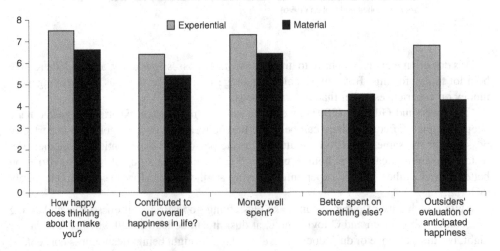

Figure 54.5   Rating of purchases.
Source: Van Boven and Gilovich (2003).

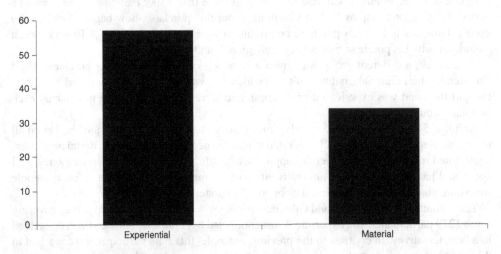

Figure 54.6   Nationwide survey – percentage reporting category as generating more happiness.
Source: Van Boven and Gilovich (2003).

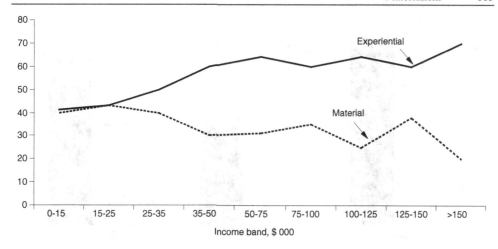

Figure 54.7 Percentage of respondents indicating that experiential or material purchase made them happier.
Source: Van Boven and Gilovich (2003).

The results were surprisingly robust across various demographic cuts, i.e. age, gender, etc. Van Boven and Gilovich found that the biggest demographic split revolved around income. Those with the lowest income were equally likely to rate material or experiential purchases as most important for happiness. As one moves up the income scale, so experiential purchases increasingly dominate people's happiness (Figure 54.7). By the time people are earning $25,000+ experiential purchases are considerably more likely to add to happiness than material purchases. This makes good sense from a Maslowian[2] point of view. Individuals with little or no discretionary income must allocate the dominant proportion of their resources towards meeting the basic needs of life, and thus may have fewer opportunities to worry about the relative benefits of experiences and possessions on the path to happiness.

WHY EXPERIENCES OVER POSSESSIONS?

The evidence seems clear. Experiences add more to our happiness than possessions. *So to increase happiness concentrate on experiences (diving, safari, concerts) rather than the next new house, fast car or flash watch.*

The inquisitive among you may wonder why experiences seem so much better for us than material possessions. Van Boven and Gilovich suggest three possible reasons. Firstly, *experiences seem to be open to positive review.* When looking back, experiences may receive favourable treatment. For instance, I've recently returned from diving in the Red Sea. The boat we were living on was an unmitigated disaster, from fires in the engine room to diesel fumes being pumped into the cabin. However, looking back the things I remember most were a couple of stunning dives, so the experience already seems better than the reality. We create

---

[2] Maslow argued that people had a pyramid of desires, or hierarchy of needs. They worked their way up the hierarchy. As each level is achieved so the next level becomes desirable. So you start with the physiological needs (i.e. oxygen, water, food, temperature), then progress to the safety needs and so forth.

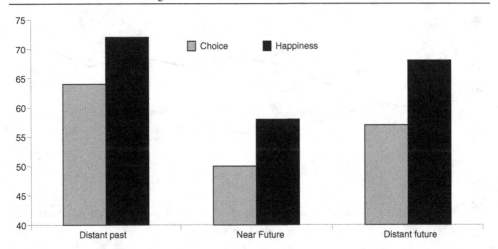

Figure 54.8 Percentage of respondents choosing the experiential purchase and saying it made them happier.
Source: Van Boven and Gilovich (2003).

our own revisionist histories with experiences. This isn't available to a solid hard material possession.

To illustrate this point Van Boven and Gilovich asked around 100 students to select from various pairs (such as a pair of leather boots or a dinner and a comedy show) the purchase that would make them happiest on various time horizons (either one year in the past, one year in the future, or the next few days). Figure 54.8 reveals the results they uncovered. It shows both the percentage of respondents choosing the experiential (non-materialistic) option under each time horizon, and the percentage of respondents that said the experiential option made them happier. When dealing with distant temporal horizons a greater proportion chose the experiential option.

The results do throw up an interesting conundrum for choice theorists and those who believe in rational behaviour. In all cases the percentage of respondents *saying* that the experience would make them happier than the possession was larger than the percentage of people *choosing* the experience over the possession! So much for people choosing what makes them happier!

Although not mentioned by Van Boven and Gilovich, experiences may also be more robust to hedonic adaptation. Simply put, hedonic adaptation (or the hedonic treadmill as it is sometimes more prosaically called) means that we are very good at quickly assimilating our current position, and then judging it as the norm. Hence, only changes from our "normal" level get noticed.

Material possessions are likely to be assimilated relatively quickly. We get used to our new house, and our new car. At first, we might be out washing the car every weekend, but then 6 months later we have become accustomed to the car, the kids have scuffed up the seats in the back, and the boot is full of dog hairs. Hedonic adaptation at work.

Experiences, on the other hand, may not be subject to such a process. Experiences tend to be relatively unique, each concert you go to is different, every dive I do has different elements. These novel elements help to prevent the hedonic adaptation process from kicking in.

Secondly, *experiences are more central to one's identity*. As Van Boven and Gilovich note, a person's life is the sum of his experiences. We are defined by the experiences we have had. The accumulation of a broad range of experiences helps to create a richer more rewarding life. Material possessions don't integrate into a person's sense of self in the same fashion. They tend to remain peripheral to the individual.

Van Boven and Gilovich asked a random sample of nearly 80 people at shopping malls in New York and New Jersey to think about one experiential and one material purchase they had made and been happy with. They were then asked which of the two had played a greater role in defining "who you are" in life. Of the respondents, 89% said the experiential purchase was more self-defining.

Finally, Van Boven and Gilovich suggest that *experiences may have greater 'social value'*. Experiences are often social events in their own right; in as much as many experiences involve other people, material possessions clearly do not.

Bragging about one's new Ferrari is unlikely to endear you to many people. However, chatting about your experiences on the Machu Picchu trail, the highways of Pakistan, or indeed picnics at Wedding Rock and near death experiences (see *Global Strategy Weekly*, 20 October 2005) are likely to be more interesting. As has been shown previously, people thrive on stories (see *Global Equity Strategy*, 27 April 2005).

CONCLUSIONS

The evidence reviewed in this chapter suggests that materialistic pursuits pose a significant stumbling block on the path to happiness. The more people aspire to materialistic goals, the less satisfied they appear to be with life, and the greater the risk that they may develop mental health problems.

The good news is that redirecting consumption towards experiences rather than possessions seems to be capable of increasing people's happiness. However, there are at least two obvious barriers that could prevent people following such advice. Firstly, we appear to have very limited self-insight, so we may well be unaware of just how materialistic our own goals are. As Van Boven (2005) notes:

> Although we can easily see that our coworker's penchant for buying the newest, most expensive technological gizmos derives from her materialistic desires, it may seem that we acquire our own laptops, cell phones and personal digital assistants out of nonmaterialistic desires to make work more efficient and to maintain contact with friends and family.

A second potential problem to overcome is that many of us seem to have a very decadent definition of "needs". People very often talk of needing the latest fashionable clothes, or needing the newest, trendiest technological toy. This is often exacerbated by an insistence on social comparisons, keeping up with the Joneses. Happiness should be an *absolute* concept, but all too often people view it relatively. Breaking these shallow frames may be an important first step on the road to true sustainable happiness.

References

Abreu, D. and Brunnermeier, M. (2002) Synchronization risk, and delayed arbitrage, *Journal of Financial Economics*, 66(2-3), 341–360.

Abreu, D. and Brunnermeier, M. (2003) Bubbles and crashes, *Econometrica*, 71(1), 173–204.

Ackert, L.F. and Church, B.K. (2001) The effects of subject pool, and design experience on rationality in experimental asset markets, *The Journal of Psychology and Financial Markets*, 2(1), 6–28.

Akers, K. and Staub, R. (2003) Regional Investment Allocations in a Global Timber Market. *Journal of Alternative Investments*, 5(4), Spring, 73–87.

Alexander, M.A. (2000) *Stock Cycles*. iUniverse.

Anderson, L. and Holt, C. (2005) Information cascade experiments. In Plott, C. and Smith, V. (eds) *The Handbook of Experimental Economics Results, Vol 1*. Amsterdam: Elsevier Science.

Anderson, S.W., Bechara, A., Damasio, H., Tranel, D. and Damasio, A.R. (1999) Impairment of social and moral behaviour related to early damage in human prefrontal cortex, *Nature Neuroscience*, 2(11), 1032–1037.

Ariely, D. and Loewenstein, G. (2006) The heat of the moment: the effect of sexual arousal on sexual decision making. *Journal of Behavioural Decision Making*, 19, 87–98.

Ariely, D., Gneezy, U., Loewenstein, G. and Mazar, N. (2005) Large stakes and big stakes. Working paper.

Ariely, D., Loewenstein, G. and Prelec, D. (2003) Coherent arbitrariness: Stable demand curves without stable preferences, *Quarterly Journal of Economics*, 118(1), 73–105.

Arnott, R. and Bernstein, P. (2002) What risk premium is normal? *Financial Analysts Journal*.

Ashenfelter, O., Ashmore, D. and LaLonde, R. (1995) Bordeaux wine vintage quality and the weather, *Chance*, 4, 7–14.

Ashraf, N., Camerer, C.F. and Loewenstein, G. (2005) Adam Smith, behavioural economist, *Journal of Economic Perspectives*, 19(3), 131–146.

Asness, C. (1997) The interaction of value and momentum strategies, *Financial Analysts Journal*, March/April.

Assness, C.S., Krail, R.J. and Liew, J.M. (2001) Do hedge funds hedge? *Journal of Portfolio Management*, 28(1), 6–19.

Asness, C.S., Liew, J.M. and Stevens, R.L. (1997) Parallels between the cross-sectional predictability of stock and country returns. *Journal of Portfolio Management*, Spring.

Asness, C.S., Porter, R.B. and Stevens, R.L. (2004) Predicting stock returns using industry-relative firm characteristics. Working paper, University of Florida.

Baker, M.P. and Wurgler, J.A. (2006) Investor sentiment and the cross-section of stock returns, *Journal of Finance*, 61(4), 1645–1680.

Bali, T.G., Demirtas, K.O. and Hovakimian, A.G. (2006) Corporate financing activities and contrarian investment. Available from www.ssrn.com.

Ball, S, Bazerman, M. and Carroll, J. (1991) An evaluation of learning in the bilateral winners' curse, *Organizational Behaviour and Human Decision Processes*, 48.

Bandura, A. (1999) Moral disengagement in the perpetration of inhumanities, *Personality and Social Psychology Review*, 3(3), 193–209.

Bandura, A., Underwood, B. and Fromson, M.E. (1975) Disinhibition of aggression through diffusion of responsibility and dehumanization of victims, *Journal of Personality and Social Psychology*, 9, 253–269.

Barber, B.M., Odean, T. and Zheng, L. (2001) The behavior of mutual fund investors. Unpublished paper.

Baumeister, R.F. (2003) The psychology of irrationality: Why people make foolish, self-defeating choices, in Brocas, I. and Carrillo, J. (eds) *The Psychology of Economic Decision Volume 1: Rationality and Well-Being*. Oxford University Press, Oxford.

Bebchuk, L.A., Cohen, A. and Ferrell, A. (2004) What matters in corporate governance, DP 491. Available from www.ssrn.com.

Bechara, A., Damasio, H., Damasio, A.R., Loewenstein, G. and Shiv, B. (2004) Investment behaviour and the dark side of emotion. Unpublished paper.

Bechara, A., Damasio, H., Damasio, A.R., Loewenstein, G. and Shiv, B. (2005) Investment behaviour and the negative side of emotion, *Psychological Science*, 16(6), 435–439.

Bechara, A., Damasio, H., Tranel, D. and Damasio, A.R. (1997) Deciding advantageously before knowing the advantageous strategy, *Science*, 275, 1293–1294.

Beilock, S.L. and Carr, T.H. (2001) On the fragility of skilled performance: What governs choking under pressure? *Journal of Experimental Psychology: General*, 130, 701–725.

Beilock, S.L. and Carr, T.H. (2005) When high-powered people fail, *Psychological Science*, 16, 101–105.

Beilock, S.L., Kulp, C.A., Holt, L.E. and Carr, T.H. (2004) More on the fragility of performance: Choking under pressure in mathematical problem solving, *Journal of Experimental Psychology: General*, 133, 584–600.

Berkelaar, A. and Kouwenberg, R. (2000) *From Boom 'til Bust: How Loss Aversion Affects Prices*. Econometric Institute working paper. Available from www.ssrn.com.

Bertrand, M. and Mullainathan, S. (2004) Are Emily and Greg more employable than Lakisha and Jamal? A field experiment on labour market discrimination. MIT Department of Economic working paper no. 03–22.

Bhattacharya, U. and Galpin, N. (2005) Is stock-picking declining around the world? Available from www.ssrn.com.

Blanchard, O.J. and Watson, M.W. (1982) Bubbles, rational expectations and financial markets. In Wachtel, P. (ed.) *Crises in Economic and Financial Structure: Bubbles, bursts and shocks*. Lexington Books: Lexington.

Blanchflower, D.G. and Oswald, A.J. (2004) Money, Sex and Happiness: An Empirical Study. *Scandinavian Journal of Economics*, 106(3), 393–416.

Bogle, J. (2005) The mutual fund industry 60 years later: For better or worse? *Financial Analysts Journal*, 61(1), 15–24.

Brandes Institute (2004) Concentrated portfolios: An examination of their characteristics and effectiveness (September). Available from http://www.brandes.com/Institute/BiResearch/.

Brandes Institute (2006) *Death, Taxes and Short-Term Underperformance*.

Brown, S.J., Goetzmann, W.N. and Kumar, A. (1998) The Dow Theory: William Peter Hamilton's track record re-considered, *Journal of Finance*, 53(4), 1311–1333.

Bruce, R.S. (1935) Group judgements in the field of lifted weights and visual discrimination, *Journal of Psychology*, 117, 1935–1936.

Brunnermeier, M.K. and Nagel, S. (2003) Hedge funds and the technology bubble. *Journal of Finance*, 59(5), 2013–2040.

Caginalp, G., Porter, D. and Smith, V.L. (2000) Overreaction, momentum, liquidity and price bubbles in laboratory and field asset markets, *Journal of Psychology and Financial Markets*, 1(1), 24–48.

Cain, D.M., Loewenstein, G. and Moore, D.A. (2005) The dirt on coming clean: Perverse effects of disclosing conflicts of interest, *Journal of Legal Studies*, 34, 1–25.

Camerer, C. (1989) Bubbles and fads in asset prices, *Journal of Economic Surveys*, 3(1), 3–41.

Camerer, C.F., Ho, T. and Chong, J.-K. (2003) A cognitive hierarchy theory of one-shot games and experimental analysis, *The Quarterly Journal of Economics*. Available from http://www.hss.caltech.edu/~camerer/.camerer.html.

Camerer, C.F., Loewenstein, G.F. and Prelec, D. (2004) Neuroeconomics: How neuroscience can inform economics, *Economic Perspectives*.

Camerer, C.F., Loewenstein, G.F. and Weber, M. (1989) The curse of knowledge in economic settings: An experimental analysis, *Journal of Political Economy*, 97(5), 1232–1254.

Carlson, K.A. and Russo, J.E. (2001) Biased interpretation of evidence by mock jurors, *Journal of Experimental Psychology: Applied*, 7(2), 91–103.

Carroll, J., Winer, R., Coates, D., Galegher, J. and Alibrio, J. (1988) Evaluation, diagnosis, and prediction in parole decision making, *Law and Society Review*, 17, 199–228.

Caruso, E.M., Epley, N. and Bazerman, M.H. (2005) The costs and benefits of undoing egocentric responsibility assessments in groups. *Journal of Personality and Social Psychology*, 91, 857–871.

Chan, L., Karceski, J. and Lakonishok, J. (2003) The Level and Persistence of Growth Rates, *Journal of Finance*, 58, April.

Chan, L.K.C., Dimmock, S.G. and Lakonishok, J. (2006) Benchmarking money manager performance: issues and evidence. NBER working paper 12461.

Chan, K. and Kot, H.W. (2002) Price reversal and momentum strategies. Working paper.

China effect convulses commodity markets, *Financial Times*, 15 November 2003.

Chugh, D., Bazerman, M. and Banaji, M. (2005) Bounded ethicality as a psychological barrier to recognizing conflicts of interest. To appear in Moore, D. Cain, D., Loewenstein, G. and Bazerman, M.H. (eds) Conflicts of Interest: Problems and Solutions from Law, Medicine and Organizational Settings. Cambridge University Press: London.

Clarke, R., de Silva, H. and Thorley, S. (2006) Minimum variance portfolios in the US equity market, *Portfolio Management*, Fall.

Clouse, R. and Small D. (2000) The Limit is the Federal Reserve Act Places on the Monetary policy actions of the Federal Reserve, Annual Review of Banking Law, 19, 553–579.

Cohen, R.B. and Polk, C.K. (1998) The impact of industry factors in asset-pricing tests.

Cremers, M. and Petajisto, A. (2006) How active is your fund manager? A new measure that predicts performance. Available from www.ssrn.com.

Cutler, D.M., Poterba, J.M. and Summers, L.H. (1989) What moves stock prices? *Journal of Portfolio Management*, Spring.

Damasio, A. (1994) *Descartes' Error: Emotion, Reason and the Human Brain*. Putnam Publishing.

Damasio, A. (2003) *Looking for Spinoza: Joy, Sorrow and the Feeling Brain*. Harvest Books.

Damasio, H., Grabowski, T., Frank, R., Galaburda, A.M. and Damasio, A.R. (1994) The return of Phineas Gage: Clues about the brain from the skull of a famous patient, *Science*, 264, 1102–1105.

Dandy, J., Brewer, N. and Tottman, R. (2001) Self-consciousness and performance decrements within a sporting context. *Social Psychology*, 141(1), 150–152.

Dasgupta, H., Prat, A. and Verardo, M. (2006) The price of conformism. Available from www.ssrn.com.

Davis, F.D., Lohse, G.L. and Kottemann, J.E. (1994) Harmful effects of seemingly helpful information on forecasts of stock earnings, *Journal of Economic Psychology*, 15, 253–267.

Dawes, R.M. (1989) *House of Cards: Psychology and Psychotherapy built on Myth*. Free Press.

Dawes, R.M., Faust, D. and Meehl, P.E. (1991) Clinical versus actuarial judgement, *Science*, 243, 1668–1674.

DePaulo, B.M., Lindsay, J.L., Malone, B.E., Muhlenbruck, L., Charlton, K. and Cooper, H. (2003) Cues to deception, *Psychological Bulletin*, 129, 74–118.

DeVaul, R.A., Jervey, F., Chappell, P., Carver, P., Short, B. and O'Keefe, S. (1957) Medical school performance of initially rejected students, *Journal of American Medical Association*, 257, 47–51.

Dichev, I.D. (1998) Is the risk of bankruptcy a systematic risk? *Journal of Finance*, 53(3), 1131–1147.

Diener, E. and Oishi, S. (2000) Money and happiness: Income and subjective well-being across nations. In Diener, E. and Suh, E.M. (eds) Cross-cultural psychology of subjective well-being. MIT Press: Boston.

DiFonzo, N. and Bordia, P. (1997) Rumour and prediction: making sense, (but losing dollars) in the stock market, *Organizational Behaviour and Human Decision Processes*, 71, 329–353.

Dinkelman, T., Levinsohn, J.A. and Majelantle, R. (2006) When knowledge is not enough: HIV/AIDS information and risky behaviour in Botswana. NBER working paper.

Ditto, P. and Lopez, D. (1992) Motivated skepticism: Use of differential decision criteria for preferred and non-preferred conclusions, *Journal of Personality and Social Psychology*, 63, 568–584.

Dohmen, T.J (2005) Do professionals choke under pressure? Working paper.

Dreman, D. and Lufkin, E. (2000) Investor overreaction: evidence that its basis is psychological, *Journal of Psychology and Financial Markets*, 1(1), 61–75.

Dukes, W. and Zhuoming, P. (2006) How do practitioners value common stocks? *Investing*, Fall.

Dunn, E.W. and Laham, S.A. (2006) A user's guide to emotional time travel: Progress on key issues in affective forecasting. In Forgas, J. (ed.) Hearts and Minds: Affective influences on social cognition and behavior. (Frontiers of Social Psychology series). Psychology Press: New York.

Dunn, E.W., Wilson, T.D. and Gilbert, D.T. (2003) Location. Location, location: The misprediction of satisfaction in housing lotteries, *Personality and Social Psychology Bulletin*, 29, 1421–1432.

Dunning, D., Johnson, K., Ehrlinger, J. and Kruger, J. (2003) Why people fail to recognize their own incompetence, *Current Directions in Psychological Science*, 12(3), 83–87.

Edwards, W. (1968) Conservatism in human information processing. Reprinted in Kahneman, D., Slovic, P. and Tversky, A. (1982) *Judgement under Uncertainty: Heuristics and Biases*. Cambridge University Press: New York.

Eisenberger, N.I. and Lieberman, M.D. (2004) Why rejection hurts: a common neural alarm system for physical and social pain, *Trends in Cognitive Sciences*, 8(7), 294–300.

Ekman, P. (2003) *Emotions Revealed: Understanding Faces and Feelings*. Orion Books.

Englich, T. and Mussweiler, T. (2001) Sentencing under uncertainty: Anchoring effects in the courtroom, *Journal of Applied Social Psychology*, 31, 1535–1551.

Englich, T., Mussweiler, T. and Strack, F. (2005) Playing dice with criminal sentences: the influence of irrelevant anchors on experts' judicial decision making, *Personality and Social Psychology Bulletin*, 32, 188–200.

Ennis, R.M. (2002) Reintegrating the equity portfolio, in *Equity Portfolio Construction*, AIMR.

Epley, N. and Dunning, D. (2000) Feeling 'Holier than thou': Are self-serving assessments produced by errors in self- or social prediction? *Journal of Personality and Social Psychology*, 79(6), 861–875.

Epley, N. and Gilovich, T.D. (2001) Putting adjustment back in the anchoring and adjustment heuristic: An examination of self-generated and experimenter-provided anchors, *Psychological Science*, 12(5), 391–396.

Epstein, S. (1990) Cognitive-experiential Self-theory. In L. Pervin (Ed.), Handbook of personality theory and research: Theory and research (pp. 165–192). Guilford Publications, Inc.: New York.

Erb, C.B. and Harvey, C.R. (2005) The tactical and strategic value of commodity futures. Working paper. Available at: *http://faculty.fuqua.duke.edu/~charvey/Research/Working_Papers/W77_The_tactical_and.pdf*.

Evans, J.ST.B.T. and Curtis-Holmes, J. (2005) Rapid responding increases belief bias: evidence for the dual process theory of reasoning, *Thinking and Reasoning*, 11(4), 382–389.

Evans, J.ST.B.T., Barston, J.L. and Pollard, P. (1983) On the conflict between logic and belief in syllogistic reasoning, *Memory and Cognition*, 11(3), 295–306.

Fama, E.F. (1998) Market efficiency, long-term returns and behavioral finance. Available from www.ssrn.com.

Fama, E.F. and French, K.R. (2004) The capital asset pricing model: Theory and evidence. Available from www.ssrn.com.

Fama, E.F. and French, K.R. (2006) Migration. Available from www.ssrn.com.

Fischhoff, B. (1975) Hindsight ≠ foresight: The effect of outcome knowledge on judgement under uncertainty, *Journal of Experimental Psychology: Human Perception and Performance*, 1, 288–299.

Franciosi, R., Kujal, P., Michelitsch, R., Smith, V. and Deng, G. (1996) Experimental tests of the endowment effect, *Journal of Economic Behaviour and Organization*, 30(2), 213–226.

Frazzini, A. (2004) The disposition effect and under-reaction to news. Yale IFC working paper. Available from www.ssrn.com.

Frederick, S. and Loewenstein, G. (1999) Hedonic adaptation. In Kahneman, D., Diener, E. and Schwarz, N. (eds) *Well-Being: The Foundations of Hedonic Psychology*. Russell Sage: New York.

Frederick, S. (2005) Cognitive reflection and decision making, *Economic Perspectives*, 19(4), 25–42.

Friesen, G.C. and Sapp, T. (2006) Mutual fund flows and investor returns: an empirical examination of fund investor timing ability. Available from www.ssrn.com.

Froot, K.A. and Obstfeld, M. (1991) Intrinsic bubbles: The case of stock prices, *American Economic Review*, 81(5), 1189–1214.

Froot, K.A., Scharfstein, D.S. and Stein, J.C. (1992) Herd on the street: Information inefficiencies in a market with short-term speculation, *Journal of Finance*, 47(4), 1461–1484.

Gilbert, D.T. (1991) How mental systems believe, *American Psychologist*, 46, 107–119.

Gilbert, D.T. (1993) The assent of man: Mental representation and the control of belief. In Wegner, D.M. and Pennebaker, J. (eds) *The Handbook of Mental Control*. Prentice-Hall: New York.

Gilbert, D.T. and Gill, M.J. (2000) The momentary realist, *Psychological Science*, 11(5), 394–398.

Gilbert, D.T., Krull, D.S. and Malone, P.S. (1990) Unbelieving the unbelievable: Some problems in the rejection of false information, *Journal of Personality and Social Psychology*, 59, 601–613.

Gilbert, D.T., Tafarodi, R.W. and Malone, P.S. (1993) You can't not believe everything you read, *Journal of Personality and Social Psychology*, 65(2), 221–233.

Glaser, M., Langer, T. and Weber, M. (2005) Overconfidence of professionals and lay men: Individual difference within and between tasks. University of Mannheim working paper. Available from www.ssrn.com.

Global Equity Strategy (various issues).

Global Strategy Weekly (various issues).

Gneezy, U. and Rustichini, A. (2000a) Pay enough or don't pay at all, *The Quarterly Journal of Economics*, August, 791–810.

Gneezy, U. and Rustichini, A, (2000b) A fine is a price, *Journal of Legal Studies*, 29(1), 1–17.

Goel, V. and Dolan, R.J. (2003) Explaining modulation of reasoning by belief, *Cognition*, 87, B11–22.

Goldberg, L.R. (1968) Simple models or simple processes? Some research on clinical judgements, *American Psychologist*, 23, 483–96.

Goyal, A. and Wahal, S. (2005) The selection and termination of investment management firms by plan sponsors. AFA 2006 Boston Meetings Paper. Available from www.ssrn.com.

Graham, J.R. and Harvey, C.R. (2005) Expectations, optimism and overconfidence. Unpublished paper.

Graham, J.R., Harvey, C.R. and Rajgopal, S. (2005) *The Economic Implications of Corporate Financial Reporting*. Available from www.ssrn.com.

Grantham, J.R. (2006) Oh Brave New World I., October.

Green, J.D., Nystrom, L.E., Engell, A.D., Darley, J.M. and Cohen, J.D. (2004) The neural bases of cognitive conflict and control in moral judgement, *Neuron*, 44, 389–400.

Green, J.D., Sommerville, R.B., Nystrom, L.E., Darley, J.M. and Cohen, J.D. (2001) AN fMRI investigation of emotional engagement in moral judgment, *Science*, 293(14), 2105–2108.

Grinold, R.C. (1989) The fundamental law of active management, *Journal of Portfolio Management*, Spring.

Grinold, R.C. and Kahn, R.N. (2000) *Active Portfolio Management*. A Quantitative Approach for Producing Superior Returns and Selecting Returns and Controlling Risk. McGraw-Hill.

Grosskopf, B. and Nagel, R. (2001) Rational reasoning or adaptive behaviour? Evidence from two-person beauty contest games. Available from www.ssrn.com.

Grosskopf, B. and Bereby-Meyer, Y. (2002) Overcoming the winner's curse: An adaptive learning perspective. AoM Conflict Management Division 2002 meetings No 13496. Available from ssrn.com.

Grossman, S. and Stiglizt, J. (1980) On the impossibility of informationally efficient markets, *American Economic Review*, 70.

Grove, W.M. and Meehl, P.E. (1996) Comparative efficiency of formal (mechanical, algorithmic) and informal (subjective, impressionistic) prediction procedures: The clinical–statistical controversy, *Psychology, Public Policy and Law*, 2, 293–323.

Grove, W.M., Zald, D.H., Lebow, B.S., Snitz, B.E. and Nelson, C. (2000) Clinical versus mechanical prediction: A meta-analysis, *Psychological Assessment*, 12, 19–30.

Haidt, J. (2001) The emotional dog and its rational tail: A social intuitionist approach to moral judgement, *Psychological Review*, 108, 814–834.

Handzic, M. (2001) Does more information lead to better informing? *Informing Science, Challenges to Informing Clients: A Transdisciplinary Approach*, June, 251–256.

Haney, C., Banks, W.C. and Zimbardo, P.G. (1973) A study of prisoners and guards in a simulated prison, *Naval Research Reviews*, 9, 1–17. Office of Naval Research: Washington DC.

Hare, R.D. (1999) *Without Conscience: The Disturbing World of the Psychopaths Among us*. Guidlford Press.

Hastie, R. and Pennington, N. (2000) Explanation-based decision making. In Connolly, T., Arkes, H. and Hammond, K.R. (eds) *Judgement and Decision Making: An Interdisciplinary Reader, 2nd Ed.* Cambridge University Press: New York.

Hastie, R., Schkade, D.A. and Payne, J.W. (1997) *Juror Judgements in Civil Cases: Assessing Punitive Damages*. Center for Research on Judgement and Policy.

Heath, F. and Gonzalez, R. (1995) Interaction with others increases decision confidence but not decision quality, *Organisation Behaviour and Human Decision Processes*, 61, 305–326.

Henry, R.A. (1989) Accuracy and confidence in group judgement, *Organisational Behaviour and Human Decision Processes*, 43, 1–28.

Hightower, R. and Sayeed, L. (1995) The impact of computer-mediated communication systems on biased group discussion, *Computers in Human Behaviour*, 11(1), 33–44.

Hirota, S. and Sunder, S. (2003) Stock market as a beauty contest: investor beliefs and price bubbles sans dividend anchor. Available from www.ssrn.com.

Hirshleifer, D. (2001) Investor psychology and asset pricing, *Journal of Finance*, 56(4), 1533–1597.

Houge, T. and Loughran, T. (2000) Cash flow is king, *Journal of Psychology and Financial Markets*, 1(3&4), 161–175.

Houge, T. and Loughran, T. (2006) Do investors capture the value premium? *Financial Management*, 35(2), 5–19.

Hsu, J.C. and Campollo, C. (2006) New frontiers in index investing: An examination of fundamental indexation. Available from www.researchaffiliates.com.

Hunt, L.H. and Hoisington, D.M. (2003) Estimating the stock/bond risk premium, *Journal of Portfolio Management*, Winter.

Jacobsen, B. and Visaltanachoti, N. (2006) The Halloween effect in US sectors. Working paper. Available from www.srrn.com.

Jolls, C. (1998) Stock repurchases and incentive compensation. NBER working paper 6467.

Kahn, R. (2002) What plan sponsors need from their active equity managers. In *Equity Portfolio Construction*. AIMR.

Kahneman, D., Knetsch, J. and Thaler, R. (1990) Experimental tests of the endowment effect and the Coase Theorem, *Political Economy,* 98(6), 1325–1348.

Kahneman, D., Krueger, A., Schkade, D., Schwarz, N. and Stone, A. (2003) *Measuring the Quality of Life*, unpublished working paper.

Kasser, T. and Ryan, R.M. (1996) Further examining the American dream: Differential correlates of intrinsic and extrinsic goals. *Personality and Social Psychology Bulletin*, 22, 280–287.

Kasser, T. and Ryan, R.M. (2001) Be careful what you wish for: Optimal functioning and the relative attainment of intrinsic and extrinsic goals. In Schmuck, P. and Sheldon, K. (eds) *Life-Goals and Well Being*. Hogrefe: Gottingen.

Kassin, S.M. and Fong, C.T. (1999) I'm innocent: Effects of training on judgements of truth and deception in the interrogation room, *Law and Human Behavior*, 23(5) 499–516.

Kassin, S.M., Meissner, C.A. and Norwick, R.J. (2005) I'd know a false confession if I saw one: A comparative study of college students and police investigators, *Law and Human Behavior*, 29, 211–228.

Keen, S. (2001) Debunking economics: The Naked Emperor of the Social Sciences. Zeb Books.

Kirby, R. (1976) You need more than numbers to measure performance. In Ellis, C. and Vertin, J. (eds) *An Investor's Anthology: Original Ideas from the Industry's Greatest Minds*. John Wiley & Sons, Ltd: New York.

Klein, G. (1999) *Sources of Power: How People Make Decisions*. MIT Press.

Knutson, B. and Peterson, R. (2005) Neurally reconstructing expected utility, *Games and Economic Behavior*, 52, 305–315.

Koehler, D.J. and Poon, S.K. (2006) Self-predictions overweight strength of current intentions, *Journal of Experimental Social Psychology,* 42, 517–524.

Kruger, J. and Dunning, D. (1999) Unskilled and unaware of it: How difficulties in recognizing one's own incompetence lead to inflated self-assessments, *Journal of Personality and Social Psychology*, 77, 1121–1134.

Langer, E.J., Blank, A. and Chanowitz, B. (1978) The mindlessness of ostensibly thoughtful action: The role of placebic information in interpersonal interaction, *Journal of Personality and Social Psychology*, 36(6), 635–642.

Langer, E.J. (1975) The illusion of control, *Journal of Personality and Social Psychology*, 32(2), 311–328.

Langer, E.J. and Roth, J. (1975) Heads I win, tails it's chance: The illusion of control as a function of the sequence of outcomes in a purely chance task. *Journal of Personality and Social Psychology*, 32(6), 951–955.

Lau, R. and Russell, D. (1980) Attributions in the sports pages, *Journal of Personality and Social Psychology*, 39(1), 29–38.

Ledoux, J. (1996) *The Emotional Brain*. Simon & Schuster.

Lee, I.H. (1998) Market crashes and informational avalanches, *Review of Economic Studies*, 65.

Leeper, M.R., Lord, C.G. and Ross, L. (1979) Biased assimilation and attitude polarization: The effects of prior theories on subsequently considered evidence, *Journal of Personality and Social Psychology*, 37, 2098–2109.

Leli, D.A. and Filskov, S.B. (1981) Clinical–actuarial detection and description of brain impairment with the Wechsler-Bellvue Form 1, *Clinical Psychology*, 37, 623–629.

Lewis, M. (2003) *Moneyball: The Art of Winning an Unfair Game*. Norton.

Lie, E. (2001) Financial flexibility and the corporate payout choice. Unpublished working paper, College of William and Mary, VA.

Lieberman, M.D., Gaunt, R., Gilbert, D.T. and Trope, Y. (2002) Reflexion and reflection: A social cognitive neuroscience approach to attributional inference, *Advances in Experimental Social Psychology*, 34, 199–249.

Lieberman, M.D., Ochsner, K.N., Gilbert, D.T. and Schacter, D.L. (2001) Do amnesiacs exhibit cognitive dissonance reduction? The role of explicit memory and attention in attitude change, *Psychological Science*, 12, 135–140.

Lo, A.W. and Repin, D.V. (2002) The Psychophysiology of Real-Time Financial Risk Processing. *Journal of Cognitive Neuroscience*, 14, 323–339.

Lo, A.W., Repin, D.V. and Steenbarger, B.N. (2004) Fear and greed in financial markets: A clinical study of day-traders. MIT Sloan working paper no. 4534–05. Available from www.ssrn.com.

Loewenstein, G. and Adler, D. (1995) A bias in the prediction of tastes, *Economic Journal*, 105(431) 929–37.

Loewenstein, G., Nagin, D. and Paternoster, R. (1997) The effect of sexual arousal on expectations of sexual forcefulness, *Journal of Research in Crime and Delinquency*, 34(4), 443–473.

Lowenstein, L. (2004) Searching for rational investors in a perfect storm. Columbia Law and Economics working paper no 255. Available from www.ssrn.com.

MacCoun, R. (2002) Comparing micro and macro rationality. In Gowda, M.V.R. and Fox, J. (eds) *Judgements, Decisions and Public Policy*. Cambridge University Press: New York. (Also available from http://ist-socrates.berkeley.edu/~maccoun/index.html#B).

Malmendier, U. and Tate, G.A. (2004) *Superstar CEOs*. Available from www.ssrn.com.

Markowitz, H. (2005) Market efficiency: A theoretical distinction and so what? *Financial Analysts Journal*, 61(5) 17–30.

Martin, F. (2006) *Speculative Contagion*. AuthorHouse.

McClure, S.M., Laibson, D.I., Loewenstein, G. and Cohen, J.D. (2004) Separate neural systems value immediate and delayed monetary targets, *Science*, 306, 503–507.

McKinsey Quarterly (January 2006) Weighing the pros and cons of earnings guidance.

Meissner, C.A. and Kassin, S.M. (2002) He's guilty: Investigator bias in judgements of truth and deception, *Law and Human Behavior*, 26(5), 469–480.

Mellstrom, C. and Joannesson, M. (2006) Crowding out in blood donation: Was Titmuss right? Working paper.

Miller, G. (1956) The magic number seven plus or minus two, *Psychological Review*, 63, 81–97.

Milgram, S. (1974) *Obedience to Authority: An Experimental View*. HarperCollins.

Minahan, J.R. (2006) The role of investment philosophy in evaluating investment managers: A consultant's perspective on distinguishing alpha from noise, *Investing*, Summer.

Moll, J., Oliveira-Souza, R., Bramati, I.E. and Grafman, J. (2002) Functional networks in emotional moral and non-moral social judgements, *Neuroimage*, 16(3a), 678–695.

Montier, J. (2002) *Behavioural Finance: Insights in Irrational Minds and Markets*. John Wiley & Sons Ltd: Chichester.

Moore, D., Loewenstein, G., Tanlu, L. and Bazerman, M. (2004) Auditor independence, conflict of interest and unconscious intrusion of bias.

Morck, R. (2004) Behavioral finance in corporate governance – independent directors and non-executive chairs. HIER working paper 2037.

Mulligan, E.J. and Hastie, R. (2005) Explanations determine the impact of information on financial investment judgements, *Journal of Behavioural Decision Making*, 18(2), 145.

Muraven, M. and Baumeister, R.F. (2000) Self-regulation and depletion of limited resources: Does self-control resemble a muscle? *Psychological Bulletin*, 126(2), 247–259.

Nagel, R. (1995) Unravelling in guessing games: An experimental study, *American Economic Review*, 85, 1313–1326.

Nagel, R., Bosch-Domènech, A., Satorra, A. and Garcia-Montalvo, J. (1999) One, two, (three) infinity: Newspaper and Lab Beauty-Contest Experiments. Available from www.ssrn.com.

Nisbett, R.E. and Wilson, T.D. (1977) Telling more than we know: Verbal reports on mental processes, *Psychological Review*, 84(3), 231–259.

Nisbett, R.E., Caputo, C., Legant, P. and Maracek, J. (1973) Behaviour as seen by the actor and as seen by the observer. *Journal of Personality and Social Psychology*, 27, 154–164.

Northcraft, G.B. and Neale, M.A. (1987) Experts, amateurs, and real estate, *Organizational Behaviour and Human Decisions Processes*, 39, 84–97.

Odean, T. (1998) Are investors reluctant to realize their losses?, *Journal of Finance*, October, 53(5), 1775–1798.

Odean, T. (1998) Volume, volatility, price and profit when all traders are above average, *Journal of Finance*, 53(6), 1887–1934.

Ono, K. (1987) Superstitious behaviour in humans, *Journal of Experimental Analysis of Behaviour*, 47, 261–271.

Oskamp, K. (1965) Overconfidence in case-study judgements, *Journal of Consulting Psychology*, 29, 261–265.

Pennington, N. and Hastie, R. (1986) Evidence evaluation in complex decision making, *Journal of Personality and Social Psychology*, 51(2), 242–258.

Pennington, N. and Hastie, R. (1988) Explanation-based decision making: the effects of memory structure on judgement, *Journal of Experimental Psychology: Learning, Memory and Cognition*, 14(3), 521–533.

Petty, R.E., Cacioppo, J.T., Strathman, A.J. and Priester, J.R. (1994) To think or not to think. In Shavitt, S. and Brock, T.C. (eds) *Persuasion: Psychological insights and perspectives*. Allyn & Bacon: Boston, MA.

Petty, R.E., Wells, G.L. and Brock, T.C. (1976) Distraction can enhance or reduce yielding to propaganda, *Journal of Personality and Social Psychology*, 34, 874–884.

Philips, T.K. (1999) Why do valuation ratios forecast long-run equity returns?, *Journal of Portfolio Management*, Spring.

Piotroski, J.D. (2000) Value Investing: The use of historical financial information to separate winners and losers, *Journal of Accounting Research*, 38, 1–14.

Plous, S. (1991) *The psychology of judgement and decision-making*. McGraw Hill.

Presson, P. and Benassi, V. (1996) Illusion of control: A meta-analytic review, *Journal of Social Behavior and Personality*, 11(3), 493–510.

Pronin, E., Lin, D.Y. and Ross, L. (2002) The bias blind spot: Perceptions of bias in self versus others, *Personality and Social Psychology Bulletin*, 28, 369–381.

Pronin, E., Wegner, D.M., McCarthy, K. and Rodriguez, S. (2006) Everyday magical powers: The role of apparent mental causation in the overestimation of personal influence, *Journal of Personality and Social Psychology*, 91, 218–231.

Rau, R., Patel, A., Osobov, I., Khorana, A. and Cooper, M. (2001) The game of the name: Value changes accompanying dot.com additions and deletions. Unpublished working paper.

Read, D. and Van Leeuwen, B. (1998) Predicting hunger: The effects of appetite and delay on choice, *Organizational Behaviour and Human Decision Processes*, 76, 189–205.

Ross, L., Amabile, T.M. and Steinmetz, J.L. (1977) Social roles, social controls, and biases in social perception processes, *Journal of Personality and Social Psychology*, 35, 485–494.

Rothchild, J. (1998) *The Bear Book: Survive and Profit in Ferocious Markets*. John Wiley & Sons, Inc: Hoboken.

Russo, J.E. and Schoemaker, P.J.H. (1989) *Decision Traps: Ten Barriers to Brilliant Decision Making and How to Overcome Them*. Simon & Schuster.

Schkade, D.A. and Kahneman, D. (1998) Does living in California make people happy? A Focusing Illusion in Judgement of Life Satisfaction, *Psychological Science*, 9(5), 340–346.

Schnabel, I. and Shin, H.S. (2003) Foreshadowing LTCM: The Crisis of 1763. Unpublished paper.

Shefrin, H. and Statman, M. (1985) The disposition to sell winners too early and ride losers too long: Theory and evidence, *Journal of Finance*, 40(3), 777–790.

Sheldon, K.M. and Kasser, T. (1998) Pursuing personal goals: Skills enable progress, but not all progress is beneficial, *Personality and Social Psychology Bulletin*, 24, 1319–1331.

Sheldon, S., Lyubomirsky, K.M. and Schkade, D. (2003) Pursuing Happiness: The Architecture of Sustainable Change. *Review of General Psychology*, 9, 111–131.

Shiller, R.J. (1981) Do stock prices move too much to be justified by subsequent changes in dividends? *American Economic Review*, 71, 421–436.

Shiller, R.J. (1984) Stock prices and social dynamics, *Brookings Papers on Economic Activity*, 2, 457–510.

Shiller, R.J. (1987) Investor behavior in the October 1987 Stock Market Crash: Survey evidence. Reprinted in Shiller, R.J. (1989) *Market Volatility*. MIT Press.

Shiv, B., Loewenstein, G. and Bechara, A. (2005) The dark side of emotion in decision-making: when individuals with decreased emotional reactions make more advantageous decisions, *Cognitive Brain Research*, 23, 85–92.

Shleifer, A. (2000) *Inefficient Markets: An Introduction to Behavioural Finance*. Oxford Univeristy Press.

Shynkaruk, J.M. and Thompson, V.A. (2006) Confidence and accuracy in deductive reasoning, *Memory and Cognition*, 34(3), 619–632.

Simons, D.J. and Chabris, C.F. (1999). Gorillas in our midst: Sustained inattentional blindness for dynamic events, *Perception*, 28(9), 1059–1074.

Simonsohn, U., Karlsson, N., Loewenstein, G. and Ariely, D. (2004) The tree of experience in the forest of information. Available from www.ssrn.com.

Skinner, B.F. (1947) Superstition in the pigeon, *Journal of Experimental Psychology*, 38.

Slovic, P. (1973) Behavioral problems adhering to a decision policy. Unpublished paper.

Slovic, P. and Fischhoff, B. (1977) On the psychology of experimental surprises. *Journal of Experimental Psychology: Human Perception and Performance*, 3, 544–551.

Smith, P. and Bond, M. (1994) *Social Psychology across cultures: analysis and perspective*. Allyn and Bacon.

Stephens, C.P. and Weisbach, M.S. (1998) Actual share reacquisitions in open-market repurchase programs, *Journal of Finance*, 53(1), 313–333.

Stasser, G. and Titus, W. (2003) Hidden profiles: a brief history, *Psychological Inquiry*, 14, 304–313.

Stasson, M.F. and Ono, K. Zimmerman, S.K. and David, J.H. (1988) Group consensus processes to cognitive bias task, *Japanese Psychological Research*, 30, 68–77.

Stotz, O. and von Nitzsch, R. (2005) The perception of control and the level of overconfidence: Evidence from analysts earnings estimates and price targets, *Behavioural Finance*, 6(3).

Stout, J.C., Busemeyer, J.R., Lin, A., Grant, S.R. and Bonson, K.R. (2004) Cognitive modelling analysis of the decision-making processes used by cocaine abusers, *Psychonomic Bulletin and Review*, 11, 742–747.

Sunstein, C.R. (2004) Group judgements: deliberation, statistical means and information markets. Chicago Law School working paper.

Surowiecki, J. (2004) The wisdom of crowds. Anchor.

Taleb, N. (2005) *The Scandal of Prediction*.

Taleb, N. (2007) *The Black Swan: The Impact of the Highly Improbable*. Random House.

Tenbrunsel, A.E. and Messick, D.M. (2004) Ethical fading: the role of self-deception in unethical behaviour, *Social Justice Research*, 17(2), 223–236.

Tetlock, P.E. (2002) Theory-driven reasoning about plausible pasts and probable futures in world politics. In Gilovich, T., Griffin, D. and Kahneman, D. (eds) *Heuristics and Biases: The Psychology of Intuitive Judgement*. Cambridge University Press.

Thaler, R.H. and DeBondt, N.F.M. (1985) Does the stock market overreact? *Journal of Finance*, 40, 793–805.

Tirole, J. (1982) On the possibility of speculation under rational expectations, *Econometrica*, 50(5), 1163–1182.

Tirole, J. (1985) Asset bubbles and overlapping generations: A synthesis, *Econometrica*, 53, 1071–1100.

Titman, S., Wei, K.C.J. and Xie, F. (2004) Capital Investments and Stock Returns. *Journal of Financial and Quantitative Analysis*, 39, 677–700.

Torngren, G. and Montgomery, H. (2004) Worse than chance? Performance and confidence among professionals and laypeople in the stock market, *Behavioural Finance*, 5(3).

Tversky, D.W. and Griffin, A. (1992) The weighing of evidence and the determinants of confidence, *Cognitive Psychology* 24, 411–435.

Tversky, A. and Kahneman, D. (1974) Judgement under uncertainty: Heuristics and biases, *Science*, 185, 1124–1131.

Tversky, A. and Kahneman, D. (1983) Extension versus intuitive reasoning: the conjunction fallacy in probability judgement, *Psychological Review*, 90, 293–315.

Tweedy Browne (1998) *10 Ways to Beat an Index*. Available from www.tweedy.com.

Tyska, T. and Zielonka, P. (2002) Expert judgements: Financial analysts versus weather forecasters, *Psychology and Financial Markets*, 3(3), 152–160.

Van Boven, L. (2005) Experientialism, materialism, and the pursuit of happiness, *Review of General Psychology*, 9, 132–142.

Van Boven, L. and Gilovich, T. (2003) To do or to have? That is the question, *Personality and Social Psychology*, 85, 1193–1202.

Van Boven, L. and Kane, J. (2005) Predicting feelings and choices. Unpublished paper.

Van Boven, L. and Loewenstein, G. (2003) Social projection of transient drive states, *Personality and Social Psychology Bulletin*, 29, 1159–1168.

Van Knippenberg, A., Dijksterhuis, A. and Vermeulen, D. (1999) Judgement and memory of a criminal act: the effects of stereotypes and cognitive load, *European Journal of Social Psychology*, 29, 191–202.

Vansteenkiste, M., Duriez, B., Simons, J., and Soenens, B. (2005) Materialistic values and well being amongst business students: further evidence for their detrimental effect, *Applied Social Psychology*, 36(12), 2892–2908.

Vuolteenaho, T. (2006) Beta arbitrage as an alpha opportunity. Arrowstreet Capital white paper.

Westen, D., Blagov, P., Feit, J., Arkowitz, P and Thagard, P. (2004) When reason and passions collide: emotional constraint satisfaction in motivated political reasoning. Unpublished paper.

Westen, D., Blagov, P., Harenski, K., Kilts, C. and Hamann, S. (2005) An fMRI study of motivated reasoning: Partisan political reasoning in the U.S. Presidential Election. Unpublished paper.

Wilson, T.D., Wheatley, T.P., Meyers, J.M., Gilbert, D.T. and Axsom, D. (2000) Focalism: A source of durability bias in affective forecasting, *Personality and Social Psychology*, 78, 821–836.

Wittenbaum, G.M. and Park, E.S. (2001) The collective preference for shared information, *Current Directions in Psychological Science*, 10, 70–73.

Wittenbaum, G.M., Hubbell, A.P. and Zuckerman, C. (1999) Mutual enhancement: Toward an understanding of the collective preference for shared information, *Journal of Personality and Social Psychology*, 77, 967–978.

Wolford, G.L., Miller, M.B. and Gazzaniga, M.S. (2000) The Left Hemisphere's Role in Hypothesis Formation, I, *Journal of Neuroscience*, 20, RC63, 1–6

Yaniv, I. and Kleinberger, E. (2000) Advice taking in decision making: Egocentric discounting and reputation formation, *Organizational Behavior and Human Decision Processes*, 83, 260–281.

Zimbardo, P. (2005) You can't be a sweet cucumber in a vinegar barrel. Interview with *Edge*, January 19.

Index

abnormal returns 249–51, 254–7, 384–6, 450–2, 575–80, 608
Abreu, D. 504
absence of evidence, evidence of absence 227
absolute alpha 240–6, 489–91
    see also alpha
absolute returns 240–6, 296–7, 469, 489–91
    see also returns
absolute-value contrasts, sector-relative factors 399–403
absolute/relative concepts, happiness 656, 665
Abu Ghraib 599, 601–3
accounting regimes
    bubbles 466
    sector-relative factors 395–6, 398–403
    unconscious biases 612, 622–8
accruals, cash flows 489–90
accuracy factors
    confidence 528
    information 135–7
Ackert, L.F. 513–14
acquisitions, learning from mistakes 65–7
actions, corporate managers 355–65
active fund managers 119–20, 225–33, 238–46, 373–4, 419, 489
    see also fund managers; stock pickers
    efficient markets 119–20, 225–7
    performance issues 225–33, 373–4, 419
active share
    average/aggregate active share 231–2
    concepts 225, 227–33
    definition 227
    persistence levels 231–2
    statistics 227–33
activism, shareholders 607–8
actor/observer bias *see* fundamental attribution error
acts of omission, unethical behaviour 628–9
addicted persons 47–53
    see also drug...
ADHD (attention deficit hyperactivity disorder) 179–86, 367

advantageous comparisons, moral-disengagement factors 608–9
Africa 168
agency issues, principal–agent problems 284–5
agriculture 591
    see also commodities
Aklerof, George 431
alcoholics 47–50
    see also drug...
Alexander, Michael 566–7
allure of growth 189–96
    see also stories
alphas
    see also information ratios
    alternative investments 245
    arbitrage 221
    bubbles 469, 489–91
    change needs 235–46
    cheap countries 410, 419–21
    concepts 183–5, 221, 225–33, 235–46, 267, 299, 333–6, 383–5, 410, 419–21, 425–35, 469, 489–91
    critique 425–35
    fund managers 183–5, 221, 228–9, 235–46, 267, 299, 383–5
    hedge funds 245, 343–4, 433–4, 489
    quant models 267
    statistics 228–9, 299, 333–6, 383–6
    zero sum games 241–2
alternative investments
    see also commodities; hedge funds
    alphas 245
    critique 245, 587–96
    returns 587–96
    risks 587–96
Altman's Z-scores 449–50, 461–2, 478–80, 489
altruism, happiness 652–3
Amazon 165
ambiguity-aversion bias 20
AMEX 428
amnesics, cognitive dissonance 585–6

amphetamines 47
  see also drug...
amygdala 6, 9
analysts 106–19, 121, 123–30, 174–5, 179–86,
    282–4, 286–7, 307, 315–17, 367–74, 459,
    521–8
  belief bias 521–8
  conflicts of interest bias 611–12, 621–2
  favoured stocks 123–4, 127–30, 521
  forecasts 106–19, 121, 129–30, 283–4, 307,
    315–17, 330, 459
  short-termism 174–5, 179–86, 282–3, 293,
    297–300, 367–74, 459
  valuation methods 123–30, 288
anatomy of value 310–12
anchoring/salience bias
  see also heuristic-simplification bias
  concepts 20, 25–7, 87–92, 99–100, 105–6, 120,
    168, 211–13, 239, 288–9, 499–500, 509–10,
    516–17, 627
  dividends 100, 288–9
  examples 25–7, 87–92, 99–100, 105–6, 120, 168,
    288–9, 627
  group-based decisions (wrath) 211–13
  legal experts 99–100, 120
  test 87, 120
anger 6–7
  see also emotions
announcements
  dividend payments 23, 37–8
  share repurchases 532–3, 543–7, 551–2
anterior cingulate cortex 6, 300
Antrim, Minna 76
Antunes, Rui 307–28, 329–36, 407–8, 429, 551–2
APT (arbitrage pricing theory) 432
arbitrage 221, 286–7, 367–74, 375, 377–86,
    428–31, 432, 504–5
  alphas 221
  betas 428–31
  big picture 377
  bonds 441–2
  critique 221, 286–7, 367–74, 375, 377–86, 504
  growth investors 380–3
  near-rational bubbles 504–5
  value added 369–74
  value investors 377–86
arbitrage pricing theory (APT) 432
arbitrary bubbles 497–8
  see also bubbles
Ariely *et al* 26–7, 37, 42–4, 635–8
Arnott, Rob 429–30, 433
Arthur Andersen 622
Ashenfelter *et al* 263–5
Ashraf *et al* 650, 653
Asness *et al* 245, 383, 397–8, 405, 407–8
Aspirations Index 657–60
asset allocations 209–15, 235–46, 261, 431–2,
    471–91

  see also strategic...; tactical...
  bubbles 487–91
asset fire sales, bubbles 480–1
asset price bubbles *see* bubbles
asset-allocation committees
  see also group...
  critique 209–15
assimilation bias
  capital punishment 148–9
  concepts 19–21, 148–51
  examples 148–51
attention deficit disorder 655, 661
attention deficit hyperactivity disorder (ADHD)
    179–86, 367
audio tests, lie-detection experiments 153–4, 156
auditors, unconscious biases 612, 622–8
Australia 430, 605
Austria 257, 605
authority figures
  electric-shock experiments 151–3, 599, 604–8
  obedience tendencies 143, 151–3, 292, 599,
    604–8
availability bias 20, 293, 301
avarice, seven sins 97, 101, 177–86

backward induction 164–5
backwardation 588, 591–5
bad behaviour 75, 151–3, 463, 466–7, 482–3,
    599–609, 627–9
  Abu Ghraib 599, 601–3
  concepts 151–3, 599–609, 627–9
  corporate malfeasance 75, 153, 463, 466–7,
    482–3, 599, 601–9
  dissenting voices 606–7, 629
  electric-shock experiments 151–3, 599, 604–8
  ethics 608–9, 627–9
  fundamental attribution error 152–3, 599, 601–9
  groups 608–9, 611–12, 619–20
  Milgram's experiments 151–3, 599, 604–8
  moral-disengagement factors 608–9, 627–9
  situational/dispositional perspectives 601–9,
    628–9
  USA 601–9
  Zimbardo's prison experiment 602–3
bad years 240–1, 271, 278, 295, 296–7, 337–8,
    344–5, 367, 388, 393
balance sheets 271, 275–6, 435–6, 469, 489–91
balanced funds
  change needs 235–46
  critique 244–5
Bali *et al* 355–64
Bandura, Albert 608–9
bargain hunters 307–28, 337–53
Barra values 228
basal ganglia 6, 14, 298
basketball players, incentives 640
Basle agreement 439
bathroom scales, feedback distortions 63–4, 72–6

Baumeister, R.F. 11–13
Bayes' theorem 93, 116, 509
Bazerman, Max 65, 611
bear markets 57, 235, 239–42, 252–4, 261, 279,
    426, 435, 463–7, 469, 483–8, 495, 506, 507,
    514–17, 570–1
'beating the gun' difficulties 161–75, 182–3, 185–6,
    241, 497
beauty contest analogy
    investor behaviour 90–2, 101, 161–75, 440–1
    strategic thinking 165–75, 440–1
Bebchuk, L.A. 608
Bechara *et al* 49–53, 66–7, 447–8
BEER 488
behaviour contrasts, knowledge 293, 295–6
behavioural activities, happiness 647, 652–3
behavioural economics
    historical background 281
    incentives 631–43
behavioural errors 289, 360–1
Behavioural Finance Compendium 49
behavioural psychology 25, 71–6, 293–304,
    359–60, 447
    see also psychology
    bad behaviour 75, 151–3, 463, 466–7, 482–3,
        599–609, 627–9
    hindsight bias 25
behavioural stumbling blocks, value investors
    293–304
behaviouralism 71–2
Beilock *et al* 641–3
Belgium 247, 257, 409
belief bias
    concepts 521–8
    definition 521, 523
    System X 524–8
    Zen of investing 521–2, 528
beliefs
    Cartesian systems 197, 199–205
    cognitive dissonance 19–21, 581–6
    concepts 19–21, 197–205, 521–8, 581–6
    corrected beliefs 197, 200–5
    distractions 197–8, 200–5
    empirical evidence 200–3
    exclusion strategy 198, 204–5
    exposure controls 198, 204–5
    false beliefs 197–205
    libraries 200
    myths 199, 519–96
    naïve beliefs 203–5
    philosophy 197–205
    Spinozan systems 197–205
    testing structures 200–1
    unbelieving strategy 197–8, 204–5
    understanding 197–205
    valid beliefs 523–4
believing everything you read (sloth), seven sins 97,
    101, 187–205

benchmarking 102, 179, 181–4, 221, 225–33,
    240–6, 274–5, 393, 429–30, 484
    see also indexing; passive investing
    change needs 240–6
    peer groups 484
Bernanke, Ben 55, 57, 61
Bernstein, Richard 252–3
Bertrand, M. 618–19
best value investors 183–4, 271–8, 293–304, 375–86
    see also successful investors
    bad years 271, 278, 295, 296–7, 337–8, 344–5
    behavioural stumbling blocks 293–304
    business risks 271, 275–6, 295
    cash holdings 271, 276–7, 295
    closed funds 272, 278, 295
    concepts 183–4, 271–8, 293–304
    highly concentrated portfolios 271, 273–6, 295
    information 271, 274–5, 276, 295
    key traits 271–8, 295
    profit margins 271, 275–6, 295, 449–50
    time horizons 271, 277, 293, 295, 297–300,
        375–6
betas 219, 222, 230–1, 245, 291, 333–6, 346–9,
    355–6, 361–4, 410, 419–21, 425–35, 445–52
    see also volatility
    arbitrage 428–31
    cheap countries 410, 419–21
    critique 219, 222, 230–1, 291, 355–6, 361–4,
        425–35
    fund management groups 231
    hedge funds 245, 433–4, 589
    net equity issuance 355–6, 361–4
    returns 428–35
    risks 425–6, 428–35, 445–52
    statistics 231, 333–6, 346–9, 410, 419–21,
        428–35
Bhattacharya, U. 230
biases 17–36, 44–6, 63–76, 99–215, 521–8, 601–9,
    611–29
    see also heuristic-simplification...; *individual
    biases*; self-deception...
    auditors 612, 622–8
    concepts 17, 19–46, 63–76, 509–17, 521–8,
        601–9, 611–29
    conflicts of interest bias 611–12, 621–7
    corporate managers 143–57, 459
    definition 19
    empathy gaps 37–46
    ethics 611–29
    fund managers 79–94, 99–215, 521–8
    fundamental attribution error 152–3, 599, 601–9
    groups 209–15, 619–20
    impact bias 37–46
    in-group bias 611–12, 619–20
    overclaiming credit 611–12, 620–1
    rebias considerations 36
    reduction techniques 24, 44–6, 63–4, 69, 76, 102,
        106, 219–22, 611, 629

biases (*Cont.*)
  self-vs-others perceptions 19, 35, 44
  seven sins of fund managers 95–215
  susceptibilities 19–21
  test 79–94, 109–10, 120
  types 19–20, 617–29
  unconscious biases 611, 615, 617–29
  veil of ignorance 629
  written records 24, 63–4, 69–70, 76
big picture, arbitrage 377
bills of exchange 465
bipolar disorder (manic depression) 275
'black box' terminology, quant models 260, 269
blood donors
  good intentions 303–4
  incentives 638–9
Bloomberg 254

the body
  the brain 7, 85–6
  emotions 7
Bogle, John 181, 277
bonds 107–9, 238–42, 280, 290, 362–3, 431, 441–2,
    462–3, 465, 469–91, 499, 573–80
  see also debt
  arbitrage 441–2
  default premiums 362–3
  economic cycles 576–80
  equities 239, 241, 280, 290, 431, 462–3, 469–91,
    499, 573–80
  forecasts 107–9
  returns 238–40, 241, 462–3, 487–8, 573–80
bookmakers' experiment, illusion of knowledge
    20–1, 133, 135–7
booms
  see also bubbles
  concepts 455–67, 469–91, 493–506
Boorstin, Daniel 20, 135
Bordeaux wines, quant models 259, 263–5
borderline mental disorder 655, 661
Bordia, P. 192–3
bottom-up value opportunities 290, 393
bounded awareness 199
bounded ethicality, concepts 611–12, 617–27
bounded rationality, concepts 168–75, 611–12,
    617–27
the brain
  beliefs/understanding 197–205
  the body 7, 85–6
  damage 7–11, 47–53, 262, 447, 616–17
  emotions 6–11, 13–15, 75–6, 85–6, 297–300, 527
  plasticity 15
  quant models 262
  reasoning systems 5–7, 75–6, 85–6, 297–300,
    445, 527
  working memory 631, 640–3
The Brandes Institute 274–5, 367, 370–2
breadth of call

concepts 242–5
definition 242
British railway boom 466, 507
Brunnermeier, M. 504
bubbles 25, 55, 59–61, 70, 164–5, 274, 278, 342–3,
    395–7, 439, 455–67, 469–91, 493–506, 507–17
  alphas 469, 489–91
  arbitrary bubbles 497–8
  asset allocations 487–91
  asset fire sales 480–1
  balance sheets 469, 489–91
  capital expenditure 481–3, 490–1
  cash flows 478–83
  causes 455, 457, 466–7, 471–6
  composite bubbles 500–3
  concepts 455–67, 469–91, 493–506, 507–17
  credit-creation stage 455, 457–9, 473–6
  critical stage 455, 457, 459–63, 477–84
  cynical bubbles 55, 59–61, 164–5, 439, 493–506
  danger triggers 503–5
  de-bubbling processes 469–91, 493–4, 500–6,
    509–17
  deflation 469, 473, 479–84, 487–9, 507
  displacement stage 455, 457, 466–7, 473–4
  dividends 471–3
  dot.com bubble 25, 70, 478, 495, 499
  earnings quality 469, 489–91
  echoes 471–2, 503, 505, 507–17
  economics 471–3, 503, 511–17
  empirical evidence 466–7, 506, 507–17
  euphoria stage 455, 457, 459–60, 476–7
  experiences 471–2, 503, 513–14
  fad bubbles 493–6, 499–503
  financial-distress stage 455, 457, 459–63,
    477–84, 514–17
  fundamentals 498–500, 514–15
  goodwill write-downs 459
  historical background 463–7
  inflation 479–88, 507
  information-dispersion factors 504–5
  informational bubbles 493, 496, 499–500
  initial public offerings 477–9
  inside information 459–63, 466–7, 477–84
  intrinsic bubbles 493, 496, 498–503
  Japan 466–7, 472–91, 507, 510–11
  laboratory conditions 471–2, 503, 511–17
  lenders/buyers of last resort 465–7, 486
  long-only portfolios 489, 491
  major bubbles 466–7, 507, 509–10
  market shares 479–80
  monetary policies 457–9, 473–6
  new era thinking 476–7, 493, 499–503, 516
  overvaluations 493–6
  positive feedback 457–9, 473–6, 504–5
  post-bubble winners 484–6
  precipitating factors 455, 457, 466–7, 471–6
  psychology 493–506, 507–17
  rational/near-rational bubbles 493, 496–8, 500–6

regression analysis 509–16
revulsion stage 455, 457, 463–7, 483–6, 507, 509, 514–17
stages 455–67, 473–86
stock pickers 469–91
survival strategies 465–7, 469–91, 513–17
swindles 463, 466–7, 482–3
synchronizing events 504–5
technical analysis 507, 514–17
types 493–506
UK 466, 507, 510
USA 455–67, 472–91, 507, 510–11
volumes 455, 463–7, 479–91
budgets, risks 439–40
Buffett, Warren 276–7, 338, 345
bull markets 247, 252–7, 261, 279, 282, 290, 435, 444, 463–7, 469, 483–8, 495–6, 501–2, 506, 507, 514–17, 529–40, 567–8
myths 529–40
valuation levels 517, 567–8
Burger, Warren 622
Bush, George 74–6
business risks
see also balance sheets; profit margins; risks
best value investors 271, 275–6, 295
concepts 271, 275–6, 295, 445–6, 448–52, 461–2, 478–9
definition 445, 448–9
measures 449–50, 461–2
statistics 449–50
Z-scores 449–50, 461–2, 478–80, 489
Business Week 531
buybacks 355–65, 529–47, 549–56
see also share repurchases
buyers of last resort, bubbles 465–7, 486

C System see System C
Caginalp et al 471, 503, 512
Cain et al 626–7
calibration curves, overconfidence bias 109–12, 117–18
call options 535–40
see also options
Camerer et al 10–11, 168–71, 174
Canada 116, 118
canonization processes 215
cap-weighted market indexes, critique 429–31, 432–3
capacity levels
Japan 481–3
USA 481
capital asset pricing model (CAPM) 425–35
see also alphas; betas
assumptions 425, 429–32
concepts 425–35
critique 425–35
current situation 432–5
failings 431–2

historical background 427
origins 427
in practice 427–31
statistics 428–35
capital expenditure, bubbles 481–3, 490–1
Capital Guardian Fund 434
capital structures, sector-relative factors 395, 398–403
capitulation concepts 463–7, 483–6
see also revulsion...
CAPM see capital asset pricing model
career risks, fund managers 337–8, 342–3, 373–4
Carlson, K.A. 149–51
Carroll et al 263
Carter, Rita 11
Caruso et al 620–1
cascades bias 20, 209, 213–14, 500
cash flows 123, 125, 400–3, 478–83, 487–8, 489–91
accruals 489–90
bubbles 478–83, 489–91
commodities 590
models 123
sector-relative factors 400–3
cash markets 247, 271, 276–7, 295, 460–7
categorization bias 20
Catholic Church 58
CEOs
see also corporate managers
compensation 30, 179, 181–2, 529–40, 633–4, 643
confidence levels 541, 547
cronies 607
stock-related compensation 633–4
'ceteris paribus' ego defence 117–19
CFOs
see also corporate managers
Duke Survey of CFOs 145–8
short-termism 181–2, 369–70
Chan et al 128–30, 384–5
Chancellor, Edward 467, 555–6
change needs 235–46
charities, incentives 631, 634–5, 639
cheap countries 243–5, 247–8, 256–7, 405–21
concepts 247, 257, 405–21
critique 247, 257, 405–21
dividend yields 405, 408–21
long-only strategy 405, 408–9, 412–21
long/short portfolios 405–21
momentum factors 405–21
performance issues 247, 257, 405–21
PEs 405, 408–21
price to book ratios 405, 408–21
risks 405–21
strategy information 409–21
value investors 405–21
cheap sectors 387–93
see also sectors

cheap sectors (*Cont.*)
   cheap stocks 307–28, 333–6, 337–53, 382–3,
      391–3, 405–21, 446, 450–2
   chemicals sector, seasonal results 61
   Chicago National Activity Index 362
   child care centres, incentives 638–9
   Chile 248, 257
   China 189–90, 194–6, 248, 257, 498, 510, 594
      growth stories 189–90, 194–6, 594
      intrinsic bubbles 498
choking under pressure 631–43
choosers, endowment effect 31–2
Christ, Jesus 58
Christianity 58, 199, 215
Church, B.K. 513–14
CIA 214
circumstances, happiness levels 650–2
Clark *et al* 429–30
Clinton, Bill 149
Clipper 273–4
closed funds, best value investors 272, 278, 295
closet indexing 225–33, 241–2, 393
   see also indexing
   ascendancy 230–1, 238
   betas 231
   critique 225–33, 241–2, 393
   statistics 230–1, 393
clues, lies 156–7
cobweb models 590
cocaine 13–14, 47–50
   see also drug misuse
cognitive activities, happiness 647, 652–3
cognitive dissonance
   concepts 19–21, 581–6
   definition 581, 583–4
   examples 584, 585
cognitive hierarchy model, games 169–75
cognitive psychology
   dual process theories of thought 5–15, 74–6,
      85–94, 281, 297–300, 445–52, 524–8, 585,
      615–19
   recent developments 5
   self-control 11–15, 609, 640–3
Cognitive Reflection Task (CRT) 85–94
Cohen, R.B. 655, 660–1
collateral returns, commodities futures 587–8,
   591–5
Columbia University 273
commercial paper 465
committees 209–15
   see also group...
commodities 274, 498–9, 587, 590–6
   see also alternative investments
   cash flows 590
   concepts 587, 590–6
   critique 590
   forecasts 594–5
   indexes 587, 590–5

   returns 587–8, 590–6
   risks 590–1
   speculation 592–4
   statistics 590–5
   volatility 590–1
common investment pitfalls, maxims 17, 35–6
communication bias 212–14
community dimension, Aspiration Index 657–60
commuting, happiness 652
competitive advantages 221
completely redundant asset pricing (CRAP) 425–
   35
completions, share repurchases 543–7, 551–2
composite bubbles 500–3
   see also bubbles
comprehension *see* understanding
computers, redundant workers 259–60, 269
Conan Doyle, Arthur 309, 407, 549, 551
concentrated stock-pickers
   betas 231
   critique 225–6, 228–33, 271, 273–6, 295
conduct disorder 661
confidence
   see also overconfidence bias
   accuracy factors 528
   CEOs 541, 547
confirmation bias
   see also self-deception...
   concepts 20, 23–4, 83–4, 100, 143–57, 339
   examples 23–4, 83–4, 100
   test 83–4
conflicts of interest bias 611–12, 621–7
conformist approaches 247–57
   see also herd...
Confucius 135
consensus views
   asset prices 249
   critique 247–57
conservatism bias 20, 116, 507, 509–17
construction sector, seasonal results 61
consumer sector, seasonal results 61
contagion bias 20
contango 588, 591–5
contrarian approaches
   concepts 219–22, 247–57, 285–6, 300
   critique 247–57, 285–6, 300
   long large caps/short small caps 255–7
   overweight cash 254–5
   performance issues 251–7
   quality issues 252–3
   social pain 300
copper 592
   see also metals
core/satellite structures 243–5
Cornwell, Patricia 200
corporate governance 151, 284–5, 535–40, 597–643
   codes of ethics 607–8
   concepts 599, 607–9

dissenting boards 607–8
Higgs report 607
situational factors 599
corporate malfeasance 75, 153, 463, 466–7, 482–3,
    599, 601–9
    see also bad behaviour
corporate managers
    see also management; meeting companies...
    actions 355–65
    ADHD epidemic 179
    biases 143–57, 459
    compensation 30, 179, 181–2, 529–40, 633–4,
        643
    confidence levels 541, 547
    conflicts of interest bias 621–2
    dissenting voices 606–7
    Duke Survey of CFOs 145–8
    inside information 247, 253–4, 355–65, 459–63,
        477–84
    meeting companies 100, 140, 141–57, 355–7, 365
    obedience tendencies 143, 151–3, 292, 599,
        604–8
    options 30, 179, 181–2, 529–40, 633–4
    overconfidence bias 143–57, 459
    risky investments 535–40
    short-termism 179, 181–2
    stock sales levels 254
    stock-related compensation 633–4
    volatility increases 535–40
corrected beliefs
    see also beliefs
    Spinozan concepts 197, 200–5
corrective waves, technical analysis 515–16
correlations
    capital asset pricing model 427–35
    good/bad times 442–4
    hedge funds 587, 589
    risk models 437, 439–44
    statistics 407–8, 442–4, 487–8, 589
cost of capital, returns 55–7, 181–2, 565–6
crack 47
    see also drug misuse
CRAP (completely redundant asset pricing) 425–35
crashes 441–2, 455–67, 469–91, 493–506, 507–17
    see also bubbles
    danger triggers 503–5
    empirical evidence 466–7, 506, 507–17
CRB index 587, 590–1
credit-creation stage, bubbles 455, 457–9, 473–6
Cremers, Martijn 225–6, 227–33
cricket 211
criminal recidivism
    see also fraud
    quant models 259, 263
critical stage
    see also financial-distress stage
    bubbles 455, 457, 459–63, 477–84
CRT (Cognitive Reflection Task) 85–94

CSI (TV series) 156
cue-competition bias 20
cumulative normal charts 566–9
curse of knowledge, concepts 167–8
cyclically adjusted PEs, critique 329–36
cynical bubbles 55, 59–61, 164–5, 439, 493–506
    see also near-rational...
    concepts 493–506
    danger triggers 503–5
Czech Republic 257

Da Vinci Code 55, 58
daily fluctuations, Dow theory 514–16
damaged brains
    detection processes 262
    emotions 7–11, 47–53, 447, 616–17
    investor behaviour 47–53, 447
    quant models 262
Damasio, Antonio 616–17
Dandy *et al* 640
DAPM (Deranged Anticipation and Perception
    Model) 427
Darwin, Charles 200
Dasgupta *et al* 247, 249–51
Datastream 554
Davis *et al* 133–4, 139–40
DCF (discounted cash flow) 123, 125, 487–8, 561
DDM (dividend discount model) 123, 125–7, 495–6
de-bubbling processes 469–91, 493–4, 500–6,
    509–17
    see also bubbles
Dead Sea Scrolls 268
the Dean of Wall Street 331–6
    see also Graham...
debasing considerations, forecasts 120–1
debt 247, 253–5, 362–3, 449–52, 457–9, 469–78,
    536–40
    see also bonds; leverage
    default premiums 362–3
    deflationary debt spirals 469, 473, 479–84,
        487–9, 507
    margin debt levels 247, 253–5
    to equity ratios 536–7
    to total capital employed 536–7
decision accuracy, illusion of knowledge 138–9
decision-making
    concepts 3, 5–15, 63, 67–76, 189–96, 209–15,
        615–17, 627–9
    damaged brains 7–11, 47–53, 447, 616–17
    emotions 3–15, 40–6, 75–6, 614–17
    empathy gaps 37–46
    explanation-based decision-making 189–96, 301
    group-based decisions 98, 101, 207–15
    information 133–40, 145, 367–9, 409–21, 504–5,
        617
    jurors 191–3, 521–2, 528, 611
    motivated reasoning 73–6
    self-attribution bias 24, 44, 63, 67–9, 76

decision-making (*Cont.*)
  stories 189–96, 219–22, 293, 301
  survival instincts 17–36
  unethical behaviour 627–9
  veil of ignorance 629
default premiums, debt 362–3
deflation 469, 473, 479–84, 487–9, 507
degenerate panic 463–7, 472–3, 483–6
  see also revulsion...
dehumanization, moral-disengagement factors
    608–9
delayed gratification, concepts 297–300
Democrats 74–6, 149
Denmark 257, 409
DePaulo *et al* 156–7
dependent mental disorder 655, 661
depression 653
Deranged Anticipation and Perception Model
    (DAPM) 427
Descartes, Rene 197–205
detection, lies 97, 100, 143–5, 153–7
DeVaul, Robert 263
devil's advocates, group-based decisions (wrath)
    209, 215
Diagnostic and Statistical Manual of Mental
    Disorders 660
Diener, E. 651
DiFonzo, N. 192–3
dilution
  concepts 549, 553–61
  definition 553
  measures 554–5
  statistics 549, 553–61
dimensions, information 23–4
Dinkelman *et al* 295–6
disclosures, conflicts of interest 626–7
discounted cash flow (DCF) 123, 125, 487–8, 561
the dismal years 240–1, 388, 393
displacement stage, bubbles 455, 457, 466–7, 473–4
dispositional perspectives 33, 601–3, 628–9
  see also fundamental attribution error
  bad behaviour 601–3, 628–9
dissenting voices, bad behaviour 606–7, 629
distortion levels, information 149–51
distractions
  beliefs 197–8, 200–5
  incentives 631, 640–3
Ditto, P. 73–5
diversified stock-pickers
  betas 231
  critique 225–6, 228–33, 244–5, 273, 274–5,
    395–6
dividend discount model (DDM) 123, 125–7, 495–6
dividend yields
  see also earnings yields
  cheap countries 405, 408–21
  concepts 237–9, 288–9, 297–300, 331, 337–53,
    398–403, 405, 529–40, 541–7, 552–61, 563–72

critique 529–40, 541–7, 565–72
declining trends 529–40
low returns 563–72
sector-relative factors 398–403
share repurchases 529–40, 541–56
statistics 529–40, 541–7, 552–61, 563–72
dividends 23, 37–8, 100, 204, 237–9, 284–5, 288–9,
    290, 297–300, 331–6, 337–53, 471–3, 529–40,
    541–7, 563–72
  anchoring/salience bias 100, 288–9
  announcements 23, 37–8
  bubbles 471–3
  critique 529–40, 541–7, 565–72
  declining trends 529–40
  expected values 471–2
  GDP growth 204
  myths 529–47
  payout ratios 541, 546–7, 566
  retained earnings 284–5, 290, 472–3, 531–40
  statistics 529–40, 541–7, 552–61, 563–72
  total payout statistics 539–40, 541–7, 552–6
DJ-AIG 591
doctors, calibration curves 110–11
Dohmen, T.J. 640
Dolan, R.J. 527
dollar/yen carry trade (October 1998) 441–2
dominated strategies, iterated dominance 91–2,
    164–75
Donaldson, Thomas 608
dopamine effects 13–14, 75–6, 287, 297–300
  drug misuse 13–14
  rewards 13, 75–6, 297–300
  short-term gains 13–15, 287, 297–300
dot.com bubble 25, 70, 478, 495, 499
Dow theory 507, 514–16
  see also technical analysis
downside risks
  see also risks; semi-variance
  concepts 445–52
DPS/EPS/GDP growth statistics 549–61
dreams, nightmares 189, 191
Dreman, D. 449–51
drug misuse 13–14, 47–53
  see also cocaine
  addicted persons 47–53
  dopamine effects 13–14, 75–6
dual process theories of thought
  concepts 5–15, 74–6, 85–94, 281, 297–300,
    445–52, 524–8, 585, 615–19
  neuroscience 5–6, 75–6, 85, 297–300, 445–52,
    527, 615–16
Duke Survey of CFOs 145–8
Dukes *et al* 123, 125–6
Dunn *et al* 39–40, 45, 46
Dunning, D. 105, 115, 613–14
durables sector, seasonal results 61
dynamic hedging, critique 441–2, 444
dynamic loss aversion

see also loss-aversion...
bubbles 501–2

earnings
 see also dividend...; profit...
 cyclical earnings 541–7
 retained earnings 284–5, 290, 472–3, 531–40,
   552–6
 share repurchases 544–7, 549–61
 US trend statistics 544–7
earnings growth
 CEO confidence levels 547
 GDP growth 551–61
 global returns 309–28
 payout ratios 546–7, 566
 statistics 309–28, 360–1, 459–63, 531–40, 544–7,
   551–61
earnings per share (EPS) 128–9, 133–4, 139, 271,
   276, 315–28, 459, 549–61
 dilution statistics 549–61
 GDP growth 549–61
earnings quality, stock-selection criteria 469,
   489–91
earnings yields
 see also dividend yields
 concepts 537–40, 544–7, 552–6, 565–7
 cyclical earnings 541–7
 Little Book strategy 337–53
 retained earnings yield 537–40, 552–6
 statistics 537–9, 544–7, 552–6
EBAY 165
Ebbers, Bernie 153, 601, 606
EBIT/EV
 Little Book strategy 337–53
 PE contrasts 341, 345–9
echoes, bubbles 471–2, 503, 505, 507–17
economics
 see also GDP...
 bubbles 471–3, 503, 511–17
 cobweb models 590
 economic cycles/returns 573–80
 experimental economics 471–2, 503, 511–17
 forecasts 107–8, 135, 283–4
 historical background 281
 incentives 631, 633–4, 635–6, 643
 market/economy links 552–3, 573–80
 sector rotation strategies 579–80
Economist 439–40
Edwards, Albert 240, 290, 388, 393, 486, 505, 510,
   568, 649
Edwards, Ward 76, 509
EEGs (electroencephalograms) 5
efficient frontiers 238–9
efficient market hypothesis (EMH) 100, 119–20,
   135, 225–7, 238–9, 359–60, 361–5, 427,
   499–500
ego defence mechanisms, experts 105, 114–19
EI *see* emotional intelligence

Eisenberger, N.I. 300
Ekman, Paul 7
electric-shock experiments, authority figures 151–3,
   599, 604–8
electroencephalograms (EEGs) 5
Elliot Wave theory 507, 515–16
 see also technical analysis
Ellis, Charles 241
emerging equity markets 189–90, 194–6, 247–8,
   256–7, 457–9, 474, 587, 589
EMH (efficient market hypothesis) 100, 119–20,
   135, 225–7, 238–9, 359–60, 361–5, 427,
   499–500
emotional intelligence (EI), concepts 46
emotions 3–15, 19–21, 37–46, 75–6, 85–94,
   297–300, 521–8, 611–29
 see also anger; feelings; happiness; sadness
 biases 19–21, 37–46, 75–6
 the body 7
 the brain 6–11, 13–15, 75–6, 85–6, 297–300, 527
 concepts 6–15, 37–46, 75–6, 297–300, 521–8,
   614–17
 damaged brains 7–11, 47–53, 447, 616–17
 decision-making 3–15, 40–6, 75–6, 614–17
 definitions 6–7
 empathy gaps 37–46
 ethics 611–29
 experiences 10–11, 28–9, 39
 facial expressions 7
 forecasts 39, 42
 impact bias 37–46
 moral judgements 611–12, 614–29
 primacy 5–15
 risks 7–11
 self-control 7–15, 20, 609
 smiling exercises 7
 System X 5–6, 14, 25, 74–6, 85–94, 281,
   297–300, 445–52, 521–8, 585, 615–19, 641
empathy gaps
 see also endowment effect
 concepts 37–46, 617
 definition 37, 39, 45
 emotional intelligence 46
 examples 37, 39–42, 45
 food experiment 41–2, 45
 investor behaviour 37–8, 40–6
 reduction techniques 44–6
 sexual stimuli 42–3
empirical sceptics 219–22, 228–9, 633
empiricists 219–22, 228–9, 309–28
EMU 116, 118
endogenous/exogenous assumptions, risks 437,
   440–4
endowment effect
 see also empathy gaps; loss-aversion...
 concepts 30–5, 42–3, 286
energy 587, 590–2
 see also commodities

Englich *et al* 99, 120
enjoying the moment, happiness 647, 653
Enron 75, 466, 482, 622
enterprise considerations 185–6, 281–2
enterprise value (EV), *Little Book* strategy 337–53
envy, seven sins 97, 100–1, 159–75
Epley, N. 613–14
EPS *see* earnings per share
equities
    see also dividend...; returns
    bonds 239, 241, 280, 290, 431, 462–3, 469–91, 499, 573–80
    bubble echoes 471–2, 503, 505, 507–17
    economic cycles 573–80
    forecasts 107–9, 283–4
    issuance processes 355–65
    junk equities 247, 251–2, 279, 290
equity markets 55–61, 247, 253–4, 279
    see also financial...
    fear and greed index 59–61, 247, 253–4, 279
    seasonal results 55–61
ethical fading, concepts 627–9
ethics 278, 597–643
    see also moral...
    auditors 612, 622–8
    bad behaviour 608–9, 627–9
    biases 611–29
    blindspot 611, 613–14
    bounded ethicality 611–12, 617–27
    codes 607–8
    combating unethical behaviour 629
    concepts 607–8, 611–29
    conflicts of interest 611–12, 621–2
    euphemistic labels 608–9, 628
    groups 608–9, 611–12, 619–20
    implicit attitudes 611, 617–20, 629
    in-group bias 611–12, 619–20
    overclaiming credit 611–12, 620–1
    perceptual causation 628–9
    psychology 611–29
    representations of the self 629
    self-deception bias 627–9
    slippery slopes 628
    unbounded objectivity 611–12, 629
    unconscious biases 611, 615, 617–29
euphemistic labels, moral-disengagement factors 608–9, 628
euphoria stage, bubbles 455, 457, 459–60, 476–7
Europe
    bargain hunters 311–17, 324–6
    beta studies 429–30
    earnings optimism 584
    growth investing 311–17, 324–6
    Little Book strategy 337–53
    net equity issuance 363–5
    sector-relative factors/ absolute-value contrasts 400–3
    value investing 311–17, 324–6

EV *see* enterprise value
Evans *et al* 523–6
evidence 191–2, 227, 466–7, 506, 507–17, 575, 638–40
    see also information
    absence of evidence 227
    beliefs 200–3
    bubbles 466–7, 506, 507–17
    crashes 466–7, 506, 507–17
    incentives 633–40
    rationality 191–2, 575
evidence of absence, absence of evidence 227
ex-ante IRs 243–4, 297
ex-post IRs 243–4
excess volatility 279, 282–3, 367–8, 370–4
    see also volatility
exclusion strategy, beliefs 198, 204–5
excuses 55–61, 101, 115–16, 189–205
    see also stories
exercising benefits, happiness 647, 652–3
exogenous assumptions, risks 437, 440–4
Expansion 170–1
expected values, dividend distributions 471–2
expensive countries, cheap countries 405–21
experiences
    bubbles 471–2, 503, 513–14
    direct/general experience 269
    emotions 10–11, 28–9, 39
    happiness 655–65
    hedonic adaptation 664–5
    identity 665
    learning 63–76, 503, 513–14
    materialism 661–5
    positive reviews 655–6, 663–5
    recency-effect bias 28–9, 301
    weightings 269
experimental economics 471–2, 503, 511–17
experts
    ego defence mechanisms 105, 114–19
    overconfidence bias 21–3, 105, 110–21, 259–60, 268–9, 293, 301–2, 369–70, 439–44, 469, 477, 497–500
explanation-based decision-making 189–96, 301
    see also stories
explicit-monitoring theory, incentives 631, 640–1
exposure controls, beliefs 198, 204–5
extrinsic aspirations 657–60

facial expressions, emotions 7
fad bubbles 493–6, 499–503
    see also bubbles
fallacy of composition, concepts 481–2
false beliefs 197–205
    see also beliefs
false consensus effect, smoking 167
Fama, E.F. 231, 289, 378–9, 427, 428, 432
fame dimension, Aspiration Index 657–60
FASB 30, 536
fashions 493–6, 499–503, 657–60, 665

fears 6, 9–11, 49–53, 55, 59–61, 247, 253–4, 279, 447
   fear and greed index 59–61, 247, 253–4, 279
   neuroscience 6, 9–11, 49–53, 447
Federal Reserve Bank 57, 116–17, 457–8, 465–7, 474–6, 477, 581
feedback distortions, concepts 63–4, 72–6
feelings
   see also emotions
   impact bias 37–46
Fibonacci lines 515
Fidelity Magellan fund 231–3
Fielding, Henry 499
financial markets
   bear markets 57, 235, 239–42, 252–4, 261, 279, 426, 435, 463–7, 469, 483–8, 495, 506, 507, 514–17, 570–1
   bubbles 25, 55, 59–61, 70, 164–5, 274, 278, 342–3, 395–7, 439, 455–67, 469–91, 493–506
   bull markets 247, 252–7, 261, 279, 282, 290, 435, 444, 463–7, 469, 483–8, 495–6, 501–2, 506, 507, 514–17, 529–40, 567–8
   economic cycles 573–80
   economy/market links 552–3, 573–80
   fear and greed index 59–61, 247, 253–4, 279
   largest market moves 59
   momentum factors 55–61, 106, 120–1, 123–4, 129–30, 161–75, 231, 238–9, 261, 281–2, 375–86, 405–21, 459–67
   myths 199, 519–96
   near-random moves 55–61
   noise generators 55–61, 139–40, 143–5, 271, 276, 301–2, 377–86, 565
   random moves 55–61, 138–9
   reflation trades 437, 439–44, 498, 581, 584–6
   rumours 192–3
   seasonal results 55–61
   sentiments 59–66, 254–7, 279, 463–7, 483–6, 506, 565–6
financial risks
   see also leverage; risks
   concepts 445–6, 449–52
   definition 446, 449–50
financial-distress stage
   see also critical stage
   bubbles 455, 457, 459–63, 477–84, 514–17
First Eagle Gold 273–4, 278
Fischhoff, Barach 70
Fisher, Irvine 472–3
fMRI (functional magnetic resonance imaging) 5, 527
food experiment
   empathy gaps 41–2, 45
   self-control 12–13
food sector, seasonal results 61
football penalty kicks, incentives 639–40
forecasts 17–39, 97, 99–100, 103–30, 133–4, 139–40, 148, 185–6, 242–5, 283–4, 314–17, 330–1, 336, 501–2, 594–5
   analysts 106–19, 121, 129–30, 283–4, 307, 315–17, 330, 459
   bonds 107–9
   commodities 594–5
   critique 99–100, 105–21, 139–40, 148, 283–4, 314–17, 331, 336, 501–2
   debasing considerations 120–1
   economics 107–8, 135, 283–4
   ego defence mechanisms 105, 114–19
   emotions 39, 42
   equities 107–9, 283–4
   errors 139–40
   growth investors 314–15
   guesses 111–13, 163–75
   inflation 107
   information coefficient 242–5, 410
   input ratings 112–13, 127–8
   laypeople/professionals comparisons 111–14
   overconfidence bias 99–100, 105–21, 148, 301–2
   seven sins 97, 99–100, 103–30, 148, 283–4
   statistics 107–21, 594–5
   uses 119–21
   weathermen 110–11, 117–19
Fortune 10 buy-and-forget portfolio 275
forward PE valuation method 123, 125–30, 256–7, 569–70
FPA Capital 273–4, 276
framing bias
   see also heuristic-simplification...
   concepts 20, 29–30, 87–9, 199, 375, 499–500, 665
   examples 29–30, 87–9, 199
   test 87–9
France 247, 257, 409, 430, 549, 556, 559
   cheap countries 247, 257, 409
   dilution statistics 549, 556, 559
   EPS/DPS/GDP growth statistics 556, 559
Franklin, Benjamin 76
fraud 75, 463, 466–7, 482–3, 601
   see also bad behaviour; swindles
   bubbles 463, 466–7, 482–3
Frazzini, Andrea 34–5
Frederick, Shane 85
French, K. 231, 378–9, 389, 428, 432
Friesen, G.C. 372–4
Frost, Alfred 515
FSA 357
FT 170–1, 194, 439
FTSE 350–3
Fuller & Thaler 259, 267
fun, stumbling blocks 303, 344
functional magnetic resonance imaging (fMRI) 5, 527
fund managers 13, 21–3, 33–5, 51–3, 79–94, 95–215, 221, 225–33, 238–46, 247–56, 271, 278, 286–7, 295, 296–7, 337–53, 367, 388, 393, 437–44, 521–8
   see also active...; investment banks
   active share 225, 227–33

fund managers (*Cont.*)
    alphas 183–5, 221, 228–9, 235–46, 267, 299,
        383–5
    bad years 240–1, 271, 278, 295, 296–7, 337–8,
        344–5, 367, 388, 393
    bargain hunters 307–28
    belief bias 521–8
    best value investors 271–8, 293–304
    biases 79–94, 99–215, 521–8
    breadth of call 242–5
    bullish attitudes 247, 252–7, 261
    career risks 337–8, 342–3, 373–4
    conflicts of interest bias 611–12, 621–2
    conformist approaches 247–57
    contrarian approaches 219–22, 247–57, 285–6
    corporate managers 143–57
    dreams/nightmares 189, 191
    ego defence mechanisms 105, 114–19
    good intentions 294, 303–4
    groups 231
    hiring/firing decisions 373–4
    Keynes's beauty contest analogy 90–2, 101,
        161–75, 440–1
    league table 183–4
    loss-aversion/prospect-theory bias 33–5, 86,
        89–90, 293, 296–7, 445–52, 501–3
    outperforming sold stocks 247, 249–50, 375–6
    overconfidence bias 21–3, 99–101, 105–21,
        133–40, 143–57, 259–60, 268–9, 290, 293,
        301–2, 307, 312, 369–70, 439–44, 469, 477,
        497–500
    past performance 27–8, 226, 231–3
    performance issues 27–8, 179–86, 221–2,
        225–33, 238–9, 369–74
    quant models 259, 267–9, 312, 337–8
    remuneration methods 181, 183, 244, 272
    risk exposures 174–5, 184–6
    risk models 439–44
    selection criteria 238, 286, 299, 373–4, 376,
        469–91
    self-control 13
    seven sins 95–215, 273
    sheep index 251
    short-termism 174–5, 179–86, 282–3, 287, 293,
        297–300, 367–74, 504–5
    skills 227–33, 278, 293, 301–2
    successful investors 183–4, 219–22, 241–2,
        271–8
    test 79–94, 120
    time horizons 174–5, 179–86, 271, 277, 287, 293,
        297–300, 375–86, 439–44, 497–8
    types 119–20, 227–33
    underperformance issues 179–86, 225–33, 238,
        271, 278, 299–300, 311–12, 314, 344–5, 357,
        370–2, 379, 450–2
fundamental analyses 55–6
fundamental attribution error, concepts 152–3, 599,
    601–9

Fundamental Indices
    see also indexes
    returns/risks statistics 429–33
fundamentals, bubbles 498–500, 514–15
future losers, past winners 129–30
futures
    see also options
    backwardation 588, 591–5
    commodities futures 587, 590–6
    concepts 590–6
    contango 588, 591–5

G&D PEs *see* Graham and Dodd PEs
GAAP 536, 538, 584
Gage, Phineas 616–17
gains, loss-aversion/prospect-theory bias 20, 30–5,
    42–3, 51–2, 86, 89–90, 293, 296–7, 445–52
Galpin, N. 230
gamblers' fallacy, concepts 84–5
gambling analogy, risks 437, 440–4
game theory 167–75
    see also Nash equilibrium
games
    learning 173–5
    thinking steps 168–75
GDP considerations
    see also economics
    booms 458–9
    debt levels 477–8
    dividend growth 204
    earnings growth 551–61
    economic cycles 576–80
    emerging equity markets 189–90, 194–6
    investment levels 458–9, 475–7
    market/economy weights 552–3
    statistics 552–61, 594
genetically determined set point, happiness levels
    649–50, 652
geographic diversification 244
geometric returns 240–1
Germany 296, 409, 430, 443, 488, 549, 556, 558,
    605, 640
    dilution statistics 549, 556, 558
    EPS/DPS/GDP growth statistics 556, 558
    'get-even-itis' investors 501–5
    see also loss-aversion...
Gilbert, Daniel 197, 199–205
Gilovich, T. 655, 661–5
Glaser *et al* 112–13
Glass-Steagall Act 466
Global Quant team 123, 126–7, 329, 331, 339, 377,
    407–8, 429
global returns 309–28
gluttony
    see also illusion of knowledge
    seven sins 97, 100, 131–40
GMO 429
Gneezy, U. 633–4, 638–9

God 199
  see also religion
Goel, V. 527
Goetzmann *et al* 407
gold 510, 512, 592
  see also metals
Goldberg, Lewis 261
Goldfarb, Bob 273–4
good intentions 294, 303–4
good things in life, happiness 647, 653
goodwill write-downs 459, 537–8
Gorbachev, M. 117
Gordon growth model 565–6
governance issues 151, 284–5
Goyal, A. 299–300, 373–4
Graham, Ben 219–21, 271, 273, 275–6, 279–92,
    307, 318, 329–36, 337, 431, 434, 445, 447–9,
    450
  arbitrage views 286–7
  behavioural errors 289
  beta views 291, 431, 434
  contemporary environment 279, 289–90
  contrarian views 285–6
  forecasting views 283–4
  history views 280, 291–2
  Keynes 279–92
  margin-of-safety views 290–1, 307, 318,
    450
  overcomplication views 291
  price/value relativity views 288–9
  principal–agent problems 284–5
  professional investors 286–7
  speculation/investment views 279, 281–3
  time horizons 287
  valuation views 279–80, 288, 335
  views on the nature of investment 279–92, 431,
    434, 445, 447–9
  volatility views 279, 282–3
  writings 281
Graham and Dodd PEs 219, 221, 255–6, 273,
    329–36, 485–6, 569–71, 581–6
  concepts 329–36, 485–6, 569–71, 581–6
  critique 329–36, 485–6, 569–71, 581–6
  definition 331
  long-only portfolios 333–6, 581–6
  long/short portfolios 332–6
  performance issues 329–36, 485–6
  statistics 331–6, 485–6
Graham, J.R. 146–8
Grantham, Jeremy 429
greater fool markets 493, 496–8, 502–6, 563
  see also rational/near-rational bubbles
greed 55, 59–61, 247, 253–4, 279
Greenblatt, Joel 219, 221, 296–7, 337–53
Greene *et al* 615–16
Greenspan, Sir Alan 466, 471, 516
Grice, Dylan 481
Grinold, R.C. 242

Grosskopf, B. 168
groups 209–15, 608–9, 611–12, 619–20
  anchoring/salience bias 211–13
  asset-allocation committees 209–15
  bad behaviour 608–9, 611–12, 619–20
  biases 209–15, 619–20
  cascades bias 209, 213–14
  communication bias 212–14
  critique 209–15, 608–9, 611–12, 619–20
  devil's advocates 209, 215
  ethics 608–9, 611–12, 619–20
  hidden information 209, 212–13
  ideals/reality contrasts 209
  in-group bias 611–12, 619–20
  moral-disengagement factors 608–9, 611–12,
    619–20
  performance issues 211–12
  polarization problems 209, 214–15
  respect benefits 209, 215
  secret ballots 209, 215
  seven sins 98, 101, 207–15
  social-status factors 213–14
  statistical groups 211–12
groupthink dangers 209, 214–15, 500
Grove *et al* 259, 266, 269
growth investors 204, 219–22, 280, 307–28,
    355–65, 375–86, 429–35, 450–2
  arbitrage 380–3
  beliefs 204, 219
  critique 307–28, 375–86
  disappointing realities 314–15
  forecasts 314–15
  momentum strategies 381–2
  net equity issuance 355–65
  patience 219–22, 280, 344, 357, 375–86
  PE values 309–28
  returns 309–28, 375–86, 450–2
  risk-adjusted returns 318
  sectors 387, 390–3
  siren calls 312, 365
  statistics 309–28, 375–86, 450–2
  valuations 312–14, 450–2
  value investors 317–18, 375–86
growth stories 189–96, 219–22, 280, 293, 301, 307,
    365
  see also stories
GSCI 587, 590–5
GTAA 222
guesses 111–13, 163–75
Gurkas 70

Haidt, J. 615
halo effects 19
Hamilton, William 514–15
Hamlet (Shakespeare) 191
Handzic, Meliha 133, 137–8
hanging sentence, paradox of the unexpected
    hanging 165

happiness 6–7, 39–40, 645–65
  see also emotions
  absolute/relative concepts 656, 665
  achievable goals 647, 653
  altruism 652–3
  Aspirations Index 657–60
  behavioural activities 647, 652–3
  benefits 649–50
  circumstances 650–2
  cognitive activities 647, 652–3
  commuting 652
  concepts 647–53, 655–65
  determinants 649–53
  enjoying the moment 647, 653
  exercising benefits 647, 652–3
  experiences 655–65
  genetically determined set point 649–50, 652
  good things in life 647, 653
  hedonic adaptation 651–3, 655–6, 664–5
  improvement tips 647–53, 655, 657, 660–5
  intentional activities 652–3, 655–65
  jobs 647, 649–51, 653, 657
  married persons 649, 650
  materialism 647, 650–1, 653, 655–65
  mental disorders 655, 660–5
  money 647, 650–1, 653, 655–65
  personal benefits 649–50, 655–65
  personality traits 649–50
  psychology 647–53, 655–65
  the pursuit 655–65
  relationships 647, 649–51, 652–3, 655–65
  religious beliefs 650
  rules 647–53, 655, 657
  self-esteem 658–9
  sex 647, 652–3
  sleep 647, 653
  social rewards 649–51, 656–65
  statistics 650–2, 657–65
  studies 650–2, 657–65
  tips 647–53, 655, 657, 660–5
  volitional activities 652–3
Hare, Robert 617
Harvey, C.R. 146–8
Hastie, R. 191–2, 193–4
HealthSouth 601
hedge funds 245, 343–4, 370–1, 433–4, 439–44,
    489, 498, 500–1, 587, 589, 595
  see also alternative investments
  alphas 245, 343–4, 433–4, 489
  betas 245, 433–4, 589
  concepts 587, 589, 595
  correlations 587, 589
  critique 245, 343–4, 370–1, 433–4, 439–44, 489,
    498, 500–1, 587, 589, 595
  leverage long funds 245, 489
  risk models 439–44
  time horizons 370–1, 489
  volatility 587, 589

hedge perspectives, inside information 359
hedonic adaptation
  experiences 664–5
  happiness 651–3, 655–6, 664–5
herd behaviour 13, 14–15, 20–1, 212–14, 251–7,
    282–3, 293, 300, 441, 493, 504–5
  see also groups; social...
Hester, William 541, 547
heuristic-simplification bias
  see also anchoring...; framing...; loss-aversion...;
      representativeness...
  concepts 19–21, 25–30, 84–94, 99–100
  test 84–94
heuristics, definition 19
hidden information 209, 212–13
Higgs report 607
highly concentrated portfolios, best value investors
    271, 273–6, 295
hindsight bias
  see also overconfidence...; self-deception...
  concepts 17, 20, 25, 63, 69–71, 291, 509–17
  dot.com bubble 25, 70
  examples 70–1, 291
  learning from mistakes 63, 69–71
hiring/firing decisions, performance issues 373–4
Hirshleifer, David 427
  historic volatility 437–44
  see also volatility
  risk models 437–44
  statistics 439–40
histrionic mental disorder 655, 661
HIV/AIDS 293, 295–6
HML, fund management group factor betas 231
holiday experiences 663–5
holistic aspects, reasoning 6, 616
Holland see Netherlands
Hong Kong 248, 257, 409, 430
hostile-media bias 24
  see also confirmation bias
House (TV series) 156
Hüber, Manfred 171–2
Hudson, George 466
human judgements, quant models 264, 266
Hungary 248, 257
hurdles, learning 63–76
Hussman Funds 541, 546–7
Hussman, John 546–7, 572
Hussman PEs 495, 571–2
hyperbolic discounting 20, 287
  see also self-control

'I was almost right' ego defence 117–19
IAT (implicit attitude tests) 611, 618–19, 629
IC see information coefficient
ICAPM (intertemporal CAPM) 430
ideas, concepts 197–205
identity, experiences 665
'if only' ego defence 116–19

illiquid assets 245, 247
illusion of control 20, 22–3, 63, 71–3, 82–3, 102,
    185–6, 301–2, 493, 496–8, 500
  see also overconfidence. . . ; overoptimism. . .
  concepts 20, 22–3, 63, 71–3, 82–3, 102, 185–6,
    301–2
  examples 22–3, 72–3, 82–3, 301–2
  learning from mistakes 72–3
  portfolios 63, 73
  test 82–3
illusion of knowledge 20–3, 82–3, 97, 100, 105–21,
    131–40, 185–6, 301–2, 369, 493, 496–8, 500
  see also overconfidence. . . ; overoptimism. . .
  bookmakers' experiment 20–1, 133, 135–7
  concepts 20–3, 82–3, 97, 100, 105–21, 131–40,
    185–6, 301–2, 369
  examples 20–3, 82–3, 112, 135–40
  test 82–3
image dimension, Aspiration Index 657–60, 665
imitation bias 20
immediacy effects 13–14
impact bias
  concept 37–46
  definition 37, 39, 45
  emotional intelligence 46
  examples 37, 39–40, 45
  investor behaviour 44–6
  reduction techniques 44–6
  romantic relationships 37, 45
implicit attitude tests (IAT) 611, 618–19, 629
implicit attitudes
  see also unconscious biases
  concepts 611, 617–20, 629
impulsive behaviour 14, 299
in-group bias, concepts 611–12, 619–20
inattentional blindness, concepts 30, 199
incentives 181, 183, 631–43
  basketball players 640
  blood donations 638–9
  charities 631, 634–5, 639
  child care centres 638–9
  choking under pressure 631–43
  concepts 181, 183, 631–43
  critique 631–43
  distraction theory 631, 640–3
  economics 631, 633–4, 635–6, 643
  evidence 633–40
  experiments 633–8, 640–3
  field evidence 638–40
  football penalty kicks 639–40
  motivation 631–43
  psychology 631–43
  self-focus theory 631, 640–1
  working memory 631, 640–3
incest, moral judgements 614–15
income statements, Japanese bubble 477, 487
indexes 230–1, 301, 307, 309–15, 329, 331–5, 375,
    377, 408–9, 429–35, 553–61, 587, 590–5

cap-weighted market indexes 429–31, 432–3
commodities futures 587, 590–5
critique 429–31, 433–5, 587, 590–5
dilution 553–61
indexing 179, 181–2, 219, 221, 225–33, 235–46,
    278, 373, 393, 429–32, 489
  see also benchmarking
  active share 225, 227–33
  ascendancy 230–1, 238
  change needs 240–6
  closet indexing 225–33, 241–2, 393
  critique 225–33
  performance issues 225–33, 278, 373, 429–32
  statistics 228–33, 278, 393
India 70, 257, 635
inertia, quant models 259–60, 269
inflation 55–61, 107, 479–88, 507, 573–80, 588, 594
  bubbles 479–88, 507
  forecasts 107
  interest rates 588, 594
  USA 55–61, 107, 573–80
information
  see also biases; evidence
  accuracy impacts 135–7
  beliefs 197–205
  best value investors 271, 274–5, 276, 295
  calibration curves 109–12, 117–18
  cascades 500
  cheap countries 409–21
  decision-making 133–40, 145, 367–9, 409–21,
    504–5, 617
  dimensions 23–4
  dispersion issues 504–5
  distortion levels 149–51
  efficient market hypothesis 100, 119–20, 135,
    225–7, 361–5, 427, 499–500
  familiar formats 55
  hidden information 209, 212–13
  illusion of knowledge 20–3, 82–3, 97, 100,
    105–21, 131–40, 185–6, 301–2, 369, 493,
    496–8, 500
  inside information 247, 253–4, 355–65, 459–63,
    477–84
  knowledge contrasts 133
  overload problems 19, 100, 133–40, 143–57
  placebic information 57–9, 101
  qualities 17, 20–3, 35–6, 167
information coefficient (IC)
  concepts 242–5, 409–10
  definition 242, 410
information ratios
  see also alphas
  concepts 183–5, 240–5, 278, 333–6, 409–21
  definition 242, 419
  performance issues 242–5, 278, 333–6, 409–21
informational bubbles 493, 496, 499–505
  see also bubbles
initial public offerings (IPOs) 357, 477–9

input ratings, forecasts 112–13, 127–8
inside information 247, 253–4, 355–65, 459–63,
        466–7, 477–84
    bubbles 459–63, 466–7, 477–84
    concepts 355–65, 459–63, 477–84
    definition 357
    hedge perspectives 359
    initial public offerings 357, 477–8
    net equity issuance 355–65
    returns 355–65
    usage 357–9, 459–63, 477–84
insider sales to purchases ratio 247, 253–4, 460–2
institutional fund managers 181–2, 247, 249–50,
        286–7, 483–4, 500–1
    see also fund managers
    outperforming sold stocks 247, 249–50
    time horizons 181–2
insula 14
intentional activities, happiness 652–3, 655–65
interest rates 57, 425–35, 457–9, 474–83, 588
    capital asset pricing model 425–35
    inflation 588, 594
internal rates of return 181–2
Internet 194, 457, 466, 473, 477
intertemporal CAPM (ICAPM) 430
intrinsic aspirations 657–60
intrinsic bubbles 493, 496, 498–503
    see also bubbles
intuitive reasoning 6–16, 85–94, 112, 615–17
    see also emotions
investment, speculation contrasts 279, 281–3, 459
investment banks 51–3, 439–44
    see also fund managers
    bullish attitudes 247, 252–7
    risk models 439–44
investment games, learning from mistakes 66–7
investment levels, GDP 458–9, 475–7
investment perspectives, risk elements 445–6,
        448–52
investment pitfalls, maxims 17, 35–6
investment processes 219–22, 271–8
investment strategies
    cheap countries 243–5, 247–8, 256–7, 405–21
    cyclically adjusted PEs 329–36
    Graham and Dodd PEs 219, 221, 255–6, 273,
        329–36, 485–6, 569–71, 581–6
    Little Book strategy 221, 261, 296–7, 337–53
    momentum strategies 106, 120–1, 123–4,
        129–30, 161–75, 231, 238–9, 261, 281–2,
        375–86, 459–67
    net equity issuance 355–65
    patience 219–22, 280, 297–300, 344, 357, 375–
        86
    sector-relative factors 395–403
    trailing earnings 106, 120–1, 123, 125–7, 329–36,
        345–6, 377, 569–72, 575–80, 583–6
    value-based strategies 120–1
    Zen of investing 521–2, 528

investor behaviour
    see also fund managers
    addicted persons 47–53
    anchoring/salience bias 25–7, 87–92, 99–100,
        105–6, 288–9, 499–500
    best value investors 271–8, 293–304, 375–6
    biases 79–94, 99–215
    damaged brains 47–53, 447
    empathy gaps 37–8, 40–6
    'get-even-itis' investors 501–5
    herd instincts 14–15, 251–7, 282–3, 293, 300,
        441, 493, 504–5
    impact bias 44–6
    Keynes's beauty contest analogy 90–2, 101,
        161–75, 440–1
    loss-aversion/prospect-theory bias 32–4, 86,
        89–90, 293, 296–7, 445–52, 501–3
    maxims 17, 35–6
    momentum effects 55–61, 106, 120–1, 123–4,
        129–30, 161–75, 231, 238–9, 261, 281–2,
        375–86, 459–67
    overconfidence bias 21–3, 99–101, 369–70
    quantitative approaches 102
    representativeness bias 27–8, 84–5
    seven sins 95–215, 273
    short-termism 13–15, 179–86, 282–3, 287, 293,
        297–300, 367–74, 504–5
    stories 55–61, 97, 101, 125, 187–205, 219–22,
        293, 301, 307, 357, 365, 575, 665
    successful investors 183–4, 219–22, 241–2,
        271–8
    synchronizing events 504–5
    Zen of investing 521–2, 528
Investors Intelligence 247, 253, 279
IPOs (initial public offerings) 357, 477–9
IQ-style test, incentives 633–4
Iraq 214, 599
irrational behaviour 12–13, 501–2, 509–17
irrelevant information, anchoring/salience bias
        25–7, 87–92, 120
ISM 573–80
Israel 633–4, 638
'It just hasn't happened yet' ego defence 117–19
Italy 409, 430, 605
iterated dominance, concepts 91–2, 164–75

Jacobsen, B. 60–1
James, William 7
Janis, Irving 214–15
Japan 235, 239, 248, 256–7, 296, 311–17, 326–8,
        337–53, 396, 401–2, 430, 433, 466–7, 472–91,
        507, 510–11, 549, 556, 560, 573–80, 584
    bargain hunters 311–17, 326–8
    bubbles 466–7, 472–91, 507, 510–11
    capacity levels 481–3
    correlation statistics 443, 487–8
    dilution statistics 549, 556, 560
    dollar/yen carry trade (October 1998) 441–2

earnings optimism 584
economic cycles/returns 573–80
EPS/DPS/GDP growth statistics 556, 560
growth investing 311–17, 326–8
liberalization considerations 466–7, 472–91
Little Book strategy 337–53
management techniques 476–7
Recruit Cosmos 482
returns 576–80
sector-relative factors/absolute-value contrasts
    401–3
value investing 311–17, 326–8
Jaws (film) 29, 301
Jensen, Michael 535
Jesus Christ 58
jobs
    happiness 647, 649–51, 653, 657
    redundant workers 259–60, 269
Johannessen, M. 638–9
Jordan 605
Journal of Investing 221
J.P. Morgan 467
Judaism 199
junk equities 247, 251–2, 279, 290
jurors
    belief bias 521–2, 528
    decision-making 191–3, 521–2, 528, 611
    stories 191–3

Kahn, R. 241–2, 419
Kahneman, Daniel 23, 25, 29, 30, 31, 84, 120, 168,
    471, 652
Kant 614
Kasser, Tim 655, 657–9
Kassin *et al* 153–7
Keen, Steve 472–3
Keynes, John Maynard 14, 55, 59, 90–2, 161–75,
    179, 182–3, 185–6, 219, 221, 247, 249, 251,
    257, 274, 279–92, 299–300, 303, 344, 393,
    434, 440–1, 450, 481, 491, 493, 497, 505–6,
    565
    arbitrage views 286–7
    beauty contest analogy 90–2, 101, 161–75, 440–1
    behavioural errors 289
    Ben Graham 279–92
    beta views 291, 434
    contemporary environment 279, 289–90
    contrarian views 285–6
    deflation 481
    forecasting views 283–4
    history views 280, 291–2
    margin-of-safety views 290–1
    overcomplication views 291
    price/value relativity views 288–9
    principal–agent problems 284–5
    professional investors 286–7, 303, 344
    speculation/investment views 279, 281–3, 497,
        506
    time horizons 287
    valuation views 279–80, 288
    views on the nature of investment 279–92, 434,
        450, 481, 491, 493, 506, 565
    volatility views 279, 282–3
    writings 281
Kidd, Joseph 135
Kindleberger, Charles 455, 457, 459, 463, 467,
    472–3, 499
King, Martin Luther 110
Kirby, Bob 434
Klarman, Seth 276
Klein, Gary 617
knowing, knowledge 135
knowledge
    behaviour contrasts 293, 295–6
    curse of knowledge 167–8
    illusion of knowledge 20–3, 82–3, 97, 100,
        105–21, 131–40, 185–6, 301–2, 369, 493,
        496–8, 500
    information contrasts 133
    knowing 135
Koehler, D.J. 303–4
Korea 248, 257
Kozlowski, Dennis 601

laboratory conditions, bubbles 471–2, 503, 511–17
Lancetti, Sebastian 123, 126–7, 129, 337–53, 356,
    363–4, 375–86, 433
Langer, Ellen 55, 57–8, 72–3
Lao Tzu 105, 107, 657
Lapthorne, Andy 255–6, 395–403, 551–2
large cap portfolio bets 247, 250–7
last resort buyers/lenders, bubbles 465–7, 486
lateral temporal cortex 6
Lau, R. 68–9
Lay, Ken 75
laypeople/professionals comparisons
    forecasts 111–14
    lie-detection experiments 153–4
learning 9–10, 20, 24, 63–76, 94, 173–5, 339, 581–
    6
    acquisitions example 65–7
    difficulties 9–10, 24, 63–76, 339, 581–6
    experiences 63–76, 503, 513–14
    feedback distortions 63–4, 72–6
    from mistakes 63–76
    games 173–5
    hindsight bias 63, 69–71
    hurdles 63–76
    illusion of control 72–3
    investment games 66–7
    limits 63–76, 173–5
    plasticity 15
    reflective practices 94
    self-attribution bias 20, 24, 63, 67–9, 76
    self-deception bias 20–4, 63–76
    Skinner's pigeons 71–3

Lee, I.H. 500
Leeper *et al* 148–9
legal experts
   anchoring/salience bias 99–100, 120
   stories 189, 191–2
Legg Mason Value 273–4, 276
lenders of last resort, bubbles 465–7, 486
leverage 245, 363–4, 446, 449–52, 459–60, 476–83, 489, 536–40
   see also debt; financial risks
   critique 449–52, 459–60, 476–83, 536–40
   hedge funds 245, 489
   measures 536
   statistics 536–7
   value stocks 363
libraries, beliefs 200
Lieberman *et al* 300, 585
lies
   clues 156–7
   detection 97, 100, 143–5, 153–7
   laypeople/professionals lie-detection comparisons 153–4
   truth 97, 100, 143–5, 153–7
lightning strikes, recency-effect bias 28–9, 301
limited resources
   self-control 11–15, 609, 640–3
   working memory 631, 640–3
liquidity, monetary policies 457–9, 473–6
Little Book strategy 221, 261, 296–7, 337–53
   backtesting results 337–53
   concepts 337–40
   core concepts 339–40
   critique 339–45
   definition 339–40, 345–6
   future prospects 344–5
   long/short portfolios 343–4
   methodology and data 339–40
   performance issues 337–53
   PEs 341, 345–9
   quality issues 341–2
   results 340–1, 345–9
   sectors 350–3
   stock lists 350–3
Livermore, Jesse 243
livestock 591
   see also commodities
Lo *et al* 39
log earnings 546–7
logic 5–6, 169–70, 521–8, 611, 615–17, 631
   see also System C
long large caps/short small caps, contrarian approaches 255–7
long value short growth strategies 355
long-only constraints, shorting 242–4
long-only portfolios 242–4, 333–6, 405, 408–9, 412–21, 447, 489, 491, 581–6, 608–9
   bubbles 489, 491
   cheap countries 405, 408–9, 412–21
   Graham and Dodd PEs 333–6, 581–6

long-run returns 237–9, 367–74
   see also time horizons
long-term growth rates (LTG) 128–9
long/short portfolios 255–7, 332–6, 343–4, 398–403, 405–21, 469, 489–91, 587, 589, 608–9
   cheap countries 405–21
   Graham and Dodd PEs 332–6
   Little Book strategy 343–4
   sector-relative factors 398–403
Longleaf Partners 273–4
Lopez, D. 73–5
Lord *et al* 149
losers/winners long-term performance in momentum strategies 129–30
loss-aversion/prospect-theory bias
   see also heuristic-simplification. . .
   concepts 20, 30–5, 42–3, 51–2, 86, 89–90, 293, 296–7, 445–52, 501–3
   examples 30–5, 86, 89–90, 296–7, 447
   investor behaviour 32–4, 86, 89–90, 293, 296–7, 445–52, 501–3
   test 89–90
lovers, overoptimism bias 83
low returns 563–72
   see also returns
Lowe, Janet 281
Lowenstein 273, 276, 278, 650–1
LSE 298
LSV 259, 267
LTCM 244, 441–2, 450, 457, 474
LTG (long-term growth rates) 128–9
luck, self-attribution bias 24, 36, 63, 67–9
Lufkin, E. 449–51
lust, seven sins 97, 100, 140, 141–57
Lyubomirsky, Professor 649

McCallum rule 474
McClure *et al* 297–9
Dr McCoy approach, dual process theories of thought 5, 615–16
machines sector, seasonal results 61
McKinsey 369–70
McNealy, Scott 531
magical thinking 301–2, 499–500
management
   see also corporate managers; fund. . .
   options 30, 179, 181–2, 529–40, 633–4
   principal–agent problems 284–5
Manias, Panics and Crashes (Kindleberger) 472–3
manic depression (bipolar disorder) 275
Mankiw, Greg 227, 229–30
MAR (minimal acceptable return) 448
margin debt, levels 247, 253–5
margins of safety, concepts 273–5, 290–1, 307, 318, 446, 450–2
market caps, volumes 463–5
market power 165–6

market risk
  see also financial markets; volatility
  critique 271, 275–6, 295
market shares, bubbles 479–80
Markowitz, Harry 425, 427, 431
Markowitz Optimization (MO) 425, 427, 431
married persons, happiness 649, 650
Martin, Frank 445–52
Marx, Karl 457, 509, 516
Maslow's needs 663
materialism
  experiences 661–5
  happiness 647, 650–1, 653, 655–65
  mental disorders 655, 660–5
  problems 660
  studies 660–5
maxims, common investment pitfalls 17, 35–6
MCI (monetary conditions indicator) 573–80
mean-reversion 27–8
mean-variance efficient portfolios 427–35
medial temporal lobe 6
Meehl, Paul 266, 269
meeting companies (lust)
  see also corporate managers
  fund managers 100, 140, 141–57, 355–7,
    365
  time-wasting exercises 143–57, 355–7,
    365
Mellstrom, C. 638–9
memory
  recency-effect bias 28–9, 301
  working memory 631, 640–3
mental disorders 261–2, 655, 660–5
  see also neurosis; psychosis
  happiness 655, 660–5
Merrill Lynch 252–3
Merton scores 449–50
Messick, D.M 627–8
meta-analysis, quant models 266
metals 510, 512, 591–2
  see also commodities
  bubbles 510, 512
Microsoft 553
Milgram, Stanley 143, 151–3, 599, 604–8
Minahan, John 221, 222
minimal acceptable return (MAR) 448
Minnesota Multiphasic Personality Inventory
    (MMPI) 261–2
Minsky, Hyman 457, 463, 467, 472–4, 499
mistakes
  learning from mistakes 63–76
  seven sins 95–215
MIT 85–6, 636–7
MMPI (Minnesota Multiphasic Personality
    Inventory) 261–2
MO (Markowitz Optimization) 425, 427, 431
Modigliani and Miller (M&M) 427, 531
Moll *et al* 615–16
momentary realists 7

momentum strategies
  cheap countries 405–21
  critique 129–30, 161–75, 231–3, 238–9, 261,
    281–2, 375–86, 387–93, 459–67
  financial markets 55–61, 106, 120–1, 123–4,
    129–30, 161–75, 231–3, 238–9, 261, 281–2,
    375–86, 405–21, 459–67
  growth investors 381–2
  past prices 106, 120–1, 123–4, 129–30
  sectors 387–93, 395–403
  value investors 383–6, 387–93
  winners/losers long-term performance 129–30
monetary conditions indicator (MCI) 573–80
monetary policies, bubbles 457–9, 473–6
money
  happiness 647, 650–1, 653, 655–65
  utility concepts 13–14
Monty Hall problem 92–4
Monty Python (TV series) 425, 649
mood bias 20
Moore *et al* 622–7
moral judgements
  see also ethics
  bounded ethicality 611–12, 617–27
  concepts 611–29
  emotions 611–12, 614–29
  origins 614–17
  psychopaths 617
  rationality 614–15
moral-disengagement factors
  see also ethics
  bad behaviour 608–9, 627–9
Morck, R. 606–7
Morocco 257
mortgages 465
motivated reasoning, concepts 73–6
motivations 13, 73–6, 631–43
  concepts 13, 73–6, 631–43
  critique 631–43
  incentives 631–43
  need to belong 13
moving averages
  critique 331–6, 581
  Graham and Dodd PEs 329–36, 569–71, 581–6
MSCI indices 230–1, 301, 307, 309–15, 329, 331–5,
    375, 377, 408–9, 429–30
Mullainathan, S. 618–19
Mulligan, E.J. 193–4
muscle analogy, self-control 11–13
Mutual Beacon 273–4
mutual funds 33–5, 179, 181–2, 183–4, 225–33,
    271, 273, 276–7, 367, 372–4, 377–8, 425–6,
    432
  evolution 229–31, 425–6
  loss-aversion/prospect-theory bias 33–5
  structural decline 425
  time horizons 179, 181–2, 183–4, 277, 367,
    372–4, 377–8
myths 199, 519–96

Nagel *et al* 167–8, 171–2, 174
naïve beliefs 203–5
    see also beliefs
narcissistic mental disorder 655, 661
NASDAQ 428
Nash equilibrium 164, 165, 169
    see also game theory
NcClure *et al* 297–8
near-random moves, financial markets 55–61
near-rational bubbles 493, 496–8, 500–6
    see also bubbles; cynical...
    concepts 493, 496–8, 500–6
    danger triggers 503–5
need to belong 13
net equity issuance 355–65
    see also inside information
    betas 355–6, 361–4
    concepts 355–65
    critique 359–65
    Europe 363–5
    USA 357–63, 364
net fixed capital, *Little Book* strategy 339–53
net repurchase yields, statistics 551–61
net share buybacks, statistics 529, 533–40
net working capital, *Little Book* strategy 339–53
Netherlands 247, 257, 409, 605
neuroscience 3–15, 75–6, 297–300, 527, 615–16
    concepts 3, 5–15, 75–6, 297–300, 527, 615–16
    dopamine effects 13–14, 75–6, 287, 297–300
    dual process theories of thought 5–6, 75–6, 85,
        297–300, 445–52, 527, 615–16
    fears 6, 9–11, 49–50, 447
    plasticity 15
    reasoning systems 5–7, 75–6, 85–6, 297–300,
        527, 615–16
    recent developments 5
    short-termism behaviour 13–15, 287, 293,
        297–300
neurosis 259, 261–2, 655, 660–5
new era thinking, bubbles 476–7, 493, 499–503, 516
New Zealand 257
nightmares, dreams 189, 191
Nikkei 467
NIPA profits 549–54
Nisbett *et al* 601, 615
Nocera, Joe 99
noise generators, financial markets 55–61, 139–40,
    143–5, 271, 276, 301–2, 376–86, 565
Norway, cheap countries 247, 257, 409
NPVs 182
NYSE 179, 181–2, 276–7, 298, 367, 369, 377–8,
    428, 463–4, 486

Oak Value 273–4
Oakmark Select 273–4
obedience tendencies
    electric-shock experiments 151–3, 599, 604–8
    power figures 143, 151–3, 292, 599, 604–8

Odean, T. 33–4
OECD 576
off-index positions 219, 221
Oishi, S. 651
Ono, K. 71–2
operating performance, statistics 449–50
optimal equity allocations 238–9
optimistic views
    earnings optimism 581–6
    selling opportunities 254
options
    see also futures
    critique 535–40, 633–4
    earnings' impact 536–7
    expensing impacts 536–8
    management options 30, 179, 181–2, 529–40,
        633–4
    valuations 535–6
    volatility 535–40
Opus Dei 58
orbitofrontal cortex 298–9
order-of-information effects, stories 193–4, 301
Oskamp, K. 135–7
OTC securities 245
outperformance 241–2, 247, 249, 259–69, 295, 307,
        310–12, 340–53, 357, 373–4, 375–6, 381–2,
        405–21, 450–2
    see also performance issues
    quant models 259–69, 340–53
Oval 211
overclaiming credit bias 611–12, 620–1
overconfidence bias
    see also hindsight...; illusion...;
        self-deception...
    accuracy factors 528
    calibration curves 109–12, 117–18
    concepts 20–3, 33–4, 63, 71–3, 99–101, 105–21,
        133–40, 143–57, 164–5, 168–75, 259–69, 290,
        293, 301–2, 307, 312, 318, 369–70, 439–44,
        469, 477, 497–500, 528
    corporate managers 143–57, 459
    experts 21–3, 105, 110–21, 259–60, 268–9, 293,
        301–2, 369–70, 439–44, 469, 477, 497–500
    forecasts 99–100, 105–21, 148, 301–2
    quant models 259–60, 268–9, 301–2
    test 109–10, 113–14
overoptimism bias
    see also illusion...; self-deception...
    concepts 20–3, 33, 63, 71–3, 82–3, 99–101, 105,
        109–21, 143–57, 211, 307, 312, 318, 459–60,
        469, 476–8, 489–90, 493, 497–505, 571–86
    examples 20–3, 82–3
    lovers 83
    test 82–3
overreactions to news, intrinsic bubbles 498–9
overtrading problems 97, 101, 177–86, 290,
        459–60, 476–8
overweight cash, contrarian approaches 254–5

ownership factors
    endowment effect 30–6, 42–3, 286
    principal–agent problems 284–5

pain of regret 484
Pakistan 248, 257, 665
panic 463–7, 472–3, 483–6
    see also revulsion. . .
paradox of the unexpected hanging 165
paranoia 261, 655, 661
parietal cortex 14, 299
passive investing 235–46, 429–30
    see also benchmarking; indexing
    change needs 235–46
past performance 27–8, 226, 231–3
past winners, future losers 129–30
patience 219–22, 280, 297–300, 344, 357, 375–86
pattern-spotting abilities 47–8
payout ratios
    earnings growth 546–7, 566
    statistics 541, 545–7
payouts
    concepts 539–40, 541–7, 552–6, 566
    total payout statistics 539–40, 541–7, 552–6
PE *see* price/earnings ratio
Pearson, Karl 575
peer groups, benchmarking 484
Pennington, N. 191–2
pension funds 235, 243–4, 299, 374, 590, 594–5
perceptual causation, unethical behaviour 628–9
performance issues
    see also returns
    active fund managers 225–33, 373–4
    bargain hunters 307–28, 337–53
    cheap countries 247, 257, 405–21
    choking under pressure 631–43
    contrarian approaches 251–7
    the dismal years 240–1, 388, 393
    fund managers 27–8, 179–86, 221–2, 225–33,
        238–9, 369–74
    Graham and Dodd PEs 329–36, 485–6, 569–71,
        581–6
    hiring/firing decisions 373–4
    incentives 181, 183, 631–43
    indexing 225–33, 278, 373, 429–32
    information ratios 242–5, 278, 333–6, 409–21
    Little Book strategy 337–53
    net equity issuance 355–65
    outperformance 241–2, 247, 249, 259–69, 295,
        307, 310–12, 340–53, 357, 373–4, 375–6,
        381–2, 405–21, 450–2
    past performance 27–8, 226, 231–3
    quant models 259–69, 312
    risks 447–52
    sector calls 387–93
    stock pickers 225–33, 238, 329–36, 387–93
    time horizons 174–5, 179–86, 277, 369–74,
        375–86

value/growth contrasts 317–18
    working memory 631, 640–3
persistence levels
    abnormal returns 249–51
    active share 231–2
personal benefits
    Aspiration Index 657–60
    happiness 649–50, 655–65
personality traits, happiness 649–50
Peru 248, 257
pessimistic viewpoints 254, 501–3, 649
PET (positron emission topography) 5
Petajisto, Antti 225–6, 227–33
Petty *et al* 200–2
Philips, Thomas K. 565–6
philosophy, beliefs 197–205
photocopier queues, placebic information 57–8,
    101
pigeons 47–53, 71–3
Piotroski, Joseph 312, 379, 449–50, 489
placebic information 57–9, 101
plan sponsors, needs 241–2, 244–5, 299–300
plasticity, learning concepts 15
polarization problems, group-based decisions 209,
    214–15
politics 74–6, 149
Ponzi scheme 466
Poon, S.K. 303–4
The Pope 215
Popper, Karl 24, 83
portable alphas
    see also alphas
    concepts 426, 432–5
portfolios 27–8, 63, 73, 129–30, 225, 227–33, 271,
    273–6, 309–28, 395–403, 553–61
    active share 225, 227–33
    bargain hunters 307–28, 337–53
    best value investors 271, 273–6, 295
    capital asset pricing model 427–35
    dilution 549, 553–61
    Fortune 10 buy-and-forget portfolio 275
    global returns 309–28
    Graham and Dodd PEs 332–6, 485–6
    highly concentrated portfolios 271, 273–6, 295
    illusion of control 63, 73
    long-only portfolios 242–4, 333–6, 405, 408–9,
        412–21, 447, 489, 491, 581–6, 608–9
    long/short portfolios 255–7, 332–6, 343–4,
        398–403, 405–21, 469, 489–91, 587, 589,
        608–9
    mean-reversion 27–8
    rebalances 244–5, 553–4
    sector-relative factors 395–403
    winners/losers long-term performance in
        momentum strategies 129–30
positive feedback
    bubbles 457–9, 473–6, 504–5
    VaR models 439–40

positive reviews, experiences 655–6, 663–5
positron emission topography (PET) 5
possessions
    see also materialism
    happiness 647, 650–1, 653, 655–65
power figures, obedience tendencies 143, 151–3,
    292, 599, 604–8
Prechter, Robert 515–16
prefrontal cortex 6, 14, 298–9, 527
premiums, value investors 310–12, 331–2, 384–6,
    391
price bubbles see bubbles
price to book ratios 389, 395, 398–403, 405, 428–9
    cheap countries 405, 408–21
    sector-relative factors 398–403
price to cashflow, sector-relative factors 400–3
price/earnings ratio (PE) 123, 125–30, 139, 195–6,
    219, 221, 237–9, 255–6, 307–28, 329–36, 341,
    375–6, 398–403, 451–2, 477, 563, 566–72
    see also share prices
    bargain hunters 307–28
    cheap countries 405, 408–21
    cyclically adjusted PEs 329–36
    EBIT/EV contrasts 341, 345–9
    forward PE valuation method 123, 125–30,
        256–7, 569–70
    Graham and Dodd PEs 219, 221, 255–6, 273,
        329–36, 485–6, 569–71, 581–6
    Hussman's PEs 495, 571–2
    Japanese bubble 477
    Little Book strategy 341, 345–9
    sector-relative factors 398–403
    statistics 307, 309–28, 375–6, 408–9, 421, 450–2,
        566–72
    trailing PE valuation method 123, 125–7, 331–6,
        345–6, 377, 569–72
pride
    see also forecasts
    seven sins 97, 99–100, 103–30
primacy of emotions 5–15
primary trends, Dow theory 514–16
principal–agent problems 284–5
principle component analysis 510–11
processing efficiency, illusion of knowledge 137–8
profit and loss statements 30
profit margins, best value investors 271, 275–6, 295,
    449–50
profit warnings 23, 37–8
profitable reinvestment theory, critique 284–5
profits
    see also earnings
    contrarian approaches 251–3
    retained earnings 284–5, 290, 472–3, 531–40
Pronin et al 301–2
propositions, distractions 197–8, 200–5
prospect-theory bias 20
psychology
    bubbles 493–506, 507–17
    ethics 611–29

happiness 647–53, 655–65
incentives 631–43
risks 20, 30–5, 42–3, 51–2, 86, 89–90, 293,
    296–7, 445–52
psychopaths 617
psychosis 259, 261–2, 617
purchasing managers, quant models 264–6
the pursuit of happiness 655–65

quality issues
    contrarian approaches 252–3
    junk equities 247, 251–2, 279, 290
    Little Book strategy 341–2
quant models
    see also Little Book strategy
    alphas 267
    Bordeaux wines 259, 263–5
    concepts 221, 259–69, 312, 337–53
    criminal recidivism 259, 263
    fund managers 259, 267–9, 312, 337–8
    human judgements 264, 266
    inertia problems 259–60, 269
    meta-analysis 266
    neurosis/psychosis diagnosis 259, 261–2
    outperformance 259–69, 340–53
    overconfidence bias 259–60, 268–9, 301–2
    performance issues 259–69, 312
    purchasing managers 264–6
    redundant workers 259–60, 269
    self-serving bias 259–60, 268–9
    statistics 259
    university admissions 259, 263
    usage 259, 261–4, 267–9
Quant team 123, 126–7, 329, 331, 339, 377, 407–8,
    429
quantitative approaches, investor behaviour 102

racism, implicit attitudes 611, 618–19
railway boom, UK 466, 507
random moves, financial markets 55–61, 138–9
random walks 138–9
rational/near-rational bubbles 493, 496–8, 500–6
    see also bubbles
rationality 12–13, 164–75, 189–96, 473, 493,
    496–8, 500–3, 614–15, 617–27, 664–5
    bounded rationality 168–75, 611–12, 617–27
    evidence 191–2, 575
    moral judgements 614–15
    stages 191–2
rats 47–8
Rau et al 478
reactionary change 235–46
reactive devaluations 19–21
reading
    see also stories
    believing everything you read (sloth) 97, 101,
        187–205
real dividend growth 237–9
realists, momentary realists 7

reasoning
    dual process theories of thought 5–15, 74–6, 85–94, 281, 297–300, 445–52, 524–8, 585, 615–19
    iterative dominance 169–70
    motivated reasoning 73–6
    neuroscience 5–7, 75–6, 85–6, 297–300, 527, 615–16
rebalances 244–5, 553–4
rebias considerations 36
recency-effect bias, concepts 28–9, 301
Recruit Cosmos 482
redundant information 133–40
redundant workers
    computers 259–60, 269
    quant models 259–60, 269
reflation trades, risk managers 437, 439–44, 498, 581, 584–6
reflective practices 94, 616–17
    happiness 647, 652–3
    reflexive contrasts 94
reflexive reasoning 6–16, 85–6, 94, 616–17
    see also emotions
regression analysis
    bubbles 509–16
    economic cycles/returns 576–8
regret theory 20
rejection 13, 14, 300
    see also social pain
relationships
    Aspiration Index 657–60
    happiness 647, 649–51, 652–3, 655–65
relative returns 240–6, 286, 333–6, 344, 434–5
relative valuation method 123, 125–6
religion 58, 199, 215, 650
remuneration methods, fund managers 181, 183, 244, 272
representations of the self, ethics 629
representativeness bias
    see also heuristic-simplification...
    concepts 20, 27–8, 84–5, 284, 360–1, 498–500, 509–17
    examples 27–8, 84–5, 360–1
    test 84–5
Republicans 74–6, 149
repurchases see share repurchases
Research Affiliates 429–30
respect benefits, group-based decisions (wrath) 209, 215
responsibility issues, moral-disengagement factors 608–9, 628–9
retail investors, returns-chasing behaviour 372–4
retained earnings, critique 284–5, 290, 472–3, 531–40, 552–6
retained earnings yield 537–40, 552–6
    see also earnings yields
    concepts 537–40, 552–6
    statistics 537–40, 552–6
retracements, technical analysis 515–16

return on assets (ROA), Little Book strategy 340–53
return on capital (ROC)
    definition 339–40
    Little Book strategy 337–53
returns
    see also dividend...; performance issues; profit...
    abnormal returns 249–51, 254–7, 384–6, 575–80, 608
    absolute returns 240–6, 296–7, 469, 489–91
    alternative investments 587–96
    bad years 240–1, 271, 278, 295, 296–7, 337–8, 344–5, 367, 388, 393
    betas 428–35
    bonds 238–40, 241, 462–3, 487–8, 573–80
    capital asset pricing model 427–35
    cheap countries 247, 257, 405–21
    commodities 587–8
    component parts 531–40, 563, 565
    contrarian approaches 251–3
    cost of capital 55–7, 181–2, 565–6
    cumulative normal charts 566–9
    cyclically adjusted PEs 329–36
    the dismal years 240–1, 388, 393
    economic cycles 573–80
    emerging equity markets 189–90, 194–6, 247–8, 256–7
    global returns 309–28
    Graham and Dodd PEs 329–36, 569–71
    growth investors 309–28, 375–86, 450–2
    inside information 355–65
    Little Book strategy 337–53
    long-run returns 237–9, 367–74
    low returns 563–72
    net equity issuance 355–65
    persistence levels 249–50
    relative returns 240–6, 286, 333–6, 344, 434–5
    risks 47–8, 86–7, 181–3, 184–6, 219–22, 247, 251–2, 290, 318, 346–9, 359–60, 401–3, 408–21, 445–52
    sector-relative factors 395–403
    sentiments 254–7, 463–7, 483–6, 565–6
    time horizons 174–5, 179–86, 271, 277, 369–74, 375–86, 565
    total payout statistics 539–40, 541–7, 552–6
    transition probabilities 378–9
    valuations 237–9, 288, 531–40, 565–72
    value investors 309–28, 375–86, 387–93, 450–2
returns-chasing behaviour, retail investors 372–4
reverse-engineering benefits, valuations 17, 27
revolutionary change 235–46
revulsion stage, bubbles 455, 457, 463–7, 483–6, 507, 509, 514–17
rewards, dopamine effects 13, 75–6, 297–300
Rhea, Rupert 514–15
ride-your-winners/sell-your-losers maxim 17, 33–6, 40–1
right lateral prefrontal cortex 527
risk exposures, fund managers 174–5, 184–6

risk managers
   concepts 219–22, 273–4, 393, 437–44
   correlations 437
   critique 219–22, 273–4, 393, 437–44
   reflation trades 437, 439–44, 498, 581, 584–6
   safeguard systems 437–44
   VaR models 437, 439–44
risk models
   see also Value-at-Risk (VaR) models
   crash of 1987 441–2
   critique 437–44
   dollar/yen carry trade (October 1998) 441–2
   dynamic hedging 441–2, 444
   endogenous/exogenous assumptions 437, 440–4
   LTCM 441–2
   Russian default (August 1998) 441–2
risk tolerance 59, 86–7
risk-free rates 425–35, 448, 535
risks
   see also business. . . ; financial. . . ; valuation. . . ;
      volatility
   alternative investments 587–96
   assessments 174–5, 184–6, 219–22, 271, 273–5,
      276, 290–1, 445–52
   betas 425–6, 428–35, 445–52
   budgets 439–40
   capital asset pricing model 427–35
   cheap countries 405–21
   commodities 590–1
   concepts 219–22, 247, 251–2, 271, 273–5, 276,
      290–1, 427–35, 437–44, 445–52, 587–96
   critique 445–52
   definitions 219, 222, 445–52
   downside risks 445–52
   elements 445–52
   emotions 7–11
   endogenous/exogenous assumptions 437, 440–4
   gambling analogy 437, 440–4
   investment perspectives 445–6, 448–52
   nature 219, 222, 437–42
   performance measurement 447–52
   psychology 20, 30–5, 42–3, 51–2, 86, 89–90,
      293, 296–7, 445–52
   returns 47–8, 86–7, 181–3, 184–6, 219–22, 247,
      251–2, 290, 318, 346–9, 359–60, 401–3,
      408–21, 445–52
   sector-relative factors 397–8, 401–3
   Sortino ratios 445, 448–52
   types 445–52
   value investors 318, 359–60, 450–2
   VaR models 437, 439–44
   variance 431–5, 448–52
risky investments, volatility increases 535–40
rituals 71–2
ROA *see* return on assets
robber barons 549–61
ROC *see* return on capital

ROE 137–8, 449–50, 565–7
roll returns, commodities futures 587–8, 591–5
Roman Catholic Church 58
romantic relationships, impact bias 37, 45
Ross *et al* 601–2
rotations 256–7, 397–403, 573–80
Rothchild, John 477
rules, happiness 647
rumours 189–96
   see also stories
Rumsfeld, Donald 149
Russell
   1000 433
   2000 228
   3000 346
Russell, D. 68–9
Russian default (August 1998) 441–2
Russo, J.E. 149–51
Rustichini, A. 633–4, 638–9
Ryan, Richard 655, 657–9

S&P500 25, 108–9, 127–8, 227–8, 231, 237–8, 252,
      370–1, 433, 439–40, 461–3, 478–80, 495,
      501–6, 511–15, 529–34, 538–41, 546, 552–5,
      568, 581
   see also Standard and Poor's. . .
sadness 6–7
   see also emotions
safety margins, concepts 273–5, 290–1, 307, 318,
      446, 450–2
Samuelson, Paul 303
Sapp, T. 372–4
Sarbanes & Oxley legislation 466
scepticism 197–205, 219–22, 228–9, 633
Scott, F.C. 274
Scrushy, Richard 601
SDC (Securities Data Company) 533
seasonal results 55–61
SEC 357, 532
secondary reactions, Dow theory 514–16
secret ballots, group-based decisions (wrath) 209,
      215
secretaries, placebic information 57–9
sector-neutral strategies 221–2
sector-relative factors
   absolute-value contrasts 399–403
   accounting regimes 395–6, 398–403
   backtests 395–403
   capital structures 395, 398–403
   concepts 395–403
   dividend yields 398–403
   methodology 398
   PEs 398–403
   price to book ratios 398–403
   price to cashflow 400–3
   regional results 399–403
   results 398–403

returns 395–403
  risks 397–8, 401–3
  small/large caps 395–403
sectors
  betas 231
  cheap sectors 387–93
  concepts 228–33, 387–93, 395–403, 484–6,
    552–61, 573–80
  critique 228–33, 387–93, 395–403
  economic cycles 579–80
  growth investors 387, 390–3
  industry-relative factors 395–403
  Little Book strategy 350–3
  market/economy links 552–4, 573–80
  momentum strategies 387–93, 395–403
  performance issues 387–93
  post-bubble winners 484–6
  rotations 256–7, 397–403, 573–80
  value investors 387–93, 395–403
Securities Data Company (SDC) 533
*Security Analysis, and the Rediscovered Ben
  Graham* (Lowe) 281, 329, 331, 337, 339
self-attribution bias
  see also self-deception...
  concepts 20, 24, 33, 44, 63, 67–9, 76
  decision matrices 24, 69
  decision-making 24, 44, 63, 67–9, 76
  examples 67–9
  learning from mistakes 20, 24, 63, 67–9, 76
self-control
  biases 20
  concepts 11–15, 20, 287, 609, 640–3
  emotions 7–15, 20, 609
  food experiment 12–13
  fund managers 13
  limited resources 11–15, 609, 640–3
  muscle analogy 11–13
self-deception bias
  see also confirmation...; hindsight...;
    illusion...; overconfidence...;
    overoptimism...; self-attribution...
  concepts 19–24, 63–76, 82–4, 99–101, 143–57,
    611–12, 613–14, 627–9
  corporate managers 143–57, 459
  examples 19–24, 82–4, 613–14
  learning 20–4, 63–76
  reduction techniques 611, 629
  test 82–4
  unethical behaviour 627–9
  veil of ignorance 629
self-esteem
  fragility 24, 67–8
  happiness 658–9
  self-control 12–13
self-focus theory, incentives 631, 640–1
self-fulfilling prophecies 185–6
self-interests 19–20

self-serving bias 19–21, 259–60, 268–9
self-vs-others perceptions, biases 19, 35, 44
sell-your-losers/ride-your-winners maxim 17, 33–6,
  40–1
semi-variance
  see also downside risks
  Sortino ratios 448–52
sensory cortex 6
sentiments
  financial markets 59–61, 254–7, 279, 463–7,
    483–6, 506, 565–6
  returns 254–7, 463–7, 483–6, 565–6
  stock pickers 255–7
  valuation/sentiment matrix 565–6
Sentix 171–3
Sequoia Fund 273
set point, happiness levels 649–50, 652
seven sins
  believing everything you read (sloth) 97, 101,
    187–205
  forecasts (pride) 97, 99–100, 103–30, 148, 283–4
  fund managers 95–215, 273
  group-based decisions (wrath) 98, 101, 207–15
  illusion of knowledge (gluttony) 97, 100, 131–40
  meeting companies (lust) 100, 140, 141–57,
    355–7, 365
  short time horizons and overtrading (avarice) 97,
    101, 164–5, 174–5, 177–86, 282–3, 287, 293,
    297–300, 367–74, 439–44, 459–60, 476–8,
    497–8
  thinking that you can outsmart everyone else
    (envy) 97, 100–1, 159–75
sex, happiness 647, 652–3
sexism, implicit attitudes 611, 618–19
sexual stimuli, empathy gaps 42–3
sexually aggressive behaviour 11
Shakespeare, William 189, 191
share options *see* options
share prices 25–7, 123, 125–30, 139, 195–6, 219,
  221, 237–9, 249, 255–6, 288–9
  see also price...; volatility
  anchoring/salience bias 25–7, 288–9
  consensus views 249
share repurchases 355–65, 529–61
  see also buybacks
  announcements 532–3, 543–7, 551–2
  completions 543–7, 551–2
  critique 529–40, 541–7, 549–56
  dividend yields 529–40, 541–56
  earnings 544–7, 549–61
  myths 529–40
  net figures 529, 533–40, 543–7, 551–2
shareholders
  activism 607–8
  corporate governance 607–8
  principal–agent problems 284–5
  total payout statistics 539–40, 541–7, 552–6

shark attacks, recency-effect bias 28–9, 301
Sharpe, Litner and Treynor 427
Sharpe ratios 240–1, 445, 448
sheep index
    see also herd...
    fund managers 251
Sheldon et al 649–52, 655
Sherlock Holmes 309, 407, 549, 551
Shiller, Robert 282, 370, 495–9
Shiv et al 49–53
short run 239–46, 367–74
    see also time horizons
short small caps, contrarian approaches 255–7
short time horizons and overtrading (avarice),
        seven sins 97, 101, 164–5, 174–5, 177–86,
        282–3, 287, 293, 297–300, 367–74, 439–44,
        459–60, 476–8, 497–8
short-term gains, dopamine effects 13–15, 287,
        297–300
short-term moves 235–46
short-termism behaviour 13–15, 179–86, 282–3,
        287, 293, 297–300, 367–74, 504–5
    see also time horizons
    critique 179–86, 282–3, 287, 293, 297–300,
        367–74
    neuroscience 13–15, 287, 293, 297–300
shorting 235–46, 472
    bad reputation 243
    change needs 235–46
    costs 243
    critique 235, 243–4
Shynkaruk, J.M. 526–8
SIA survey, expected returns 501–2
SIC (Standard Industrial Classification) 389,
        398
Simonsohn et al 269
'single prediction' ego defence 117–19
siren calls 312, 355, 365
situational perspectives
    see also fundamental attribution error
    bad behaviour 151–3, 599–609, 628–9
size issues, sector-relative factors 395–403
skills
    fund managers 227–33, 278, 293, 301–2
    overconfidence bias 20–3, 33–4, 63, 71–3,
        99–101, 105–21, 293, 301–2
    self-attribution bias 24, 36, 63, 67–9, 76
Skinner, B.F. 71–3
sleep, happiness 647, 653
slippery slopes, unethical behaviour 628
sloth, seven sins 97, 101, 187–205
Slovic, Paul 20–1, 70–1, 133, 135–7
small cap portfolio bets 247, 250–7, 395–403
SMB, fund management group factor betas 231
smiling exercises, emotions 7
Smith, Adam 281, 459, 505, 647, 650, 653
Smith, Vernon 471–2, 503, 512
smoking, false consensus effect 167

Snijders, Professor Chris 264
social pain 14, 213–14, 293, 300
    see also herd behaviour
    contrarian approaches 300
social rewards, happiness 649–51, 656–65
social-interaction bias
    see also herd...
    concepts 19–21
social-status factors, group-based decisions (wrath)
        213–14
Sortino ratios
    concepts 445, 448–52
    definition 448
    Sharpe ratios 448–9
South Africa 116, 118
South Sea bubble 466, 507, 510
Soviet Union 116, 118
Spain 247, 257, 409, 605
speculation 179, 185–6, 277, 279, 281–3, 367–9,
        459–67, 473, 497, 506, 515–16, 592–4
    commodities 592–4
    concepts 179, 185–6, 277, 279, 281–3, 367–9,
        459–67, 497, 506
    critique 279, 281–3, 367–9, 459–67, 473, 497,
        506
    enterprise 281–2
    investment contrasts 279, 281–3, 459
Speculative Contagion (Martin) 448–9
speed dating 649
Spektrum 170–1
Spinoza, Benedict 197–205
Mr Spock approach, dual process theories of
        thought 5, 615–16
spot returns, commodities futures 587, 591–5
Sri Lanka 257
standard deviation 237–9, 240–1, 318, 411–21,
        445–52, 590–1
    see also variance; volatility
Standard Industrial Classification (SIC) 389, 398
Standard and Poor's quality rankings 251–2
    see also S&P...
Star Wars (film) 124, 130
statistical groups
    see also group...
    performance issues 211–12
statistical models
    see also quant...
    concepts 261–9
status quo bias
    see also loss-aversion...
    concepts 30–5
stereotypes 611, 618–20
    see also implicit attitudes
Stigler, George 261
Stigler, Stephen 575
stock pickers 119–20, 225–33, 238–9, 255–7,
        301–2, 329–36, 375–86, 387–93, 395–403,
        469–91

see also active fund managers
active share 225, 227–33
bubbles 469–91
concepts 119–20, 225–33, 238–9, 255–7, 301–
    2, 329–36, 375–86, 387–93, 395–403, 469–
    91
critique 225–33, 301–2, 329–36, 387–93, 469–
    91
cyclically adjusted PEs 329–36
Little Book strategy 221, 261, 296–7, 337–53
performance issues 225–33, 238, 329–36, 387–
    93
sector-relative factors 395–403
sentiments 255–7
types 225, 227–33
stockbrokers
see also fund managers
dreams/nightmares 189, 191
stop-loss systems 379–80, 441–3
stories 55–61, 97, 101, 125, 187–205, 219–22, 293,
    301, 307, 357, 365, 575, 665
see also excuses; explanation-based
    decision-making; reading
acceptance problems 55–61, 97, 101, 187–205,
    575
China 189–90, 194–6, 594
critique 187–205, 219–22, 293, 301, 307, 357,
    365, 575, 665
decision-making 189–96, 219–22, 293, 301
emerging equity markets 189–90, 194–6
jurors 191–3
order-of-information effects 193–4, 301
strategic asset allocations (SAA)
change needs 235–46
valuations 238–9
strategic diversification 244
strategic thinking
beauty contest analogy 165–75, 440–1
thinking steps 168–75, 440–1
strokes 53
style rotations 256–7, 397–403, 573–80
successful investors 183–4, 219–22, 241–2, 271–
    8
see also best value investors
key traits 271–8, 295
Summers, Larry 55, 59
Sun Microsystems 531
Sunstein, Professor 211–12
superstitions 71–2
Surowiecki, James 211
survival instincts 17–36
Sweden 638–9
swindles 75, 463, 466–7, 482–3, 601
see also bad behaviour; fraud
bubbles 463, 466–7, 482–3
Switzerland 257, 409
syllogisms 521–6
synchronizing events, concepts 504–5

System C, dual process theories of thought 5–6, 14,
    74–6, 85–94, 281, 297–300, 525–7, 585–6,
    615–19, 641
System X
belief bias 524–8
dual process theories of thought 5–6, 14, 25,
    74–6, 85–94, 281, 297–300, 445–52, 521–8,
    585, 615–19, 641
moral judgements 615–19

t-stats 333–6, 399–403, 409–10, 575–80
TAA enzymes 73–5
tactical asset allocations (TAA)
concepts 239–45, 261
critique 261
Taleb, N. 227
Tasker, Peter 148, 381, 476–7, 481, 484
Taylor rule 458, 474–5
technical analysis
see also Dow theory; Elliot Wave theory
bubbles 507, 514–17
concepts 514–17
Telecoms sector, USA 390–2
Templeton, Sir John 14, 221, 247–9, 254, 257, 300,
    434–5
Tenbrunsel, A.E. 627–8
test, biases 79–94, 109–10, 120
Tetlock, Philip 105, 115–19
Texas, USA 263
Thailand 248, 257, 510
thalmus 6
theology 199
The Theory of Moral Sentiments (Smith) 281, 650,
    653
thinking steps, games 168–75
thinking that you can outsmart everyone else (envy),
    seven sins 97, 100–1, 159–75
Third Avenue Value Fund 276
Thompson, V.A. 526–8
Thomson Financial 533, 537, 554–60
timber, alternative investments 245
time horizons 97, 101, 123, 125–30, 164–5, 174–5,
    177–86, 271, 277, 287, 293, 297–300, 329–36,
    375–86, 439–44, 473, 484–5, 497–8, 565–7,
    575–80
see also short-termism behaviour
best value investors 271, 277, 293, 295, 297–300,
    375–6
critique 179–86, 271, 277, 287, 293, 297–300,
    329–36, 375–86, 439–44, 497–8, 565–7
deflation 484–5
economic cycles/returns 575–80
fund managers 174–5, 179–86, 271, 277, 287,
    293, 297–300, 375–86, 439–44, 497–8
hedge funds 370–1, 489
mutual funds 179, 181–2, 183–4, 277, 367,
    372–4, 377–8
patience 219–22, 280, 297–300, 344, 357, 375–86

time horizons (*Cont.*)
  performance issues 174–5, 179–86, 271, 277, 369–74, 375–86
  returns 174–5, 179–86, 271, 277, 369–74, 375–86, 565
  short time horizons and overtrading 97, 101, 164–5, 174–5, 177–86, 282–3, 287, 293, 297–300, 367–74, 439–44, 459–60, 476–8, 497–8
  statistics 179–86, 271, 277, 297–300, 367–86
  valuations 123, 125–7, 565–7
Tirole, J. 407
Titman *et al* 490–1
TMT bubble 25, 70, 274, 278, 395, 397, 606
Tobin's Q 477
'torpedo' risks 314
torture 151–3, 599
total payout statistics, shareholders 539–40, 541–7, 552–6
total return valuation method 125–7, 433–5
tracking error 227–33, 247, 273–4, 425–35
trading range environments, economic cycles 579–80
traditions 509
trailing earnings, investment strategies 106, 120–1, 123, 125–7, 329–36, 345–6, 377, 569–72, 575–80, 583–6
trailing PE valuation method 123, 125–7, 331–6, 345–6, 377, 569–72
training, deception training 154–6
transition probabilities, returns 378–9
trend earnings, critique 571–2, 581–6
trend reversals 124, 129–30
truth, lies 97, 100, 143–5, 153–7
Turkey 248, 257
Tversky 23, 25, 29, 30, 31, 84, 120, 168
Tweedy Browne 271, 273–4, 278
Tyco 482, 601
Tyska, T. 117–19

UK 247, 256–7, 296, 337–53, 401–3, 407–9, 430, 443, 466, 507, 510, 549, 556–7, 605
  bubbles 466, 507, 510
  cheap countries 247, 257, 407–9
  correlation statistics 407–8, 443
  dilution statistics 549, 556–7
  EPS/DPS/GDP growth statistics 556–7
  Little Book strategy 337–53
  railway boom 466, 507
  sector-relative factors/ absolute-value contrasts 401–3
  South Sea bubble 466, 507, 510
  USA correlated returns 407–8
UMD, fund management group factor betas 231
UN 168
unbelieving strategy, beliefs 197–8, 204–5
unbounded objectivity 611–12, 629

unconscious biases
  see also implicit attitudes
  concepts 611, 615, 617–29
underperformance issues 179–86, 225–33, 238, 271, 278, 299–300, 311–12, 314, 344–5, 357, 370–2, 379, 450–2
understanding
  beliefs 197–205
  concepts 197–205
unethical behaviour, *see also* bad behaviour; ethics
university admissions, quant models 259, 263
unpacking practices, overclaiming credit bias 620–1
upside risks
  see also risks
  concepts 445–52
USA 55–61, 107, 151–3, 235–46, 263, 271, 273–4, 276–9, 296, 311–17, 321–3, 337–53, 370–4, 377–86, 400–3, 407–9, 430, 448–50, 455–67, 472–91, 507, 510–11, 529–72, 584, 601–9, 650–2, 661–3
  bad behaviour 601–9
  bargain hunters 311–17, 321–3
  beta studies 428–9
  bubbles 455–67, 472–91, 507, 510–11
  business risk studies 449–50
  capacity levels 481
  correlation statistics 407–8, 443, 488
  deflation 481–2, 507
  dilution statistics 549–61
  dollar/yen carry trade (October 1998) 441–2
  earnings optimism 584–6
  electric-shock experiments 151–3, 599, 604–8
  EPS/DPS/GDP growth statistics 554–6
  growth investing 311–17, 321–3
  happiness studies 650–2, 661–3
  inflation 55–61, 107, 573–80
  Little Book strategy 337–53
  low returns 563–72
  net equity issuance 357–63, 364
  portfolio concentration 271, 273–4
  sector-relative factors/ absolute-value contrasts 400–3
  Sharpe/Sortino ratios 448–9
  short-term performance 370–2
  Telecoms sector 390–2
  UK correlated returns 407–8
  valuations 563–72
  value investing 311–17, 321–3
utility concepts 13–14

valid beliefs, belief bias 523–4
valuation risks
  concepts 271, 276, 445–6, 450–2
  definition 446, 450
  statistics 450–1

valuations 17, 25–7, 123–30, 146–8, 237–9, 271,
    276, 282–3, 288, 335, 377, 395–403, 445–52,
    531–40, 563–72
  analysts 123–30, 288
  anchoring/salience bias 25–7, 288–9
  bull markets 517, 567–8
  critique 123–30, 282–3, 288, 312–14, 335, 377,
    395–403, 445–52, 565–72
  Graham and Dodd PEs 219, 221, 255–6, 273,
    329–36, 485–6, 569–71, 581–6
  growth investors 312–14, 375–86, 450–2
  historical factors 569–72
  low returns 563–72
  methods 123–30, 271, 276, 288, 569–71
  options 535–6
  returns 237–9, 288, 531–40, 565–72
  reverse-engineering benefits 17, 27
  sector-relative factors 395–403
  time horizons 123, 125–7, 565–6
  USA 563–72
  valuation/sentiment matrix 565–6
value added 242–5, 330, 336, 369–74, 387–93, 409,
    433–4
value investors 219–22, 271–8, 280, 293–304,
    307–28, 355–65, 375–86, 387–93, 429–35,
    450–2
  see also best value investors
  anatomy of value 310–12
  arbitrage 377–86
  bad states of the world 362–3
  bargain hunters 307–28, 337–53
  behavioural stumbling blocks 293–304
  cheap countries 405–21
  cheap stocks 307–28, 333–6, 337–53, 382–3,
    391–3, 405–21, 446, 450–2
  concepts 271–8, 295, 307–28, 450–2
  critique 307–28, 375–86
  global returns 309–28
  good intentions 294, 303–4
  growth investors 317–18, 375–86
  key traits 271–8, 295
  Little Book strategy 221, 261, 296–7, 337–53
  momentum strategies 383–6, 387–93
  net equity issuance 355–65
  patience 219–22, 280, 344, 357, 375–86
  PE values 309–28
  premiums 310–12, 331–2, 384–6, 391
  returns 309–28, 375–86, 387–93, 450–2
  risk-adjusted returns 318, 450–2
  risks 318, 359–60, 450–2
  sectors 387–93, 395–403
  statistics 309–28, 375–86, 389–93, 450–2
  stop-loss systems 379–80, 441–3
value issuers (VI), inside information 358–65
value repurchases (VP), inside information 355–
    65
value traps 312

Value-at-Risk (VaR) models
  see also risk models
  critique 437, 439–44
  LTCM 441–2
  positive feedback 439–40
  usage 439–40
  vicious circles 439–40
value-based strategies, uses 120–1, 219–22
value-oriented approaches 219–22
Van Boven, L. 655, 661–5
Van Knippenberg et al 611, 619–20
Vanguard Legend 181
Vansteenkiste et al 658
VaR models see Value-at-Risk. . .
variance
  see also standard deviation
  mean-variance efficient portfolios 427–35
  risks 431–5, 448–52
  Sortino ratios 448–52
veil of ignorance, decision-making 629
ventral medial prefrontal cortex (VMPFC) 527
video tests, lie-detection experiments 153–4
Vietnam War 214
Visaltanachoti, N. 60–1
VMPFC (ventral medial prefrontal cortex) 527
volatility
  see also betas; historic. . . ; market risk; risks
  commodities 590–1
  concepts 219–22, 271, 274–6, 279, 281–2, 367–8,
    433–4, 437–44, 445–52, 535–40, 587, 589
  corporate managers 535–40
  critique 219, 222, 271, 274–6, 279, 281–2, 295,
    367–8, 445–52, 535–40
  excess volatility 279, 282–3, 367–8, 370–4
  hedge funds 587, 589
  increases 535–7
  price/fundamental contrasts 367–8, 370–1
  risky investments 535–40
  share options 535–40
volitional activities, happiness 652–3
volumes
  bubbles 455, 463–7, 479–91
  market caps 463–5
voodoo experiment 301–2
VP (value repurchases) 355–65

Wahal, S. 299–300, 373–4
wealth dimension, Aspiration Index 657–60
Wealth of Nations (Smith) 281, 650
weathermen, forecasts 110–11, 117–19
weightings, experiences 269
well-being 645–65
  see also happiness
Westen et al 74–6, 149
Wharton 608
Whitman, Marty 276
wide mandates, change needs 235–46

Wilde, Oscar 76
Williams, John Burr 123, 125
Wiltshire 5000 228
wines, quant models 259, 263–5
Winners and Losers 381
winners/losers long-term performance in
      momentum strategies 129–30
Winning the Loser's Game (Ellis) 241
Wittenbaum *et al* 213
Wolford *et al* 52–3
working capital 279–80, 290
working memory
   capacity test 642
   incentives 631, 640–3
WorldCom 466, 482, 601
Worldscope data 363–4
wrath, seven sins 98, 101, 207–15

written records, biases 24, 63–4, 69–70, 76
WYSIWYG 29–30

X System *see* System X
Y2K 457–8, 474
Yahoo Behavioural Finance group 172
yield curves
      dollar/yen carry trade (October 1998) 441–2
      economic cycles 576–80
yield forecasts, bonds 107–9

Z-scores 449–50, 461–2, 478–80, 489
Zen of investing 521–2, 528
zero leverage, net equity issuance 363–4
zero sum games, alphas 241–2
Zielonka, P. 117–19
Zimbardo, Philip 599, 602–3

Index compiled by Terry Halliday